About Pearson

Pearson is the world's learning company, with presence across 70 countries worldwide. Our unique insights and world-class expertise comes from a long history of working closely with renowned teachers, authors and thought leaders, as a result of which, we have emerged as the preferred choice for millions of teachers and learners across the world.

We believe learning opens up opportunities, creates fulfilling careers and hence better lives. We hence collaborate with the best of minds to deliver you class-leading products, spread across the Higher Education and Test Preparation spectrum.

Superior learning experience and improved outcomes are at the heart of everything we do. This product is the result of one such effort.

Your feedback plays a critical role in the evolution of our products and you can contact us - reachus@pearson.com. *We look forward to it.*

What the reviewers say about this book ...

Economics is an ever dynamic and ever evolving subject. For someone who is not from Economics background, its subject matter remains abstruse and challenging. The lucid analysis of complex economic issues is the highlight of the book and will go a long way in establishing it the finest book on 'Indian Economy'.

—Dr Piyush Singla, IAS

A timely treatise for civil services aspirants, also for those who have not studied economics ever. It has been long required as there was no dependable manuscript available on this very subject.

—Mitesh Jain, IPS

The lucid style, concept development, chapter summary and MCQs are the highlights of the book. The book will be extremely helpful for economics optional, general studies and other competitive examinations. Congratulations to Dr Madhur Mohit Mahajan for bringing a phenomenal manuscript.

—Gagandeep Gambhir, IPS

The book is unique in itself and caters to the need of both prelims and mains examination. A perfect treat for UPSC aspirants.

—Parul Kush, IPS

The realm of Indian Economy is vast and vibrant and requires in-depth analysis of key economic issues. The book offers a wonderful read for the students preparing for university examinations, UGC and civil services.

—Deepti Uppal, IAS

Indian economy is a crucial subject for the preparation of civil services and other competitive exams. The book will offer a one stop solution to all aspirants to cover this vast subject.

—Kashish Mittal, IAS

In university or competitive exams, one needs to refer to a plenty of books and other material to cover the vast dimensions of Indian economy. This book addresses the long felt need for an authentic guide on the complex economic issues.

—Dr Gaurav Uppal, IAS

The book is both simple and effective. The concept development and analysis is marvellous. Highly recommended for those who want to know and understand Indian Economy.

—Lalit Jain, IAS

The book is remarkable in its lucidity and pinpointed focus on the essential. The study of Indian economy can often to be overwhelming due to the overload of statistics and data trends in most books on the subject. This book familiarizes the student with only most relevant data, weaving it beautifully with the concepts and models driving the evolution of Indian economy.

—Vrinda Shukla, IPS

Rich and illuminating account of the concepts and issues concerning Indian Economy.

—Ritika Narula, Indian Economics Services

A splendid read for crisp insights on Indian Economy.

—Shailesh Nawal, IAS

The book provides an articulate analysis of intricate problems of Indian Economy. An indispensable book for those who want to choose civil services as their career.

—Ketan Bansal, IPS

Essential reading for anyone who wants to understand Indian Economy and its dynamism.

—Dr Aman Puri, Indian Foreign Services

An indispensable book for economics optional & general studies, university and UGC exams.

—Sunil Choudhary, IPS

A treasure for optional and general studies students.

—Vikas Kumar, IRS

Dr Mahajan has done full justice to the subject. The book is unique and superior to any other book available on the subject in the market.

—Sabya Sachi Raman Mishra, IPS

The book is good in approach and coverage. A dependable manuscript.

—Dr Deepak Kumar, IPS

Many other books available on the title of 'Indian economy' are factual and lack in-depth analysis of its various dimensions. The present book methodically explains the concepts and provides analytical framework to the dynamic issues of Indian economy.

—Sanjay Kumar, IPS

Congratulations to Dr. Madhur for bringing this valuable book to the students.

—Prem Malik, IRS

INDIAN ECONOMY

Third Edition

Madhur M. Mahajan
Assistant Professor, PG Dept. of Economics,
GGDSD College, Chandigarh
(Affiliated to Panjab University, Chandigarh)

Pearson

Senior Editor—Product: Anindita Malhotra
Senior Editor—Production: C. Purushothaman

ISBN 978-93-615-9555-4

First Impression

Published by Pearson India Education Services Pvt. Ltd, CIN: U72200TN2005PTC057128.

Head Office: 1st Floor, Berger Tower, Plot No. C-001A/2, Sector 16B, Noida - 201 301, Uttar Pradesh, India.
Registered Office: Featherlite, 'The Address' 5th Floor, Survey No 203/10B, 200 Ft MMRD Road, Zamin Pallavaram, Chennai – 600 044.
Website: in.pearson.com, Email: companysecretary.india@pearson.com

Compositor: DigiWorld Creative, Pune, Maharashtra
Printer: Rahul Print O Pack

To Ninaad

Brief Contents

CONTENTS

PREFACE TO THE THIRD EDITION

It gives me immense pleasure to bring out the third edition of this popular book. As Indian Economy is ever-evolving and ever-dynamic subject, my efforts have been to incorporate in this book the latest trends and issues pertaining to our economy. In the present third edition of the book, some significant changes and additions have been made in the chapters. Among them, mention may be made of the following::

- **The data of all the chapters has been revised** so as to make the reader abreast of the latest trends in the Indian Economy.
- The new booklet titled **Indian Economy - Ready Reckoner** has been prepared and it will be supplied free of cost as complementary reading for the students. It will contain latest statistics of Indian Economy, Economic Survey, Budget, Chapter-wise Multiple-choice Questions and their Answer Keys for quick revision. The booklet will be immensely helpful for the students who want themselves enriched with latest data of Indian Economy and for those who are preparing for competitive exams.

With the changes I hope the students will find the book more useful for them. The book intends to meet the requirements of undergraduate and postgraduate students of Economics, Commerce and Business Management, and candidates preparing for Indian Economic Service and other competitive examinations. I will greatly appreciate the suggestions for further improvement of the book from fellow teachers and students. The author can be approached at madhurm2100@gmail.com

Madhur M. Mahajan

PREFACE TO THE SECOND EDITION

It gives me immense pleasure to bring out the second edition of this popular book. As Indian Economy is ever-evolving and ever-dynamic subject, my efforts have been to incorporate in this book the latest trends and issues pertaining to our economy. In the present second edition of the book, some significant changes and editions have been made in the chapters. Among them, mention may be made of the following:

- **The data of all the chapters has been revised** so as to make the reader abreast of the latest trends in the Indian Economy.
- **Chapter 2:** *The impact of COVID-19 on Indian Economy* has been added.
- **Chapter 14:** *Political Economy of Farm Laws* has been explained in detail with its merits and demerits.
- **Chapter 30:** *The Economic Survey 2021–22 and Budget 2022–23* have been added and analysed in detail in question and answer format.

With the changes I hope the students will find the book more useful for them. The book intends to meet the requirements of MA (Economics), MCom, MBA and related courses, BA/B.com (Hons) and candidates preparing more competitive examinations such as IAS, IES, State Public Service Commissions and NTA UGC NET/ JRF Exams etc. I will greatly appreciate the suggestions for further improvement of the book from fellow teachers and students. The author can be approached at madhurm2100@gmail.com

Madhur M. Mahajan

PREFACE TO THE FIRST EDITION

For students who are studying in college, university or are preparing for varied competitions, including prestigious exams like civil services, a good grasp and understanding of Indian economy is paramount and more generally for appreciating how Indian economy works. I have seen many civil services aspirants struggling to get familiar with the vast and complex issues of 'Indian Economy'. Similar is the fate of university and college students. Though there are good books available in the market, most of them are factual in nature that bombard the reader with a plethora of data or expound the various economic issues in a very intricate manner. For a general reader who wants to acquaint with wide-ranging dimensions of Indian economy, it remains a distant dream. No doubt there are wonderful research papers and reports but reading them all is something extremely difficult and they also remain outside the ambit of students because of lack of time or awareness. The present book is a humble attempt to address such problems.

The present work is the culmination of my teaching and understanding of Indian economy for the past 13 years. The book covers the syllabus of civil services optional and general studies, graduate and post-graduate courses of Indian universities, Indian economic services, UGC and other competitive exams. An attempt has been made to first discuss the concepts and then analytically explain the trends and direction of Indian economy. The chapter summary at the end of every chapter provides the crux of the whole chapter and will be a significant help to revise the chapter in a short span of time especially before the exams. The multiple-choice questions at the end of every chapter will broaden the objective understanding of the reader. Glossary at the end of book will help the students to understand the various complex terms associated with Indian economy.

I am thankful to team 'Pearson' who painstakingly worked day and night for the accomplishment of this project. Special thanks to Anindita Malhotra, Editor—Higher Education and C.Purushothaman, Senior Editor—Productions for their efficiency and cheerful disposition. I want to extend my gratitude to my parents and brother Munish who had been an inspiring force behind this monumental work. I am indebted to my wife Dr Babita for her consistent support during the writing of the book. I am thankful to my little son and best friend 'Ninaad' who gives me meaning to work hard and smile, and despite my best efforts to play and enjoy with him, understood me, whenever I was busy in this project. I feel blessed for the light shown by my 'Gurus' and 'almighty', and bow my head in deep reverence and gratitude.

I will welcome and appreciate suggestions from teachers and students for further improvement of the book.

Madhur M. Mahajan

About the Author

Dr Madhur M. Mahajan is an Assistant Professor at PG Dept. of Economics, GGDSD College Chandigarh, affiliated to Panjab University Chandigarh. He did his post-graduation in Economics and Ph.D. in international trade from Department of Economics, Panjab University Chandigarh.

Dr Mahajan has over 18 years of vast teaching and research experience and is guiding research on various dimensions of Indian Economy and Health Economics including Economics of Happiness, Economic Burden of Health, Affordability of Health and Health Efficiency. He has published numerous papers in esteemed international and national journals and presented papers in international and national conferences/seminars. He has organized numerous panel discussions/seminars and lectures on various economic issues and frequently appears in television discussions/debates.

CHAPTER 1

Few Basic Concepts and Nature of Indian Economy

The first lesson of economics is scarcity: there is never enough of anything to fully satisfy all those who want it. The first lesson of politics is to disregard the first lesson of economics.

—Thomas Sowell

Introduction

For those who are born and living in India, the economy is providing abundant goods and services to choose from. People get jobs, start new business venture, travel and communicate with anybody anywhere within the India and outside, and yet many of us have no idea how it all works. From the agriculture production by a farmer in some remote Indian village to the sale and purchase of derivatives in Bombay stock exchange, economics has countless dimensions and a serious seeker of the subject needs to be fully informed about the nuances of Indian economy. One of the main tasks in this very book is to make us understand how Indian economy works, how well it works, and what can be done when it does not work well.

This chapter addresses the following key issues:

- Economics and Economic problems
- Microeconomics and Macroeconomics
- Capitalism, Socialism, and Mixed economy
- Input and Output
- Nature of Indian Economy

What Is Economics?

We all know that human wants are unlimited but resources are limited. This is also called "basic economic problem." Wants generate demand and resources generate supply. Consider a world without scarcity. If infinite quantities of all goods and services were easily produced and all demands were easily met, would there be any economic problem? Businesses would not worry about cost of labor or availability of raw material; the governments would not worry about taxes and subsidies and other economic policies; consumers would not worry about prices and availability issues. It is because there would not have been any demand and supply problem.

For example, we all need oxygen to survive. But do we pay for that? Absolutely no! It is because there is abundant oxygen available in the atmosphere for all of us. But if you want to scale Mount Everest or if you are an astronaut, you will surely carry oxygen cylinder along and it will cost you as well. Therefore, "Economics is the study of how societies use scarce resources to produce valuable commodities and distribute them among different people."[1] Economics thus addresses the basic economic problem of rational management of resources or the problem of optimum utilization of resources. This economic problem poses three important questions to policymakers and economists of all the nations worldwide. These questions are (1) what to produce? (2) how to produce? and (3) for whom to produce?

Let us look more closely to these questions:

1. *What to produce?*
   Immediately after independence, India confronted with the problem of food grain shortage and started importing wheat from the United States under 1954 food aid program[2] (PL 480).* But after the war with Pakistan during 1965, the changing geopolitics led to the scrapping of food aid by the United States and India faced the urgent need of going for some out of box measures to increase agriculture production. New agriculture strategy (green revolution) in the form of HYV seed technology was adopted in 1966 in the three states of Punjab, Haryana, and western Uttar Pradesh. To address the problem of "what to produce," green revolution was a clear-cut choice of the policymakers of that time.
2. *How to produce?*
   In any economy, the government or policymakers determine who will do the production and with what techniques? Whether the country should go for labor-intensive techniques or capital-intensive techniques? Obviously, a capital-rich nation (or labor scarce nation) should go for capital-intensive techniques and a labor surplus nation (or capital deficit) country should go for labor-intensive techniques. For example, Mahatma Gandhi National Rural Employment Guarantee Act (MNREGA) was launched in India in the year 2006 to produce rural assets by labor-intensive techniques. India being a labor surplus country requires labor absorbing techniques, and for that, the government has envisaged 60:40 wage-material ratio under MNREGA at district level.
3. *For whom to produce?*
   The government needs to take a decision regarding who will be the beneficiaries of production activities. How will be national income divided between different residents of the country? For example, bank nationalization of 1969 was announced by the government so as to make the institutional credit available to common man. Before 1969, Indian banking was class banking, as it addressed credit needs of few rich private sector corporates. Bank nationalization was a move to transform Indian banking from class banking to mass banking. If poverty is high, the government may think of effective public distribution system. Pradhan Mantri Ujjwala Yojana (providing LPG connections to women of BPL families) and Deendayal Upadhyaya Gram Jyoti Yojana (for rural electrification) are few other examples.

The Two Branches of Economics: Microeconomics and Macroeconomics

The effective birth of economics as a separate discipline may be traced to the year 1776, when the Scottish philosopher Adam Smith published "An Enquiry into the Nature and Causes of the Wealth of Nations."[3] There are two major branches of economics: Microeconomics and

*The P.L. 480 agreements aimed at supply of surplus agricultural commodities from the United States against payment of the rupee equivalent of the dollar cost of these commodities plus 50% of the ocean freight cost.

BOX 1.1 Water-diamond Paradox

The classical economist, *Adam Smith*, the father of economics, in his famous book *An Enquiry into the Nature and Causes of Wealth of Nations* has tried to explain the problem of scarcity with the help of famous *water-diamond paradox*. According to him, water is very essential for life but has very little or no value. But diamond is not essential and is very costly. The price is not determined by total utility or total satisfaction gained from a product but depends upon the satisfaction derived from each additional unit of the commodity, which is called marginal utility. Since water is available in abundance, its marginal utility is less. It is because each additional unit of water that becomes available can be applied to less urgent uses as more urgent uses for water are satisfied. Therefore, with increase in the supply of water, each additional unit of water becomes worth less to people. On the other hand, diamonds are in such low supply that the usefulness of one additional diamond is greater than the usefulness of one additional glass of water, which is in abundant supply. Hence, diamonds are most costly than water.

Source: Smith, A. (2007). *An enquiry into the nature and causes of wealth of nations*. Metalibri, p.26.

macroeconomics. Microeconomics studies the behavior of individual entities, households, firms, and markets. Adam Smith is considered as the founder of the field of microeconomics. Macroeconomics on the other hand studies the overall performance of the economy. Macroeconomics in its modern form can be attributed to John Maynard Keynes who published his revolutionary "General Theory of Employment, Interest, and Money" in the year 1936. Macroeconomics examines a wide variety of areas, such as how total investment and consumption are determined, how central bank manages money and interest rates, what causes international financial crisis, and why nations grow rapidly while others stagnate.[4]

Capitalism, Socialism, and Mixed Economies

The questions of what, how, and for whom are answered by different economic systems differently. Capitalism also called as market economy is an economic system in which private firms and individuals make the major decisions regarding production and consumption. There is little government intervention or central planning, and price- and output-related decisions are taken by demand and supply forces (price mechanism). On the other hand, socialism is a school of thought in which means of production are owned by the government. All production and distribution decisions are taken by the government, and individuals rely on the state for everything from food to healthcare. It is the government that determines output and pricing levels of these goods and services. Socialist economies are also called command economies. North Korea, Cuba, and former Soviet Republic can be placed in the category of socialism. A mixed economic system is a system that combines the aspects of both capitalism and socialism. A mixed economic system protects private property and allows a level of economic freedom in the use of capital, but also allows for the governments to interfere in economic activities in order to achieve social aims. In fact, all economies of the world are mixed economies, though economies may tilt toward capitalism and socialism. There has never been a 100% capitalist economy (although 19th century England came close). There has never been a 100% socialist economy either as market forces always work in some form or other. However, Indian economy since independence is envisaged as a mixed economy by the planners and started its march toward capitalism since 1991 economic reforms.

INPUTS AND OUTPUTS

To answer the question of what, how, and for whom, every country needs to make a choice regarding inputs and outputs. Inputs are the goods and services that can be used to produce goods and services. For example, bricks, sand, cement, labor, glass, and wood are inputs required to manufacture building. Outputs are various useful goods or services that are produced with the help of inputs in the production process and can be consumed or employed in further production. For example, biscuits are the output that can be consumed by consumer and photo state machine (which is also the output) can be used for copying the documents. Another term for inputs is factor of production. Factors of production can be broadly classified into four broad categories: Land, labor, capital, and entrepreneurship. The payment made for the use of factors of production is called factor cost or factor income.

1. Land—also called as natural resource—represents the gift of nature and consists of land used for agriculture, constructing factories or roads, some useful raw materials like iron ore and copper, and energy resources like hydroelectricity and petrol. The payment made for the use of land or land resources is called rent.
2. Labor represents human time spent in the production, for example, teaching in schools, ploughing the land, and working in industries. Labor gets wages as factor income. Wages are high in labor deficit countries (in Canada, Australia, the United States, and European Union) and low in labor surplus nations (China, India, Bangladesh, etc.).
3. Capital signifies the machines or durable goods which are produced to produce further goods and services. For example, washing machine, photo state machine, roads, automobiles, and buildings. Capital is also called financial wealth or investment which is used to start and maintain business. Interest is paid for the use of capital. In the developed countries which are capital rich, the interest is low. In the developing countries like India which are capital scarce, the interest rate is comparatively high.
4. Entrepreneurship signifies the capability of an entrepreneur to visualize operations of business and take risks. Entrepreneur combines the other factors of production, viz., land, labor, and capital, to produce goods and services. For his services, entrepreneur gets profit.

ECONOMIC GROWTH AND DEVELOPMENT

Traditionally, economic development has been considered as synonymous with economic growth. Modern view, however, tries to differentiate between growth and development. Let us have a look.

- Economic growth means a sustained increase in country's output and measured in terms of gross domestic product or growth per capita. Economic development on the other hand measures the technological and institutional change by which increase in output takes place.

- Economic growth is a narrow concept as it measures the quantitative change in the economy in terms of increase in output. Economic development on the other hand is a broader concept and measures change in composition and distribution of national and per capital income. Economic development is determined by the improvement in life expectancy rate, infant mortality rate, literacy rate, and poverty rates. Economic development, thus, measures both the quantitative and qualitative aspects of change in national income.
- Economic growth is a short period process and is measured annually. Economic development on the other hand is a long-term process and takes place over the period of time.
- Economic growth is a continuous process and is measured in terms of sustained indicators like Gross Domestic Product (GDP). Economic development is a discontinuous process involving periods of expansion and of recession, reflecting the existence of business cycles[5].
- Economic growth as a concept is related with the developed countries. For the developed economies, development is not the problematic issue as such economies have already attained the qualitative targets and reached the pinnacle of institutional and technological progress over the period of time. For such countries, the major challenge is to attain a minimal required level of GDP growth so that economy does not plunge into recession. However, the major challenge for the developing countries like India is to undergo technological and institutional change so as to attain quantitative and qualitative progress.

BOX 1.2 Few Prominent Schools of Economics

Mercantilism: Mercantilism is a school of thought which dominated European thought between the 16th and 18th centuries. Mercantilists believed that precious metals, such as gold and silver, were crucial to nation's wealth and prosperity. If a nation did not possess mines or have access to them, precious metals should be obtained by trade. The major pioneers of mercantilism were Thomas Mun in England, Jean-Baptiste Colbert in France, and Antonio Serra in Italy.

Physiocrats: This school of thought was founded in the 18th century France by François Quesnay. The school believes that the government policy should not interfere with the operation of natural economic laws and that land (agriculture) is the source of all wealth. Physiocrat is regarded as the first scientific school of economics.

Classical economics: Classical economics is a school of economic thought that originated during the late 18th century Britain with Adam Smith and that reached maturity in the works of David Ricardo and John Stuart Mill. The theories and models of classical school emphasized economic growth and economic freedom, stressed laissez-faire ideas, and free competition. Classical economics introduced labor theory of value, assumed full employment situation under market economy, and hailed trade as an engine of growth.

Marxian economics: Marxian school of economics thought was mainly developed by Karl Marx, and to a lesser extent, by Friedrich Engels in the mid-19th century. The Marxian economics analyzes the process of economic evolution through crisis in capitalism and its doom. It studies the distribution of the surplus product and surplus value in various types of economic systems, the nature and origin of economic value and analyzes the impact of class and class struggle on economic and political processes.

Keynesian economics: Keynesian economics represents the body of ideas set forth by John Maynard Keynes in his popular book "General Theory of Employment, Interest and Money" published in 1936 and remained the dominant school of macroeconomics and guided the economic policy framework of most Western governments until the 1970s. Keynesian economics is a short-run demand side theory which believed that "full employment" is an exception and economic disequilibrium (because of the change in aggregate demand) can be corrected by suitable policy response and government intervention.

Chicago School of Economics: Chicago school of economics was developed by Department of Economics at the University of Chicago and emphasizes free-market principles. It was founded in the 1930s, mainly by Frank Knight, and subsequently, developed by Gary S. Becker, Ronald Coase, Milton Friedman, Merton Miller, and George Stigler. At the heart of the Chicago school's approach is the belief in laissez-faire as it rejected Keynesianism in favor of monetarism. Until the mid-1970s, it turned to new classical macroeconomics profoundly based on the concept of rational expectations.

Sources:

1. Landreth, H., Colander, D.C. *History of economic thought*, 4th ed. Houghton Mifflin Company.
2. Backhaus, J.G. (2012). *Handbook of the history of economic thought*. Springer.

TYPES OF ECONOMIES

International economic institutions and economists classify countries around the world based on their level of economic and industrial development. Let us have a look at this.

Developed economies: A developed economy is one which has high per capita income, developed financial markets, and high level of human development. Such nations are characterized by higher level of productivity in agriculture, industry, and services. The United States, Canada, Japan, and countries of European Union can be placed under this category.

Emerging economies: The term "emerging markets" dates back to 1981 and was invented by Antoine van Agtmael. The emerging market has many things in common with the developed countries but lack in certain standards to be termed as developed economies. For example, China, India, Brazil, Russia, and South Korea are termed as leading emerging markets in the world.[6]

Developing economies: Developing countries have low levels of living and productivity, high population growth, underdeveloped industry, and reliance on agriculture and exports for economic sustainability. The difference between the developing nations and the emerging nations is that the latter are growing rapidly and becoming more important in world economics, while the developing nations are struggling and still need help from trade partners around the world.

Frontier economies: Frontier markets are smaller, more undeveloped, and riskier than emerging markets. They are economically less developed than the emerging economies. Frontier markets are thus the developing markets but better than the least developed markets.[7] Examples of frontier economies are Sri Lanka, Argentina, and Ghana.

Least developed economies: The least developed economies are the countries characterized by massive poverty, low level of human development, and economic vulnerability. In 2018, 47 nations were classified by UN as the least developed countries (LDCs)—Angola, Nigeria, Afghanistan, and Myanmar are the examples of LDCs.

NATURE OF INDIAN ECONOMY

India—A Lower Middle-income Country

The World Bank classifies the world's economies into four income groups—high, upper-middle, lower-middle, and low. This assignment is based on GNI per capita which is calculated using the Atlas method.* For the current 2024 fiscal year, low-income economies are defined as those with a GNI per capita of $1,135 or less in 2022; lower middle-income economies are those with a GNI per capita between $1,136 to $4,465; upper middle-income economies are those with a GNI per capita between $4,466 and $13,845; high-income economies are those with a GNI per capita of $13,846 or more. Out of 218 countries, there are 26 low-income economies, 54 lower-middle-income economies, 54 upper-middle-income economies, and 83 high-income economies. With GNI per capita income of $2,410, India is classified as a lower-middle income country.[8]

Third Largest and Fastest Growing Economy

At the time of independence, India was a backward nation with very less growth rate. The government through five-year plans tried to address such problems by laying down targets and ensured the allocation of funds for the development of different sectors. Till the first five plans, the average GDP growth was around 3.5%, and as a result, Indian economy failed to take off. During the post-reform period, the growth rate picked up, especially during 2004–2008, the country witnessed an average growth rate reaching an unprecedented high of 8.8% a year. Reaching an aspirational growth rate of 8% or higher and sustaining such growth momentum requires contributions from all domestic sectors and support from the global economy. While India's growth has been well diversified, the pace of growth acceleration has differed across sectors. The acceleration of value added has been fastest in services, followed by industry, and there has been no evident pattern of acceleration in agriculture.[9] As per world economic outlook 2023 report, India is the world's third largest economy in terms of purchasing power parity (PPP), after the China and the United States. India has become the fifth largest in terms of nominal GDP. India is forecast to overtake the Germany to become the world's fourth largest economy in 2024 and projected to surpass Japan to feature at the second position in the Asia-Pacific region by 2025.[10]

Higher Population Growth and High Dependency Ratio

World Bank noticed population growth rate of 1% in 2020. Population of India has increased from nearly 38 crore in 1951 to 143.87 crore in April 2024.[11] The country is passing through the third stage of demographic transition which is characterized by falling birth rate and death rate.[12] Higher population puts pressure on limited resource base of the country and causing deprivations to the masses that result into low per capita income of the nation. The pressure of population has also resulted in higher dependency ratio as well. Dependency ratio is (No. of

* A country's national income is converted into U.S. dollars using the Atlas conversion factor, which uses a three-year average of exchange rates adjusted for the difference between the rate of inflation in the country and international inflation. The resulting GNI in U.S. dollars is divided by the country's midyear population to obtain the GNI per capita.

persons in age group 0–14 years + No. of persons in age group 65 years or more) ÷ No. of persons in age group 15–64 years.[13] Dependency ratio gives the proportion of persons whom the persons in economically active age group need to support. Dependency ratio of India fell gradually from 79.1 in 1970 to 47.5 ratio in 2022.[14]

Wide Scale Poverty and Unemployment

Almost 72 years have elapsed since India got independence but we are still the home for the world's largest number of poor people. On the basis of NSSO 68th round, 29.5% of population in India was below poverty line during 2011–12. Around 27.5% of India's population was multi-dimensionally poor in 2015 as per Multi-Dimensional Poverty Index and the number has come down to 14.96% for the period 2019–21. Unemployment rate in India marginally increased to 8% during the fiscal 2023–24 as compared to 7.6% in 2023–24. According to CEIC's economic database, India's Labor Force Participation Rate increased to 42.4% in Dec 2023, compared with 41.3% in the previous year.[15] The labor force participation rate for females has also revealed a declining trend. But what is more worrisome is the rise in educated unemployment in India. An ed-tech and skill development company of India, ImaginXP recently conducted a survey that showed that 33% educated youth in India are unemployed due to lack of future-ready skills for most of them, despite getting a degree.[16]

Low Level of Savings and Investment

Savings are vital as they lead to investment and cause increase in gross domestic product. In the western world, the private sector contributes almost 80% of total savings and household and the government sector does rest of the savings. However, in India, it is household sector which contributes around 60% in total domestic savings. During 1990–91, situation was worse as household sector contributed as high as 84% of total savings. The problem with household sector savings is that in a country like India the per capita income is low that results in higher consumption pattern and low savings. Further, it also indicates poor business and entrepreneurship profile of the country. However, in the past few decades, especially after the post-reform period, the private sector participation in the economy has increased multi-fold resulting in the increasing share of private sector and the decreasing share of household sector in aggregate domestic savings. Further, investment profile of the country has improved over the past few decades but it still lacks in certain aspects. The gross domestic capital formation in India has decreased from 39% in 2011–12 to around 30.9% in 2023–24 (Projected). Finance holds the key to India's long-term sustainable growth. As the economy becomes larger and market-oriented, the financial sector needs to play a critical role in channeling savings into productive investments. For example, the two biggest challenges of investment in India at present are investment in infrastructure and in micro, small, and medium enterprises.[17]

Low Level of Human Development

The term human development denotes the process of widening people's choices and the level of their achieved wellbeing. India has emerged as the third largest and one of the fastest growing economies but its human development report card is dismal. The low level of human development gets reflected into poor education, lack of affordability and accessibility to basic healthcare facilities, and lower level of economic well-being, which ultimately results in lower productivity of the nation as a whole. India's Human Development Index (HDI) rank is 134 out of 193 nations for the year 2022. As per Inequality adjusted HDI, India experiences a loss of 26.8% due to inequality in the distribution of the HDI dimension indices. The status of women in India is also not good which is reflected through different indices. For every 100,000 live births, 174 women die from pregnancy-related causes; and the adolescent birth rate is 23.1 births per 1,000 women of ages 15–19. Female participation in the labor market is 37% compared to 78.5 for men for 15 years and above.[18]

From Agriculture Predominance to Service Led Growth

The share of agriculture as a percentage of GVA has come down from 53% in 1950–51 to around 18.3% in 2022–23. On the contrary, the share of services has increased from 30.3 to 53% during the same period. This transition of economy from agriculture to service sector is called service led growth phenomenon. Generally, as an economy progresses, it transmutes itself from an agriculture-based economy to an industrialized economy and finally into a service led economy. But in Indian case, the industrial development could not take place as envisaged by our policymakers. The contribution of industry in country's GDP has increased from 16.6% in 1950–51 to nearly 28% in 2022–23. In contrast, in China, the share of agriculture, industry, and services is 7.2, 40.7, and 52.2%, respectively.[19] One more thing which has serious implication is the share of respective sectors in employment. For example, in the United States, agriculture contributes 4% of GDP and absorbs 4% of country's workforce. In the United Kingdom too, agriculture contributes 2% of GDP and provides employment to around 2% of the workforce. Comparatively, agriculture in India contributes 18.3% of GVA and employs around 43.4% of country's workforce. Thus, the service sector which generates maximum national income provides lesser employment, a phenomenon called as "jobless growth."

Summary

1. Human wants are unlimited but resources are limited. Wants generate demand and resources generate supply. Economics is the study of how societies use scarce resources to produce valuable commodities and distribute them among different people.
2. There are two major branches of economics: Microeconomics and macroeconomics. Microeconomics studies the behavior of individual entities, households, firms, and markets. Adam Smith is considered as the founder of the field of microeconomics. Macroeconomics on the other hand studies the overall performance of the economy. Macroeconomics in its modern form can be attributed to John Maynard Keynes.
3. Capitalism also called as market economy is an economic system in which private firms and individuals make the major decisions regarding production and consumption. Socialism is a school of thought in which means of production are owned by the government. A mixed economic system is a system that combines the aspects of both capitalism and socialism.
4. Inputs are the goods and services that can be used to produce goods and services. Another term for inputs is factor of production. Factors of production can be broadly classified into four broad categories: Land, labor, capital, and entrepreneurship.
5. Economic growth means a sustained increase in country's output that measures the quantitative change in the economy, and is a short term and continued process. Economic development on the other hand is a broader concept and measures the change in composition and the distribution of national and per capital income. It measures the qualitative change in the economy and is a long term and discontinuous process. Economic growth is usually distinguished from economic development, the latter term being restricted to economies that are close to the subsistence level and the former with the developed economies.
6. The developed economies are highly industrialized advanced economies. The emerging markets have not yet become advanced but are in the process to become developed in due course of time. The developing nations are struggling economies and still need help from trade partners around the world. Frontier markets are countries that are better established than LDCs but still less established than the emerging markets. The least developed economies are the counties characterized by massive poverty, low level of human development, and economic vulnerability.
7. The World Bank assigns the world's economies into four income groups—high, upper-middle, lower-middle, and low. As per World Bank definition, India is classified as a lower-middle income country.
8. India is the world's third largest economy in terms of PPP and the sixth largest in terms of nominal GDP. India has also emerged as one of the fastest major economies of the world. Population of India has increased from nearly 38 crore in 1951 to 136 crore in June 2019. Dependency ratio gives the proportion of persons whom the persons in economically active age group need to support. In India, the dependency ratio is high though it has shown declining trend. India has 29.5% of population below poverty line during 2011–12 as per NSSO 68th round and 27.5% of population multi-dimensionally poor in 2015 as per Multi-Dimensional Poverty Index. Unemployment rate in India as per the current daily status was 5.6% as per NSSO 68th round for the year 2011–12. The rising female unemployment rate and educated unemployment rate is another cause of worry for the policymakers. In India, household sector contributes around 60% of domestic savings. Since per capita income in India is low, the overall saving rate is also low. The human development performance of India is also below satisfaction. India's HDI rank is 130 out of 189 nations for the year 2017. Though the share of agriculture as a percentage of GDP has come down from 53% in 1950–51 to around 15% in 2017–18, the share of employment has not decreased. Services contribute maximum in country's GDP (53%) but it is agriculture that provides employment to 45% of workforce.

Endnotes

1. Samuelson, P., Nordhaus, W. (2005). *Economics*, 18th ed. Tata McGraw-Hill Publishing Company Limited, p.4.
2. Laxminarayan, H. (1960). Indo-US food agreement and state trading in food grains. *EPW* Vol. 12, Issue No. 39.
3. Blaug, M. *Economics*. Encyclopedia of Britannica. Retrieved from https://www.britannica.com (Accessed on March 10, 2016).
4. Samuelson, P., Nordhaus, W. (2005). *Economics*, 18th ed. Tata McGraw Hill, p.4.
5. Alcouffe, A., & Ferrari, S. Growth versus development from Schumpeter to Georgescu-Roegen, retrieved from https://halshs.archives-ouvertes.fr (Accessed on February 4, 2015).
6. Roberts, J., Kayande, U., Srivastava, R.K. (2015). *What's different about emerging markets, and what does it mean for theory and practice?, Customer needs and solution*, Vol. 2, Issue 4, pp.245–250, December 2015.
7. Ins and outs, *The Economist*, September 20, 2008.
8. Information retrieved from https://data.worldbank.org (Accessed on April 8, 2024).
9. India's Growth Story, *India Development Update*, World Bank, March 2018.
10. The Economic Times, June 3, 2019.
11. Population India. Retrieved from https://www.worldometers.info (Accessed on April 8, 2024).
12. For detailed discussion of demographic transition model, refer to Chapter India's Population and Demographic Dividend.
13. Census of India 2011. *Report on Post Enumeration Survey*, Government of India.
14. India dependency ratio. Retrieved from https://www.statista.com/ (Accessed on March 30, 2024).
15. Data accessed from https://www.cmie.com visited on 9 April 2024
16. Retrieved from India Today https://www.indiatoday.in/education accessed on 10 Jan, 2022
17. Patnaik, I., & Pandey, R. (2019). *Savings and capital formation in India*. NIPFP Working paper no. 271.
18. *PLFS, Annual Report, MOSPI, 2022–23.*
19. Retrieved from https://www.statista.com (Accessed on March 15, 2019).

CHAPTER 2

NATIONAL INCOME, SAVINGS, AND CAPITAL FORMATION

If a man were to hire a housekeeper or cook, national income and employment will go up; but if he were to marry her and she continued to do the same work, national income and employment will go down. These things are paradoxes.

—**A.C. Pigou**

INTRODUCTION

National income estimates are the most comprehensive measures of aggregate economic activity in an economy. National income accounts have multiple roles: First, they provide an excellent approximation of a nation's available economic resources and actual output. This is invaluable for setting government fiscal and monetary policy, and for evaluating the impacts of governmental policies. Second, national income accounts provide a precise understanding of the current state of national economic demand, supply, and inflation. This creates a sound basis for current business and financial decision-making. Third, the national income framework has proved a useful basis for long-term forecasting of economic activity and for business and government planning at multi-year horizons. Finally, the statistics is used for international and interregional cost sharing and aid agreements.[1]

This chapter addresses the following aspects of national income:

- National Income Indicators
- Circular Flow of National Income
- Methods of Measuring National Income in India
- Characteristic Features of National Income in India
- Trends of National Income in India
- State Domestic Product: Features and Trends
- Savings and Capital formation in India

WHAT IS NATIONAL INCOME?

National income is the sum value of all goods and services produced in a nation in a single financial year. Goods mean all tangible commodities like clothes, cars, motorbikes, food items, electronic goods and so on, whereas, services refer to all intangible items like banking, health, insurance, consultancy, education, etc. In India, the government's financial year runs from April 1 to March 31. For example, the financial year for 2024–25 will start from April 1, 2024 to March 31, 2025. Central Statistical Office (CSO) computes national income and classifies Indian economy into three parts, that is, primary sector, secondary sector, and tertiary sector. Primary sector constitutes (a) agriculture, (b) forestry, and (c) fishing; secondary sector comprises (a) mining and quarrying, (b) manufacturing, (c) electricity, gas and water supply, and (d) construction activities; and tertiary sector includes (a) trade, hotel, transport, and communication, (b) financing, insurance, real estate and business services, and (c) community, social and personal services. The aggregated value of product in all these sectors in a financial year will be national income or gross domestic product (GDP) or gross value added (GVA).*

Before discussing other aspects of national income, let us understand the national income indicators.

National Income Indicators

Gross Domestic Product (GDP): GDP is one of the popular measures of national income worldwide. It is the sum total of all the final goods and services produced in a nation in a single accounting year. So, the aggregate of all final goods and services produced in agriculture and allied sectors, industry and services sectors will constitute national income in India.

Gross National Income (GNP): GDP is an incomplete measure as it does not take into account the factor income** of Indian working in abroad or profits earned by Indian companies in abroad who send a part of such income to India in the form of remittances. Similarly, foreign nationals and multi-national companies working in India send remittances and profits back to their home nations and therefore, such income needs to be deducted from the GDP. The macroeconomic indicator that takes into account net factor income from abroad is known as Gross National Product (GNP).

GNP = GDP + Net factor income from abroad.

where Net factor income from abroad = Factor income earned by the domestic factors of production employed in the rest of the world – Factor income earned by the factors of production of the rest of the world employed in the domestic economy.

Net National Product (NNP)

We know that part of the capital goods or machinery gets consumed during the year due to wear and tear and is called depreciation. Naturally, depreciation does not become part of anybody's income. If we deduct depreciation from GNP, the measure of aggregate income that we obtain is called Net National Product (NNP).

Thus, **NNP** = GNP – Depreciation
And similarly, **Net Domestic Product (NDP)** = GDP – Depreciation

*The terms GDP and GVA though similar are different in a technical sense. It will be elaborated later.

**Returns received on factors of production: rent is a return on land, wages on labor, interest on capital, and profit on entrepreneurship. For details, please see Chapter 1, Few Basic Concepts and Nature of Indian Economy.

GDP at Market Price/Factor Cost: GDP can be calculated at market price or factor cost. Market price includes indirect taxes that accrue to the government. Market price does not include subsidies that are given by the government to citizens. When indirect taxes (such as excise, custom, and service tax) are imposed on goods and services, their prices go up. Similarly, there may be subsidies granted by the government on the prices of some commodities so as to provide relief to the common citizen. For example, in India petrol is heavily taxed by the government, whereas cooking gas or railway ticket for passenger class is subsidized. We have to deduct indirect taxes and add subsidies to the GDP evaluated at market price in order to calculate that part of GDP that actually accrues to the factors of production in the form of rent, wages, interest, and profits. The measure that we obtain by doing so is called Gross Domestic Product at factor cost (FC).

Thus, **GDP at FC** is = GDP at MP – Indirect taxes + Subsidies
where FC = factor cost, and MP = market price
Similarly, **GDP at MP** = GDP at FC + Indirect taxes – Subsidies
And, GNP at FC = GNP at MP – Indirect taxes + Subsidies
or, GNP at MP = GNP at FC + Indirect Taxes – Subsidies
or, NNP at FC = NNP at MP – Indirect taxes + Subsidies
or, NNP at MP = NNP at FC + Indirect taxes – Subsidies

In technical sense, the national income is NNP at FC. But since the data regarding depreciation are not documented across many countries in the world due to existence of large-scale unorganized sector, GDP and GNP is preferred over NNP.

Gross Value Added: The CSO has adopted the concept of **Gross Value Added (GVA)** in January 2015. The concept of GVA at basic prices follows from the United Nation's System of National Accounts (SNA) introduced in 1993 and carried forward in an identical fashion in SNA 2008 as a part of revision of compilation and classification systems.

As we discussed earlier, GDP at factor cost represents what the producers in the economy make from industrial activity wages, profits, rents, and capital called "factors of production." Aside from these costs, producers may also incur other expenses such as property tax, stamp duties, and registration fees before sale. These are included in the GDP, but not in the GVA. Essentially, GVA captures what accrues to the producer, before a product is sold.[2] GVA is defined as the value of output less the value of intermediate consumption.

GVA at factor cost (earlier referred to as GDP at factor cost) = GVA at basic prices – Production taxes less Production subsidies*

GVA at basic prices = GDP (at market prices) – Product taxes + Product subsidies**

---

*Production taxes or production subsidies are paid or received with relation to production and are independent of the volume of actual production. Some examples of production taxes are land revenues, stamps and registration fees, and tax on profession. Some production subsidies include subsidies to railways, input subsidies to farmers, subsidies to village and small industries, administrative subsidies to corporations or cooperatives, etc.

**Product taxes or subsidies are paid or received on per unit of product. Some examples of product taxes are excise tax, sales tax, service tax, and import and export duties. Product subsidies include food, petroleum and fertilizer subsidies, interest subsidies given to farmers, households, etc. through banks.

National Income at Current Prices and Constant Prices

National Income at Current Prices

If goods and services produced in a year are valued at current prices, that is, prices prevailing in that particular year, we get national income at current prices. For example, if the goods and services produced in 2024–25 are valued at prices prevailing in 2024–25, then it will be called national income at current prices for the year 2024–25. National income at current prices is called nominal national income.

National Income at Constant Prices

If goods and services produced in a year are valued at constant prices, that is, prices of the base year, we get national income at constant prices. For example, the CSO treats 2011–2012 as the base year in India, and if the goods and services produced in 2024–25 are valued at prices prevailing in 2011–2012 (**base year prices**), then it will be called national income at constant prices for the year 2024–25. It is change in volume of physical output produced during the year, which affects national income at constant prices because prices remain constant. National income at constant prices is also called real national income.

Per Capita Income

Per capita income is an average earning of individuals in an economy. It is national income divided by population of the country. Per capita income is useful indicator for measuring country's income profile and change in living standard. However, it fails to give the accurate measure of quality of life because it ignores income inequality. For example, despite the fact that Goa is the richest state in India in terms of per capita income, we do not know the true picture of the living conditions of the entire population. As per 2nd advanced estimates of National Statistics Office, the per capita GDP at current prices is projected to be ₹1,83,236 during 2023–24 and ₹1,06,134 at constant prices during the same period.

Circular Flow of National Income

As our heart beats, it pumps blood through a system of blood vessels, that is, arteries, veins, and capillaries, the blood is circulated to and away from the heart and hence the system is called the blood circulatory system. Similarly, as an economy functions, the income flow takes place among various sectors of the economy. Taking simply, let us assume that there are two sectors of the economy, firms or producer, and households or consumer. There are four factors of production viz. Land, Labor, Capital, and Entrepreneurship, which contribute in the production of goods and services. All these factors in lieu of services supplied get some return called factor earnings or factor payments. Land gets rent, labor gets wages, capital gets interest, and entrepreneurship gets profit. The factors of production produce goods and services and use their remuneration (factor earnings) to purchase the goods and services, which they assisted in producing. The aggregate spending (consumption) by the households of the economy is equal to the aggregate expenditure on goods and services produced by the firms in the economy. The entire income of the economy, therefore, comes back to the producers in the form of sales revenue. However, in this entire case study we have assumed that there is no leakage (in terms of savings or imports) from the system, as this is a simple circulation flow model and we take into consideration only firms and household sector. This aggregate amount of money that is flowing in the form of spending or factor payments is called national income.

Methods of Measuring National Income in India

National income can be measured in three ways.

Expenditure Method

To calculate GDP under expenditure method, we combine consumption, investment, government spending, and net exports. Under this everything that the private sector, including consumers and private firms, and government spend in a year, must add up to arrive at the GDP value. This method produces nominal GDP, which must then be adjusted for inflation to result in the real GDP. This method is used in calculating national income in construction sector.

Hence, $GDP \equiv C + I + G + X - M$

where C = the final consumption expenditure on the goods and services incurred by household sector and firms.

I = the final investment expenditure incurred by all the firms and government.

G = the expenditure that the government makes on the final goods and services produced by firm.

X – M = Net exports (Exports – Imports).

Product Method

Under this method of measuring national income, the total production of all final goods and services produced in a year is added to reach an aggregate value from which the value of intermediate goods is deducted to arrive at the GDP value. For example, in the manufacturing of car, intermediate goods are steel, glass, rubber, etc. If car showroom price is ₹10 lakhs (which is the final value), then the consumption expenditure made on the purchase of car company on steel, glass, and rubber will be intermediate consumption expenditure. The only and major problem with this method that there may be some error of double counting due to which the accurate value of national income may not be derived. This method is used in calculating national income in agriculture sector.

Income Method

This method is used to measure national income at distribution level. The sum of final expenditures in the economy must be equal to the incomes received by all the factors of production taken together. The revenues (factor income) earned by all the firms put together must be distributed among the factors of production as wages, profits, interest earnings, and rents.

GDP = Wages + Profit + Interest + Rent

This is the most popular and most widely measure of national income.

Characteristic Features of National Income in India

India: Among the Largest Economies of the World

GDP is a significant yardstick to measure the size of an economy. India is the world's third largest economy in terms of purchasing power parity (PPP),* after China and the United States. In fact, the size of Indian economy is almost three times the size of the UK economy and more than two times the size of German economy. GDP comparisons using PPP are better than that of nominal GDP when assessing a nation's economic strength because PPP takes into account the relative cost of local goods, services, and inflation rates of the country, rather than using international market exchange rates that may distort the real differences in per capita income (Table 2.1).

However, in terms of nominal GDP, India's national income was worth $2,940,428 million for 2021, according to the projections of the IMF's World Economic Outlook for October, 2021.

TABLE 2.1 GDP Ranking of Top 10 Nations (2023)

In Terms of Nominal GDP			In Terms of PPP		
Ranking	Country	Millions of International Dollars	Ranking	Country	Millions of International Dollars
1	The United States	26,949,643	1	China	32,897,929
2	China	17,963,171	2	The United States	26,949,643
3	Japan	6,272,363	**3**	**India**	**13,119,622**
4	Germany	4,429,838	4	Japan	6,495,214
5	India	3,732,224	5	Germany	5,537,992
6	**The United Kingdom**	**3,332,059**	6	Russia	5,326,855
7	France	3,049,016	7	Indonesia	4,393,370
8	Brazil	2,616,157	8	Brazil	4,101,022
9	Italy	2,408,655	9	The United Kingdom	3,871,790
10	Russia	2,288,428	10	France	3,868,619

Source: World Economic Outlook, IMF, October, 2023

Sectoral Change in National Income

Poorer the nation, higher is the share of agriculture sector in GDP and richer the nation, higher is the share of services sector in GDP.[3] It simply suggests that in the development process, the share of agriculture falls and that of industry and services rises. For example, in 1950–1951, agriculture was a dominant sector in the Indian economy and accounted for 53.1% of GDP. The share of industry and services was 16.6 and 30.3%, respectively. After independence and with the start of planning process, the share of agriculture declined and that of industry and services increased. In 1980–1981, the services sector with a share of 38% out surpassed agriculture sector (whose share was 36.1%) and became the largest contributor in India's GDP. The industry

*For detailed discussion on Purchasing Power parity, please refer to Chapter 19, Balance of payment, Foreign Investment and Exchange Rate System.

remained at the third slot with 25.9% share. After 1980, there was a clear and significant compositional shift in favor of services sector. From Table 2.2, the following observations can be made with regard to sectoral changes in national income.

1. The post-reform period witnessed decrease in the sectoral share of agriculture and increase in sectoral share of both industry and services.
2. Despite increase in the share of manufacturing, this sub-sector of industry has failed to grow up to desired limits and is a cause of concern both for robust economic growth and for increasing ample economic opportunities.
3. The financing, insurance, real estate, and business services constitute the largest share among the services.

TABLE 2.2 Sectoral Contribution in GDP (in%)

	Share in GDP 2004–2005 Prices			Share in GVA 2011–2012 Prices	
Activity	1950–1951	1980–1981	2000–2001	2019–20	2023–24 (Second Advanced Estimates)
1. Agriculture, forestry, and fishing	53.1	36.1	22.3	14.64	14.07
2. Industry	16.6	25.9	27.3	30.2	30.82
a. Mining and quarrying	1.9	2.6	3	2.67	2.15
b. Manufacturing	9.2	14.1	15.5	17.42	17.17
c. Electricity, gas, and water supply	0.3	1.5	2.2	2.32	2.36
d. Construction	5.2	7.7	6.6	7.8	9.13
3. Services	30.3	38	50.4	55.2	54.73
a. Trade, hotels, transport, Communications and services related to broadcasting	11.3	16.9	21.6	19.38	18.68
b. Financing, real estate, and professional services	8.5	8.2	14.1	21.92	23.28
c. Public administration, defense, and other services	10.4	12.9	14.7	13.86	12.77

Source: Economic survey for many years

Steep Increase in Per Capita National Income

Per capita national income is total national income divided by total population of the country. By allocating total production to each head of population, shows the extent to which the total production of a country can be shared by its population. The growth in real GDP per capita indicates the pace of income growth per head of the population. As a single composite indicator, it is a powerful summary indicator of economic development.[4] In 1950–1951, India's per capita national income at 2004–2005 prices was ₹7,513 and has risen to ₹1,06,134 in 2023–2024 at 2011–2012 prices. The per capita income at current prices for the year 2023–24 is reported to be 1,83,236 as per advanced estimates. The growth rate of per capita income during 1951–1980 was below 2% and picked up after 1980s. During 1980s and 1990s, the per capita income growth crossed 3%

mark but remained modest comparing to the growth rate of many Southeast Asian economies. However, the impact of economic reform placed Indian economy in the higher growth trajectory as the country's per capita income experienced more than 5% growth rate after 2000–2001.

Fast Growing Economy

The poorest countries tend to have the lowest growth; the wealthiest next; the middle-income countries highest. Angola's total GDP growth fell from 4.8 in the 1960s to –9.2 in the 1970s; and that of Iran's fell from 11.3 to 2.5, comparing the same two periods. However, the per capita income of four East Asian countries "miracles" of South Korea, Taiwan, Hong Kong, and Singapore grew at a rate of 7.0%, 6.5%, 6.8%, and 7.5%, respectively, during 1960–1980.[5] However, the matured economies of the United States, Japan, the United Kingdom, Germany, and France are growing at a rate of less than 2%. The lower growth rate of India's GDP during 1960–1980 too explains the above phenomenon. The historical evolution of all the major economies of the world reveals that growth rate accelerates during the first stage of development process, eventually peaks and then starts falling. The counties that are ranked high in per capita income experienced lower growth rate and vice versa, whereas the middle income and fast emerging economies are somewhere in the center. In 2024 and 2025, emerging and developing economies are projected to grow at the rate of 4.1 and 4.2% respectively (in terms of real GDP), whereas the advanced economies will grow at the rate of 1.5 and 1.8% respectively during the same period. The real GDP growth of the world is projected to be 3.1 and 3.2% respectively for the year 2024 and 2025.[6]

During the pre-reform period, the share of agriculture and allied activities in India, has declined considerably from 53.1% in 1950–1951 to 36.1 in 1980–1981. The launching of reforms and adoption of LPG policies after the economic crisis of 1991 paved the way for good economic outcomes and higher GDP growth rates. During the eighth five-year plan (1992–1997), ninth five-year plan (1997–2002) and 10th five-year plan (2002–2007), the growth rate of economy was 6.7, 5.3, and 7.6%, respectively. The economy witnessed rapid strides in growth rate during 2004–2005 to 2009–2010 due to conducive economic policies and economic boom worldwide. The average growth rate during this time was above 8% but the expansion dwindled in the aftermath of global financial crisis and Euro Zone crisis. The country was again set to recovery path since 2013–2014 and emerged as the fastest growing economy (at the growth rate of 7.6%) in the world outpacing China during 2015–2016. As per IMF projections Indian economy will grow at 7.6% (fastest in the major economies) during the financial year 2024–25.[7]

Trends of National Income in India

1951–1980: The Phase of Modest Growth Rate

The growth rate of India's national income during the first five-year plan (1951–1956) was quite encouraging as the actual growth (4.6%) was greater than that of desired growth (2.1%). But the progress in national income could not be sustained in the subsequent plans and realized growth was less than the targeted growth during second, third, and fourth five-year plan, respectively. The country experienced a sluggish growth rate during the first three decades after independence that largely covered first four five-year plans. Professor Raj Krishna, coined the term "Hindu rate of growth" in 1978 to characterize the slow growth and to explain it against the backdrop of socialistic economic policies.[8] The term refers to the low annual growth rate of the planned economy of India, which stagnated around 3.5 per cent during 1950s to 1980s, while per capita income growth averaged 1.3%. It was only during sixth five-year plan (1980–1985) and later plans that India was able to break the jinx of Hindu Rate of Growth. No five-year plan before 1980 witnessed growth rate of above 5%.

1980–90: The Phase of Economic Buoyancy and Recovery

The decade of 1980s covered sixth and seventh five-year plans and during these plans country attained growth rate of 5.3 and 5.8%, respectively. Three reasons can be attributed to higher growth in 1980s as compared to the decade of 1970s. First, higher government expenditure (mainly via deficit financing) provided a much required fiscal stimulus to the economy. Second, liberalized import policies of the government increased imports of capital goods and raw materials for manufacturing that provided boost to the production of luxury articles. However during early 1990s, the country fell into crisis due to internal and external imbalances.* During 1990–1992, the country also abandoned its regular five-year planning and declared plan holiday.

1992 Onwards: Post-Reform Period

During the eighth plan period, that is, from 1992–1997, the national income growth was 6.5% as compared to the target of 5.6%. The major reason of high growth rate in eighth plan was acceleration in the inflow of foreign capital, which is the direct fallout of new economic policy of 1991.[9] However, the growth rate dipped in the ninth five-year plan (1997–2002) to 5.4%, mainly, on account of failure of manufacturing and agriculture sectors. Both manufacturing and agriculture registered a modest growth rate of 3.3 and 2.5%, respectively. The 10th plan (2002–2007) witnessed a great turnaround with 7.6% growth rate and major reason for this reversal was accelerated growth of services, construction, and manufacturing sectors. In fact, during 2002–2003 to 2006–2007, India recorded GDP growth rate of 8.6%, making it world's second fastest growing economy after China. This emboldened the government to set an economic growth target of 9% during 11th five-year plan (2007–2012). However, the actual growth rate was around 7.8%, despite the double impact of global financial crisis and euro zone crisis. The target growth rate for 12th five-year plan (2012–2017) was 8% but the actual growth rate was 6.8%. India's GDP growth has averaged 7.3% for the period from 2014–2015 to 2017–2018, which is the highest among the major economies of the world. The growth was around 4 percentage points higher than global growth average of during 2018–19 to 2019–20 and nearly 3 percentage points more than the average growth achieved by emerging market and developing economies.[10] The economy suffered a setback during covid pandemic as growth rate turned negative and recorded –7.3% GDP growth. However the economy recovered the very next year and recorded 7.2% growth rate. The projected growth rate by IMF for India is 7.6% for the year 2024 and with this figure, India will be the fastest growing major economy of the world surpassing china which is projected to grow at 4.6% in 2024.

State Domestic Product: Features and Trends

There is variation in growth performance across states in both periods, with some states growing faster than others, but the degree of dispersion in growth rates increased very significantly in the 1990s. During the decade of 1980s the 14 largest states of India grew at the rate of 5.24% and during 1990s the growth rate marginally increased to 5.9%. At that time national income grew at the rate of 5.47 and 6.50%, respectively.[11] During the first decades of 2000s, the growth rate accelerated very fast and few laggard states like Bihar, Chhattisgarh, Odisha, and Madhya Pradesh did exceptionally

---

* For details, kindly see Chapter 29, Economic Reforms and Globalization.

TABLE 2.3 State-wise Income Profile 2022–23 at Constant Prices

States/UTs	Per Capita Net State Domestic Product at Factor Cost (Constant Prices)	States/UTs	Per Capita Net State Domestic Product at Factor Cost (Constant Prices)
Andaman and Nicobar Islands	163138	Maharashtra	138490
Andhra Pradesh	123526	Manipur	49602
Arunachal Pradesh	111776	Meghalaya	65114
Assam	69826	Mizoram	129785
Bihar	31280	Nagaland	70020
Chandigarh	219778	Odisha	87361
Chhattisgarh	83511	Puducherry	155246
Delhi	271019	Punjab	123614
Goa	310201	Rajasthan	86134
Gujarat	170384	Sikkim	259938
Haryana	181961	Tamil Nadu	166727
Himachal Pradesh	152376	Telangana	169006
Jammu and Kashmir	77891	Tripura	91853
Jharkhand	60033	Uttar Pradesh	47066
Karnataka	176383	Uttarakhand	158245
Kerala	148810	West Bengal	75561
Madhya Pradesh	65023		

Source: Handbook of Statistics on Indian States, 2022–23
*The data for Underlined states is for the year 2021–22.

well. During Period 2012–19, Mizoram has the highest average growth rate of 12.56%, followed by Tripura (9.94%), and Gujarat (9.83%). Six states/UTs grew by an average of above 8 percent per year between fiscals 2013 and 2019. Sixteen states have grown faster than India's average 6.95 percent at constant prices. The five slowest growing states are Meghalaya (3.17%), Puducherry (4.69%), West Bengal (5.16%), Nagaland (5.46%), and Goa (5.48%). At constant 2011–12 prices, Mizoram has attained the highest GSDP growth rate of 14.07%, followed by Bihar(10.47%) among 23 Indian states and union territories data available for 2019–20.[12] It can be seen from Table 2.3 that Goa, Sikkim, and Haryana are the richest states in India in terms of per capita income. Bihar, Uttar Pradesh, and Manipur are the three poorest states in India.

Savings and Capital Formation in India

When a substantial part of national income is saved and invested, it leads to general increase in production of goods and services, and capital enrichment, and creates a sound base for overall development and progress of the economy. Let us have a brief discussion on domestic savings and capital formation.

Domestic Saving

Total domestic saving is measured as the excess of national income over consumption and taxes. National disposable income can be divided into two parts: (i) consumption and (ii) savings.

Saving is that part of national disposable income, which is not spent on consumption. Thus, income is identically equal to consumption plus savings.

Thus, Saving = Disposable Income – Consumption Expenditure

The rate of saving or saving rate is expressed as a percentage of GDP at market price. This can be measured as follows:

$$\text{Rate of Saving} = \frac{\text{Gross Domestic Savings}}{\text{Gross Domestic Product}} \times 100$$

Gross Domestic Saving consists of savings of household sector, private corporate sector, and public sector. The household sector contributed nearly 74% of total nation's savings during 1950–1951 and its share went up to 91% during 1990–1991. The unnecessary policy of control and regulations during pre-reform period impacted private sector growth and productivity and consequently the share of private corporate savings declined during the first two decades after independence. The share of private corporate sector increased from 6.8% during 1950–1951 to 12% during 1990–1991. However, the post-reform period witnessed decline in the share of household sector and increase in the share of private sector. The impact of new economic policies is clear indicator of the fact that the policies of liberalization, privatization, and globalization have increased private sector activity tremendously. The share of public sector savings has also become negligible over the period of time and declined from 18.9% during 1950–1951 to 4.9% in 2018–19 (Table 2.4).

The saving rate (which is measured in terms of GDP) of the country has increased from 9.5 of GDP during 1950–1951 to 22.9% during 1990–1991. The saving rate peaked at 36.8% during 2007–2008 but declined thereafter. During 2021–22 and 2022–23, the saving rate was reported to be 32.5% for both the years. The share of household, private and government sector in the gross domestic savings is 62.5, 33.97 and 3.53 percent respectively during 2019–20. However, the sectoral saving rates had some unprecedented outcomes during 2020–21 due to covid outbreak. The government savings turned negative due to over spending during 2020–21. The saving rate forecast for 2020–21 and 2021–22 is 27.1 and 27.2%, respectively.[13]

TABLE 2.4 Sectoral Share of Gross Domestic Savings

Year	Household Sector	Private Corporate Sector	Public Sector
1950–1951	74.3	6.8	18.9
1970–1971	91.0	5.4	3.6
1990–1991	84.0	12.0	4.0
2010–2011	68.7	23.6	7.7
2018–2019	60.3	34.7	4.9
2019–2020	62.5	33.97	3.53
2020–2021	78.5	35.52	−14.02

Source: Economic Survey, 2022–23.

Reasons for Low Savings in India

1. **Lower level of per capita income:** In India around 29% of population is below poverty line and equal proportion of population is marginally above poverty line. The low per capita income signifies low level of disposable income, which, in turn, discourages savings.
2. **Poor banking habits:** India has second largest unbanked population in the world. Schemes like Jan Dhan Yojana and demonetization encouraged opening up of bank

accounts and therefore, the number of people with bank accounts grew from 53% in 2014 to 80% in 2017. In 2017, 191 million Indians did not have bank account in India, that is, one in every five Indians did not have a bank account.[14]

3. **Increase in unproductive expenditure:** The post-reform period in India has led to increase in conspicuous consumption. The consumerism and demonstration effect has enhanced consumption patterns in the country while discouraging savings.
4. **Low private corporate-sector savings:** The private sector was subject to multiple controls and regulations and was not allowed to grow during pre-reform period. However, the post-reform period has witnessed a spectacular growth in private sector share in savings. In many developed countries like the United States, the United Kingdom, Germany, and France, the share of private corporate sector is as high as 80% of domestic savings. The household and government sectors contribute a minuscule share in overall savings. The trends in India with regard to increasing share of private corporate sector and that of decreasing share of household sector in overall savings are in line with the experience of developed world and augurs well for the future growth and development of the nation.
5. **Low public-sector savings:** The public sector in India during the pre-reform phase was characterized by wrong pricing policy, underutilization of capacity, lower productivity, and perpetual loss-making. The poor performance of public-sector enterprises and their incapability to generate savings made them handicapped and dependent on fresh budgetary allocation every year.

Capital Formation in India

The term capital formation means investment and leads to addition to physical stock or productive capacity of the economy. Capital goods are those goods that are used in the further production of goods and services. Therefore, the term Gross Domestic Capital Formation (GDCF) signifies production of more capital goods, such as machines, tools, factories, buildings, raw materials, and fuels, which are to be further used in producing more goods.

The rate of GDCF is expressed as a percentage of GDP at market price. This can be measured as follows:

$$\text{Rate of Capital Formation} = \frac{\text{Gross Domestic Capital Formation}}{\text{Gross Domestic Product}} \times 100$$

The rate of capital formation in India has witnessed a fluctuating trend. It increased from 9.3% during 1950–1951 to 26% during 1990–1991. It dipped to 24.3% during 2000–2001 and moved up further to 39% during 2011–2012. It showed a declining trend and reached at 30.7% during 2019–20.[15] The rate of GCF to GDP is 32.2% during 2022–23 as against 32.4% in the 2021–22.

Few Concerns Related to Capital Formation in India

1. **Lower GDCF as compared to newly emerged economies:** In India the rate of gross capital formation remained less for a larger period of time since independence. Many newly emerged economies like South Korea, China, Taiwan, Thailand, and Malaysia experienced more than 30% rate of GDCF much before India could do so. The higher rate of GDCF enabled these nations to make faster growth in their respective economies in very less period of time. India's investment rate reached a peak of 38% of GDP

in 2007–2008. With an incremental capital–output ratio (ICOR) of 4, it was not surprising that a high growth rate close to 9.4% was achieved. One sees a steady decline in the investment rate since then, though an exception in 2011–2012 (rate of GDCF was 39% in 2011–2012). With low investment rate, it is simply impossible to achieve a growth rate in the range of 8–9%.[16]

2. **Incremental capital-output ratio:** The ICOR is the amount of capital required to produce one unit of output. The higher the ICOR, the less efficient we are in the use of capital. The ICOR in India was 3.5% during 1950s and shot up to 6.65% during 1970s. Since then it has come down and at present it is hovering around 4%. Lower ICOR indicates that capital is being employed productively. There are some signs of improvement in domestic productivity in the post-reform period. Cross-country comparisons too indicate that ICOR has been among the lowest in India. This is especially true of the period since the 1980s onward. Various reform measures aimed at increasing the competitiveness appear to be having the desired impact on the productivity of the Indian economy.[17]

Suggestions to Raise Capital Formation in India

Following suggestions are made to increase GDCF in India:

1. **Increase in Savings:** Indian economic growth has been largely enabled by the availability of domestic savings. The continuous acceleration of its growth over the decades has been accompanied by a sustained increase in the level of domestic savings, expressed as a proportion of GDP. But for last few years gross domestic saving rate has fallen below 30%, which is a matter of grave concern. In order to achieve 10% plus growth, we will need to encourage the continuation of growth in savings in each of the sectors: households, private corporate, public corporate, and the government.
2. **Continuance of Reforms:** To enhance GDCF, government needs to push up reforms, simplify procedures, and enlarge competition. Some significant steps have been taken in this regard in recent years such as moving forward on the GST Bill, passing of the Bankruptcy Act, and enlarging the scope of foreign direct investment. All viable-stalled projects must be brought to completion. Further government also needs to address the twin balance sheet problem. If corporate balance sheets are weak, automatically the banks' balance sheets also become weak. Really speaking, it is two sides of the same coin.[18]
3. **Conducive Monetary Policy:** It is well-known fact that cheap monetary policy incentivizes investment activity. But if there is high persistent inflation rate, then RBI needs to tighten monetary policy. Increase in interest rates then will discourage investment activity. Indian inflation, though low now by our own historical standards, is still higher than world inflation, and hence needs to be brought down further. It is only when there is a further secular reduction in inflation and inflation expectations over the medium term that Indian interest rates can approach international levels on a consistent basis. Hence, it is necessary for us to improve our understanding of the structure of inflation in India: how much can be done by monetary policy and how much through other actions in the real economy so that leads and lags in supply and demand in critical sectors can be removed, particularly in infrastructure.[19]

4. **Revitalizing the PSUs**: The policy mechanism needs to reform public sectors in such a way; they could generate more savings rather than being a burden on exchequer. The major reasons for the poor performance of PSUs were longer gestation period than expected, underutilization of installed capacity and poor efficiency. Government initiated plethora of reforms for the improvement of efficacy in PSUs during post-reform period. Although the number of loss making units has decreased and net profit of PSEs has increased, the reform process must continue so that PSUs could generate large surplus to be utilized for future investment.

Impact of COVID-19 on Indian Economy

The impact of coronavirus pandemic on India has been largely disruptive in terms of economic activity as well as a loss of human lives. Almost all the sectors have been adversely affected as domestic demand and exports sharply plummeted with some notable exceptions where high growth was observed. Let us have a brief discussion of impact of COVID-19 on Indian Economy.

Impact on Sectoral Growth Rate

As per economic survey 2021–22 GDP during the financial year 2020–21, contracted by 6.2 %. It is the most severe contraction from the time India got its independence. The reasons behind this trajectory are obvious – lockdown leading to the closing of business units, increasing unemployment rate and a significant decline in domestic consumption. For the financial year 2021–22, the Government has anticipated growth of 9.2 %. But the rating agencies across the globe have downgraded it due to the impact of the second wave of COVID-19. Moody's initially projected 13.7 % of growth for FY 2021–22, but later lowered it to 9.3 %. The same goes with S&P Global Rating. They have lowered the 11 % growth to 9.8 % in case of moderate impact of the second wave, but for a worst-case scenario, it would be 8.2 %. The ideas around new covid variants are not helping the situation at all.[20] Let us discuss the sectoral impact of COVID-19 on Indian Economy.

Agriculture

In the first wave, the country went through a prolonged national lockdown and a significantly lower number of peak cases. Agriculture further benefited from good monsoon and cheaper and higher availability of labor. Reflecting on the GDP figures, our agricultural economy grew by 3.4% while the overall economy contracted with –6.2% in FY21. The second wave had seen stricter and there were longer lockdowns in the rural parts of the country. Due to the lockdowns, APMC Mandis in Gujarat, Rajasthan, Maharashtra and other parts of the country were closed during the peak harvesting season. As farmers were not prepared for the ensuing chaos crops were left to rot in the fields. It also adversely hit the vegetable vendors, processing industries and other industries. *Despite covid pandemic, the agriculture sector has experienced buoyant growth in the past two years. The sector accounted for a sizeable 18.8 per cent (2021–22) in Gross Value Added of the country registering a growth of 3.6 per cent in 2020–21 and 3.9 per cent in 2021–22.*

BOX 2.1 Different Recession and Recovery Shapes

'V' shape recession and recovery

Under this type, the economy goes down and starts recovering after it hits the bottom. The economy suffers a sharp decline for a brief period with a clearly defined trough, followed by a strong recovery and while resembles a 'V' shape in charting. The recoveries that followed the recessions of 1920–21 and 1953 in the United States are classic examples of V-shaped recoveries.

'U' shape recession and recovery

A U-shaped recovery describes a type of economic recession that takes longer than the V shaped recovery that charts a U shape. Under this GDP, employment, and industrial output sharply decline and remain depressed typically over a period of one to two years before start recovering. The 1973-75 recession in the United States can be cited as a notable example of 'U' shaped recovery. The crisis began with the onset of oil crisis of 1973 that led to one of the worst stock market downturns in modern history, which affected all the major stock markets in the world.

W-shape recession and recovery

In this type, the economy goes down, recovers with a short period of growth, then goes down again before finally recovering, giving a "down up down up" pattern resembling letter W in charting. It is also called double-dip recession. The US economy during January to July 1980 experienced the initial recession, then entered recovery for almost a full year before dropping into a second recession in 1981 to 1982. The Euro-zone crisis of early 2010 is another example of W-shaped recovery.

L-shape recession and recovery

This is the most brutal of the different shapes of recession. When depicted as a line chart, graphs of major economic performance may visually resemble the shape of the letter "L" during this period. Under this the economy undergoes a severe recession and does not return to trend line growth for many years. The classic example of an L-shaped recession occurred in Japan following the bursting of the Japanese asset price bubble in 1990. The Greek economy recession (2007–2016) is another example of L-shaped recession and recovery.

K- shape recession and recovery

A K-shaped recession is a two-stage recession, where one part of society experiences V-shaped recession, while other parts of society experience a slower more protracted L-shaped recession pattern resembling letter K in charting. The term "K-shaped" recovery became popular in during the sharp recession in the U.S. that accompanied the COVID-19 pandemic and was used to describe the uneven economic recovery across different sectors, industries, and groups of people in the economy. Even in India many economists predicted the 'K' shape recovery of Indian Economy.

Source: Shape of a recession, New York Times, 11 January 2009; What shape is your recession? FP. October 12, 2010.

Manufacturing

The manufacturing sector contracted with –7.2% growth rate during the pandemic times. In manufacturing, some of the most affected industries have been metals and chemical products, motor vehicles, machinery and equipment, textiles, etc. Almost exclusively supplying to other

TABLE 2.5 Impact on GDP Growth

Time Period	Agriculture GDP Growth	Manufacturing GDP Growth	Services GDP Growth	Overall GDP Growth
2020–21 (Indicating the impact of First wave)	3.6%	–7.2%	–8.4%	–6.2%
2021–22 Impact of Second wave	Lower than wave- I	Lower than wave-I	Significantly lower than wave-I	8.2% to 9.3% (Overall growth due to base effect but reduced forecast by rating agencies)

Source: Economic Survey 2020–21, RBI Monthly Bulletins: March 2021, April 2021, May 2021.

industries, the MSME (Micro, Small and Medium Enterprises) sector is labour-intensive and the lifeline of India's manufacturing sector. Production cuts in the manufacturing sector have had a percolating negative impact on the component industries, predominantly suspending operations of MSMEs engaged in the small and spare parts manufacturing.[21] The pharmaceutical industry has been on the rise since the start of the COVID-19 pandemic, especially in India, the largest producer of generic drugs globally. With a market size of $55 billion during the beginning of 2020, it has been surging in India, exporting Hydroxychloroquine and other drugs to the world, esp. to the US, UK, Canada, and the Middle East.[22]

Services

The services sector was the hardest hit and experienced negative 8.4% growth rate during the first wave, but it is expected to be the least hit from wave 2 from an output standpoint. Global COVID-19 curbs restricted international demand for Indian services. The contribution of the Aviation Sector and Tourism to our GDP stands at about 2.4% and 9.2% respectively. The Tourism sector served approximately 43 million people in FY 18–19. Aviation and Tourism were the first industries that were hit significantly by the pandemic. The common consensus seems to be that COVID will hit these industries harder than 9/11 and the Financial Crisis of 2008. These two industries have been dealing with severe cash flow issues since the start of the pandemic and are staring at a potential 38 million layoffs, which translates to 70 per cent of the total workforce. The impact is going to fall on both, white as well as blue-collar jobs. The first wave required a steep learning curve for the organizations to develop infrastructure and processes for remote working. For the employees, first wave lockdowns were a new paradigm, and it took them some time to adjust to work from home and be productive. Prolonged lockdown and unlocking phases during the first wave ensured that both the employer and employee got into a rhythm and the productivity started reaching pre-COVID levels.[23]

Impact on Employment

The strict nationwide lockdown to contain the virus spread had led to widespread unemployment in the country. The lockdown had not only impacted gig workers, but many white-collar jobs were also lost, especially in sectors like aviation, tourism, travel and hospitality. Household incomes fell sharply as a result of jobs losses and subsequently led to a critical demand crisis. While some jobs have been restored, India's employment level is far from what it used to be before the pandemic in 2020.[24]

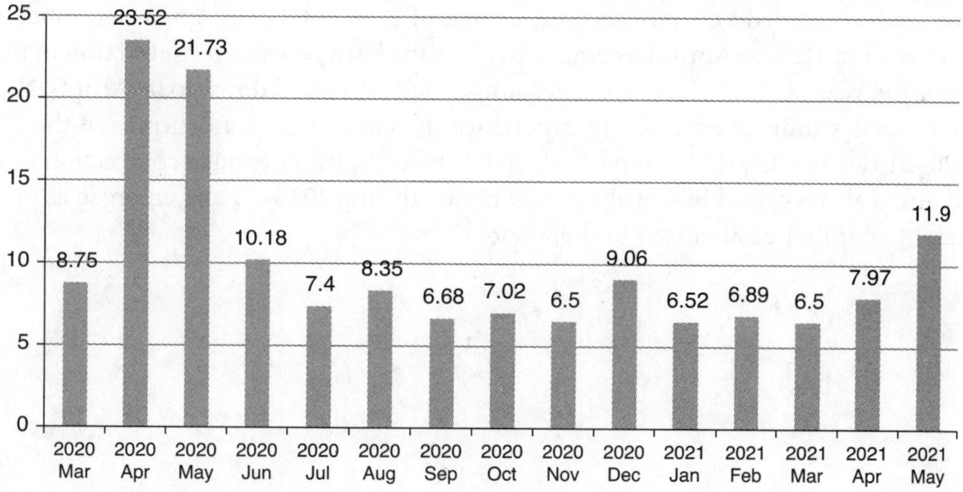

FIGURE 2.1 Unemployment Rate in India

Source: CMIE, Unemployment Rate in India

Experts said that the CMIE data indicated improvement in the unemployment scenario from July 2020 onwards, but there is a need for consistency which would only come after an increase in buoyancy in the manufacturing and services sectors.[25]

Impact on Poverty

A new Pew Research Center analysis finds that the middle class in India is estimated to have shrunk by 32 million in 2020 as a consequence of the downturn, compared with the number it may have reached absent the pandemic. This accounts for 60% of the global retreat in the number of people in the middle-income tier. Meanwhile, the number of people who are poor in India is estimated to have increased by 75 million because of the COVID-19 recession. This, too, accounts for nearly 60% of the global increase in poverty.[26] The indicated that the first wave of the coronavirus pandemic may have doubled poverty in India. The pandemic disrupted almost all industries last year, resulting in massive job losses across the formal and informal sectors of the economy. The Pew Research categorised income levels in India — $2 or less per day (poor), $2.01 to $10 per day (low income), $10.01 to $20 per day (middle income), $20.01 to $50 per day (upper middle income) and $50 or higher (high income). It estimated that the number of poor people — with income less than $2 (₹150) or less in a day — in the country increased from 6 crores to 13.4 crores. Therefore, the number of poor people increased in India by almost 7.5 crores last year. As the economy plunged into a recession in 2020, India's vast middle-class also shrank by 3.2 crores in numbers — to 6.6 crores from the pre-pandemic level of 9.9 crores.

Impact on Trade and Balance of Payment

The cumulative value of merchandise exports during April–March 2020–21 has been estimated at $290.63 billion compared to $313.36 billion during April–March 2019–20, which is a negative growth of -7.26%, which is fairly moderate given the prevailing global situation. The merchandise trade deficit between 2019–20 and 2020–21 declined from $161.35 billion to $98.56 billion.

Moreover, India recorded a current account surplus of 1.7% of GDP in April–December 2020 as against a deficit of 1.2% in April–December 2019 on the back of a sharp contraction in the trade deficit. For the year 2019-20 the current account deficit narrowed down to 0.9% of GDP. As per advance estimates India is expected to experience the current account surplus in the financial year 2020–21 due to COVID 19 impact which has resulted into the huge contraction of import demand. India also received FDI of about $ 59 Billion during 2020–21 and emerged as one of the most sought after FDI destinations in the world.

Summary

1. National income is the sum value of all goods and services produced in a nation in a single financial year. In India national income is calculated by Central Statistical Organization (CSO) and for that it classifies Indian economy into three parts, that is, primary sector, secondary sector, and tertiary sector. There are various national income indicators that reflect nation's economic health in one way or other. For example, GDP is the aggregate of all final goods and services produced in agriculture and allied sector, industry, and services sector. GNP is more comprehensive indicator as it also takes into account net factor income from abroad and adds it into GDP. To calculate NNP or NDP we need to deduct depreciation values from GNP and GDP.
2. National income can be calculated at market price or factor cost. At market price it is inclusive of indirect taxes less subsidies. However, at factor cost it is inclusive of subsidies minus indirect taxes. National income will be called nominal national income, if it is calculated at price prevailing in that year only. If national income is calculated at base-year prices then it will be called real national income.
3. There are three methods of measuring national income in India viz. expenditure method, product method, and income method. National income with expenditure method is calculated by adding up the final consumption expenditure on the goods and services incurred by household sector, firms, and government; the final investment expenditure incurred by all the firms and government, and net exports (Exports-Imports). Under product method, the total production of all final goods and services produced in a year is added to reach an aggregate value from which the value of intermediate goods is deducted to arrive at the GDP value. Under income method, national income is the factor income earned by all the economic agents in the form of wages, profits, interest earnings, and rents.
4. India is world's third largest economy in terms of purchasing power parity index but sixth largest in terms of nominal GDP. There is sectoral change in the national income of India since independence. At present services is the largest contributor in national income followed by industry and agriculture. India's per capita income has increased at a faster pace during post-reform period. Today the country is among the fastest growing economies of the world.
5. The period from 1951–1980 is considered as the period of the modest growth rate. The growth rate of India stagnated around 3.5% during 1950s to 1980s, a phenomenon termed as Hindu rate of Growth by Professor Raj Krishna. The period between 1980 and 1990 is called the period of economic buoyancy and recovery. The post-reform period witnessed spectacular increase in India's GDP growth. India's GDP growth has averaged 7.3% for the period from 2014–2015 to 2017–2018, which is the highest among the major economies of the world.
6. Saving is that part of national disposable income, which is not spent on consumption. Thus, income is identically equal to consumption plus savings. The rate of saving or saving rate is expressed as a percentage of GDP at market price. The share of household sector, private corporate sector, and public sector in nation's total savings is 60.3, 34.7 and 4.9% respectively. There are certain reasons for low savings in India, they are lower per capita income, poor banking habits, increase in unproductive expenditure, low private corporate-sector savings, and low public-sector savings.
7. The term capital formation means investment and leads to addition to physical stock or productive capacity of the economy. The rate of GDCF is expressed as a percentage of GDP at market price. There are few concerns related with GDCF. For example, India's GDCF is low as compared to newly emerged economies. Despite a comfortable level of ICOR, growth rate cannot become high unless there is adequate rate of GDCF in the country. To increase the GDCF the policy action must focus toward raising the saving rate, push up reforms, conducive monetary policy, and increase in public sector productivity and efficiency.

Endnotes

1. Nakamura, L.I. (2006). National income accounts, Federal Reserve Bank of Philadelphia, Working paper no. 06-11, Retrieved from philadelphiafed.org (Accessed on March 12, 2017).
2. Merwin, R. (2017, March 6). *All you want to know about GVA*. The Hindu Business Line.
3. Echevarria, C. (1997). Changes in sectoral composition associated with economic growth. *International Economic Review, 38*(2), 431–452.
4. Growth and Development. Retrieved from www.un.org (Accessed on June 30, 2017).
5. Lucas, R.E. JR. (1988). *On the mechanics of economic development*. Journal of Monetary Economics, 22, 3–42.
6. IMF (Jan 2024).*World Economic Outlook,* IMF. Retrieved from http://www.imf.org (Accessed on Feb 1, 2024)
7. 'IMF raises India's FY24 growth forecast to 6.7% from 6.3%', Business Standard, Jan 30, 2024.
8. Siva, M. (June 8, 2013). The Hindu Business Line. *What's a 'Hindu' rate of growth*. Retrieved from https://premium.thehindubusinessline.com (Accessed on 16 July, 2019)
9. Jalan, B. (1993). *India's Economic Policy. Preparing for 21st Century*, Penguin. New Delhi,
10. Economic Survey, 2017–18, p.1.
11. Ahluwalia, M.S. (2005). State-level performance under economic reforms in India. Retrieved from-http://planningcommission.nic.in (Accessed on December 22, 2018)
12. Economic Survey 2020–21, Volume 2, A-18.
13. RBI (2020). *Survey of Professional Forecasters on Macroeconomic Indicators– Results of the 64th Round.* Retrieved from www.rbi.org (Accessed on April 9, 2021)
14. India has second largest unbanked population in the world, *The Times of India*, June 15, 2018.
15. Survey of Professional Forecasters on Macroeconomic Indicators - Results of the 64th Round. Retrieved from www.rbi.org (Accessed on April 9, 2021).
16. Rangarajan, C. (2017, April 3). *Sharpen the focus on growth*. The Hindu.
17. Mohan, R. *The growth record of the Indian economy, 1950–2008: A story of sustained savings and investment*. Retrieved from https://www.rbi.org. (Accessed on March 15, 2018)
18. Rangarajan, C. (2017, April 3). *Sharpen the focus on growth*. The Hindu.
19. Mohan, R. The growth record of the Indian economy, 1950–2008: A story of sustained savings and investment. Retrieved from https://www.rbi.org (Accessed on March 15, 2018).
20. Impact on Indian economy after the COVID-19 second wave. Financial Express, June 21, 2021.
21. The Impact of COVID-19 on India's Manufacturing Sector, The Wire, 10 May 2021.
22. Impact of Covid-19 on Indian economy, The Times of India, October 4, 2020.
23. Impact of Covid-19 on Indian economy, The Times of India, October 4, 2020.
24. India Today, 12 April 2021.
25. Business Standard, March 24, 2021.
26. In the pandemic, India's middle class shrinks and poverty spreads while China sees smaller changes, retrieved from https://www.pewresearch.org (Accessed on 26 June 2021)

CHAPTER 3

Human Development and Happiness Economics

What can be added to the happiness of the man who is in health, who is out of debt, and has a clear conscience?

—Adam Smith

Introduction

The concept of human development has become popular in recent years among those seeking an alternative to Gross Domestic Product (GDP) per capita as a measure of the quality of life. The national income figures or growth figures, though useful do not reveal the composition of income or the real beneficiaries and people often value achievements that remain obscured in the growth figures. The difference between economic growth and human development is that the former focuses exclusively on the expansion of only one choice, that is, income while the latter concentrates on all human choices whether economic, social, cultural, or political. Of course, people also want higher incomes as one of their options but it is not the sum total of their lives. It is a means, not an end. Well-being of a society depends on the uses to which income is put, not on the level of income itself. For example, Saudi Arabia has a per capita income five times that of Sri Lanka but a much lower literacy rate. IMR in Brazil is four times higher than that in Jamaica though Brazil has double the per capita income. Oman has three times the per capita income of Costa-Rica but about one-third its literacy rate and 7 less years of life expectancy. Life expectancy of black males in harbor in New York City is lower than that in Bangladesh or Sudan. Such examples remind us that the end of development must be human well-being because people are the real wealth of a nation.

The following topics will be covered in this chapter:

- HDI and Its Calculation
- Difference Between HDI and GNP as a Measure of Development
- Inequality Adjusted Human Development Index
- Gender Empowerment Index
- Multi-dimensional Poverty Index
- Happiness Index and Its Critical Evaluation

Human Development

Human development is a process of enlarging people's choices. In principle these choices can be infinite and change over time. But at all levels of development, the three essential ones are for people to lead a long and healthy life, to acquire knowledge, and to have access to resources needed for a decent standard of living. If these essential choices are not available, many other opportunities remain inaccessible. The term human development thus denotes both the process of widening people's choices and the level of their achieved well-being. It also helps to distinguish clearly between two sides of human development. One is the formation of human capabilities, such as improved health or knowledge. The other is the use that people make of their acquired capabilities, for work or leisure.[1] Over the years, efforts have been made to measure human development using different indices. Let us discuss them one by one.

Human Development Index

The search for a comprehensive measure that could capture the various dimensions of development led to the definition and formation of Human Development Index (HDI) by the United Nations Development Programme (UNDP) in its Human Development Report (HDR) published in 1990. The report was first launched in 1990 by the world-renowned Pakistani Economist Mahbub ul Haq (project director of the report), Indian Nobel laureate Amartya Sen, and few other noted economists of the world.

The HDI captures the three essential components of human life—longevity, knowledge, and basic income, for a decent living standard.

- A long and healthy life: life expectancy at birth;
- Access to knowledge: mean years of schooling and expected years of schooling;
- A decent standard of living: GNI per capita (PPP US$).

HDR 2014 introduced four cut-off points for the countries vis-à-vis their achievements in human development (Table 3.1).

Out of 7.4 billion people in the world, around one-third live in low human development condition. A total of 22% of such deprived human beings live in very high and high human development countries, whereas, 45% live in medium human development countries and 33% in low human development countries.[2]

How Is HDI Calculated?

The HDI is the geometric mean of normalized indices measuring achievements in each dimension. Prior to HDR 2010, simple arithmetic mean of the three dimension indices is used to be taken. There are two steps to calculate HDI.

TABLE 3.1 Categories of Human Development

Country/Group	Index Value
Very high human development	0.800 and above
High human development	0.700–0.799
Medium human development	0.550–0.699
Low human development	Below 0.550

Source: HDR, Statistical updates, 2018, p.3.

Step 1: The first step of calculating the HDI is to create three separate indices for each of the three dimensions, that is, long and healthy life, knowledge, and standard of living.

Step 2: The geometric mean of these three indices is calculated to get global HDI.*

Long and healthy life: The long and healthy life dimension uses life expectancy at birth as its indicator. The life expectancy index is calculated using a minimum value of 20 years and a maximum value of 85 years. These maximum and minimum values are fixed goalposts adopted in the 2014 HDR. The minimum value for life expectancy (20 years) is based on long-run historical evidence, which shows that if a society or a sub-group of society has a life expectancy below the typical age of reproduction, then that society would fail to reproduce itself. The minimum level of 20 years is, therefore, the life expectancy needed for society to survive.[3] The maximum value is fixed at 85 years, as that can be interpreted as an aspirational goal for societies.[4]

Knowledge: The education component of the HDI is measured by two indicators: mean years of schooling for adults aged 25 years and older and the expected years of schooling for children of school entering age. Mean years of schooling simply mean duration of schooling at each level of education. Expected years of schooling estimates are based on two factors: enrolment by age at all levels of education and the number of children of school age in the population for each level of education. The two indicators are first normalized using a minimum value of 0 and maximum value of 15 for mean years of schooling and 18 for expected years of schooling. As societies can exist without formal education, the minimum value of 0 years is used for both education variables. The maximum values were set to aspirational fixed goalposts in the 2014 HDR. Both indicators are then combined to produce an education index with the help of arithmetic mean.

Decent standard of living: The decent standard of living component is measured on the basis of income, and the income is measured using the natural logarithm of Gross National Income (GNI) per capita adjusted by purchasing power parity (PPP). In a globalized world, differences are often large between the income of a country's residents and its domestic production. Some of the income residents' earn are sent abroad, some residents receive international remittances, and some countries receive sizeable aid flows. For example, because of large remittances from abroad, GNI of India greatly exceeds GDP. For this component, the minimum value is PPP \$100, this low value is set on the basis of low income level of subsistence economies which is not captured in the official data. The maximum value is set at PPP \$75,000 and it is believed that above this income level there is virtually no gain in human development and well-being (Table 3.2).[5]

Having defined the minimum and maximum values, the sub-indices are calculated as follows:

$$\text{Dimension index} = \frac{\text{Actual value} - \text{Minimum value}}{\text{Maximum value} - \text{Minimum value}}$$

*Since 2010, geometric mean instead of arithmetic mean is being used to compute HDI. It is because poor performance in any dimension is directly reflected in the geometric mean. Further, the geometric mean also reduces the level of substitutability between dimensions and at the same time ensures that a 1% decline in the index of, say, life expectancy has the same impact on the HDI as a 1% decline in the education or income index.

TABLE 3.2 Goalposts for Calculating the HDI

Dimension	Indicator	Observed Maximum	Minimum
Health	Life expectancy (years)	85	20
Education	Mean years of schooling	15	0
	Expected years of schooling	18	0
Standard of living	Per capita income (PPP 2011 $)	$75,000	$100

Source: UNDP (2014), Technical Note 1. p.2.

The HDI is the geometric mean of the three dimension indices. Let us take the example of India to understand how HDI is calculated for all countries (Table 3.3).

Calculation of Dimension Indices

- Life expectancy index $= \dfrac{68.8-20}{85-20} = 0.751$

  Mean years of schooling index $= \dfrac{6.4-0}{15-0} = 0.427$

- Expected years of schooling index $= \dfrac{12.3-0}{18-0} = 0.683$
- Education index $= \dfrac{0.427+0.688}{2} = 0.556$
- Income index $= \dfrac{In(6{,}353) - In(100)}{In(75{,}000) - In(100)} = 0.627$
- Human development index $= \sqrt[3]{0.751 \times 0.556 \times 0.627} = 0.640$

India's HDI value for 2022 as per HDR 2023–24 was 0.644 and its rank was 134 out of 193 countries (Table 3.4).

India's HDI value for 2022 was 0.644—which put the country in the medium human development category. Between 1990 and 2022, India's HDI value increased from 0.427 to 0.644, an increase of 51.1% (Table 3.5). All the dimensions of HDI for India have increased since 1990, which is a positive sign in terms of human development achievements as India has moved up the scale from a low human development country to medium human development country. But

TABLE 3.3 Dimensions for India

Dimension	Value
Life expectancy	67.7
Mean years of schooling	6.57
Expected years of schooling	12.6
Per capita income (PPP$)	$6,951
HDI value	0.644

Source: Calculation by author, data taken from UNDP website.

TABLE 3.4 Some Key HDI Statistics 2022 data as Per HDR 2023–24

Country	HDI Value for 2019	Rank for 2019
India	0.644	134
Best performer in the world (Switzerland)	0.967	1
Worst performer in the world (Somalia)	0.380	193
World average	0.739	

Source: HDR Statistical updates, 2023, UNDP.

TABLE 3.5 India's HDI Trends

Year	Life Expectancy at Birth	Expected Years of Schooling	Mean Years of Schooling	GNI Per Capita (2011 $)	HDI Value
1990	57.9	7.6	3.0	1,733	0.427
1995	60.4	8.2	3.5	2,015	0.460
2000	62.6	8.3	4.4	2,470	0.493
2005	64.6	9.7	4.8	3,157	0.535
2010	66.6	10.8	5.4	4,357	0.581
2015	68.3	12.0	6.3	5,691	0.627
2016	68.6	12.3	6.4	6,026	0.636
2017	68.8	12.3	6.4	6,353	0.640
2019	69.7	12.2	6.5	6,681	0.645
2022	67.7	12.6	6.6	6,951	0.644

Source: HDR Report for various years.

India's HDI value of 0.644 is below than that of world average of 0.739, which indicates India's deprivation in comparison to other countries of the world.

Why the Concept of HDI Is superior to GNP?

HDI does not replace GNP but is the extension of later. It is superior to the GNP on the following grounds.

First, GNP is a single dimension as it takes into account only growth of real output ignoring other significant dimensions of human life. Income or wealth is significant but cannot constitute a direct measure of the overall well-being. HDI on the other hand is considered as a multi-dimensional concept of development that combines health, education, and per capita income to form a composite index.[6] It has been noticed that human progress may be lacking in some societies despite rapid GNP growth or high per capita income levels unless some additional steps are taken.

Second, income is a means, not an end. It may be used for essential medicines or narcotic drugs. However, the ultimate purpose of the entire exercise of development is to treat men, women, and children-present and future generations-as ends, to improve the human conditions, to enlarge people's choices.

Third, present income of a country may offer little guidance to its future growth prospects. If it has already invested in its people, its potential income may be much higher than what its current income level shows, and vice versa. The success story of East Asian nations' viz. Singapore, Philippines, Thailand, and Cambodia is the best example to validate the above viewpoint. On the contrary, multiplying human problems in many industrial-rich nations show that high income levels, by themselves, are no guarantee for human progress.

Fourth, human development gaps between the nations are more manageable than widening income disparities. Since 1960, average life expectancy has increased by around 20 years, adult literacy by 45%, and child mortality rates have been halved. The international gaps among these indicators are closing while in case of GNP per capita it is widening. While average income per head in the less developed nations is 6% of that in the developed nations, life expectancy is 80%, literacy is 60%, and nutrition is 85%.

Last, HDI can be disaggregated by gender (women empowerment measures), ethnic group (tribal area development), or geographical region (desert or hill area development) and in many other ways to present relevant policy measures and the "danger points" of explosion. GNP does not provide for the same.

Other Human Development Indices

HDR 2010 introduced three new development indices viz. Inequality Adjusted Human Development Index (IHDI), Gender Inequality Index (GII), and Multi-dimensional Poverty Index (MPI). HDR 2014 introduced Gender Development Index (GDI).

Inequality Adjusted Human Development Index

Introduced by HDR 2010 and published by UNDP, IHDI is a measure of the average level of human development of people in a society once inequality is taken into account. It captures the HDI of the average person in society, which is less than the aggregate HDI when there is inequality in the distribution of health, education, and income. Under perfect equality, the HDI and IHDI are equal; the greater the difference between the two, the greater the inequality. IHDI for 2022 is estimated for 193 countries, capturing the losses in human development due to inequality in health, education, and income.

Generally, countries with less human development also have more multi-dimensional inequality and thus larger losses in human development due to inequality, while people in developed countries experience the least inequality in human development. Life expectancy averages 79.5 years in very high human development countries, compared with 60.8 in low human development countries. The East Asia and the Pacific Region perform well on the IHDI, particularly in access to healthcare and education, and former socialist countries in Europe and Central Asia have relatively egalitarian distributions across all three dimensions. Country wise there are vast inequalities in human development parameters. For example, life expectancy at birth (years) in Hong Kong is 84.1, whereas in Sierra Leone it is 52.2 years. Expected years of schooling (years) in Australia is 22.9, whereas it is 4.9 in South Sudan. Similarly, mean years of schooling in Germany is 14.1 but only 1.5 in Burkina Faso. The estimates of gross national income per capita for 2021 are (2011 PPP) $97,262 in Qatar but merely $1,013 in Central African Republic.[7] According to Oxfam International reports, only eight men own the same wealth as the 3.6 billion people who make up the poorest half of humanity and that "82% of all global wealth in the last year went to the top 1%, while the bottom half of humanity saw no increase at all."

India's HDI value for 2022 is 0.644 and IHDI value is 0.444. It simply means that when the value is discounted for inequality, the HDI falls to 0.444, a loss of 31.1% due to inequality in the distribution of the HDI.

The Gender Inequality Index

The GII reflects women's disadvantages in three dimensions: reproductive health, empowerment, and economic activity. It is published by UNDP and was introduced in 2010 HDR. The reproductive health is measured by maternal mortality and adolescent fertility rates; empowerment is measured by the share of parliamentary seats held by women and attainment at secondary and higher education by each gender; and economic activity is measured by the labor market participation rate for each gender. It ranges from 0, where women and men fare equally, to 1, where one gender fares as poorly as possible in all measured dimensions. India has a GII value of 0.437, ranking it 108 out of 193 countries in the 2022 index. In India, 14.6% of parliamentary seats are held by women, and 41% of adult women (% ages 25 and older) have reached at least a secondary level of education compared to 58.7% of their male counterparts. For every 100,000 live births, 103 women die from pregnancy-related causes; and the adolescent birth rate is 16.3 births per 1,000 women of ages 15–19. Female participation in the labor market is 28.3 compared to 76.1 for men.[8]

Gender Development Index

Introduced by HDR 2014 and published by UNDP, GDI is based on the sex-disaggregated HDI, and is defined as a ratio of the female to the male HDI. The GDI measures gender inequalities in achievement in three basic dimensions of human development: health (measured by female and male life expectancy at birth), education (measured by female and male expected years of schooling for children and mean years for adults aged 25 years and older), and command over economic resources (measured by female and male estimated GNI per capita). The 2022 female HDI value for India is 0.582 in contrast with 0.684 for males, resulting in a GDI value of 0.852.[9]

Multi-dimensional Poverty Index

The global MPI was first developed in 2010 by Oxford Poverty & Human Development Initiative (OPHI) and the UNDP and for the UNDP's flagship Human Development Reports. Like development, poverty is multi-dimensional—but this is traditionally ignored by headline income measures of poverty. Introduced for the first time in the 2010 HDR, the Global MPI complements monetary measures of poverty by considering overlapping deprivations suffered by individuals at the same time. The index identifies deprivations across the same three dimensions as the HDI is based on 10 indicators and shows the number of people who are multi-dimensionally poor. Health is measured with the help of two indicators: nutrition and child mortality. Education is measured with the help of two indicators: years of schooling and school attendance. Standard of living is measured with the help of six indicators: cooking fuel, sanitation, drinking water, electricity, housing and assets. If someone is deprived in 33% or more of 10 (weighted) indicators, the global index identifies them as "MPI poor," and the extent–or intensity–of their poverty is measured by the number of deprivations they are experiencing. MPI can be deconstructed by region, ethnicity, and other groupings as well as by dimension and indicator, making it a useful tool for policymakers.[10]

Global MPI is an international measure of multidimensional poverty covering many developing countries. It utilises the National Family Health Survey (NFHS) which is conducted under the aegis of Ministry of Health and Family Welfare (MoHFW) and International Institute for Population Sciences (IIPS). India is one of the 25 nations that have successfully halved their global multidimensional poverty Index values within 15 years. In India the incidence of poverty fell from 55.1% (645 million) in 2005/06 to 16.4% (230 million) in 2019/21.[11]

WORLD HAPPINESS INDEX

In fact, the roots of World Happiness Index (WHI) can be traced back to 1972, when Bhutanese King Jigme Singye Wangchuck propounded the concept of Gross National Happiness (GNH) to measure contentment and happiness. The four pillars of GNH are sustainable development, preservation and promotion of cultural values, conservation of natural environment, and establishment of good governance. The GNH concept inspired the modern political happiness movement and in July 2011, the UN General Assembly adopted a resolution by placing happiness on the global development agenda.[12] Consequently, the first World Happiness Report was released on April 1, 2012. The world happiness report is an annual publication of the Sustainable Development Solutions Network (SDSN) and the Global Happiness Council (GHC).

Six factors are used to predict happiness across the nations. These variables are levels of GDP, life expectancy, generosity, social support, freedom, and corruption. Using Gallup World Poll methodology, life-evaluation questions are asked to respondents. Respondents are asked to think of a ladder, with the best possible life for them being a 10, and the worst possible life being a 0. They are then asked to rate their own current lives on that 0–10 scale.

As per World Happiness Report, 2024, out of 143 nations which were ranked on the basis of happiness, Finland with happiness index of 7.741 ranks one and Afghanistan with 2.523 ranks last. India with index score of 4.054 was ranked at 126th position.

Importance/Merits of Happiness Index

Following are the merits of happiness index.

Useful Policy Tool

Can finding out what makes us happy as individuals help us prosper better as nations? Current advances in development thinking seem to suggest this is the case. Many governments worldwide have taken strides in this regard. After Bhutan's efforts to measure happiness through ***GNH*** in 1977, many advanced and emerging economies such as England, Brazil, and Mexico have shown keen interest in measuring well-being of their citizens. Such national efforts are also supported by policy-oriented data presentations like the OECD Better Life Index and the New Economics Foundation's Happy Planet Index. Member States are encouraged to explore options for measuring happiness and well-being with a view to guiding their public policies.

This so-called well-being perspective on development offers interesting advantages, first by directly focusing on what matters to people at the grassroots level, by emphasizing attention to local, participatory development and "direct giving." Happiness Index through its well-being perspective offers potential advantages, including insights into what matters to people directly, and a comprehensive and relatively non-judgmental view on development.[13] Second, well-being approach to development presents the potential to overcome the powerful distinction between "developed" and "developing" countries. This would be the case if a well-being lens opens space to recognize culturally specific values and development processes that reflect the respect for diversity in people's wants and needs.

An alternate to Other Measures of Development

The quest for material development, even if it leads a nation to the pinnacle of progress, will be meaningless, if the citizens remain unhappy, depressed, and discontented. In a time of economic, social, and environmental crises, it seems self-evident that we need to critically examine and complement the conventional yardsticks for development, such as GDP growth. Notwithstanding the rapid strides in GDP growth and human development levels, the few economies of the world (including India) have demonstrated the declining level of happiness. The phenomenon of rapid economic growth occurring at the time of declining levels of subjective well-being is known as the "Unhappy Growth" paradox.[14] Easterlin Paradox (formulated in 1974 by Richard Easterlin) also implies that if each individual in society becomes richer by the same degree then no individual is any better off (in subjective well-being terms) than they were prior to their income increasing.[15] In simple words, subjective well-being at the national level does not rise with income.* UN General Assembly adopting a 2011 resolution titled *Happiness: Towards a Holistic Approach to Development* states that "the pursuit of happiness is a fundamental human goal" and that "the gross domestic product indicator by nature was not designed to and does not adequately reflect the happiness and well-being of people in a country".[16]

Lifestyle Problems and Happiness

Mental illness is one of the main causes of unhappiness in the world. It produces nearly as much of the misery that exists as poverty does, and more than is caused by physical illness. According to WHO, depression is the leading cause of ill health and disability in the world with more than 300 million people worldwide have a diagnosis of depression. Treating depression should be a top priority for every government, as this would save billions because mental illness is a major block on the economy. Research suggests that depression is the main illness among people of working age. It reduces national income per head by some 5%—through non-employment, absenteeism, lowered productivity, and extra physical healthcare costs. What makes the matter worse is that, even in high-income countries, nearly 50% of people with depression do not receive treatment and drugs prescribed are often ineffective.[17] The United States offers a typical example of declining happiness because of lifestyle problems. The United States ranks 19th as per 2021 WHR (it was ranked 14th in 2016 WHR). American happiness is being undermined by three distinct health epidemics. These three epidemics are obesity, depression, and opioid addiction and all of these are mutually reinforcing. Obesity causes depression and depression can lead to obesity. Depression and substance abuse are also bi-causal.[18] The major reasons for deteriorating American social system are high income inequality, inadequate healthcare system, corporate deregulation,** and

---

*At a point in time, happiness varies directly with income both among and within nations, but over time happiness does not trend upward as income continues to grow. It is because the marginal gain in happiness begins to decrease beyond a particular point.

**For example, the obesity epidemic can be linked directly to the fast-food industry, which makes aggressive use and promotion of sugar additives and other obesogenic processed foods, and the opioid epidemic can be traced in part to the lobbying and direct marketing of major pharmaceutical companies that charge exorbitant prices despite the evidence of very limited and inadequate market competition over prices.

excessive use of the information and communications technology.* World Happiness Report 2018 states that "programs of positive psychology and wellness at schools, workplaces, and in the community can help individuals to change their own behaviours, overcome addictions, and pursue life strategies to bolster their personal well-being and the well-being of friends, family, and community. The evidence is large and growing that such life-change strategies can be highly effective."[19]

Demerits/Drawbacks of Happiness Index

Following critical points can be mentioned that disapprove relevance of Happiness Index.

It Is Not Easy to Measure Subjective Well-Being

Happiness rankings are generally based on surveys that ask questions on what most academics in the field call subjective well-being. The distinctive characteristic of subjective well-being is that it is based on how people evaluate their lives from their own perspectives. Subjective well-being is generally related to both temporary moods, as well as broader perspectives on quality of life. The difference between questions on temporary moods and those on one's broader perspective on life is, however, not always clear and many researchers tend to use them interchangeably or have an unstated preference for one rather than the other.

The Statistics Problem

To find out the concrete happiness solutions, one needs to get statistics/data that is certain, truthful, and far from prejudices. Following points can be mentioned in this regard. First, while certain governments such as those of Bhutan, Brazil, Mexico, and the United Kingdom conduct surveys on life satisfaction and thereby collect a significant amount of national data, there is not much globally comparable data available. Certain sources, such as the Gallup World Poll collects data through surveys in over 160 countries, do offer some insights into how people evaluate their own lives. However, much more research is clearly needed before moving toward international comparisons of scores on subjective well-being indicators. Second, a nation is a heterogeneous unit with diversified religious and ethnic groups. Aggregating individual scores into a single one that represents an entire nation can be problematic in the sense that it neglects the cultural diversity that exists within nations. However, culture and context are known to be key determinants of how people respond to happiness surveys and importantly on how people understand well-being.[20] It is clear from the above discussion that the most well-known application of well-being data, so-called happiness rankings, is limited in this regard. If we are to truly take the well-being lens on development seriously, we need to find ways to improve our measures of happiness and well-being and present data in a constructive manner.

Making Happiness Index More Comprehensive

Few economists argue that finding the "happiest" country is not the only or even the most relevant question to ask when we apply a well-being lens to the development debate. The goal

---

*Depressive tendencies may lead to excessive use of mobile phone/new technologies, while screen time may itself be addictive and/or linked to increased loneliness and alienation.

of policymaking should be allocating resources toward collecting more and better data, and presenting that data in a constructive manner. Happiness rankings result in a hierarchical representation of nations which does not do justice to the potential of well-being approaches to development. They are currently not based on comprehensive measurement toolkits and therefore, greatly oversimplify the complex experience of well-being. It is further argued that the question of how to make use of well-being data in such a way that it is constructive for policymaking deserves further exploration.

Beyond Happiness Index

There is currently no universal agreement on how well-being should be measured and how it should be used to guide policymaking. The debate is lively and ongoing. Some interesting alternatives to happiness approaches exist. The indigenous understanding of Buen Vivir* is an example of an alternative view on well-being, in which personal well-being is seen as inseparable from the well-being of others and of nature. The Well-being and Poverty Pathways research group at the University of Bath has developed a model of well-being which moves away from the narrow psychological and individualistic focus of happiness, and sees well-being as grounded in the wider political, cultural, and relational context.

*Etymologically, *buen vivir* means good living, which describes a way of doing things that is community-centric, ecologically balanced, and culturally sensitive. The movement advocates legal standing for the natural environment. Ecuador became the first country in the world to codify the Rights of Nature and to inform a more clarified content to those rights

Summary

1. Human development denotes both the process of widening people's choices and the level of their achieved well-being.
2. HDI was first published in 1990 by noted Pakistani economist Mahbub ul Haq, Indian Nobel laureate Amartya Sen, and other noted economists of the world. The HDI captures the three essential dimensions of human life—longevity, knowledge, and decent living standard. Longevity is measured in terms of life expectancy at birth; knowledge is measured in terms of mean years of schooling and expected years of schooling; and decent standard of living is measured in terms of GNI per capita (PPP US$). The separate indices for three dimensions are constructed and geometric means of such indices yield HDI.
3. GNP is a single-dimensional concept as it includes only income. On the contrary, HDI is multi-dimensional, which not only includes income but also other dimensions such as health and knowledge. Income is a means, not an end. High income levels, by themselves, are no guarantee for human progress. But if a nation invests in its people, its potential income may be much higher than what its current income level shows, and vice versa. Further, human development gaps between the nations are more manageable than widening income disparities. HDI can be disaggregated by gender, ethnic group, or geographical region and in many other relevant policy measures, whereas, GNP does not provide for the same. Apart from HDI, there are some other measures of development viz. IHDI, GII, GDI, MPI, and WHI.
4. IHDI measures the level of human development when inequality is accounted for. It captures the HDI of the average person in society, which is less than the aggregate HDI when there is inequality in the distribution of health, education, and income. It was introduced by HDR 2010 and is published by UNDP.
5. The GII reflects women's disadvantages in three dimensions: reproductive health, empowerment, and economic activity. The reproductive health is measured by maternal mortality and adolescent fertility rates; empowerment is measured by the share of parliamentary seats held by women and attainment at secondary and higher education by each gender; and economic activity is measured by the labor market participation rate for each gender. It was introduced by HDR 2010 and is published by UNDP.
6. Introduced in HDR 2014, the GDI measures gender inequalities in achievement in three basic dimensions of human development: health (measured by female and male life expectancy at birth), education (measured by female and male expected years of schooling for children and mean years for adults aged 25 years and older), and command over economic resources (measured by female and male estimated GNI per capita). It is published by UNDP.
7. The MPI was first developed in 2010 by OPHI and the UNDP and for the UNDP's flagship Human Development Reports. First published in HDR 2010, MPI identifies deprivations across the same three dimensions as the HDI based on 10 indicators and shows the number of people who are multi-dimensionally poor.
8. World Happiness Report was first published in 2012 and it annually constructs world Happiness Index which measures happiness among more than 150 nations on the basis of six factors viz. levels of GDP, life expectancy, generosity, social support, freedom, and corruption. It is an annual publication of the SDSN and the GHC. A useful policy tool, WHI helps governments to directly focus on what matters to people at the grassroots level, by emphasizing attention to local, participatory development, and "direct giving." It offers an alternate viewpoint on development (other than GNP and HDI) and addresses lifestyle problems like depression more effectively. It also provides a spiritual dimension to development perspective. However, happiness is a subjective phenomenon and it is not easy to measure subjective well-being. Another problem is regarding difficulty in collecting data and whatever data is collected may not be true representative for the whole nation which consists of too many heterogeneous diversified population groups. It is also argued that happiness index oversimplifies the complex experience of well-being and thus deserves further exploration. Few also contend to move beyond happiness index and construct an index which is wider in terms of political, cultural, and relational context.

Endnotes

1. UNDP. *Human Development Report 1990*, OUP, p.10.
2. Human Development. *Human Development Report 2016*. UNDP, p.53.
3. Riley, J.C. (2005). *Poverty and life expectancy*. Cambridge: Cambridge University Press.
4. UNDP. *Human Development Report, 2016*. Retrieved from http://hdr.undp.org (Accessed on December 15, 2017).
5. Kahneman, D., & Deaton, A. (2014). High income improves evaluation of life but not emotional wellbeing. Psychological and cognitive sciences. *Proceedings of National Academy of Sciences*, *107*(38), 16489–16493.
6. Anand, S., & Sen, A. (2004). The income component of the human development index. *Journal of Human Development*, *1*(1).
7. "World Economic Outlook - GDP per capita". International Monetary Fund. April 2021. Retrieved 10 April 2021.
8. HDR (2023–24) *Statistical update*, Technical Notes, p.295.
9. HDR (2023–24) *Statistical update*, Technical Notes, p.5.
10. UNDP. Human Development Reports. The 2023 Global Multidimensional Poverty Index (MPI). Retrieved from http://hdr.undp.org (Accessed on April 15, 2023).
11. Global Multidimensional Poverty Index. (2023). Retrieved from https://ophi.org.uk/multidimensional-poverty-index/ (Accessed on April 15, 2023).
12. Alkire, S. (2011). *The Gross National Happiness Index of Bhutan*. Paper Presentation, Centre of Bhutan Studies.
13. van Dijk, N., Spencer, L., Ramirez, V. (2014). *Happy country, happy government: How useful are international happiness rankings?* United Nations Research Institute for social development. Retrieved from http://www.unrisd.org/happiness. (Accessed on February 1, 2019).
14. Graham, C., & Lora, E. (Eds.), (2009). *Paradox and perception: Measuring quality of life in Latin America*. Washington, DC: The Brookings Institution Press.
15. Easterlin, R.A. (1974). Does economic growth improve the human lot? Some empirical evidence. *Nations and Households in Economic Growth*, *89*, 89–125.
16. Alkire, S. (2011). *The Gross National Happiness Index of Bhutan*. Paper Presentation, Centre of Bhutan Studies.
17. Rachel Roberts, *Independent*. Friday 31 March, 2017.
18. Sachs, J.F. (2018). *America's health crisis and the Easterlin Paradox*. WHR.
19. Sachs, J.D. (2018). *America's health crisis and the Easterlin Paradox*. WHR.
20. Christopher, J. (1999). Situating psychological well-being: Exploring the cultural roots of its theory and research. *Journal of Counseling and Development*, *77*, 141–152.

CHAPTER 4

Natural Resources, Environment, and Sustainable Development

There is no 'Plan B' because we do not have a 'Planet B.' We have to work and galvanize our action.

—Ban Ki-moon

Introduction

A resource is anything we get from the environment to meet our needs and wants. Natural resources, as conventionally understood, include all those objects and products that human labor combined with inputs of capital and enterprise, can extract from nature and make use of them to produce more goods and services. Natural resources are not static in nature; they are dynamic and keep on changing. As the process of economic development gathers momentum, the demand for natural resources increases; it becomes critical that both the urgency and temptation to exploit natural resources to the hilt for the sake of short-term gains are avoided; instead a holistic view is taken, so that the interests of the future generations are not compromised. "Sustainable development" should be the goal.

In this chapter, we will address the following issues:

- Natural Resources in India
- Sustainable Developmental and Global Concerns
- Sustainable Development and India
- Environment Degradation and Policies in India

Natural Resources in India

Natural resources are both biotic (forests and wildlife) and abiotic (water, soil, air, and minerals) in nature. Let us have an idea regarding natural resources in India.

Land

India measures 3,214 km from north to south and 2,933 km from east to west with a total land area of 32,87,782 km^2 and a coastline measuring 7,516.5 km, plus 1,197 islands. It is the seventh largest landowner in the world after Russia, Canada, China, the United States, Brazil, and Australia in that order. In brief, India is a vast country and has a considerable strategic significance on account of its location, size and economic resources (Table 4.1).

TABLE 4.1 Land Utilization in India 2013–2014

Land Use	Million Hectare	As a Percentage of Total Geographical Area
Geographical area	328.7	–
Forests	71.8	21.9
Area under non-agricultural uses	26.9	8.2
Barren and unculturable land	16.9	8.2
Not available for cultivation	43.9	13.3
Culturable wasteland	12.38	3.76
Fallow lands	24.8	7.5
Net area sown	141.4	43
Total cropped area	200.8	61.1
Area sown more than once	59.4	18.1
Agricultural land/arable land	181.8	55.3
Cultivated land	155.6	47.3

Source: Computed by author from All India level Pattern of Land Utilization From 2000–2001 to 2013–2014 retrieved from https://data.gov.in. (Accessed on April 4, 2019).

Following observations can be made with regard to land use in India:

1. India is the country of 1.35 billion people. The arable land per capita in the country is 0.14 hectares, less than world average. In the United States, arable land per capita is 0.59 hectares, whereas the world average is 0.22 hectares.
2. Forests in India constitute 71.8 million hectares of land and has increased from 14% in 1951 to 22% in 2013–2014 as a percentage of total geographical area.
3. Area under non-agricultural uses, that is, for industry and housing, and land occupied by villages, towns, roads, railways or under water, that is, rivers, lakes, canals, tanks, ponds, etc. is nearly 8.2%.
4. Barren and unculturable land area includes land covered by mountains, deserts, etc. and comprises 8.2% of total geographical area.
5. Land not available for cultivation includes forest area under non-agriculture use, barren and unculturable land. As a percentage of total geographical area, this type of land has reduced from 17% in 1950–1951 to 13.34% in 2013–2014.
6. Culturable wasteland includes land available for cultivation, whether taken up or not taken up for cultivation once, but not cultivated during the last 5 years or more in succession including the current year for some reason or the other. Such land may be either fallow or covered with shrubs and jungles which are not put to any use. Such type of land has reduced from 8% of total geographical area in 1950–1951 to 3.76% in 2013–2014. Reclamation of waste and fallow lands was relatively rapid during the 1950s due to land reform measures such as abolition of Zaminadari system and conferment of ownership rights to tenants. The dispossessed Zamindars reclaimed land which had been left to them for "personal cultivation," while their former tenants reclaimed waste and fallow lands to which they had acquired rights. The process was aided by loans and subsidies from the government.

7. Fallow land is used for farming but left uncultivated to let it recover its fertility. Fallow land is of two types viz. current fallow and fallow other than current fallow. Fallow of 1 year is called "current fallow" while that of 2–5 years is classified as "fallow other than current fallow." Fallow land is 7.55% of total land area.[1]
8. Net sown area is the proportion of the total areas of the country which is used for growing crop. In India, net sown area is around 43% of total geographical area.
9. Total cropped area is net sown area plus area sown more than once and thus constitutes 61.1% of total geographical area.
10. The "area sown more than once" is 18% of geographical area and has also shown a significant rise during the last five decades. It is because the land for non-agricultural uses is constantly increasing. Further fragmentation of land holdings and increase in irrigation cover has also contributed to this trend.
11. Arable land is land capable of ploughing and growing crops and thus is called agricultural land. It comprises 55.31% of total geographical area of the country.
12. Cultivated land is land used for growing crops. It is 47.32% of total geographical area.

Soil

The soil is the biologically active upper layer of earth and is characterized by the mixture of organic matter, minerals, gases, liquids, and organisms that together support life. Over 90% of the world's food comes from the soil and less than 10% comes from both inland water and the oceans. The cropping pattern of the country is greatly influenced by the soils and the elements of the physical environment. The Indian Council of Agricultural Research (ICAR) divides the soils found in the country into eight major groups, which are as follows:

Alluvial soils are widespread in the northern plains and the river valleys and cover around 40% of the area of the country. They are depositional soils, transported and deposited by rivers and streams. These soils are suitable for the cultivation of almost all kinds of cereals, pulses, oilseeds, cotton, sugarcane, and vegetables.

Black soils are found in Deccan Plateau which includes parts of Maharashtra, Madhya Pradesh, Gujarat, Andhra Pradesh, and some parts of Tamil Nadu. Known for their fertility, black soils give good yields despite continued cultivation and without proper manuring. Cotton, cereals, oilseeds, and many kinds of vegetables and citrus fruits are some of the crops suited to black soils.

Red soil develops on crystalline igneous rocks in areas of low rainfall in the eastern and southern part of the Deccan Plateau, parts of Odisha and Chhattisgarh and in the southern parts of the middle Ganga plain.* Almost all kinds of crops can be grown on red soil, although it seems to be more suitable for the cultivation of rice, ragi, tobacco, and vegetables.

Laterite soils develop in areas with high temperature and high rainfall. They are suitable, among others, for rice and sugarcane.

Arid soils range from red to brown in color and found in western Rajasthan. Due to the dry climate, high temperature, and accelerated evaporation, they lack moisture and humus.

---

*The soil develops a reddish color due to a wide diffusion of iron in crystalline and metamorphic rocks. It looks yellow when it occurs in a hydrated form.

Saline soils contain a larger proportion of sodium, potassium, and magnesium, and thus, they are infertile, and do not support any vegetative growth. Saline soils are prominently found in western Gujarat, deltas of the eastern coast, and in Sunderbans area of West Bengal.*

Peaty soils are found in the areas of heavy rainfall and high humidity, where there is a good growth of vegetation. Peaty soils cover northern part of Bihar, southern part of Uttaranchal, and the coastal areas of West Bengal, Odisha, and Tamil Nadu.

Forest soils are formed in the forest areas where sufficient rainfall is available.

Soil Erosion

The destruction of the soil cover is described as soil erosion. Various factors have been reported to cause soil erosion in India. Wind erosion takes place in arid and semi-arid regions. Water erosion is more frequent in the regions of heavy rainfall and takes place mainly in the form of sheet and gully erosion. Sheet erosion is not easily noticeable as it takes place on the flattened land due to heavy shower and is harmful because it removes the finer and more fertile top soil. Localized soil waterlogging and salinity cause serious damage to the soil fertility and are prominent in 27% of irrigate area of the country. Chemical fertilizers in the absence of organic manures harden the soil and reduce its fertility in the long run. The green revolution belt experiences this type of soil damage. Human settlements are responsible for soil erosion to a great extent as forest and other natural vegetation is removed for human settlement, cultivation, grazing animals, and various other needs. Deforestation is another chief cause of soil erosion. For example, Kerala lost 906,440 hectares of forest land, more than 50% of its forest area between 1973 and 2016.[2] According to 2015 report of Indian Institute of Remote Sensing, the estimated amount of soil erosion that occurs in India was 147 million hectares, out of which 94 million hectares was claimed by water erosion, 16 million hectares by acidification, 14 million hectares by flooding, and 9 million hectares by wind erosion. Out of the total eroded soil, 29% was lost into sea and 61% was relocated.

Soil Conservation

Soil conservation is a methodology to maintain soil fertility, prevent soil erosion and exhaustion, and improve the degraded condition of the soil. Following measures can be applied for controlling erosion and restoring the productivity of eroded lands:

1. To stop faulty practices and checking cultivation on slopes. For example, lands with a slope gradient of 15–25% should not be used for cultivation. If such land is to be used, terraces should carefully be made.
2. To regulate over-grazing and shifting cultivation practices.
3. To disseminate education among people with regard to the positive benefits of contour bunding, contour terracing, regulated forestry, cover cropping, mixed farming, crop rotation, etc.
4. Efforts should be made to prevent gully erosion and control their formation.

---

*In the areas of green revolution, the fertile alluvial soils are becoming saline because of over irrigation. Over irrigation causes water logging under dry climatic conditions which promotes capillary action, resulting in the deposition of salt on the top layer of the soil.

5. Developing shelter belts of trees and agro-forestry from encroachment by sand dunes in arid and semi-arid regions.
6. Lands not suitable for cultivation should be converted into pastures for grazing. Experiments have been made to stabilize sand dunes in western Rajasthan by the Central Arid Zone Research Institute (CAZRI).
7. Government of India established All India Soil Survey Organisation in 1956 with the headquarters at the Indian Agricultural Research Institute, Nagpur. The Government established National Bureau of Soil Survey and Land Use Planning (NBSS&LUP) at New Delhi in 1976. The NBSS&LUP is one among the chain of ICAR Institutes.[3] The Central Soil Conservation Board, set up by the Government of India, has prepared a number of plans for soil conservation in different parts of the country. These plans are based on the climatic conditions, configuration of land, and the social behavior of people.

Water

India receives an average annual precipitation of 4,000 billion cubic meters (BCM) which is the principle source of fresh water in the country.

Surface Water Resources

Rivers, lakes, ponds, and tanks are the four major sources of surface water. In the country, there are about 10,360 rivers and their tributaries longer than 1.6 km each. The mean annual flow in all the river basins in India is estimated to be 1,869 km^3. However, due to topographical, hydrological, and other constraints, only about 690 km^3 (32%) of the available surface water can be utilized. The Ganga, the Brahmaputra, and the Barak rivers have 60% of the total surface water resources.[5]

Groundwater Resources

The total replenishable groundwater resources in the country are about 432 km^3. The Ganga and the Brahmaputra basins have about 46% of the total replenishable groundwater resources. The level of groundwater utilization is relatively high in the river basins lying in north-western region and parts of south India. The groundwater utilization is very high in the states of Punjab, Haryana, Rajasthan, and Tamil Nadu. However, there are states like Chhattisgarh, Odisha, Kerala, etc., which utilize only a small proportion of their groundwater potentials. States such as Gujarat, Uttar Pradesh, Bihar, Tripura, and Maharashtra are utilizing their groundwater resources at a moderate rate. If the present trend continues, the demands for water would need the supplies and such situation, will be detrimental to development, and can cause social upheaval and disruptions.

Some Concerns Related With Water Resource

India is suffering from the worst water crisis in its history and millions of lives and livelihoods are under threat. Following points of concern can be mentioned in this regard:

1. India has only about 4% of the world's renewable water resources but is home to nearly 18% of the world's population.
2. Per capita annual water availability reduced from 1,816 m^3 in 2001 to 1,544 m^3 in 2011.[4]

3. Currently, 600 million Indians face high to extreme water stress and about 2 lakh people die every year due to inadequate access to safe water. The crisis is only going to get worse. By 2030, the country's water demand is projected to be twice the available supply, implying severe water scarcity for hundreds of millions of people and an eventual 6% loss in the country's gross domestic product (GDP).
4. The average annual precipitation in India is estimated to be about 4,000 BCM. After accounting for evaporation and evapo-transpiration, the average annual water availability has been assessed as 1,869 BCM. It is estimated that owing to topographic, hydrological, and other constraints, the utilizable water is 1,123 BCM, which comprises of 690 BCM of surface water and 433 BCM of replenishable groundwater resources.

National Water Policy, 2012

Ministry of Water Resources has evolved the Draft National Water Policy (2012) to meet the present challenges in the water sector. The salient features of the Draft National Water Policy (2012) are as follows[6]:

1. emphasis on the need for a National Water Framework Law;
2. comprehensive legislation for optimum development of inter-state rivers and river valleys;
3. evolving a system of benchmarks for water uses for different purposes to ensure efficient use of water;
4. setting up of Water Regulatory Authority in each state;
5. incentivizing recycle and reuse of water;
6. community participation in management of water resources projects and services;
7. incentivizing water saving in irrigation through methods like aligning cropping pattern with natural resource endowments, micro-irrigation, automated irrigation operation, evaporation–transpiration reduction, etc.;
8. undertaking conservation of rivers, river corridors, water bodies, and infrastructure in a scientifically planned manner through community participation; and
9. arresting declining groundwater levels in overexploited areas.

Composite Water Management Index

The National Institute for Transforming India (NITI) Aayog has developed the Composite Water Management Index (CWMI) to enable effective water management in Indian states in the face of this growing crisis. The objective of the index is (1) providing the states a benchmark for performance on key water indicators; (2) inculcating a culture of constructive competition among states by identifying high-performers and under-performers; and (3) identifying areas for deeper engagement and investment on the part of the states.[7]

The Index comprises 9 broad sectors covering 28 indicators which are as follows:

1. Source augmentation and restoration of water bodies (weight 5%)
2. Source augmentation (groundwater) (weight 15%)
3. Major and medium irrigation—supply-side management (weight 15%)
4. Watershed development—supply-side management (weight 10%)
5. Participatory irrigation practices—demand-side management (weight 10%)

6. Sustainable on-farm water use practices—demand-side management (weight 10%)
7. Rural drinking water (weight 10%)
8. Urban water supply and sanitation (weight 10%)
9. Policy and governance (weight 15%)

High performer states will be those which score more than 65% and medium performer states will be those which score between 50 and 65%. The states achieving less than 50% score will be low performer (Table 4.2).

TABLE 4.2 Ranking of States According to Composite Water Index Scores (2018)

Non-Himalayan States			North-eastern and Himalayan States		
Rank	**States**	**Water Index Scores**	**Rank**	**States**	**Water Index Scores**
1	Gujarat	75	1	Himachal Pradesh	59
2	Andhra Pradesh	74	2	Uttarakhand	53
3	Madhya Pradesh	70	3	Tripura	49
4	Goa	60	4	Assam	31
5	Karnataka	59	5	Sikkim	28
6	Tamil Nadu	58	6	Nagaland	26
7	Haryana	58	7	Meghalaya	26
8	Maharashtra	56	8	Arunachal Pradesh	22
9	Punjab	52			
10	Telangana	50			
11	Rajasthan	47			
12	Kerala	45			
13	Chhattisgarh	45			
14	Odisha	39			
15	Uttar Pradesh	39			
16	Bihar	38			
17	Jharkhand	34			

Source: Composite Water Management Index, August 2019, Niti Aayog, retrieved from https://www.niti.gov.in/sites/default/files/2019-08/CWMI-2.0-latest.pdf (accessed on March 14, 2021).

Forests

Forests are the green lungs of the nation and provide various ecological services like clean air, water, maintenance of soil-moisture regime by checking soil erosion, etc. Forests directly sequester carbon dioxide from atmosphere and play a critical role in checking global warming and climate change. Forests check extension of sand-dunes preventing desertification. Healthy forest eco-systems are necessary for reversal of land degradation in the country.[8] Forests produce the requisite raw materials for industries, defense, communications, and domestic use; contribute to the country's exports and create a large volume of employment in the primary, secondary, and tertiary sectors. Washington-based World Watch Institute hailed forests as the "great chemical factory of the natural world," as 40% of the prescription drugs have active ingredients derived from wild plants, animals, or micro-organisms, many of them from forests. Among other things, forests maintain ecological balance by providing shelter both to wildlife and birds, and finally add to the aesthetic beauty of the country.

Russia, Brazil, Canada, and the United States together account for nearly 50% of global forest area. Russia alone accounts for 20% of global forest area, whereas India accounts for 2% of global forest area. However, in terms of percentage of country area, Brazil is at the top, as it has 58% of country's area under forests. As per India State of Forest Report (ISFR), 2019 total forest cover is 7,12,249 km^2, which is 21.67% of total geographical area of India (Table 4.3). Forest cover is classified into three density classes viz. very dense forest (canopy density >70%), moderately dense forest (canopy density 40–70%), and open forest (canopy density 10–40%). India is endowed with rich forest types such as tropical wet evergreen forests, tropical moist deciduous forests, tropical dry deciduous, sub-tropical dry evergreen forests, Himalayan moist temperate forests, sub-Alpine and Alpine scrub forests. India is also enriched with 95,027 km^2 of tree cover which is 2.89% of total geographical area of India.

Among states, Madhya Pradesh has the maximum forest area (77,482 km^2), followed by Arunachal Pradesh (66,688 km^2) and Chhattisgarh (55,611 km^2). However, as a percentage of state's geographical area Mizoram has highest forest cover of 85.41%. Haryana has the least forest area of 1,588 km^2 and forest cover which comes at 3.62% of state's geographical area. Among UTs Andaman & Nicobar has maximum area under forests (6,743 km^2), whereas Lakshadweep tops in terms of forest cover which is 90.33% of total geographical area.[9]

TABLE 4.3 Forest Cover of India

Area (km^2)	Percentage of Total Geographical Area
Very dense forests	3.02
Moderately dense forests	9.39
Open forests	9.26
Total forest cover	21.67

Source: State of Forest Report, Govt of India, 2021.

Draft National Forest Policy, 2018

The ministry of environment, forest, and climate change has framed a new draft National Forest Policy, 2018 in March 2018. It is slated to replace the National Forest Policy, 1988. Following are the highlights of draft National Forest Policy, 2018[10]:

1. Bringing a minimum 33% of India's total geographical area under forest cover through scientific interventions.
2. Promoting public–private participation models for undertaking afforestation and reforestation activities in degraded forest areas and forest areas available with Forest Development Corporations and outside forests.
3. Strengthening wildlife management by addressing the issues of human–animal conflict.
4. Monitoring and managing of population of wildlife on a long-term basis within and outside forests for maintaining the balance.
5. Safeguarding forest land by exercising strict restraint on diversion for non-forestry purposes, and strict oversight on compliance of the conditions.

6. Adopting adequate measures to safeguard ecosystems from forest fires, map the vulnerable areas, and develop and strengthen early warning systems and methods to control fire, based on remote sensing technology and community participation.
7. Managing trees outside forests by promoting agro-forestry and farm forestry and promoting urban greens which include woodlands, wetlands, parks, wood in institutional areas, gardens, avenue plantations, block plantations, etc. in such areas;
8. Developing a national forest ecosystems management information system.

Minerals

A mineral is a natural substance of organic or inorganic origin with definite chemical and physical properties. Minerals are a valuable natural resource being the vital raw material for the core sectors of the economy. India produces as many as 95 minerals, which include 4 fuel, 10 metallic, 23 non-metallic, 3 atomic, and 55 minor minerals* (including building and other materials). Metallic minerals are the sources of metals and are further divided into ferrous and non-ferrous metallic minerals. For example, iron ore is ferrous metallic mineral, and copper and bauxite are non-ferrous metallic minerals. Non-metallic minerals are categorized into organic and inorganic. Organic non-metallic minerals are coal and petroleum. Whereas inorganic non-metallic minerals which are also called minor minerals are mica, limestone, graphite, etc. The value of metallic minerals, non-metallic, and minor minerals in 2016–2017 is ₹40,017 crore, ₹7,414.53 crore, and ₹52,810 crore, respectively. India's ranking in 2015 as compared to world production was second in barytes, and talc/steatite/pyrophyllite, third in chromite, coal and lignite, and zinc (slab), fourth in kyanite/andalusite/sillimanite, fifth in iron ore and steel (crude), sixth in bauxite ore, seventh in manganese ore, and eighth in aluminum. Rajasthan is the leader in mineral production and has the share of 20.26% in the national output. Next in order is Odisha with a share of 17.77% followed by Andhra Pradesh (9.45%).

Minerals are generally concentrated in four broad belts in India.

The North-Eastern Plateau Region covers Chota Nagpur Plateau (Jharkhand), Odisha Plateau, West Bengal, and parts of Chhattisgarh. The minerals found in this region are iron ore, coal, manganese, bauxite, mica, etc.

The South-Western Plateau Region extends over Karnataka, Goa and contiguous Tamil Nadu uplands, and Kerala. This region is rich in ferrous metals and bauxite. It also contains high-grade iron ore, manganese, and limestone.

The Western Region extends along Aravalli in Rajasthan and part of Gujarat. The minerals found in this region are copper, zinc, sandstone, granite, marble, gypsum, dolomite, limestone, etc. Gujarat is known for its petroleum deposits.

The Himalayan Region is another mineral belt where copper, lead, zinc, cobalt, and tungsten are known to occur. They occur on both the eastern and western parts.

---

*Minor minerals means building stones, gravel, ordinary clay, ordinary sand other than sand used for prescribed purposes.

National Mineral Policy 2019

Government approved National Mineral Policy 2019 in February 2019. The objective of policy is to ensure transparency, better regulation and enforcement, balanced social and economic growth as well as sustainable mining practices.

Following are the salient features of policy[11]:

1. introduction of Right of First Refusal for Reconnaissance permit to Prospecting Licence (RP/PL) holders;
2. encouraging the private sector to take up exploration;
3. auctioning in virgin areas for composite RP cum PL cum ML (mining lease) on revenue share basis;
4. encouragement of merger and acquisition of mining entities;
5. transfer of mining leases and creation of dedicated mineral corridors to boost private sector mining areas;
6. to grant status of industry to mining activity to boost financing of mining for private sector and for acquisitions of mineral assets in other countries by private sector;
7. long-term import–export policy for mineral that will help private sector in better planning and stability in business;
8. rationalizing reserved areas given to PSUs which have not been used and to put these areas to auction, which will give more opportunity to private sector for participation;
9. making efforts to harmonize taxes, levies, and royalty with world benchmarks to help private sector;
10. maintenance of database of mineral resources; and
11. use of coastal waterways and inland shipping for evacuation and transportation of minerals.

SUSTAINABLE DEVELOPMENT

The term sustainable development was first used and described by Brundtland Commission* in its report *Our Common Future*. According to Brundtland Commission report, "Sustainable development is development that meets the needs of the present without compromising the ability of future generations to meet their own needs."[12] Sustainable development recognizes that growth must be both inclusive and environmentally sound to reduce poverty and build shared prosperity for today's population and to continue to meet the needs of future generations. The three pillars of sustainable development are economic growth, environmental protection, and social inclusion—carry across all sectors of development, from cities facing rapid urbanization to agriculture, infrastructure, energy development and use, water availability, and transportation. The goals of sustainable development seem to conflict with each other in the short term. For example, industrial growth might conflict with preserving natural resources. Yet, in the long term, utilization of natural resources, not exploitation, will help ensure sustainable and

* World Commission of Environment and Development (the Brundtland Commission) was headed by Gro Harlem Brundtland. She served three terms as Prime Minister of Norway and as Director-General of the World Health Organization from 1998–2003.

equitable growth. Economic development is about promoting inclusive growth and providing incentives for businesses and other organizations to adhere to sustainability guidelines. Social development is about awareness of and legislative protection of the health of people from pollution and other harmful activities of business along with encouraging people to participate in environmental sustainability. Environmental protection defines how to protect ecosystems, air quality, integrity, and sustainability of our resources, and focuses on the elements that place stress on the environment. It emphasizes that technology will drive our greener future and will protect the environment of the future from potential damage that technological advances could potentially bring.[13]

Sustainable Development Goals

The Sustainable Development Goals (SDGs) are a collection of 17 global goals set by the United Nations General Assembly in 2015 for the year 2030. The goals are broad based and inter-dependent. The SDGs are[14] (1) no poverty; (2) zero hunger; (3) good health and well-being; (4) quality education; (5) gender equality; (6) clean water and sanitation; (7) affordable and clean energy; (8) decent work and economic growth; (9) industry, innovation, and infrastructure; (10) reducing inequality; (11) sustainable cities and communities; (12) responsible consumption and production; (13) climate action; (14) life below water; (15) life on land; (16) peace, justice, and strong institutions; and (17) partnerships for the goals.

Global Awakening Toward Sustainable Environment

The beginning of modern environment movement can be attributed to Rachel Carson who in her best-known book *Silent Spring* (published in 1962) documented the adverse environmental effects caused by the indiscriminate use of pesticides.[15] It was followed by *Club of Rome* (which was founded by politicians, public servants, diplomats, scientists, economists, and business leaders from around the globe in 1968) that got wide public attention through its report on *Limits to Growth* in 1972. *UN Conference on the Human Environment (1972)* was held in Stockholm and famously known as Stockholm Conference. It was the UN's first major conference on international environmental issues and led to the establishment of the United Nations Environment Programme (UNEP). *World Commission on Environment and Development (1987)* also known as Brundtland Commission, prepared a report titled *Our Common Future* and developed the theme of sustainable development. *UN Conference on Environment and Development (1992)* held in Rio de Janeiro and also known as the Earth Summit or Rio Conference, led to the establishment of the "Commission on Sustainable Development." It also resulted in the adoption of three major agreements such as Rio Declaration,* Agenda 21,** and Statement of Forest Principles.*** It also led to two multilateral treaties such as United Nations Framework Convention on Climate Change (UNFCCC) and Convention on Biological

---

* A series of principles defining the rights and responsibilities of states on environment and development.

** A global plan of action to promote sustainable development.

*** A set of principles to underpin the sustainable management of forests worldwide.

Diversity. *World Summit on Sustainable Development (2002)* was held in Johannesburg, and is also called Rio + 10 or Johannesburg Summit. It led to three key outcomes such as a political declaration, the Johannesburg Plan of Implementation, and a range of partnership initiatives. Key commitments included those on sustainable consumption and production, water and sanitation, and energy. *UN Conference on Sustainable Development (2012)* took place at Rio de Janeiro and is known as Rio + 20, led to the outcome document titled *The Future We Want*. It resulted in a focused political outcome document which contains clear and practical measures for implementing sustainable development. *UN Sustainable Development Summit (2015)* was held in New York, and led to the adoption of *Transforming Our World: The 2030 Agenda for Sustainable Development*.

Paris Agreement

At the Paris climate conference (COP21) in December 2015, 195 countries adopted the first-ever universal, legally binding global climate deal. Countries furthermore aimed to reach "global peaking of greenhouse gas (GHG) emissions as soon as possible." The agreement has been described as an incentive for and driver of fossil fuel divestment. The Paris deal is the world's first comprehensive climate agreement.

Following are the salient features of Paris Agreement[16]:

1. A long-term goal of keeping the increase in global average temperature to well below 2°C above pre-industrial levels
2. To aim to limit the increase to 1.5°C, since this would significantly reduce risks and the impacts of climate change
3. The Paris Agreement requests each country to outline and communicate their post-2020 climate actions, known as their "Nationally determined contributions" (NDCs)
4. The developed countries will continue to support developing countries by mobilizing USD 100 billion per year by 2020 and extend this until 2025. A new and higher goal will be set for after this period
5. This strategy involved 20/20/20 targets, namely reduction of GHG emissions (by 20%), the increase of renewable energy share (to 20% on the basis of consumption), and the increase of energy efficiency, thus, saving up to 20% in the energy consumption
6. Target of "global peaking of GHG emissions as soon as possible."

Why Is Sustainable Environment Important for Us?

1. *Human-generated emissions cause global warming*: Carbon dioxide, nitrous oxide, and methane are gases that collect in the atmosphere and prevent heat radiating from Earth's surface into space, creating what's known as the greenhouse effect. Carbon dioxide (the chief contributor to climate change) is up by 40%, nitrous oxide by 20%, and methane by a whopping 150% since 1750—mainly from the burning of dirty fossil fuels. In 2017, China, the United States, the EU 28, India, Russia, and Japan—the world's largest CO_2 emitters—emitted 68% of total global fossil CO_2. China and the United States emitted 29.4 and 14.3% of CO_2, respectively, whereas India with 6.8% of global emissions is the

fourth largest contributor.[17] Around 90 fossil fuel companies are responsible for 63% of CO_2 emissions from human activities.[18]

2. *Global warming threatens climate systems*: Hotter temperatures—both on land and at sea—alter global weather patterns and change how and where precipitation falls. Those shifting patterns exacerbate dangerous and deadly drought, heat waves, floods, wildfires, and storms, including hurricanes. They also melt ice caps, glaciers, and layers of permafrost, which can lead to rising sea levels and coastal erosion. Warmer temperatures impact whole ecosystems as well, throwing migration patterns and life cycles out of whack. For example, early spring can induce trees and plants to flower before bees and other pollinators have emerged. While global warming may equate to longer growing seasons and higher food production in some regions, areas already coping with water scarcity are expected to become drier, creating the potential for drought, failed crops, or wildfires.
3. *Climate change endangers human health*: Extreme heat contributes directly to cardiovascular deaths and respiratory disease. High temperatures also reduce air quality by creating more smog, pollen, and other airborne allergens—all of which can trigger asthma, which afflicts 235 million people around the world. Extreme heat can also exacerbate drought, leading to malnutrition and famine. Changing weather patterns can impact sources of fresh water and food. While drought creates water scarcity, floods can contaminate drinking water supplies, increasing the risk of waterborne diseases and illnesses spread by disease-carrying insects, such as mosquitoes. Extreme weather and rising seas can destroy homes, public infrastructure, and entire ways of life—forcing people to move or migrate, displacing whole populations, and increasing the threat of civil unrest. Indeed, the World Economic Forum ranks extreme weather, natural disasters, and our collective failure to mitigate and adapt to climate change as among the greatest threats facing humanity in the coming decade. We're already experiencing some of those dangers. In the United States, 16 extreme weather-related disasters cost the country a record-breaking $306 billion in damages.

Sustainable Development and India

According to India's Biennial Update Report (BUR), India emitted 2.1 billion tonnes of CO_2 equivalent in 2010 from energy, industrial processes and product use, agriculture and waste sectors. The share of energy in GHG emissions is 71% and that of agriculture is 18%. Industry and waste contribute around 8 and 3% of GHG emissions, respectively. According to the 2011 Census data, around 49% of households still use firewood for cooking while only 29% use LPG or PNG for cooking purposes. Within the energy mix of the country, coal accounts for nearly 55% of the total primary energy supply, followed by oil at 30%, and natural gas at 9%. Only 2% of total primary energy is supplied by renewable energy sources.

The World Bank Group commissioned a study to look at the likely impacts of temperature increases from 2°C to 4°C in three regions South Asia, South East Asia, and Sub-Saharan Africa. The scientists used the best available evidence and supplemented it with advanced computer simulations to arrive at likely impacts on agriculture, water resources, cities, coastal ecosystems, etc. Some of their findings for India are summarized in Table 4.4.

TABLE 4.4 Impact of Climate Change on Indian Economy

Threats	Impact of Climate Change
Extreme heat	■ Unusual and unprecedented spells of hot weather. ■ Under 4°C warming, the west coast and southern India are projected to shift to new, high-temperature climatic regimes with significant impacts on agriculture.
Changing rainfall patterns	■ A 2°C rise in the world's average temperatures will make India's summer monsoon highly unpredictable. ■ India's northwest coast to the southeastern coastal region could see higher than average rainfall. ■ Dry years are expected to be drier and wet years wetter.
Droughts	■ Droughts are expected to be more frequent in some areas, especially in north-western India, Jharkhand, Odisha, and Chhattisgarh. Crop yields are expected to fall significantly because of extreme heat by the 2040s.
Groundwater	■ Falling water tables can be expected to reduce further on account of increasing demand for water from a growing population, more affluent life styles, as well as from the services sector and industry.
Glacier melt	■ At 2.5°C warming, melting glaciers will threaten the stability and reliability of glacier-fed rivers, particularly the Indus and the Brahmaputra. ■ Alterations in the flows of the Indus, Ganges, and Brahmaputra rivers could significantly impact irrigation, affecting the amount of food that can be produced in their basins as well as the livelihoods of millions of people.
Sea-level rise	■ With India close to the equator, it would see much higher rises in sea levels than higher latitudes. ■ Sea-level rise and storm surges would lead to saltwater intrusion in the coastal areas, impacting agriculture, degrading groundwater quality, contaminating drinking water, and possibly causing a rise in diarrhea cases and cholera outbreaks, as the cholera bacterium survives longer in saline water.
Agriculture and food security	■ Above 34°C, India has experienced negative effect on wheat yields, and rising temperatures can only aggravate the situation. ■ Under 2°C warming by the 2050s, the country may need to import more than twice the amount of food grain than would be required without climate change.
Energy security	■ The increasing variability and long-term decreases in river flows can pose a major challenge to hydropower plants and increase the risk of physical damage from landslides, flash floods, glacial lake outbursts, and other climate-related natural disasters. ■ Decreases in the availability of water and increases in temperature will pose major risk factors to thermal power generation.
Water security	■ Urbanization, population growth, economic development, and increasing demand for water from agriculture and industry are likely to aggravate the situation further. ■ An increase in variability of monsoon rainfall is expected to increase water shortages in some areas.
Health	■ Climate change is expected to have major health impacts in India—increasing malnutrition and related health disorders such as child stunting—with the poor likely to be affected most severely. Child stunting is projected to increase by 35% by 2050 compared to a scenario without climate change. ■ Malaria and other vector-borne diseases, along with and diarrheal infections which are a major cause of child mortality, are likely to spread into areas where colder temperatures had previously limited transmission.
Migration and conflict	■ The Indus and the Ganges-Brahmaputra-Meghna Basins are major trans-boundary rivers, and increasing demand for water is already leading to tensions among countries over water sharing. ■ Climate change impacts on agriculture and livelihoods can increase the number of climate refugees.

Source: Tabulated by author from the information retrieved from World Bank (2013). *Turn down the heat: Climate extremes, regional impacts, and the case for resilience*. Retrieved from https://www.worldbank.org (accessed on June 6, 2017).

India's Actions on Sustainable Development and Climate Change

1. *National Action Plan on Climate Change (NAPCC)*: National Action Plan on Climate Change (NAPCC) was launched in June 2008, and includes eight national missions: Jawaharlal Nehru National Solar Mission, National Mission for Enhanced Energy Efficiency, National Water Mission, National Mission for a Green India, National Mission on Sustainable Habitat, National Mission for Sustainable Agriculture, National Mission for Sustaining the Himalayan Ecosystem, and National Mission on Strategic Knowledge for Climate Change. Each mission is anchored under a Ministry, which is responsible for its implementation and lays down the budget provisions and actionable priorities for it.[19]
2. *National Green Corridor Program*: National Green Corridor Program (NGCP) was introduced in 2013 to address the fluctuations/variability in the renewable power supply. The Power Grid Corporation of India is developing the inter-state transmission corridor and the state transmission utilities are responsible for setting up and strengthening the intra-state transmission infrastructure. The cost to develop the corridor is estimated as $380 billion. The inter-state transmission projects of the Green Corridor are likely to be completed by 2018. As per transmission Works under Green Energy Corridor–II, the Government has an ambitious plan to establish total 1,00,000 MW Solar and 60,000 MW Wind generation capacity by 2022.[20]
3. *R&D for Clean Coal Technologies*: In 2016, R&D Project for "Development of Advanced Ultra Supercritical (Adv. USC) Technology for Thermal Power Plants" on a Mission Mode, at an estimated cost of ₹1,554 crore has been approved by the Cabinet Committee on Economic Affairs.
4. *National Green Highways Mission*: Introduced in 2015, the scheme aims at plantations, transplantations, beautification, and maintenance for sustainable environment and inclusive growth. The scheme is implemented by Ministry of Road Transport and Highways to develop green corridors along 1 lakh km network of National Highways.
5. *Faster Adoption and Manufacturing of Hybrid & Electric Vehicles (FAME India)*: The Faster Adoption and Manufacturing of (Hybrid &) Electric Vehicles (FAME) India was launched in 2015 to promote eco-friendly vehicles in the country. The scheme will help in addressing the issue of environmental pollution and fuel security. The scheme is being administered by the Heavy Industries Ministry. This scheme has two components: FAME India-I and FAME India-II. The FAME India-I scheme was introduced for the period April 1, 2015 to March 31, 2019 with total outlay of ₹895 crores. The FAME India-II scheme has become operational w.e.f. April 1, 2019 for the period of 3 years and has an outlay of ₹10,000 crore.[21] Through the scheme, the Government plans to support 10 lakhs two wheelers, 5 lakhs three wheelers, 55,000 four wheelers, and 7,000 buses. The scheme proposes support for setting up of charging infrastructure whereby about 2,700 charging stations will be set up in metros, other million-plus cities, smart cities, and cities of hilly states across India.[22]
6. *National Clean Energy and Environment Fund*: Introduced in 2010–2011, National Clean Energy and Environment Fund (NCEF) was created out of cess on coal produced/imported ("polluter pays" principle) for the purposes of financing and promoting clean energy initiatives, funding research in the area of clean energy or for any other purpose relating thereto. Subsequently, the scope of the Fund has been expanded to include clean environment initiatives also. The coal cess which was collected at $50 per tonne since

June 22, 2010 was increased to $400 per tonne in the Union budget 2016–2017, and the same has been renamed as "Clean Environment Cess."[23]

Air Pollution and Control Measures in India

Around 92% of people worldwide do not breathe clean air. Air pollution costs the global economy $5 trillion every year in welfare costs and ground-level ozone pollution is expected to reduce staple crop yields by 26% by 2030. According to Global Burden of Disease estimates for the year 2017 the early deaths related to PM 2.5* in India are the second highest in the world and ozone-related deaths are the highest in the world. Long-term exposure to air pollution can lead to symptoms and conditions affecting human health. This mainly affects the respiratory and inflammatory systems, but can also lead to more serious conditions such as heart disease.

Initiatives on Air Pollution Mitigation

1. National Ambient Air Quality Standards envisaging 12 pollutants have been notified under EPA, 1986 and 115 emission/effluent standards for 104 different sectors of industries, besides 32 general standards for ambient air have also been notified.
2. A nation-wide program of ambient air quality monitoring known as National Air Quality Monitoring Programme (NAMP) launched with the network of 691 manual operating stations all over India.
3. With reference to vehicular pollution, the steps taken include introduction of cleaner/alternate fuels like gaseous fuel (CNG, LPG etc.), ethanol blending, universalization of BS-IV by 2017; leapfrogging from BS-IV to BS-VI fuel standards by April 1, 2020; ongoing promotion of public transport network of metro, buses, e-rickshaws and promotion of carpooling; streamlining granting of 'Pollution Under Control Certificate', lane discipline, vehicle maintenance, etc.
4. National Air Quality Index (AQI) was launched by the Prime Minister in April 2015 starting with 14 cities and now extended to 34 cities.
5. A 'Graded Response Action Plan' for control of air pollution in Delhi and NCR region has been notified. This plan specifies actions required for controlling particulate matter (PM emissions from various sources) and prevents PM10 and PM2.5 levels to go beyond "moderate" national AQI category.
6. Central Pollution Control Board has issued a comprehensive set of directions for implementation of 42 measures to mitigate air pollution in major cities including Delhi and NCR comprising of action points to counter air pollution in major cities which include control and mitigation measures related to vehicular emissions, re-suspension of road dust and other fugitive emissions, bio-mass/municipal solid waste burning, industrial pollution, construction and demolition activities, and other general steps.
7. Educating school children to go for pollution-free Diwali.

Waste Management in India

There are about 41,523 industries in the country generating about 7.90 million tonnes of hazardous waste annually, out of which landfillable waste is about 3.32 million tonnes (42.02%),

* PM 2.5 is fine particulate matter with a diameter of 2.5 μm or less.

incinerable waste is about 0.60 million tonnes (7.60%), and recyclable hazardous waste is about 3.98 million tonnes (50.38%). Many steps have been taken by the government with regard to waste management in the country.[24]

1. GIS Based National Hazardous Waste Information System has been launched.
2. Treatment, Storage and Disposal Facilities (TSDFs) for Hazardous Wastes in different cities of the country.
3. e-Waste rules notified in 2011, and as per these rules, the producers are required to collect e-waste generated from the end of life of their products by setting up collection centers or take back systems either individually or collectively. e-Waste recycling can be undertaken only in facilities authorized and registered with State Pollution Control Boards/Pollution Control Committee.
4. The Batteries (Management & Handling) Rules, 2001 was notified in May 2001 to regulate the collection, characterization, and recycling as well as import of used lead acid batteries in the country.
5. The municipal areas of the country generate 133,760 metric tonnes per day (TPD) of plastic waste, of which only 91,152 TPD waste is collected and 25,884 TPD treated. The government has notified the Municipal Solid Wastes (Management and Handling) Rules, 2000 for management of the municipal solid waste.
6. Around 4.16 tonnes of biomedical waste is generated per day. There are 190 Common Bio-Medical Waste Treatment and Disposal Facilities in operation and 29 are under construction. The waste is required to be managed as per the Biomedical Waste (Management and Handling) Rules, 1998.
7. The Indian coal has high ash content of the order of 30–45%, generating large quantity of fly ash at coal/lignite-based thermal power stations in the country causing pollution of air and water. The Government issued Notification on fly ash utilization in 1999 with an aim to achieve 100% utilization in a phased manner. The objective of the notification is to encourage utilization of ash in the manufacture of building materials and construction activity. The fly ash utilization in the country has been increased to 57.63% in 2013–2014. However, the utilization has not reached 100%.

India's Post-2020 Climate Goals

For post-2020 period, in response to the decisions of the Conference to the Parties, India submitted its nationally determined contributions (NDC) to the UNFCCC on October 2, 2015, outlining the climate actions intended to be taken under the Paris Agreement. The eight goals put forth by India in its NDC are as follows[25]:

1. To put forward and further propagate a healthy and sustainable way of living based on traditions and values of conservation and moderation.
2. To adopt a climate-friendly and a cleaner path than the one followed hitherto by others at corresponding level of economic development.
3. To reduce the emissions intensity of its GDP by 33–35% by 2030 from 2005.
4. To achieve about 40% cumulative electric power installed capacity from non-fossil fuel–based energy resources by 2030 with the help of transfer of technology and low-cost international finance including from Green Climate Fund (GCF).
5. To create an additional carbon sink of 2.5–3 billion tonnes of CO_2 equivalent through additional forest and tree cover by 2030.

6. To better adapt to climate change by enhancing investments in development programs in sectors vulnerable to climate change, particularly agriculture, water resources, Himalayan region, coastal regions, health and disaster management.
7. To mobilize domestic and new and additional funds from developed countries to implement the above mitigation and adaptation actions in view of the resource required and the resource gap.
8. To build capacities, create domestic framework and international architecture for quick diffusion of cutting edge climate technology in India and for joint collaborative R&D for such future.

Summary

1. A natural resource is something that is found in nature and can be used by people for different activities. Earth's natural resources include light, air, water, plants, animals, soil, stone, minerals, and fossil fuel.
2. India's total geographical area is 328.7 million hectares. Out of this, arable land is 55.3%, total cropped area is 61.1%, and net sown area is 43%.
3. The soil is the biologically active upper layer of Earth. ICAR has divided soils in India into eight major groups. These are alluvial soil, black soil, red soil, laterite soil, arid soil, saline soil, peaty soil, and forest soil. The destruction of the soil cover is described as soil erosion. Soil erosion can take place through wind, water, etc. Soil conservation is a practice to prevent soil loss through erosion or fertility loss. To promote soil conservation, government has taken various steps such as establishing All India Soil Survey Organisation, National Bureau of Soil Survey and Land Use Planning, and Central Soil Conservation Board.
4. Water resources can be tapped from surface water and groundwater. India has only about 4% of the world's renewable water resources but is home to nearly 18% of the world's population. The per capita water availability in India is 1,544 m^3. Government announced National Water Policy, 2012 to promote efficient and sustainable use of water in the country. To promote competitive efficiency among the states, Niti Aayog has also come out with Composite Water Management Index in 2018. The Index comprises 9 broad sectors covering 28 indicators. Gujarat, Madhya Pradesh, and Andhra Pradesh are the three leading states on the basis of performance in Composite Water Management Index.
5. India accounts for 2% of global forest area. The forest and tree cover constitutes 21.54% of total geographical area of India. Among states, Madhya Pradesh has the maximum forest area and Mizoram has the highest forest cover. Haryana has the least forest area and forest cover. The draft National Forest Policy, 2018 aims at bringing a minimum 33% of India's total geographical area under forest cover through scientific interventions.
6. India produces as many as 95 minerals, which include 4 fuel, 10 metallic, 23 non-metallic, 3 atomic, and 55 minor minerals. Rajasthan is the leader in mineral production followed by Odisha and Andhra Pradesh. Government approved National Mineral Policy, 2019 in February 2019 with the objectives of ensuring transparency, better regulation and enforcement, balanced social and economic growth as well as sustainable mining practices.
7. Sustainable development is development that meets the needs of the present without compromising the ability of future generations to meet their own needs. The term sustainable development was first used and described by Brundtland Commission in its report "Our Common Future." The United Nations General Assembly adopted 17 broad-based and interdependent goals in 2015 to be achieved in 2030. Many efforts have been made worldwide to spread awareness about sustainable development.
8. The beginning of modern environment movement can be attributed to Rachel Carson's book *Silent Spring*, published in 1962, followed by Club of Rome (1968) and Stockholm Conference (1972). Earth Summit (1992) led to the establishment of the "Commission on Sustainable Development." Rio + 10 (2002) and Rio + 20 (2012) led to further pledge to save environment. UN Sustainable Development Summit (2015) was held in New York and led to the adoption of "Transforming our world: the 2030 Agenda for Sustainable Development." Paris deal (2015) is the world's first comprehensive climate agreement. Under this, parties to the UNFCCC reached a landmark agreement to combat climate change and to accelerate and intensify the actions and investments needed for a sustainable low carbon future.
9. India with 6.8% of global emissions is the fourth largest contributor of CO_2 emissions. Within the energy mix of the country, coal accounts for nearly 55% of the total primary energy supply, followed by oil at 30%, and natural gas at 9%. India's actions on Sustainable Development and Climate Change include National Action Plan on Climate Change (NAPCC), National Green Corridor Program (NGCP), R&D for Clean Coal Technologies, National Green Highways Mission, FAME India scheme, and National Clean Energy and Environment Fund. To control air pollution, government has taken various measures viz. National Ambient Air Quality Standards, National Air Quality Monitoring Programme, introduction of cleaner/alternate fuels, National Air Quality index, Graded Response Action Plan, directions from Central Pollution Control Board and spreading awareness.

Waste management measures taken by government include GIS Based National Hazardous Waste Information System, Treatment, Storage and Disposal Facilities, e-waste rules, The Batteries (Management & Handling) Rules, 2001, Municipal Solid Wastes (Management and Handling) Rules, 2000, Biomedical Waste (Management and Handling) Rules, 1998, and fly ash utilization.

Endnotes

1. Pandeya, G., & Ranganathanb, T. (2018). Changing land-use pattern in India: has there been an expansion of fallow lands? *Agricultural Economics Research Review*, *31*(1), 113–122.
2. Remote sensing data shows massive erosion of forests in Kerala. *Livemint*, May 23, 2017.
3. Retrieved from https://www.nbsslup.in (Accessed on March 12, 2019).
4. Lahiry, S. (2017). Why India needs to change the way it manages water resources. *Down to Earth*.
5. Press Information Bureau, Government of India, Ministry of Water Resources, May 11, 2015.
6. National Water Policy. (2012). *Government of India Ministry of Water Resources*. Retrieved from http://mowr.gov.in (Accessed on March 14, 2019).
7. Composite Water Management Index, June 2018, Niti Aayog. Retrieved from http://social.niti.gov.in (Accessed on March 14, 2019).
8. Retrieved from http://moef.gov.in.
9. State of Forest Report, 2017, pp.27–29.
10. Draft National Forest Policy, 2018, F. No. 1-1/2012-FP (Vol.4) Government of India Ministry of Environment, Forest and Climate Change, Forest Policy Division.
11. National Mineral Policy 2019. Retrieved from https://mines.gov.in (Accessed on March 18, 2019).
12. Report of the World Commission on Environment and Development: Our Common Future. Retrieved from http://www.un-documents.net (Accessed on March 19, 2019).
13. Shah, M.M. (2008). Sustainable development. *Encyclopaedia of Ecology*.
14. UNDP. *Sustainable Development Goals* Retrieved from https://www.undp.org (Accessed on February 18, 2018).
15. Griswold, E. How 'Silent Spring' ignited the environmental movement. *The New York Times*, September 21, 2012.
16. *Paris Agreement*. Retrieved from https://unfccc.int (Accessed on March 20, 2019).
17. Fossil CO_2 emissions of all world countries-2018 Report, Publications Office of the European Union, 2018.
18. Vidal, J., & Vaughan, A. Paris climate agreement may signal end of fossil fuel era. *The Guardian*, December 13, 2015.
19. Pandve, H.T. (2009). India's National Action Plan on climate change. *Indian Journal of Occupational and Environmental Medicine*, *13*(1), 17–19.
20. Green Corridor. Retrieved from https://powermin.nic.in (Accessed on May 6, 2019).
21. Cabinet approves Scheme for FAME India Phase II, *Press Information Bureau, Government of India*, February 28, 2019.
22. Ghosh, M. How FAME 2 scheme aims to promote the use of electric vehicles in India. *Livemint*, March 12, 2019.
23. Climate Change, Sustainable Development and Energy, Economic Survey, Chapter 5, 2017–18.
24. *Waste Management*. Retrieved from http://moef.gov.in (Accessed on March 25, 2019).
25. *Nationally Determined Contribution*. Retrieved from http://moef.gov.in (Accessed on May 26, 2019).

CHAPTER **5**

INDIAN INFRASTRUCTURE

You and I come by road or rail, but economists travel on infrastructure.

—Margaret Thatcher

INTRODUCTION

Infrastructure development is critical to delivering growth, reducing poverty, and addressing broader development goals. Infrastructure affects growth and development in two ways—by directly boosting economic activity and raising productivity. Yet, there is often a tendency to under-invest in infrastructure because of following three factors. First, infrastructure comprises large up-front investments, involving a large gestation period, which means returns may take decades to accrue. Second, the risk of uncertain returns is high in long-term and large investments. Third, the social benefit of infrastructure investment is larger than private returns generated for the operator (infrastructure creates so-called "positive externalities"). Consequently, infrastructure may be ignored if left to the market forces.[1] Therefore, it is imperative at the level of policy-making that government directly intervenes or makes some regulations with regard to infrastructure development. According to Global Infrastructure Outlook, around US $4.5 trillion worth of investments is required in India till 2040 to develop infrastructure to improve economic growth and community well-being.[2]

This chapter will be centered on the following key areas:

- Types of transport, characteristics, problems, policy issues with regard to road, railway, waterways, and airports.
- Types of energy, characteristics, problems, and policy issues.
- Types of communication, characteristics, problems, and policy issues.

ECONOMIC AND SOCIAL INFRASTRUCTURE

Infrastructure can be classified as "economic infrastructure" and "social infrastructure." Economic infrastructure (which constitutes around 13% of GDP) comprises transport, energy, and communication. On the other hand, social infrastructure comprises sectors like health, education, etc., which require relatively lesser capital investments. In this chapter, our discussion of Indian infrastructure will be limited to only economic infrastructure. Economic infrastructure can be broadly classified into three parts: transport, energy, and communication (Figure 5.1).

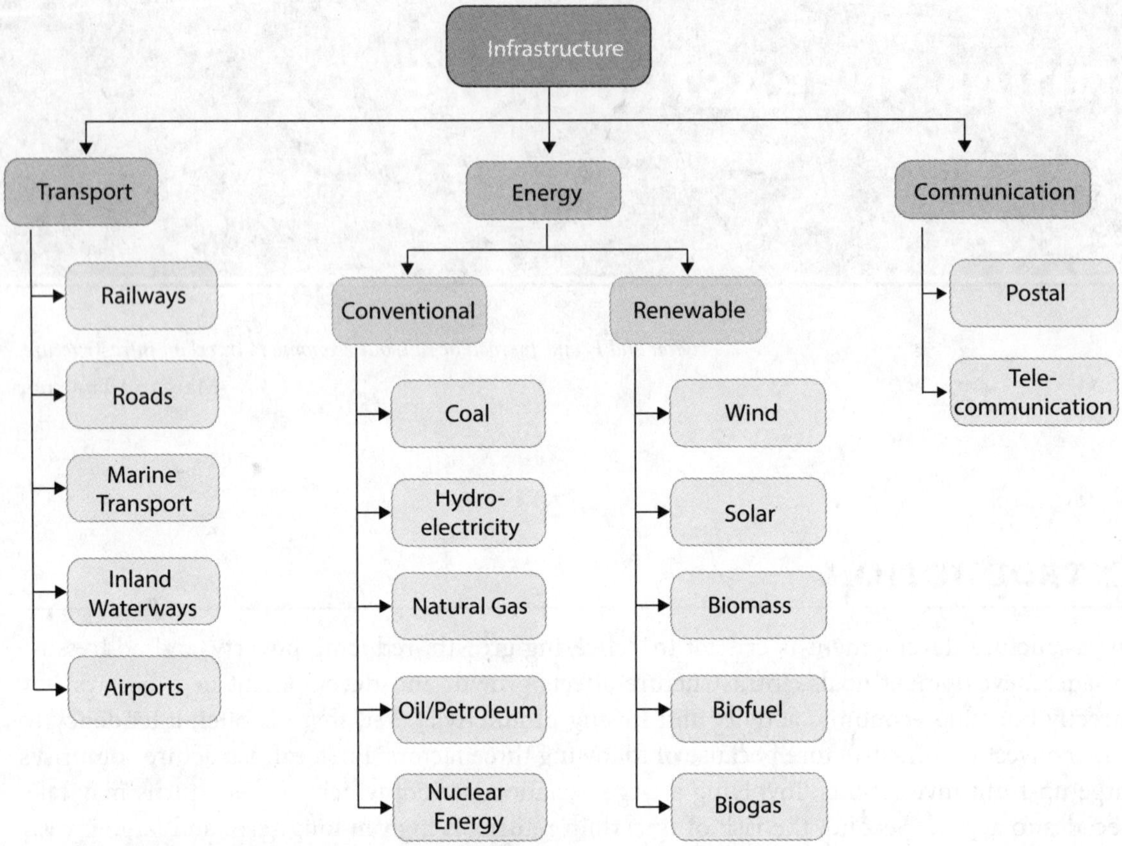

FIGURE 5.1 Economic Infrastructure Types

TRANSPORT

The development of transport infrastructure plays an important role in the growth process through increasing mobility of resources and increasing factor productivity. Transport has recorded a substantial growth over the years both in spread of network and in output of the system. It also provides a vital link between production centers, distribution areas, and the ultimate consumers. The present transport system of the country comprises several modes of transport including rail, road, coastal shipping, air transport, inland waterways transport (IWT), etc.

Indian Railways

Indian Railways is the lifeline of the nation. It traverses the length and breadth of the country providing the required connectivity and integration for balanced regional development. First proposal for Indian Railways was mooted in Madras (now Chennai) in 1932 but idea remained on paper. The idea got materialized after 21 years and the first passenger line measuring 20 miles opened in 1853 connecting the port of Bombay to Thana. The initial advocates for developing railways were mercantile firms in London and Manchester with trading concerns in India.[3] The expectation was that railways would lower transport costs and allow English merchants easier access to raw cotton from India. Simultaneously railways would open Indian markets to British-manufactured products such as cotton textiles. By the early 1900s, India had the fourth largest rail network in the world and was far ahead of China. Much has changed during last three decades and Indian Railways has its own mix of highs and lows.

Features of Indian Railways

1. Indian Railways is the third largest rail network in terms of length (measured in kilometers) after the United States and China.[4] It is one of the largest transportation and logistics networks of the world that runs around 22,600 trains. It runs about 13,600 trains to carry over 23 million passengers per day connecting about 8,000 stations spread across the sub-continent. It runs about 9,146 freight trains per day carrying about 3 million ton (MT) of freight every day. Its network of 68,000 route kilometers (RKM) is more than one and half times the circumference of the earth.[5]
2. Indian Railways is divided into 18 zones that are further sub-divided into 70 divisions. Northern Railway is the largest zone of Indian Railways.
3. There are 14 undertakings under the administrative control of the Ministry of Railways. Some of them are RITES Ltd., IRFC, IRCTC, etc. The Government has proposed to set up a newly specialized university at Vadodara, Gujarat.
4. The railway operates services on three gauges—the broad gauge (1.676 m), the meter gauge (1.00 m), and the narrow gauge (0.762 and 0.610 m). The broad gauge network is the largest operating system (56,000 km) in the country and accounts for the bulk of traffic, both freight and passenger.
5. Around 1.6 million people work for Indian Railways, making it the seventh-largest employer in the world.[6]
6. As of 30th April 2024, Indian Railways has electrified more than 95% of the total broad-gauge route kilometers.

Problems of Indian Railways

Under Investment and Lack of Capacity Addition The legacy of inadequate allocation is reflected in the fact that the share of railways in total plan outlay (12th five-year plan) is currently only 5.5% vis-à-vis about 11% for the other transport sectors and its share in overall development expenditure has remained low at below 2% over the past decade.[7] If we compare Indian case with that of China, Chinese investment in railways has outstripped Indian Railways. For example, during the period 2005–2012, China has invested around three times as much as India on average as a proportion of GDP. In per-capita terms, China has invested on average 11 times as much over the same period even though both countries have similar populations. There are many consequences of low public investment.

First, expansion pace of Indian Railways has slowed down. In 1990 Indian rail network of about route 62,211 km was more than that of Chinese rail network of 57,900 RKM. By 2019, the situation was reversed in favor of China with the country's network expanding to over 139,000 RKM, while India's route length grew marginally to 68,000 km. China aims to expand its railway network to 150,000 km by 2020, including 30,000 km of high-speed rail.[8]

Second, capacity addition in Indian road sector has been far above than that of Indian Railways and it has led to significant shift of passenger and freight traffic to road sector. The share of railways in freight traffic is around 30%, whereas in other countries like China, Russia, and Canada, the share is as much as 51, 65, and 66%, respectively.[9]A study by Mckinsey (2010) has

*In China investment in railways is done by both central and provincial governments (unlike the case of India where investment is done by only central government) and in freight railways coal companies are also investors as they are the freight users. A part of the freight tariff is earmarked as a Railway Construction Fund (RCF) that is used only for infrastructure capital spending. Furthermore, the railway has been corporatized and market borrowings are raised via debts to meet investment requirements.

predicted fall in share of railways in freight traffic to 25%. The need of the hour is to frame certain bold and accelerated scheme of investment in dedicated freight corridors (DFCs) that can parallel the golden quadrilateral (as in the case of road transportation), along with associated industrial corridors. Such an initiative will transform Indian manufacturing industry with "Make in India" becoming a reality. With lack of capacity addition, the share of railways in the GDP has declined to stand at around 1% in recent years.

Congestion and Low Speed Congestion takes place because of lack of multiple tracks and common corridor for both freight and passenger traffic. It also results into lower speed of trains and the speed of the average freight train has remained virtually constant between 2000–2001 and 2012–2013 at around 24–25 km/h. For example, in contrast, in China, the maximum speed of freight trains was 80 km/h around 2008–2009, and the maximum train speed that was around 80–100 km/h in 1991 was raised in stages to 160 and 200 km/h on the most popular passenger corridors by 2008 and is above 300 km/h at present. The distance between Beijing and Shanghai is 1,318 km and the bullet train has reduced the travel time to under 4 hours and 30 minutes and it also makes China's high-speed rail the fastest in the world. Congestion and stretching of capacity go together and on high-density network routes, over 65% of total sections (161 out of 247) are running in India at a capacity of 100% or above. With passenger trains utilizing around 65% of the network capacity, the above situation imposes constraints on the running of heavy freight trains and high-speed passenger trains as passenger traffic is generally accorded priority.

Price Distortions Two major sources of revenue for railways are passenger tariffs and freight charges. For many decades, due to political compulsions, passenger fares have been deliberately kept low and to cover the losses fright rates were kept high. Passenger tariffs have not kept pace with general rate of inflation in the economy and a persistent larger gap between the index of consumer prices and that of passenger rates has emerged over the years. In contrast, the freight rate index moves more closely with wholesale price index. The profits generated via freight services have cross-subsidized passenger services and Indian freight rates remain among the highest in the world. This trend along with inefficiency and stressed capacity has largely undermined the competitiveness of Indian Railways vis-à-vis other countries of the world. For example, China carries about thrice as much coal freight per hour vis-à-vis India at half the cost and at 30% less time.

Lack of Cleanliness Maintaining a clean and hygienic environment in station premises and in trains by Indian Railways is imperative since an average of 2.30 crore passengers frequent the railway stations and travel in the trains every day all over the country. The challenge of sanitation arises because of many reasons viz. open defecation on the track and near stations, solid waste on the track, sanitary disposal on platform, spitting on platform, open drain near platform, garbage near the station, and overflowing dustbins. A survey of over 12,000 respondents conducted by research firm Market Xcel found that "unclean toilets" followed by "unclean coaches" were the main issues that travellers had with the Railways.[10]

Accidents Safety has been one of the biggest concerns in the Indian Railways system. While the number of accidents has gone down over the last few years, the number still remains over 100 accidents a year. Major reasons of accidents are derailments, level crossing, collision and fire in train, etc. Six of every 10 rail accidents in India have happened because of mistakes by or the negligence of railway staff, according to a study by NITIAayog.[11] Such lapses include carelessness in working, poor maintenance, adoption of short-cuts, and non-observance of laid down safety rules and procedures, and signaling errors for which loco-pilots (train-operators) are responsible. Another reason as per the Standing Committee on Railways is defect in the track or rolling stock. Of the total track length of 121,000 km in the country, 4,500 km should be renewed annually. However, the speed of renewal is desperately slow. The Standing Committee had recommended that Indian Railways should switch completely to the Linke Hoffman Busch (LHB) coaches as they do not pile upon each other during derailments and hence cause lesser casualties.[12] According to an estimate in April 2018, there are 3,479 unmanned crossings on the entire broad gauge network throughout India and majority of these are believed to be functioning mainly in the northern and north-eastern parts of the country. The figures of similar unmanned crossings existing on the meter gauge and narrow gauge railway lines serving different parts of the country are not known.[13] In 2012, a Committee headed by Mr. Anil Kakodkar had estimated that the total financial cost of implementing safety measures over the 5-year period (2012–2017) was likely be around ₹1 lakh crore.

BOX 5.1 National Rail Plan

To develop capacity- both infrastructure and rolling stock- ahead of demand, the Ministry of Railways has developed a National Rail Plan (NRP). Following are the key features:

1. It aims at developing adequate rail infrastructure by 2030 to cater to the projected traffic requirements up to 2050.
2. An attempt has been made to map the entire transport infrastructure of the country on a common platform.
3. It has assessed the existing passenger and freight traffic carried on all modes and forecast the growth for the period 2030 to 2050 and then strategize a significant modal shift to rail. The objective is to increase the modal share of rail in freight from the current level of 27 per cent to 45 per cent.
4. Innovative financing has been devised to fund priority projects. Indian Railway Finance Corporation (IRFC) is mobilizing resources with sufficient moratorium period and projects are being targeted to be completed well before the expiry of the moratorium period. These priority projects are being planned in such a way that they will provide enough return to service the debt.

Source: Economic Survey, 2020–21, p. 297

Government Policy with Regard to Railways

Rationalization of Freight Tariff The share of Indian Railways in freight movement has been declining over a period of time primarily due to non-competitive tariff structure. While the passenger fare had remained more or less flat, the freight fare has increased sharply over the year and as a consequence the freight traffic has shifted to road transport system that is more flexible and cost effective. To make rail transportation attractive and arrest the declining trend of rail share, various initiatives were taken in 2016–2017, which include tariff rationalization, classification of new commodities, new policy guideline for station to station rates, expansion of freight basket through containerization, withdrawal of dual freight policy for export of iron ore, rationalization of coal tariff, policy guidelines of Merry Go Round System, and Liberalized Automatic Freight Rebate scheme for traffic loaded in empty flow directions, etc.[14]

Increase in Capital Investment in Railways Greater public investment in the railways would boost aggregate growth and the competitiveness of Indian manufacturing substantially. China invests 11 times as much in per-capita terms and underinvestment in the Indian Railways is also indicated by congestion, strained capacity, poor services, and weak financial health. Budget 2018–2019 allocated ₹1.48 lakh crore for Indian Railways and most of the amount will be dedicated to capacity creation.

Station Redevelopment "Station Redevelopment" is the biggest non-fare revenue-generating project for redeveloping railways stations in the country. The stations to be redeveloped will provide world class amenities and services to passengers. The station redevelopment has been undertaken through various modes such as Zonal Railways, Indian Railway Stations Development Corporation Ltd. (IRSDC), JV with Smart City SPVs, Railway Public Sector Undertaking (PSU), and Co-operation with State Government.[15] The Union Cabinet approved Railways' proposal in 2018 for redevelopment around 400 stations by inviting open bids from interested parties with their designs and business ideas.[16]

Metro Rail System The metro rail network in the country is increasing with the mass rapid transit system emerging as one of the best solutions for urban transportation.[17] Following the success of the Delhi Metro, many cities have implemented or are planning for metro rail systems. The Government of India has been providing financial assistance to cities for improving public transport including metro rail projects. There are 425 km of metro rail systems operational in the cities of Delhi, Noida, Gurugram, Kolkata, Mumbai, Chennai, Bengaluru, Hyderabad, Jaipur, Lucknow, and Kochi and another about 684 km are under construction in various cities by December 2017. As metro rail projects are highly capital intensive, it is difficult to fund metro rail projects from Government exchequer only. In this context, in order to create an ecosystem for proliferation of metro rail in country, the Government of India has notified Metro Rail Policy, 2017.[18] The policy seeks to "enable realization of growing metro rail aspirations of a large number of cities but in a responsible manner" and requires a higher than before commitment from states and public–private partnership (PPP), in terms of comprehensive transit plans and funding obligations. The new policy was prepared by the Ministry of Urban Development in consultation with different states and makes the private sector's participation mandatory for seeking the central government's assistance.[19]

Road Transport

Road transport is a critical infrastructure for economic development of a country. It provides the arterial network to facilitate trade, transport, social integration, and economic development. It is used for the smooth conveyance of both people and goods. Transportation by road has the advantage over other means of transport because of its easy accessibility, flexibility of operations, door-to-door service, and last mile connectivity and reliability. Consequently, passenger and freight movement in India, over the years, have increasingly shifted toward roads vis-a-vis other means of transport.[20]

Features of Indian Roads:

1. India has about 67 lakh km of road network, which is the second largest in the world. India's road density at 1.70 km/km^2 of area is higher than that of Japan (0.91 km/km^2), the United States (0.68 km/km^2), China (0.47 km/km^2), Brazil (0.18 km/km^2), and Russian Federation (0.08 km/km^2).[21]
2. The road network of the country constitutes National Highways (NH), State Highways (SH), District Roads, Rural Roads, Urban Roads, and Project Roads.* The Ministry of Road Transport & Highways is primarily responsible for the development and maintenance of NH. All roads other than the NH are with the state governments (Table 5.1).

---

*Project roads largely include roads built/coming under the purview of central and state government agencies and departments. These include roads of Forest Departments, Irrigation Departments, Electricity Departments, roads in coal fields and coal mines of Coal India Ltd., roads under the plant areas of Steel Authority of India Limited (SAIL), National Mineral Development Corporation (NMDC), Sugarcane Departments of States/UT and Border Roads Organisation (BRO).

TABLE 5.1 Indian Road Length (2023)

Roads	Road Length (in KMS)	Percentage of Total
National Highways	1,46,145	2.19
State Highways	1,79,535	2.69
Other Roads*	63,45,403	95.12
Total	66,71,083	100

*Other Roads include District Roads, Rural Roads, Urban Roads, and Project Roads.

Source: Ministry of Road Transport & Highways, Govt of India, 2023, data accessed from https://pib.gov.in on 25 April, 2024.

TABLE 5.2 Lane-wise Break-up of National Highways, 2023

Number of Lanes	Length (km)	Percentage of Total
Single lane/intermediate lane	14,870	10
Two-lane	85,096	58
Four-lane and above	46,179	32
Total	146,145	100

Source: National Highway Statistics accessed from https://pib.gov.in as on 20th April, 2024.

3. The total road length of the country increased significantly from 3.99 lakh km in 1951 to 66.7 lakh km in 2023, growing at a compound annual growth rate (CAGR) of more than 4% during the year 1951–2023. The state-wise break-up shows that Maharashtra accounted for the largest share (12.49%) in total network of roads, followed by Uttar Pradesh (8.57%), Karnataka (7.22%), Madhya Pradesh (6.86%) and Assam (6.76%). Moreover, Maharashtra accounted for the largest share (13.52%) in the total length of NHs followed by Uttar Pradesh, Rajasthan, Madhya Pradesh and Karnataka.
4. As on 2016, two-lane NHs constituted the largest share of NHs, that is, 58% in the total length of NHs. This was followed by four-lane and above NHs (comprising of 32% of the total length of NH). The share of less than two-lane NHs during 2023 was 10% (Table 5.2). National Highway network increased by about 60% from 91,287 km in 2014 to 1,46,145 km in year 2023.
5. The pace at which roads have been constructed has grown significantly from 12 kms per day in 2014–15 to 30 kms per day in FY23.

Problems of Indian Road Sector

Problems With National Highways NH that constitutes 1.8% of total road length bears around 40% of traffic burden. Further compared to international standards, the condition of Indian highways is below average. There have been following constraints in the expansion and upgradation of NH: (1) lack of availability of land, (2) significant increase in land acquisition costs, (3) lack of equity with developers, (4) too many bottlenecks and checkpoints on NHs—could adversely impact benefits of GST, (5) higher cost of financing, (6) lesser traffic growth than expected, and (7) shortfall in funds for maintenance.[22]

Traffic Congestion Traffic congestion during peak hours in four major cities—Delhi, Mumbai, Bengaluru, and Kolkata—costs the economy ₹1.47 lakh crore annually, according to a study conducted by global consultancy firm.[23] Traffic congestion costed New Delhi close to ₹54,000 crore in the year 2013. Furthermore, the major detrimental effects arising due to increasing congestion levels include the people spending more time in traffic, leading to productivity losses, vehicles spending more time idling, releasing more pollutants into the air, increasing fuel wastages due to frequent traffic jams, and stalling at signals.[24] The trucking sector contributes 4.5–5% to the GDP and is the lifeline of the economy transporting goods from one point to another on a 24/7 basis. On an average, for a truck, it takes 3 days to cover 1,380 km on Delhi to Mumbai highway at an average speed of 17 km per hour. Though road freight volumes are rising at a CAGR of 9.08% and the population of vehicles is increasing at a CAGR of 10.76%, road length is widening at a CAGR of 4.01%.[25]

Poor Quality of Roads The economic costs of poor road maintenance are borne primarily by road users. When a road is allowed to deteriorate from good to poor condition, each dollar saved on road maintenance increases vehicle operating cost by between $2 and $3. Far from saving money, cutting back on road maintenance increases the cost of road transport and raises the net cost to the economy as a whole.[26] Nearly 40% of roads, including rural, intra-district, and state highways, are not metalled outlining the limitations in connectivity but also offering hope that road development in remote areas can be a major employment generator for many years to come. Just five states of India—Maharashtra, Uttar Pradesh, Karnataka, West Bengal, and Assam—account for 43% of the road network reflecting the huge imbalances in the road network of the country.[27]

Issues Regarding Road Safety In India, more than 150,000 people are killed each year in traffic accidents. That is about 400 fatalities a day and far higher than developed countries of the world. Besides human errors, the poor quality of roads can be attributed to higher number of road accidents in India.[28] The maximum number of road accidents—about 2 Lakh—occur on two-lane roads. At 33.8%, two-wheelers accounted for the highest share in the total number of road accidents followed by cars, jeeps, and taxis at 23.6%. According to a World Bank estimate, road accidents cost India about 3% of its gross domestic product every year.[29]

Government Policy With Regard to Road Transportation

The Government's focus on constructing NH in Indian States has a significant impact on trade and per capita income. Two interesting relationship can be established as follows[30]:

- Higher the density of NH, higher the Interstate Trade (Export + Import) as % of Gross State Domestic Product (GSDP) in Indian States.
- A positive relationship exists between density of NHs and the per capita income in Indian States. Higher the density of NH, higher the per capita GSDP.

For the last few years government has initiated many reform measures in road transport sector. Followings are the highlights.

National Highway Development Project (NHDP) National Highway Development Project (NHDP) was launched in 1998 by NHAI with the objective of developing roads of international standards that facilitate smooth flow of traffic. The NHDP represents 49,260 km of roads and highways work and construction in order to boost economic development of the country. The Government planned to end the NHDP program in early 2018 and consume the ongoing projects under a larger Bharatmala project. NHDP has been implemented in seven phases. Under first phase the government introduced two ambitious projects: Golden Quadrilateral (GQ) and North South-East West (NS-EW) corridor. GQ network comprises a total length of 5,846 km, which connects the four major cities of Delhi, Chennai, Mumbai, and Kolkata. NS-EW corridor connects Srinagar in the north to Kanyakumari in the south and Silchar in the east to Porbandar in the west.

Bharatmala Pariyojana Bharatmala Pariyojana is a new umbrella program for the highways sector, which was launched on July 31, 2015. It focuses on optimizing efficiency of freight and passenger movement across the country by bridging critical infrastructure gaps through effective interventions such as development of Economic Corridors, Inter Corridors and Feeder Routes, National Corridor Efficiency Improvement, Border and International Connectivity Roads, Coastal and Port Connectivity Roads, and Greenfield Expressways. A total of around

24,800 km is being considered in Phase I of Bharatmala. In addition, Bharatmala Pariyojana phase I also includes 10,000 km of balance road works under NHDP, taking the total to 34,800 km at an estimated cost of ₹535,000 crore.[31]

Road Safety The Government has approved a National Road Safety Policy. This Policy outlines various policy measures such as promoting awareness, encouraging safer road infrastructure including application of intelligent transport, enforcement of safety laws, and trauma care. The Government has constituted the National Road Safety Council as the apex body to take policy decisions in matters of road safety. The important schemes on road safety operated by the Ministry include publicity measures and awareness campaign on road safety, Scheme for Setting up Institutes for Driving Training, Refresher Training of Drivers in Unorganized Sector and Human Resource Development, National Highways Accident Relief Service Scheme (NHARSS), setting up of inspection and certification centers and road safety and pollution-testing equipment and program implementation.[32]

e-tolling In order to remove traffic bottle neck at toll plazas and ensure seamless movement of vehicles and hassle-free collection of toll, the Government has implemented a nationwide Electronic Toll Collection based on passive Radio Frequency Identification (RFID) conforming to EPC Gen-2, ISO18000-6C standards. It provides for electronic collection of toll through FASTags. The project was first launched in 2015.[33]

National Green Highways Project The Ministry of Road Transport and Highways (MoRTH), Government of India, has promulgated Green Highways (Plantations, Transplantations, Beautification, and Maintenance) Policy-2015 on September 29, 2015 to develop green corridors along NH for sustainable environment and inclusive growth. Road-side plantations have immense potential to enhance the green cover of nation and generate employment opportunities for rural community. Green Highways Division under NHAI has been entrusted with the task of planning, implementation, and monitoring road-side plantations along 1 lakh km network of NH, which would in turn generate 1 lakh direct employment opportunity in plantations sector in next 10 years.[34]

Water Transport: Maritime & Inland Waterways

Water transport can be discussed in two parts: marine transport and Inland water transport (IWT).

Marine Transport

Maritime transport is a critical infrastructure for the economic development of a nation. It comprises of ports, shipping, shipbuilding and ship repair, and IWT systems. India has a huge coastline spanning 7,516.6 km, forming one of the biggest peninsulas in the world. The importance of this sector can be ascertained from the fact that around 95% of India's trading by volume and 70% by value are done through maritime transport. It influences the pace, structure, and pattern of development.

Features of Shipping and Port Sector

1. There are 13 major ports and about 200 non-major ports in the country. All major ports are administered by central government, whereas the intermediate and minor ports are

TABLE 5.3 Major Ports in India

Ports	State	Year of Establishment/ Declaration as Major Port
Kandla Port	Gujarat	1950
Mumbai Port	Maharashtra	1873
Jawaharlal Nehru Port Trust (JNPT) (also known as NhavaSheva)	Maharashtra	1989
Mormugao Port	Goa	1963
New Mangalore Port (Panambur Port)	Karnataka	1974
VO Chidambaranar Port (Tuticorin Port)	Tamil Nadu	1974
Cochin Port	Kerala	1928
Chennai Port	Tamil Nadu	1881
Kamarajar Port (Ennore Port)	Tamil Nadu	1999
Visakhapatnam Port	Andhra Pradesh	1933
Paradip Port	Odisha	1966
Kolkata Port	West Bengal	1870
Port Blair port	Andaman and Nicobar	2010

Source: Indian Port Association database.

administered by respective state governments. Kamarajar Port (Ennore Port) is the major port but it is a non-governmental port (corporate port) (Table 5.3).

2. India's shipping tonnage has increased from 1.92 lakh gross tonnage (GT) during independence time to about 130 lakh GT during 2023. India has one of the largest merchant shipping fleet among the developing countries and ranks 17th in the world in terms of size of shipping fleet. The maritime sector not only facilitates transportation of national and international cargoes but also provides a variety of other services such as cargo-handling services, shipbuilding and ship repairing, freight forwarding, light house facilities, and training of marine personnel.
3. Jawaharlal Nehru Port Trust (JNPT) continued to be the leading container handling port in the country with a share of about 44% followed by Chennai (24%) and the remaining share of 32% being handled by other major ports.[35] The major items in Cargo Traffic include POL, Coal, Fertilizer, and other cargo.
4. As on December 31, 2023, India had a fleet strength of about 1500 vessels with gross registered tonnage (GRT) of 12.35 million. The age profile of Indian merchant shipping vessels indicates that about 40.1% of the fleet was above 20 years of age.

Problems of Shipping and Port Sector

1. As many as 12 out of India's 28 states have a shoreline, spreading across 7,517 km and about 200 small harbors. Despite a strong platform, the Government has so far failed to transform coastal shipping into a lucrative business opportunity in India.
2. Most cargo that can be transported via costal shipments is still being transported through traditional modes like Rail and Road. The Government regulations are not

coastal-shipping friendly yet. Although India has 14,500 km of navigable waterways, large cargo vessels are unable to use them due to insufficient draught. Furthermore, as these rivers are extensively used for irrigation and electricity generation, the capacity for cargo transportation is severely restricted even further.[36]

3. The port productivity and efficiency also depend upon the quality and reliability of road and rail connectivity, and adequate storage and handling facilities. The lack of expressway connectivity between major ports as well as industrial clusters, and high fuel cost makes hinterland transportation inefficient and slow. Also, the container freight stations and business need to be organized efficiently through good management practice in space utilization, adoption of technology for track and trace, etc.[37]
4. A new study "Port Logistics: Issues & Challenges in India" by Dun and Bradstreet looks into various roadblocks and suggests policy recommendations to resolve the challenges across ports in India. The study introduces a "Port Performance Index" as an attempt to benchmark performance of various ports by combining qualitative perception of stakeholders with quantitative outcome-based data. Looking at 13 major ports, 3 ports (JNPT, Kamarajar, Vizag) have received "Good" score; 7 ports (Cochin, Kandla, Paradip, Chennai, Mormugao, New Mangalore, and VOC) have received "Average" score; and 3 ports (Haldia, Kolkata, and Mumbai Port) have received "Poor" score. Five issues, namely port congestion, customs clearance, shipping line issues and charges, documentation and paperwork, and regulatory clearance, are the most common problems across ports.[38]

Government Policies With Regard to Shipping and Port Sector The salient features of India's shipping policy are the promotion of national shipping to increase self-reliance in the carriage of country's overseas trade and protection of stakeholder's interest in India's foreign trade. For last few years the Government has undertaken following steps to promote India's marine transportation:

Sagarmala Program The Sagarmala project was launched by Indian Prime Minister, on April 14, 2016 at the Maritime India Summit 2016. It is the flagship program of the Ministry of Shipping to promote port-led development in the country through harnessing India's 7,500 km long coastline, 14,500 km of potentially navigable waterways, and strategic location on key international maritime trade routes. The main vision of the Sagarmala Program is to reduce logistics cost for international and domestic trade, industry and infrastructure with minimal infrastructure investment.[39] The four components of Sagarmala Program are port modernization and new port development, port connectivity enhancement, port-linked industrialization and coastal community development.[40]

Port Development The following initiatives have been taken to improve the performance of Major Ports:

1. Major Ports have been benchmarked to international standards and 116 initiatives were identified of which 86 initiatives have been implemented and remaining will be implemented by 2019.
2. RFID System to reduce dwell time, transaction time, and ease congestion has been operationalized in all the Major Ports.
3. Direct port delivery and direct port entry initiated at Major Ports for EXIM containers.

Port Efficiency Efficiency at ports has an important bearing on the transaction cost of the shipping lines. The Average Turnaround Time improved from 4.24 days in 2000–2001 to 2.11 days during 2016–2017. In the Maritime Agenda 2010–2020, a target of 3,130 MT port capacity has been set for the year 2020. The proposed investment in major and non-major ports by 2020 is expected to be around ₹277,380 crore. FDI up to 100% under the automatic route is permitted for construction and maintenance of ports.[41]

Shipbuilding and Ship-Repair Industry Shipbuilding is a manufacturing industry endowed with the unique feature of having nearly 65% value addition coming from other technology/ancillary industries. In India, there are 27 shipyards comprising 6 under Central Public Sector, 2 under State Governments, and 19 under Private Sector Undertakings. Shipbuilding industry employs over 30,000 people directly. However, over the years, the industry has developed a large number of ancillary units and subcontractors around them employing lakhs of people. Globally, the shipbuilding industry is dominated by three countries, namely South Korea, China, and Japan, which together have more than 90% share of the shipbuilding market. Major shipbuilding nations support their industry through direct financing and fiscal incentives. The Indian share in the global ship repair market continued to be low as there was very little capacity addition. Indian ship owners continued to rely on overseas repair facilities owing to insufficient capacity and high level of taxation.[42] However, it is important to note that India is located strategically on the international trade route, whereby it can attract ships plying from west to east in the trade route for its ship-repair activity. Geostrategic location of India, abundance of labor, and quality of work are the strengths for the ship-repair business.[43]

Maritime Clusters Clusters induce innovations, create employment opportunities, attract foreign investors, and also spark new ideas. Shipbuilding clusters and maritime parks are some of the concepts practiced in top maritime nations. The Government has identified two major maritime clusters in Tamil Nadu and Gujarat similar to the global success stories in Japan and South Korea. These clusters will focus on developing various components of the maritime cluster such as ship building and ancillary services, maritime services, and promoting maritime tourism and marine products. Given the manufacturing strength, size of the ports, and synergies with other steel ancillaries, both the identified locations for maritime clusters can attract business and improve the overall economics for the cluster participants.[44]

Indian Maritime University Indian Maritime University (IMU) was set up in 2008 in Chennai with campuses at Chennai, Kolkata, and Visakhapatnam as a Central University. The existing seven government and government-aided maritime training and research institutes have been merged with the IMU. The University aims to achieve academic and research excellence in merchant navy, ship design, ship building and repair, supply chain management, and hydrography.

Inland Water Transport

IWT is a method of transporting cargo over rivers, backwaters, canals, and creeks. It provides a cost-effective, logistically efficient, and environment-friendly mode of transport.

Features of Inland Waterways

1. Water transportation cost is barely 50 paise a km in comparison to ₹1 by railways and ₹1.5 per km through roads. About 55 MT of cargo is being moved annually by IWT, a fuel efficient and environment-friendly mode.

2. Inland waterways comprising rivers, lakes, canals, creeks, backwaters, etc., extend to about 14,500 km in the country. Of this 5,200 km of the rivers and 4,000 km of canals can be used by mechanized craft.
3. The National Waterways Act, 2016 came into force in April 2016. The Act seeks to develop inland waterways in 24 states of India.
4. There are 111 National Waterways in the country today, after 106 waterways were declared as National Waterways, as per the National Waterways Act, 2016. The five National Waterways existed before the enactment of Act.

Problems of Inland Waterways

1. Approximately 90% of freight in India currently moves via land transport (road, rail, pipelines). More than 40% transportation is done through the inland waterways in China, Korea, and European nations, while in India a meagre 3.5% was done through this channel, which has now gone up to 6%.[45]
2. In India, river water is a state subject. River linkages and water sharing arrangements will have to be worked out between states to estimate the quantum of water required on a time basis throughout the year to maintain the minimum depth of water in the canals for navigability, besides ensuring that drinking, irrigation and other demands of water do not get impacted.
3. Inland waterways require long-term vision for the development of dams, bridges, and other in-way infrastructures. For example, the road and rail bridges with low vertical clearances may hinder the passage of larger ships on the waterways.
4. Higher water salinity, especially in the coastal regions and estuaries, and constant inflow of silt in the rivers can be problematic. Along with the minimal water flow continuous dredging is desired as the rivers bring a large amount of siltation.[46]
5. The cost savings from water transportation would never be realized unless vessels are able to load to their full tonnage. This is possible only if the rivers are deepened between 2.5 and 4.5 m and if return cargo is made available for the vessel to avoid wasteful return trips.
6. Indian rivers are locational, cover small geography, and undergo huge seasonal fluctuations because of their ephemeral nature (especially the non-Himalayan rivers). Some of the rivers generally remain dry, which make them unsuitable for navigation. There is a need to develop water reservoirs for the conservation of rainwater to feed such rivers.
7. The financing requirement for IWT is huge and open-ended. The heavy investment will be needed for construction of locking barrages to hold water for vessel movement, concretization, and building of embankments to create port terminals and procure equipment, including dredgers, shipping vessels, and barges of different sizes and require river ports with their support infrastructure—road and rail connectivity, warehouses, and other services.[47]

Policy Issues with Regard to Inland Waterways

1. According to Integrated National Transportation Waterway Grid Study, an indicative investment of ₹22,763 crore is required to develop infrastructure such as fairway, terminals, ports, road, and rail connectivity. This public investment is expected to attract private investment of about ₹65,600 crore on inland shipbuilding, ship repair, and cargo movement in the IWT Sector by the end of 2023.

2. India's first multi-modal inland waterways hub in Varanasi was inaugurated by Prime Minister in November 2018. This is the first of the four multi-modal terminals being constructed on the National Waterway-1 (river Ganga) as part of the World Bank-aided *Jal Marg Vikas project* of the Inland Waterways Authority of India. The total estimated cost of the project is ₹53.6918 billion, which will be equally shared between the Government of India and the World Bank. The project entails construction of three multi-modal terminals (Varanasi, Sahibganj, and Haldia), two inter-modal terminals, five roll-on-roll-off (Ro-Ro) terminal pairs, new navigation lock at Farakka in West Bengal, assured depth dredging, integrated vessel repair and maintenance facility, differential global positioning system (DGPS), river information system (RIS), and river training. The project aims at developing the stretch of the river between Varanasi and Haldia for navigation of large vessels weighing up to 1,500–2,000 ton.[48]
3. Private sector participation is being encouraged in the inland waterways to promote investment and innovation. A MoU has been signed between Inland Waterways Authority of India (IWAI) and Maruti Suzuki India Ltd for transportation of cars through inland vessels. The private sector can participate in many potential areas like terminal and warehousing facilities, mechanization of the cargo-handling system, installation of the new navigational aids, deploying low draft barges and vessels, and maintenance of the existing fairways.
4. Inland waterways offer millions of job opportunities in the coming years. Professionals and technocrats will get job opportunities in the form of marine managers, naval architect, ship and port safety officer, port inspectors, ship surveyors, cargo managers, marine chartering, cargo brokers, and many others. In Uttar Pradesh alone the National Waterway-1 is proposed to generate employment to 5 lakh workers.

Air Transport

Air transport is an important enabler to achieving economic growth and development. Air transport facilitates integration into the global economy and provides vital connectivity on a national, regional, and international scale. It helps generate trade and promote tourism, and create employment opportunities.[49]

Features of Air Transport

1. India's first commercial civil aviation flight took off from Allahabad for Naini over a distance of 10 km in 1911. Tata airline (first commercial airlines of India) was founded by J.R.D. Tata in 1932 in an airline, which later became Air India in 1946.
2. India is the third largest and the fastest growing domestic aviation market in the world in terms of number of domestic tickets sold. There are more than 20 airlines that are operational in India, including Air India and Pawan Hans PSUs, listed companies viz. SpiceJet, IndiGo Airlines, Jet Lite, Air India Express, and Jet Airways, and private airlines, such as GoAir, Air Asia, Vistara, and IndiGo.
3. The total number of scheduled operational airports in India has increased from 74 in 2014 to 149 in 2023, of which about about 34 are international airports and rest are domestic airports.[50] The Indira Gandhi Airport at New Delhi is the busiest airport in the country in terms of passenger traffic since 2009 and the second busiest airport in the country in terms of cargo traffic after Mumbai.

4. The Freight traffic stood at 3.15 million metric tonnes in FY23. The Freight traffic in airports in India has the potential to reach 17 MT by FY40. In FY23, the number of aircraft movements stood at 2.5 million. The total passenger traffic stood at a 327.28 million in financial year 23.
5. By 2036, India is estimated to have 480 million flyers, which will be more than that of Japan (just under 225 million) and Germany (just over 200 million) combined. India ranks fourth in world aviation market followed by the United States, China, and the United Kingdom. India is expected to overtake the United Kingdom to become the third largest air passenger market by 2025.[51]

Problems of Indian Air Transport Sector

1. While the domestic demand for air travel has increased considerably in the last few years, the Government has done little to actually help it achieve its true potential. The Government has not reduced the jet fuel prices in proportion to the fall in international crude oil prices. As a result, flying by air is expensive for an average Indian. Only about 2% of the Indian population currently travels by air.[52]
2. A majority of India's new and aspirant airlines appear to be facing major cash and operational issues, delaying salaries, putting off aircraft induction, grounding planes, and cancelling flights, leading to questions about whether they can cope in a sector that demands patience to deal with bureaucratic delays and the ability to overcome lobbying by incumbents.[53] No wonder, the employees of such airlines are relinquishing their jobs and are joining the other airlines. The failure of incumbent airlines also discourages ready-to-join players to make entry in India's much sought after transport sector.
3. One of the biggest challenges facing the aviation sector in India is to be able to provide regional connectivity. What is hampering the growth of regional connectivity is the lack of airports and quality infrastructure. The need for improved aviation infrastructure extends beyond the construction of new airports—existing metro airports also require significant modernization and upgrading.[54]

Government Policies With Regard to Air Transport Sector

Airport Authority of India (AAI)

Airports Authority of India (AAI) was established in April 1995. AAI under the Ministry of Civil Aviation is a Mini-Ratna-Category-I PSE involved in building, upgrading, maintaining, and managing airports infrastructure across the country. It provides air traffic management services over Indian airspace and adjoining oceanic areas.[55]

Regional Connectivity Scheme—"Ude Desh ka Aam Naagrik" (RCS-UDAN)

To make flying accessible and affordable for the masses in the regionally important cities, the RCS-UDAN scheme was launched in October 2016. This is a first-of-its-kind scheme globally to stimulate regional connectivity through a market-based mechanism. Twenty-seven states/union territories have already signed MOUs with the Central Government under RCS-UDAN. Many private sector airlines are actively participating under this scheme. The Government has awarded

325 routes to airlines as well as helicopter operators with the objective of enhancing flight services to hilly and remote areas. Under the scheme airline operators have to offer half of their seats at discounted rates and helicopter operators can offer up to 13 seats at lower fares with the government providing Viability Gap Funding (VGF) or subsidy to airlines and helicopter operators.[56]

Airport Development

The Government has granted in-principle approval for setting up 18 greenfield airports in the country. The Government has granted "site clearance" for five greenfield airports: Machiwara in Punjab, Itanagar in Arunachal Pradesh, Jamshedpur in Jharkhand, Alwar in Rajasthan, and Kothagudem in Telangana.[57]

Investment Initiatives

The Government of India has raised the FDI limit for 49–100% in scheduled and non-scheduled air transport services, FDI in scheduled airlines up to 49% permitted under automatic route and FDI beyond 49% through government approval. For NRIs, 100% FDI will continue to the allowed under automatic route.[58] In July 2020, the government notified changes in FDI norms on civil aviation, which will permit non-resident Indian nationals to own 100% stake of Air India. FDI inflows in air transport (including air freight) between April 2000 and December 2023 stood at US $3.83 Billion. India is estimated to see an investment of US$25 billion in the next decade in the airports sector, and traffic growth of 13%, according to Morgan Stanley. Capex plans to the tune of ₹65,000 crore have been finalized by AAI with ₹17,500 crore for the next 5 years and around ₹22,000 crore for brownfield expansion in Delhi, Mumbai, Hyderabad, and Bengaluru by private operators and around ₹21,000 crore for greenfield airports.

National Civil Aviation Policy, 2016

The National Civil Aviation Policy, 2016 aims to take flying to the masses by making it affordable and convenient, establish an integrated eco-system that will lead to significant growth of the civil aviation sector to promote tourism, employment, and balanced regional growth, enhance regional connectivity through fiscal support and infrastructure development, and enhance ease of doing business through deregulation, simplified procedures, and e-governance. The policy is very comprehensive, covering 22 areas of the Civil Aviation sector. The broad areas covered by policy are:[59] regional connectivity scheme; 5/20 requirement—under which airlines can now commence international operations provided that they deploy 20 aircraft or 20% of total capacity; bilateral traffic rights with SAARC nations; encouraging private sector participation in airport development; encouraging the helicopter passenger services in the country; providing incentives to promote maintenance, repair, and overhaul business; promoting aviation education and skill building and; hybrid till policy & greenfield airports.

ENERGY

Energy access is the "golden thread" that weaves together economic growth, human development, and environmental sustainability. It is one of the most critical components of infrastructure crucial for the economic growth and welfare of nations.

Characteristic Features of Energy in India

1. With total electricity generation of nearly 1600 TWh in March 2021, India was the third largest producer and the third largest consumer of electricity in the world, behind China and the United States. India generates about 71 per cent of electricity through coal and lignite followed by hydroelectricity (Table 5.4).
2. Industry is the biggest consumer of electricity in India (42.7%), followed by domestic, agriculture, and commercial uses (Table 5.5).
3. Renewable energy sources (RES) include wind power, solar energy, geothermal energy, bio energy, and small hydro-plants. According to the Ministry of New and Renewable Energy (MNRE), the hydroelectric plants with capacity of 25.00 MW and below are considered as RES. In India RES constitute 10% of electricity production, whereas the rest 90% is produced by non-RES.
4. Electricity demand in the country has increased rapidly and is expected to rise further in the years to come. In order to meet the increasing demand for electricity in the country, massive addition to the installed generating capacity is required. India ranks third among 40 countries in EY's Renewable Energy Country Attractiveness Index, on back of strong focus by the government on promoting renewable energy and implementation of projects in a time bound manner. India has moved up 73 spots to rank 26th in the World Bank's list of electricity accessibility in 2017.

The followings are the primary energy sources:

Thermal Energy: Fossil fuels (e.g., coal, natural gas, crude oil, and its products), nuclear fuels, biomass (including wood), geo thermal energy, industrial by products [e.g., liquefied petroleum gas (LPG), coke oven gas, and blast furnace gas], etc.

Hydropower: Hydropower energy excluding pumped storage operation.

Non-conventional energy: Solar energy, wind power, wave power, tidal power, animal draught.

TABLE 5.4 Mode-wise Gross Electricity Generation in India 2022–23

Mode	GWh	In Percentage
Coal/lignite	1,182,096	73.07
Hydro	162,099	10.02
Renewable energy sources (RES)	203,552	12.58
Gas	23,885	3.50
Nuclear	45,861	2.83
Diesel	320	0.02

Source: Growth of Electricity Sector in India from 1947–2023, Ministry of Power, Government of India, Oct, 2023.

TABLE 5.5 Electricity Energy Consumption in India (in Million Units)

Category	2022–23 (GWh)	2022–23 (%)
Industrial	595,000	42.40
Domestic	362,000	27.21
Agriculture	240,800	17.16
Commercial	105,100	7.49
Misc	75,500	5.38
Traction	25,000	1.78
Total	1,403,400	100%

Source: Growth of Electricity Sector in India from 1947–2023, Ministry of Power, Government of India, Oct 2023.

CONVENTIONAL ENERGY

Coal

Coal is the only natural resource and fossil fuel available in abundance in India. The systematic exploration of coal in India started about 172 years back sometimes in the year 1845.

Features of Coal Energy Resource

1. India is the third largest producer of coal in the world. The total estimated coal resources in the country 315.149 billion ton. Every year about 3–5 billion ton of resources are being added through fresh exploration to the Coal Inventory of India.[60] With the present rate of around 0.8 Mt average daily coal extraction in the country, the reserves are likely to last over a 100 years.
2. Coal is one of the primary sources of energy, accounting for about 73% of the total energy consumption in the country. The energy derived from coal in India is about twice that of energy derived from oil, as against the world, where energy derived from coal is about 30% lower than energy derived from oil.
3. State-wise distribution of Indian coal shows that Jharkhand tops the list with 82.44 billion ton followed successively by Odisha (77.28 billion ton), Chhattisgarh (56.66 billion ton), West Bengal (31.67 billion ton), Madhya Pradesh (27.67 billion ton), Telangana (21.46 billion ton), Maharashtra (12.26 billion ton), and others. A glimpse at the coal-field-wise distribution of Indian coal resource suggests that five coalfields—Talcher (51.16 billion ton), Mand-Raigarh (30.06 billion ton), Raniganj (26.84 billion ton), Ib-River (26.12 billion ton), and Godavari (23.04 billion ton) are sharing nearly 50% of total resources of the country.[61]
4. The Coal India Ltd. (CIL) contributes around 86% of coal production in India. CIL is the largest company in the world in terms of coal production.

Problems in the Coal Sector

Supply Constraints

Many private sector steel, power, and aluminum producers facing a shortage of the coal in the plants and are forced to shut or pare operations. Many reasons can be attributed to the supply-side bottlenecks. First, poor rail connectivity is a major constrains, which leads to inadequate evacuation. Second, the 2014 Supreme Court judgment on the coal scam and the subsequent decisions of de-allocation implemented by the Ministry of Coal have made both mining and acquisition of this mineral a sticky affair in India. Third, there has been a swift decline in the energy production in hydel and nuclear plants. Coal-fired generating stations, which were battling low electricity demands, are caught unaware by the sudden explosion of power demand.

Corruption and Scams

The Government allocated 208 coal blocks with geological surveys of about 50,000 MT to various public/private companies during 2004–2009. A report by the Comptroller and Auditor General

(CAG) of India found such allocation inefficient and illegal and estimated loss to the exchequer to the tune of ₹1.86 lakh crore. The central point of the CAG report that showed improper allocation was that the Government had the authority to allocate the coal blocks. However, this was to be done via competitive bidding. But the Government chose to take another route and avoided competitive bidding. Hence, the revenue secured from the allottees for allocation was much less than what could have been if there was competitive bidding—hence presumptive loss to the exchequer. Coalgate, as it was popularly known snowballed into a huge political scandal, which pulled top leaders and bureaucrats from the previous UPA regime into the probe.[62] As mentioned earlier, it affected the smooth bureaucratic function in allocation and subsequent mining and acquisition.

Environmental Challenges

Environmental activists have long sought to depict coal as a "dirty" fuel. In recent times policy-makers as well as activists have questioned the viability of coal as a sustainable energy source, certainly in the context of the greenhouse effect and global climate change. There is a need for balance between mining and environmental requirements. The rapid, unchecked, and sometimes biased activities result in air, water, and noise pollution, land degradation, health hazards, loss of forest wealth and agricultural land, drying of wells, and rehabilitation problems leading to large-scale environmental deterioration. In addition, due to excessive mining, chances of accidents increase, which lead to misery and tragedy.[63]

Social Challenges

Social impact of coal development deserves serious, systematic, and sympathetic consideration. There have been unsatisfactory mining practices in the past looking at today's standards and still today such practices are continuing. Like the environmental impacts, the social impacts of mining are often difficult to quantify and because of this perhaps, little attention has been paid to this aspect. The mindless mining in the country has led to the problem of mining-induced displacement and resettlement. Research has found few other social implications like joblessness, homelessness, marginalization, food insecurity, loss of common lands and resources, increased health risks, social disarticulation, the disruption of formal educational activities, and the loss of civil and human rights. Certain groups—especially indigenous people, the elderly, and women—have been found to be more vulnerable to displacement-induced impoverishment risks.[64]

Policy Issues in the Coal Sector

In September 2014, the Supreme Court had cancelled 204 coal mines allocated to the different government and private companies since 1993 under the provisions of Coal Mines (Nationalisation) Act, 1973. To bring transparency and accountability, the Coal Mines (Special Provisions) Bill 2015 was passed by the Parliament, which was notified as an Act in March 2015. During March 2018, the Cabinet Committee on Economic Affairs approved a methodology to auction coal blocks for commercial mining.

Followings are the features and benefits associated with new coal distribution policy[65]:

1. The new policy will promote efficiency in the coal sector by moving from an era of monopoly to competition. India is said have coal reserves of up to 300 billion ton. The new coal distribution methodology gives the highest priority to transparency, ease of doing business, and ensuring that natural resources are used for national development.

2. While coal mines were till now auctioned for captive power generation, they will now be sold in an e-auction to private domestic and global miners. It will increase competitiveness and allow the best possible technology into the sector. The higher investment will create direct and indirect employment in coal bearing areas, especially in the mining sector and will have an impact on economic development of these regions.
3. The move will also lead to greater energy security as 70% of India's electricity is generated from thermal power plants. Under the proposed commercial mining policy, mining companies will have the ability to set their own sale price for coal. It will set a benchmark for CIL and force it to be more competitive. The reform will ensure assured coal supply, accountable allocation of coal, and affordable coal leading to affordable power prices for consumers. It will also help India's dependence on coal imports and thus save valuable foreign exchange.
4. The entire revenue from the auction of coal mines for sale of coal would accrue to the coal-bearing states. This methodology shall incentivize them with increased revenues, which can be utilized for the growth and development of backward areas and their inhabitants including tribals. States in eastern part of the country viz. West Bengal, Odisha, Jharkhand, Chhattisgarh, and Madhya Pradesh will be especially benefited.

Hydroelectricity

The earlier uses of hydropower could be traced back to sixth century B.C. at Mesopotamia and ancient Egypt, besides peninsular India and Sri Lanka. The world's first modern electrical power generation on a commercial scale is just 130 years old, which was constructed in England in 1881 by utilizing the water potential of river Wey at Godalming Surrey. Hydropower plants all over the world produce about 24% of the world's electricity. Asia accounted for 24% of the world's hydropower generation, followed by North America with 23% and Europe with 20%.

Features of Hydroelectric Power in India

1. India's first hydropower generation plant named Sidrapong on Teesta river at Darjeeling became operational in 1897 with an electricity generating capacity of 130 kW.
2. India is the seventh largest producer of hydroelectric power in the world with installed capacity of 44,594 MW. However, India's hydroelectric power potential is estimated at 148,700 MW at 60% load factor. The top three producers of hydroelectric power are China, Canada and Brazil.
3. The small hydropower potential of the country has been assessed at 6,781.81 MW of installed capacity.
4. India's hydropower development potential lies in the key basins of Brahmaputra Basin (66 GW), Indus Basin (34 GW), Ganga Basin (21 GW), and the rivers of South India (24 GW).
5. The public sector dominates the energy production in India with a share of nearly 89% in the total installed capacity (Table 5.6).

Challenges and Problems of Hydropower Projects

There are a number of problems and challenges in the hydropower sector that discourage hydropower producers to participate in hydro-development of the country.

TABLE 5.6 Top 10 Largest Dams in India

Name of the Dam	Opening Year	Installed Capacity (MW)	State
Tehri Dam	2006	2,400	Uttarakhand
Koyna Hydroelectric Project	1964	1,960	Maharashtra
Srisailam	1981	1,670	Andhra Pradesh
Nathpa Jhakri	2004	1,500	Himachal Pradesh
Sardar Sarovar Dam	2017	1,450	Gujarat
Bhakra Nangal Dam	1963	1,325	Himachal Pradesh
Chamera Dam	1994	1,071	Himachal Pradesh
Sharavathi Project (Linganamakki Reservoir)	1964	1,035	Karnataka
Indira Sagar Dam	2005	1,000	Madhya Pradesh
Karcham Wangtoo Hydroelectric Plant	2011	1,000	Himachal Pradesh

Source: Ministry of Power, Government of India.

1. Long gestation period mainly because of delay in land acquisition, time consumption in project clearance, and huge capital intensive nature of the project.
2. Technical constraints due to complex geological nature of the projects.
3. Inter-state disputes as water is a state subject.
4. Financial constraints.
5. Involvement of multiplicity of agencies in the hydro-sector such as Ministry of Environment & Forests.
6. The issue of resettlement and rehabilitation.

Government Policies with Regard to Hydroelectricity The Government has come out with various policies for the development of hydroelectricity. National Policy (1998) on Hydropower was announced to undertake measures for the exploitation of vast hydro-electric potential in the country. Subsequently government also announced The Electricity Act, 2003; The National Electricity Policy, 2005; National Tariff Policy, 2006. For a more transparent and participative rehabilitation and resettlement process, government announced National Resettlement and Rehabilitation (R&R) Policy, 2007. Mega Power Projects Policy, 2008 and Land Acquisition Act, 2014 were announced to speed up hydroelectricity generation in India.[66]

Small Hydropower Programs

MNRE has been vested with the responsibility of developing Small Hydro Power (SHP) projects up to 25 MW station capacities. The estimated potential for power generation in the country from such plants is about 20,000 MW. Most of the potential is in Himalayan States as river-based projects and in other states on irrigation canals. The SHP program is now essentially private investment driven. Projects are normally economically viable and private sector is showing lot of interest in investing in SHP projects. The viability of these projects improves with increase in the project capacity. The Ministry's aim is that at least 50% of the potential in the country is harnessed in the next 10 years.[67] The Government has classified hydro-plants on the basis of their station capacity. The hydro-plants up to the station capacity of 100 KW are classified as micro-hydro-projects, from 101–2,000 KW as mini-hydro-projects and from 2001–25,000 KW as small hydro-projects.

A key benefit of small hydropower generation is that it can deliver local energy to remote communities, which are unlikely to get connected to the main electricity grid due to setup costs. Due to small size and investment, such units get easy access to finance as well. The incentive in returns is another motivating factor as it costs ₹9 crore to develop a plant that produces 1 MW. Once a unit starts generating electricity, the Government pays ₹3.27 per Watt to buy the energy, and guarantees to continue doing so for 40 year. Within 5–7 years, the cost is recovered.[68] SHP is a clean energy source as it does not produce waste in the rivers, or air pollution and renewable. Small hydropower plants ensure a minimum flow downstream, ecological, or reserved flow that guarantees fish life.[69] Finally, there is no problem of resettlement and rehabilitation in the construction of small dams as in the case of large dams.

Natural Gas

Natural gas occurs deep beneath the earth's surface. Natural gas consists mainly of methane, a compound with one carbon atom and four hydrogen atoms. If it occurs in coal deposits, it is called coalbed methane. If it occurs in the tiny pores (spaces) within some formations of shale, sandstone, and other types of sedimentary rock, it is called shale gas or tight gas.[70] Natural gas*, in itself, might be considered an uninteresting gas—it is colorless, shapeless, and odorless in its pure form. Quite uninteresting—except that natural gas is combustible and when burned it gives off a great deal of energy with fewer emissions than many other sources. Found in reservoirs underneath the earth, natural gas is often associated with oil deposits. Compared to other fossil fuels, natural gas is cleaner burning and emits lower levels of potentially harmful by-products into the air.[71]

Features of Natural Gas in India

Followings are the characteristic features of natural gas in India.

1. India's natural gas production in 2017 was reported to be 32.64 billion cubic meter (BCM), out of which 22.01 BCM was offshore production and 10.63 BCM was onshore production.[72]
2. The development of natural gas industry in the country started in 1960s with discovery of gas fields in Assam and Gujarat. After discovery of South Basin fields by ONGC in 1970s, natural gas assumed importance. The exploration activities in India were earlier carried out only by the national oil companies viz. Oil and Natural Gas Commission (ONGC) and Oil India Ltd (OIL). Later private companies were allowed to enter into exploration through joint venture.
3. Natural gas available in India can broadly be classified into two categories, viz. (1) Domestic Natural Gas and (2) Imported Re-gasified Liquefied Natural Gas (RLNG). Supply and distribution of domestically produced gas is being carried out under the policy guidelines issued by the Government Policies from time to time. The import of RLNG falls under

* Natural gas is considered "dry" when it is almost pure methane, having had most of the other commonly associated hydrocarbons removed. When other hydrocarbons are present, the natural gas is "wet."

the list of Open General License Item and the marketers are free to import LNG and sell the RLNG to customers.

4. Natural Gas Infrastructure in India can be classified under three categories.
   a. *Natural Gas Pipelines* At present, country is having about 16,470 km long natural gas pipeline network in operation.
   b. *Liquid Natural Gas (LNG) Re-gasification Terminals* At present, four LNG terminals are operational on the western coast of the country viz. Hazira, Kochi, Dhabol, and Dahej.
   c. *City Gas Distribution (CGD) Infrastructure* In year 2007, Government of India established Petroleum and Natural Gas Regulatory Board (PNGRB) that regulates the City Gas Distribution (CGD) network [including piped natural gas (PNG) network]. CGD sector has four distinct segments—compressed natural gas (CNG) predominantly used as auto-fuel, and PNG used in domestic, commercial, and industrial segments.

Challenges of Natural Gas in India and Policy Implications

Domestic Production and Consumption The share of natural gas in the country's primary energy mix declined from 10% in 2009 to 6.7% in 2023 compared with the global average of 24%, mainly due to a sharp drop in domestic supplies. The Government has set a target to raise the share of natural gas in energy mix to 15% in 2030. Furthermore, India's 39 m^3 per capita of natural gas consumption lags far behind the world average of 469 m^3 per capita. The consumption ratio of oil to gas for India stands at 4.72 against a global ratio of 1.38, indicates that we are more dependent on crude oil and comparatively less on natural gas.[73] India's natural gas demand has been mainly affected by lower availability and price affordability; inadequate transmission and distribution infrastructure; and limited gas import facilities.

National Gas Grid The Government has envisaged developing an additional 15,000 km long pipeline network to have an ecosystem of National Gas Grid in the country.

The aims and objectives of National Gas Grid are as under[74]:

1. To remove regional imbalance within the country with regard to access of natural gas and provide clean and green fuel throughout the country.
2. To connect gas sources to major demand centers and ensure availability of gas to consumers in various sectors.
3. Development of CGD networks in various cities for supply of CNG and PNG.

The 2,650 km Jagdishpur-Haldia and Bokaro-Dhamra Pipeline (JHBDPL) natural gas pipeline project, popularly known as Pradhan Mantri Urja Ganga of Eastern India, has already been under construction. This project will connect eastern part of the country with National Gas Grid and will ensure the availability of clean and eco-friendly fuel, natural gas, to the industrial, commercial, domestic, and transport sectors in the states of Uttar Pradesh, Bihar, Jharkhand, Odisha, and West Bengal.[75]

Liberalization of Gas Pricing Supplies to India's gas market are categorized into two segments: domestically produced and imported (via LNG) gas. The price of domestic gas is lower than that of LNG and is defined by the Government's adopted indexation formula. The Government of India has liberalized domestic gas pricing in a phased manner. The price of imported LNG is higher than that of domestic gas. The Government does not exercise any control on LNG imports and the marketing of RLNG.[76]

Schemes for the Consumers

Pratyaksh Hanstantrit Labh (PAHAL) Scheme The Pratyaksh Hanstantrit Labh (PAHAL)-Direct Benefits Transfer for LPG (DBTL) scheme was launched on June 1, 2013 and it required the consumer to mandatorily have an Aadhaar number for availing LPG subsidy. The Government has comprehensively reviewed the scheme and after examining the difficulties faced by the consumer substantively modified the scheme and re-launched it in November 2014.[77] The purpose of the scheme is to cut subsidy leakages, but not subsidies themselves. PAHAL has entered into Guinness Book of World Records being largest Direct Benefit Transfer (DBT) Scheme.

LPG Connections to BPL Houses—Pradhan Mantri Ujjwala Yojana Pradhan Mantri Ujjwala Yojana is an ambitious social welfare scheme of the Government launched on May 1, 2016 from Ballia in Uttar Pradesh. Under the scheme, the Government aims to provide LPG connections to Below Poverty Line (BPL) households in the country. The scheme is aimed at replacing the unclean cooking fuels mostly used in the rural India with the clean and more efficient LPG. Ujjwala Yojana is aimed at providing 5 crore LPG connections in the name of women in BPL households across the country.[78]

OIL/PETROLEUM

Due to its high energy density, easy transportability, and relative abundance, oil has been the world's leading source of energy since the mid-1950s. Termed as Black Gold, it is the world's leading fuel, accounting for a third of global energy consumption.

Features of Petroleum Energy

1. Oil production in India is done both onshore and offshore areas. 49% of oil is produced onshore whereas 51% is produced offshore. Onshore production comes primarily from three states viz. (Gujarat, Assam, and Rajasthan, which account for more than 95% of onshore output). Offshore production is concentrated in the Mumbai high field, south of Gujarat state, in shallow waters.[79]
2. India had estimated crude oil reserves of 604.10 MT. The largest reserves are found in the Western Offshore (39.60%), and Assam (26.48%). India produced 35.68 MT of crude oil during 2017–2018, which is nearly 0.9% of world production. India's crude oil import dependence is 82.8% of total oil consumption in the country. India produced 254.3 MT of petroleum products in 2022–23 and among petroleum products, high-speed diesel oil accounted for 42.08%, followed by Motor Gasoline. India is the second largest refiner in Asia after China, and is emerging as a refinery hub with refining capacity exceeding demand.
3. Various PSUs are engaged in the exploration, production or refinery functions are Balmer Lawric & Co. Limited, Bharat Petroleum Corporation Limited, Biecco Lawrie Co. Limited, Chennai Petroleum Corporation Limited, Engineers India Limited, Gas Authority of India Limited, Hindustan Petroleum Corporation Limited, Indian Oil Corporation Limited, Numaligarh Refinery Limited, Oil India Limited (OIL), and Oil and Natural Gas Corporation Limited (ONGC).[80]

4. ONGC Videsh Limited (OVL), which is wholly owned subsidiary and overseas arm of Oil and ONGC, was created with an objective of acquiring overseas assets, including exploration, development, and production of oil and gas. Presently, it has participated in 39 E&P projects in 18 countries.
5. There are 23 crude oil refineries in India, of which 18 are state-owned, 3 are privately owned, and 2 were joint ventures. The refinery of Indian Oil Corporation is the largest in the country.

Government Policy Regarding Petroleum Sector

1. In order to provide energy security and a buffer from supply-side disruption of crude oil, Government of India has established Strategic Petroleum Reserve (SPR) facilities at three locations viz. Visakhapatnam (Andhra Pradesh), Mangaluru, and Padur in Karnataka. These facilities, which have total capacity of 5.33 MMT, are being managed by Indian Strategic Petroleum Reserve Limited (ISPRL).
2. Exploration and production sector was opened up after implementation of New Exploration Licensing Policy (NELP), which provides an equal platform to both public and private sector companies in exploration and production of hydrocarbons. The Government has allowed 100% foreign direct investment (FDI) in many segments of the sector, including natural gas, petroleum products, and refineries, among others. Today, it attracts both domestic and foreign investment, as attested by the presence of Reliance Industries Ltd (RIL) and Cairn India.[81]
3. The Government has introduced Hydrocarbon Vision 2030 for north east. The Vision aims at doubling oil and gas production by 2030, making clean fuels accessible, fast-tracking projects, generating employment opportunities, and promoting cooperation with neighboring countries, and targets an investment of ₹1.30 lakh crore till 2030 in north east India.[82]
4. India has 26 sedimentary basins covering an area of 3.14 million km^2 spread over onshore, shallow water, and deep water. Nearly 48% of total sedimentary basin area does not have adequate geo-scientific data. As a base to launch future exploration and production (E&P) activities, the Government has approved complete mapping of sedimentary basins that would be instrumental in increasing investments in domestic production of oil and gas. The project is being implemented by OIL and ONGC at an estimated cost of ₹2,932.99 crore.[83]

Nuclear Energy

In India the Atomic Energy Commission was set up to frame policies with respect to the development of atomic energy in the country. The Government established the department of atomic energy in 1954 with Dr Homi Bhabha its secretary. The atomic energy program, which was initiated in a modest manner initially, has now grown as a wide spectrum, multi-dimensional multidisciplinary with 63 organizations under DAE.[84] In India, nuclear power is the fifth largest source of electricity after coal, gas, hydroelectricity, and wind power. India has 22 nuclear reactors in operation in 7 nuclear power plants, having a total installed capacity of 6,780 MW as on March 2023 (Table 5.7). Nuclear power produced a total of 43 terawatt hours (TWh) and supplied nearly 3.5% of power in the country in 2022.[85]

TABLE 5.7 Operational Nuclear Power Plants in India

Nuclear Power Plant	State	Installed Capacity (MW)
Kudankulam	Tamil Nadu	2,000
Tarapur	Maharashtra	1,400
Rawatbhata	Rajasthan	1,180
Kaiga	Karnataka	880
Kakrapar	Gujarat	440
Kalpakkam	Tamil Nadu	440
Narora	Uttar Pradesh	440
Total		**6,780**

Source: Department of Atomic Energy, retrieved from http://www.dae.nic.in/?q=node/171

The five nuclear power plants/reactors with 6,700 MW capacity are under construction and will be operational soon. Ten planned nuclear power plants with total installed capacity of 39,800 MW are also coming up at Jaitapur and Tarapur (Maharashtra), Chutka and Bhimpur (Madhya Pradesh), Kovvada and Kavali (Andhra Pradesh), Chennai (Tamil Nadu), Gorakhpur (Haryana), Kaiga (Karnataka), and Mahi Banswara (Rajasthan). India has signed civil nuclear agreements with 14 countries: Argentina, Australia, Canada, Czech Republic, France, Japan, Kazakhstan, Mongolia, Namibia, Russia, South Korea, the United Kingdom, the United States, and Vietnam. Despite not being a party to the Non-Proliferation Treaty (NPT), India carries out nuclear commerce with other countries. Since 2008 the 48-nation NSG has granted a waiver to India allowing it to access civilian nuclear technology and fuel from other countries.

Apart from generation of electricity, the Department of Atomic Energy has been actively engaged in supplying radio isotopes to hospital and industry, in the use of radiation technologies for preventing spoilage of marine foods, spices, and for enhancing the shelf life of onions, mangoes, and other food articles, as well as in sterilization of medical products.[86]

Renewable Energy in India

The World Energy Forum has predicted that fossil-based oil, coal, and gas reserves will be exhausted in less than another 10 decades. Fossil fuels account for over 79% of the primary energy consumed in the world, and 57.7% of that amount is used in the transport sector and are diminishing rapidly. The exhaustion of natural resources and the accelerated demand of conventional energy have forced planners and policymakers to look for alternate sources.[87] After the ratification of Paris agreement, the focus of the Government has shifted to clean energy. With the increased support of government and improved economics, the sector has become attractive from investors perspective. As India looks to meet its energy demand on its own, which is expected to reach 15,820 TWh by 2040, renewable energy is set to play an important role. The country ranks 4th in the world in terms of total installed wind power capacity. Total installed renewable energy capacity (including large hydro-projects) in India touched 114.43 GW as of May 2018, which is around 33% of total energy capacity of the country.

Renewable energy resource in India can be discussed in the following sections.

Wind Energy

Winds are generated by complex mechanisms involving the rotation of the Earth, heat energy from the Sun, the cooling effects of the oceans and polar ice caps, temperature gradients between land and sea, and the physical effects of mountains and other obstacles. Wind is a widely distributed energy resource. Wind energy is being developed in the industrialized world for environmental reasons and it has attractions in the developing world as it can be installed quickly in areas where electricity is urgently needed. In many instances, it may be a cost-effective solution if fossil fuel sources are not readily available. In addition, there are many applications for wind energy in remote regions, worldwide, either for supplementing diesel power (which tends to be expensive) or for supplying farms, homes, and other installations on an individual basis.[88]

The availability of wind varies for different regions. Wind resources can be exploited mainly in areas where wind power density is at least 400 W/m^2 at 30 m above the ground. India is the fourth largest wind power producer in the world, after China, the United States, and Germany. The Wind Resource Assessment (WRA) Programme being coordinated by the National Institute of Wind Energy (NIWE), Chennai has so far been covered in 29 states and 3 union territories involving establishment of about 836 dedicated wind-monitoring stations. The wind potential at 80 m height has been estimated at 102,788 MW.

Policy Initiatives

Draft Wind-Solar Hybrid Policy

Research has demonstrated that the wind and solar are almost complementary to each other and hybridizing of two technologies would help in minimizing the variability apart from optimally utilizing the infrastructure, including land and transmission system. The Government announced a national wind-solar hybrid policy, which seeks to promote new projects as well as hybridization of the existing ones. The Government has set an ambitious target of achieving 175 gigawatt (gw) of installed capacity from RES by 2022, which includes 100 gw of solar and 60 gw of wind power capacity.[89]

Competitive Bidding

The wind power projects in the country are installed on the basis of commercial viability through tariff-based competitive bidding process. As on date, the bids for setting up of wind power projects of aggregate 8,389.90 MW capacity have been finalized through Solar Energy Corporation of India Ltd. (SECI) and National Thermal Power Corporation Ltd. (NTPC) by December 2018. The Government has issued guidelines under Section 63 of the Electricity Act, 2003 providing a framework for procurement of wind power through a transparent process of bidding including standardization of the process and defining of roles and responsibilities of various stakeholders. These guidelines would enable the distribution licensees to procure wind power at competitive rates in a cost effective manner.

Incentives by the Government

The Government is promoting wind power projects in entire country by providing various fiscal and financial incentives such as accelerated depreciation benefit and concessional custom duty exemption on certain components of wind electric generators.

Other Measures

In addition to fiscal and other incentives as stated earlier, following steps also have been taken to promote installation of wind capacity in the country[90]:

- Technical support including wind resource assessment and identification of potential sites through the NIWE.
- In order to facilitate inter-state sale of wind power, the inter-state transmission charges and losses have been waived off for wind and solar projects to be commissioned by March 2022.

Solar Energy

The Earth receives an incredible supply of solar energy. The Sun, an average star, is a fusion reactor that has been burning over 4 billion years. It provides enough energy in 1 minute to supply the world's energy needs for 1 year. In 1 day, it provides more energy than our current population would consume in 27 years. In fact, the amount of solar radiation striking the Earth over a 3-day period is equivalent to the energy stored in all fossil energy sources.[91] Notwithstanding the above benefits, 80% of the present worldwide energy use is based on fossil fuels.

Solar energy has the following benefits in India:

1. India is endowed with vast solar energy potential. About 5,000 trillion kWh per year energy is incident over India's land area with most parts receiving 4–7 kWh/m^2 per day. Hence both technology routes for conversion of solar radiation into heat and electricity, namely solar thermal and solar photovoltaics, can effectively be harnessed providing huge scalability for solar in India.
2. Solar also provides the ability to generate power on a distributed basis and enables rapid capacity addition with short lead times. Off-grid decentralized and low-temperature applications will be advantageous from a rural electrification perspective and meeting other energy needs for power and heating and cooling in both rural and urban areas.
3. From an energy security perspective, solar is the most secure of all sources, since it is abundantly available. Theoretically, a small fraction of the total incident solar energy (if captured effectively) can meet the entire country's power requirements. It is also clear that given the large proportion of poor and energy un-served population in the country, every effort needs to be made to exploit the relatively abundant sources of energy available to the country. While, today, domestic coal-based power generation is the cheapest electricity source, future scenarios suggest that this could well change.
4. The highest annual radiation energy is received in western Rajasthan while the north-eastern region of the country receives the lowest annual radiation. India has a good level of solar radiation, receiving the solar energy.

Policy Action for the Development of Solar Energy

Following schemes/policy action has been taken by the Government to promote solar energy in the country.

1. National Solar Mission (NSM), launched on January 11, 2010, had set a target for development and deployment of 20 GW solar power by the year 2022. The Cabinet in its meeting held on June 17, 2015 had approved revision of target under NSM from 20 to 100 GW.

2. World's largest solar park named "Shakti Sthala" was launched in Karnataka in March 2018 with an investment of ₹16,500 crore (US$2.55 billion).
3. Scheme for setting up 1,000 MW of Grid-Connected Solar PV Power Projects by the Central Public Sector Undertakings (CPSUs) and the Government of India organizations with VGF.
4. Scheme for setting up 300 MW of Grid-Connected Solar PV Power Projects by Defence Establishments and Para Military Forces with VGF.
5. Pilot-cum-demonstration projects for development of grid connected solar PV power plants on canal banks and canal tops.
6. Bundling Scheme—15,000 MW grid-connected solar PV power plants through NTPC Ltd/NVVN.
7. VGF Scheme for setting up of 2,000 MW of Grid Connected Solar PV Power Projects through SECI.
8. VGF Scheme for setting up of 5,000 MW of Grid Connected Solar PV Power Projects through SECI.
9. Installation of grid connected solar rooftop power plants.
10. The Government has provided custom and excise duty benefits to the solar rooftop sector, which, in turn, will lower the cost of setting up as well as generate power, thus boosting growth.
11. Off-grid Solar PV scheme.

Biomass Power

Biomass has always been an important energy source for the country considering the benefits it offers. It is renewable, widely available, carbon-neutral, and has the potential to provide significant employment in the rural areas. About 32% of the total primary energy use in the country is still derived from biomass and more than 70% of the country's population depends upon it for its energy needs. MNRE has realized the potential and role of biomass energy in the Indian context and hence has initiated a number of programs for promotion of efficient technologies for its use in various sectors of the economy to ensure derivation of maximum benefits. Biomass power generation in India is an industry that attracts investments of over ₹600 crore every year, generating more than 5,000 million units of electricity and yearly employment of more than 10 million man-days in the rural areas. For efficient utilization of biomass, bagasse-based cogeneration in sugar mills and biomass power generation have been taken up under biomass power and cogeneration program. Biomass materials that can be used for power generation include bagasse, rice husk, straw, cotton stalk, coconut shells, soya husk, de-oiled cakes, coffee waste, jute wastes, groundnut shells, and saw dust. The current availability of biomass in India is estimated at about 500 million metric tonnes per year. Studies sponsored by the ministry have estimated surplus biomass availability at about 120–150 million metric tonnes per annum covering agricultural and forestry residues corresponding to a potential of about 18,000 MW. This apart, about 5,000 MW additional power could be generated through bagasse-based cogeneration in the country's 550 sugar mills.[92]

Biofuel

A number of transportation fuels can be produced from biomass, helping to alleviate demand for petroleum products and improve the greenhouse gas emissions profile of the transportation sector. Ethanol from corn and sugarcane, and biodiesel from soy, rapeseed, and oil palm dominate the current market for biofuels, but a number of companies are moving forward aggressively to develop and market a number of advanced second-generation biofuels made from non-food feedstocks, such as municipal waste, algae, perennial grasses, and wood chips. These fuels include cellulosic ethanol, bio-butanol, methanol, and a number of synthetic gasoline/diesel equivalents.[93]

Benefits/Features of Biofuels

Followings are the benefits of biofuels:

1. The ethanol supply will reduce import dependence on petroleum products and hence will save valuable foreign exchange. For example, the ethanol supply during the year 2017–2018 of around 150 crore liters of ethanol resulted into savings of over ₹4,000 crore of forex.
2. The biofuel is also a cleaner source of energy. It is estimated that 1 crore liter of E-10* saves around 20,000 ton of CO_2 emissions. In the year 2017–2018, there was lesser emissions of CO_2 to the tune of 30 lakh ton in the country. By reducing crop burning and conversion of agricultural residues/wastes to biofuels there will be further reduction in Green House Gas emissions.
3. Prolonged reuse of cooking oil for preparing food, particularly in deep-frying, is a potential health hazard and can lead to many diseases. Used cooking oil is a potential feedstock for biodiesel and its use for making biodiesel will prevent diversion of used cooking oil in the food industry.
4. Annually, around 62 MMT of municipal solid waste gets generated in India. There are technologies available that can convert waste/plastic, municipal solid waste (MSW) to drop in fuels. One ton of such waste has the potential to provide around 20% of drop in fuels.
5. By adopting 2G technologies, agricultural residues/waste that otherwise are burnt by the farmers can be converted to ethanol and can fetch a price for these waste if a market is developed for the same. Also, farmers are at a risk of not getting appropriate price for their produce during the surplus production phase. Thus, conversion of surplus grains and agricultural biomass can help in price stabilization.
6. Biofuels in India are of strategic importance as it augers well with the ongoing initiatives of the Government such as Make in India, Swachh Bharat Abhiyan, Skill Development and offers great opportunity to integrate with the ambitious targets of doubling of Farmers Income, Import Reduction, Employment Generation, Waste to Wealth Creation.[94]

National Policy on Biofuels–2018

The Union Cabinet, chaired by the Prime Minister Shri Narendra Modi, has approved National Policy on Biofuels–2018. Followings are the salient features of the policy:

1. The Policy categorizes biofuels as "Basic Biofuels"—First Generation (1G) bioethanol and biodiesel, "Advanced Biofuels"—Second Generation (2G) ethanol, and MSW to drop-in

*E10 Ethanol is a low-concentration biofuel blend consisting of 10% ethanol and 90% gasoline.

fuels—Third Generation (3G) biofuels, bio-CNG, etc. to enable extension of appropriate financial and fiscal incentives under each category.

2. The Policy expands the scope of raw material for ethanol production by allowing use of sugarcane juice, sugar-containing materials like sugar beet, sweet sorghum, starch-containing materials like corn, cassava, damaged food grains like wheat, broken rice, rotten potatoes, unfit for human consumption for ethanol production.
3. Farmers are at a risk of not getting appropriate price for their produce during the surplus production phase. Taking this into account, the Policy allows use of surplus food grains for production of ethanol for blending with petrol with the approval of National Biofuel Coordination Committee.
4. With a thrust on Advanced Biofuels, the Policy indicates a VGF scheme for 2G ethanol bio-refineries of ₹5,000 crore in 6 years in addition to additional tax incentives, higher purchase price as compared to 1G biofuels.
5. The Policy encourages setting up of supply-chain mechanisms for biodiesel production from non-edible oilseeds, used cooking oil, short gestation crops.

Biogas

Biogas is produced through anaerobic digestion, the bacterial fermentation of organic material. Biogas is often produced from animal and agricultural wastes. The energy produced can be used directly for lighting, for producing heat, and as a fuel source for fuel cells.

Followings are the benefits associated with biogas:

1. It provides clean gaseous fuel for cooking and lighting.
2. Digested slurry from biogas plants is used as enriched bio-manure to supplement the use of chemical fertilizers.
3. It improves sanitation in villages and semi-urban areas by linking sanitary toilets with biogas plants.
4. Biogas plants help in reducing the causes of climate change.

National Biogas and Manure Management Programme (NBMMP) is a Central Sector Scheme, which provides for setting up of Family-Type Biogas Plants mainly for rural and semi-urban/households. A family-type biogas plant generates biogas from organic substances such as cattle dung, and other bio-degradable materials such as biomass from farms, gardens, kitchens, and night soil wastes.

Communication

Communication signifies imparting or exchanging of information by speaking, writing, or using some other medium like electronic or digital media. If transport implies the conveyance of goods, the communication implies conveyance of information. The important means of communication are postal services, telephone services, television, Internet, etc.

Postal Services

The first post office of the country was opened in the year 1727 in Kolkata. With around 155,000 post offices at the end of 2018, India has largest postal network in the world. On an average a post office serves around 7,800 persons and covers an area of 21.56 km^2. Around 10% of post offices are located in urban area and 90% are located in rural areas.[95] The postal index code (PIN) was introduced in 1972 and quick mail service was initiated in 1975. The speed post was introduced in 1986. The postal department has undergone mechanization and computerization in its postal operation to provide better services to its customers. There are nine PIN regions in the country; the first eight are geographical regions, and the ninth is reserved for the Army Postal Service (APS). The country has been divided into 23 postal circles, each circle headed by a Chief Postmaster General.

Telecommunication

Telecommunication means communication over a distance and is realized by cable, telephone, or broadcasting.

Telephony

Landline Before the New Telecom Policy was announced in 1999, only the Government-owned BSNL and MTNL were allowed to provide land-line phone services through copper wire in India with MTNL operating in Delhi and Mumbai and BSNL servicing all other areas of the country. Due to the rapid growth of the cellular phone industry in India, landlines are facing stiff competition from cellular operators, with number of wireline subscribers fell from 37.90 million in December 2008 to 31.2 million in December 2023. This has forced land-line service providers to become more efficient and improve their quality of service.

Mobile Telephony and Internet The liberal and reformist policies of the Government of India have been instrumental along with strong consumer demand in the rapid growth in the Indian telecom sector. The Government has enabled easy market access to telecom equipment and a fair and proactive regulatory framework (under TRAI) that has ensured availability of telecom services to consumer at affordable prices. Because of easy FDI norms, telecommunication has become the third largest recipient of FDI in the country and fifth largest employment generator in the country. India is currently the world's second largest telecommunication market after China with a subscriber base of 1.158 billion. According to report prepared by GSM Association (GSMA) in collaboration with the Boston Consulting Group (BCG), the Indian mobile economy is growing rapidly and will contribute substantially to India's Gross Domestic Product (GDP) in the years to come. With 94 crore Internet subscribers (66% of population), as of December 2023, India ranks as the world's second largest market in terms of total Internet users and app downloads globally. The Government announced National Digital Communication Policy in 2018 with an aim to attract $100 billion worth of investment and generating 4 million jobs by the year 2022.[96] In 2023, India accounted for about 26 billion (10%) of 257 billion global app installs.

Broadcasting

Television In India television broadcasting began in India in 1959 by Doordarshan. Though, the private channels were allowed to broadcast in India in the early 1990s and Supreme Court finally ended the state's legal monopoly over the airwaves in 1995.[97] As per the latest Broadcast India Survey, the country now has 217 million TV homes, up from 183 million in 2016. The BI-2023 survey also notes that the television viewership in India, measuring an average minute audience (AMA) is approximately 1.5 trillion in 2023.[98] As on 31 October 2018, the country has around 905 TV channels out of which about 890 are private channels.[99]

Radio The first radio program was broadcast by the Radio Club of Bombay in June 1923, Vividh Bharati was started on October 1957 and the first ever FM service was started in Madras on July 1977. The number of radio stations went up from six in 1947 to 481 by March 2023. All India Radio is the largest radio network in the world.[100]

Summary

1. Infrastructure affects growth and development in two ways—by directly boosting economic activity and raising productivity. Economic infrastructure (which constitutes around 13% of GDP) comprises transport, energy, and communication.
2. Indian Railways is the third largest rail network in the world and runs around 19,000 trains daily. The railway is divided into 17 zones; operates services on three gauges; and is seventh largest employer in the world. Certain problems: under investment, lack of multiple tracks and common corridor for both freight and passenger traffic, congestion and low speed of trains, price distortion, lack of cleanliness and safety concerns due to higher incidence of accidents. The initiatives taken by government are freight tariff rationalization, increased capital investment for capacity creation, emphasizing station redevelopment and introducing metro rail network on the lines of New Delhi to other prominent cities of the country.
3. India has the world's second largest road network and road density of 1.70 km/ km^2 of area. Indian road network comprises NH, State Highways, District Roads, Rural Roads, Urban Roads, and Project Roads. India has nearly 56 lakh km of road network, and state of Maharashtra accounts for the largest share (13.04%). Problems of road transport are: higher burden on NHs, traffic congestion, poor quality of roads and accidents. The Government initiated certain schemes for the development of roads in India. For example, NHDP, Bharatmala Pariyojana, Nation-wide Electronic Toll Collection, Green Highways Policy.
4. India has a huge coastline spanning 7,516.6 km and to serve this vast peninsula, there are 13 major ports and about 200 non-major ports in the country. Among the major ports, Kamarajar Port (Ennore Port) is a corporate port. India has the world's 17th largest shipping fleet with fleet strength of 1,371 vessels in 2017. Jawaharlal Nehru Port Trust (JNPT) with 44% share is the leading container handling port in the country. Problems of marine transport are: lack of lucrative business opportunities, non-connectivity between ports and industrial clusters, inadequate storage and handling facilities, etc. The Government has introduced various programs in the recent past viz. Sagarmala project 2016, the maritime agenda 2010–2020 efforts for shipbuilding and ship repair, establishment of IMU to foster academic and research excellence.
5. Inland waterways transport (IWT) is a cost-effective, logistically efficient, and environment-friendly mode of transport. The National Waterways Act, 2016 seeks to develop 111 inland waterways in 24 states of India. The shortcomings of IWT are: inter-state river disputes, road and rail bridges with low vertical clearances; higher water salinity, especially in the coastal regions; ephemeral nature of non-Himalayan Rivers; loading the vessels to their full tonnage in to and fro journey; and, huge financial implications. India's first multi-modal inland waterways hub in Varanasi was inaugurated by Prime Minister in November 2018. Private sector/foreign direct investment is being encouraged in many potential areas.
6. Air transport is important because it helps generate trade, promote tourism, and create employment opportunities. With 126 airports and more than 20 airlines in operation, India is the third largest and fastest growing aviation market in the world. The problems faced by air transport system are: (1) costliest mode of transport because of higher jet fuel prices; (2) financial crunch, operational issues, and bureaucratic hurdles faced by both incumbent and new airlines; (3) lack of regional connectivity due to inappropriate infrastructure. Many steps have been taken by the Government in the promotion of air transport. Examples are: RCS-UDAN scheme, raising the FDI limit, government approving setting up of 18 greenfield airports, The National Civil Aviation Policy, 2016.
7. India is the third largest producer and the third largest consumer of electricity in the world. The conventional sources of energy in India are coal, hydroelectricity, oil/petroleum, and nuclear energy. India is the third largest producer of coal in the world. Coal constitutes 67% of total energy consumption. Jharkhand has the largest reservoirs of coal. The coal sector faces several challenges viz. supply-side constraints, corruption and scams, environmental challenges, and social challenges. In order to bring transparency in coal segment, the Coal Mines (Special Provisions) Act was enacted in 2015 followed by new coal distribution policy, 2018.

8. India is the seventh largest producer of hydroelectric power in the world. The public sector dominates in energy production with 89% share. Hydropower projects suffer from certain bottlenecks like long gestation period, technical constraints, economic constraints, and problems related with rehabilitation problems. In order to promote hydropower in the country, parliament has enacted different legislations from time to time. The Government is promoting Small Hydro Power (SHP) up to 25 MW station capacities. The estimated potential for power generation in the country from such plants is about 20,000 MW.
9. Natural gas also called coal-bed methane consists mainly of methane, a compound with one carbon atom and four hydrogen atoms. Natural gas infrastructure comprises Natural Gas Pipelines, Liquid Natural Gas (LNG) Re-gasification Terminals, and City Gas Distribution (CGD) Infrastructure. The Government is creating 15,000 km National Gas Grid in the country, liberalized gas pricing and introduced many schemes such as Pahal, Ujjwala Yojana.
10. Around 49% of India's petroleum oil is produced onshore whereas 51% is produced offshore. India had estimated crude oil reserves of 604.10 million ton and 23 crude oil refineries. To promote oil sector, the Government has established Strategic Petroleum Reserve facilities at three locations, implementation of New Exploration Licensing Policy, Hydrocarbon Vision 2030 for North East, and mapping of sedimentary basins.
11. The nuclear power is the fifth largest source of electricity after coal, gas, hydroelectricity, and wind power. India has 22 nuclear reactors in operation in 7 nuclear power plants, having a total installed capacity of 6,780 MW, 5 will be operational soon (6,700 MW) and 10 are coming up (39,800 MW).
12. Renewable energy comprises wind energy, solar energy, biomass, biofuel, and biogas. India is the fourth largest wind power producer in the world and at 80 m height there is estimated potential of generating 102,788 MW of wind energy. The Government has taken various steps like Draft Wind-Solar Hybrid Policy, competitive bidding, and incentive measures to promote wind energy in the country. India is endowed with vast solar energy potential. About 5,000 trillion kWh per year energy is incident over India's land area with most parts receiving 4–7 kWh per m^2 per day. National Solar Mission was launched in 2010. World's largest solar park named "Shakti Sthala" was launched in Karnataka in March 2018. About 32% of the total primary energy use in the country is still derived from biomass. The current availability of biomass in India is estimated at about 500 million metric tonnes per year. Ethanol from corn and sugarcane, and biodiesel from soy, rapeseed, and oil palm dominate the current market for biofuels. However, the second-generation biofuels are being made from non-food feedstocks, such as municipal waste, algae, perennial grasses, and wood chips. The Government has announced National Policy on Biofuels–2018 to promote biofuels in the country. Biogas is often produced from animal and agricultural wastes and is a clean source of energy. Government is promoting biofuel through National Biogas and Manure Management Programme.
13. Communication mainly comprises postal services and telecommunication. With around 155,000 post offices at the end of 2018, India has largest postal network in the world. India's telecommunication sector that mainly comprises landline, mobile telephony, Internet, and broadcasting has become the most vibrant sector in the economy during the post-reform period.

Endnotes

1. Economic Survey, 2017–2018, p.11, Chapter 8.
2. G20 (2017). Global infrastructure outlook. Retrieved from https://outlook.gihub.org/ (Accessed on January 4, 2019)
3. Thorner, D. (1955). The pattern of railway development in India. *Far Eastern Quarterly, XIV*, 201–206.
4. Retrieved from http://indianrailways.gov.in/ (Accessed on April 15, 2024) and https://www.investindia.gov.in/sector/railways accessed on 15 April, 2024.
5. Indian Railways (February 2015). Lifeline of the nation. A White Paper, Ministry of Railways, Government of India, New Delhi.
6. *Indian Railway*. Retrieved from https://economictimes.indiatimes.com (Accessed on June 12, 2019).
7. Economic Survey, 2014–2015, p.91.

8. *China to expand railway network to 150,000 km by 2020*. retrieved from https://www.reuters.com (Accessed on March 8, 2019).
9. Amos, P. (2011). Freight railways governance, organization and management: An international round-up. World Bank Paper submitted to NTDPC.
10. Lack of hygiene emerges as main complaint of train travellers, The Hindu Business Line, June 2012.
11. Why the railways suffer on an average 100 accidents a year, Jyotika Sood, retrieved from www.livemint.com (Accessed on May 25, 2018).
12. *What explains the high number of railway accidents?* Retrieved from https://thewire.inderailment (Accessed on May 25, 2018).
13. *3,479 unmanned level crossings on Indian Railways broad gauge network*, retrieved from http://www.newindianexpress.com (Accessed on December 12, 2018).
14. Economic Survey, 2017–2018, p.138.
15. Economic Survey, 2017–2018, p.139.
16. Press note, Indian Railways, retrieved from http://pib.nic.in (Accessed on May 12, 2018).
17. Sood J. *How metro rail networks are spreading across India*, https://www.livemint.com (Accessed on May 11, 2018).
18. Economic Survey, 2017–2018, p.139.
19. *Metro Rail Policy 2017*. Retrieved from http://mohua.gov.in (Accessed on January 14, 2019).
20. *Statistical Year Book (2017)*. Retrieved from http://www.mospi.gov.in9 (Accessed on November 14, 2018).
21. Basic road statistics of India, 2015–2016, *Ministry of Road Transport and Highways*, Government of India and data accessed from https://pib.gov.in/PressReleaseIframePage.aspx?PRID=1993425 as on 24 April 2024.
22. *Ibid.*
23. Dash, D.K. Traffic congestion costs four major Indian cities ₹1.5 lakh crore a year, *Times of India*, April 26, 2018.
24. Davis, J., et al (2017). *Congestion costs incurred on Indian Roads: A case study for New Delhi*, Accessed from https://arxiv.org (Accessed on May 14, 2018).
25. *Traffic jams and delays cost nearly ₹40 billion annually*, retrieved from https://www.indiatoday.in (Accessed on December 12, 2018).
26. Heggie, I.G., & Vickers, P. (1998). Commercial management and financing of roads, Technical Paper 409, World Bank, Washington, DC.
27. Dash, D.K., 40% roads in India not metalled, 78% NHs have one or two lanes: Data, October 17, 2016, *Times of India*, April 26, 2018.
28. *Economic Times*, January 10, 2018.
29. Gupta,M.D. Road accidents killed 17 people every hour in India in 2016, Delhi most unsafe. *Hindustan Times*, September 6, 2017.
30. Economic Survey, 2017–2018, p.133.
31. Press release, Ministry of Road Transport & Highways, October 25, 2017, retrieved from http://pib.nic.in (Accessed on February 18, 2018).
32. Press Information Bureau, Government of India, Ministry of Road Transport & Highways, retrieved from http://pib.nic.in (Accessed on March 29, 2019).
33. India Year Book, Ministry of Information and Broadcasting, Publication Division, Government of India.
34. *National Green Highway*. Retrieved from http://nationalgreenhighway.org (Accessed on June 6, 2019).
35. Annual Report 2016–2017, Ministry of Shipping, Government of India, New Delhi, p.6.
36. Mishra, B. Indian shipping industry—A perspective. *Sea News*, January 5, 2018.
37. *A white paper on seaport: Challenges and issues in India (2018)*. CII Institute of Logistics, Confederation of Indian Industry.
38. *Dun & Bradstreet releases 'Port Logistics: Issues & Challenges in India' report (2018)*. Retrieved from http://pib.nic.in (Accessed on November 12, 2018).
39. Economic Survey, 2017–2018, p.141.
40. Sagarmala. Retrieved from http://sagarmala.gov.in (Accessed on January 8, 2019).
41. Annual Report 2016–2017, Ministry of Shipping, Government of India, New Delhi, p.6.
42. India Year Book, 2017–2018.
43. Economic Survey, 2017–2018, p.141.
44. *Indian maritime sector—on the cusp of revolution*, Retrieved from http://www.forbesindia.com (Accessed on February 6, 2019).
45. *The Economic Times*, July 25, 2016.
46. Inland Waterways. Retrieved from https://www.marinerdesk.com (Accessed on March 6, 2019).
47. *Ibid*
48. Business Standard (2018). *Modi inaugurates India's first multi-modal inland waterways hub in Varanasi*. PTI, November 12, 2018. Retrieved from https://www.business-standard.com (Accessed on March 6, 2019)

49. *Air Transport.* Retrieved from http://www.worldbank.org (Accessed on January 16, 2019).
50. *Airports in India.* Retrieved from https://www.aai.aero (Accessed on January 16, 2019).
51. Data accessed from https://pib.gov.in/PressRelese as on 27 Feb, 2024.
52. *The challenges facing India's civil aviation sector,* Accessed from https://indianexpress.com (Accessed on January 19, 2019).
53. Chowdhury, A. India's new airlines face major cash, operational challenges. *Economic Times,* October 12, 2015.
54. Montgomery, E.(2008). *Infrastructure in India, a vast land of construction opportunity.* Pricewater house Coopers.
55. *Airports Authority of India.* Retrieved from https://www.aai.aero/en (Accessed on February 19, 2019).
56. Indian Aviation Industry, Retrieved from https://www.ibef.org (Accessed on February 20, 2019).
57. Economic Survey, 2017–2018, p.140.
58. India Year book, 2018, p.481.
59. National Civil Aviation Policy, 2016: sailent fatures, retrieved from http://pib.nic.in (Accessed on March 4, 2019)
60. Press Information Bureau, Government of India, Ministry of Coal, March 7, 2018, retrieved from http://pib.nic.in (Accessed on February 21, 2019).
61. Indian Coal and Lignite Resources-2017, Government of India, Geological Survey of India.
62. *What is coal scam?* Retrieved from https://indianexpress.com (Accessed on February 21, 2019).
63. Singh, Gurdeep (2006). Environmental and social challenges facing the coal industry. *Proceedings of International Coal Congress & EXPO 2006*, December 11–13, New Delhi, pp.301–310.
64. Singh, Environmental and social challenges facing the coal industry. *Proceedings of International Coal Congress & EXPO 2006,* December 11–13, New Delhi, pp.301–310.
65. *Coal Mining.* Retrieved from https://www.businesstoday.in (Acccessed on March 16, 2019).
66. *Hydroelectricity.* Retrieved from https://powermin.nic.in (Accessed on June 8, 2019)
67. *Small Hydropower.* Retrieved from https://mnre.gov.in (Accessed on February 16, 2019).
68. Is small-scale hydro the answer to India's clean energy needs? *The Guardian,* November 26, 2016.
69. *Hydropower.* Retrieved from https://hub.globalccsinstitute.com (Accessed on February 16, 2019).
70. *Natural Gas.* Retrieved from https://www.eia.gov (Accessed on March 15, 2019)
71. NaturalGas.org. Background. Retrieved from http://www.naturalgas.org (Accessed on March 6, 2019).
72. Abdi, B. First growth in India's natural gas production in six years. *The Economic Times,* April 25, 2018.
73. Shunmugam, V., Mukherjee, J. Energising India's natural gas market. *Financial Express,* February 21, 2018.
74. Press Information Bureau, Government of India, Ministry of Petroleum & Natural Gas, May 13, 2015.
75. Economic Survey, 2017–2018, p.146.
76. *Gas market in India, overview and future* (2018). Outlook.Joint study by PhD Chamber and Earnest & Young", 2018.
77. Petroleum. Retrieved from http://petroleum.nic.in (Accessed on February 26, 2019).
78. *Pradhan Mantri Ujjwala Yojana.* Retrieved from http://www.pmujjwalayojana.in/ (Accessed on February 26, 2019).
79. Annual Report, 2017–2018, Ministry of Petroleum and Natural Gas, Government of India.
80. *Petroleum.* Retrieved from http://www.petroleum.nic.in/ (Accessed on February 26, 2019).
81. *Oil & Gas Industry in India* https://www.ibef.org (Accessed on February 26, 2019).
82. Annual Report, 2017–2018, Ministry of Petroleum and Natural Gas, Government of India.
83. Economic Survey, 2017–2018, p.146.
84. Jain, S.K. Nuclear power—An alternative (2018). Accessed from http://www.npcil.nic.in (Accessed on February 27, 2019).
85. *Atomic Energy.* Retrieved from https://pris.iaea.org (Accessed on February 28, 2019).
86. Srinivasan, M.R. India's atomic energy program. Press Information Bureau, Government of India, August 17, 2017.
87. Kumar et al. (2010). Renewable energy in India: Current status and future potentials. *Renewable and Sustainable Energy Reviews, 14,* 2434–2442.
88. Kumar et al. (2010). Renewable energy in India: Current status and future potentials. *Renewable and Sustainable Energy Reviews, 14,* 2434–2442.
89. *National Wind-Solar Hybrid Policy.* https://economictimes.indiatimes.com (Accessed on February 28, 2019).

90. Press Information Bureau, Government of India, December 27, 2018.
91. *Solar Energy*. http://www.altenergy.org (Accessed on February 28, 2019).
92. *Biomass Power*. Retrieved from https://mnre.gov.in (Accessed on March 2, 2019).
93. *Biofuel*. Retrieved from https://www.eesi.org (Accessed on March 2, 2019).
94. Cabinet approves National Policy on Biofuels–2018. Press Information Bureau, Government of India, May 16, 2018.
95. India Post, Annual Report, 2017–2018.
96. *Telecommunication*. Retrieved from https://www.ibef.org (Accessed on March 2, 2019).
97. Television: The daily theatre in our lives. *Livemint*, August 12, 2011.
98. Information retrieved from https://www.barcindia.co.in/data-insights as on 27 April, 2024.
99. *Television*. https://mib.gov.in (Accessed on March 2, 2019).
100. India 2018. A reference annual, Publications Division, Ministry of Information and Broadcasting, Government of India.

CHAPTER 6

India's Population and Demographic Dividend

We control the growth of every other species, except our own.
—David Rockefeller

Introduction

The growth of the human population over the past 60–70 years has been unprecedented. The population growth has been beyond Earth's sustainable means. We are consuming more resources than our planet can regenerate, with devastating consequences. It took humanity 2 lakh years to reach one billion and only 200 years to reach seven billion. We are still adding an extra 80 million each year and are headed towards 10 billion by 2050. More population means demand for more food, water, sanitation, homes, public services, and amenities—but it is becoming difficult with finite resources of earth. It has been suggested that if everyone on the planet consumed as much as the average American citizen, four Earths would be needed to sustain them.

This chapter proposes to discuss the following:

- Demographic transition theory
- World Population trends
- Characteristic features of India's population
- Population Policies in India
- Indian Population: Demographic disaster or Demographic dividend

Demographic Transition Theory

In 1929, American demographer, Warren Thompson, proposed the theory of demographic transition after observing changes, or transitions, in birth and death rates in industrialized societies over the previous 200 years. The theory has been further developed by Adolphe Landry and Frank W. Notestein. According to the theory, every country passes through the five different stages of demographic transition (Figure 6.1).

First stage is the stage of high birth rate and high death rate, which results in stationary population growth. This stage occurs primarily in traditional societies with marked absence of widespread education and scientific knowledge. India before independence can be placed in this stage.

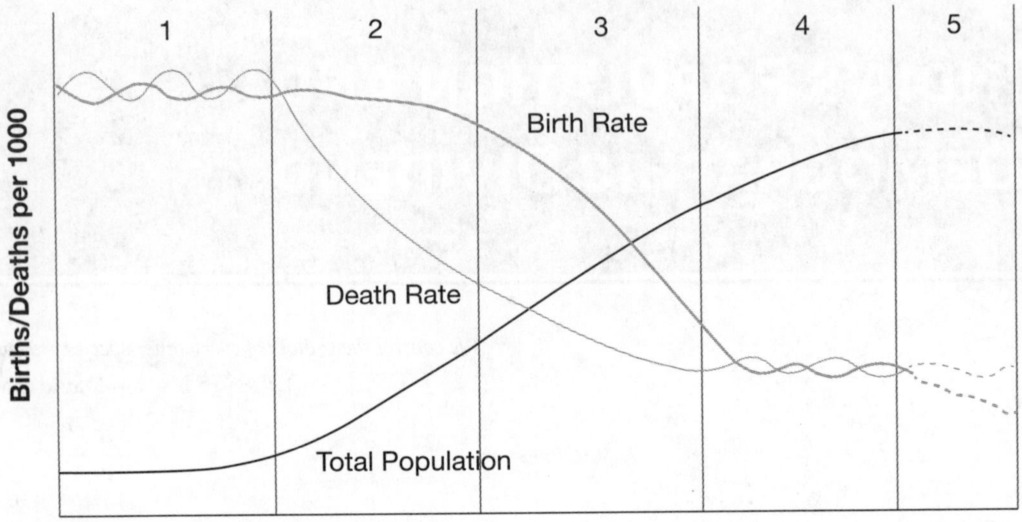

FIGURE 6.1 Demographic Transition Model

Source: Adolphe Landry and Frank W. Notestein

Second stage is the stage of falling birth rate and death rate but the fall in death rate is steeper and the gap between birth and death rates signifies a natural increase in population or population explosion. It happens because of the improvement in medical facilities and increase in awareness among masses. India after independence can be placed in this stage).

Third stage is the stage where both birth rate and death rate continue falling but the fall in birth rate is steeper and population keeps on increasing at an alarming rate. At the tail end of third stage, birth rate and death rate become equal. In this stage, birth rate falls due to various fertility factors such as access to contraception, increase in wages, urbanization, increase in the status and education of women, and other social changes. China is at the tail end of the third stage with 0.5% population growth, whereas India is at the beginning of the third stage with 1.2% growth rate.

Fourth stage is the stage of low birth rate and low death rate, which results in low stationary population growth. Birth rate may drop to well below replacement level as has happened in many advanced Western countries that have achieved zero or near zero growth rate of population.

Fifth stage is the stage of negative population growth rate. It is the stage where death rate is greater than the birth rate and there is a natural decrease in the population size. Of the 230 countries for which data is available, 196 countries had a positive population growth and 34 countries showed a decline. Population growth rate of few countries, viz. Japan (−0.12), Lithuania (−1.63), and Latvia (−1.18) can be placed under this category.

World Population Trends

Before the start of the demographic transition, life was short, births were many, growth was slow, and the population was young. From 1 A.D. to 1000 A.D., world population hardly grew at all (Table 6.1). The transition began around 1800 with declining mortality in Europe and spread to all parts of the world and is projected to be completed by 2100. This global demographic transition has brought momentous changes, reshaping the economic and demographic life cycles of individuals and restructuring populations.[1] According to UN Report, the world's population numbered nearly 7.6 billion as of mid-2017. Sixty per cent of the world's people live in Asia (4.5 billion), 17% in Africa (1.3 billion), 10% in Europe (742 million), 9% in Latin America and the Caribbean (646 million), and the remaining 6% in Northern America (361 million) and Oceania (41 million). China (1.4 billion) and India (1.3 billion) remain the two most populous countries of the world, comprising 19 and 18% of the global total, respectively. At the global level, the number of men and women are roughly equal, with the male population being slightly larger than the female population. Currently, in 2017, there are 102 men for every 100 women.[2]

According to World Population Prospects (the 2017 revision) of UN, the future of world population will have following characteristics:

- The world's population is projected to increase by slightly more than one billion people over the next 13 years, reaching 8.6 billion in 2030, and to increase further to 9.8 billion in 2050 and 11.2 billion by 2100.
- Africa will be the largest contributor to the world population with the addition of 2.2 billion people during 2017–2050 followed by Asia (addition of 750 million people). After 2050, Africa will be the largest contributor to population growth.
- The global fertility rate is projected to fall from just over 2.5 births per woman in 2010–2015 to around 2.4 in 2025–2030, and 2.0 in 2095–2100.
- The world life expectancy at birth is projected to rise from 71 years in 2010–2015 to 77 years in 2045–2050.
- During 1950 and 2015, the regions of Europe, Northern America, and Oceania were net receivers of international migrants, while Africa, Asia, Latin America, and the Caribbean were net senders with the volume of net migration generally increasing over time. In the

TABLE 6.1 Global Population Trends Over the Transition: Estimates, Guesstimates, and Forecasts

Year	Population (in Crores)	Population Growth Rate (%/Year)	Life Expectancy (Years at Birth)	Total Fertility Rate (Births per Woman)
1 AD	16.8			
1000	26.5			
1700	68	0.50	27	6
1800	98	0.51	27	6
1900	162.3	0.56	30	5.2
1950	252	1.80	47	5
2000	607	1.22	65	2.7
2017	755	1.09	70.5	2.5
2050	977	0.33	74	2
2100	1,118	0.04	81	2

Source: Carl Haub, World population history, Population Reference Bureau, Washington, DC, the USA; Lee, R. (2003). The demographic transition: Three centuries of fundamental change. *Journal of Economic Perspectives, 17*(4), 167–190; World population prospects, the 2017 revision (2017). UN, New York.

future (2015–2050), the top net receivers of international migrants (more than 100,000 migrants annually) will be the United States, Germany, Canada, the United Kingdom, Australia, and the Russian Federation. The top net senders of more than 100,000 migrants annually constitute countries like India, Bangladesh, China, Pakistan, and Indonesia.

- The world's working population (aged between 15 and 64 years) has increased from 58% in 1960 to around 66% in 2016.
- Globally, population aged 60 years or above is growing faster than all younger age groups and is growing at a rate of about 3% per year. By 2050, all regions of the world except Africa will have nearly a quarter or more of their populations aged 60 years and above. The number of aged people in the world is projected to be 1.4 billion in 2030 and 2.1 billion in 2050, and could rise to 3.1 billion in 2100.

Characteristic Features of Indian Population

The office of the Registrar General of India conducts an all-India census of population every 10 years. The country's first all-India census was completed in 1872 during British rule. Thereafter, decennial censuses have been organized in the years ending in "1," that is, 1881, 1891, 1901, 1911, 1921, etc. The last such census, that is, 15th census was completed in March, 2011. The census in India is conducted under the Census Act, 1948, which makes it obligatory for the public to provide all answers correctly and fully.

The following are the characteristic features of the Indian population:

Size and Growth of Population

India has 2.4% of the world's total area but the home for nearly 17.5% of population. The population of India is 121.09 crore as per 2011 census and is almost equal to a combined population of the United States, Indonesia, Pakistan, Bangladesh, and Japan. In the year 2025, India is projected to surpass China in world population. At the beginning of 20th century, population of India was 23.84 crores. After 1921, the year of great divide*, Indian population grew at an alarming rate. India was the first country in the world to establish a government family planning program way back in 1952. However, the expected decline in the population growth rate was not achieved in response to the government's family planning programme. The high growth rate of population during 1961–2001 reflects population explosion as average annual growth was almost 2% and above (Table 6.2).

The crude birth rate (CBR)** and crude death rate (CDR)*** in India was 39.9 and 27.4, respectively, during 1950–1951 and came down to 20.4 and 6.4 in the year 2016. Both the CBR and CDR of the country have fallen since 1921 but the fall in CDR is steeper and the resultant gap has produced natural increase in population number.

---

* Before 1921, the population of India was not stable, sometimes it increased and at other times it decreased. The population growth during 1911–1921 was negative and after 1921, there has been considerable and continuous increase in the population and, therefore, the year 1921 is called the year of great divide.

** The crude birth rate is the annual number of live births per 1,000 people.

*** The crude death rate is the total number of deaths per year per 1,000 people.

TABLE 6.2 Population Size and Growth Rate

Census Year	Population (in Crores)	Decadal Growth (%)	Average Annual Growth Rate (%)
1901	23.84		–
1911	25.21	5.7	0.56
1921	25.13	−0.3	−0.03
1931	27.90	11.0	1.04
1941	31.87	14.2	1.33
1951	36.11	13.31	1.25
1961	43.92	21.64	1.96
1971	54.82	24.80	2.20
1981	68.33	24.66	2.22
1991	84.64	23.87	2.16
2001	102.87	21.54	1.97
2011	121.09	17.72	1.64

Source: Census of India, 2011 and United Nations Department of Economic and Social Affairs/Population Division World Population Prospects: The 2017 Revision.

Density of Population

The density of population is calculated as a ratio of the number of persons per square kilometer of land area. According to the 2011 census, the density of population in the country is 382 (Table 6.3). No doubt, India is one of the densely populated countries in the world. However, based on the available evidence, it is not possible to establish any indisputable relationship between the density of population and the level of economic development. A country like Myanmar with a population density of 202 has a per capita income of only $2,520 in terms of PPP as against $6,500 in India. On the contrary, Japan with a density of 336 has a per capita income of $43,000. Similarly, less densely populated countries show both high and low levels of development. Australia with a density of only 3.2 persons per square kilometer has a per capita income of $50,000, which is among the highest in the world. On the other hand, Mali with a density of 15 has a per capita income of only $2100.

TABLE 6.3 Density of Population (Percentage Share)

Census Year	Density of Population (Per Square Kilometer)
1901	77
1911	82
1921	81
1931	90
1941	103
1951	117
1961	142
1971	177
1981	216
1991	267
2001	325
2011	382

Source: Census of India, 2011

The density of population helps to determine the magnitude of the burden that the land is being called upon to carry and to determine the future potentials of growth. It is in this sense that we found India is already a densely populated country and more additions are likely to add only more to the burden on land. In fact, whether a geographical area is overpopulated, underpopulated or optimally populated is determined on the basis of population number and carrying capacity of the region. An area is overpopulated if the size of the population is greater than the carrying capacity or resource base of the region. There exists an uneven nexus between population and resource size. An underpopulated region will have lesser population size comparable to resources. An optimally populated region makes the best use of its resources so its people can enjoy a high quality of life.

Age Composition of Indian Population

There has been a gradual decline in the share of population in the age group 0 -14 from 41.2–29.5% during 1971–2011, whereas, the proportion of economically active population (15–59 years) has increased from 53.4–62.5% during 1971–2011. This chunk of population provides us with huge prospective demographic dividend only if such a large number of people is turned into a productive human resource. On account of better education, health facilities and increase in life expectancy, the percentage of elderly population (60+) has gone up from 5.3–8.0%, respectively, during the periods under reference. The proportion of young children in the age group 0–4 years and also the proportion of population in the age group 0–14 years are higher in rural areas than in urban areas for both males and females. According to census 2011, the mean age at effective marriage for female has improved from 19.3 years in 1990 to 21.2 years in 2011.

Sex Composition of Indian Population

Sex composition of the human population is one of the basic demographic characteristics, which is extremely vital for any meaningful demographic analysis.[3] Sex ratio is used to describe the number of females per 1000 males. In India sex ratio has reduced from 972 in 1901 to 943 in 2011 (Table 6.4). The sex ratio differs among different states; while it is as high as 1,084 in Kerala, it is as low as 879 in Haryana as per 2011 census. The decline in juvenile sex ratio over the last five decades despite the improving socioeconomic characteristics reinforces the existence of gender discriminatory practices, which starts even before birth.[4] The major factors responsible for low sex ratio in India are increased discrimination of females in providing the minimum nutrition, access to health, and other amenities; female selective termination of pregnancy; and increase in the proportion of male selective migrants from other countries; etc.

TABLE 6.4 Sex Composition of Indian Population

Census Year	Sex Ratio in India
1901	972
1911	962
1921	955
1931	950
1941	945
1951	946
1961	941
1971	930
1981	934
1991	927
2001	933
2011	943

Source: Census of India, 2011

Life Expectancy and Mortality Rates

The mean expectation of life at birth is the best statistical measure of the health conditions and of the general level of mortality of a country. If the death rate is high and/or death occurs at an early age, life expectancy will be low; on the other hand, if the death rate is low and/or death occurs at an advanced age, life expectancy will be high. During the last few decades, the death rate in India has recorded a perceptible fall; this is reflected in the rising life expectancy in the country. Life expectancy at birth currently is being estimated 66.4 years for males and 69.6 years for females and 67.9 overall for the period 2010–2014.[5] The rising life expectancy has some social implications as well: (1) It creates pressure on the job market. As persons reaching retirement age remain fit to work, they seek an extension of their jobs or fresh employment. (2) As the elderly continue to live longer, the number of joint or multigenerational families tends to increase. However, the average size of households has not increased significantly over the last five decades and the total number of households has risen sharply. This is not really surprising because the tolerance limits for the strain arising out of joint family living have gone down. The mortality rates for India have also declined significantly. The infant mortality rate in India has come down from 129 per 1,000 live births in 1971 to 34 per 1000 live births in 2017. Maternal mortality rate has also come down from 254 per 1,00,000 live births during 2004–2006 to 130 per 1,00,000 live births during 2014–2016.

TABLE 6.5 Religion-wise Population (Percentage Share)

Religion	1951	1991	2011
Hinduism	84.1	81.53	79.8
Islam	9.8	12.61	14.23
Christianity	2.3	2.32	2.30
Sikhism	1.79	1.94	1.72
Buddhism	0.74	0.77	0.70
Jainism	0.46	0.40	0.37
Zoroastrianism	0.43	0.44	0.9
Others/religion not specified	0.13	0.08	NA

Source: Census of India, 2011, Govt. of India

Religious Composition of Population

There is a continuous decline in the Hindu population of the country as a proportion of Indian population from 84.1% in 1951 to 79.8% in 2011. The Muslim population has increased from 9.8% in 1951 to 14.23% in 2011. The age share of the Christian population has remained constant since independence. The proportion of Sikhs, Buddhists, and Jains also decreased marginally since independence (Table 6.5).

State-wise Distribution of Population

In India, the combined population of five states of Uttar Pradesh, Maharashtra, Bihar, West Bengal, and Andhra Pradesh is equal to almost 50% of the entire population of the country. Uttar Pradesh with 16.49% of total population tops the chart. Sikkim has a total population of around 6.07 lakhs constituting 0.05% of the total population and ranks last among the states. In union territories, Chandigarh has the highest population of 10.54 lakhs constituting 0.09% of population, and Lakshadweep has the lowest population of 64,429 persons constituting 0.01% of population (Table 6.6).

TABLE 6.6 State-wise Total and Percentage Population, 2011

State	Total Population	Total %	State	Total Population	Total %
Uttar Pradesh	1,99,581,477	16.49	Jammu & Kashmir	12,548,926	1.04
Maharashtra	1,12,372,972	9.29	Uttarakhand	10,116,752	0.84
Bihar	1,03,804,637	8.58	Himachal Pradesh	6,856,509	0.57
West Bengal	91,347,736	7.55	Tripura	3,671,032	0.30
Andhra Pradesh	84,665,533	7.00	Meghalaya	2,964,007	0.24
Madhya Pradesh	72,597,565	6.00	Manipur	2,721,756	0.22
Tamil Nadu	72,138,958	5.96	Nagaland	1,980,602	0.16
Rajasthan	68,621,012	5.67	Goa	1,457,723	0.12
Karnataka	61,130,704	5.05	Arunachal Pradesh	1,382,611	0.11
Gujarat	60,383,628	4.99	Puducherry	1,244,464	0.10
Odisha	41,947,358	3.47	Mizoram	1,091,014	0.09
Kerala	33,387,677	2.76	Chandigarh	1,054,686	0.09

State	Total Population	Total %	State	Total Population	Total %
Jharkhand	32,966,238	2.72	Sikkim	607,688	0.05
Assam	31,169,272	2.58	Andaman & Nicobar Islands	379,944	0.03
Punjab	27,704,236	2.29	Dadra & Nagar Haveli	342,853	0.03
Chhattisgarh	25,540,196	2.11	Daman & Diu	242,911	0.02
Haryana	25,353,081	2.09	Lakshadweep	64,429	0.01
NCT of Delhi	16,753,235	1.38	**Total**	**1,210,193,422**	**100**

Source: Census of India, 2011

Population Policies in India

Background

Population policy represents a strategy for achieving a particular pattern of population change. Population policy can be categorized as: anti-natalist and pro-natalist. Anti-natalist policies are adopted through liberalization of abortion laws, raising the age of marriage, provision of contraceptive services, nutrition and health services for mother and child, etc. Indian population policy can be placed under this category. Anti-natalist policies, on the other hand, emphasize disincentives to childbirth to discourage large families. Singapore and China can be placed under this category. In India, the first reference to family planning was mentioned in 1916 by P.K. Wattal in his book, "The Population Problem in India." Raghunath Dhondo Kave opened the country's first birth control center in Bombay in the year 1925. The Health Survey and Development Committee appointed in 1943 with Sri Joseph Bhore as a chairman is a milestone in the evolution of Family Planning policy in independent India. India was the first country in the world to launch an official Family Planning Programme in 1952.[6] Central Family Planning Board was formed in 1956 to strengthen the family planning programme. After 1952, the death rate declined sharply but it was not accompanied by a similar fall in birth rate, resulting in population explosion. In 1976 during emergency, the government came out with National Population Policy. The policy emphasized raising the age of marriage and increasing female education in the country. Taking advantage of the emergency conditions in the country, a massive drive for compulsory sterilization was undertaken during 1976–1977 and a total of 8.2 million sterilizations were carried out as against the target of 4.3 million. The Family Planning Programme was renamed as the Family Welfare Programme by Janata Government in 1977. A more comprehensive national population policy was adopted in 1986, by the government. It was promoted on a voluntary and democratic basis as a "movement of the people, by the people, for the people." An expert group on National Population Policy headed by Dr. M.S. Swaminathan was appointed in 1993 to prepare a draft on national population policy. The expert group submitted its report in 1994 and recommended the formation of a Population and Social Development Commission[7].

National Population Policy 2000

The government announced a new population policy in 2000. The "long-term objective" is to achieve a stable population by 2045, at a level consistent with the requirements of sustainable economic growth, social development, and environmental protection. The "immediate objective" of the NPP 2000 is to address the needs for contraception, health care infrastructure, and health personnel, and to provide integrated service delivery for basic reproductive and child health care. The "medium-term objective" is to bring the TFR to replacement levels by 2010, through vigorous implementation of inter-sectoral operational strategies. The policy includes freezing the number of seats in Lok Sabha at the current level of 543, which is based on the 1971 census till 2026. To achieve these objectives, the NPP has envisaged the following 14 sociodemographic goals for 2010:[8]

1. Addressing the unmet needs for basic reproductive and child health services, supplies, and infrastructure.
2. Make school education up to the age of 14 years, free and compulsory and reduce drop-outs at primary and secondary school levels to below 20% for both boys and girls.
3. Reduce infant mortality rate to below 30 per 1000 live births.
4. Reduce the maternal mortality rate to below 100 per 100,000 live births.
5. Achieve universal immunization of children against all vaccine-preventable diseases.
6. Promote delayed marriage for girls, not earlier than the age of 18 and preferably after 20 years of age.
7. Achieve 80% institutional deliveries and 100% deliveries by trained persons.
8. Achieve universal access to information/counseling, and services for fertility regulation and contraception with a wide basket of choices.
9. Achieve 100% registration of births, deaths, marriage, and pregnancy.
10. Contain the spread of AIDS, and promote greater integration between the management of reproductive tract infections and sexually transmitted infections and the National AIDS Control Organization.
11. Prevent and control communicable diseases.
12. Integrate Indian Systems of Medicine (ISM) in the provision of reproductive and child health services, and in reaching out to households.
13. Promote vigorously the small family norm to achieve replacement levels of TFR.
14. Bring about convergence in implementation of related social sector programs so that family welfare becomes a people-centered Programme.

BOX 6.1 Few Important Steps/Measures to Control Population Growth by Government of India

1. **Jansankhya Sthirata Kosh (JSK):** The Government of India had set up a National Population Stabilization Fund (NPSF) or JSK in the year 2004–2005 with a one-time grant of ₹100 crores in the form of a corpus fund. JSK can raise contributions from organizations and individuals that support population stabilization. JSK has implemented two schemes, namely, Santushti and Prerna. JSK is also running a call center for providing free advice on reproductive health, family planning, maternal health, and child health, etc.
2. **Santushti Strategy:** Under this strategy, Jansankhya Sthirata Kosh, invites private sector gynecologists and vasectomy surgeons to conduct sterilization operations in Public–Private Partnership mode. The private hospitals/nursing homes that achieved a target of 10 or more tubectomy/vasectomy cases in a month are suitably awarded as per strategy.
3. **Prerna Strategy:** JSK has launched Prerna strategy for helping to push up the age of marriage of girls and delay in first child and spacing in second child in the interest of health of young mothers and infants. Couples who adopted this strategy were awarded suitably.

4. **Accredited Social Health Activist (ASHA):** ASHA is a trained female community health activist. Selected from the community itself and accountable to it, the ASHA works as an interface between the community and the public health system. Functions of ASHA include delivery of contraceptives at doorstep of beneficiaries, counselling newly married couples to ensure delay in childbirth up to 2 years after marriage and couples with 1 child to have spacing of 3 years after the birth of first child. At present, there are over 9 lakh ASHAs. The ASHA scheme is presently in place in 33 states (except Goa, Chandigarh, and Puducherry).

Sources:

1. Paul, et al. (2013). *Functioning of accredited social health activists (ASHAS) in ICDS: an evaluation" Health and Population—* Perspectives and Issues 36 (3&4), 78–89.
2. National Population Policy, Ministry of Health and Family Welfare, Press Information Bureau, 11 December, 2015.

Is India's Huge Population a Demographic Disaster or Demographic Dividend?

Population growth and its relation to economic growth has been a matter of debate for over a century. The early Malthusian view was that population growth is likely to impede economic growth because it will put pressure on the available resources, result in a reduction in per capita income and resources; this, in turn, will result in deterioration in quality of life. Contrary to the Malthusian predictions, several of the East Asian countries have been able to achieve economic prosperity and improvement in quality of life in spite of population growth. This has been attributed to the increase in productivity due to the development and utilization of innovative technologies by the young educated population who formed the majority of the growing population.

Let us discuss both the viewpoints in detail.

Population as a Demographic Disaster

Poverty, Unemployment, and Low Level of Human Development

Growing population has forward and backward linkages with the other economic dynamics particularly poverty and unemployment. In fact, all the underdeveloped countries of the world are characterized by high population growth and high incidence of poverty and unemployment. The whole planning effort in India critically failed in achieving the most important social and human values of any society normally cherished, namely, to have an educated and healthy population. In large regions of the country, illiteracy, especially among women, continued to be still rampant. In terms of absolute numbers, the number of illiterates, the total number of infant deaths, and the total number of malnourished or partially hungry persons have all risen since independence. The failure to eradicate illiteracy, to improve the status of women in society and to assure access to health care also accounted for the failure to reduce the rate of population growth. The unemployment problem remains unsolved and agriculture still sustains 45% of Indian workforce, which is unproductive and generates lower per capita income. The population pressure and rampant problem of unskilled labor have caused non-absorption of rural labor into industry and services. The real shortcomings of population policy lie in its overall neglect of social sector planning and thus in its failure to integrate population issues with the development programmes and policies.[9]

Adverse Land–Man Ratio

While India accounts for a meager 2.4% of world's surface area of 135.79 million square kilometers, it supports and sustains a whopping 17.5% of the world population. As such among the 10 most populous countries in the world, only Bangladesh has a high population density compared to India. When the population grows, the gains from economic growth are wasted on supporting the growing population. Had India's population growth been modest, the country's development performance would have looked far more impressive. Increasing population is the prime factor for land fragmentation and lower productivity in Indian agriculture. The situation has been aggravated due to intensification of domestic competition for land for non-agricultural uses. Accelerated GDP growth demands more roads, dams, airports, industrial estates, and housing. The mindless acquisition of agricultural land in the name of planned development or industrial growth would adversely affect the future availability of food. Prime land must be conserved for agriculture and not diverted for non-agricultural uses.[10]

Environmental and Ecological Consequences

Rapid population growth, developmental activities either to meet the growing population or the growing needs of the population as well as changing lifestyles and consumption patterns pose a major challenge to preservation and promotion of ecological balance in India. Some of the major ecological adverse effects reported in India include:[11]

1. Pressure on the forests due to unbridled deforestation and jungle fire. The per capita forest biomass in the country is only about 6 tonnes as against the global average of 82 tonnes;
2. Adverse effect on the diversity of species;
3. Conversion of habitat to some other land use such as agriculture, urban development, and forestry operation. Around 80% of freshwater marshes and lakes in the Gangetic flood plains have been lost in the last 50 years;
4. Commercial needs and fuelwood requirements lead to tropical deforestation and destruction of mangroves. India lost 40% of its mangrove area during the last century;[12]
4. Intense grazing by domestic livestock;
5. Poaching and illegal harvesting of wildlife;
6. Increase in agricultural area, high use of chemical fertilizers, pesticides, and weedicides; water stagnation, soil erosion, soil salinity, and low productivity;
7. High level of biomass burning causing large-scale indoor pollution;
8. Increase in commercial activities such as mining and unsustainable resource extraction;
9. Degradation of coastal and other aquatic ecosystems from domestic sewage, pesticides, fertilizers, and industrial effluents;
10. Overfishing in water bodies and introduction of weeds and exotic species;
11. Diversion of water for domestic, industrial, and agricultural uses leading to increased river pollution and decrease in self-cleaning properties of rivers;

12. Increasing water requirement leading to tapping deeper aquifers that have high content of arsenic or fluoride resulting health problems;
13. Disturbance from increased recreational activity and tourism causing pollution of natural ecosystems with wastes left behind by people.

Urbanization

At present 54% of the world population lives in urban areas. By 2050, this share is forecast to increase to 66%. That equates to an additional 2.4 billion people living in urban centers—an increase of 1,93,000 persons per day for the next 33 years[13]. In India 17% of population lived in cities in 1951, 32.7% in 2015, and by the year 2050, 50.3% of population is projected to reside in cities. The process of urbanization in India has continued to be top-heavy, oriented toward large cities. This is consistent with the fact that larger cities are generally more efficient in generating growth and attracting investments.[14] Migration has been affected by both pull and push factors. A recent study by Rural Development and Migration Commission has reported that 734 villages in Uttarakhand have been deserted and more than 3.83 lakh people have left their villages in the last 10 years. Around 1,19,000 people have permanently migrated from their villages, while 3,84,000 persons from 6338 gram panchayats were forced to leave in search of jobs.[15] Urbanization has both economic and social consequences. Poor air and water quality, insufficient water availability, waste-disposal problems, high-energy consumption, increase in crime rate, problem of housing and slums are exacerbated by the increasing population density and demands of urban environments.[16]

Food Security

Technological innovations in agriculture and increase in area under cultivation have ensured that so far, food production has kept pace with the population growth. However, it is estimated that the global population will grow to 9 billion by 2050 and the food and nutrition security could become critical in many parts of the world especially in the developing countries and pockets of poverty in the developed countries. In India, one of the major achievements during the last seven decades has been the green revolution and self-sufficiency in food production. Though the food grain production has increased by more than five times, yet it is a matter of concern that the per capita availability of certain cereals and pulses has decreased or remained stagnant since 1951. Increase in purchasing power and shift in food habits will escalate demand for food products and hence their prices.

Population as a Demographic Dividend

The term "Demographic Dividend" refers to the accelerated economic growth that a country can achieve when it has a low dependency ratio or, in other words, when the proportion of its population that is of working age is greater than the proportion of its population that does not work (e.g., children and the elderly). This population structure frees up household and state resources that would otherwise be used to support dependent groups. These resources can then be invested to improve productivity and to generate economic growth.[17] In simple words, demographic dividend is a window of opportunity opens up toward the development of a nation as a consequence of rapid demographic transition.

The three main factors that contribute to the demographic dividend of the country is as follows:

1. **Lower fertility rate:** There are empirical evidences that fertility decline has led to demographic change accompanied by greater female participation in the labor force.[18] Lower fertility rate leads to smaller family size which also means increase in spending on rearing and educating the children, which are the future productive human resource. On the contrary if fertility rate is high, countries will have a difficult time investing in the human capital needed to secure the well-being of its people and to stimulate economic growth. The total fertility rate in a specific year is defined as the total number of children that would be born to each woman if she were to live to the end of her childbearing years and give birth to children in alignment with the prevailing age-specific fertility rates. Assuming no net migration and unchanged mortality, a total fertility rate of 2.1 children per woman ensures a broadly stable population.[19] The total fertility rate for India, measured as the number of children born to a woman, has fallen from 4.97 during 1975–1980 to 2.3 for the current period of 2015–2020. By 2025–2030, it was expected to go down to 2.1 and slide to 1.86 during 2045–2050 and 1.78 during 2095–2100.[20] Lowering fertility requires stronger policy intervention and the two most important methods are increasing access to family planning services and improving girls' access to education.
2. **Increase in working age population and fall in dependency ratio:** India is undergoing a major demographic transition. The transition started about 40 years ago and will likely last another 30 years. According to some estimates, about a quarter of the projected increase in the global population aged 15–64 years between 2010 and 2040 will occur in India. The working-age ratio in the country is set to rise from about 64% currently to 69% in 2040, reflecting the addition of just over 300 million working-age adults. This would make India—by an order of magnitude—the largest single positive contributor to the global workforce over the next three decades.[21] Cross-country evidence suggests that productivity is an increasing function of age, with the age group 40–49 years being the most productive because of work experience. The poorer nations have a lower proportion of 40-year-old workers than the richer nations in every year.[22] Nearly half the additions to the Indian labor force over the period 2011–2030 will be in the age group 30–49 years, even while the share of this group in China, Korea, and the United States will be declining. India will be expanding its most productive cohorts even when most developed countries and some developing countries like China will be contracting theirs in the coming decades can be another source of advantage.[23]
3. **Growth in labor productivity:** The research has proved that fruits of demographic dividend are channeled through the increase in labor productivity, which depends upon three factors. First, more physical capital employed per worker. It results from greater saving and investment. Second, more human capital per worker. It comes from better education as smaller families lead to greater spending on education per child. Third, greater total factor productivity (TFP). It measures how productive the job intrinsically is, capturing aspects such as the technology used, efficiency with which the work is carried out, and use of hard-to-measure aspects of work such as tacit knowledge, organizational capabilities, and trust.

Lessons from China and East Asia

There are empirical evidences that fertility decline leads to demographic change and accompanied by greater female participation in the labor force. For example, both India and China established world's earliest national family planning programmes, in 1952 and 1956, respectively. China launched one-child policy norm with the campaign of "later, longer, fewer" in 1979 that led to a precipitous decline in fertility and a sharp rise in the working-age share of the population. Meanwhile, India's family planning program led to political backlash that ultimately set back its family planning efforts and pushed India's demographic trajectory out of phase with China's. India had 66% higher per capita income than China in 1980, but by the early 1990s China overtook India. In 2008, the situation was decisively reversed with per capita income doubled in China than India.

If India needs to follow the similar path, it needs to concentrate on increasing savings and investment, escalating budget on education and raising TFP. Major increase in China's TFP has come as workers migrate from low-productivity sectors like agriculture to high-productivity sectors like manufacturing.[24] The process of inter-sector migration has started in India and it is expected that the share of employment in agriculture will come down to about 40% by 2020 and that in industry will rise. But the problem is that while industry is creating jobs, these have been relatively low-productivity jobs as much of the labor has been absorbed in construction sector. As a result, per capita income in India has not benefited as much from inter-sectoral migration of workers out of agriculture as other Asian countries had.[25]

Demographic Dividend: Challenges and Road Ahead

Notwithstanding the favorable demographic character of a nation, the benefits of demographic dividend are not realized automatically and depend much upon a right economic policy framework. Labor input to economic growth is not only determined by the size of the working-age population but also depends on labor market participation, that is, the proportion of the working-age population actually employed and the nature of working regulations. Keeping the above facts in the mind, the policy framework needs to focus upon three things.

First, India has amongst the lowest women's labor force participation rates (LFPR) in the world. Not only women's participation rates are low but have been showing a declining trend since 2004–2005. Women's LFPR dropped from 42.7% in 2004–2005 to 31.2 in 2011–2012 and further to 27.4% in 2015–2016. Participation rates are even lower in urban areas and among educated women, and when women work they tend to end up in marginal jobs, often in home-based work (as contributing family worker/unpaid worker) and the domestic work sector. Research has proved the positive correlation between female literacy and their labor force participation and for that there is a need to develop a holistic approach to empower the girls while looking at barriers that are keeping girls from school. By investing in a young adolescent girl's education and health, and reducing the risk of early marriage and early pregnancy, she has greater opportunities to find a path out of poverty, lead a healthier life and become an asset to her family, community, and society.

Second, despite remarkable economic growth during the past three decades, the majority of Indian workers are engaged in informal employment. Roughly, 85% of the workforce is engaged in the informal sector. Among wage employees outside of agriculture, more than three-quarters have no written contract, 70% are not eligible for any paid leave, and 74% are not covered by social security benefits. India's high rate of informality is a drag on its economic development and a source of considerable inequity. Productivity differences between workers in the formal and informal sectors are large suggesting that moving a worker from an informal to a formal firm would bring about sizeable gains from improved allocation of resources. Research suggests that an informal job in the formal sector has double the value added than an informal job in the informal sector. And considerably, the productivity per worker in a formal job within the formal sector is almost 10 times than in an informal job in the formal sector. Not only that informal worker earns less but he/she is also subject to violations of basic human rights such as realistic, sound and safe work environment. Lack of job security and poor safety nets make informally employed workers extremely vulnerable to shocks such as illnesses and loss of income. Consequently, a strong correlation exists between informality and poverty in India. It is therefore, essential that consensus building on labor market reforms should start soon. India needs many more firms in the formal sector, especially firms that continue growing and creating productive jobs. The government should continue to create a minimum safety net for informal workers by, for example, extending the reach of Ayushman Bharat—National health protection mission, National pension scheme, and introducing certain unemployment insurance schemes.

Third, the services sector in India remains the most dynamic one and growth is very high, but that growth is not matched by commensurate growth in employment. It generates 53% of country's GDP but employs 28% of India's workforce. In most other economies, the share of services in gross value added is more or less similar to its share in total employment. But India remains exception to this. Despite India climbing 30 positions in the ease of doing business ranking in 2018, some impediments to business creation such as regulatory hurdles and access to funding, infrastructure and labor regulations remain common between services and industry. For example, more than one-fourth of retail stores in India report labor laws as a constraint for their businesses. But what stands out for the services sector is the importance of education and skilling. Suitable higher education is important for high-end knowledge-based services such as IT, software development, and finance. Mid-level services such as retail trade, hotels, and restaurant services also require adequate skilling of the labor force.

Finally, the urgency to put in place appropriate policies is magnified by the reality that what follows the demographic dividend is a time when aging population begins to increase again because of increasing longevity and decreasing fertility. Inevitably, the demographic fizz that made its way through the most fruitful working years creating the demographic dividend grows old and retires. With a disproportionate number of old people relying upon a smaller generation following behind them the demographic dividend becomes a liability. With each generation having fewer children, population growth slows, stops, or even turns negative and this trend may be deemed a demographic burden. This phenomenon is being noticed most dramatically in Japan, Germany, and few other European countries with younger generations essentially abandoning many parts of the country. Other regions, notably Europe and North America, will face similar situations in the near future, with East Asia to follow suit. As per 2011 census, India had 90 million elderly persons (above 60 years) in 2011 and the number is projected to be 173 million by 2026 and 315 million by 2050. While only 8% of population was above 60 years in 2011, as much as 20% of population is expected to be above 60 years in 2050. Time has come when we stop labeling older people as burden but assuming them as potential resource and creating opportunities for them across the sectors. Another policy intervention requires considerable ingenuity to increase the ability to save for old age. This, in turn, would require improving the quality of education as better education will increase productivity, thereby enhancing the level of incomes and savings.

Not all countries, which have undergone demographic transition, have been able to transform their economies. Sri Lanka in South Asia underwent demographic transition at the same time as Southeast Asian countries but has not achieved the economic transition. It is now realized that population growth or demographic transition can have favorable impact on economic growth only when there are optimal interventions aimed at human resource development (HRD) and appropriate utilization of available human resources. For India, the current phase of demographic transition with low dependency ratio and high working age group population thus represents both a challenge and an opportunity.

Summary

1. The theory of demographic transition was given by Warren Thompson in 1929 and later developed by Adolphe Landry and Frank W. Notestein. There are five stages as per theory: First stage of high birth and death rate; second stage of falling birth and death rate with fall in death rate being steeper than birth rate; third stage of falling birth and death rates; fourth stage of low birth and death rate and fifth stage of negative growth rate where death rate turns greater than birth rate.
2. The global population has increased from 16.8 crores in 1 A.D. to 750 crores in 2017. Indian population has increased from 23.84 crores in 1901 to 121.09 crores in 2011. The crude birth rate and crude death rate in India was 39.9 and 27.4 respectively during 1950–1951 and came down to 20.4 and 6.4 in the year 2016. The density of population has increased from 77 in 1901 to 382 in 2011. Economically active population (15–59 years) comprises 62.5% of population in 2011. Sex ratio has declined from 972 in 2001 to 943 in 2011. Life expectancy at birth currently is being estimated 66.4 years for males and 69.6 years for females and 67.9 overall for the period 2010–2014. The Hindu population and Muslim population in India constitutes nearly 94% of total population. Uttar Pradesh with 16.49% of population is the most populous state in the country.
3. Population policy represents a strategy for achieving a particular pattern of population change. India was the first country in the world to launch an official Family Planning Programme in 1952. A number of population policy measures were adopted by the government after independence. The population policy 2000 envisages the "long-term objective" of achieving a stable population by 2045; the "immediate objective" of addressing the needs for contraception, health care infrastructure, and health personnel, and to provide integrated service delivery for basic reproductive and child health care; and the "medium-term objective" to bring the TFR to replacement levels by 2010, through rigorous implementation of inter-sectoral operational strategies. The policy includes freezing the number of seats in Lok Sabha at the current level of 543, which is based on the 1971 census till 2026. To achieve this objective, the NPP has envisaged the 14 socio-demographic goals for 2010.
4. Population can be a demographic disaster or demographic dividend. The negative implications of population are: poverty, unemployment, and low level of human development; adverse land–man ratio, which affects land productivity due to fragmentation and this ratio is further aggravated by diversion of land for other uses; challenge to preservation and promotion of ecological balance; massive and fast increasing urbanization and food security issues because of demand and supply mismatch.
5. Demographic dividend is a window of opportunity opens up toward the development of a nation as a consequence of rapid demographic transition. The three main factors that contribute to the demographic dividend are (1) lower fertility rate; (2) increase in working age population and fall in dependency ratio; and (3) growth in labor productivity. The lessons from Chinese growth escalation and East Asian turnaround have demonstrated that much of the increase in per capita income has come from greater labor productivity which in turn depends upon more physical capital employed per worker, more human capital per worker, and greater total factor productivity. To tap the demographic dividend, the policy framework needs to focus on three things. First, increasing the women LFPR, second, a transition from informal to formal employment set-up, promoting labor-absorbing service sector and channelizing the potential of the old aged population.

Endnotes

1. Lee, R. (2003). The demographic transition: Three centuries of fundamental change. *Journal of Economic Perspectives, 17* (4) pp. 167-190.
2. World population prospects, the 2017 revision. (2017). UN, New York.
3. Census of India. (2001). *Sex composition of the population, Chapter 6.*
4. Chakarborty & Sinha. (2006). *Determinants of declining child sex ratio in India: An empirical investigation.* New Delhi: National Institute of Public

Finance and Policy. Retrieved from https://mpra.ub.uni (Accessed on November 16, 2017).

5. *Life Expectancy*. Retrieved from https://niti.gov.in (Accessed on April 6, 2019).
6. Srinivasan, S. (2007). Population policy and programme in India: A review. *Social Change*, 37 (1).
7. Chaudhry, M.D. (1989). *Population and Environment, 11*, 101. https://doi.org (Accessed on October 14, 2017).
8. National Population Policy, (2002). Department of Family Welfare, Ministry of Health and Family Welfare, Govt. of India, Reprint.
9. Krishnan, T.N. (1992). Population, poverty and employment in India. *EPW, 14*.
10. Bhalla, S. (2015) Notes on land, long run food security and the agrarian crisis in India. Retrieved from https://ideas.repec.org (Accessed on June 27, 2017).
11. Planning Commission (2006). *Population growth trends, projections, challenges and opportunities.*, retrieved from http://planningcommission.nic.in (Accessed on May 6, 2018).
12. Sahu, S.C., Suresh, H.C., Murthy, I.K, & Ravindranath, N.H (2015). Mangrove area assessment in India: Implications of loss of mangroves. *Journal of Earth Science & Climatic Change*, ISSN: 2157-7617.
13. UNCTAD (2018) *Handbook of Statistics 2017—Population*. Retrieved from http://unctad.org. (Accessed on May 6, 2018).
14. Kundu, A. (September 2011). Trends and processes of urbanisation in India. Urbanization and Emerging Population Issues - 6 IIED, UNFPA.
15. 700 Uttarakhand villages deserted in 10 years. *The Tribune*, May 06, 2018.
16. Urban Threats. (2018). Retrieved from https://www.nationalgeographic.com (Accessed on May 4, 2019).
17. Demographic Dividend. (2018). Retrieved from https://www.populationmatters.org (Accessed on June 6, 2019)
18. Bailey, M.J. (2006). More power to the pill: The impact of contraceptive freedom on women's life cycle labor supply. *Quarterly Journal of Economics, 121*, 289–320.
19. Fertility Rates. (2018). *OECD Labor Force Statistics*. Retrieved from https://data.oecd.org (Accessed on June 7, 2019).
20. *India's fertility rate more than halves over 40 years*. The Hindu. June 22, 2017.
21. Aiyar, S., & Mody, A. (2011). The demographic dividend: Evidence from the Indian States. IMF Working Paper.
22. Feyrer, J. (2007). Demographics and productivity. *Review of Economics and Statistics, 89* (1): 100–109.
23. Seizing the demographic dividend, *Economic Survey*, 2012–13, p.27.
24. IMF, World Economic Outlook. (2006). Asia rising: Patterns of economic development and growth, Chapter 3.
25. Seizing the Demographic Dividend, Economic Survey, Ministry of Finance, Govt. of India. 2012–2013, p.35.

CHAPTER 7

POVERTY AND INEQUALITY IN INDIA

A nation will not survive morally or economically when so few have so much and so many have so little.

—Bernie Sanders

INTRODUCTION

According to HDR 1997, poverty is a denial of choices and opportunities for living a tolerable life. There has been marked progress on reducing poverty over the past decades in the world. According to World Bank estimates, in 2016, less than 10% of the world's population lived on less than US$1.90 a day as compared to 35% in 1990. Despite all this, a vast majority of the global poor live in rural areas and are poorly educated, mostly employed in the agricultural sector, and over half are under 18 years of age. Access to good schools, healthcare, electricity, safe water, and other critical services remains elusive for many people, often determined by socio-economic status, gender, ethnicity, and geography. Moreover, for those who have been able to move out of poverty, progress is often temporary; economic shocks, food insecurity, and climate change threaten to rob them of their hard-won gains and force them back into poverty.[1]

This chapter devotes discussion on following topics:

- Estimation of Poverty by International Agencies
- Incidence of Poverty in India
- Estimation of Poverty in India
- Universal Basic Income and Its Critical Appraisal
- Critical Evaluation of Poverty Alleviation Measures in India
- Inequality: Extent, Causes and Solutions

ESTIMATION OF POVERTY BY INTERNATIONAL AGENCIES

World Bank's Estimates of Poverty

World Bank, in its World Development Report 1990, introduced the dollar-a-day international poverty line (IPL). The IPL is revised periodically in line with new data from the independent

International Comparison Program* (ICP), which is hosted by the World Bank. The newly updated figure of IPL is $2.15 at 2017 prices (earlier it was $1.90 at 2011 prices). It was released in 2022 and is based on ICP purchasing power parity (PPP) calculations and represents the international equivalent of what $2.15 could buy in the United States in 2017. This means that anyone living on less than $2.15 a day is considered to be living in extreme poverty. The Bank's estimates reveal that about 648 million people were living in extreme poverty in 2019. According to World Bank's estimates extreme poverty in India has declined from 21.2% of population in 2011 to 12.92% in 2021.

Multi-dimensional Poverty Index

Multidimensional Poverty Index (MPI) identifies deprivations across the same three dimensions as the Human Development Index (HDI) and with the help of 10 indicators shows the number of people who are multi-dimensionally poor (suffering deprivations in 33% or more of the weighted indicators) and the number of weighted deprivations with which poor households typically contend with.[2] According to MPI 2023 report, India is one of the 25 nations that have successfully halved their global multidimensional poverty Index values within 15 years. In India the incidence of poverty fell from 55.1% (645 million) in 2005/06 to 16.4% (230 million) in 2019/21.**

Extreme Poverty in India as per World Poverty Clock

The world poverty clock is a tool to measure poverty globally and country wise. It is created by World data Lab, Vienna, Austria and is funded by Germany's Federal Ministry for Economic Cooperation and Development. It was launched in Berlin, 2017.[3] It measures poverty on the basis of publicly available data on income distribution, production, and consumption, provided by various international organizations, most notably the UN, World Bank, and the IMF. On the basis of Indians living on less than $2.15 per day, it estimated that number of Indians who are extremely poor have fallen from 306 million in 2011 to 34 million in April 2024, which accounts for about 2% of population.[4]

Incidence of Poverty in India

Many economists, for example, Minhas, Ahluwalia, and Bardhan have endeavored to measure poverty in India but the original official poverty estimates in India, provided by the Planning Commission, were based on the Lakdawala poverty lines so named after Prof. D.T. Lakdawala who headed a 1993 expert group that recommended these lines. Because all these economists

*The ICP is a worldwide statistical initiative led by the World Bank under the auspices of the United Nations Statistical Commission, with the main objective of providing comparable price and volume measures of gross domestic product (GDP) and its expenditure aggregates among countries within and across regions. Through a partnership with international, regional, sub-regional, and national agencies, the ICP collects and compares price data and GDP expenditures to estimate and publish purchasing power parities (PPPs) of the world's economies.

**For detailed discussion of MPI, please refer to Chapter 3 'Human Development and Happiness Economics'.

applied different methodologies, the divergence in measuring the poverty estimates was quite evident. For example, Minhas, Bardhan and Ahluwalia measured all India poverty rates of 37.1, 54.0 and 56.5% respectively for the year 1967–1968.

Planning Commission has prominently attempted five times to delineate the methodology of poverty estimation in the country and for that the Commission has constituted Task Force/ Expert Group. These include the Planning Commission working group in 1962, Task Force under the chairmanship of Dr Y.K. Alagh in 1977, Expert Group under the chairmanship of Prof. D.T. Lakdawala in 1989, Expert Group under the chairmanship of Prof. S.D. Tendulkar in 2005, and Expert Group under the chairmanship of Dr C. Rangarajan in 2012. Different committees established by Planning Commission from time to time gave poverty estimates on the basis of their own methodology. The difference in methodology provided dissimilar poverty estimates. For example, on the basis of Tendulkar methodology, the poverty ratio decreased from 37.2–29.8% during 2004–05 to 2009–10. It further decreased to 21.9% in 2011–12. This initiated a debate within the country with regard to authenticity of poverty estimates, sometimes also called as 'great Indian poverty debate.' Let us have an idea of poverty estimates by different committees.

Planning Commission Working Group (1962)

The Planning Commission constituted a Working Group in 1962 to find out a desirable minimum level of living for the population. The Working Group recommended that the national minimum consumption expenditure for a household of five persons (four adult consumption units) should be not less than $100 per month at prices and for urban areas, this figure was $125 per month. The poverty line excluded expenditure on health and education, both of which, it was assumed, were to be provided by the State.

Task Force Under the Chairmanship of Dr Y.K. Alagh (1977)

The Planning Commission in July 1977 constituted the Task Force on "Projections of Minimum Needs and Effective Consumption Demand" under the Chairmanship of Dr Y.K. Alagh. The Task Force provided a quantitative measure of poverty based on poverty line corresponding to the calorie requirement. The estimated calorie norm was 2,400 kcal per capita per day in rural areas and 2,100 kcal per capita per day in urban areas. Based on the observed consumer behavior in 1973–1974, it was estimated that, on an average, consumer expenditure (food and non-food) of ₹49.09 per capita per month was associated with a calorie intake of 2,400 kcal per capita per day in rural areas and ₹56.64 per capita per month with a calorie intake of 2,100 kcal per day in urban areas. This monthly per capita expenditure (MPCE) was termed as poverty line.[5] The Task Force used the percentage distribution of persons in different expenditure classes in the NSSO data on household consumer expenditure to estimate the percentage of persons living below the poverty line (Box 7.1). The NSSO distribution of private consumption was adjusted proportionately (on pro-rata basis) to correspond to the consumption estimates of National Accounts Statistics (NAS) made by the Central Statistical Office (CSO).[6] Using the poverty line and the adjusted distribution of persons by expenditure classes for the reference year, the percentage of persons below the poverty line was estimated.

BOX 7.1 What are NSSO Surveys?

National Sample Survey Office (NSSO) comes under statistics wing of the Ministry of Statistics and Programme Implementation (MOSPI) which was established in 1999. Headed by Director General, it collects primarily data through nation-wide household surveys on various socio-economic subjects such as employment, consumption expenditure, rural and urban prices, and various other surveys viz. crop estimation surveys, Annual Survey of Industries (ASI), etc. India's official poverty estimates are based on regular consumer expenditure surveys conducted by NSSO from time to time. Pioneered by P. C. Mahalanobis in 1940s, NSSO surveys were world's first system of household surveys to apply the principal of random sampling. Large consumer expenditure surveys are conducted after every 5 or 6 years, whereas the smaller surveys are conducted annually. In the recent years, the large surveys were conducted in 1983 (Round 38), 1987 to 1988 (Round 43), 1993 to 1994 (Round 50), 1999 to 2000 (Round 55), 2004 to 2005 (Round 61), 2011 to 2012 (Round 68), and 2013 to 2014 (Round 70). On the basis of such surveys, the government publishes estimates of poverty at national, state, and sector (urban/rural) level.

Sources:

1. NSSO (2019). Retrieved from http://mospi.nic.in. (Accessed on January 8, 2019).
2. Deaton and Kozel (2005), *Data and dogma: The great Indian poverty debate*. Accessed from https://www.princeton.edu (Accessed on December 12, 2018).

Expert Group Under the Chairmanship of Prof. D.T. Lakdawala (1989)

The magnitude of difference between poverty ratios based on NSS and the NAS consumption data increased overtime and it also affected the adjustment process. A lower level of poverty leads to a lower allocation not only in the anti-poverty programmes but also in the developmental programmes as the latter also takes poverty as one of the criteria in its allocation, both inter and intra-state. Faced with these odds, the Planning Commission constituted the Expert Group under the Chairmanship of Prof. D.T. Lakdawala* in September 1989 to re-visit the methodology of poverty estimation. The Expert Group submitted its Report in July 1993 and the Government accepted the Expert Group methodology in March 1997 as the basis for computing the official estimates of poverty in India.

Lakdawala's methodology was different from Alagh's methodology on two accounts. First, the Expert Group (Lakdawala) method used state-specific poverty lines against national poverty line for estimation of poverty in the state; it thereby captured the cost of living in the states more accurately (as compared to the Alagh Committee's methodology). Second, the Expert Group (Lakdawala) used the state-wise consumption distribution of the NSSO without any adjustment to the NAS consumption. This is a major departure from the Task Force method, which did this adjustment on a pro-rata basis.[7] Using this methodology planning commission measured all India poverty ratios of 54.9, 36 and 27.5% for the years 1973–1974, 1993–1994 and 2004–2005 respectively.

---

*D.T. Lakdawala served as Professor of Economics at Mumbai University and was deputy chairman of Planning Commission (1977–1980). He died in April 1993, 2 months before the report submitted by expert group.

BOX 7.2 Difference between URP, MRP, and MMRP

Three estimates of consumption are available from the NSSO depending upon the recall (reference) period of data collection. These are: (1) Uniform Recall Period (URP), (2) Mixed Recall Period (MRP), and (3) Modified Mixed Recall Period (MMRP). In the URP, the consumption expenditure data are collected using 30-day recall period for all the items. In the MRP, the consumption expenditure data are collected using 365-day recall period for five non-food items and 30-day recall period for remaining items. In the MMRP, the consumer expenditure data are gathered from the households using the recall period of: (1) 365 days for clothing, footwear, education, institutional medical care, and durable goods; (2) 7 days for edible oil, egg, fish and meat, vegetables, fruits, spices, beverages, refreshments, processed food, pan, tobacco, and intoxicants; and (3) 30 days for the remaining food items, fuel and light, miscellaneous goods and services including non-institutional medical, rents and taxes.

Sources:

1. Meaning: URP, MRP and MMRP, Indian Express, October 7, 2015.
2. Planning Commission (2014). *Report of the expert group to review the methodology for measurement of poverty*, Government of India, New Delhi.

Expert Group—Tendulkar (2005)

The Expert Group under the chairmanship of Suresh D. Tendulkar was constituted by the Planning Commission in December 2005. It was mandated to (1) examine the issues relating to the comparability of the NSS 50th (1993–1994), NSS 55th (1999–2000), and NSS 61st (2004–2005) Round consumer expenditure data and suggest methodologies for deriving such comparability with past and future survey data; (2) review alternative conceptualizations of poverty; and (3) recommend any changes in the existing procedures of official estimates of poverty. The Expert Group submitted its recommendations to the Planning Commission in November 2009.

The Expert Group (Tendulkar) did not construct a poverty line. It adopted the officially measured urban poverty line of 2004–2005 based on Expert Group (Lakdawala) methodology and converted this poverty line (which is Uniform Recall Period (URP)-consumption based) into Mixed Recall Period (MRP) consumption (Box 7.2). Using Fisher index, national level poverty line was further disaggregated and state-wise poverty line was derived for Indian states. The poverty line in terms of MPCE was devised at ₹446.68 for rural areas and ₹578.80 for urban areas during 2004–2005. For 2011–2012, the MPCE was ₹816 for rural areas and ₹1000 for urban areas. The previous expert groups (both Alagh and Lakdawala) used calorie as a basis of measuring poverty. Tendulkar committee suggested to move away from calorie-based norms and included the certain set of goods and services that constitute a desirable national minimum standard of living. Further the previous expert groups used URP to capture the consumption patterns of households. Tendulkar committee instead suggested shifting to MRP so as to capture the household consumption expenditure of poor households on low-frequency items of purchase more satisfactorily. Tendulkar committee broadened the scope of minimum standard of living by providing greater significance to non-food items. The proposed poverty line basket (PLB) covered all the items of consumption for the construction of price indices. Private expenditure on education and health was also included. The previous practice was to omit this expenditure as providing basic healthcare and education was deemed to be the responsibility of state.

As per Tendulkar methodology, the all India poverty rate came down from 37.2% from 2004–2005 to 21.9% in 2011–2012 (Table 7.1).

Expert Group—Rangarajan (2012)

Government established an expert group under the chairmanship of Dr C. Rangarajan to review the methodology for measurement of poverty in June 2012. The expert group submitted its report in June 2014. Following are the key ingredients of Rangarajan Panel on poverty estimation.

1. **Choice of Recall Period:** The Modified Mixed Recall Period (MMRP) is considered as the better estimate as it is closer to the true value.[8] The Expert Group (Rangarajan) makes a departure from the previous poverty estimates by using MMRP estimates and hence better in approach.
2. **The New PLB and Revised Norms for Calories, Proteins, and Fats:** The new PLB includes (1) food component; (2) normative level of consumption expenditure for essential non-food item groups (education, clothing, conveyance, and house rent); and (3) residual set of behaviorally determined non-food expenditure. The Expert Group (Rangarajan) has recomputed the average requirements of calories, proteins, and fats, per capita per day at the all-India level for 2011–2012, separately for the rural and the urban populations. This has been done by reference to the 2010 ICMR norms differentiated by age, gender, and activity-status for the rural and urban population, as per the NSS 68th Round Employment–Unemployment Survey (2011–2012).[9] The new revised average calorie requirement is 2,155 kcal per capita per day in rural areas and 2,090 kcal per capita per day in urban areas. The task Force (Alagh) and Expert Group (Lakdawala) had used calorie norms of 2,400 kcal per capita per day in rural areas and 2,100 kcal per capita per day in urban areas in their estimation.
   The two factors responsible for overall lowering of estimated calorie norm are as follows:
   a. Change in the population structure/demographic pattern, which is associated with the overall rate of growth of the economy.*
   b. Changes in the lifestyle of all sections of the society, which are reflected in the reduction in proportion of population engaged as heavy workers overtime, while that of moderate or sedentary workers has increased.[10] It lowers the average calorie norm of the entire population because calorie requirement of moderate or sedentary workers is much less than that of heavy workers.
3. **Deriving the Non-Food Component of the PLB:** The non-food component of the PLB includes both normative component and observed consumption pattern of households. On the basis of this, the MPCE of ₹972 in rural areas and ₹1,407 in urban areas constitutes the new poverty lines at the all-India level as per the recommendation of the Expert Group (Rangarajan).** They translate to a monthly per household expenditure of ₹4,860 in rural India and of ₹7,035 in urban India—assuming a family of five members

* Especially in rural areas where the lowering of the estimated calorie norm from 2,400–2,155 kcal per capita per day is the outcome of change in the population structure (e.g., migration to urban areas by youngsters) and the overall lowering of the average age-sex-activity-specific calorie requirement of the individuals as determined by the ICMR.

** The MPCE includes (1) food, (2) four essential non-food items viz. education, clothing, shelter (rent), and mobility (conveyance), and (3) other non-food items.

in each case.[11] In terms of PPP values (World Bank, 2014), the PLB-MPCE translates to $2.14 per capita per day for rural India, $3.10 per capita per day for urban India, and $2.44 per capita per day for the country as a whole.*

The poverty line as per Expert Group (Tendulkar) methodology and derived from the MRP for 2011–2012 is ₹816 and ₹1,000 per capita per month for all-India rural and urban populations, respectively. The Expert Group (Rangarajan) poverty lines, based on MMRP, are thus 19% higher for rural India and 41% higher for urban India. The increase in poverty line is partly attributed to shift from MRP to MMRP.

4. **Disaggregation of National Poverty Line Into State-Specific Poverty Lines:** As discussed earlier, the all-India poverty line of ₹972 in rural areas and ₹1,407 in urban areas has been estimated from the MMRP consumption expenditure distribution of NSS 68th Round. Using the Fisher index, the inter-state price differential is calculated separately in rural and urban areas and from these the national poverty lines (separately in rural and urban areas) in 2011–2012 are disaggregated into state-specific poverty lines.
5. **Estimation of Poverty Ratio:** A comparative analysis between Expert Group (Rangarajan) method and the Expert Group (Tendulkar) method shows that the average level of poverty ratio derived from the Expert Group (Rangarajan) method is higher than that derived from the Expert Group (Tendulkar) method. The all-India poverty ratio derived from the Expert Group (Rangarajan) method is 7.6 percentage points higher in 2011–2012 than that derived by the Planning Commission using the Expert Group (Tendulkar) method (Table 7.1). It is to be noted that poverty estimates by Tendulkar committee remains the official statistics of Government of India as Government has not approved Rangarajan committee estimates as official estimates.

TABLE 7.1 Poverty Estimates by Tendulkar and Rangarajan Methodology

	Poverty Ratio			No. of Poor (Millions)		
	Rural	**Urban**	**Total**	**Rural**	**Urban**	**Total**
Tendulkar 2004–2005	41.8	25.7	37.2	326.6	80.76	407.6
Tendulkar 2011–2012	25.7	13.7	21.9	216.6	53.12	269.8
Rangarajan 2011–2012	30.9	26.4	29.5	260.5	102.5	363.0

Source: Planning Commission. (2014). *Report of the expert group to review the methodology for measurement of poverty*. Government of India. New Delhi

THE NATIONAL MULTIDIMENSIONAL POVERTY INDEX

The global Multidimensional Poverty Index (MPI) is based on the of Alkire and Foster (AF) methodology uses ten indicators covering three areas namely health, education and standard of living. The global MPI Report is jointly published by the Oxford Poverty and Human Development Initiative (OPHI) and the United Nations Development Programme (UNDP).

In 2021, NITI Aayog took a significant step by releasing the first ever MPI for India (based on NFHS 4). This initiative aims to improve India's position in globally accepted indices,

* In PPP conversion US $1= ₹15.11.

underscoring the importance of comprehensive poverty alleviation efforts. The national MPI retains all the ten indicators from the global MPI and incorporates two additional indicators, Maternal Health and Bank Accounts, in line with India's national priorities. India, comprising 36 States & Union Territories, and more than 700 administrative districts, requires a refined policy tool for data-driven decision-making and the formulation of sectoral policies at the sub-national level. In contrast to conventional monetary poverty assessments based on consumption surveys, the national Multidimensional Poverty Index (MPI) delves into deprivations up to the district level, providing a more nuanced perspective.[12]

TABLE 7.2 State wise Poverty estimates (Headcount Ratio (%))

State/ UT	2005–06	2015–16	2022–23	State/ UT	2005–06	2015–16	2022–23
Andhra Pradesh	48.80	11.77	4.19	Odisha	63.84	29.34	11.07
Arunachal Pradesh	60.67	24.23	10.05	Punjab	26.66	5.57	4.35
Assam	60.78	32.65	14.47	Rajasthan	64.15	28.86	10.77
Bihar	78.28	51.89	26.59	Sikkim	38.85	3.82	2.10
Chhattisgarh	69.78	29.90	11.71	Tamil Nadu	36.54	4.76	1.43
Goa	18.20	3.76	0.37	Telangana	-	13.18	3.76
Gujarat	39.79	18.47	9.03	Tripura	52.78	16.62	11.49
Haryana	41.84	11.88	5.30	Uttar Pradesh	69.52	37.68	17.40
Himachal Pradesh	32.23	7.59	3.88	Uttarakhand	40.38	17.67	6.92
Jharkhand	74.04	42.10	23.34	West Bengal	57.60	21.29	8.60
Karnataka	46.71	12.77	5.67	Andaman & Nicobar Islands	–	4.29	1.63
Kerala	12.31	0.70	0.48	Chandigarh	–	5.97	2.62
Madhya Pradesh	69.44	36.57	15.01	Dadra & Nagar Haveli & Daman & Diu	–	19.58	6.06
Maharashtra	40.07	14.80	5.48	Delhi	14.63	4.44	2.97
Manipur	44.13	16.96	5.37	Jammu & Kashmir	40.45	12.56	2.81
Meghalaya	62.54	32.54	25.46	Ladakh	–	12.70	1.73
Mizoram	32.95	9.78	3.77	Lakshadweep	–	1.82	0.84
Nagaland	58.82	25.16	11.76	Puducherry		1.71	0.58
India	55.34	24.85	11.28	India	55.34	24.85	11.28

Source: National Multidimensional Poverty Index, A Progress Review, 2023.

Critical Evaluation of Poverty Alleviation Measures in India

Pre-reform Phase (1947–1990)

Poverty reduction was never in the forefront of economic strategies during the first two decades after independence. The planners of that time were optimistic about the positive impact of industrialization (Mahalanobis Strategy) and were confident that spillovers will reduce poverty and generate more employment opportunities. But it did not happen and the economic growth did not take place as per desired targets. The lower GDP growth coupled with higher population growth produced a typical demand and supply mismatch resulting in lower per capita income and massive poverty.

The decade of 1970s witnessed first ever assault on poverty as fifth 5-year plan introduced poverty alleviation as one of the principal objectives. Many programs such as Small Farmers' Development Agency (SFDA), Marginal Farmers' and Agricultural Laborers' Development Agency (MFAL), Drought Prone Area Development Program (DPAP), Cash Scheme for Rural Employment (CSRE), Pilot Intensive Rural Employment Project (PIREP), and Food for Work Program (FWP) were initiated to alleviate poverty in the country. However, these programs suffered from three major shortcomings. First, they did not cover the whole country and were confined to certain parts and groups. Second, programs operated simultaneously for the same target group and hence were overlapping in nature. Third, they were mere subsidy giving programs and failed to directly alleviate poverty in the country.

The government tried to correct this mistake during and after sixth 5-year plan by introducing schemes that were comprehensive in nature. For directly alleviating poverty and promoting self-employment, government started a plenty of programs in 1970s and 1980s such as Integrated Rural Development Program (IRDP), National Rural Employment Program (NREP), Rural Landless Employment Guarantee Program (RLEGP), Training of Rural Youth for Self-Employment (TRYSEM), and so on.* It was assumed that the poor possessed neither any productive assets nor any special skills. The programs were designed to help the poor by creating new assets for them or by providing necessary skills to them. The critics, however, lambasted the government for failing to classify the poor in terms of common characteristics and their requirements. There are two categories of poor, one who can take up self-employment and the other who cannot but can be provided with wage employment. Each category needs to be dealt separately by appropriate policy measure.[13] A good poverty alleviation strategy demands integration of both self-employment and wage-employment approach.

Post-reform Phase (1991 Onward)

Expansion of employment opportunities and augmentation of productivity and income level of both the underemployed and unemployed poor were made the principal instruments for achieving the goal of poverty reduction during eighth 5-year plan. However, this strategy could show the required results only in the medium and long term. Therefore, during the short period, poverty was targeted through special employment programs. Further, rapid growth of GDP produces a larger expansion of production and income which, if the growth process is sufficiently inclusive, will directly raise the standard of living of large section of population via generation of huge employment opportunities and other income-enhancing activities. The higher growth enhances government revenue which can be used in funding the various poverty alleviation programs.[14] Ninth 5-year plan also continued with trickle down efforts as well as poverty alleviation programs. The 10th 5-year plan continued with trickle down approach with a difference to achieve faster reduction in poverty rate by redressal of regional imbalances for which aggregate growth rate target was broken down state-wise. The 11th 5-year

*All such programmes were later modified and renamed. For example, IRDP was restructured and renamed as Swarnajayanti Gram Swarojgar Yojna (SGSY), TRYSEM and EAS as Sampoorna Grameen Rozgar Yojna (SGRY).

plan also relied on trickle down but emphasized that higher growth must be better balanced to rapidly create jobs in the industrial and services sector. The plan also underlined shifting the surplus agricultural labor into a non-agricultural activity that can provide higher real income per head. The 12th 5-year plan highlighted "faster, sustainable, and more inclusive growth." It was recognized that while the objective of development is broad-based improvement in the economic and social conditions of our people, rapid growth of GDP is an essential requirement for achieving this objective. To ensure that growth is more inclusive, the 12th plan emphasized (1) faster growth in agriculture and (2) faster growth in the manufacturing sector as a whole, including MSMEs.

During the recent past, the government has taken comprehensive steps to reduce poverty in the country. A plethora of skill development programs have been initiated besides certain schemes wherein persons can avail financial help to start their own ventures. Schemes such as Ujjawala (to provide subsidized LPG connections to poor households), Pradhan Mantri Awas Yojna (for rural and urban housing), and Deendayal Upadhyaya Gram Jyoti Yojana (for rural electrification) can help people to avail basic facilities to get rid of poverty.

Qualitative Aspects of Poverty

Poverty is also a qualitative phenomenon. Policy issues need to address the following three viewpoints.

1. There are three useful analytical categories in terms of which deprivations in any society, including India can be discussed. They are positive freedom, negative freedom, and discrimination.[15] Positive freedom is the "capability to function," that is the ability to lead a good life or certain power individuals enjoy or enabled by society.[16] For example, access to good health, efficient public distribution system and better education facilities can be described as positive freedom. Negative freedom is concerned with absence of restraint or protection from coercion. That is, an individual should not be subjected to any hindrance in the pursuit of his desired goals including the goal of avoiding deprivation. Discrimination pertains to inequitable distribution of freedoms across individuals on the basis of caste, religion, age, gender, or region. For example, *dalits* are still subjected to caste atrocities; religious minorities are subjected to appeasement or live in the fear of getting lynched; women are discriminated against intra-family distribution of resources or inequitable wages in labor market, forced prostitution, triple talaq or dowry deaths, and so on.
2. Poverty is more of social marginalization of an individual, household, or group in the community/society rather than inadequacy of income to fulfill the basic needs. Indeed, inadequate income is, therefore, one of the factors of marginalization but not the sole factor. The goal of poverty alleviation program should not aim merely increasing the income level of individual, household, or group, but mainstreaming marginalized in the development process of the country.[17]
3. Given that raising per capita income (or output) is the most crucial factor in reducing poverty, controlling population growth also has a significant role to play in the fight against poverty, at least in a surplus labor economy like India, where the marginal contribution of labor to output is close to zero. The government should, therefore, actively promote smaller family norms and try to move toward a zero population-growth target for the country at the earliest.[18]

UNIVERSAL BASIC INCOME

The idea of a universal basic income (UBI)—an unconditional cash payment paid to everyone—has been gaining a lot of attention recently. UBI is a regular fixed cash transfer payment provided by the government to every citizen, regardless of whether he or she is rich or poor and/or wishing to be engaged in paid employment.

The idea of a basic income is found on the three following characteristics.[19]

Universality: a basic income should be open to all population (however, some basic income proponents advise to start in a specific domain and then "universalize" gradually over time);

Individuality: a basic income should be designed to cater to individuals, not households, since it is considered a truly individual right;

Un-conditionality: a basic income should be unconditional (or it should employ conditions that do not violate inclusiveness).

Arguments in Favor of UBI

Following are the points in favor of UBI in India.

Freedom and Justice

Freedom is the basic and the most intrinsic human need. Basic income would induce a shift from the psychology of scarcity to the psychology of abundance that can improve social cohesion as it produces initiative, faith in life, and solidarity.[20] UBI can also give people a greater sense of freedom and justice over their life through a variety of mechanisms. First, the guarantee of an income can motivate people to make meaningful work choices not driven simply by financial needs but also by affinity and interest. Second, it can improve people's well-being by making them more independent of coercive and punitive policies that can negatively affect their mental well-being. Third, the UBI would help to address concerns of justice, as everybody in a society should have a right to a minimum income and a good life. For many other proponents of the UBI, this measure has the fundamental role of promoting two levels of justice: providing fundamental rights to individuals and securing social interests, such as fostering a community's sense of well-being.[21]

Poverty Reduction

UBI is more feasible in a country like India, where it can be pegged at relatively low levels of income but still yield following welfare gains.

1. One of the strongest arguments in favor of the UBI is that it could help to eradicate poverty, regardless of what the causes of poverty are. In fact, if the basic income were set above the poverty line, it should theoretically lead to the complete elimination of absolute poverty. Though a basic income helps to treat the symptoms rather than the causes of poverty, yet, for the people living in poverty, a basic income would provide material relief, thus contributing to satisfy their basic needs.[22]

2. For families, the UBI scheme gives parents the capacity to invest in the human capital of their children. This investment would help break the vicious cycle of poverty that they are entrapped in, and in particular inter-generational poverty.
3. Greater income security for the poor may create further positive outcomes, such as increased levels of entrepreneurship and of business creation. Alternatively, the additional income flow from the transfer may allow poor people to obtain other investments and work opportunities that were previously limited by credit constraints, including education, training, and migration, which produces positive spillover effects for human and economic development.[23]
4. Since the money under UBI is provided universally as a "right of citizenship" rather than as a targeted benefit, the stigma and shame typically attached to receiving benefits from the state should not be there.[24]
5. Compared to targeted welfare policies, the government needs not to push or check the minute working of UBI, as it is not required to monitor people's behavior.
6. Unlike other schemes, the transfers under UBI would help strengthen social solidarity and cohesion, which are particularly relevant in small and poor communities, and avoid alienation and distrust.[25]

Optimum Allocation and Efficient Welfare Solution

In many developing countries including India, there are plethora of welfare schemes which suffer from complex, bureaucracies, and administrative costs of implementation. UBI would help consolidate several different policies and targeted schemes into one single entity, and would require lower administrative efforts, thus helping government to gather a clearer idea of the overall redistributive effects and costs of its welfare system. For example, according to budget 2016–2017, there are about 950 central sector and centrally sponsored sub-schemes in India accounting for about 5% of the GDP by budget allocation. A large majority of these are small in terms of allocation with the top 11 schemes accounting for about 50% of total budgetary allocation. Most of the central sector schemes are continuing for at least 15 years and 50% of them were over 25 years old.[26] The misallocation can be captured from the disproportionate allocation of resources in different regions. In India, the poorest districts are the ones grappling with inadequate funds. Another reason for misallocation is ineffective implementation; richer districts have better administrative capacities to effectively implement schemes. A natural consequence of misallocation is "exclusion error"—genuine poor find themselves unable to access program benefits. An estimate of the exclusion error from 2011–2012 suggests that 40% of the bottom 40% of the population are excluded from the PDS. The corresponding figure for 2011–2012 for MGNREGS was 65% The states of Bihar, Madhya Pradesh, Rajasthan, Odisha, and Uttar Pradesh despite accounting for over 50% of the poor in the country, spent nearly 30% on MNREGS during 2015–2016.

UBI will address such issues in the following manner:

1. If poor constitute the bottom 40% (in terms of consumption expenditure), the top 60% of the population will also gain access to the UBI. Since UBI is universal and all individuals are targeted, exclusion error (poor being left out) is zero though inclusion error (rich gaining access to the scheme) is 60%.
2. UBI will do away with administrative inefficiencies as it would simply lead to transfer of resources from the government to citizens, making beneficiaries to withdraw money

from their accounts as and when they please, without any bureaucratic interference causing no administrative burden.

3. Since resources are to be transferred directly into the accounts of beneficiaries, discretionary powers of authorities are eliminated; diversion is nullified; making welfare policy corruption free.

Reducing Income Inequality

As UBI scheme would be financed through a progressive income tax or by cutting subsidies favoring the richer class, it would help to reduce income inequalities.[27] Further it would help increase the bargaining strength of poor workers as they could refuse to accept degrading or unhealthy working conditions and low wages. It would not only force employers to improve working conditions but also make jobs more attractive.[28] The UBI would also help minimize the impact of digitalization and automation on job loss and resultant inequalities. The basic income would not only turn out as an insurance against the technology-induced job losses but also help to reduce public resistance to technological innovation by providing basic life security.[29]

Gender Equality

In a country like India where labor force participation rate of female workers is quite dismal, the UBI could provide a ray of hope. Interestingly the female employment in urban India has also witnessed a declining trend and whenever (majority of) women work they end up working as domestic help or as a marginal worker. Since women perform the majority of unpaid work, especially in the household, the transfers through UBI would result in an improvement of women's bargaining position in the household and would promote a decrease in gender inequality.[30] It may also have the additional effect of helping to modify traditional definitions of what constitutes meaningful work. Another advantage to women would be that UBI is granted to individuals and not households, and hence, basic income could provide greater income security and autonomy for women.[31] But the success of gender equality would be largely determined by the awareness of women with regard to banking services and financial inclusion efforts of the government with regard to females.

Increase in Financial Inclusion

Demand and supply side factors play a significant role to bring improvement in financial inclusion across the country. While on the demand side, there is a need for behavioral change on the part of account holders so that they use their accounts more often, on the supply side, banks need to find it profitable to provide access to banking services. Banks have been making use of Bank correspondents (BCs) to fill the gap in unbanked area. BCs work on the basis of commissions they receive from banking sector and higher amount of commission motivate them and bring effectiveness in their working. UBI would lead to increase in the volume of transactions and revenue from government transfers along with a corresponding decrease in per unit fixed costs, thereby increasing the profitability of BCs and expanding their coverage. A fixed basic income would enhance the consumption expenditures of the rural India and it would also lead to increase in institutional credit thereby, reducing dependence of farmers on moneylenders or other non-institutional sources. According to a study by Debt and Investment Survey (2013), it is evident that as farmers' consumption expenditure increase beyond a certain level, the proportion of farmers taking informal loans fall and that of formal loans rise.

Arguments in Disfavor of UBI

UBI as a "Negative Incentive"

In our modern societies, work has been a central principle of organization; it contributes to people's routines, feelings of self-worth and personal satisfaction, socialization processes and their establishment of an identity and role in the society.[32]

There are three propositions in this regard.

1. The free money makes people lazy and they drop out of the labor market.
2. In India, the LFPR for females is already low and it may enhance the gendered division of labor if more women than men decide to reduce their labor market participation.[33]
3. Few opponents argue that people should have the obligation to contribute back to a society that provides them with payments. With a basic income, people could choose to do nothing at all but still receive the transfer. This argument is defined as *"the reciprocity objection."*[34]

The Costing Problem

The direct burden of UBI signifies the cost burden. UBI would be an expensive affair in high populous countries like India and also because of its universal nature. Few estimates have predicted the annual financial burden of UBI to be more than 5% of GDP. There will be cases where PDS or fertilizer subsidies do reach most beneficiaries which will then have to be taken into account if a measure of UBI as a replacement program is to be calculated. This is a complicated task because there will be a number of general equilibrium effects which will need to be considered. For example, replacing the PDS will increase market prices of cereals the poor face. Similarly, phasing down MGNREGS might reduce market wages for rural casual labor. Calculating these effects and hence the exact magnitude of subsidies will help refine any costing of the UBI.[35] Further, the process of determining a UBI amount is not a one-time exercise: as the UBI is a cash transfer, its "real" value tends to be determined by inflation in the economy. Over time, the same amount of cash transfer may not buy the same amount of goods. Therefore, UBI transfers will require regular indexing so that the amount gets revised periodically. Politics can play a huge role in determining the exact amount each time it is up for revision and so it is important to set up a sufficiently politically neutral mechanism to do so.

Other Problems

There are certain other problems associated with UBI, which are as follows:

1. In a country like India where government is providing multiple subsidies and is running plethora of social sector schemes, taking away such subsidies is politically difficult for any government. Without a clearer understanding of its larger economy-wide implications, it would be an administrative challenge as well.
2. Universal programmes are—as previously mentioned—an excellent option for remedying social exclusion and for reaching economically vulnerable groups. The universal nature of the initiative, however, entails that beneficiaries will include people who do not need this form of public help; a problem defined as the *leakage* of benefits to the non-poor.
3. Once introduced, it may become difficult for the government to wind up a UBI in case of failure.
4. It may lead to increase in conspicuous consumption as households, especially male members, may spend this additional income on wasteful activities.

UBI Experiments Around the World

UBI has been experimented in different countries on small scale as a pilot project. Few examples are Winnipeg and Manitoba in Canada (families with under 58-year-old persons, incomes lower than US$13,000); India (100 families of West Delhi and few villages of Madhya Pradesh); Namibia (Residents of the Otjivero-Omitara village); and Kenya (Residents of Rarieda village). On January 1, 2017, Finland became first country in the Europe to launch and experiment UBI for 2 years on pilot basis. The following lessons were learnt from such experiments. First, it is important to ensure consistent political will to implement and sustain an UBI scheme; second, unconditional cash grant transfers enable beneficiaries to identify their particular needs and priorities and a broad support from civil society was crucial for success because it allowed for stronger lobbying mechanisms to the government.

Guiding Principles for Setting Up a UBI in India

Economic Survey 2016–2017 prepared a roadmap of introducing UBI and suggested three principles in this regard.[36]

De Jure Universality, de Facto Quasi-universality

If universality has powerful appeal, it will also elicit powerful resistance. Keeping in mind the fiscal costs, the notion of transferring even some money to the well-off may be difficult. It is, therefore, important to consider ideas that could exclude the obviously rich, that is, exclusion of the non-deserving persons. It can be done in following four ways:

1. Define the non-deserving based on ownership of key assets such as automobiles or air-conditioners or bank balances exceeding a certain size.
2. Adopt a "give it up" scheme wherein those who are non-deserving chose to opt out of the programme just as in the case of LPG and are given credit for doing so.
3. Introduce a system where the list of UBI beneficiaries is publicly displayed; this would "name and shame" the rich who chose to avail themselves of a UBI.
4. Develop a system where beneficiaries regularly verify themselves in order to avail themselves of their UBI—the assumption here is that the rich, whose opportunity cost of time is higher, would not find it worthwhile to go through this process and the poor would self-target into the scheme.

Gradualism

The UBI must be embraced in a deliberate, phased manner. A key advantage of phasing would be that it allows reform to occur incrementally—weighing the costs and benefits at every step. Following points of concern need mention here:

1. UBI should not replace the current schemes but it must be in addition to current schemes. It is because it will give people choice, in negotiating with the administrators who are currently supposed to be giving them benefits.
2. In the beginning, UBI for women can be started at pilot basis. It can not only reduce the fiscal cost of providing a UBI but can also have large multiplier effects on the household.

Giving money to women also improves the bargaining power of women within households and reduces concerns of money being splurged on conspicuous goods.

3. Another approach is to phase in a UBI for certain vulnerable groups—widows, pregnant mothers, the old, and the infirm—first. This would serve as a means for the state to serve the most vulnerable. Furthermore, these are also easily identifiable groups of individuals.

UBI and Redistributive Resource Transfers to States

A number of state governments receive large amounts of transfers that may not prima facie increase growth or consumption. The UBI offers a possible way-around: a part of the redistributive resource transfers may be transferred by the center directly into beneficiaries' accounts in the form of a pilot UBI programme.

Inequality in India

In 1776, when Adam Smith wrote *The Wealth of Nations*, the richest country in the world was approximately four times wealthier than the poorest. Today, the world's richest country is more than 400 times richer than the poorest.[37] The term inequality refers to cross-sectional distribution of income or wealth at any particular period, or changes of income and wealth over longer periods of time among individuals in a group, among groups in a population, or among countries. Economists are interested to understand the gains of growth and distribution of income so as to analyze the welfare impact of development in a proper perspective. There is now a greater understanding of the negative effects of inequality and the nature of economic growth that leads to it. That is why there is clear shift in the policy discourse to "inclusive growth."

Extent of Income Inequality During Pre-reform India

Different economists/reports/surveys have estimated extent of inequality in India.

1. A study by Lucas Chancel and Thomas Piketty in 2017 found that the top 1% of Indian population had 23% share in India's National Income in 1923. It came down to 6.2% in 1982–1983 but again started increasing thereafter. It abruptly increased during the post-reform period and increased to nearly 21.3% in 2014–2015. In India, the average income of top 0.001% population was €11,589,000 compared to just €1,900 for bottom 50% population. The bottom 50% of population has 15.3% of income share.[38]
2. In India, top 20% of households has share of 44% in National Income or consumption, whereas bottom 20% have share of just 8.3%. The statistics from World Development Indicators, World Bank reveals that percentage share of top 20% household income or consumption has gone up from 41.4 to 44% from 1983–2012 and that of lowest 20% has increased marginally from 8.1 to 8.3% for the same period.
3. The Gini coefficient in India went up from 0.29 in 1983–1984 to 0.30 during 1993–1994. The post-reform period also witnessed increase in inequalities as Gini coefficient went up from 0.35 during 2004–2005 to further 0.36 in 2011–2012.[39] In India, most of the population is in informal sector and out of income-tax database. The Gini coefficient calculations are based on consumption-expenditure data of NSSO instead of income data (Box 7.3).

BOX 7.3 Gini Coefficient and Lorenz Curve

The Gini coefficient was introduced in 1921 by Italian statistician Corrado Gini as a measure of inequality. Gini coefficient is a popular statistical measure to gauge the rich–poor income or wealth divide. It measures inequality of a distribution—be it of income or wealth—within nations or states. It measures the extent to which the distribution of income (or, in some cases, consumption expenditure) among individuals or households within an economy deviates from a perfectly equal distribution. On the other hand, Lorenz curve is a graphical representation of the distribution of income or of wealth. It was developed by Max Lorenz in 1905. A Lorenz curve plots the cumulative percentages of total income received against the cumulative number of recipients, starting with the poorest individual or household. The Gini index measures the area between the Lorenz curve and a hypothetical line of absolute equality, expressed as a percentage of the maximum area under the line. Thus, a Gini index of 0 represents perfect equality, while an index of 1 implies perfect inequality.

Sources:

1. Farris, F.A. (2010). The Gini index and measures of inequality. *The American Mathematical Monthly*, 117(10), 851–864.
2. Catalano et al. (2009). Measuring resource inequality: The Gini coefficient. *Numeracy, 2*(2).

4. The analysis of growth incidence curves using the MPCE confirms the steep rise in inequality after 1993–1994. The growth rate of rural MPCE was 1.28% between 1993-94 and 2004–2005 and increased to 4.08% per year between 2004–2005 and 2011–2012. The corresponding growth rates for urban areas were 1.51 and 4.62% per year. While urban MPCE growth outpaced rural MPCE growth, within rural and urban areas, it was the upper deciles of MPCE which saw faster growth after 1991 as against the 1980s when lower deciles saw faster growth.[40]
5. According to Oxfam report 2023, the top 1% in India now owns more than 40.5% of total wealth in 2021 while the bottom 50% of the population (700 million) has around 3% of total wealth. The report titled "Survival of the Richest", reveals that the covid pandemic exacerbated the gap between rich and poor as billionaires in India have seen their wealth surge by 121%, while the number of hungry Indians has increased from 19 crores to 35 crores.[41]
6. The Global wealth report 2018 by Credit Suisse has given insight into adult inequalities in the country. According to the report, 91% of the adult population has wealth below US$10,000. At the other extreme, a small fraction of the population (0.6% of adults) has a net worth over US$100,000. However, owing to India's large population, this translates into 4.8 million people. The country has 404,000 adults in the top 1% of global wealth holders, which is a 0.8% share. Around, 3,400 adults have wealth over US$50 million, and 1,500 have more than US$100 million.[42]

Causes of Inequality in India

The March of Billionaires

The super-rich continue to get richer, widening the gap between them and everyone else. There are now a record 2,781 people on Forbes' World's Billionaires list, worth a record $14.2 trillion in all from 78 countries, according to Forbes magazine's World's Billionaires List 2024. There are five countries in the world with more than 100 billionaires (Table 7.3).[43]

Since the early 1990s, the number and wealth of India's billionaires has risen dramatically, in relation to India's own growth and in relation to other countries. The trend bears testimony to the fact that reforms have contributed positively in the generation of wealth in few hands. India is now an outlier with respect to the size of billionaire wealth relative to the size of the economy, especially for a relatively poor country.[44] There were two billionaires in India in the mid-1990s, worth a combined total of $3.2 billion. By 2012, there were 46, with a total net worth of $176.3 billion and in 2018, there were 119 billionaires with a total net worth of $440.1 billion. The total number of Indian billionaires rose to 140 in 2021 from 200 in 2024 and their combined wealth nearly doubled to 954 billion dollars. While the largest number of Indian billionaires (67%) is "self-made," some 33% of total billionaire wealth is

TABLE 7.3 Countries With More Than 100 Billionaires (2024)

Country	Number of Billionaires	Total Net Worth
United States	813	$5.7 TRILLION
China	406	$1.3 TRILLION
India	200	$954 BILLION
Germany	132	$644 BILLION
Russia	120	$537 BILLION

Source: Forbes' World's Billionaires Issue, 2024 and calculations by author

TABLE 7.4 Ten Richest Indians 2024

Global Rank	Name	Net Worth ($ Billions)
9	Mukesh Ambani	116
17	Gautam Adani	84
39	Shiv Nadar	36.9
46	Savitri Jindal & family	32.4
69	Dilip Shanghvi	26.9
90	Cyrus Poonawalla	21.3
92	Kushal Pal Singh	20.9
98	Kumar Birla	19.7
107	Radhakishan Damani	17.6
113	Lakshmi Mittal	16.4

Source: Forbes' World's Billionaires Issue, 2024.

in the "inherited and growing" category. Total wealth of India's billionaires is nearly one-fourth of the GVA of the country.

Monopolies and Crony Capitalism

Monopolies can use their market power to eliminate or buy off innovative market entrants, and they do not need to invest as much as potential rivals to stay on top. Monopoly power is driving extreme inequality around the world. Monopoly power is compounded by cronyism, the ability of powerful private interests to manipulate public policy.[45] Crony capitalism is defined as a system where businesses multiply their wealth not by the fair rules of the market, but through their nexus with governments. Classic examples of crony capitalism are the distribution of legal permits, licenses, land, contracts, tax breaks, and so on. It is this crony capitalism which later surfaced in the form of various scams, such as the 2G spectrum scam and the coal scam. So is the case of real estate billionaires, many of whom benefitted from cheap land allotted to them by the governments. It is worth noting here that the majority of the 12 companies which have been reported for bankruptcy proceedings in 2017 are from rent-thick sectors,* such as housing and steel. Not only have the richest benefitted from undue favors granted to them in the allocation of natural resources, they have also got easy credit from the financial sector. A look at the non-performing assets of the public sector banks has clearly established that the majority of these companies are held by the richest Indians.[46]

Inherited Wealth

Wealth inequality is greater than income inequality and evidence suggests that disparities have increased in recent decades. According to OECD report, The Role and Design of Net Wealth Taxes, rich people also have more power, influence, and opportunities and are able to generate income without having to work. Wealth—such as property, savings, share portfolios, and pensions—grows and becomes self-reinforcing because the rich have more to invest in higher yielding assets, greater financial knowhow, and better access to investment advice.[47] Around 33% of the world's extreme wealth are held by heirs. Over the next 20 years, 500 of the world's richest people will hand over $2.4 trillion to their heirs—a sum larger than the GDP of India, a country of 1.3 billion people.[48] Almost 40% of Indian billionaires have inherited their wealth and the inheritors account for almost two-thirds of the total wealth of billionaires.

Gender Bias

Globally, more men than women own land, shares, and other capital assets; men are paid more for doing the same roles as women, and men are concentrated in higher paid and higher status jobs. It is no coincidence that women are vastly over-represented in so many of the poorest paid and least secure jobs. Around the world, social norms, attitudes, and beliefs devalue the status and abilities of women, justify violence and discrimination against them, and dictate which jobs they can and cannot expect to hold.[49] India was ranked low at 140th position out of 156 countries in Global Gender Gap Index 2021 released as part of World Economic Forum's (WEF) Global Gender Gap Report 2021. At the current rate of progress, the global gender gap will take 100 years to bridge. Iceland is the most gender-equal country with score of 0.892, followed by Finland (second rank), Norway (third rank), New Zealand (fourth rank), and Sweden (fifth rank).[50] The index measures gender gap as progress toward parity between men and women in four indicators, namely (1) educational attainment, (2) health and survival, (3) economic opportunity, and (4) political empowerment. Countries are ranked on the basis of scale ranging from 0 (lowest, i.e., imparity) to 1 (highest, i.e., parity). On an average, a woman in India is estimated to earn less than quarter of annual income earned by a man. She gets paid only 60% of what her male count gets for similar work. Moreover, women account for one-third of labor force participation, but their share of daily unpaid work (household chores, childcare etc.) is 66% while it is only 12% for men. Across sectors, only 13% of senior officials, managers, and legislators are women.[51]

Unequal Distribution of the Gains From Growth

The liberalization process, which was set in motion in 1991, attracted massive capital inflows. This sets off a domestic retail credit boom, and along with fiscal concessions it created an environment

* Rent-thick sectors comprise real estate, infrastructure, construction, mining, telecom, cement, and media and characterized by dominating role of government in distributing licences, reputations of illegality, or information on monopolistic practices. According to the KPMG study, the real estate sector is perceived to be the most corrupt in India. The real estate sector is well known for the large number of unaccounted transactions, and the nexus between politicians and realtors has been well documented.

for a hike in consumption of the better-off households and "competitive consumerism." While this fueled a rapid growth of GDP, there remained an abysmally low public spending on basic facilities, insufficient employment generation, and a persistent agrarian crisis.[52] Deregulation and opening-up of reforms in India since 1980s have led to substantial increase in inequality. The growth strategy failed to include measures which would enable mass consumption of goods and as a consequence the inequalities in the system have persisted and even intensified.

Inequality in Wages

There are wide inequalities in wages on the basis of region, contract, gender, sector, and caste. The national average daily wage in 2011–2012 was estimated at ₹247 but daily wages was more than twice as high in urban areas ₹384 compared to rural areas ₹175. Average wage paid for casual work was only 36% of the compensation received by regular/salaried workers in 2011–2012. In 2011–2012, the Gender Pay Gap was 34% in India, that is, women are still getting 34% less compared to their male counterparts.[53] As per the State of Working India Report 2018, in 2015, totally 82% of men and 92% of women are earning less than ₹10,000 per month. On an average, in 2011–2012, the wage difference of regular workers (compared to the casual workers) in the organized sector was 3.1 times higher in the primary sector, 2.6 times higher in the tertiary sector, and 2.3 times higher in the secondary sector. Even among regular wage workers, more than half (57%) have monthly average earnings of ₹10,000 or less, well under the Seventh Central Pay Commission's minimum stipulated salary of ₹18,000 per month. SC and ST workers received, on an average, 15% lower wages than other workers in both public and private sectors. According to report, the SCs, STs, and OBCs earned only 56, 55, and 72%, respectively, of upper caste earnings.[54]

Measures to Address the Problems of Inequality

The problem of inequality does not have a quick-fix solution and it requires a deep surgical procedure.

Tax Policies

The international experience shows the vital role played by progressive taxation in tackling inequality. Tax policy of India is pro-rich and it is the high time that government stops corporate loan-waivers and tax write-offs to check the rising concentration of income at the top. The present policy framework of the country should be redesigned to ensure financial inclusion, tax-compliance, and introduction of wealth and inheritance tax. Therefore, India's tax policies must be framed keeping in view the following issues. First, the tax base is very low, hence not many people report incomes to tax authorities in the first place. Second, the pervasiveness of tax evasion and black money sources (particularly in property and real estate) needs accounting, to gather a more complete picture of income inequality. Finally, the CBDT should regularize these reports and also start reporting similar statistics on collection of wealth and property taxes. This will allow economists and social statisticians to start similar studies on the distribution of Indian wealth, about which very little is known.[55]

Redistributive Policies

Redistributive policies make a positive impact on poverty and unemployment reduction. The fact that the period during 2004–2011 is also the period with highest poverty reduction is then not a surprise. However, these have been achieved by enactment of several legislations which have strengthened the social protection measures for the poor. The National Food Security Act

(NFSA), Mahatma Gandhi National Rural Employment Guarantee Act (MGNREGA), Right to Education (RTE), and Forest Rights Act are legislations which have strengthened the social protection measures. These have also contributed to the improvement in income of poor through indirect income transfer.[56] Transfers on just food-related schemes have contributed to a one-third reduction in poverty headcount ratio and almost half of the total poverty reduction using the squared poverty gap measure.[57] The demand for strengthening the food schemes and the consequent pressure on the government to raise public procurement of food grains also contributed indirectly. The expenditure on MGNREGA and the rise in MSP were also instrumental in a sharp rise in casual wages during 2008–2013 which insulated the rural poor during times of high food inflation. It also explains the moderation in the rise of inequality after 2008.

Addressing Human Development Issues

Wide inequalities in people's well-being cast a shadow on sustained human development progress, with people in very high human development countries living 19 years longer, and spending 7 more years in school, than those living in the group of low human development countries. In HDI, India's position is not comparable to the other developing nations of the world. India spends less than 2% of GDP on health and less than 4% of GDP on education and fares poorly not only in comparison to poorer countries in the Sub-Saharan Africa and Bhutan but also vis-à-vis developing countries like Brazil. Access to education and health enables empowerment of people and improves productivity of workforce and ultimately increases income per capita. Further, 26.8% of India's HDI value are lost on account of inequalities—a greater loss than for most of its South Asian neighbors (the average loss for the region is 26.1%). The gender-based challenges are also evident in India, where despite considerable progress at the policy and legislative levels, women remain significantly less politically, economically, and socially empowered than men. For instance, women hold only 11.6% of parliamentary seats, and only 39% of adult women have reached at least a secondary level of education as compared to 64% males. Female participation in the labor market is 27.2% compared to 78.8 for men. On the basis of GII, India performs badly, ranking 123 out 162 countries in 2019 as per HDR, 2020. This confirms that inequality remains a challenge for India as it progresses economically, though the Government of India and various state governments have, through a variety of social protection measures, attempted to ensure that the gains of economic development are shared widely and reach the farthest first.

Land Reforms

In India, 67.1% of total operational holdings were marginal holdings but area operated under them was just 22.5% (with average holding size being just 0.39 hectare). Together marginal and small holdings* account for 85% of holdings but they operated only 44% of area. On the contrary, large holdings** were only 0.7% of the total holdings but operated 10.6% of total cultivated area. In India, the size of landholdings has shrunk because of land fragmentation which makes agriculture activity uneconomical and unproductive and also unprofitable. Though government has undertaken certain land reform measures since independence, it should encourage land consolidation and cooperative farming with full vigor. Cooperative farming will help farmers to gain the economies of large-scale production by pooling their resources jointly. It will help reducing rural inequalities.

---

* Marginal landholdings are less than 1 hectare in size and small landholdings lie between 1 and 2 hectare of land.

** Large landholdings are of the size 10 hectare or more.

Summary

1. According to Dollar a Day IPL, 21.2% Indians are below poverty line. On the basis of MPI, 27.5% of India's population is multi-dimensionally poor. The world poverty clock estimates 3.9% of population as extremely poor.
2. The first official attempt to measure poverty was made in 1962, when Planning Commission established a working group which suggested a desirable minimum level of living not less than ₹100 a month for rural areas and ₹125 per month for urban areas. In 1977, the task force under the chairmanship of Dr Y.K. Alagh was constituted which first time gave the concept of poverty line. Using NSSO and NAS data, task force defined poverty line (for whole India) at ₹2,400 kcal for rural areas and ₹2,100 kcal for urban areas. The Expert Group which was constituted under the chairmanship of Prof. D.T. Lakdawala in 1989, retained calorie-based norm of Alagh committee, went few steps further and disaggregated national poverty line (both rural and urban) into state-specific poverty lines in order to reflect the inter-state price differentials. Using NSSO data, the expert group estimated all India poverty ratio (with URP methodology) at 36% during 1993–1994 and 27.5% in 2004–2005. The Expert Group under the chairmanship of Suresh D. Tendulkar (constituted in 2003) switched over to MRP methodology from that of URP and besides calorie-based norms gave due weightage to non-food items as well. The committee estimated poverty for India at 37.2 and 21.9% for 2004–2005 and 2011–2012, respectively. Different poverty estimates by different committees initiated great Indian poverty debate in the country and consequently government constituted another expert group under Dr C. Rangarajan in 2012. The Rangarajan committee shifted to MMRP methodology, revised PLB (2,155 kcal for rural areas and 2,095 kcal for urban areas), widened PLB by including both normative component and observed consumption pattern of households. The committee estimated 29.5% poverty ratio for India during 2011–2012.
3. Poverty was never at the agenda of Indian planners during the first four 5-year plans and it was only during fifth 5-year plan that government introduced poverty alleviation as one of the principal objective. The pre-reform poverty alleviation strategy lacked integration of self-employment and wage-employment approach. The post-reform period witnessed a strategic shift in government approach to reduce poverty. Government emphasized trickle down approach in which higher GDP growth is envisaged over a period of time and if the growth process is sufficiently inclusive will directly raise the standard of living of large section of population via generation of huge employment opportunities and other income-enhancing activities. Poverty is also a qualitative aspect. It can be measured in terms of lack of freedom, deprivations, and discrimination. Mainstreaming the marginalized sections along with increase in income must be the goal of the government. Government approach to actively promote small family norms must also be at the priority list.
4. UBI is a regular fixed cash transfer payment provided by the government to every citizen, regardless of whether he or she is rich or poor and/or wishing to be engaged in paid employment. The idea of UBI is based on universality, individuality, and un-conditionality. The merits of UBI include freedom and justice, poverty reduction, optimum allocation and efficient welfare solution, reducing income inequality, gender equality, and increase in financial inclusion. However, UBI may act as negative incentive and can prove to be extremely costly. The other problems of UBI are political difficulty of withdrawing other subsidies in case of implementation of UBI, leakages due to its universal nature, difficult to withdraw in case UBI fails, and increase in conspicuous consumption. Many countries in the world, including India, have launched UBI in certain pockets. Finland is the first nation in the world to launch it countrywide.
5. The term inequality refers to cross-sectional distribution of income or wealth at any particular period, or to changes of income and wealth over longer periods of time among individuals in a group, among groups in a population, or among countries. The top 1% of Indian population has nearly 21.3% of national income in 2014–2015. The major causes of inequality in India are increase in number of billionaires, increase in monopolies and crony capitalism, inherited wealth, gender bias, unequal distribution of the gains from growth, and unequal wages. The government can address the problem of

inequality by the policies of sound taxation system which should be progressive and confirm to the principal of equity; effective redistributive policies such as NFSA and MGNREGS; raising the human development capabilities in education, health, and gender; and land reform policies especially cooperative farming that will help to solve the problem of small size of landholdings.

Endnotes

1. Poverty. (2019). Retrieved from http://www.worldbank.org (Accessed on April 28, 2019).
2. HDR (2018) *UNDP*. Retrieved from http://hdr.undp.org (Accessed on March 24, 2019).
3. World Poverty Clock. Retrieved from https://worldpoverty.io (Accessed on April 24, 2019).
4. *Ibid.*
5. Planning Commission. (1979). *Report of the Task Force on Projections of Minimum needs and Effective consumption demand", Perspective Planning Division* Government of India New Delhi.
6. *Ibid.*
7. Planning Commission. (2014). *Report of the expert group to review the methodology for measurement of poverty, Government of India*. New Delhi.
8. Deaton. A., & Kozel, V. (2005). Data and dogma: The great Indian poverty debate. *The World Bank Research Observer*, 20(2).
9. Planning Commission. (2014). *Report of the expert group to review the methodology for measurement of poverty, Government of India*. New Delhi pp.54–55.
10. Deaton. A., & Dreze, J. (2009). *Food and Nutrition in India*. EPW. XLIV. 7.
11. Rangarajan Report on Poverty. (2014). Retrieved from www.pib.nic.in (Accessed on July 26, 2017).
12. Multidimensional Poverty in India Since 2005–06, Discussion Paper, accessed from https://www.niti.gov.in as on 13 April, 2024.
13. Hirway, I. (1985). Garibi hatao: Can IRDP do it? *EPW, 20*(13), p.562.
14. Agrawal, P. (2015). *Reducing Poverty in India: The Role of Economic Growth* IEG Working Paper No. 349.
15. Subramanian, S. *Poverty*. In Basu, K. (Ed.) *Concise oxford companion to Economics*. OUP. p.544.
16. Sen, A. (1985). *Commodities and capabilities*. Retrieved from https://scholar.harvard.edu (Accessed on January 4, 2019).
17. Yesudian, C.A.K. (2007). Poverty alleviation programmes in India: A social audit. *Indian Journal of Medical Research, 126*, 364–373.
18. Agrawal, P. (2015). *Reducing poverty in India: The role of economic growth*. IEG Working Paper No. 349.
19. De Wispelaere, J., & Stirton, L. (2004). The many faces of universal basic income. *The Political Quarterly*, 266–274.
20. Fromm, E. (1966). The psychological aspects of the guaranteed income. In R. Theobald (Ed.), *The guaranteed income*. New York: Doubleday & Co.
21. UNDP. (2017). *Universal Basic Income. A policy option for China beyond 2020.*, Retrieved from www.cn.undp.org (Accessed on July 7, 2018).
22. Tobin, J. (1966). The case for an income guarantee. *Public Interest*, 31–41.
23. UNDP. (2017). *Universal Basic Income. A policy option for China beyond 2020.*, Retrieved from www.cn.undp.org (Accessed on July7, 2018).
24. Standing, G. (2008). How cash transfers promote the case for basic income. Basic Income Studies, pp.1–30.
25. Ravallion, M. (2016). *The economics of poverty: history, measurement and policy*. Oxford: Oxford University Press.
26. Economic Survey, Chapter 9, 2016–2017.
27. Ravallion, M. (2016). *The economics of poverty: History, measurement and policy*. Oxford University Press.
28. Perkiö, J. (2014). *Universal basic income: A new tool for development policy?* Kansainvalinen Solidaarisuutyo: International Security Work.
29. Sheahen, A. (2012). *Basic income guarantee: Your right to economic security*. New York: Palgrave Macmillan.
30. Robeyns, I. (2000). Hush money or emancipation fee? A gender analysis of basic income. In R. Van der Veen, & L. Groot (Eds.), *Basic income on the agenda. Policy objectives and political chances*. Amsterdam: Amsterdam University Press.
31. Pateman, C. (2004). Democratizing citizenship: Some advantages of a basic income. In E.O. Wright (Ed.), *Redesigning distribution: Basic income and stakeholder grants as cornerstones for an egalitarian capitalism*. London: Verso.
32. UNDP. (2017). *Universal Basic Income. A policy option for China beyond 2020.*, Retrieved from www.cn.undp.org (Accessed on July 7, 2018).

33. Withorn, A. (1993). Women and basic income in the US: Is one man's ceiling another woman's floor? *Journal of Progressive Human Services*, 29–43.
34. UNDP. (2017). *Universal Basic Income. A policy option for China beyond 2020.*, Retrieved from www.cn.undp.org (Accessed on July 7, 2018).
35. Economic Survey, 2016–2017, p.189.
36. Economic Survey, 2016–2017, pp.191–193.
37. Bungenberg, M. et al. (2016). *European Yearbook of International Economic Law 2016*. Springer.
38. Chancel, L., & Piketty, T. (2017). *Indian income inequality, 1922–2015: From British Raj to Billionaire Raj?* WID. World Working Paper Series N° 2017/11.
39. IMF warns of growing inequality in India and China. Live mint, May 4, 2016.
40. India Inequality Report, 2018. *Widening gaps.* Oxfam, p.23.
41. Survival of the Richest: The India Story, accessed from https://www.oxfamindia.org/ as on 13 April, 2024.
42. *Global Wealth Report 2018*. Credit Suisse, p.42.
43. *Forbes' 32nd Annual World's Billionaires Issue, 2018.* Retrieved from https://www.forbes.com (Accessed on June 6, 2019).
44. Gandhi, & Walton (2012). Where do India's billionaires get their wealth? *EPW Economic & Political Weekly*, *Xlvii*(40), 10.
45. *Reward work, not wealth*, Oxfam Briefing Paper (January 2018). Retrieved from https://www.oxfam.org/.oxfam. (Accessed on June 8, 2019).
46. Oxfam (2018). *Widening Gaps. India inequality reports*, p.35.
47. Use inheritance tax to tackle inequality of wealth, says OECD. *The Guardian*, 12 April, 2018.
48. PWC. (2017). *Billionaires insights 2017: New value creators gain momentum*. Retrieved from https://www.pwc.com (Accessed on June 8, 2019).
49. *Reward work, not wealth*, Oxfam Briefing Paper (J 2018). Retrieved from https://www.oxfam.org (Accessed on June 10, 2019).
50. *The Global Gender Gap Report 2017*. Retrieved from https://www.weforum.org (Accessed on March 16, 2019).
51. *Ibid.*
52. Widening Gaps. *India inequality reports*, Oxfam India, p.58.
53. Mind the gap. (2018). *The State of Employment in India*. Oxfam, p.14.
54. *State of Working India Report 2018*. Retrieved from https://cse.azimpremjiuniversity.edu.in (Accessed on June 8, 2019).
55. Kumar, R. (2017). *'Two Class' Distribution of Income in India, Evidence from Income Tax Data (2012–13)* (Vol. L II no 6, p.62).
56. Widening Gaps. *India inequality reports*. Oxfam India, p.68.
57. Himanshu, & Sen, A. (2013). In-kind food transfers-I. *Economic and Political Weekly*, *48*, 46–54.

CHAPTER **8**

Labor Force, Occupational Pattern, and Unemployment in India

It's a recession when your neighbor loses his job; it's a depression when you lose yours.

—Harry S. Truman

Introduction

Out of the four factors of production (land, labor, capital, and enterprise), labor is the most significant factor. It is simply because it activates the other factors of production and makes them useful in the production process. When a country makes progress and its production expands, the occupational distribution of population and employment pattern undergoes a dramatic change. But if employment does not increase considerably, it leads to serious economic consequences.

The present chapter is centered on the following key issues.

- Activity status of population
- Labor Force: Characteristic Features and Growth
- Occupational Structure in India
- Unemployment: Types, Structure, Causes, and Government Policies

Activity Status of Population

Labor force is economically active population. An economically active person is one who is engaged in some economic activity or seeks to engage him/herself in some economic activity. Accordingly, to classify a person as belonging to labor force or not during a reference period, the National Sample Survey Office (NSSO) provides three broad activity status of population.

1. Working (engaged in an economic activity), that is, "Employed."
2. Seeking or available for work, that is, "Unemployed."
3. Neither seeking nor available for work.

The individuals that fall in the broad activity status of (1) and (2) above are classified as being in the labor force and those having activity status (3) are classified as outside the labor force. Thus, labor force means total labor available in the country both working and willing to work and constitutes both employed and unemployed. Persons who were "neither seeking nor available for work" during the reference period are classified as being outside the labor force. These are students, rentiers, pensioners, those engaged in domestic duties, recipients of remittances, too young persons, etc. and casual laborers not working due to sickness (Box 8.1).

BOX 8.1 What is LFPR and WPR?

Labor Force Participation Rate (LFPR)

Labor Force Participation Rate (LFPR) is defined as the number of persons in the labor force per 1,000 persons.

$$\text{LFPR} = \frac{\text{No.of employed + No.of unemployed persons}}{\text{Total population}} \times 1{,}000$$

Worker Population Ratio

Worker Population Ratio (WPR) is defined as the number of persons employed per 1,000 persons.

$$\text{WPR} = \frac{\text{No.of employed}}{\text{Total population}} \times 1{,}000$$

The WPR for India is low in contrast to the developed nations. For example worker population ratio in India was 50.5 in 2015 but for Australia, Japan, and the United Kingdom, it was 72%, 71.7%, and 71.3, respectively, during 2013.

Characteristics of Labor Force Growth in India

1. **Labor Force Growth:** The rapid increasing labor force generates pressure for the creation of employment opportunities. In India, labor force has grown by more than two and half times during 1971–2011 (from 18.07 crore to 48.17 crore) and average rate of labor force growth during this period was 2.48% whereas average rate of population growth was around 2%. However, labor force growth in India has witnessed a declining trend over the years. For example, the average annual growth rate of labor force in India has come down from 2.96% during 1971–1981 to 1.82% during 2001–2011.
2. **Main Workers and Marginal Workers:** The Census of India classifies workers into two groups namely main workers and marginal workers. Main workers are those workers who had worked for major part of the reference period, that is, 6 months or more. Marginal workers are those workers who had not worked for major part of the reference period, that is, less than 6 months. There were 36.24 crore main workers and 11.93 crore marginal workers in India in 2011. The proportion of main workers was as high as 96.8% in 1971 and came down to 75.2% in 2011. On the other hand, proportion of marginal workers has increased from 3.2% in 1971 to 24.8% in 2011.
3. **Rural Workers and Urban Workers:** The labor force participation rate (LFPR) in India is skewed in favor of rural India (55.8) as compared to urban India (43.7) as rural India constitute around three-fourth of Indian population and provides employment to majority of Indians via agriculture. Proportion of rural worker in India has come down from 82.5 to 75% from 1971–2011 and proportion of urban worker has gone up from 17.5 to 22.6% during the same period. The trend reflects increase in urbanization in the country. The growth rate of urban workers is higher than that of rural workers mainly because people from rural areas are migrating toward cities and cities provide more and better job

opportunities than villages. The average growth rate of urban workers was 3.82% during 2001–2011 and that of rural workers was 1.16%.

4. **Male Workers and Female Workers:** In India, male workers have always accounted for more than two-third of Indian labor force. For example, male workers in 1971 were 80% of workforce and in 2011 they constituted around 69% of the workforce. In proportion of workforce, the share of females has increased from 20 to 31% during 1971–2011. Female WPR (25.8%) is much lower than male WPR (73.3%) in India mainly due to the fact that most of the women work only under economic compulsions and that is why female WPR is high among poor families, rural areas, and socially backward classes.
5. **Working Children in India:** Government has taken different measures to eliminate child labor in India and consequently the incidence of child labor has decreased by 2.6 million between 2001 and 2011. The total child population in India is 259.6 million and of these 10.1 million (3.9%) are working children in the age group of 5–14 years, either as "main worker" or as "marginal worker."[1] In addition, more than 42.7 million children in India are out of school. The five states with the highest incidence of working children are Uttar Pradesh, Bihar, Rajasthan, Maharashtra, and Madhya Pradesh; these states constitute nearly 55% of working children in India. Child labor has different ramifications in both rural and urban areas. In rural regions, the majority children are working as agricultural laborers and cultivators, whereas in urban areas, they are mostly engaged with household and informal industries.[2]

Occupational Structure in India

The occupational structure of a country is mainly function of three important factors.

1. Rapid decline in the population
2. Significant increase in agricultural productivity
3. Surge in the industrial and service sector production and productivity

In India, population grew by more than 2% during 1951–1991 and started declining thereafter. Agriculture sector remained highly unproductive on account of failure of land reform policies, outdated production techniques and disguised workforce. In the process of industrialization, surge in industrial activities and increase in agricultural productivity releases significant manpower from agriculture that could seek employment in industry and services. Indian industry in spite of good start under Mahalanobis's strategy (second 5-year plan onward) experienced slowdown during 1964–1980. The stagnation in agriculture did not allow adequate markets for industrial goods to develop and it exacerbated the slowdown process. Without growth in agriculture and industry, services too remained underdeveloped and as a result the occupational structure of pre-reform India remained almost unchanged. But economic reforms undertaken in 1990s placed Indian economy in higher trajectory of growth and Indian industry and services, particularly the private sector started absorbing the workforce. Not only the proportion of workforce in agriculture shrunk and that of industry and services grew but sub-sectors of industry and services also underwent an enormous transformation. Following discussion on sector-wise occupational change will help us to understand the issue in a better way.

Agriculture: The Mainstay of Indian Workforce

After independence during planning era, high priority was accorded to industry and it was hoped that proportion of labor force engaged in agriculture will fall considerably and will be absorbed by industry. The agricultural work force was expected to fall to 60% by the mid of 1970s but it did not happen. It was mainly due to rapid increase in population and failure of industry and services sector to absorb the ever-increasing working population. The agriculture continued to be disguisedly employed and it further lowered down agricultural productivity. The man-power planning flopped miserably as government plans and policies failed to create necessary inter-sectoral transfer of labor. During the first three decades of planning, agriculture dependence remained unchanged and it was as high as 66.8% during 1991. Post-reform India witnessed reduction in the share of agricultural workforce mainly due to vast employment opportunities in industry and services sector. During 1991–2001, agriculture dependence reduced from 66.8 to 56.7% and during 2001–2011, it further came down to 43.45% in 2019–20. (Table 8.1).

Proportion of Workforce in Industrial Sector

Industrial workforce changed very little during the pre-reform period. Share of industrial workers was 10.7% during 1951 and increased only to 12.7% during 1991. However, post-reform period witnessed a remarkable increase in the proportion of labor force employed in the industrial sector of Indian economy. The share of mining and quarrying in total employment has remained constant during both pre-reform and post-reform India. The share of manufacturing and utilities such as electricity, gas, and water supply has increased from 9% in 1951 to 10.2% in 1991 and further increased to 13.2% in 2011 and 25.2% in 2022–23. The share of construction in labor absorption was almost stagnant or increased at very slow pace during the pre-reform India.

TABLE 8.1 Occupational Structure of Working Population in India

Occupation	1951	1961	1971	1981	1991	2001	2011	2022-23
I. Agriculture, forestry and fishing	72.1	71.8	72.1	63.8	66.8	56.7	48.9	45.8
II. Industry (A+B+C)	10.7	12.2	11.1	13.6	12.7	18.2	24.4	25.2
A. Mining and quarrying	0.6	0.5	0.5	0.6	0.6	0.6	0.5	0.3
B. Manufacturing*	9	10.6	9.4	11.3	10.2	13.9	13.2	11.9
C. Construction	1.1	1.1	1.2	1.7	1.9	3.7	10.6	13
III. Services (D+E+F)	17.2	16	16.8	17.6	20.5	25.1	26.7	28.9
D. Trade and commerce	5.2	4	5.6	6.3	7.5	9.4	11.4	12.1
E. Transport, storage, and communication	1.5	1.6	2.5	2.7	2.8	4	4.4	5.4
F. Other services	10.5	10.4	8.7	8.6	10.2	11.7	10.9	11.4
Total	100	100	100	100	100	100	100	100

*Manufacturing includes electricity, gas, and water supply.

Source: Indian labor and Employment report 1951–2011. PLFS Quarterly 2021 accessed from https://mospi.gov.in on Feb 1, 2022.

However, during post-reform period the sector has grown by more than 10 times in terms of proportion of workforce. It signifies the pace of construction activities in the country under both public and private sector. It must be noted that employment elasticity of utilities and construction is also more than one for the period 1999–2000 to 2011–2012.* But we need to understand that employment in construction sector is mostly temporary, casual, and contractual. The workers are deprived of all benefits given to permanent jobs like casual and medical leaves and other social security benefits. Therefore, the current policy effort is to increase employment opportunities in the manufacturing sector. Both the National Manufacturing Policy, 2011 and Make in India aimed at creating 100 million job opportunities in manufacturing sector by 2022.

Proportion of Workforce in Service Sector

The service sector which contributes nearly 53% of GDP employs more than one-fourth of workforce. In 1951, the share of service sector as a proportion of GDP was 17.2% and it decreased to 16.8% in 1971. It increased thereafter but the pace of growth was very less. The share of services sector in the workforce increased from 20.5% during 1991 about 29% during 2022–23. In the process of economic development, the contribution of service sector in GDP and employment increases. In many developed countries, such as the United States, the United Kingdom, Australia, and Canada, the services constitute 80% of GDP and workforce, whereas agriculture contributes miniscule in terms of GDP and employment. But in countries like India productive forces are underdeveloped and technology is backward. And as long as productive forces are not developed adequately and technology does not acquire sophistication, productivity of labor remains low and inter-sectoral transfer of workforce (from agriculture to services) does not take place.

UNEMPLOYMENT

Unemployment is the situation where a person who is searching a work does not get it. Labor force means people available for work and workforce means people who actually get work. Unemployment is, therefore, the difference between labor force and workforce. The unemployment rate is the total number of unemployed people (calculated as labor force minus work force) divided by the total labor force and the ratio is expressed in percentage.

$$\text{Unemployment rate} = \frac{\text{Labor force} - \text{Work force}}{\text{Labor force}} \times 100$$

Or Unemployment rate = (Unemployed workers/Total labor force) × 100

The different types of unemployment are as follows:

1. **Voluntary Unemployment:** It is a situation when a person is unemployed not due to unavailability of jobs in the economy, but because of not being able to find employment of his/her own choice. It is an unemployment where work is available but the worker does not want to do it at prevailing wage rate.

* For understanding the concept of employment elasticity, please refer to section "causes of unemployment in India."

2. **Involuntary Unemployment:** It occurs when worker is willing to work at prevailing wage rate but does not get work. Involuntary unemployment is a serious problem with grave economic and social consequences.
3. **Frictional Unemployment:** It is a state of unemployment when people move between the jobs or remain temporarily unemployed while looking for the first job. It is a type of voluntary unemployment as people choose to remain unemployed. Frictional unemployment always exists in an economy.
4. **Structural Unemployment:** It is a long-term unemployment caused by technological shifts in the economy, which makes it difficult for workers to find job. It exists when an economy is unable to provide people with jobs that fit their skills.
5. **Cyclical Unemployment:** It is an unemployment that takes place due to change in business cycles. During boom period unemployment rate dips as production and income experiences a steep rise. During recession unemployment rises due to fall in economic activity and production.
6. **Seasonal Unemployment:** The unemployment exists during certain time of a year because of low demand. For example, agriculture experiences a lean period between harvest and next planting. Amusement parks during winter also experience seasonal unemployment.
7. **Disguised Unemployment:** It means the workers look like employed but actually they are not contributing into the production. It is because their marginal productivity is zero. Generally the public sector offices or agriculture sector experiences such type of unemployment. For example, it is seen that the whole family is engaged in the agriculture. If one or two family members leave agriculture profession and the output remains same, it means these (outgoing) members were disguisedly unemployed.
8. **Natural Rate of Unemployment:** The concept of natural rate of unemployment was developed by Milton Friedman and Edmund Phelps in the 1960s. It signifies the hypothetical unemployment rate consistent with aggregate production being at the "long-run level. That is, the unemployment that exists naturally over the period of time in an economy. It is a combination of frictional and structural unemployment.

Concept of Unemployment in India

Unemployment estimates in India are based on NSSO surveys and such surveys are conducted on quinquennial basis. In order to measure unemployment on an annual basis, Employment-Unemployment Survey is being conducted by Labor Bureau since 2009. For measuring unemployment in India, NSSO has developed and standardized three concepts of unemployment suitable to Indian conditions.[3] In a country where majority of the workers are employed in the unorganized sector and pursuing multiple activities, estimating labor force and its derivatives by a single approach is a difficult task. In such cases no single measure is appropriate to estimate the labor force parameters precisely. As per international practice, labor force related parameters can be estimated for both longer reference period and current or shorter reference periods. Let us discuss such measures.

Usual Principal Status (UPS)

Under this approach, the major time criterion based on the 365 days is used to determine the activity pursued by a person. Accordingly, the major time spent by a person (183 days or more) is used to determine whether the person is in the labor force or out of labor force. A person found unemployed under this approach reflects the chronic unemployment.[4]

Usual Principal and Subsidiary Status (UPSS) Approach or Usual Status (US) Approach

This approach is a hybrid one which takes into consideration both the major time criterion (365 days) and shorter time period (30 days or more) in any economic activity. In case of multiple subsidiary economic activities, the status of the activity in which relatively longer time has been spent will be considered.[5]

Current Weekly Status (CWS)

CWS approach to measuring unemployment uses 7 days preceding the date of survey as the reference period. A person is considered to be employed if he/she is employed for at least 1 hour on any day of the reference week. On the other hand, if a person does not get employment, but has been seeking or available for work, the person is considered as unemployed.[6]

Current Daily Status (CDS)

CDS approach to measuring unemployment seeks to ascertain the activity status of an individual for each day of the reference week. It reports time disposition of an individual on each day of the reference week. A person is classified as employed for the "full day" if he has worked for 4 hours or more during the day. If a person works for more than 1 hour but less than 4 hours he is classified as "working" (employed) for "half day." If a person is not engaged in any work even for 1 hour during the day but was "seeking/available for work" for more than 4 hours a day, then he is classified as "unemployed" for "full day."* The CDS approach of measuring unemployment is most relevant for policymaking as it is more inclusive and covers both open as well as partial unemployment.[7]

Employment Structure in India

The latest statistics on unemployment available in the country is based on NSSO 68th round survey for the period 2011–2012. Since then, no large consumer expenditure surveys results have come in public domain. The employment structure in India can be studied under following sub-sections.

Sectoral Distribution of Employment

In India, a large proportion of the workforce is still dependent on the agricultural sector with 48.9% employment share in 2011–2012. The agricultural sector still accounts for 62.7% of India's rural employment, although this share has fallen significantly, from 77.6% in 1993–1994. The share of the services sector in urban areas was 58.7% (2011–2012) compared to just 16.1% in rural regions (26.7% for all India in 2011–2012). The share of industry which consists of both manufacturing and construction stood at 24.4% in 2011–2012. In terms of employment, the manufacturing sector provides employment to 12.6% in 2011–2012 (Table 8.1).

Employment by Status

The national Sample Survey Office is conducting the Periodic Labor Force Survey (PLFS) since 2017. At present PLFS is the primary source of data for employment and unemployment situation in India. The sixth annual report was brought by NSSO based on the survey conducted during July 2022 to June 2023. Following observations can be made on the basis of PLFS survey.

---

*This approach is associated with persons-days and not to persons. The person-days in employment for each day of the reference week are aggregated to arrive at person-days of employment and unemployment (daily status) in the economy.

TABLE 8.2 Unemployment Rates According to Usual Status (ps+ss) and Current Weekly Status (CWS)

	PLFS 2022–23			PLFS 2021–22			PLFS 2020–21		
	Male	Female	Person	Male	Female	Person	Male	Female	Person
Rural									
Usual Status (ps+ss)	2.8	1.8	2.4	3.8	2.1	3.3	3.9	2.1	3.3
Current Weekly Status	4.6	4.0	4.5	6.5	4.6	6.0	7.2	4.8	6.5
Urban									
Usual Status (ps+ss)	4.7	7.5	5.4	5.8	7.9	6.3	6.1	8.6	6.7
Current Weekly Status	6.3	9.1	7.0	7.8	9.9	8.3	9.4	12.2	10.1
Rural + Urban									
Usual Status (ps+ss)	3.3	2.9	3.2	4.4	3.3	4.1	4.5	3.5	4.2
Current Weekly Status	5.1	5.1	5.1	6.9	5.8	6.6	7.8	6.6	7.5

Source: Annual Report, PLFS, 2022–23, p. 28.

- Unemployment rate (usual status) has declined in 2022-23 to 3.2% from 4.2% in 2020–21. The weekly status unemployment has also revealed declining trend from 7.5 to 5.1% during the same period.
- Urban unemployment (5.4%) is higher than that of rural unemployment (6.3%), although it has shown declining trend since 2020–21.
- Female unemployment rate is higher than that of male unemployment rate in cities whereas the situation is reverse in villages.

Employment by Religion and Caste

According to sixth PLFS survey findings, the usual status unemployment rate is highest for Sikhs (5.1%), followed by Christians (4.5%), Hindus (3.2%) and Muslims (2.4%) during 2022–23. However, it is important to note that unemployment was highest among Christians in 2020–21 (6.7%).The unemployment rate is lowest among Scheduled tribes (1.8%) and Scheduled castes (3.2%) during 2022–23. The unemployment rate among other backward classes and others was 4.2% and 5% respectively for the same period. It is also interesting to note that the unemployment rate in all the categories mentioned above has declined since 2020–21.

Employment Status by Categories

The overall proportion of informal workers in total employment (e.g., unorganized sector workers plus informal workers in the organized sector) is around 92%. The increasing casualization of the workforce (from 27.2% in 1977–1978 to 37% in 2011–2012) is a matter of grave concern especially because casual workers are subject to various kinds of exploitation and do not get benefits that generally accrue to the regular salaried class, for example, security of job, casual and medical leaves, increments and job promotions, etc. (Table 8.3). In the recent years, the increase in casual work force could have occurred due to spurt in construction activities in MNREGA in rural areas and real estate in urban areas.[8] Among the state/UT's, Arunachal Pradesh had the highest 81.2% of the workers as self-employed as compared to the lowest 15.7% in Puducherry. Chandigarh had the highest 54.2% of the workers employed on regular wage/salary basis while

TABLE 8.3 Employment Status by Categories (%)

Year	Self-employment	Regular Salaried	Casual
1977–1978	58.9	13.9	27.2
1993–1994	54.8	13.2	32
2011–2012	52	17.9	30
2015–2016	46	17	37
2022–2023	57.3	20.9	21.8

Source: NSSO various rounds, statistics 1977–2016, © Ministry of Statistics & Programme Implementation (MOSPI), Govt. of India, Annual Report, PLFS, 2022–23.

Bihar had the lowest 9.7%. Andhra Pradesh had the highest 48.5% of workers engaged in casual labor followed by Tamil Nadu (47.3%).[9]

Employment in Public and Private Sector

Employment in public sector has negative growth because of deliberate policy decision by the government. The public sector retired more number of employees than it recruited during the post-reform period. Increase in job opportunities in private sector during the post-reform period is quite visible as economy is undergoing a structural change.

State-wise Unemployment Patterns

In India, the unemployment rate exhibits wide variations across the states and UT's. Among states Goa (9.7%) had the highest unemployment rate in 2023 followed by Kerala (7%) and Haryana

TABLE 8.4 Unemployment Rate (UR) (in per cent) According to Usual Status (ps+ss) for Each State/UT

State/ UT	2022–23	State/ UT	2022–23
Andhra Pradesh	4.1	Nagaland	4.3
Arunachal Pradesh	4.8	Odisha	3.9
Assam	1.7	Punjab	6.1
Bihar	3.9	Rajasthan	4.4
Chhattisgarh	2.5	Sikkim	2.2
Delhi	1.9	Tamil Nadu	4.3
Goa	9.7	Telangana	4.4
Gujarat	1.7	Tripura	1.4
Haryana	6.1	Uttar Pradesh	2.4
Himachal Pradesh	4.4	Uttarakhand	4.5
Jharkhand	1.7	West Bengal	2.2
Karnataka	2.4	Andaman & Nicobar Islands	9.7
Kerala	7.0	Chandigarh	4.0
Madhya Pradesh	1.6	Dadra & Nagar Haveli & Daman & Diu	2.5
Maharashtra	3.1	Jammu & Kashmir	4.4
Manipur	4.7	Ladakh	6.1
Meghalaya	6.0	Lakshadweep	11.1
Mizoram	2.2	Puducherry	5.6
India	3.2	India	3.2

Source: PLFS, Annual Report. 2023, Ministry of Statistics and Programme Implementation.

(6.1%). Tripura, M.P., Jharjhand, Gujarat and Assam had lowest unemployment rate. Even the state like Goa which boasts of highest per capita income in the country has higher unemployment rate of about 10%. Kerala too that boasts of high human development is characterized by high unemployment rate. Among the Union territories, the Lakshadweep and Andaman & Nicobar Islands have highest unemployment rates whereas Dadra & Nagar Haveli & Daman & Diu and Chandigarh have lowest unemployment rates.

Causes of Unemployment in India

Following causes of unemployment in India can be analyzed.

Jobless Growth

Jobless growth means existence of high growth rate along with high unemployment rate. In the first three decades of Indian planning, the GDP growth rate was around 3–3.5%. During this period, the employment grew at a reasonable rate of 2% p.a. During 1980s and especially after the post-reform period, India experienced high GDP growth rate but employment growth registered a sharp fall. It was because labor force absorption was inadequate in industry and service sector. The service sector in India remains the most dynamic one and growth is very high, but that growth is not matched by commensurate growth in employment. In most other economies, the share of services in gross value added is more or less similar to its share in total employment.[10] But India remains exception to this. (Table 8.5).

Further, the vast scale industrial sickness in Micro, small and medium enterprises (MSMEs), stringent labor laws, and lower employment elasticity in manufacturing sector are other reasons for jobless growth.

Declining Female Employment

India is among the lowest women's LFPRs in the world. Not only women's participation rates are low but have also been showing a declining trend since 2004–2005. Women's LFPR dropped from 42.7% in 2004–2005 to 31.2% in 2011–2012 and further to 27.4% in 2015–2016. The decline in LFPR in case of rural females is possibly on account of greater number of persons opting for education/skill development. Participation rates are even lower in urban areas and among educated women, and when women work they tend to end up in marginal jobs, often in home-based work (as contributing family worker/unpaid worker) and the domestic work sector.[11]

TABLE 8.5 Performance of Services Sector: International Comparison

Country	Share of Services in GVA in 2015	Share of Services in Employment in 2016
The United States	79.3	80
China	49.7	42.4
The United Kingdom	79.9	80
India	53.2	28.6
Brazil	72	68.9
South. Korea	59.7	70.2
Mexico	60.4	61.2
World	67.2	50.9

Source: Economic Survey, 2016–2017, Part II.

Falling Employment Elasticity

Employment elasticity is a measure of the percentage change in employment associated with one percentage point change in economic growth. The aggregate employment elasticity estimates for India for the period 1993–1994 to 2011–2012 was 0.18%. It simply means that for every 10% change in real GDP, there is about 1.8% change in employment. The employment elasticity is measured by dividing percentage change in employment with percentage change in GDP, that is, $e = (\Delta L/L)/(\Delta Y/Y)$, where e denotes elasticity, L denotes employment, and Y denotes GDP of the country. While for other nations, simple percentage change is used, in case of India, since employment data is available once in 5 years, compounded annual growth rate (CAGR) approach is used.*

There is a significant decline in the employment elasticity since the decade of 1970s. During 1977–1978 to 1983–1984, the employment elasticity in India was recorded at 0.53%. It came down to 0.15% during 1993–1994 to 1999–2000. However, this trend has been reversed in the period 1999–2000 to 2004–2005. During 1999–2000 to 2004–2005, aggregate employment elasticity was estimated to be 0.5 and the overall employment growth rate accelerated to a high of 2.8% per annum during this period.[12] However, for the period 1999–2000 to 2011–2012, the employment elasticity was 0.20.

In sector-wise analysis for the period 1999–2000 to 2011–2012, it has been found that employment elasticity has been highest in case of utilities** (1.17) followed by construction (1.01). Agriculture is the only sector with negative employment elasticity (−0.08). Manufacturing employment elasticity has hovered in the range 0.29–0.33. Within manufacturing, the employment elasticity for organized manufacturing sector based on various estimates seems to be higher, in the range 0.42–0.57 for 2000s and it has risen over the previous two decades. Given the huge productivity and wage differentials between organized and unorganized sectors, greater employment generation in organized manufacturing is crucial as it has larger multiplier effects.[13] If India has to tap its vast demographic dividend, emphasis should be on industries with higher employment elasticity. On a rough basis, about 10 million people would need a job every year for the next 15 years.[14] Finding productive jobs for such huge numbers is a big challenge, and clearly the answer lies in stepping up growth, and importantly, stepping up the employment intensity of growth.

Educated Unemployment

The low demand of high-skilled workers and lack of productive job opportunities create educated unemployment. Thus, educated unemployment generally takes place due to mismatch between the job aspirations of educated and the job availability. Unemployment rate among the uneducated people is lower since they are mostly own account workers (i.e., self-employed) and engaged in other work. Most of such workers are engaged as helpers in household enterprises on an unpaid basis. However, the educated people are mostly engaged in regular salaried jobs. Thus, one of the reasons for high unemployment among educated people as against uneducated is that the educated people do not want to be underemployed or do not want to work in sub-standard informal jobs. The relationship between education and unemployment differs across the developed and

*The CAGR method gives arc elasticity of employment. An alternative way to compute the elasticity is to estimate a log linear regression equation between employment and GDP that generates the point elasticity of employment.

**Utilities include electricity, gas, water supply, sewerage, and waste management.

developing countries. In the case of developed countries, the higher the educational level, the lower is the likelihood of unemployment. However, in developing countries, what is observed is that the unemployment rate increases with an increase in the educational level.[15] Hence, there exists a negative relationship between higher education and employment rate. According to AICTE, more than 60% of the 8 lakh engineers graduating from technical institutions across the country every year remain unemployed. This is a potential loss of 20 lakh man days annually.[16]

Government Policies for Removal of Unemployment

Government policies regarding the removal of unemployment can be discussed under following four heads:

1. Policy action under five year plans
2. Major employment schemes
3. Mahatma Gandhi National Rural Employment Guarantee Scheme (MGNREGS)
4. Skill development programs

Policy Action Under 5-year Plan*

The second 5-year plan estimated a backlog of unemployment at 5 million and an annual addition of labor force at 1.5–2 million. A rate of growth of 5% p.a. was expected to generate employment opportunities for all over a period of 10 years through trickle-down effect. The plan overemphasized trickle down approach as employment removal was considered as a goal of development. It was not central in the policy framework of the government. *The third and fourth plan* did not give due importance to employment generation. *The fifth plan* re-orientated development strategy toward employment-centric growth and introduced anti-poverty schemes and employment generation programmes. Slogan of Garibi Hatao and 20-point program was highlight of this plan. *The Sixth 5-year plan* adopted wage employment programmes as a short-term measure and skill development measures as long-term measure. Many schemes for employment generation were launched during this plan. *The seventh plan* development strategy focused on generation of productive employment. The labor force was expected to be absorbed in rural development projects via enhancing the rural construction and capital formation. Self-employment and wage employment programmes were continued.

The eighth plan emphasized on promoting growth of the economy and restructuring the output composition of growth. Re-adjusting the sectoral composition of output in favor of sectors and sub-sectors having higher employment elasticity was stressed. *The ninth plan* laid emphasis on the sectors, sub-sectors, and technologies which were more labor intensive in the regions characterized by higher rate of unemployment and underemployment. *Under tenth plan* sectors of higher labor intensity were identified viz. construction, tourism; MSMEs like textiles, gems and jewellery, leather and footwear, and food processing; health and education services; rural non-farm activities; IT and financial services. The plan had a target growth rate of 8% and that was expected to generate employment of around 50 million person years. *The Eleventh plan* emphasized enhancing both quantity as well as quality of the employment. Self-employment remained the important source of labor absorption and the employment strategy was to increase

---

*For detailed discussion of 5-year plans, please see Chapter 27, Planning in India.

the proportion of regular employment with a matching reduction in the share of casual employment. *Under twelfth plan* manufacturing was considered to be the engine of growth and government aimed to create 100 million jobs by 2022. Focus remained on labor intensive manufacturing segment that includes textiles, gems and jewellery, leather and footwear, and food processing, and so on. Make in India was launched to facilitate manufacturing growth by enhancing foreign and indigenous investment. Skill development remained the central agenda of employment generation and government aims to provide 50 million people with the skill certification.

Major Employment Generation Schemes

Various unemployment removal schemes launched by government from time to time are as follows:

- The Integrated Rural Development Program (IRDP) was launched in 1978–79 to promote self-employment in rural areas.
- To train 2 lakh rural youth every year, government initiated the scheme of Training Rural Youth for Self-Employment (TRYSEM) in 1979.
- National Rural Employment Program (NREP) was launched in 1980 to provide wage employment to seasonal unemployed persons.
- The Rural Landless Employment Guarantee Program (RLEGP) was started in 1983 to provide employment to at least one member of the landless household for about 100 days in a year.
- Jawahar Rozgar Yojana (JRY)—a wage employment program was launched in 1989 for creating employment in 120 backward districts.
- Similarly, to alleviate urban unemployment Nehru Rozgar Yojana (NRY) was also launched in 1989.
- The Employment Assurance Scheme (EAS) was launched in 1993 for implementation in 1778 identified backward blocks of different states comprising drought prone areas, desert areas, tribal areas, and hilly areas. Later, the scheme was extended to the remaining blocks of the country in phased manner.
- In 1999, Jawahar Gram Samridhi Yojana (JGSY) was launched by restructuring JRY. The aim of the scheme was creation of infrastructure and durable assets so as to increase opportunities for sustained employment in rural areas.
- The Swarana Jayanti Shahari Rozgar Yojana (SJSRY) came into operation in 1997 to promote urban employment and subsumed all previous urban alleviation schemes.
- The Swarana Jayanti Gram Swarozgar Yojana (SGSY) came into operation in 1999 to promote self-employment in rural areas after restructuring IRDP and allied schemes. The scheme aimed at providing gainful employment to urban unemployed and underemployed poor.
- In 2011, SGSY was restructured as National Rural Livelihood mission (NRLM) and was subsequently renamed as Aajeevika to implement it in a mission mode in the country. In November 2015, the program was renamed Deendayal Antyodaya Yojana (DAY-NRLM). The scheme aims at creating efficient and effective institutional platforms of the rural poor, enabling them to increase household income through sustainable livelihood enhancements and improved access to financial services.[17]

Mahatma Gandhi National Rural Employment Guarantee Scheme

The National Rural Employment Guarantee Act (NREGA) was enacted in 2005 and was introduced in phased manner. It was introduced in 2006 in the most backward districts of the country in Phase I, additional 130 districts in 2007–2008 under Phase II and remaining 274 rural districts of India w.e.f. April 1, 2008 in Phase III. With the introduction of Phase III, NREGA covered all rural areas of the country. From October 2, 2009, NREGA was renamed as Mahatma Gandhi National Rural Employment Guarantee Scheme (MGNREGS).

Salient Features of MGNREGS

1. MGNREGS provides right-based framework for adult members of a rural household willing to do unskilled manual work.
2. Providing not less than 100 days of guaranteed employment in a financial year, to those who demand work.
3. At least 33% of the beneficiaries are to be women.
4. 60:40 wage and material ratio for permissible works; no contractors/machinery.
5. Work-site facilities include crèche, drinking water, first aid, and shade provided at worksites.
6. Transparency and accountability will be maintained through proactive disclosure through social audits, grievance redressal mechanism.
7. Wage rates for workers under the scheme are notified and revised annually based on Consumer Price Index-Agricultural Labor (CPI-AL).

Performance of MGNREGS

Following are the achievements of MGNREGS.

1. **Employment generation:** Till date MGNREGS has been operational in 691 districts, 6,920 blocks, and 262,610 gram panchayats. The scheme has generated 267.97 crore person days employment for the financial year 2018–2019. The permissible wage–material ratio under MGNREGS is 60:40 but the actual achievement is 71:29. [18]
2. **Wage enhancement:** 70% of the total expenditure under MGNREGS has been on wages. The average wage rate per day for the financial year 2018–2019 was ₹179.12. The Union Rural Development Ministry has increased the rate of wages for 2019–2020 in a range of 2–8.76% in most of the states. The highest wage under the MGNREGA is ₹284 in Haryana, while the lowest is ₹171 in Bihar and Jharkhand.[19]
3. **Benefit to disadvantage section:** The share of women in total employment under MGNREGS has been 54.54%. The share of SCs and STs in total employment has been 20.66 and 17.39%, respectively.
4. **Financial inclusion:** Around 99.91% of the wages were paid electronically into the Bank/Post Office accounts of MGNREGA workers through Electronic Fund Management System (eFMS).[20] In FY 2013–2014, only 37% of the wages were paid electronically.[21]
5. **Impact on migration and bargaining power of rural workers:** Rural poor benefit from MGNREGA in at least two ways: directly by earning income through participating in the programme and indirectly by earning higher wages while doing non-MGNREGA casual labor for private employers. Average wage paid under MGNREGS has increased from ₹65 in 2006–2007 to more than ₹179.12 in 2018–2019. It has pushed up the wage rate of casual workers in private sector, by restricting the supply of labor, and also reduced

short-term migration to urban areas by 10%.[22]

6. **Strengthening natural resource system and asset generation:** Since its inception MGNREGS has focused on works relating to soil and water conservation, land development and afforestation, drought proofing work, and so on. Government has issued consolidated guidelines for water conservation. Planning and monitoring framework for Natural Resource Management–related works under MGNREGA in convergence with Pradhan Mantri Krishi Sinchayee Yojana and Integrated Watershed Management Programme has been prepared.
7. **GeoMGNREGA:** Launched in 2016–2017, it is a path-breaking initiative that uses space technology for geo-tagging all assets created under MGNREGA for improved planning, effective monitoring, enhanced visibility, and greater transparency. Under this, assets are created across the country related to water harvesting, drought relief, flood control activities, and sanitation. Satellite-derived location-based services are being utilized for planning and monitoring of nearly 2 million assets annually through the use of mobile-based geo-tagging. So far, 3.3 crore assets were geo-tagged as on December 2018.[23]
8. **Skill development:** Government has taken up skill development of the MGNREGA workers through initiatives such as Bare Foot Technicians and Project LIFE (Livelihood In Full Employment) in order to move them up the skilling ladder.
9. **Good governance:** The government initiated interstate exchange programmes, a process ensuring sharing of ideas and good practices. Reduction in number of registers being maintained at Gram Panchayat level to 7 simplified registers from an average of 22 registers has been implemented. The programme is progressing toward a more independent and empowered system of social audit and internal audit to ensure growth with accountability through a trained community cadre of social auditors drawn from women SHGs.[24]

Criticism of MGNREGS

1. **MNREGS-Not benefitting workers:** MGNREGS guarantees 100 days of employment in a year. However, it has been able to provide employment for 45 and 51 days for 2017–2018 and 2018–2019, respectively. About 13.17 crore people were registered under the MGNREGA in 2017–2018. Out of these, 5.73 crore workers sought work and only 5.11 crore people were given work and only 29.60 lakh workers got full 100-day employment. Unemployment allowance was paid only to 217 workers during the year.[25]
2. **Delayed payment of wages:** A study by Azim Premji University in the year 2018 found that 78% of payments were not made on time, and as many as 45% payments did not include compensation for delayed payment as per guidelines which are 0.05% per day of the wages earned. In the financial year 2017–2018 alone, ₹11,000 crore of wages remained unpaid to workers.[26]
3. **Corruption and fund leakages:** In the initial years of MGNREGA, there were reports of rampant corruption as the process was mostly manual. Fake entries were made in job sheets to divert funds, job cards existed in non-existent names. In many cases, people held multiple cards in a bid to draw added benefits. Rural workers complain that funds that are sanctioned for public works are going into the pockets of middlemen. A study conducted by NCAER revealed that 67% of the people covered under survey had to share their guaranteed wage. In 2017, government canceled nearly a crore of fake "job cards" in the MGNREGA scheme, plugging a major source of fund leakage.[27]

Skill Development Programs

Nearly 62% of India's population is in the working age group (15–59 years), and more than 54% of the total population is below 25 years of age. According to some estimates, 109.73 million additional skilled manpower will be required across 24 key sectors by 2022. But only 4.69% of the total workforce in India has undergone formal skill training as compared to 68% in the United Kingdom, 75% in Germany, 52% in the United States, 80% in Japan, and 96% in South Korea. While the debate on the exact quantum of the challenge continues, there is no disputing fact that it is indeed a challenge of formidable proportion.[28] In the light of above, government has initiated various skill development programs in the country. Our analysis on skill development program will focus on following four policy issues.

1. National Policy for Skill Development and Entrepreneurship 2015
2. Pradhan Mantri Kaushal Vikas Yojana (PMKVY)
3. National Skill Development Mission
4. Deen Dayal Upadhyaya Grameen Kaushalya Yojana (DDU-GKY)

National Policy for Skill Development and Entrepreneurship 2015 National Policy for Skill Development and Entrepreneurship 2015 was announced by the government for providing an effective roadmap for promotion of entrepreneurship as the key to a successful skills strategy. Following are the objectives of policy. [29]

- Making quality vocational training aspirational for both youth and employers whereby youth sees it as a matter of choice and employer acknowledges the productivity linked to skilled workforce by paying the requisite premium.
- Ensure both vertical and horizontal pathways to skilled workforce for further growth by providing seamless integration of skill training with formal education.
- Focus on an outcome-based approach toward quality skilling so as to increase employability and improve productivity across primary, secondary, and tertiary sectors.
- Increase the capacity and quality of training infrastructure and trainers to ensure equitable and easy access to every citizen.
- Addressing human resource needs by aligning supply of skilled workers with sectoral requirements of industry including flagship programmes like Make in India.
- Establish an IT-based information system for aggregating demand and supply of skilled workforce which can help in matching and connecting supply with demand.
- Promote national standards in the skilling space through active involvement of employers in setting occupational standards, helping develop curriculum, providing apprenticeship opportunities, participating in assessments, and providing gainful employment to skilled workforce with adequate compensation.
- Operationalize a well-defined quality assurance framework aligned with global standards to facilitate mobility of labor.
- Leverage modern technology to ensure scale, access, and outreach, in addition to ease of delivering content and monitoring results.
- Recognize the value of on-the-job training, by making apprenticeships in actual work environments an integral part of all skill development efforts.
- Ensure that the skilling needs of the socially and geographically disadvantaged and marginalized groups (like the SCs, STs, OBCs, minorities, differently abled persons, etc.) are appropriately taken care of.

- Promote increased participation of women in the workforce through appropriate skilling and gender mainstreaming of training.
- Promote commitment and ownership of all stakeholders toward skill development and create an effective coordination mechanism.

Pradhan Mantri Kaushal Vikas Yojana (PMKVY) Launched in July 5, 2015 by government, PMKVY is the flagship scheme of the Ministry of Skill Development & Entrepreneurship (MSDE). The objective of the scheme is to enable a large number of Indian youth to take up industry-relevant skill training that will help them in securing a better livelihood. Individuals with prior learning experience or skills will also be assessed and certified under recognition of prior learning (RPL). Government has approved the scheme for another 4 years (2016–2020) to benefit 10 million youth. The scheme will be implemented through the National Skill Development Corporation (NSDC). Following are the key components of the scheme.[30]

Key Components of the Scheme

1. **Short-Term Training**: The short-term training imparted at PMKVY training centers is expected to benefit candidates of Indian nationality who are either school/college dropouts or unemployed. Apart from providing training according to the National Skills Qualification Framework (NSQF), training centers shall also impart training in Soft Skills, Entrepreneurship, Financial and Digital Literacy. Duration of the training varies per job role, ranging between 150 and 300 hours. Upon successful completion of their assessment, candidates shall be provided placement assistance by training partners (TPs). Under PMKVY, the entire training and assessment fees are paid by the government.
2. **Recognition of Prior Learning**: Individuals with prior learning experience or skills shall be assessed and certified under the RPL component of the scheme. RPL aims to align the competencies of the unregulated workforce of the country to the NSQF.
3. **Special Projects**: The Special Projects component of PMKVY envisages the creation of a platform that will facilitate trainings in special areas and/or premises of government bodies, corporates or Industry bodies, and trainings in special job roles not defined under the available Qualification Packs (QPs)/National Occupational Standards (NOSs).
4. **Kaushal and Rozgar Mela**: Social and community mobilization is extremely critical for the success of PMKVY. TPs shall conduct Kaushal and Rozgar Melas every 6 months with press/media coverage; they are also required to participate actively in National Career Service Melas and on-ground activities.
5. **Placement Guidelines**: PMKVY envisages to link the aptitude, aspiration, and knowledge of the skilled workforce it creates with employment opportunities and demands in the market. Every effort thereby needs to be made by the PMKVY training centers to provide placement opportunities to candidates, trained and certified under the scheme. TPs shall also provide support to entrepreneurship development.
6. **Monitoring Guidelines**: To ensure that high standards of quality are maintained by PMKVY training centers, NSDC and empanelled Inspection Agencies shall use various methodologies, such as self-audit reporting, call validations, surprise visits, and monitoring through the Skills Development Management System (SDMS). These methodologies shall be enhanced with the engagement of latest technologies.

National Skill Development Mission The National Skill Development Mission was launched by prime minister on July 15, 2015 on the occasion of World Youth Skills Day. Following are the salient features of mission. [31]

- To create convergence across sectors and states in terms of skill training activities.
- To consolidate, coordinate skilling efforts, and expedite decision making across sectors to achieve skilling at scale with speed and standards.
- To implement the program through a streamlined institutional mechanism driven by Ministry of Skill Development and Entrepreneurship (MSDE).
- Three tier institutional mechanism consisting of Governing Council for policy guidance at apex level, a Steering Committee and a Mission Directorate (along with an Executive Committee) as the executive arm of the Mission.
- To establish National Skill Development Agency (NSDA), National Skill Development Corporation (NSDC), and Directorate General of Training (DGT)—all of which will have horizontal linkages with Mission Directorate to facilitate smooth functioning of the national institutional mechanism.
- To propose seven sub-missions for achieving overall objectives. They are: (1) Institutional Training, (2) Infrastructure, (3) Convergence, (4) Trainers, (5) Overseas Employment, (6) Sustainable Livelihoods, and (7) Leveraging Public Infrastructure.

Deen Dayal Upadhyaya Grameen Kaushalya Yojana (DDU-GKY) The DDU-GKY was launched on September 25, 2014. It is a part of the National Rural Livelihood Mission, tasked with the dual objectives of adding diversity to the incomes of rural poor families and cater to the career aspirations of rural youth. Following are the key components of the program.[32]

- The Ministry of Rural Development (MoRD) is the implementation agency of the program.
- The program is focused on rural youth between the ages of 15 and 35 years from poor families.
- The scheme mandates a minimum salary of ₹6,000 per month for workers who have received placement after 3 months of training course and also post-placement support to candidates.
- To promote social inclusion, the scheme mandates coverage of socially disadvantaged groups—50% allocation to SC/ST groups, 15% to minorities, and 33% to women.
- DDU-GKY is applicable to entire country. Over 7.38 lakh candidates have been trained and over 3.48 lakh candidates have been placed in jobs so in the course till March 31, 2019.
- As a part of the Skill India campaign, it plays an instrumental role in supporting the social and economic programs of the government such as the Make in India, Digital India, Smart Cities and Start-Up India, Stand-Up India campaigns.
- Innovation from partners is encouraged to build scale and capacity. Partners are supported through investment, capacity building, strategies for retention, linkages to international placement, and technology support for training purposes.

Summary

1. Labor is an important input of production. Those who are available for work are called labor force and those who actually get work are called workforce. Workers can be classified as main workers, marginal workers, rural workers, urban workers male workers and female workers. Comparing the time period of 1971 with 2011, the proportion of main workers has gone down and that of marginal workers has gone up; the proportion of rural workers has gone down and that of urban workers has gone up; the proportion of male workers has gone down and that of female workers has gone up. Proportion of child labor has come down since 2001.
2. In the occupational distribution of population share of agriculture has come down from 72.1% in 1951 to 48.9% in 2011, the share of industry has gone up from 10.7 to 24.4% and share of services has gone up from 17.2 to 26.7% during the same period.
3. Unemployment refers to the difference between labor force and workforce and unemployment rate = (Unemployed workers/Total labor force) × 100. NSSO measures four different kinds of unemployment: usual principal status which seeks to measure employment based on principal activity in which person is engaged for major part of the year; usual status which measures both principal and subsidiary status; current weekly status where a person is considered to be employed if he works for at least 1 hour on any day of the reference week; and current daily status which seeks to ascertain the activity status of an individual for each day of the reference week.
4. Employment structure of India can be studied in terms of sectoral distribution of income, which shows changing employment patterns in agriculture, industry, and services; employment by status (UPS, US, CWS, and CDS), region (urban and rural), and gender (male and female); employment status by categories, covering formal and informal workers; employment in public and private sectors and state-wise unemployment patterns.
5. Government policies to tackle unemployment can be categorized into four parts: policy action under 5-year plan; major employment schemes; Mahatma Gandhi National Rural Employment Guarantee Scheme (MGNREGS), and skill development programs. Though the initial five year plans did not take concrete measures on removing unemployment, it was sixth plan when government introduced wage employment and skill employment policies. The policies kept on changing in different plans during post-reform period as well. Major employment generation policies were launched viz. IRDP, NREP, TRYSEM, JRY, SJRY etc., to alleviate unemployment problem. MGNREGS was introduced in 2008 which guaranteed minimum 100 days of employment in a year. MGNREGS has been praised worldwide for generating wage full employment, financial inclusion, empowering rural masses, and so on. It has also been criticized on the basis of unmet targets of 100 days of employment, delayed payment of wages and corruption, etc. According to some estimates, only 4.69% of the total workforce in India has undergone formal skill training. Government has initiated various skill development programs in the country viz. announcement of National Policy for Skill Development and Entrepreneurship 2015; Pradhan Mantri Kaushal Vikas Yojana; National Skill Development Mission; and Deen Dayal Upadhyaya Grameen Kaushalya Yojana.

Endnotes

1. Census of India (2011). Retrieved from http://censusindia.gov.in (Accessed on October 15, 2017).
2. India Labor Market Update ILO Country Office for India (July 2017).
3. Kindly see "Box 7.1: What are NSSO surveys?" in the chapter: Poverty and inequality in India.
4. Labor Bureau (2016). *Report on Fifth Annual Employment–Unemployment Survey (2015–2016)* Volume I, Government of India, p.25.
5. *Concepts and definitions used in NSS*. Retrieved from http://mospi.nic.in (Accessed on July 17, 2017).
6. *Ibid.*

7. *Employment and Unemployment, Situation in India, 2011–2012*, NSSO 68th Round. Retrieved from mospi.nic.in (Accessed on July 18, 2017).
8. Choudhary, S. (2011). *Employment in India: What does the latest data shows*. EPW.
9. Labor Bureau (2016). *Report on Fifth Annual Employment–Unemployment Survey (2015–2016)* Volume I, Government of India
10. *India's jobless growth in services*. Retrieved from http://www.livemint.com (Accessed on July 19, 2018).
11. *India* Labor *Market Update* ILO Country Office for India (July 2017).
12. Bhalla, G.S. (2008). Globalisation and employment trends in India. *The Indian Journal of Labor Economics, 51* (1).
13. Misra, S., & Suresh, A.K. (2014). *Estimating employment elasticity of growth for the Indian Economy*. RBI working paper series, W P S (DEPR).
14. Chakravarty, K.C. (2013). *Environmental & social sustainability: Key issues & concerns*. Yes Bank–GIZ–UNEP Sustainability Series event on Environment and Social Risk Management, Mumbai.
15. Bairagya, I.(2015). *Socio-economic determinants of educated unemployment in India*. Working paper 343. Bangalore: The Institute for Social and Economic Change.
16. 60% of engineering graduates unemployed. (2017) *The Times of India*.
17. *Deendayal Antyodaya Yojana* (2017) Retrieved from https://aajeevika.gov.in (Accessed on November 2017).
18. *MGNREGSAt a glance*. Retrieved from https://www.nrega.nic.in(Accessed on March 4, 2019).
19. Wages rise under MGNREGA with EC endorsement. (2019). *The Economic Times*.
20. *MGNREGSAt a glance*. Retrieved from https://www.nrega.nic.in (Accessed on March 4, 2019.
21. MGNREGA - Lifeline to millions, Press Information Bureau, 22 March, 2017.
22. Imbert, C., & Papp, P., (2014). MGNREGA works well for the poor. *Mint*, December, 31.
23. *GIS implementation of MGNREGA* Retrieved from https://www.isro.gov.in (Accessed on March 14, 2019).
24. *MGNREGSAt a glance*. Retrieved from https://www.nrega.nic.in(Accessed on March 4, 2019.
25. 4 reasons why MGNREGA is not benefitting workers. (2018). *Business Today*.
26. 4 reasons why MGNREGA is not benefitting workers. (2018). *Business Today*.
27. Fund leakage: Nearly a crore fake 'job cards' struck off from MGNREGA scheme (2017). The Hindustan Times, April 9, 2019.
28. *National Policy for Skill Development and Entrepreneurship 2015*. Retrieved from https://www.msde.gov.in (Accessed on December 14, 2018). p.6.
29. *National Policy for Skill Development and Entrepreneurship 2015*. Retrieved from https://www.msde.gov.in (Accessed on December 14, 2018).
30. *Pradhan Mantri Kaushal Vikas Yojana (2015)* Retrieved from https://msdegov.in. (Accessed on August 17, 2019).
31. *National Skill Development Mission* Retrieved from https://www.msde.gov.in (Accessed on March 14, 2019).
32. *Deen Dayal Upadhyaya Grameen Kaushalya Yojana* Retrieved from http://ddugky.gov.in (Accessed on March 14, 2019).

CHAPTER 9

Indian Economy During Pre-Independence Period

India is the pivot of our Empire... If the Empire loses any other part of its Dominion we can survive, but if we lose India, the sun of our Empire will have set.

—Victor Alexander Vruce

Introduction

Colonialism or imperialism is the policy or practice of acquiring complete or limited political control over another country, inhabiting it with settlers, and exploiting it economically. British imperialism was more pragmatic than that of other colonial powers. The British remained on Indian soil for around 350 years and their subjugation affected India one way or another and had many political, social, and economic implications. India which was world's largest economy in terms of GDP during ancient and medieval times was reduced to a deprived nation in the second half of the twentieth century, struggling to find its lost pride and eminence in the trails of world history.

The present chapter will focus on the following key issues:

- India economy in ancient and medieval times
- Indian economy during British times
- Impact of colonial rule in India

Indian Economy During Ancient and Medieval Times

The 5,000 years old Indus Valley civilization is characterized with early signs of economic development initiatives as evident from the major development in transport technology and other urban infrastructure. The firstly unified administration of the Indian subcontinent can be traced back to the Mauryan Empire (300 B.C.). The political unity and military security allowed for a common economic system, enhanced trade and commerce, nationally administered, and strict-but-fair system of taxation as advised by the principles in the Kautilyas's Arthashastra and establishment of a single currency across India (Box 9.1).

India's total GDP during 1 A.D. was US$33,750 million (at 1990 prices) and constituted around 32% of World GDP. By 1000 A.D., the GDP of India remained stagnant at US$33,750 million and was around 28% of world GDP. India is estimated to have had the largest economy of the ancient and medieval world between the first and fifteenth centuries A.D., controlling between one-third and one-fourth of the world's wealth. In 1526, the empire established by Babur was reported as the second largest economy in the world after China. In 1600 A.D. India's

BOX 9.1 Arthashastra

Arthashastra (in Sanskrit: "The Science of Material Gain") is attributed to Kautilya (also known as Chanakya), who reportedly was chief minister to the emperor Chandragupta (c. 300 BCE), the founder of the Mauryan dynasty. The manuscript remained prominent till the twelfth century, when it disappeared. It was rediscovered in 1904 by R. Shamasastry, who published it in 1909, though the English translation was published in 1915. The text incorporates ancient Indian wisdom and includes ancient economic and cultural details on agriculture, mineralogy, mining and metals, animal husbandry, medicine, forests, and wildlife. The manuscript deals with the way the state's economy is organized, how taxation should be arranged and distributed, how ministers should be chosen and how war should be conducted, and so on. Kautilya's political vision had a heavy influence on Chandragupta, the first Indian ruler who unified Northern India under a single political unit for the first time in history. Even today, the Arthashastra is the number one classic of diplomacy in India and, within this category, it is one of the most complete works of antiquity.

Sources:

1. Artha-shastra *Encyclopaedia Britannica* Retrieved from https://www.britannica.com (Accessed on January 17, 2016).
2. Cristian Violatti, *Ancient History Encyclopaedia* Retrieved from https://www.ancient.eu (Accessed on January 19, 2019).

GDP was US$74,250 million, which was around 22% of world GDP. India's population during 1 A.D. was around 5.5 crore and per capita income was around US$ 450. During 1600 A.D. India's population was 13.5 crore and per capita income was US $550. India's per capita GDP in 1600 A.D. was higher than that of the United States ($400) and many other nations. India's total GDP at the arrival of British (around 1600 A.D.) was US$74,250 million and that of Britain was US$6,007 million.[1]

Indian Economy During British Times

Before the advent of British, all Muslim conquerors had overthrown Indian political powers but made no basic changes in the country's economic structure; rather gradually they became the part of Indian society. However, the British economic policy made a huge transformation from a self-sustaining Indian economy to dependent colonial economy for their interest.[2] The British connection with India started in 1600 with the creation of a monopoly trading company called as the East India Company.

The British impact on the Indian economy can be discussed in the following three different phases:

Early British Period: 1600–1757 A.D.

The East India Company had started as trading organization in India since 1600 covering eastern part. The East India Company traded in some selected pockets. Initially, the company had twofold purposes: (1) finding raw material for their factories, and (2) searching market of their manufactured product. Further, the company moved ahead to acquire administrative and political power. As a trading organization, it had brought huge precious metals particularly silver and gold to India and in place of that exported Indian cotton cloths, silk, saltpeter, spices, and other goods that commanded huge demand across the world markets. The East India Company earned a good profit from these transactions and this profit was also shared with Indian manufacturers and big producers, which helped for the company's interest. In this process, the company also provided a good market for Indian products. The company was given an authorization by the British crown to export gold and silver bullion and the coins of these metals worth £30,000 per annum in exchange for goods and services from India.

From Battle of Plassey till the Sepoy Mutiny: 1757–1857 A.D.

During the early phase of company rule, there was high demand for Indian products across the world and pouring of bullions into India created a sense of jealousness among British traders. Indian products like silk, cotton, drugs, and spices were in high demand in the European market at a much higher price and the East India Company earned a considerable profit from the sale of such products in Britain. The products were exchanged for bullion. The danger of drain of treasure from the West became a nightmare for British and they termed India "sink of precious metals." In 1772, Lord Clive mentioned in his speech at House of Commons that "silver of the West and the gold of the East have for many years been pouring into that country and goods only have been sent out in return."[3] The Battle of Plassey marks a watershed as far as colonial rule in India is concerned. The Battle of Plassey was fought on June 23, 1757, at Plassey on the banks of Hooghly river in West Bengal and marks the victory of British East India Company (led by Robert Clive) over Nawab of Bengal Siraj-ud-Daulah and his French allies. Battle of Plassey paved the way for British entry into India. Thereafter, the company had acquired both economic and political power in Bengal province. That was detrimental not only for revenue collection but also to make the authoritative trade policy. This change had long-term impact on Indian farmers and traders. This period was characterized by direct plunder by East India Company under the guise of trade, exploitative land revenue policy, and corrupt and unscrupulous officers of the company making large fortunes.

British Crown Period: 1858–1947 A.D.

Following the Great Sepoy Mutiny of 1857, which is also hailed as "First war of Independence" the British crown dissolved the company and the governance of India was taken over by the British crown in 1858. The Sepoy Mutiny witnessed a larger presence of British recruits in India. There were only 31,000 British in India in 1805 (of which 22,000 were in the army and 2,000 in civil government). The number increased substantially after the mutiny and in 1931, there were 168,000 British in India. The higher ranks of the administration remained almost entirely British until the 1920s who were appointed through Indian Civil Services exam held in the United Kingdom. There was a whole hierarchy of separate bureaucracy in which the higher ranks were British, that is, the revenue, justice, police, education, medical, public works, engineering, postal and railway services, and the provincial civil services. This period was characterized by colonial exploitation through industrial and financial capital. Agriculture was commercialized, import of machine-made goods from England experienced a steep rise and heavy investments were made in plantation sectors and railways.

Impact of Colonial Rule in India

The economic policies were meant to serve the interests of the East India Company and later the British Empire. Following are the implications of British rule on India:

Impact on GDP

According to the estimates made by Angus Maddison, India's GDP was US$ 74,250 and per capita income was US$550 in 1600 A.D. In India, the first estimates of national income was made by Dadabhai Naoroji for the year 1867–1868 in his book "Poverty and Un-British Rule in India." According to him, the national income of British India was ₹340 crore and per capita income was ₹20 per annum at current prices. At 1948–1949 prices, this comes at ₹142 per annum. Other economists of time also made estimates about India's national income and results of all are almost the same. Atkinson measured India's per capita income at ₹172 and Horne measured at ₹158 for the years 1875 and 1891, respectively, at 1948–1949 prices.* Curzon estimated per capita income at ₹148 for the years 1902 at 1948–1949 prices.** However, by 1947, the per capita income increased to ₹250 per annum. India's share in the world economy was 23% in 1600 A.D. and by the time British departed in 1947, it had dropped to just 3%. Similarly, India constituted 33% of world exports in 1600 but the share declined to less than 3% in 1947. India was governed for the benefits of Britain (Table 9.1). Britain's rise for 200 years was financed by its depredations in India.[4]

TABLE 9.1 India: National Income, Per Capita Income and Population Since 1 A.D.

Year	GDP (1990 International $)	Per Capita GDP (1990 International $)	Population of India
1 A.D.	$33,750 million	$450	5.5 crore
1000 A.D.	$33,750 million	$450	7.5 crore
1600 A.D.	$74,250 million	$550	13.5 crore
1820 A.D.	$111,417 million	$533	20.9 crore
1870 A.D.	$134,882 million	$533	25.3 crore
1913 A.D.	$204,241 million	$673	30.4 crore
1950 A.D.	$222,222 million	$619	35.9 crore

Source: Tabulated by author from Maddison, A. (2001). The world economy: A millennial perspective. Development Centre Studies, OECD.Paris.

Impact on Agriculture

At the advent of British rule, there is a general consensus that the Indian economy was stable or in a state of equilibrium, often called self-sufficient village economy. Village produce were consumed and exchanged for other requirements at a local level. Therefore, the subsistence nature of agricultural production left out the scope of growth and innovation. Till late seventeenth century, the principal produce were wheat, rice, maize, millet, and tobacco apart from cash crops in the subcontinent, including high-quality cotton. From eighteenth century onward, India's per head

*At current prices, the per capita income was ₹24 and ₹28 per annum.

**At current prices, the per capita income was ₹30 per annum.

agricultural output turned lower than that of China and Japan, which was insufficient to fulfill the needs of our population. The British transformed the structure of Indian agriculture and made it weaker through land revenue policy and commercialization of agriculture. Let us discuss them.

Land Revenue Policy and Land Settlements

To conquer the vast territory of India, the British needed money and contacts. They also needed money for trade, projects of the company as well as for running the administration. Therefore, they carried out a number of land revenue experiments. Lord Cornwallis introduced the Permanent Settlement in Bengal and Bihar in 1793. Under this, Landlords or Zamindars were required to deposit a fixed amount of land revenue of £3,400,000 with the government. In return, they were recognized as hereditary owners of the land. It made British financially secured as now they knew in advance as to how much revenue was coming in from the State. The new class of Zamindars that emerged became their political allies. They supported the British in times of need and acted as a buffer between them and the peasants. In 1822, the British introduced the Mahalwari Settlement in the North-Western Provinces, Punjab, the Ganga Valley, and parts of Central India. It was the duty of village headman or Mahalwar to collect land revenue and submit to the government. The Ryotwari Settlement was introduced at the beginning of the nineteenth century in many parts of Bombay and Madras Presidencies. Here, the land revenue was imposed directly on the riots, the individual cultivators, who actually worked on the land.

Commercialization of Indian Agriculture

Another major economic impact of the British policies in India was the transformation of Indian agriculture from food grain production to commercial crop production, termed as commercialization of agriculture. Agriculture has been to some extent commercialized since ancient and medieval times but the vast scale commercialization took place after 1857. A number of factors were responsible for the commercialization of agriculture in India.[5] First, the expanding rail and road network ensured that surplus crop could be transported to areas of shortage. In addition, the development of port facilities also meant that crop could be exported. Second, the Suez Canal reduced travel time between London and India by 36 days with a distance reduction of 3,000 miles. Third, steamships also reduced travel time and storage constraints in comparison with sail-based ships. Fourth, the American Civil War reduced the supply of cotton to the British who in turn transferred their demands to Indian farmers. Fifth, the introduction of money facilitated trade, rent, and tax collection, and replaced what had been a barter economy.

The impact of the commercialization of Indian agriculture was that crop production became more specialized and localized in certain regions as sugarcane was cultivated in the Deccan, jute in Bengal, wheat in the Punjab, and cotton in Berar. British exhorted production of a large number of commercial crops such as tea, coffee, indigo, opium, cotton, jute, sugarcane, and oilseed with different intentions. For example, the market for opium was strictly controlled by British traders and the Indian opium was used to balance the trade of Chinese tea with Britain in the latter's favor. This did not leave much scope for Indian producers to reap profit. Indian farmers were forced to produce indigo on 3/20th part of their land which was sent to England and used as a dyeing agent in the textile mills. The cultivation of Indigo left the land infertile for some years, which made farmers reluctant to grow it. In the tea plantations, ownership changed frequently and the workers on these plantations worked under a lot of hardships. Commercialization of agriculture further enhanced the speed of transfer of ownership of land thereby increasing the number of landless laborers. The size of landless laborers continuously increased from 8.2 million in 1871 to 1849 million in 1951. Commercialization of agriculture promoted a new class of merchants, traders, and middlemen who made peasants dependent on them and further exploited the situation. There was a decrease in food grain production due to frequent occurrence of famines.

Deindustrialization

India's share in world manufacturing output declined from 24.5% of in 1750 to 17.6% in 1830. But by 1880, the share reduced to just 2.8%. According to Clingingsmith and Williamson India deindustrialized between 1760 and 1860, and two main periods, with very different deindustrialization causes, distinguishes that century. The first epoch ran from about 1760–1810 and was a direct result of the poor climatic conditions and an indirect result of the dissolution of the Mughal Empire. The deterioration in climatic conditions lowered agricultural productivity, raised grain prices, and thus increased nominal wages of Indian manufacturing, like textiles, lowering India's competitiveness with England and other world textile producers. During the second epoch, running from about 1810–1860, advance in productivity resulting from the adoption of the factory system due to industrial revolution brought down relative prices of British textiles. The transport revolution further lowered the price of European textile imports causing a death blow to Indian handlooms. By 1860, India had transformed from being a net exporter to a net importer of textiles. India's deindustrialization was over by the late nineteenth century.[6]

Decay of Local Industry and Crafts

Indian industry at the advent of British can be categorized in the following areas and vocations: (1) The first category includes arts and crafts activities pursued by farmers during free time and off seasons like hand spinning and weaving, jaggery making, flour grinding, rice pounding, cotton ginning, rope making, mat weaving, basket making, sericulture, tobacco making, etc. (2) The second category includes subsistence activities like blacksmith, carpenter, weaver, oil presser, potter, etc. (3) The third category pertains to village industries and comprises carpet weaving of Mirzapur and Benaras, silk weaving, metalworks, conch shell, bangles, lungis, sarees, embroidery cloths of specific places, etc. (4) The fourth category relates to urban arts and crafts and comprises textiles handicrafts, silks, woolen cloths, metal works, paper making, bangle making, etc. While at the village level, the industry was flexibly organized under individual artisan level, in cities it was organized along the lines of guilds.

After the Battle of Plassey in 1757, the British East India company occupied political power and made various economic interventions that affected the growth of the Indian Industry. These interventions included the demise of local royal dynasties and their replacement by British rule, the peace and relative security brought by British rule, the adoption of Western lifestyle by Indians and the emergence of machine manufactured goods. The end of royal families meant that there was no longer the same level of demand for traditionally produced goods, and peace and security meant that traditional weapons of warfare were no longer required.[7] The main aim of the British was to transform India into a consumer of British goods. As a result, textiles, metal-works, glass, and paper industries were soon out of work. By 1813, the Indian handicrafts had lost both their domestic and foreign markets.

The Demise of Textile Industry and Trade

Indian handloom enjoyed a big reputation in the world markets since ancient times. Indian textiles such as cotton, linen, silk, and wool were in great demand in the markets of Asia, Africa, and Europe. The industrialization of Europe, however, reversed the direction of the textile trade between Britain and India. British devised a distorted trade policy whereby English products were imported in India duty-free and Indian exports were subjected to export duty in India as well as heavy import duties in Britain. The massive import of machine-made clothes from mechanical looms in England led to the ruin of Indian handicraft industries as the British goods were sold at a much cheaper price. Besides, under the pressure of its industrialists, British government often imposed a protective tariff on Indian textiles. Consequently, within a short span of time, India from being an exporter of clothes became an exporter of raw cotton and an importer of British clothes. This reversal made a huge impact on the Indian handloom weaving industry causing its virtual collapse, generation of huge unemployment for a large community of weavers and their migration to rural areas as agricultural laborers. This, in turn, caused an increased burden on the rural economy and livelihood.

Attempts of Industrialization During Colonial Period

The first textile mills were started in the 1850s by Indian capitalists who had made their money trading with the British and had acquired education in English. The first jute mill was built in 1854 and the industry expanded rapidly in the vicinity of Calcutta. Coal mining, mainly in Bengal, was another industry, which achieved significance. Its output, which by 1914 had reached 15.7 million tonnes, largely met the demands of the Indian railways. In 1911, the first Indian steel mill was built by the Tata Company at Jamshedpur, Bihar. Indian firms in industry, insurance, and banking were given a boost from 1905 onwards by the Swadeshi movement, which was a nationalist boycott of British goods in favor of Indian enterprise.[8] But the government's role was non-cooperative. To discourage indigenous textile production, the excise duty of 5% was levied on textile manufacturing. Tata wanted to start Iron and steel plant in the 1880s but permission was not granted.

British interests were of several kinds. At first, the main purpose was to achieve a monopolistic trading position. Later, it was felt that a regime of free trade would make India a major market for British goods and a source of raw materials, but British capitalists who invested in India, or who sold banking or shipping service there, continued effectively to enjoy monopolistic privileges. India also provided interesting and lucrative employment for a sizeable portion of the British upper middle class, and the remittances they sent home made an appreciable contribution to Britain's balance of payments and capacity to save. Finally, control planning of India was a key element in the world power structure, in terms of geography, logistics, and military manpower. They introduced some British concepts of property but did not push them too far when they met vested interests. The British were not averse to Indian economic development if it increased their markets but refused to help in areas where they felt there was a conflict with their own economic interests or political security. Hence, they refused to give protection to the Indian textile industry until its main competitor became Japan rather than Manchester.[9]

Transport and Communication

India's first railway line was the Red Hill Railroad line, Madras opened in 1837 and was used for the carriage of granite stone, whereas, the first passenger railway line ran from Bombay to Thane in 1853. India's first telegraphic line from Calcutta to Agra and postal service was also opened in 1853. The main purpose for the development of railways was connecting the raw material producing areas with the exporting ports and to facilitate the movement of British goods to different parts of the country. This opened the avenue for British bankers and investors to invest surplus wealth and material in the construction of railways. Railways benefited the British capitalists in two important ways. First, it made trading in commodities much easier and profitable by connecting the internal markets with the ports. Secondly, the rail engines, coaches, and the capital input for building of rail lines came from Britain. The British capitalists who invested in railways were also guaranteed a minimum profit of 5% by the government. These companies were also given free land with a lease of 99 years. Although the railways were set up for the advantage of British trade, they also played an important role in the national awakening of the country. The extensive transport network and improved education brought people and ideas closer.[10]

English Education and New Westernized Elite

From the 1820s to the 1850s, the British demonstrated a strong urge to change Indian social institutions, and to Westernize India. One of the most significant things the British did to Westernize India was to introduce a modified version of English education. Macaulay's 1835 Minute on Education had a decisive impact on British educational policy and is a classic example of a Western approach to subjugate Indian civilization. In the words of Macaulay—*"It is impossible for us, with our limited means to attempt to educate the body of the people. We must at present do our best to form a class who may be interpreters between us and the millions whom we govern; a class of persons, Indian in blood and colour, but English in taste, in opinions, in morals, and in intellect.*[11] The English education did little to promote analytic capacity or independent thinking and produced a group of graduates with a half-baked knowledge of English but sufficiently Westernized to be alienated from their own culture.

Education for girls was almost totally ignored throughout the nineteenth century. As a result, the great mass of the population had no access to education and, at independence in 1947, 88% of Indians were illiterate. Education could have played a major role in encouraging social mobility, eliminating religious superstition, increasing productivity, and uplifting the status of women. Instead, it was used to turn tiny elite into imitating Englishmen and a somewhat bigger group into government clerks. They often acted as the agents and intermediaries of the British traders and thus made huge fortunes. The new landed aristocracy, which came into being after the introduction of Permanent Settlement, also formed a part of this new class. In urban areas, new classes emerged under British rule, that is, industrial capitalists and a new bourgeoisie of bureaucrats, lawyers, doctors, teachers, and journalists, whose social position was due to education and training rather than heredity.

Drain of Wealth

The economic drain has been envisaged as a portion of the national income of India, which was not available for capital formation or consumption by its own people rather drained away to Britain for political reasons. This drain was the unilateral transfer of wealth from India to Britain without getting an adequate economic, commercial, and material return. A number of British intellectuals have provided insights into the drain of wealth. Alexandor Dow, a military personnel, of the East India Company, was the first to estimate the annual drain from Bengal to Great Britain for about £1,477,500 including company's revenue and exports. In the words of Maddison,

> *The first generation of British rulers was rapacious. Clive took quarter of a million pounds for himself as well as a Jagir worth £27,000 a year. British salaries were high: the Viceroy received £25,000 a year, and governors £10,000. The starting salary in the engineering service was £420 a year or about sixty times the average income of the Indian labor force. Under the rule of the East India Company, official transfers to the UK rose gradually until they reached about £3.5 million in 1856, the year before the mutiny. In addition, there were private remittances.*[12]

Later on, Edmund Burke in 1783 developed this theory and explained the mechanism of economic drain in Indian situation and increasing poverty. In 1776, Philip Francis analyzed the drain economy and divided it into four major streams—firstly was the East India Company's Investment, secondly remittance to other presidencies, thirdly the transfer of private income, and fourthly, the transfer of income from private trade or investment.[13]

Later in nineteenth century, Indian intellectuals like Dadabhai Naoroji, M.G. Ranade, G.V. Joshi, Romesh Chandra Dutt, and few others also realized the impact of British rule as exploitative process and transfer of Indian economy toward Britain. Before this period, India's elite class had a positive opinion and assumed British rule as a development actor in India. But the British's exploitative policies changed this perception. Many nationalists had started reviewing such policies and the idea of economic drain had evolved to show how scrupulously the British policies were draining India and reducing it to poverty. Dadabhai Naoroji hailed as "Grand old man of India" and "Father of Indian Nationalism" put forward the "drain of wealth" theory in his book "Poverty and Un-British Rule in India." According to his estimates, the drain amounted to £50 crore from 1835–1872. R.C. Dutt elaborated drain of wealth in his book "the economic history of India." According to him "*If manufactures were crippled, agriculture overtaxed, and a third of the revenue remitted out of the country, any nation on earth would suffer from permanent poverty and recurring famines.*"[14] C.N. Vakil estimated drain of wealth from 1834–1939 worth £85 crores.[15] William Digby estimated drain of wealth between Battle of Plassey and Battle of Waterloo* in the range of £50–100 crores.[16] According to estimates by K.T. Shah and K.J. Khambata, during the early decades of twentieth century, the England appropriated nearly 10% of India's GDP annually.

During the period of direct British rule from 1858–1947, official transfers of funds to the United Kingdom by the colonial government were called the "Home Charges." Home charges included dividends to the shareholders of East India Company; interest on loans raised by Government of India in England; expenditure on British army stationed in India; expenditure on the conveyance of British army wherever it was sent to India; pensions, annuities, etc., of retired British officers; payment of guaranteed interest to railway companies; and salaries of secretary of state for India and his staff. As per estimates of Dadabhai Naoroji, from 1829–1865, India paid to Britain £10 crores as home charges. By the 1930s these home charges were in the range of £40–50 million a year.[17]

---

* The Battle of Waterloo was fought in 18 June 1815, near Waterloo in Belgium, where French Army (under the leadership of Napoleon Bonaparte) was defeated by two of the armies of the Seventh Coalition: a British-led allied army and Prussian army. The battle marked the end of Napoleon's wars and ended Napoleon's rule as Emperor of France.

TABLE 9.2 Comparative Macroeconomic Performance of India and Britain, 1600–1947

	1600 A.D.	1947 A.D.
Per Capita GDP (1990 int. Dollars)		
India	550	618
The United Kingdom	974	6,361
Population		
India	13.5 crore	41.4* crore
United Kingdom	61. 7 lakh	4.95 crore
GDP (Million 1990 int. Dollars)		
India	74,250	255,852
United Kingdom	6,007	314,969

*Including Pakistan.

Source: Tabulated by author from Maddison, A. (2001). The world economy: A millennial perspective. Development Centre Studies, OECD.Paris.

Table 9.2 reflects how Britain prospered at the cost of India's depredation. India's per capita income from 1600–1947 increased by 12%, whereas the increase for Britain for the same period was 553%. India's total GDP during 1600–1947 increased by 2.44 times, but for Britain the rise was 52 times.

Summary

1. Colonialism signifies the practice of acquiring complete or limited political control over another country, inhabiting it with settlers, and exploiting it economically. India's total GDP during 1 A.D. was US$33,750 million (at 1990 prices) and constituted around 32% of world GDP. In 1600 A.D., India's GDP was US$ 74,250 million, which was around 22% of world GDP and at this time India was the world's second largest economy after China.
2. The British impact on the Indian economy can be discussed in three different phases: Early British Period: from 1600–1757 A.D., from 1757–1857 AD, and British Crown Period: 1858 onward. The first period was marked by establishment of the East India Company in 1600 A.D. The company functioned with twofold purposes: getting raw material for their factories and searching market of their manufactured product. The second period began with the Battle of Plassey that marks a watershed as far as a colonial rule in India is concerned. This period was characterized by direct plunder by East India Company under the guise of trade, exploitative land revenue policy, and corrupt and unscrupulous officers of the company making large fortunes. The third period started when the British crushed the Sepoy Mutiny in 1857. The British crown dissolved the company and took over governance of India in its own hand. This period was characterized by colonial exploitation through de-industrialization, commercialization of agriculture, drain of wealth, and Westernizing Indian education system.
3. By the time British left, India had turned into an impoverished economy. India's share in the world GDP had declined from 23% in 1600 A.D. to 3% in 1947. India's share of world exports had also decreased from 33 to 3% during the same period. Land revenue policy of British was meant to exploit Indian peasantry. British introduced Zamindari system, Mahalwari system, and Ryotwari system to extract exorbitant land revenue from the farmers. Indian agriculture was also commercialized as farmers were lured as well as forced to produce for British factories. Transportation, trade policies, development of ports, and opening of Suez Canal sped up the process of commercialization. Commercialization produced a new class of middlemen, increased the occurrence of famines and turned farmers into landless laborers. The process of deindustrialization had started from the mid of 18th century. The fall of Mughal Empire, the decline of Indian agriculture, rise in nominal wages and drop in the competitiveness of Indian textile and an increase in transport facilities, all resulted into deindustrialization. The trade policy that was highly unfavorable for India also aided into the reduction of trade and exacerbated deindustrialization. Though some sort of industrialization took place during British times but British support was governed by their selfish interest rather than their intention to help India. The transportation system developed by the British was also characterized with the agenda to plunder India. Railways helped British to transit goods from hinterlands to ports and vice versa. It also helped British investors to earn handsome returns on their capital invested for the construction and development of Railway infrastructure. The main purpose of introducing Western education to India was to produce a group of Indians with a half-baked knowledge of English, but sufficiently Westernized to be alienated from their own culture. The drain of wealth was unilateral transfer of wealth from India to Britain without getting an adequate economic, commercial, and material return. It took place in the form of remittances, home charges, and the transfer of income from private trade or investment, etc. Many British thinkers and Indian nationalists including Dadabhai Naoroji, R.C. Dutt, and C.N. Vakil among many others estimated drain of wealth from India to Britain.

Endnotes

1. Maddison, A. (2001). The world economy: A millennial perspective. Development Centre Studies, OECD.Paris.
2. Chandra, B. (1988). India's struggle for independence, 1857–1947. New Delhi, India: Viking.
3. Roy, R.D. (1987). Some aspects of the economic drain from India during the British Rule. *Social Scientist 15* (3) 39–47.
4. Shashi, T. (2016). An era of darkness: The British Empire in India. New Delhi: Aleph Book Company.

5. Ramesh, S. (2017). China's lessons for India: Volume I. DOI. Retrieved from https://doi.org (accessed on April 1, 2019).
6. Clingingsmith, D. & Williamson, J.G. (2008). Deindustrialization in 18th and 19th century India: Mughal decline, climate shocks and British Industrial Ascent. *Explorations in Economic History* 45 (3), 209–234.
7. Ramesh, S. (2017). China's lessons for India: Volume I. DOI. Retrieved from https://doi.org (accessed on April 1, 2019).
8. Maddison, A. (2013). The economic and social impact of colonial rule in India. Routledge.
9. Maddison, A. (2013). The economic and social impact of colonial rule in India. Routledge.
10. Dhapali, B. & Kaur, A. (2015). Railway development in colonial Punjab: Social and cultural assimilation. *International Journal of Social Science and Humanities Research (3) 80-84.*
11. Excerpts taken from Edwardes, M. (1967). British India 1772–1947. London: Sidgwick and Jackson.
12. Maddison, A. (2013). *The economic and social impact of colonial rule in India*. Routledge.
13. Mishra, B., & Rastogi, S. (2017). *Colonial deindustrialisation of India: A review of Drain Theory*. South Asian Survey.
14. Dutt, R.C. (Reprint 1989). The economic history of India, Vol. II. Government of India, Publication division.
15. Vakil, C.N. (1924). Financial developments in modern India, 1860–1924, Chapter 11. Department of Economics, University of Bombay.
16. Digby, W. (1885). India for the Indians—and for England. London: Talbot Brothers.
17. Maddison, A. (2013). The economic and social impact of colonial rule in India. Routledge.

CHAPTER 10

INDIAN AGRICULTURE: PRODUCTIVITY, LAND REFORMS, AND LIVESTOCK

Earth is here so kind, that just tickle her with a hoe and she laughs with a harvest.

—Douglas Jerrold

INTRODUCTION

Indian agriculture was the most advanced agriculture before the conquest by British. In the autonomous villages, agriculture was no mere an economic activity but the basic life activity of the people. Its major function, if an integrated life activity can at all be analyzed in terms of functions, was to fulfill their life needs and the needs of the government, market and industry were all secondary to that major function. However, the continuous exploitation by British in one form or other not only destroyed this unique interdependent rural practice but made life of Indian peasantry full of misery.* By the time British left in 1947, Indian agriculture was in dilapidated condition. The major task before the newly elected government was to bring back those glorious days of Indian agriculture. In the decades following independence, the Indian agriculture went through the different phases of structural transformation that affected the rural peasantry in one way or other.

The chapter will be covering the following issues:

- Role and importance of Indian agriculture;
- Production and productivity trends in Indian agriculture;
- Land reforms and their appraisal;
- Livestock sector in India.

ROLE AND IMPORTANCE OF INDIAN AGRICULTURE

Contribution in GDP

Agriculture sector of India comprises four sub-sectors namely crops, livestock, forestry & logging and fishing & aquaculture. The share of agriculture, forestry & fishing sector in GVA has seen a steady decrease over the years from 17.8% in 2012–2013 to 15.7% in 2021–22. (Table 10.1). For the year 2019–20, the share of crops, livestock, forestry & logging and fishing & aquaculture in country's GVA is 10.7, 5.2, 1.3 and 1.2% respectively.

---

* For detailed discussion on this theme, please see the chapter 9 'India Economy during pre-independence period'.

TABLE 10.1 Trends in Agricultural Share and Growth Rate (at Constant Prices, Base Year 2011–2012)

Year	Share in GVA	Growth Rate of Agriculture
2011–2012	18.5	–
2012–2013	17.8	1.5
2013–2014	17.8	5.6
2014–2015	16.5	−0.2
2015–2016	15.4	0.6
2016–2017	15.2	6.3
2017–2018	14.9	5
2018–2019	14.4	2.9
2019–2020	14.8	4.3
2020–2021	16.3	3.6
2021–2022	15.67	3.9
2022–2023	15.34	4.7
2023–2024	14.45	0.7

Source: (1) RBI Handbook of Statistics, 2017–2018, p.7. (2) Economic Survey, Ministry of Finance, Govt. of India. 2020–2021 and 2021–22..

Within the four sub-sectors, crops* constitute nearly 60% of agriculture gross value added (GVA) and livestock constitutes nearly 25% of agriculture GVA. The share of livestock in GVA in agriculture has been rising gradually, whereas the share of crop sector in GVA has been falling.

With economic progress, the share of agriculture in national income falls. In all developed nations, the share of agriculture in GDP has become miniscule. It is not because agriculture production has not increased but only due to the much increase in relative share of industry and services. In India too, agriculture share in GDP is receding continuously since independence from more than 50% during 1951 to less than 16% at present (Table 10.1). The declining share of agriculture does not mean that the absolute value of agriculture is dropping. It only means that the overall size of the economy is growing. If we look at the production figures of various agricultural crops, they have not only registered a significant increase but also placed India amongst the ranks of largest producers (Table 10.2).

Indian planners have aimed at 4% of annual agriculture growth since the mid-1980s but many exogenous and endogenous factors come in between the attainment of the desired growth rate (Table 10.1). There are sharp fluctuations in the growth rate in agriculture and hence income of the farmers has not increased substantially or stabilized over the period of time.

*Crops include food grains, cash crops, and horticulture crops. In India, the agricultural crop year is from July to June and is divided into two main seasons—(1) Kharif and (2) Rabi based on the monsoon. The Kharif cropping season is from July to October (during the south-west monsoon) and the Rabi cropping season is from October to March (winter). The crops grown between March and June are summer crops. Pakistan and Bangladesh are two other countries that are using the term "Kharif" and "Rabi" to describe about their cropping patterns. The terms "Kharif" and "Rabi" originate from Arabic language where Kharif means autumn and Rabi means spring. Examples of Kharif crops are rice, maize, sorghum, pearl millet/bajra, finger millet/ragi (cereals), arhar (pulses), soyabean, groundnut (oilseeds), cotton, etc. The example of Rabi crops are wheat, barley, oats (cereals), chickpea/gram (pulses), linseed, mustard (oilseeds), etc.

TABLE 10.2 Leading Agriculture Export and Import Items 2022–23

Export		Import	
Commodity	**US $ Billion**	**Commodity**	**US $ Billion**
Rice	11.14	Vegetable oil	20.8
Marine Products	8.1	Fruits and vegetables	2.7
Meat, dairy & poultry products	4.03	Pulses	1.94
Spices	3.8	–	–
Rice (other than Basmati)	3.21	–	–

Source: RBI Handbook of Statistics, 2023.

BOX 10.1 Agriculture Export Policy 2018

Government announced Agriculture Export Policy 2018 with the vision, "Harness export potential of Indian agriculture, through suitable policy instruments, to make India global power in agriculture and raise farmers' income." Following are the objectives of the agriculture export policy:

- To double agricultural exports from present US$ 30+ billion to US$ 60+ billion by 2022 and reach US$ 100 billion in the next few years thereafter, with a stable trade policy regime.
- To diversify our export basket, destinations and boost high value and value-added agricultural exports including focus on perishables.
- To promote novel, indigenous, organic, ethnic, traditional, and nontraditional agri product exports.
- To provide an institutional mechanism for pursuing market access, tackling barriers, and deal with sanitary and phytosanitary issues.
- To strive to double India's share in world agri exports by integrating with global value chain at the earliest.
- Enable farmers to get benefit of export opportunities in overseas market.

Source: Cabinet approves Agriculture Export Policy, 2018, Press Information Bureau, December 06, 2018.

Agriculture Trade

The share of India's agricultural exports and imports in the world agriculture trade in 2015 were 2.26% and 1.74%, respectively. The share of agricultural exports in India's total exports is around 14% and share of agricultural imports in total imports is nearly 6%.[1] Rice, marine products and meat, dairy, and poultry products are the leading agricultural export items constituting nearly three-fourth of agricultural export revenue. India's leading import items are edible oil, pulses, and fruits and vegetables (Table 10.2). India is the world's largest importer of edible oil* and pulses.[2]

FDI in Agriculture

Agriculture has been opened up to the foreign investors in a limited manner. Government has recently allowed 100% FDI in the development and production of seeds and planting materials.

* Over 60% of total edible oil imports comprise palm oil and main exporter nation of palm oil to India is Malaysia.

In addition, 100% FDI is allowed for floriculture, horticulture, and cultivation of vegetables and mushrooms under controlled conditions. Also, 100% FDI is allowed in animal husbandry (including breeding of dogs), pisciculture, aquaculture, and services related to agro and allied sectors. Similarly, 100% FDI is allowed in the plantation sector namely tea, coffee, rubber, cardamom, palm oil tree, and olive oil tree. The food-processing sector of Agriculture has witnessed FDI equity inflow of US$ 4.99 billion during the period April 2014 to September 2021. [3]

Employment in Agriculture

Agriculture is the largest employment providing sector to the economy. As a country makes economic progress, the share of agriculture falls. For example, only 4% and 2% of population is dependent on agriculture in the United States and United Kingdom, respectively. In India too, the share of agriculture in total employment has come down from 73.9 in 1950–51 to 43.45% in 2019–20. Because of the failure of the industry and services to absorb the surplus manpower in agriculture, there is an urgent need to take up nonfarm rural livelihood initiatives at all India level. As per census 2011, out of total female main workers, 55% were agricultural laborers and 24% were cultivators. However, only 12.8% of the operational holdings were owned by women, which reflect the gender disparity in ownership of landholdings in agriculture. With growing rural to urban migration by men, there is "feminization" of the agricultural sector, with an increasing number of women in multiple roles as cultivators, entrepreneurs, and laborers. Globally, there is empirical evidence that women have a decisive role in ensuring food security and preserving local agro-biodiversity. Rural women are responsible for the integrated management and use of diverse natural resources to meet the daily household needs.[4]

Food Security

Food security encompasses three things: food availability, food accessibility, and food nutrition. India used to import wheat from the United States and Russia before the green revolution period. However, the surplus agriculture production in the country has produced the "food security cover" despite the increase in population size and growth rate. India's PDS system is the largest of its kind in the world through which government sells food grains to poor population at subsidized price. The success story of popular schemes like Antyodaya Anna Yojana, midday meal scheme, integrated child development service, and national food security scheme lies in the very fact that the country has sufficient food cover to meet the demand of its masses. Further, the increase in agriculture production has not only provided the safety cushion to large mass of population but has also made India net exporter in cereals and other agricultural items.

Backward and Forward Linkages

Agriculture generates huge backward and forward linkages. A forward linkage is created when investment in a particular project encourages investment in subsequent stages of production. For example, agriculture provides raw materials to various industries of national importance, viz. sugar, jute, cotton textile, and tea and spices industries. A backward linkage is created when a project encourages investment in facilities that enable the project to succeed. For example, agriculture generates demand for many items such as fertilizers, pesticides, seeds, and irrigation projects. Apart from such linkages, agriculture also generates demand for industrial goods and services and thus provides boost to overall economy.

Capital Formation in Agriculture

Gross Capital Formation (GCF) in agriculture takes place both in the form of public and private investment. Public investment or government investment is crucial for the development in agriculture assets and raising the productivity and growth of rural economy. Public investment in agriculture includes construction of canals; development of rural roads; improvement of land and irrigation works; R&D, power, and construction of warehouses.[5] The public GCF as a proportion of GVA in Agriculture is around 3% which is quite low. In fact, the public GCF in agriculture has revealed a declining trend during 1991 to 2014 and exhibited a rising trend in the recent years. It must be noted that a decline in public investment in agriculture has potential negative impact on agriculture growth over the longer term. A 10% decrease in public investment leads to 2.4% annual reduction in agriculture GDP growth.[6]

Agriculture and Poverty Reduction

Importance of agriculture lies in the fact that nearly 70% of population in India lives in rural areas and more than 45% of workforce thrives on it. According to world development report 2008, 1% growth in agriculture is at least two or three times more effective in reducing poverty than the same growth coming from non-agriculture sectors. But given that India is still home to the largest number of poor and malnourished people in the world, a high priority to agriculture will achieve the goals of reducing poverty and malnutrition as well as achieving inclusive growth. It is in these lines that prime minister has given the vision to double farmers' income by the year 2022 (Box 10.2).

BOX 10.2 Doubling Farmers' Income by 2022

The Prime Minister has set a target before the country to double farmers' income by 2022. To achieve this target he has also advocated a seven-point strategy. These are:

1. Special focus on irrigation with sufficient budget, with the aim of "Per Drop More Crop."
2. Provision of quality seeds and nutrients based on soil health of each field.
3. Large investments in Warehousing and Cold Chains to prevent post-harvest crop losses.
4. Promotion of value addition through food processing.
5. Creation of a National Farm Market, removing distortions, and e-platform across 585 stations.
6. Introduction of a New Crop Insurance Scheme to mitigate risks at affordable cost.
7. Promotion of ancillary activities like poultry, beekeeping, and fisheries.

Source: Annual Report, 2017–2018, Department of Agriculture, Cooperation & Farmers Welfare, Govt of India.

Changing Cropping Pattern

The cropping pattern signifies the proportion of area under different crops at a point of time, changes in this distribution over a period of time, and factors determining this change in distribution. The cropping pattern of a country is determined by natural factors like soil type, rainfall and climate conditions, and technological factors. In India, food grains are grown on nearly 75% of gross cropped area. Rice is grown on nearly on 34% of total area followed by wheat, pulses, and coarse cereals which are grown on 24, 23, and 18% of gross cropped area, respectively. In India, the cropping pattern has exhibited following trends: First, due to the adoption of high yield variety (HYV) seed technology, area under wheat and rice has increased since independence but the area under wheat has increased three times, that is, from 10 million hectares in 1950–1951 to 31 million hectares in 2017–2018. Second, area under pulses and coarse grains has considerably shrunk, mainly due to less value addition as compared to other crops. Third, area under cotton, sugarcane, oilseed, and other plantation crops like tea, coffee, potato, and rubber has increased but decreased for jute and mesta.[7]

Agricultural Production and Productivity Trends: Pre-reform Period

Agriculture performance can be discussed in terms of production and productivity. Production indicates the volume of output, whereas productivity is the output generated from the resources employed on a given piece of land.* The performance of Indian agriculture in terms of both production and productivity during the pre-reform period can be characterized by three distinct phases:

First Phase: 1949–1950 to 1964–1965

Second Phase: 1967–1968 to 1980–1981

Third Phase: 1980–1981 to 1989–1990

Phase I: 1949–1950 to 1964–1965

During the first phase, the growth rate of crop production was 3.2% which was not bad looking at the growth rate in the beginning of this century. Even the rate of growth of production of food grains was pretty high touching almost 3% per annum. However, for some significant rise in the yield per hectare for rice crop, most of other increase in production was attributable to the increase in area under the crops. The highest growth was noticed in wheat (4%) and this growth was largely contributed by growth in area under wheat. The growth rate in yield per hectare for all crops during this period was 1.3% (See Table 10.5). Despite all this, the gap between demand and supply persisted and the 1965 war with Pakistan exposed the vulnerability of India's food security system. It was the time when our late Prime Minister Shri Lal Bahadur Shastri gave the slogan of Jai Jawan-Jai Kisan.

* There are different measures of agriculture productivity and one such measure is crop yield, that is, amount of crop produced per unit or area of land production, generally, in kilograms per hectare of land.

TABLE 10.3 Trends in Agriculture Production (Million Tonnes)

Crop	1950–1951	1990–1991	2000–2001	2010–2011	2017–2018	2022–23***
Rice	20.6	74.3	85	96	112.91	135.5
Wheat	6.4	55.1	69.7	86.9	99.70	112.7
Coarse cereals	–	32.7	31.1	43.4	46.99	54.8
Pulses	8.4	14.3	11	18.2	25.23	27.5
Total foodgrains	50.8	176.4	196.8	244.5	284.83	330.54
Oilseeds	6.2	18.6	18.4	32.5	31.31	41
Sugarcane	57.1	241	296	342.4	376.91	494.23
Cotton*	3.0	9.8	9.5	33	34.89	34.35
Jute and Mesta**	3.3	9.2	10.5	10.6	10.14	9.49

Source: Economic Survey. Statistical Appendix. Department of Economic Affairs, Ministry of Finance, Govt. of India 2022–23 and Handbook of statistics on Indian Economy, RBI, 2022–23.

*In Lacs bales (Bales = 170 kg).

**In Lacs bales (Bales = 180 kg).

***Data as per 3rd advanced estimates

TABLE 10.4 Yield of Major Crops (Kilograms per Hectare)

Crop	1950–1951	1990–1991	2000–2001	2010–2011	2020–21	2022–23
Rice	668	1740	1,901	2,239	2,713	2,844
Wheat	655	2,281	2,708	2,989	3,464	3,543
Coarse Cereals	519*	900	1,027	1,531	2,146	2,321
Pulses	441	578	544	691	892	944
Total Food grains	552	1,380	1,626	1,930	2,386	2,500
Oilseeds	481	771	810	1193	1,254	1,362
Cotton	88	225	190	499	462	447
Jute	1,043	1,833	2,026	2,192	2,628	2,582

Source: Economic Survey. Statistical Appendix. Department of Economic Affairs, Ministry of Finance, Govt. of India. (2022–23) and Handbook of statistics on Indian Economy, RBI, 2022–23.

*Data pertains to the year 1961–1962

TABLE 10.5 All India Compounded Average Growth Rate in Production and Yield of Major Crops in India

Time Period	Growth Rate in Production	Growth Rate in Yield Per Hectare
Pre-Reform Period		
Phase I 1949–1950 to 1964–1965	3.2	1.2
Phase II 1967–1968 to 1980–1981	2.2	1.3
Phase III 1980–1981 to 1989–1990	3.2	2.6
Post-Reform Period		
Phase I 1990–1991 to 1999–2000	2.3	1.3
Phase II 2000–2001 to 2010–2011	3.2	2.1
Phase III 2010–2011 to 2017–2018	1.7	1.9

Source: (1) Economic survey. Department of Economic Affairs, Ministry of Finance, Govt. of India. 2018–2019, (2) Hand Book of Statistics, 2017–2018, RBI

Phase II: 1967–68 to 1980–81

During 1964 to 1967, India experienced severe drought-like situation. Government introduced new agricultural strategy, hailed as green revolution, in the mid-1960s by increasing the usage of modern technology and extension of irrigation facilities. During phase II, the rate of growth in production for all crops was 2.2% per annum, which is lower than the rate of growth of 3.2% during phase I. The contribution of annual average growth in yield per hectare during phase II was almost same at 1.3% to that of phase I. The growth rate in wheat production and yield at 5.7% and 2.6% growth rate was highest among all the crops.

Phase III: 1980–1981 to 1989–1990

For food grains as a whole as well as the two major food grain crops, viz. rice and wheat, the rates of growth in yield per hectare contributed much more to the increase in the production during the 1980s as compared to the 1970s. In fact, the period of mid-1980s is also called the golden period of Indian agriculture due to nearly 5% growth rate in agriculture production. The commercial crop production picked up during this phase and the rapid growth in area coupled with the growth in productivity was the reason for the growth in non-food grain sector. The period also started witnessing agriculture diversification as fruits and vegetable crops steadily gained ground at the cost of coarse cereals and pulses. The growth rate in crop production and yield was 3.2% and 2.6%, respectively. Oilseeds scored highest growth rate of 5.2% in production and ushered in the era of yellow revolution in the country.

Agricultural Production and Productivity Trends: Post-Reform Period

The post-reform period can be discussed in the following three different phases:

First Phase: 1990–1991 to 1999–2000
Second Phase: 2000–2001 to 2010–2011
Third Phase: 2010–2011 to 2017–2018

Phase I: 1990–1991 to 1999–2000

The acceleration witnessed in the rates of growth of production as well as productivity during the phase III of pre-reform period could not be maintained in the decade of 1990s. There were clear symptoms of a green revolution fatigue with a slowdown in the rates of growth. The growth rate in production and yield per hectare during the phase I of post reform period was 2.3 and 1.3% respectively. The deceleration in the growth rate was most marked in the rainfed areas, occurred in almost all the states and covered almost all the major subsectors, including those such as horticulture, livestock, and fisheries where growth was expected to be high.

Phase II: 2000–2001 to 2010–2011

Indian agriculture grew at a decent pace during this phase and India's crop sector experienced a growth rate of 3.2%. The productivity of the major crops was also higher than 1990s and the yield per hectare was recorded at 1.9%. The growth rate of agriculture at 4.1% per annum in the 11th plan (2007 to 2012) exceeded the targeted growth rate of 4% per annum for this plan. The high growth in production can be partially attributed mainly to the adoption of hybrid maize varieties and Bt cotton, which caused an enormous increase in the yield. The spread of green revolution to the eastern belt also yielded positive dividends.

Phase III: 2010–2011 to 2017–2018

The growth in production and yield per hectare during this phase was recorded at 1.7% and 1.9%, respectively. The growth target of 12th plan (2012–2017) was kept at 4% but the actual achievement was only 2.5%. During 2014–2015 and 2015–2016, Indian agriculture experienced a growth rate of −0.2 and 0.6 mainly due to failure of rainfall (see Table 10.1). If we remove these 2 years from the phase of 2010–2011 to 2017–2018, then the average growth rate is more than 4% which seems to be adequate.

Indian Agriculture and International Comparison

India is a typical example of higher production but low productivity. There is a number of agriculture items in which India is a leading producer or amongst the top producer nations. But in productivity, our agriculture performs very poorly and in many items agriculture productivity of the country is lower than that of world average productivity. China has nearly 18.5% of world area under paddy but produces 28% of paddy, whereas India has 27% of the world area under paddy but produces nearly 21% of paddy. In wheat too, China has 11% of the world area and produces 18% of world production (Table 10.6). However, in wheat, India uses 14% of the world area but produces 12% of total world production.[8]

TABLE 10.6 India's Position in World Agriculture Production in 2020

Item	Per Cent Share in the World	Next to	India's Rank
Total area (million hectares)	2.4	Russian Federation, Canada, United States, China, Brazil, Australia	7th
Arable land	11.20	United States	2nd
Total population	17.81	China	2nd
Rural Population	26.35		1st
Wheat	14.25	China	2nd
Rice (paddy)	24.25	China	2nd
Pulses	25.88		1st
Groundnut	18.50	China	2nd
Sugarcane	19.87	Brazil	2nd
Tea	20.16	China	2nd
Coffee (green)	2.96	Brazil, Vietnam, Colombia, Indonesia, Honduras, Ethiopia, Uganda, Peru	9th
Jute and jute-like fibers	48.42	Bangladesh	2nd
Cotton	24.43*	China	2nd
Tobacco unmanufactured	13.18	China, Brazil	3rd
Fruits and vegetables	11.89	China	2nd
Milk	22.99	–	1st

Source: Department of Agriculture, Cooperation & Farmers Welfare. "*Agriculture Statistics at a glance*," 2023, Govt. of India.

*Data is for 2017.

TABLE 10.7 World Productivity Levels, 2020 (Yield in Kg/hectare)

Paddy		Wheat		Pulses	
China	7,161	Germany	7,819	Canada	2,212
India	**4,138**	**India**	**3,440**	**India**	**743**
World average	4,717	World average	3,474	World average	986
Maize		**Sugarcane**		**Groundnut**	
United States	10,761	USA	85,400	United States	4,273
India	**3,006**	**India**	**80,497**	**India**	**2,063**
World average	5,815	World average	70,483	World average	1,767

Source: Department of Agriculture, Cooperation & Farmers Welfare. "*Agriculture Statistics at a glance*," 2023, Govt. of India.

India is world's largest producer, consumer, and importer of pulses but in terms of productivity it is just one-third of Canada. India's position in many agriculture products is either first or second. The major reason is the arable land that is next only to United States and because agriculture is still practiced at large scale in the rural belts of India. But it is the lower productivity of Indian agriculture that is a matter of concern for both farmers and policymakers. It may be noticed that India's productivity is lesser than even the world average except in the case of sugarcane (Table 10.7).

Causes of Low Productivity of Indian Agriculture

Small Size of Landholdings

There are five main categories of landholdings: (1) marginal landholdings (<1 hectare), (2) small landholdings (1 to 2 hectares), (3) semi-medium landholdings (2 to 4 hectares), (4) medium landholdings (4 to 10 hectares), and (5) large landholdings (10 hectares and above). The average size of landholding in India is 1.15 hectares, which is far below the developed countries of the world. In India, marginal landholdings constitute 67% of total and small landholdings constitute 18% of total landholdings. Together small and marginal landholdings makeup 85% of total landholdings in the country but account for nearly 45% of land area under agriculture.[9] This is a well-established fact that smaller the land size, lesser the productivity and vice versa. It is because small land size makes mechanized agriculture difficult and sometimes leads to wastage of land.* The result of situation assessment survey (SAS) of farmers conducted in 2013 revealed that positive net income accrues only to the farmers with landholding of more than 1 hectare. The major reason for smaller landholdings is land fragmentation that takes place due to laws of inheritance, pressure of population on land, decline in joint family system, farmers' indebtedness that forces them to sell the pieces of land, etc.

* For example, in Punjab 6% of land is wasted because cultivation is not possible due to smaller land size.

Population Pressure on Land

Heavy pressure of population causes low land man ratio and adversely affects agriculture productivity. In 1901, 163 million people were dependent on agriculture. In 2011, about 263 million workers, or three-fourth of the rural working population was employed in agriculture. Heavy pressure of population has led to subdivision and fragmentation of land holdings and thus reduced per capita cultivable land and productivity of land.

Inadequate Irrigation Facilities

Irrigation and productivity go hand in hand. In India, only 50% of gross cropped area is under irrigation and rest of the area is rain fed. Even more than 80% of rainfall occurs in the 3 months, June, July, and August, which makes other months rainfall deficient. In the areas where irrigation development has potential are not fully utilized due to defective management. Inefficiencies in irrigation and unequal regional spread of irrigation affect the farm productivity adversely. In many areas, the inefficient use of water has led to overexploitation of groundwater and has thus affected the water ecosystem.**

Land Degradation

Land degradation means deterioration of the original quality of land and deterioration or total loss of the production capacity of the soil. Nearly half of the country's 329 million hectares of land has become degraded. Almost 44% of the India's land suffers from high degradation resulting in 33 to 67% yield loss while 5% is so damaged that it has become unusable. Major reasons for land degradation are soil erosion, waterlogging, over dosage of pesticides, imbalanced fertilizers use and shifting cultivation and grazing, etc. A study found that more intensive application of inputs such as fertilizer in search of better yield in the short-run results in soil degradation. That is, efforts to bring in 1% more yield can, in fact, reduce soil degradation by about 0.9%. The study also found that a larger operated area, and a higher number of different crops grown, both increase degradation. This hints at sustainable land management practices reducing erosion.[10] A study by Delhi-based The Energy and Resources Institute (TERI) estimated that the economic losses from land degradation in 2014–15 stood at 2.2% of India's GDP or ₹2,61,000 crores for that year.[11]

Low Fertilizer Consumption

Not only imbalanced fertilizer use reduces productivity by degrading the land but lower fertilizers usage also affects productivity adversely. Low and imbalanced consumption of fertilizer is another factor of low productivity. The average consumption of fertilizers in India was around 135 kg per hectare in 2016, whereas the world average is 141 kg per hectare. In comparison, Pakistan consumes 208 kg per hectare and China consumes 400 kg per hectare.[12] There

** For detailed discussion on irrigation, please see chapter 11, Agriculture inputs and green revolution.

are three major types of nutrients used as fertilizers: Nitrogen (N), Phosphate (P), and Potassium (K). While the recommended ratio of NPK fertilizers is 4:2:1, this ratio in India is currently at 6.7:2.4:1. An imbalanced use of urea may lead to a loss of fertility in the soil over a period of time, affecting productivity.

Inadequate Access to Credit and Insurance

Access to agricultural credit is linked to the holding of land titles. As a result, small and marginal farmers, who account for more than half of the total land holdings, and may not hold formal land titles, are unable to access institutionalized credit. Farmers may require credit for short-term uses such as purchasing inputs, weeding, harvesting, sorting, and transporting, or long-term uses such as investing in agricultural machinery and equipment, or irrigation. In a study, it has been found that larger the land size, greater the access from the formal source of credit and smaller the land size, greater the access from the informal source of credit. For example, small farmers (land size less than 1 hectare) take 63% of loan from informal sources whereas large farmers (land size more than 10 hectares) take 22% of credit from informal sources.[13] Poor coverage of crops and livestock underinsurance has also been the cause of low productivity. As of 2011, about 10% of Indian farmers were covered under a crop insurance scheme. Some persistent issues with the crop insurance system include unawareness about insurance schemes, inadequate coverage of insurance schemes, assessment of the extent of damages in case of crop losses, and untimely settlement of claims.[14]

Lower Level of Research and Development

Research expenditure on agriculture requires special significance not only because of its impact on productivity but also the millions of Indians depend in this sector. Also, when the country expects around 1.63 billion stomachs to feed by 2050 with ever-shrinking cultivable land due to rising urbanization, research in agriculture is anything but a luxury.[15] Research reveals that every rupee spent on agricultural research and development, yields better returns (11.2), compared to returns on every rupee spent on fertilizer subsidy (0.88), power subsidy (0.79), education (0.97), or on roads (1.10).[16] India currently spends 0.30% of agriculture GDP on agricultural research, which is just half the share invested by China (0.62%). Reduced research in agriculture for identification of HYV seeds in different crops has severely affected country's productivity.

Lack of Technological Upgradation

Indian agriculture is still traditional in many respects. Wooden ploughs and bullocks are still used by a majority of farmers. We can count a number of issues related to poor technological dissemination in Indian agriculture. These are (1) Inadequate availability and high costs of modern inputs; (2) The irrigated component of total cropped area and the progress achieved in intensive cultivation of land are still at very modest levels; (3) Slower dispersion of agricultural technology to the farmers, especially marginal and small farmers; and (4) Limited and poor post-harvest technology.

Measures to Improve Productivity in Indian Agriculture

Technical measures are related with technique of production and agriculture inputs.

Adoption of HYV Seeds

According to research, seeds account for nearly one-fourth of agricultural productivity. After examining the soil conditions and irrigation facilities in a given area, the farmers must be educated about the best seed usage. In fact, the efficacy of various agricultural inputs such as fertilizers, irrigation, pesticides, and even the methods of sowing and manuring, depend much upon the quality of HYV seeds. This is well-known fact how Bt cotton* transformed Indian cotton productivity. The introduction of Bt cotton led to a dramatic increase in production across the cotton producing states and soon Bt cotton took over most of the acreage under cotton cultivation. Cotton production rose from 14 million bales in the pre-Bt year of 2001–2002 to 35 million bales in 2017–2018, a rise of almost 150%. India is expected to overtake China as the biggest cotton producer in the world very soon.

Enhancing Per Capita Fertilizer Consumption

The elasticity of output with respect to fertilizer usage is estimated to vary between 0.1345 and 0.700 among different states of the country. In fact, the research has proved that fertilizer consumption is one of the most significant factors to raise agricultural productivity in the country.[17] Government needs to plug in vast inter-state variations in the fertilizer usage, guide the farmers regarding the ideal application of NPK ratio, and extend soil health card policy throughout the country.

Spread of Irrigation

The coverage of irrigation in various states varies from 14 to 97% and the elasticity of crop output with respect to irrigation is estimated to vary between 0.303 and 1.004. There is ample evidence that the states which have comprehensive irrigation network experience higher yield in agriculture production. In India, only 50% of gross cropped area is irrigated and the rest is rainfed. There is a huge gap between the ultimate irrigation potential and actual utilization and the efforts must be to fully utilize the irrigation potential of the country. India receives scanty rainfall in most of the months and therefore, the country needs effective policies to enhance water efficiency, rainwater harvesting, adoption of modern irrigation technology, and integrated management of land and water resources. Various schemes like command area development program, accelerated irrigation benefit program, micro irrigation schemes, and Pradhan Mantri Krishi Sinchayee Yojana have been launched during the past few decades.

---

* Bt cotton was the first genetically modified crop to be approved for cultivation in India in 2002, with the introduction of Monsanto's GM cotton seeds. Bt stands for *Bacillus thuringiensis*, a bacterium that produces toxins harmful to a variety of insects, including bollworms that attack cotton. Bt cotton was created by introducing genes from the bacterium into the cotton seed, creating a crop resistant to this pest.

Increase in Consumption of Power

Energy consumption and agricultural productivity go hand in hand because higher energy consumption promotes irrigation and mechanized farming and thus agricultural productivity. There are vast inter-state variations in the usage of power in agriculture. Motor-driven water abstraction and conveyance requires a reliable energy source—or a reliable combination of energy sources. Apart from diesel and electric source of power, India can also opt for solar-powered irrigation systems as practiced in Egypt, Senegal, Honduras, Nepal, and Zambia. The other viable options are effective use of wind power operated pumps and natural gas operated pumps for water extraction.

Agriculture Finance and Marketing

Agriculture finance is vital to fulfill the input demands of the farmers. The mounting farmers' deaths due to suicide that mainly take place due to the problem of debt trap speak volumes about the significance of agricultural credit. The financial inclusion of small and marginal farmers needs to be addressed urgently so as to make them free from the clutches of moneylenders and other forms of informal credit. The interest subvention scheme, different types of crop insurance schemes and Kisan credit card scheme are the steps in the right direction. Apart from finance, agriculture marketing is another significant area that needs special emphasis. India has a poor record in the postharvest management of its crops and that leads to sheer wastage of farmer's hard work and resources. Though the government has recently taken numerous steps to strengthen agricultural marketing, efforts must be their right implementation and ensuring remunerative returns to the farmers, especially small and marginal.

Land Reforms

Land reforms in India have not delivered satisfactorily. India needs focused land reform measures that should enhance agriculture production and productivity and generate sufficient income to the farmers. Land size and land productivity are positively correlated. The endeavor of the new age land reforms must be focused on enhancing productivity through land consolidation and cooperative farming. Such measures will go a long way to enhance the productivity of Indian agriculture via the adoption of mechanized farming. The farmer–corporate ties should also be nurtured through contract farming models. This will help farmers to adopt state-of-art technology in agriculture along with the assurance of remunerative returns.

Integrated Management of Land and Water Resources

The over dosage of pesticides, wrong application of fertilizers, mono crop culture, and other problems like water logging, land salinization, and human-induced water erosion has damaged the soil fertility of land in India. Inefficient water management practices have also caused dip in the water table and wastage of water resources. Sustainable land management practices help to work against this kind of degradation, such as feeding the soil with organic manure, or usage of a well-working drainage system, which prevents loss of water and increases water-use efficiency. Therefore, the urgency of integrated management of land and water management resources becomes indispensable. Farmers need to be made aware of sustainable land practices.

BOX 10.3 Soil Health Card Scheme

The soil health card scheme was introduced by Government of India on February 19, 2015. A soil health card is intended to provide each farmer with information regarding the status of his/her soil as well as providing advice on fertilizer usage and other nutrient recommendations that maintain soil health in the long run. The soil health card is a printed report containing information on soil health through 12 parameters, including soil information on macro- and micronutrients, pH levels, and organic content. The government intends to issue the cards to 14 crore farmers.

Source: Department of Agriculture, Cooperation & Farmers Welfare, Ministry of Agriculture, GOI.

Government's soil health card is a remarkable step in this direction (Box 10.3). Further watershed management programs, rainwater harvesting and schemes to replenish the water aquifers should need priority efforts on the part of the government.

Land Reforms in India

Land reform as a phenomenon signifies an arrangement by which farmers hold or control land and the conditions that must be observed for its use and occupancy. Land reforms are visualized as an instrument of social justice as they seek to do away with exploitative relationships characterized by sharp class division between rich landowning classes and impoverished peasants with no security of tenure. Although land reforms are popularly understood to mean redistribution of land, their scope is much wider.

System of Land Tenure in British India

During pre-independent India, to consolidate their position, the British regularized the revenue collection system by working out different settlements with the different sections of the peasantry in different regions.

Permanent Settlement System or Zamindari System for assessing land revenue was first introduced by the Lord Cornwallis in 1793. Under this Zamindars (Landlords) were declared full proprietors of the large areas of land and the task of collecting rent from the farmers was entrusted to them. Zamindars acted as the intermediary between government and peasants and the share of government in total revenue collected was kept at 10/11th, the balance going to Zamindars as remuneration. Zamindari system was prevalent in the states of West Bengal, Bihar, Odisha, Uttar Pradesh, Madhya Pradesh, and Andhra Pradesh.

Mahalwari system was introduced by Lord William Bentinck in the year 1833. Under this system, it was the duty of village headman or Lambardar to collect the land revenue and submit with the government. The state's share of the revenue was 66% of the rental value. This system was introduced in regions of North-West Frontier, Agra, Central Province, Gangetic Valley, Punjab, etc.

Ryotwari system was introduced by Sir Thomas Munro in the late eighteenth century. Ryot means peasant cultivator and it was his duty to pay land revenue directly to the government. The rates were 50% in dry land and 60% in wetland. The system was initially introduced in Tamil Nadu and was later extended to Maharashtra, East Punjab, Assam, and Coorg.

By the time the British rule came to an end, the different types of settlement systems had given rise to an agrarian structure in which unproductive interest groups held the reins. Simultaneously, the concentration of land in the hands of a few continued to grow and landlessness, hunger, unemployment, and indebtedness reached unprecedented heights. Eviction and insecurity of tenancy aggravated the problems, which needed to be addressed immediately in independent India.

Components of Land Reforms

Following are the components of land reforms (Figure 10.1).

Abolition of Intermediaries

At the time of independence, 57% of the area of the country was under the Zamindari system. Zamindars were patronized and promoted by the British for their vested interest. So immediately after independence, legislations were passed in many states to abolish Zamindari system. Steps taken by the respective state governments included: all rights of Zamindars and Jagirdars were abolished and a ban on further acquisition of land was imposed; abolition of intermediary tenures was effected on payment of compensation to the landowners; the vast mass of the peasantry was freed from all illegal exactions in cash, kind and services; land records were created and survey and settlement was carried out in these areas; holdings were demarcated on the basis of the individual as a unit. Around 173 million acres of land was acquired from intermediaries and as a consequence, 2 crore tenants were brought into direct relationship with state.

Tenancy Reforms

Tenants were subject to pay higher rent to the landlords and lived under fear of eviction in case of nonpayment of rent. So, the government introduced three major measures under tenancy reforms:

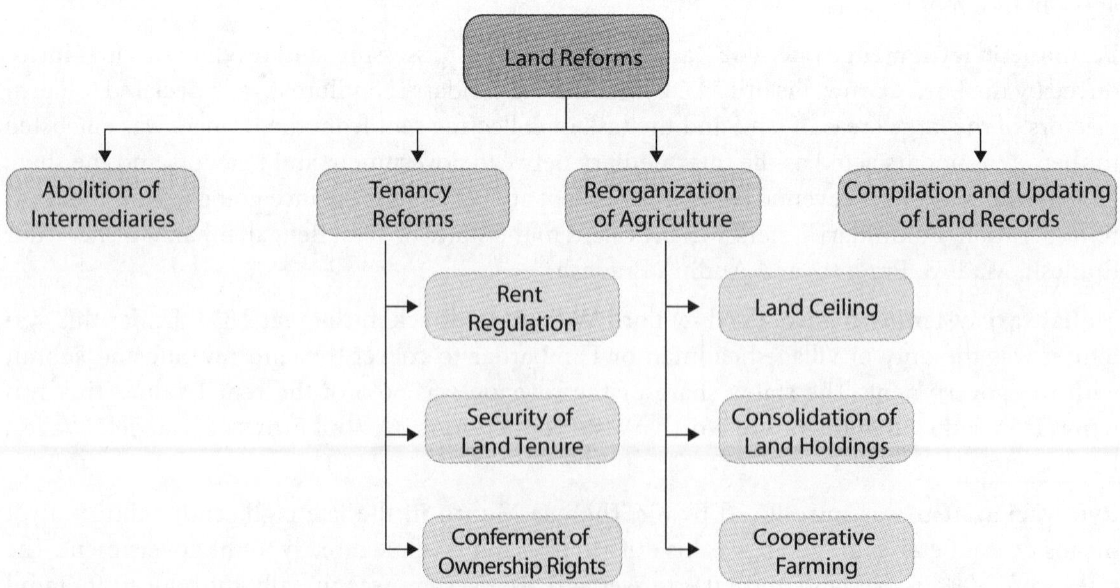

FIGURE 10.1 Components of Land Reforms

Regulation of Rent The rent signifies the extractions made by the landowning section from the nonowner cultivators, be it tenants or share-croppers. In pre-independent India, the rent charged by Zamindars from tenants was exorbitant and varied from 34 to 75% in different parts of the country. In Punjab, it has been estimated that as much as 80% of the produce was extracted from tenants in the form of rent. To regularize it, the first five-year plan stated that the maximum rent should be fixed at one-fourth or one-fifth of the total produce. Legislations were enacted after 1947 to regulate the limit of rents and reduce the burden on tenants.

Security of Tenure The most important and probably the most significant provision for regulating tenancy has been the measure of security to the tenants. Such security provides incentive for carrying out improvements in land, increase its productivity, and enable the tenant to retain an equitable share of the produce. Legislation for security of tenure had three essential aims, they were (1) ejectments do not take place except in accordance with the provisions of the law; (2) land may be resumed by an owner if at all, for personal cultivation only; and (3) in the event of resumption, the tenant is assured of a prescribed minimum area.

Conferment of Ownership Rights to Tenants The ultimate objective of tenancy reform is to confer ownership rights on tenants and share-croppers who are tilling the soil, so that the absentee landlordism is completely eliminated. Throughout the country, around 12 million tenants acquired ownership rights over 15 million hectares of land. In a number of states, governments followed two ways for bringing tenants of non-resumable lands into direct relationship with the government: (1) by declaring tenants owners and requiring them to pay compensation to earlier owners in suitable installments; (2) through the acquisition of the rights of ownership by the government on payment of compensation to the earlier owners and transfer of ownership to tenants.

BOX 10.4 Operation Barga

Launched in 1978 by West Bengal Government, Operation Barga was an agricultural tenancy Law that regulated rents and security of tenure of sharecroppers (Bargadars). Under these laws, if tenants get registered with the Department of Land Revenue, they would be entitled to permanent and inheritable tenure on the land they share-cropped as long as they paid the landlord at least 25% of output as rent. After the launching of Operation Barga, there was a significant improvement in the terms of tenants' contracts and more secure tenure as names of approximately 1.5 million bargadars were recorded. Operation Barga has been marked as one of the most successful land reform programs in India.

Sources:

1. Chattopadhyay, S. (1979). Operation Barga. *Social Scientist*, 8(3), 41–48. doi:10.2307/3520390
2. Mukhopadhyay, A. (1979). West Bengal-Operation Barga. *EPW*. Vol. 14, Issue No. 37

Reorganization of Agriculture

Ceiling on Land Holdings A ceiling on land holding means statutory absolute limit on the amount of land which an individual may hold. The main purpose of the ceiling law is to eliminate the excessive ownership of land. It is because the larger agriculture area of the country is owned by privileged class that functions merely as absentee landlords but their land is cultivated by landless laborers. According to FAO, redistribution of only 5% of farmland in India, coupled with improved access to water could reduce poverty by 30%.[18] To bring uniformity in different policies regarding the imposition of ceilings being pursued by states, a conference of chief ministers was called in July 1972. Based on the consensus at the conference, a new policy on land ceilings was evolved. The main features of the new policy were as under:

1. Lowering of ceilings to 18 acres of wetland and 54 acres of unirrigated lands;
2. The family (not the individual) will be the unit for determining land holding—the family will constitute five persons and will include husband, wife, and minor children.
3. To insulate the measure from judicial intervention, the jurisdiction of civil courts was barred and most of such laws were included in the ninth schedule of the constitution, which places them beyond any challenge in courts of law on grounds of infringement of fundamental rights.
4. All exemptions for modern and mechanized farms should be abolished.

Land Consolidation Under this, a farmer can be given one consolidated land holding equal to the total of the land in different scattered plots under his possession. The major case for land consolidation is rooted in the logic that it will not only help reverse the problem of land fragmentation but also help adoption of mechanized agriculture and increase in land productivity. In India, bulk of the land consolidated has been in Punjab, Haryana, Maharashtra, Uttar Pradesh, Bihar, and Odisha. Many states in India have passed legislation to prevent subdivision and fragmentation of land beyond a certain minimum limit, known as "standard area." The states that have made necessary provisions in Consolidation Acts are Assam, Bihar, Gujarat, Rajasthan, Andhra Pradesh, Uttar Pradesh, and West Bengal.

Cooperative Farming

This measure is also advocated to help solve the problem of land fragmentation. Under this farmers are encouraged to join hands and pool their land and other resources together. The benefits associated with cooperative farming are:

- It enables the farmers to reap all the benefits of large-scale farming.
- The cooperative societies can purchase all the agriculture inputs like seeds, fertilizers, manures, etc., in the bulk and procure them to the farmers at cheaper rates.
- Certain expensive agriculture implements and machines like tractors, harvesting machines, etc., which small farmers cannot purchase can now be bought on a collective basis by the cooperative society and can even be rented out.
- Agriculture can be planned in a scientific manner and new and innovative practices can be implemented.
- The marketable surplus of food grains and industrial raw materials can be obtained more easily from the large farms and can be transported to the market on a bulk basis. Thus, it solves the problem of transportation and sale as in the case of small farmers.
- It is easier to obtain agriculture data from large cooperative societies, which is not only reliable but also important for ideal agriculture planning and policy making.
- The cooperatives help ushering in the idea of people participation, collective action and mutual cooperation which go a long way in strengthening the democracy.

Compilation and Updating of Land Records

A land record management system is a pre-condition for an effective land reform programme. The lack of a comprehensive land rights database was one of the main reasons for the concealment of land, which has hampered the land reforms programme. The lack of land records hampered land ceiling and tenancy reforms and thus affected the government's intention to end the dominance of landlordism in rural India. In 1987–1988, a centrally sponsored scheme for Strengthening of Revenue Administration and Updating of Land Records (SRA&ULR) was introduced in Odisha and Bihar. The scheme was extended to other states in 1989–1990. It provides funds for survey and resettlement operations, training for revenue and settlement staff, facilities for modernization of survey and settlement operations and strengthening of revenue machinery at the village level.

Critical Evaluation of Land Reforms in India

Impact on Landlessness

The cumulative impact of land reform on rural landlessness has been negligible. The Draft Land Reforms Policy, using NSSO data (2003–2004), notes that while one-third of all rural households are landless, those near to landlessness (less than 0.4 hectares) add up one-third more. The next 20% hold less than 1 hectare. In other words, 60% of the country's population has rights over only 5% of the country's land, whereas 10% of the population has control over 55% of the land.[19] Many field studies show that while the possession of land added to their social standing and self-confidence, very often they were unable to cultivate it because supporting credit or grants were not available for land development and input costs.[20]

Impact on Poverty and Productivity

A study by Besley and Burgess on the impact of land reforms in 16 major Indian states reveals that abolition of intermediaries led to a significant reduction in poverty but did not impact productivity. Further, imposing a ceiling on landholdings does not seem to have had much effect on either poverty or productivity, while land consolidation had a positive effect on productivity without having any effect on poverty. They also concluded that land reforms did not have much effect on the distribution of land and seem to have operated mainly through altering the contractual relations in agriculture.[21] Another study by Banerjee, Gertler, and Ghatak, however, maintains that tenancy reforms improved agricultural productivity mainly due to operation Barga. They compared the growth in productivity in West Bengal districts with that in the districts in the neighboring country, Bangladesh. Except for religion and political boundaries, the two regions are very similar in terms of agroclimatic conditions, prevalence of tenancy, and agricultural technology. Indeed, for the same period under study, agricultural productivity in both regions (and much of Eastern India) grew in part due to the belated arrival of the Green Revolution, however, the authors find that even though the rate of adoption of HYV rice was faster in Bangladesh than in West Bengal, the rate of growth in rice productivity was higher in West Bengal. They attribute this difference to the implementation of tenancy reform. But it must be noted that tenancy reforms were not implemented with so much zeal in other Indian states except West Bengal.[22] Hence, the evidence suggests that land reforms had a negative effect on poverty, while the effect on productivity is mixed. In states where these measures were strongly implemented, the effect of land reform on productivity seems positive.

Problems in Abolishing the Intermediaries

The important land reform measure "abolition of intermediaries" met with limited success due to the typical feudal powers enjoyed by the landlords in rural India. Landowners naturally resisted the implementation of these reforms by directly using their political clout and also by using various methods of evasion and coercion, which included registering their own land under names of different relatives to bypass the ceiling, and shuffling tenants around different plots of land, so that they would not acquire incumbency rights as stipulated in the tenancy law.[23] For example, under land reform, it was maintained that landlords could resume land for "personal cultivation." The term "personal cultivation" was not clear and landlords tried to maximize their gains through such loopholes.

Problems with Tenancy Reforms

The tenancy reforms comprised regulation of rent, security of land tenure, and conferment of ownership rights. The rent regulation legislation was not passed by every state and even in the states it was passed, the rent charged was very high. Because of the strong socioeconomic and political hold of the landowners in the countryside, they have been able to extract considerably more rent from the peasants than the rent fixed by legislators. Further, the right of resumption combined with flaws in the definition of personal cultivation rendered all tenancies insecure. Many landlords compelled their tenants to give up the tenancies on their own accord. In this manner, they succeeded in circumventing the tenancy laws because no law can help the tenants if they give up their right voluntarily. Laws related to the security of land tenure can be implemented effectively only if correct and up-to-date land records are available. A tenant can claim his right only if his name appears on such land records. However, in many states, no records of tenancy exist or are incomplete or out of date. Farmers were unwilling to purchase land from the government as they lacked funds. Another reason for such unwillingness was more basic and reflected dominant controlling power of landowners over tenants.

Problems with Land Consolidation

The land consolidation efforts of the government also did not yield productive results. There was a nexus between village headman, Patwaris (land record officer), and politicians. The rich farmers took away fertile lands and the lands located near highways. The poor farmers were unaware about such things and were left with the option of buying unirrigated lands and hence did not come forward. Agriculture cooperatives also did not succeed. Rich farmers formed cooperatives and took away all the benefits provided to cooperatives by the government.

Lack of Political Will

Enactment of progressive measures of land reforms calls for hard political decisions and effective political support, direction, and control. The lack of political will is amply demonstrated by the large gaps between policy and legislation and between law and its implementation. In no sphere of public activity in our country since independence has the hiatus between percept and practice, between policy pronouncement and actual execution been as great as in the domain of land reforms.[24] Not only political masters were unwilling to go for wholehearted land reforms, but they also discouraged able and efficient bureaucrats to implement land reforms strictly by transferring them or creating undue pressure on them. This dampened the spirits of dynamic administrators and had an overall demoralizing effect on bureaucracy.

Livestock Sector in India

Under the Constitution of India, livestock development falls within the jurisdiction of the State Government. However, the Central Government supplements and complements the efforts of the State Governments through different schemes and programmes apart from creating an enabling environment to promote sustainable growth of the sector. Let us discuss the role and importance of the livestock sector in Indian economy.

Role and Importance of Livestock in India

Contribution to GDP

Livestock is an integral part of India's agricultural economy and plays a multifaceted role in providing livelihood support to the rural population. Livestock sector is significant to Indian economy in a way that it contributes 4.5% of GVA and nearly 26% of agriculture GVA. The total output worth was higher than the value of food grains. Livestock sector grew at an annual rate of 5.3% during 1980s, 3.9% during 1990s, and 3.6% post 2000 period. Despite deceleration, growth in livestock sector remained around 1.5 times larger than in the crop sector, which implies its critical role in cushioning agricultural growth.

Employment

The agricultural sector engages about 57% of the total working population and about 73% of the rural labor force. Livestock employed 8.8% of the agricultural workforce albeit it varied widely from 3% in Northeastern states to 40–48% in Punjab and Haryana. It is estimated that about 70 million rural households own livestock of one species or the other. Animal husbandry promotes gender equity as women constitute about 69% of the workforce. The share of women employment in livestock sector is around 90% in Punjab and Haryana where dairying is a prominent activity and animals are stall-fed.[25]

Structural Change in Demand Pattern

The livestock sector is experiencing a steady structural change in its demand pattern because of change in utility and increase in income. The non-food functions of livestock are becoming weaker as the importance of livestock as a source of "draught power" has declined considerably due to mechanization of agricultural operations and declining farm size. Use of dung manure is increasingly being replaced by chemical fertilizers. On the contrary, their importance as a source of quality food has increased. Sustained increase in per capita income and economic growth, a fast-growing urban population, burgeoning middle-income class, changing lifestyles, increasing proportion of women in workforce, improvements in transportation and storage practices, and rise of supermarkets especially in cities and towns are fuelling rapid increases in consumption of animal food products. Global market for animal products is expanding fast and is an opportunity for India to improve its participation in global market.[26]

Equitable Growth

Research has established that livestock development has been an important route for the small and marginal farmers to escape poverty and inequality because the growth in livestock sector is demand-driven, inclusive and pro-poor. Incidence of rural poverty is less in states like Punjab, Haryana, Jammu & Kashmir, Himachal Pradesh, Kerala, Gujarat, and Rajasthan where livestock accounts for a sizeable share of agricultural income and employment. Distribution of livestock is more equitable than that of land. The marginal farm households (≤1.0 hectare of land) who comprised 48% of the rural households controlled more than half of country's cattle and buffalo and two-thirds of small animals and poultry as against 24% of the land. They contributed about 16% to their income, more so in states like Gujarat (24.4%), Haryana (24.2%), Punjab (20.2%), and Bihar (18.7%).

TABLE 10.8 Problems and Policy Options in Indian Livestock Sector

Problem Area	Constraints	Policy Options/Suggestions
1. Breeding of animals	■ Poor productivity ■ Failures to genetically upgrade indigenous cattle and streamline AI (artificial insemination) services and support system. ■ Slow progress in the area of bull production and evaluation. ■ Most government AI centers are still stationary due to deficiency of manpower and transport facility.	■ For achieving the targeted growth rate of 5–6% in milk production, provision should be made for production of required good quality semen from high genetic sources. ■ Existing semen stations should be strengthened and upgraded. ■ AI delivery should be made at farmers' doorstep. Larger focus should be on field progeny testing for quality bull production.
2. Small ruminants	■ Shrinking and degrading pastures coupled with limitations of fodder, lack of sufficient veterinary care, and apathy to assisted reproductive technologies have been the major constraints. ■ The potential of raising Pashmina goats', viz. Changthangi in Ladakh and Chegu in Himachal Pradesh remains under exploited.	■ Profitability in sheep and goat would largely come from increased meat and to some extent wool/hair production. ■ The focus should be to adopt commercial production systems, application of assisted reproductive technologies, provision of improved quality feed and fodder, and health care, establishment of ultramodern meat processing plants and developing adequate market linkages.
3. Piggery	■ Pigs are mostly concentrated in NE and eastern states, but insufficient production is not able to meet the pork requirement of NE states. ■ High cost of concentrate feed, non-availability of swine fever vaccine and quality germplasm, lack of organized slaughter, and market facilities have been the major constraints.	■ A mission on pig production has already been initiated in Northeastern region and other eastern states. ■ Strengthening/establishment of pig breeding units, arranging feed inputs, quality germplasm, vaccines and diagnostics, processing plants, and developing market linkages should remain policy issues.
4. Poultry	■ Failed to diversify in favor of duck, quail, turkey, and emu production. ■ Rural poultry sector, however, needs financial, infrastructure and technological support to raise the present 2% growth rate to 3%.	■ For increasing growth rate from present 2–3% in rural poultry, a rural poultry mission project with focus on providing low input birds and bird diversification should be initiated. ■ Threatened breeds with unique characteristics should receive priority. There must be at least one farm for each breed in its native tract.
6. Feed and fodder problems	■ Deficiency of dry fodder, concentrates, and green fodder currently is 10, 33, and 35%, respectively. ■ Only 25% of forage seeds are available, that too of 15–20 years old varieties.	■ The policy should address the shortages of quality fodder seed production, and nutritional enhancement of crop by-products with effective institutional interventions. ■ A comprehensive strategy for rejuvenation of natural grasslands/pastures/common property resources for enhancing their productivity is also required.
7. Inadequate infrastructure	■ Organized slaughtering facilities are too inadequate. ■ Lack of access to organized markets and meager profits distract farmers from investing in improved technologies and quality inputs. Informal market intermediaries often exploit the producers.	■ Suitable incentives should be provided for setting up of rural abattoirs, establishment of new and modernization of existing slaughter houses, meat processing units, and high-value by-product plants for ensuring quality meat production. Rearing of buffalo male calves for meat should receive priority. ■ Well-equipped laboratories for testing adulterants, antibiotics residues, and foodborne pathogens should be established to enhance the safety and quality of animal feeds and foods.

Problem Area	Constraints	Policy Options/Suggestions
8. Lack of government support	■ Livestock sector receives only about 12% of the total public expenditure on agriculture and allied sectors and about 4–5% of the total institutional credit flowing to agriculture and allied sectors. Only 6% of the animal heads (excluding poultry) are provided insurance cover. ■ Livestock extension remains grossly neglected. Only about 5% of the farm households in India access information on livestock against 40.4% for crop farming.	■ The share of animal husbandry in agricultural credit should be increased at least to 10% and the interest rate on animal husbandry credit should be at par with crop loan. ■ The facility of the Kisan credit cards and insurance has already been provided by the government. ■ Livestock economics, business management, and market intelligence should be strengthened.
9. Health issues	■ Frequent outbreaks of diseases like FMD, BQ, PPR, Brucellosis, Swine fever, avian influenza, etc. continue to reduce productivity and production.	■ Immunization programs should be the national commitment with 100% central funding. ■ A comprehensive national network of diagnostic laboratories should be established. The vaccine and diagnostic production should be privatized with suitable incentives. ■ Mobile veterinary services should be introduced and treatment provided at cost. ■ A veterinary drug control authority should be put in place.
10. Lack of appropriate Veterinary infrastructure	■ Veterinary infrastructure, in general, is poor, inadequate, and need strengthening. ■ Only 50% veterinarians are employed against the required jobs and in case of para-vets only 20% are working.	■ Dedicated Krishi Vigyan Kendras (KVKs) exclusively for livestock should be established for training and demonstration. ■ Para-vets should receive larger focus in respect of trainings and delivery of technologies. ■ Public-Private-Partnership (PPP) in extension should be promoted for convergence and sharing of resources. ■ The issue of shortage of manpower in veterinary and animal sciences should be addressed on priority. ■ Veterinary colleges/veterinary universities should receive special grants to develop appropriate infrastructure to meet the manpower shortage in a given time frame.
11. Milk adulteration	■ Testing of milk for safety and quality parameters at the collection centers is almost non-existent. ■ Lack of proper anerobic waste treatment and dairy byproduct utilization are the other concerns. ■ Due to quality concerns of milk, value addition and export potential has not been fully exploited.	■ Government regulation since 2011 requires that all individual milk producers (except those who are members of a dairy cooperative) be registered with the local authority. This scheme is expected to help ensure milk quality and safety. ■ Quality control is possible only through well-equipped laboratories and trained technical manpower.

Source: Department of Agriculture, Cooperation & Farmers Welfare (2018). "Agriculture Statistics at a glance," 2016, Govt. of India.

* Data for 2014-15 retrieved from United States Department of Agriculture website https://pecad.fas.usda.gov/ (accessed on April 6, 2019).

BOX 10.5 Few Important Government Schemes for the Development of Livestock Sector

National Livestock Mission

The National Livestock Mission (NLM) was launched in 2014–15 and covers all the activities required to ensure quantitative and qualitative improvement in livestock production systems and capacity building of all stakeholders. The mission has four sub-missions: (1) sub-mission on fodder and feed development; (2) sub-mission on livestock development; (3) sub-mission on pig development in northeastern region; and (4) sub-mission on skill development, technology transfer, and extension.

Livestock Health and Disease Control scheme

It is a centrally sponsored scheme launched by DADF since August 2010. The scheme envisages prevention, control, and containment of animal diseases of economic importance, e.g., foot and mouth disease (FMD), Peste des petits ruminants (PPR), brucellosis, anthrax, hemorrhagic septicemia (HS), black quarter (BQ), classical swine fever, new castle disease (Ranikhet), avian influenza (AI), etc.

Schemes on Dairy Development

Government of India is making efforts for strengthening infrastructure for production of quality milk, procurement, processing and marketing of milk, and milk products through following dairy development schemes:

- National Programme for Dairy Development (NPDD)
- National Dairy Plan (Phase-I)
- Dairy Entrepreneurship Development Scheme(DEDS)
- Support to Dairy Cooperatives
- Dairy Processing and Infrastructure Development Fund (DIDF)

Rashtriya Gokul Mission

Rashtriya Gokul Mission was launched in December 2014 with an outlay of ₹2,025 crores for development and conservation of indigenous breeds through selective breeding especially for genetic upgradation of 11.3 crores low milk yield nondescript bovine population. Project period is from 2014–2015 to 2019–2020.

Extension of Kisan Credit Card Scheme to Livestock Farmers

In the interim budget 2019–2020, government announced extending the Kisan credit card scheme to livestock farmers for their working capital requirements.

National Livestock Policy, 2013

National Livestock Policy, 2013 was approved by Government of India in April 2013 after wide consultations with states and other stakeholders. The primary focus of this policy is on increasing livestock productivity and production in a sustainable manner, while protecting the environment, preserving animal biodiversity, ensuring biosecurity, and farmers livelihood. The policy seeks to redress several challenges that confronted the livestock sector, viz. prevalence of animal diseases, inadequate availability of feed and fodder for livestock and issues relating to biosecurity and sustainability. The policy emphasizes on strengthening infrastructure and services, reorientation of breeding policy for livestock, control and eradication of infectious diseases, and strengthening institutional credit and livestock insurance.

Source: *Department of Animal Husbandry and Dairying, Ministry of Agriculture*, GOI. Retrieved from http://www.dahd.nic.in/ (accessed on December 11, 2018).

Summary

1. Indian agriculture has come a long way since independence. The characteristics of Indian agriculture include: around 15% contribution in GVA (though it has declined since independence); unstable agricultural growth rate; around 14% export share as a percentage of total exports and around 6% import share as a percentage of total imports; allowing 100% FDI in the selected sectors with in the agriculture; self-reliant agriculture which has resulted into food security; huge backward and forward linkages; declining public investment in agriculture (which is around 3% of agriculture GVA); and contribution of agriculture in reducing rural poverty.
2. The journey of Indian agriculture since independence can be broadly categorized under pre-reform period and post-reform period. During pre-reform period, there are three different phases. During the first phase (1949–1950 to 1964–1965), the compound annual growth rate (CAGR) in crop production was around 3.2% and growth rate in yield per hectare for all crops during this period was 1.3% and most of increase in production was attributable to the increase in area under the crops. During the second phase (1967–1968 to 1980–1981) the growth rate in production for all crops was 2.2% per annum and annual average growth in yield per hectare was 1.3%. During the third phase (1980–1981 to 1989–1990) the growth rate in production and yield for major crops increased to 3.2% and 2.6%, respectively. The post-reform period also witnessed vast fluctuation in growth rates. The first phase (1990–1991 to 1999–2000) witnessed decrease in growth rate in production and yield (2.3 and 1.3%, respectively) reflecting the signs of green revolution fatigue. Agriculture sector demonstrated resurgence during the first decade of twenty-first century (2000–2001 to 2010–2011) and experienced growth rate of 3.2% and 2.1%, respectively, in production and yield. However, the growth momentum could not be sustained in the third phase (2010–11 to 2017–18) and growth dipped to 1.7% and 1.9%, respectively, for production and yield.
3. In terms of agriculture production, India ranks among the top producers in many agricultural commodities but country's productivity in many agricultural goods is lower than that of world average except in the case of sugarcane. The causes of low agricultural productivity in India are: lower size of landholdings; pressure of population on land causing fragmentation of land holdings; inadequate irrigation facilities; degradation of land causing severe loss in yield; low fertilizer consumption that lead to low productivity; inadequate access to formal credit, especially to small farmers and miniscule coverage of farmers under crop insurance; lower investment in agricultural research and lack of technological upgradation. The measures suggested to improve productivity of Indian agriculture are enhancing the usage/consumption of HYV seeds, fertilizers, power, and irrigation, so as to raise overall productivity; providing the access to formal credit and insurance, so as to make farmers capable to purchase inputs and minimizing risk; providing marketing facilities, so as to help farmers earn remunerative returns; land reforms with special emphasis on consolidation, cooperative farming; and contract farming and integrated management of land and water resources, so as to make agriculture more sustainable.
4. The components of land reforms are (1) abolition of intermediaries which envisaged ending of landlordism in the country; (2) tenancy reforms that include regulation of rent (fixation of rent through state legislations), security of land tenure (by making eviction process difficult and illegal) and conferment of ownership rights to tenants (making tiller the ultimate owner of the land); (3) reorganization of agriculture that includes land ceiling (fixation of maximum size of land holding taking family as a unit), land consolidation and cooperative farming (to overcome the limitation of land fragmentation); and, (4) compilation and updating of land records. The critical evaluation of land reforms in India suggests that their impact on landlessness has been negligible. However, on poverty and productivity the research has confirmed varied outcomes. The other components of land reforms like abolition of intermediaries and tenancy reforms also failed because of corruption and dominant feudal rural setup. Land consolidation and cooperative farming suffered due to nexus between officials and rich farmers. Political unwillingness to pursue land reforms effectively also created a big logjam.
5. The livestock sector is a significant component of Indian agriculture. It contributes nearly 26% of

agriculture GVA; provides employment to 8.8% of the total workforce, and 69% of the female workforce; has emerged as an important source of quality food with changing demand patterns and promotes equitable growth. However, the livestock in India suffers from certain problems like poor productivity; shrinking and degrading pastures along with dearth of feed and fodder; unproductive poultry and piggery sector; inadequate slaughtering facilities and unorganized market structure; dismal credit, extension and health services; insufficient veterinary staff and problems of milk adulteration. Government has tried to address such problems through a variety of measures and introduced schemes like National Livestock Mission, Livestock Health & Disease Control scheme, schemes on dairy development, Rashtriya Gokul Mission, Extension of Kisan credit card scheme to livestock farmers, and National Livestock policy, 2013.

Endnotes

1. WTO. *Trade Statistics Review, 2017*. Retrieved from. https://www.wto.org (Accessed on November 16, 2018).
2. Cooking oil imports up 10% in FY'18. *The Times of India*. April 16, 2018.
3. Economic Survey 2020–21, p. 256, Govt. of India
4. *Economic Survey*, Department of Economic Affairs, Ministry of Finance, Govt. of India. 2017–18.
5. Department of Agriculture, Cooperation & Farmers Welfare (2018). *Annual Report 2017–18.*, Govt. of India.
6. Gulati, A., & Bathla, S. (2002). Capital formation in Indian agriculture: Trends, composition and implications for growth. *NABARD, Occasional paper 24*, Mumbai.
7. Economic Survey, *Statistical appendix*. Department of Economic Affairs, Ministry of Finance, Govt. of India 2017–18.
8. Department of Agriculture, Cooperation & Farmers Welfare (2018). *"Agriculture Statistics at a glance," 2016*, Govt. of India. p.252.
9. Department of Agriculture. *State of Agriculture in India, 2017–18*, Govt. of India.
10. Mythili, G., & Goedecke, J. (2016). Economics of land degradation in India. In E. Nkonya, A. Mirzabaev & J. von Braun (Eds.), *Economics of Land Degradation and Improvement–A Global Assessment for Sustainable Development*. Cham: Springer
11. Jain, N. *Why land degradation in India has increased and how to deal with it*. Mongabay, October 3, 2018.
12. Fertilizer consumption. Retrieved from https://data.worldbank.org (Accessed on April 16, 2019).
13. RBI (2015). *Report of the Committee on Medium-term Path on Financial Inclusion*, Retrieved from https://rbidocs.rbi.org (Accessed on May 16, 2017).
14. Department of Agriculture. *State of Agriculture in India, 2017–18*, Govt. of India. P.7
15. The Hindu Business Line, October 11, 2018.
16. Gulati, A., Ferroni, A., & Zhou, Y. (2018). *Supporting Indian farms the smart way*. New Delhi: Academic Foundation.
17. Chand, R., Raju, S.S., & Pandey, L.M. (2007). Growth crisis on agriculture. *EPW* p.2532.
18. Dogra, B. (2002). *Land reforms, productivity and farm size. EPW*, February 9, p.533.
19. Mander, H. (2013). *Reviving land reforms? EPW xlviii(35)*, p.14.
20. Iyer, K. G. (1997). *Implementation of the land ceiling programme*. In A. Aziz & S. Krishna (Eds.), *Land Reforms in India*. Vol. 4. Karnataka, New Delhi: Sage.
21. Besley, T., & Burgess, R. (2000). Land reform, poverty reduction, and growth: Evidence from India. *Quarterly Journal of Economics, 115* (2), 389–430.
22. Banerjee, A. V., Gertler, P. J., & Ghatak, M. (2002). Empowerment and efficiency: Tenancy reform in West Bengal. *Journal of Political Economy 110* (2), 239–280.
23. Land reform in India (2007). In K. Basu (Ed.), The *Oxford companion to economics in India*. New Delhi: Oxford University Press.
24. Planning Commission (1973)."Report of the task force on agrarian relations," Retrieved from http://krishikosh.egranth.ac.in (Accessed on February 16, 2018).
25. Department of Animal Husbandry, Dairying & Fisheries (2013). *National livestock policy, 2013*, p.5. Retrieved from www.dahd.nic.in (Accessed on April 6, 2017).
26. "Planning Commission. *Report of the working group on animal husbandry & dairying 12th five year plan* Retrieved from https://www.india.gov.in/ (Accessed on December 16, 2017).

CHAPTER **11**

AGRICULTURE INPUTS AND GREEN REVOLUTION

If agriculture goes wrong, nothing else will have a chance to go right in the country.

—M.S. Swaminathan

INTRODUCTION

Long-time back, in 1798, the great classical economist T.R. Malthus in his famous work "An Essay on the Principle of Population" had predicted the doom of world civilization because of ever increasing population number that will create a mismatch between demand and supply of agriculture products. But Malthus failed to foresee technological change which was bound to revolutionise agriculture practises worldwide, around one and half century later. The green revolution strategy for food crop productivity growth was explicitly based on the premise that, given appropriate institutional mechanisms, technology spill-over across political and agro-climatic boundaries could be captured.[1] In India, the phenomenon of green revolution is identified with country being catapulted from a chronically food deficient country, with a begging bowl image, to one which was self-sufficient and which became over time even surplus in food.[2]

This chapter will discuss the following topics:

- Agriculture Inputs and Their Importance in Indian Economy
- Green Revolution: Its Advantages and Disadvantages
- Second Green Revolution and Its Opportunities & Challenges

AGRICULTURE INPUTS

The backbone of agricultural development is to facilitate access of farmers to modern agricultural inputs. These agricultural inputs range from improved seeds, fertilizers, and crop protection chemicals to machinery, irrigation, credit, and knowledge. In this section, we will be discussing four critical inputs of agriculture: Seeds, fertilizers, pesticides, and irrigation.

Seeds

Seeds are the primary basis for human sustenance. They are critical to successful crop production and inevitably, farm productivity and profitability. Seeds efficacy of other agricultural inputs in enhancing productivity and production, such as fertilizers; pesticides and irrigation is largely determined by the quality of seed. Quality of seed accounts for 20–25% of productivity. It is, therefore, important that quality seeds are made available to the farmers of the country.[3]

Areas of concern

The followings are the areas of concern with regard to seeds in India:

Affordability: Pollinated varieties can be developed by farmers from their own harvested crops. But for high yield variety (HYV) seeds, farmer has to depend on the market for each crop. In India majority of the farmers are marginal or small who cannot afford high cost of hybrid seeds affecting the viability of farming.

Availability: India has skewed availability of certified quality seeds. Except wheat and rice, the availability of quality seeds is not sufficient.[4] While there is a demand for banning noncertified seeds, facilitating more players private and public and competition in the market for seeds would improve availability of quality seeds at lower/competitive prices.

Research and technology for seed development: Developing improved seeds is a complex research-and-development process. Seeds should be accessible in time, affordable and meet the true needs of farmers and markets.[5] Inadequate research and genetic engineering has been a constraint in the development of seeds/seed technologies in major crops during the past few decades in India. There is need to encourage participation of both private and public sectors in seed research so as to cover all agricultural segments/crops.

GM crops and seeds: Many environmentalists have raised concerns about environmental and ethical issues in cultivation of GM crops, risks to the food chain, disease spread and cross pollination that have resulted in their non-introduction. These issues needs to be debated, tested, evaluated, so that introduction of hybrids is facilitated at the earliest.

Policy Measures

In the past few years, the following steps have been taken for the promotion of seeds in India:

First, FDI is permitted up to 100% under the automatic route in development and production of seeds and planting material subject to certain conditions.

Second, the Indian Seed program recognizes three generations of seeds, namely, breeder, foundation, and certified seeds. The Department of Agriculture and Co-operation is implementing a Central Sector Scheme as "Development and Strengthening of Infrastructure Facilities for Production and Distribution of Quality Seeds" since 2005–2006 for the whole country. The objective of the ongoing scheme is to ensure production and multiplication of high-yielding certified/quality seeds of all crops in sufficient quantities and to make the seeds available to farmers, including those in remote areas, who were unable to easily access by rail/road on time and at affordable price.

Third, India is the world's biggest cotton producer with 8 million farmers buying 50 million seed packets of 450 g each annually to plant on 12.26 million hectares (mh) of land. In exercise of the powers conferred by the Cotton Seeds Price (Control) Order, 2015, the Government has slashed Bt cotton seed prices which will benefit millions of cotton cultivators in the country.[5]

Fourth, the Pardarshi Kisan Seva Yojana (PKSY) was launched in September 2014 and rolled out in April 2015 in Uttar Pradesh for the distribution of hybrid seeds through Direct Benefit Transfer (DBT). The aim of the scheme was to target the intended beneficiaries and prevent diversion of subsidized seeds, corruption, and manipulation.

Fertilizers

Once crops are harvested for human consumption, the natural supply of nutrients in the soil must be refilled. Fertilizer is the single most important input underlying the growth in food and other crops during last four decades, and it holds key to future growth in agricultural output in the country. It has been estimated that an increase in fertilizer consumption of 40–60 kg/ha can yield an additional 30–45 million tonnes of food grains. The application of fertilizers on agriculture lands increased after the introduction of HYV program in the country way back in 1966. In India during 2016-17, the total fertilizer production, consumption and imports were 179.49, 259.49 and 78.35 Lakh ton respectively.

Problems in Fertilizer Usage

The problems regarding fertilizers consumption in Indian agriculture are as follows:

Discrepancies in the use of fertilizers: There are discrepancies in the use of fertilizers on the basis of chemical ratios. The current consumption ratio of nitrogen, phosphorus, and potassium (NPK) is 6.7:2.4:1 against their desirable ratio of 4:2:1. The situation is grimmer in major agricultural states like Punjab and Haryana where NPK use ratios are as high as 31.4:8.0:1 and 27.7:6.1:1, respectively.[6] The imbalanced nutrient use coupled with neglection of organic matter has resulted in multi-nutrient deficiencies in Indian soils. As nutrient additions do not keep pace with nutrient removal by crops, the fertility of land is falling rapidly under intensive agriculture and demonstrating the signs of fatigue, especially in the Indo-Gangetic plains.

Low fertilizer consumption: India's average fertilizer consumption of 137.2 kg/ha is even less than that of world average of 140 kg/ha. In India, fertilizer consumption is highly skewed. Out of 766 districts in the country, about 300 districts account for consumption of 85% of all of the country's fertilizers. Telangana has the highest consumption of fertilizer (269 kg/ha) followed by Punjab (249 kg/ha) and Andhra Pradesh (226 kg/ha). Puducherry tops among UTs with the consumption of 262 kg/ha, while Manipur with 0 kg/ha and Arunachal Pradesh with 0.56 kg/ha are the least consumers of fertilizers.[7]

Flaw in nutrient-based subsidy (NBS) scheme: The NBS, which is sought to deregulate subsidy on non-urea fertilizers, was expected to reduce the subsidy burden substantially. But the immediate result of NBS was a sharp rise in fertilizer prices, particularly for phosphoric and potassic fertilizers which caused a sharp decline in the use of phosphoric and potassic fertilizer mix, with the increase in urea consumption. Although urea prices remained administered, the surge in demand for urea led to the sale of urea in the black market at twice the administered prices, which also caused severe shortage of urea in the market. The net result has been an overall increase in fertilizer prices, with neither the government benefiting due to subsidy reduction nor the farmer benefiting, as fertilizer prices more than doubled in the last 4 years. But an unintended consequence of the rise in urea price has been the sharp reduction in fertilizer consumption in the country for the first time in the last three decades.[8] The fertilizer consumption fell down from 281 LT in 2010–2011 to 259 LT in 2016–2017.

Huge dependence on imports: In India, around 259 LT of fertilizer was consumed in the year 2016–2017, out of which around 70% was produced within the country and 30% was imported. Since sufficient potassic mineral deposits are not present in the country for producing potassic fertilizers, India imports 100% of its potassic requirement from Canada, Belarus, CIS, Jordan, Israel, the United Kingdom, and Germany (Table 11.1).[9]

Impact on health and environment: Excessive use of fertilizers may pollute the underground water with nitrate and it is so much hazardous to humans or livestock. Many studies in the medical world are associated with high levels of chemical fertilizers (sodium nitrate) in groundwater with the prevalence of gastric cancer, testicular cancer, kidney-related problems, and the development of methemoglobinemia, otherwise known as Blue Baby syndrome. Scientists also claim that chemical fertilizers do not help replenish soil nutrients and its fertility contrary to the popular belief, but replenish only nitrogen, potassium, and phosphorous. And we know phosphorous does not dissolve in water and its overuse may cause hardening of soil.

Important Government Schemes

NBS scheme: The Government launched NBS scheme w.e.f. April 1, 2010. The main aim of the policy was to improve agricultural productivity, ensure the balanced use of N, P, and K fertilizers, growth of indigenous fertilizer industry and to contain the fertilizer subsidy bill. The policy allowed the manufacturers of P and K fertilizers to fix their maximum retail prices at reasonable levels. The subsidy provided would be based on per kilogram of the nutrient. The policy also provided for an additional subsidy to be paid to indigenous manufacturers of fertilizers.[10]

The city compost scheme: The city compost scheme was launched by Government of India (GOI) in 2016. The scheme aims to convert all organic wastes generated in cities into compost or biogas and market the compost with the help of fertilizer companies to benefit farmers.[11]

DBT in Fertilizer sector: The GOI has introduced DBT system for fertilizer subsidy from October 2016. Under the proposed fertilizer DBT system, 100% subsidy on various fertilizer grades shall be released to the fertilizer companies on the basis of actual sales made by the retailers to the beneficiaries. The Sale of all subsidized fertilizers to farmers/buyers will be made through Point of Sale devices installed at each retailer shop and the beneficiaries will be identified through Aadhar card, Kisan Credit Card (KCC), voter identity card, etc.[12]

Pesticides

The term pesticide covers a wide range of compounds including insecticides, fungicides, herbicides, rodenticides, molluscicides, nematicides, and plant growth regulators. The production of pesticides started in India in 1952 with the establishment of a plant for the production of BHC near Calcutta. The per hectare consumption of pesticides in India is among the lowest in the world and currently stands at 0.6 kg/ha against 5–7 kg/ha in the United Kingdom and at almost 20 times, that is, 13 kg/ha in China. Pesticides have been an integral part of the process by reducing losses from the pest and insect attack that can markedly reduce the amount of harvestable produce. Production and productivity have increased tremendously because of pesticide usage during the post-Green Revolution period in India. Severe infestation of weeds, particularly in the early stage of crop establishment, ultimately accounts for a yield reduction of 40%. Herbicides provide both an economic and a labor benefit.[13]

Drawbacks of Pesticides

Following are the drawbacks of pesticide usage.

First, there is a high occurrence of generalized symptoms (headache, nausea, vomiting, fatigue, and irritation of skin and eyes) besides psychological, neurological, cardio, respiratory, and gastrointestinal symptoms because of pesticide exposure.[14] Every year, there are about 10,000 reported cases of pesticide poisoning in India according to National Crime Record Bureau (NCRB). There are numerous class-I pesticides which are extremely toxic and have been banned worldwide but still widely prevalent in India.[15]

Second, pesticides can contaminate soil, water, turf, and other vegetation. In addition to killing insects or weeds, pesticides can be toxic to a host of other organisms including birds, fish, beneficial insects, and non-target plants. Pesticide sprays can directly hit non-target vegetation, or can drift or volatilize from the treated area and contaminate air, soil, and non-target plants.[16]

Third, groundwater pollution due to pesticides is a worldwide problem. Apart from nitrate contamination, the presence of fluoride, iron, arsenic, and heavy metals has also touched worrying levels in India. Punjab which was once called food basket of India has turned into disease basket. The water quality index of 80% of the samples in Malwa region of Punjab was found to be unfit for drinking. In fact, the high degree of the presence of insecticides and toxic substances in the ground water has led to the proliferation of cancer villages in the region and outbreak of mental disorders among kids and newborns.[17]

Fourth, heavy treatment of soil with pesticides can cause populations of beneficial soil microorganisms to decline.

Government Policies

1. The Insecticides Act, 1968 regulates import, manufacture, sale, transportation, distribution, and use of insecticides with a view to prevent risk to humans or animals.
2. The Integrated Pest Management scheme was launched by GOI in 1985. It is an eco-friendly approach which aims at keeping pest population at below economic threshold levels by employing all available alternate pest control methods and techniques such as cultural, mechanical, and biological with emphasis on the use of bio-pesticides and pesticides of plant-origin like Neem formulations. The use of chemical pesticides is advised as a measure of last resort when pest population in the crop crosses economic threshold levels.[18]
3. Sub Mission on Plant Protection and Plant Quarantine has been established to minimize loss to quality and yield of agricultural crops from the ravage of insect pests, diseases, weeds, nematodes, rodents, etc.[19]
4. To monitor the quality of pesticides, the Central Insecticides Laboratory has been established at Faridabad. Besides a number of regional level and state level laboratories have also been established.

Irrigation

India accounts for about 17% of the world's population but only 4% of the world's fresh water* resources. Further, large chunk of people (almost three-fourth of total population) reside in rural

*Fresh water is naturally occurring water on Earth's surface in ice sheets, ice caps, glaciers, icebergs, ponds, lakes, rivers and streams, and underground as groundwater in aquifers and underground streams. Altogether, (groundwater) aquifers store 97% of the planet's (available) freshwater.

regions and significant proportion of workforce (nearly 48%) is engaged in farm and farm-related activities. The huge demand and supply gap requires suitable policy efforts to expand irrigation network in the country. Despite massive investments in irrigation projects over the years, the gross irrigated area as a percentage of gross cropped area has increased from 17% in 1950–1951 to 55% in 2022–23 (115 mh of total 210 mh gross sown area).

There are mainly three sources of irrigation, viz., Wells and tube wells, Canal, and Tank.

Well and tube well Irrigation: Well irrigation is popular in areas where sufficient sweet ground water is available. These areas include a large part of the Great Northern Plain, the deltaic regions of the Mahanadi, the Godavari, the Krishna, and the Cauvery, parts of the Narmada and the Tapi valleys and the weathered layers of the Deccan Trap and crystalline rocks, and the sedimentary zones of the Peninsula. However, due to rocky structure, uneven surface, and lack of underground water, the greater part of the Peninsular India is not suitable for well irrigation. Large dry tracts of Rajasthan, the adjoining parts of Punjab, Haryana, and Gujarat and some parts of Uttar Pradesh have brackish ground water which is not fit for irrigation and human consumption and hence unsuitable for well irrigation. Groundwater accounts for 43% of the water used for irrigation globally but in India well irrigation accounts for 63.7% share.

Canal Irrigation: Canals used to be the most important source of irrigation up to 1960s, but in the 1970s they yielded first place to wells and tube wells and now constitute the second most important source of irrigation in India. The percentage of canal irrigation area to total irrigated area in the country has fallen from about 39.77% in 1951 to 26.18% in 2016. The main concentration of canal irrigation is in northern plains due to perennial waters of Himalayas. Peninsular and western Indian rivers are ephemeral and water for irrigation is not available throughout the year. Further, the rocky and uneven terrain of peninsular India makes canal digging difficult and costly affair. However, limited canal irrigation is done in the coastal and the delta regions in South.

Tank Irrigation: A tank consists of water storage which has been developed by constructing a small bund of earth or stones built across a stream. Tank irrigation is popular in the peninsular India especially in Tamil Nadu and Andhra Pradesh where canal and well irrigation are practically difficult due to hard and rocky terrain. The share of tank irrigation has come down from 14% during 1960–1961 to 3.5% during 2015–2016.

The other sources accounted for 6.7% of total irrigation in the country.

Importance of Irrigation

There are various reasons why irrigation is an important input for Agriculture in general in India.

First, there is a positive correlation between irrigation infrastructure and yield. A study found that the per-hectare yield of foodgrains on irrigated land was two to six times higher than the yields on un-irrigated land.[20] The states which have higher proportion of foodgrain area under irrigation have the higher productivity.

Second, India is a tropical and sub-tropical country and 80% of the annual rainfall is received in less than four months, that is, between June and September. Several regions in the country face acute water stress chronically. These include districts of South and North Interior Karnataka; Rayalseema in Andhra Pradesh; Vidarbha and Marathwada in Maharashtra; and western Rajasthan and Bundelkhand region of Uttar Pradesh and Madhya Pradesh. Low and erratic rainfall for consecutive years in these districts have rendered water-harvesting structures

TABLE 11.1 Sources of Irrigation in India (2016)

Source	% Share
Wells and tube wells	63.7
Canal	26.18
Tank	3.5
Other	6.7

Source: Department of Agriculture & Farmers Welfare (Agriculture Census 2015–16).

devoid of water and the conservation measures almost unviable. The water storage in reservoirs has depleted leading to scarcity of drinking water. The moisture index in the majority of these districts is in the range of –85 to –50% denoting that natural precipitation is highly inadequate to support the arable cropping.

Third, the main channel through which irrigation impacts on land productivity is via its effect on cropping intensity (number of cropping seasons).[21] Inadequate rainfall makes multiple cropping almost difficult or impossible. Many countries including China have lesser arable land but have larger productivity. Irrigation, thus, can promote multiple cropping which will go a long way in increasing both the production and the productivity of agriculture crops.

Fourth, the high yield variety (HYV) of seeds and chemical fertilizers require a substantial amount of water at regular intervals of time. Indeed, that is the reason why Green Revolution in the beginning years remained restricted to the states which had higher irrigation infrastructure.

Fifth, Agriculture production and productivity is subject to monsoon vagaries, and erratic rainfalls affecting both yield and farm income. A study by Gandhi and Bhamoriya for the period 1971–1984 found that the degree of instability of agriculture output was less than half of that in unirrigated areas.[22]

Sixth, irrigation delivers various direct and indirect benefits to the masses. People in the irrigated area can benefit directly by increased and more stable incomes from increased cropping intensities, improved yields, new farm enterprise/technology mixes, diversification of cropping patterns, and the appreciation of the value of land with access to irrigation. Indirectly, they benefit from an increase in farm incomes/wages, lower food prices, better nutrition, and more water for domestic uses that can improve health.[23] Bhatia and Malik estimated that the irrigation multiplier for the Bakhra irrigation command in the Haryana, which assessed the indirect benefits of backward and forward linkage, is about 1.90—which means every ₹100 that the project generates as a direct benefit will yield another ₹90 as an indirect benefit.[24] The rural poor can further benefit from employment-intensive construction, operation, and maintenance practices (as undertaken under MGNREGA or AIBP or CADPs).

Characteristics and Problems of Irrigation in India

1. *Underutilization of Irrigation Potential:* India has ultimate irrigation potential of 139.9 mh, out of which irrigation potential created is 113 mh (81%) and 87 mh of irrigation potential is utilized (77%). The underutilization of irrigation potential created is due to the slow pace of the Command Area Development Programme, depletion of professional staff in state irrigation agencies, and paucity of unplanned funds available for irrigation departments.[25] This necessitates review and restructuring of the underlying institutional setup in the irrigation sector.

2. *Inefficiencies in Irrigation:* As per the international norms, a country is classified as water stressed and water scarce if per capita water availability goes below 1,700 and 1,000 m^3, respectively. With 1,544 m^3 per capita water availability, India is already a water-stressed country and moving toward water scarcity.[26] As compared to countries like China, Brazil, and the United States, India uses two to four times water to produce one unit of major food crops.[27] These variations imply that if India attains water use efficiency of those countries, it can save at least half of water presently used for irrigation purposes. Irrigation consumes about 84% of total available water. Industrial and domestic sectors consume about 12 and 4% of total available water, respectively. Most of the horticulture crops and livestock products are more water intensive as compared to food grains (except rice). Further preference to have fresh fruits and vegetables in all the seasons is resulting in increase in their cultivation in off season requiring much higher use of water. The amount of water required to produce a unit of animal origin products (chicken, mutton, and eggs) is much higher than plant origin products (cereals, pulses, and oilseeds).
3. *Unequal Regional Spread of Irrigation:* Around 49% of country's area under food grains is irrigated. Punjab has the highest area under food grains irrigated (98.7%), whereas Assam (4.6%) has the least. The states with the highest irrigation percentage are the states with the highest yield. The positive correlation between irrigation and yield gets reflected in terms of Punjab and Haryana which are ranked number one and two, respectively, in productivity. Further northern states which are located in the great Indian planes, viz., Punjab, Haryana, and Uttar Pradesh have generated huge irrigation potential. Western states like Maharashtra, Rajasthan, and Gujarat have proportion of irrigation area even lesser than the national average of 49.8%. Similarly, eastern states (like Assam, Jharkhand, and Chhattisgarh) and southern states (like Karnataka) too suffer from scant irrigated area.
4. *Overexploitation of Water Resources:* Over-dependence on groundwater beyond sustainable level use (because of underdeveloped canal and other modes of irrigation) has resulted in a significant decline in the groundwater table. India is the world's largest user of groundwater and, since the 1980s, its groundwater levels have been dropping. The severity of the problem is particularly acute in the northwest, where levels have plunged from 8 m below ground to 16m, so that water needs to be pumped from even greater depths.[28] Groundwater is depleting at an alarming rate in different parts of the country and the water level is going down. A study in Tamil Nadu found that over a period of 11 years, from 2002–2012, ground water depletion has taken place at the rate of 21.4 $km^3 yr^{-1}$, which is 8% more than the annual recharge rate (19.81 $km^3 yr^{-1}$).[29] * A world bank study in Jalandhar highlighted groundwater depletion at an alarming rate (36%), and in few parts, water has gone down by over 30 m.[30]

Government Policies on Irrigation

The Government has devised many schemes and proposals for the development of irrigation in the country since independence. During 1950–1951, irrigation schemes were categorized into major, medium, and minor. Since 1978, the new classification redefined major schemes as those

*The study used remote sensing data from NASA's Gravity Recovery and Climate Experiment and the Global Land Data Assimilation Systems to assess the total change in groundwater storage across the state of Tamil Nadu.

having culturable command area* (CCA) of more than 10,000ha, medium irrigation schemes as those having CCA between 2,000 ha and 10,000 ha, and minor schemes as those having CCA of less than 2,000 ha. In 1974–1975, the Government launched Command Area Development Programme to bridge/narrow the gap between irrigation potential created and actually utilized in major and medium irrigation schemes. The program was restructured and renamed as Command Area Development and Water Management Programme (CADWMP) since April 1, 2004, and the scheme was further restructured and was thrown to states to implement in 2008–2009. In 1995–1996, Rural Infrastructure Development Fund (RIDF) was created with NABARD, and under this, state governments were provided loans to finance their rural infrastructure projects including irrigation, soil conservation, and water management. In 1996–1997, Accelerated Irrigation Benefit Programme (AIBP) was initiated by GOI, and under this, the central government provided financial assistance to the states in terms of loans for early completion of selected large irrigation and multi-purpose projects. In January 2006, a centrally sponsored scheme on Micro Irrigation (MI) was launched for promoting water-use efficiency by adopting drip and sprinkler irrigation. In June 2010, the scheme was rechristened as the National Mission on Micro Irrigation (NMMI).

During July 1, 2015, Pradhan Mantri Krishi Sinchayee Yojana (PMKSY) was launched as a national mission to improve the effectiveness in irrigation and ensure better utilization of the water resources in the country. The objectives of PMKSY are to achieve the convergence of investments in irrigation at the field level, expand the cultivable area under assured irrigation, improve the on-farm water use efficiency to reduce wastage of water, enhance the adoption of precision-irrigation and other water saving technologies, enhance the recharge of aquifers and introduce the sustainable water conservation practices by exploring the feasibility of reusing treated municipal waste water for peri-urban agriculture, and attract greater private investment in precision irrigation** system. Various ongoing schemes have been amalgamated into PMKSY, viz., AIBP, River development & Ganga, Integrated Watershed Management Programme (IWMP), and the Onfarm Water Management (OFWM). The scheme is implemented by Ministries of Agriculture, Water Resources, and Rural Development.[31]

Massive investments have been made by the government in irrigation development of the country and investment expenditure escalated from ₹442 crore during first five-year plan to ₹422,012 crore during 12th five-year plan. PMKSY has been approved for implementation across the country with an outlay of ₹50,000 crore in 5 years. Because of extensive efforts, irrigation infrastructure in India has seen substantial expansion over the years. The total irrigation potential created from major, medium, and minor irrigation schemes has increased from 22.6 mh during pre-plan period to 113 mh at the end of the 11th plan. It represents 81% of India's ultimate irrigation potential estimated at 139.9 mh.

Suggestions to Improve Irrigation in India

1. *Emphasizing MI:* Looking at water crisis all around, micro irrigation is an idea whose time has come and deserves greater attention. MI involves irrigation practices through

---

*Culturable command area (CCA) is the area which can be irrigated from an irrigation scheme and is fit for cultivation.

**Also called site-specific irrigation, it is a tool of precision farming that involves the delivery of irrigation water in optimum amount over an entire field. Under this, the water will be applied directly where it is needed, therefore, saving water and preventing excessive water runoff and leaching. Drip irrigation is part of precision irrigation.

sprinkler and drip irrigation. In 2015, the share of sprinkler and drip irrigation was 56.4 and 43.6%, respectively, in the country. MI can save 22–40% of water across different horticulture crops. India, with arable land of 140 mh, has huge potential for MI. Task-force on MI, 2004 estimated a potential of 27 mh for drip irrigation and 42.5 mh for sprinkler irrigation with total potential of 69.5 mh.[32]

2. *The prudent agronomic practices:* It is high time that water saving agronomic practices can be readily implemented across different parts of the country. In India, production of 1 kg of rice requires estimated 3,000–5,000 L of water. This makes a very unbalanced sustainability equation: pitting the need for food security against the requirements of water for drinking, cooking, washing, bathing, and sanitation.[33] An International Rice Research Institute paper, which reviewed 44 studies from different countries, showed 12–33% lower irrigation water use in direct seeded rice than in flooded transplanting. As most rice in India is grown using transplantation, it is important that the practice of direct seeding is encouraged. The objective of sustainable increase in agriculture productivity through genetic improvement of food crops is quite possible. Biotechnology and appropriate mix of better agronomic practices, and improved agriculture extension services, can ensure better yields while using the same amount of water.
3. *Lessons from Israel:* India's annual per capita availability of water is less than 1,500 m^3 but still much higher than that of Israel which has per capita water availability of less than 200 m^3. Still Israel exports high-value agri-produce to Europe and many other parts of the world. The country is known as the land of innovations in water management, be it drip irrigation, recycling of urban wastewater for the use in agriculture or desalinization of seawater for drinking purposes. Almost 62% of the irrigation water used in Israel comes from recycled and brackish water, thus saving potable water for domestic use. Such recycling endeavors—of course with proper treatment that make wastewater safe—have relevance in India.[34]

Green Revolution

The agricultural sector of India during the British colonial period was totally stagnant or even a negative growth was recorded in the first half of 20th century.[35] The post-second world war period witnessed medical breakthrough that brought down death rate worldwide and many countries experienced rapid increase in population producing mismatch between demand and supply. From the time of independence in 1947 until 1965, agricultural production in India was unable to meet the country's needs. Severe droughts in the mid-1960s threatened famine which was averted only by substantial shipments of food grains from the United States. By the late 1960s, however, it had begun to look as if salvation was at hand.[36] The demand and supply mismatch necessitated a major breakthrough in agriculture. Earlier, in April 1959, a team of expert sponsored by ford foundation submitted a report titled "India's food crisis and steps to meet it." The report suggested focused efforts in selected regions of the country via stress on modern inputs such as fertilizers, credit, and market facilities. On the basis of this report, the Government in 1960 introduced Intensive Area Development Program in seven districts of seven states. The seven districts were West Godavari in Andhra Pradesh, Shahabad in Bihar, Raipur in Madhya Pradesh, Thanjavur in Tamil Nadu, Ludhiana in Punjab, Aligarh in Uttar Pradesh, and Pali in Rajasthan. Among these districts, the first four were selected for rice, next two were selected for wheat, and the last one was selected for millets. This program was later extended to whole of India by selecting one district from each state. In 1965, the Government widened its agriculture intensification efforts by selecting 114 districts of the country and labeled the new program as intensive agriculture area program (IAAP). During this time, Professor Norman Borlaug along with his associates was developing HYV seeds in Mexico.* The success of Mexican agriculture and some other countries prompted South Asian and few South East Asian nations to adopt HYV seed technology. In India, the new agriculture strategy or Green Revolution was introduced in the Kharif season of 1966 and was implemented in the form of a package program since it depended crucially on regular and adequate irrigation, fertilizers, HYV seeds, pesticide, and insecticides. The Green Revolution was introduced in a total area of 1.89 mh comprising the three states of Punjab, Haryana, and western Uttar Pradesh.

The term Green Revolution was coined by Sir William Gaud, former director US Agency for International Development in 1968. Green Revolution signifies a general increase in Agriculture production and productivity. Norman Ernest Borlaug, an American biologist, humanitarian, and Nobel Laureate, took the initiative of developing the high yielding varieties of cereal grains that led to major paradigm shift in agriculture production and productivity. Norman Borlaug is hailed as "the father of Green Revolution," "agriculture's greatest spokesperson," and "the man who saved a billion lives." The noted agriculture scientist M.S. Swaminathan is hailed as the father of Green Revolution in India. M.S. Randhawa, the former civil servant, botanist, and historian is called the father of Green Revolution in Punjab.

Positive Impact of Green Revolution

The following are the positive implications of Green Revolution:

1. **Increase in the production and productivity of food grains:** The rapid increase in agricultural output resulting from the GR came from an impressive increase in yields per hectare.[37] The following points can be mentioned in this regard:

   Firstly, between 1960 and 2000, yields in all developing countries rose to 208% for wheat, 109% for rice, 157% for maize, 78% for potatoes, and 36% for cassava.[38] The research has revealed that 55% of India's output growth is accounted for an increase in average crop yield, 13% by expanding land in production and 32% by re-allocating resources to produce higher valued commodities. In fact, India was among the first countries to show the impact of the GR varieties on rice yields, with China and other Asian countries experiencing later.

   Secondly, one of the best measures to analyze the impact of Green Revolution is total factor productivity (TFP).** The country experienced strong average annual TFP growth of 3.60% in the 1980s, then growth slowing to 1.32% in the 1990s, but then again accelerating to 3.08% between 2000 and 2008. For the entire 1980–2008 period, India's average

---

*In 1960, the Philippines government with Ford and Rockefeller Foundations established International Rice Research Institute (IRRI). In 1961, the Rockefeller funded Centre in Mexico was renamed as CIMMYT (Centro International de Mejoramiento de Maiz Y Trigo or the International Maize and Wheat Improvement Centre) where Dr Norman Borlaug developed some of his famous HYV seeds such as *Lerma Rojo 64, Siete Cerros, Sonora 64,* and *Super X.*). Thus, two institutions, CIMMYT and IRRI, played a major role in the development of wheat and rice varieties, respectively.

**TFP is the measure of economic productivity that determines how efficiently and intensely the inputs are utilized in the production process. The long-run growth in income per capita in an economy is driven by growth in TFP.

annual TFP growth rate has been 1.9%. Among Indian states, only Odisha has achieved TFP growth of less than 1% on average each year, whereas Andhra Pradesh and Kerala have achieved TFP growth exceeding 3% per year. All remaining states achieved productivity growth rates between 1% per annum and 3% per annum over the reference period.[39]

2. **Increase in input usage:** The Green Revolution was a technology package and it contained improved varieties of seeds, chemical fertilizers, pesticides, and irrigation. The high yielding varieties demanded more usage of fertilizers and it was supported by the subsidy policy on fertilizers. Research has proved a long run relationship between fertilizer consumption and food grain production in India. Fertilizer consumption increased rapidly during Green Revolution years. The all India average consumption of fertilizers has increased by more than 14 times since independence. However, with the introduction of new agricultural policy where the greater emphasis is given on promotion of organic cultivation, there is a considerable reduction in the growth rate of chemical fertilizer consumption after 2000–2001. In India, high yield varieties adoption was strongly correlated with water supply. Rural India witnessed a widespread agricultural development in the 1980s, mainly due to the diffusion of private tube-wells. As a result of this diffusion, the production of rice, the main staple food in the eastern and southern India, increased rapidly and contributed to higher rural incomes and lower poverty.
3. **Self-reliance in agriculture and food security:** The major breakthrough of Green Revolution because of enhanced agriculture production was non-dependence on imports which also saved country's valuable foreign exchange reserves. As discussed earlier, India used to import cereals from the United States, Russia, and few other nations during the pre-Green Revolution period. Almost after five decades, the country has not only turned self-reliant but also exports have registered a remarkable growth. Agriculture exports constitute 14% of country's export and cereals are the largest agriculture export item followed by marine products and spices. Before Green Revolution, famine had become regular feature because of low productivity and a number of uncertainties associated with agriculture. India attained food security in 1982 with cereals production stabilizing around the annual requirement of the population.[40] The increase in agriculture production helped the policy makers to intensify efforts in food procurement and distribution to the poor and needy. The surplus agriculture production was diverted through a vast network of Public Distribution System, Antodhaya Ann Yojna, and mid-day meal scheme. Green Revolution has not only reduced frequent incidences of hunger but also changed the consumption patterns of rural households. A 10-year study in the southern India found that the increased rice production resulting from the spread of HYVs accounted for about one-third of the substantial increase in energy and protein consumption of both farmers and landless workers.[41] In fact, there is a marked increase in protein and fat intake during the post-Green Revolution phase across all income groups, suggesting that all consumers have benefitted from nutritional improvements.
4. **Backward and forward linkages:** Backward linkages in agriculture signify the inputs or industrial products that aids in the development of agriculture. For example, seeds, fertilizers, pesticides, insecticides, tractors and machinery, and irrigation act as an input, and hence, higher demand for such products intensified their output and growth and generated employment opportunities for millions. Forward linkages on the other hand are connected with those industries that use agriculture products as raw material. For example, sugar mills, cotton textile/jute textile industry, tea, rubber, coffee, and other plantation industries.

5. **Changes in income and lifestyle of the farmers:** Green Revolution brought a significant change in the income and lifestyle of the farmers both directly as well as indirectly. The following points can be mentioned in this regard:
First, in different parts of the country, agricultural growth during the 1980s was accompanied by a substantial increase in labor productivity. Consequently, along with an increase in off-farm job opportunities in the rural areas, agricultural wages started to rise. In just 10 years, that is, during 1977/1978 to 1987/1988 agricultural wages in India grew by 47% for male workers and 37% for female workers in real terms.[42] In India, it is estimated that a 1% increase in agricultural value added per hectare leads to a 0.4% reduction in poverty in the short run and 1.9% reduction in the long run, the latter arising through the indirect effects of lower food prices and higher wages.[43] As per NSSO data, the poverty situation in India improved sharply after the mid-1970s; the poverty head count ratio declined from more than 55% in 1973–1974 to 35% in 1989–1990.
Second, the post-Green Revolution phase has brought a significant change in the modern agriculture practices and opened few new vistas in the field of agriculture. Organic farming, and contract farming, and farmers' experimentation in the field of agriculture diversification became possible because of the increase in yield, outlook, and market practices. For example, in the coarse cereals production regions (mainly central India), as farmers faced decreased demand, they substituted more remunerable oil seed crops for coarse cereals, which contributed to higher rural incomes in this region especially in Madhya Pradesh, Gujarat, and Maharashtra.
6. **Spread of Green Revolution:** The Punjab, Haryana, and western Uttar Pradesh experienced an accelerated growth rate during 1965–1980 and turned into role model for rest of the Indian states. The period between 1980–1983 and 1990–1993 marks a turning point in India's agricultural development as the country experienced 3.37% growth rate in crop production. It was the time when states like West Bengal experienced high growth rate of nearly 6%. Odisha and central region also witnessed an accelerated growth rate during this period. The southern region comprising the states of Andhra Pradesh, Tamil Nadu, Karnataka, and Kerala experienced growth rate of nearly 3.5% during this period as compared to the growth rate of 1.8% during 1965–1980. The major reason for the development of eastern region was wider adoption of new technology and inputs such as HYV seeds, fertilizers, and credit. The chief factor responsible for the growth of agriculture in the southern India was faster growth of non-foodgrains, a phenomenon hailed as Rainbow Revolution[44] (see Box 11.1). The post-reform period witnessed a remarkable increase in growth of western states like Maharashtra and Gujarat; eastern states like Arunachal Pradesh, Manipur, Mizoram, Tripura, and Chhattisgarh; and states of central and southern region. Though there was a dip in growth rates during 1990s (1.8%), however, high growth rate was experienced during 11th and 12th five-year plans (around 3.5%). If states like Gujarat and Maharashtra experienced hike in growth due to adoption of Bt Cotton, then the other states experienced increase in growth rate due to increase in public and private investment expenditure, dissemination of technology, increase in remunerative returns to the farmers, and improvement in terms of trade of agriculture sector.[45]

Drawbacks of Green Revolution

1. **Green Revolution and regional inequalities:** Technological changes in the Indian agriculture had widened economic disparities between different regions, between big and

BOX 11.1 Rainbow Revolution

The concept of Rainbow revolution is an integrated development of crop cultivation, horticulture, forestry, fishery, poultry, animal husbandry and food processing industry. Following are different colors of rainbow revolution in India.

Revolution	Production
Blue Revolution	Fish production
Brown Revolution	Leather/non-conventional(India)/Cocoa production
Golden Revolution	Overall Horticulture development/Honey Production
Golden Fiber Revolution	Jute Production
Green Revolution	Food grains
Gray Revolution	Fertilizer production
Pink Revolution	Meat Production
Red Revolution	Tomato production
Round Revolution	Potato production
Silver Fiber Revolution	Cotton production
Silver Revolution	Egg production
White Revolution	Milk/dairy production
Yellow Revolution	Oil seeds production

Source: Kurukshetra, Vol. 60, No. 2, December 2011; The Hindu, March 29, 2016; The Deccan Herald, March 19, 2011.

small farmers, and between landholders and land-less workers. Green Revolution was a package program and was based on "betting on the strong" approach, and therefore, the disparity was inherent in it. The Green Revolution was crop specific and region specific, that is, the benefits of the new technology were mainly limited to the few crops, such as wheat, rice, sugarcane, and few agriculturally developed regions, having adequate irrigation facilities. Most of the crops and rain-fed agricultural regions did not get sufficient benefits from HYV technology and caused serious distress to the farmers. In fact throughout the world, where the new technology was adopted, its benefits accrued to the farmers of already developed regions, and not to the farmers of the poorest and least developed regions. For example, delay in the introduction of private tube wells due to dominance of small and marginal farmers and shortage of capital was the reason that why Green Revolution could not be accepted in the eastern region of the country for a longer period of time.[46] Besides, there is conflicting evidence as to whether Green Revolution had "spread effect" or has intensified income differences across regions. Since this seed-fertilizer technology was not suited to agriculture of the unirrigated and rainfed regions, to a greater extent it contributed to inter-regional income disparities and caused serious distress to the farmers. In fact, the Green Revolution technology worked effectively on those farms which possessed controlled production environment, such as good quality soils, better irrigation facilities and markets. Since this environment is not sufficiently available in the agriculturally backward regions, farmers of these regions could not get much benefit from the new technology; rather, they lost competitiveness and remained in the disadvantaged position as compared to the farmers in the developed regions.

2. **Green Revolution and interpersonal inequalities:** Green Revolution as discussed earlier was a package program and only rich farmers could afford it. Research reveals that Green Revolution has widened the gap between the rich and the poor, that is, the rich have become richer and the poor have become poorer. Green Revolution was crop specific as

it benefited a particular class of farmers and geographical regions growing a particular crop. The major benefits in the crop section accrued to wheat and rice growers. Moreover, as per a study in Punjab in 1967, around two-third of the farmers in the state had land size of 10 acres or less. But the Green Revolution was viable only for the farmers who owned land size more than 20 acres as only such farmers could afford to purchase new inputs and adopt mechanized farming.[47] In short, small farmers were just not equipped to keep up with the pace of the Green Revolution. The small, poor peasants who have restricted access to credit, technical knowledge, and the material means of production are unable to innovate as easily or as quickly as those who are landed, liquid, and literate.

3. **The question of sustainability:** Unintended consequences in water use, soil degradation, and chemical runoff have had serious environmental impacts beyond the areas cultivated. The following points can be mentioned in this regard:
First, groundwater depletion takes place when withdrawal is more than its replenishment. Groundwater depth depends on rainfall, pattern of available water resources utilization, existing cropping pattern, and energy policy of the state.[48] Because HYV seeds are water sensitive, exponential growth of tube wells in Indo-Gangetic plains, agricultural subsidy on critical inputs,* and lack of effective regulation on sustainable groundwater usage have contributed to rapid depletion of ground water resources. For example, about 97% of total annual groundwater draft in Punjab is consumed by the agriculture sector. However, the ground water stressed blocks in the country have been found in the seven states of Rajasthan, Tamil Nadu, Andhra Pradesh, Maharashtra, Madhya Pradesh, Gujarat, and Rajasthan.
Second, crops remove substantial quantity of major nutrients from soil, particularly, in high input intensive rice-wheat systems. Scientist after conducting diagnostic surveys in north western India confirmed that higher amounts of fertilizer need to be applied for getting the same level of yield as that achieved in the 1970s and early 1980s. But the farmers have been removing more nutrients than the amount added externally through fertilizers. Surveys have also reported declining trends in potassium and zinc in Indian soils. Due to all such factors, the land productivity has either become stagnant or going down. According to the Working Group Report on "Natural Resource Management" the estimated loss to the economy on account of soil degradation during 1980s and 1990s ranged from 11 to 26% of GDP.
Third, use of farm yard manure and green manure has declined due to various reasons like decline in draught animals (as they have been replaced by machines), change in the cropping pattern from legume crops to rice, wheat, sugarcane, and other commercial crops. It is also argued that Green Revolution technology could not promote crop-diversification but rather encouraged the crop-concentration.
Fourth, biodiversity is necessary for sustaining the rural livelihoods and achieving the food security. But the use of HYV seeds displaced indigenous species and agricultural system that had been built up over generations. This has led to loss of biodiversity and agricultural genetic resources aggravating the genetic vulnerability of many valuable gene pools.
Fifth, in order to avoid crop failure, farmers are frequently applying poisonous pesticides and insecticides, a practice that has made lands drug addict. Lands are demanding more but delivering less.

*The policy incentives such as subsidies for water pumps and electricity subsidies accelerated high level of tube well constructions by farmers. However, it was found that when incentives were corrected, farmers quickly changed behavior and adopted more sustainable practices. For example, the removal of pesticide in Indonesia in the early 1990s led to a dramatic drop in insecticide use.

Sixth, since HYV seeds are highly susceptible to diseases, poisonous chemicals are used both extensively and intensively for plant protection without realizing their health hazards.

4. **Capitalistic farming:** In India, the size of landholding has contracted because of pressure of population and laws of inheritance. Small and marginal farmers in order to increase the production and productivity in such fragmented lands are looking for viable mechanized system of farming. The availability of institutional credit and subsidy to the farm sector motivates these divided holdings to increase investment in farm machinery. However, research has proven that this type of private investment in agriculture is not desirable, as it increases the unit cost of cultivation, reduces competitiveness of small farmers, and enhances indebtedness among them. Green Revolution also reduced a substantial amount of work force from the lands as machines replaced men. For example, a tractor replaces 25% of the farm labor. Indian tractor industry has emerged as the largest in the world and account for one-third of total global production. In 1960–1961, about 93% of farm power was coming from animal sources, which has reduced to less than 10% during 2018–2019. On the other hand, mechanical and electrical sources of power have increased from 7% to more than 90% over the same period.
5. **Undesirable social consequences:** A lot of research has been done with regard to social consequences of Green Revolution. Farmers were left discontented and indebted as a result of degraded soil and pest-ridden crops. It not only had negative consequences for the ecology of the villages but had social implications as well. Before the Green Revolution, agriculturalists relied on mutual relationships within their villages. Farming was their livelihood and the way that they connected with each other. But Green Revolution transformed the entire village setup into cash-centric. After the introduction of Green Revolution technology, they found themselves solely dealing with banks and agribusiness, thus weakening relationships within villages. For example, the farmers of Punjab found themselves in the midst of increasing conflict that was converging and intensifying tensions. There was class conflict, pauperization of the lower peasantry, conflicts over water resources, and mechanization displacing labor. There was also conflict related with religious and cultural relations among different people. The Green Revolution commercialized all relations and "created an ethical vacuum where nothing is sacred and everything has a price,"[49] Another study found certain grim evidences regarding increasing number of suicides by the farmers.[50] The Green Revolution brought about an increasingly commercialized version of agriculture that was difficult for small and marginal farmers to keep up with. Because of this, they encountered increasing amounts of debt, insufficient means of support, and the incapacity to care for the needs of themselves and their families. This resulted in distress and humiliation which often pushed these farmers to suicide.[51] Various studies have highlighted problems pertaining to economic misery of local labor stemming from crop monoculture and in-migration of labor. Green Revolution affected production and productivity of Punjab agriculture and attracted a lot of migrants from the states of Uttar Pradesh, Bihar, and Madhya Pradesh. The migration is believed to have depressed wage rate of labor by about 30% in the case of paddy and nearly 20% in the case of wheat.[52] Though it helped the farmers as their product become more competitive, it harmed the local labor. The crime rate in various forms has gone up because it is easy for the migrants to commit crime as their background is unknown and they have access to employers' secrets.[53]

Second Green Revolution

The country has made great strides toward increasing food grains production since the mid-1960s. Today, India ranks high in the production of various commodities such as milk, wheat, rice, fruits, and vegetables. However, the agriculture sector in India is at a crossroad with rising demand for food items and relatively slower supply response in many commodities resulting in frequent spikes in food inflation. The technological breakthrough achieved in the 1960s is gradually waning. A report from professional services firm Grant Thornton in collaboration with FICCI has predicted spike in demand for food grains to 355 million tonnes by 2030. The need for a second Green Revolution is being experienced more than ever before.[54] The second Green Revolution is a transformation in agricultural production/productivity so as to sustain the growing demand by addressing various contemporary issues. It is a smarter revolution that will need to consider many more variables, such as global warming, new types of nonpetroleum energy, better irrigation practices, and inclusive growth while addressing the problems of small and marginal farmers.[55] The second Green Revolution encompasses both opportunities as well as challenges. Let us ponder over them.

Opportunities and Challenges

1. *Agro-forestry on degraded land:* If the first Green Revolution is charged with the impact of creating vast inequalities, the second Green Revolution must be remembered for creating sustainable and egalitarian agriculture practices by generating employment for small and marginal farmers owning low fertile lands, deprived of irrigation. A study in Rajasthan and Odisha indicates the high potential of agroforestry systems to restore the productivity of degraded lands through assisted regeneration of native vegetation and planting of trees, especially fodder, fuel, and multi-purpose species.[56] Such lands can be profitably used for the establishment of drought-tolerant fruit crops and agri-horti-pastures. Tree-based farming has the ability to withstand the vagaries of nature, provides year-round employment while protecting the soil from erosion and runoff of rain water, improves soil fertility, and increases the water table while absorbing atmospheric carbon dioxide all-round the year. Farmers can earn a regular handsome income from crops like mango, cashew, custard apple, amla, and tamarind once the orchards start bearing fruits. Apart from food grains and vegetables, there are many under-utilized plant species having food, medicinal, and nutraceutical uses which can be planted as inter-crops to fetch premium price in the local markets. Apart from unirrigated lands, there are large stretches of wastelands in India. Among the estimated 40–50 mh of wastelands, more than 9 mh are sodic wastelands. Most of these lands had been fertile irrigated fields which turned sodic due to excessive use of water for irrigation and poor drainage facilities. In many areas of Punjab, the village lands have turned barren due to waterlogging.[57] This has seriously affected agriculture production and caused unemployment in the region. With reclamation of sodic lands, it is possible to enhance food production by 50–75 million tonnes/annum, while creating employment for 8–10 million people. Similarly, several million hectares of ravine lands remaining idle for decades can be brought under agri-silvi-pasture system while improving the local economy and the biodiversity.[58]

2. *Livestock development:* Livestock development is another area which can help ushering in second Green Revolution significantly. It has been documented that more than 50% of country's cattle and buffalo and two-thirds of small animals and poultry are owned by marginal farmers only. It is simply because such farmers consider livestock as an important asset for earning their livelihood as well as supplementary income. India has the largest population of livestock in the world, but its production potential has not been optimally tapped so far. For the last few years, income increase has altered the demand pattern of Indians. The demand for milk is steeply rising and is expected to reach 180 million tonnes/year and the demand for meat is also expected to increase by three to four folds by this period. Further, dairy husbandry is the only program where poor families are able to build new assets every year in the form of crossbred cows which also have a handsome value at market place. There is a need to improve the production and productivity of livestock sector through supply of superior quality feeds and fodder, promotion of forage shrubs and trees on degraded lands and backyards, treatment of agricultural by-products to improve the nutritional qualities, and establishment of decentralized complete feed production units, strengthening veterinary health care through an extensive network of vets and para-vets. There is also scope for promoting sheep and goat husbandry, piggery and poultry for farmers who are unable to adopt dairy husbandry. Livestock being the major source of organic manure, animal husbandry should be an integral part of agriculture. The tree-based farming particularly agri-horti-pastoral system linked with livestock development can help in boosting the agricultural production while providing gainful self-employment to small farmers.[59]
3. *Efficient management of water resources:* The experience learnt from the first Green Revolution is well-known and the total benefits of Green Revolution could not be achieved due to improper management of water resources. The indiscriminate irrigation practices in many parts of the country have turned ground water polluted and arsenic prone. Water has become a scarce "economic commodity." Global warming is leading to a huge scarcity of water and this may affect many of the vulnerable regions of the world. With increasing exploitation of natural resources and environmental pollution, the atmospheric temperature is expected to rise by 3–5°C in the next 75–100 years. If it happens, the perennial rivers of Himalayas may dry up and suppress agricultural production by 40–50%. Global warming will cause erratic rainfall and the water requirement for crops is likely to increase due to a significant increase in evaporation and transpiration losses. In India, 85% of water resource is used for irrigation purpose and most of the irrigation water is inefficiently utilized and wasted. Therefore, greater awareness needs to be created to make efficient use of water resources and to prevent global warming through environmental protection as an integral part of Green Revolution.
4. *Virtual water trade:* In addition to the "real" water market, there exists, though somewhat dormant at present, another large market of "virtual water." The virtual water concept was introduced by a British geographer John Anthony Allan. Virtual/embedded water is the amount of water used in the production of food, energy, and other products. For example, the average virtual water content of paddy and wheat in India is 2,850 and 1,654 m^3/ton, respectively, against the world average of 2,291 and 1,334 m^3/ton for such crops.[60] For example, to produce 1 ton of wheat in India, say, 1,654 m^3 of water is required. That means, 1,654 m^3 of water get embedded in 1 ton of wheat. Thus, if India exports 1 ton of wheat to the United States, then there is a virtual flow of 1,654 m^3 of water from India to the

United States. Large parts of North and South America, Australia, Asia, and Central Africa are net exporters of virtual water. Most of Europe, Japan, North and South Africa, the Middle East, Mexico, and Indonesia, in contrast, are net importers of virtual water.[61] The developed countries have taken a conscious decision to save their scarce water resources by shifting the burden of cultivation to developing countries which can be proved with the help of water import dependence (WID) ratio. WID is the ratio between "water footprint" of a country's import and its total water footprints.* The higher the ratio, the more a country depends on outside water sources. During 1997–2001, the "water import dependence" of the Netherlands, the United Kingdom, Japan, and Germany were 82, 70, 64, and 53%, respectively. The corresponding figures for India, Bangladesh, China, and Brazil are 2, 3, 7 and 8%. Keeping the above challenge in mind, India needs to devise its water conservation policy and agriculture trade policy in such a manner that huge quantities of scarce water should not be transferred to importing countries. In fact, the country needs to promote the export of such agriculture goods which use less virtual water.

5. *Thrust on biotechnology:* The opportunities arising from the GE of crops and other tools of biotechnology are expected to provide answers to the productivity problems of agriculture, environmental degradation, climate change, and sustainability. The varied technologies in the realm of biotechnology and their potential make them eminently suited to the development of not just cereal crops in irrigated areas, but also dry-land crops, fruits and vegetables, livestock, fisheries, and forestry. These developments can improve food security in India, which is witnessing a diet diversification from food grains to fruit and vegetables, milk, and livestock.[62] Therefore, the Government needs to step up R&D budget of agriculture universities and should exhort agriculture research bodies to collaborate with foreign research bodies so as to develop new varieties of seeds.** The importance of biotechnology in ushering the second Green Revolution was emphasized by ICAR in its "Agricultural Policy: Vision 2020." But it is also being alleged that India has been conducting research on biotechnology without having a proper national policy in place. For example, many scientists and activists have voiced their concerns over the hurried introduction of genetically modified brinjal.*** They have raised long-term safety concerns, besides apprehension that India could lose the 2,500 varieties of brinjal it currently has. Bowing to public resistance, the Government put on hold the commercial cultivation of BT Brinjal.
6. *Capacity building:* Building capabilities at the grass root level especially of women and weaker rural households must be the central point of second Green Revolution. In India, 65–70% of the labor in crop production is contributed by women. Not only in India but across the world, women's contributions to agriculture are significant. The FAO estimates that if women had the same access to productive resources as men, they could increase yields on their farms by 20–30%. This could raise in total the agricultural output in developing countries by up to 4%, which could in turn reduce the number of hungry people

---

*A country's "Water Footprint" is the volume of water used to produce goods and services, including imports that people consume.

**Government has allowed 100% FDI in development and production of seeds and planting material.

***Bt Brinjal is a GM crop developed by Maharashtra Hybrid Seeds Company in collaboration with Monsanto. The insertion of the gene gives Brinjal plant resistance against lepidopteron insects like the Brinjal Fruit and Shoot Borer that cause up to 20% damage in the crops.

in the world by 12–17%—that is, 100–150 million people.[63] Women should be encouraged to form the self-help groups to connect them with micro-credit. Similarly, the poor farmers who comprise 65–70% of rural families, have been experiencing failures, are likely to develop a dependency syndrome and thus need regular support and peer group pressure to take active part in various development initiatives. Presently, the organizations which deal with agricultural extension, input supply, credit, and marketing at the village level are extremely weak and should be taken over by the People's Organizations. In rural India, where the poor and illiterate people are lacking initiatives, any approach with a "supply push" is not likely to work as most of the BPL families are not able to take advantage of various development schemes. There is an urgent need to create a "demand pull" through awareness among the poor about various opportunities and motivate them to take active part in socio-economic development. Such people should demand for the services to fulfill their needs, instead of the donors and traders imposing their ideas and products in rural areas. They need hand holding in the initial stage, and subsequently, the organizations of local people—self-help groups and federations—can take the responsibility of mentoring and facilitation. The people should own their programs.[64]

Summary

1. The four critical inputs of agriculture are seeds, fertilizers, pesticides, and irrigation.
Seeds: Quality of seed accounts for 20–25% of productivity. However, there are few concerns like affordability, availability, emphasis on seed R&D, and impact of GM crops on environment. Many schemes have been introduced, which are 100% FDI approval in seed R&D, infrastructural development, slashing of Bt cotton prices, and introduction of PKSY.
Fertilizers: Fertilizer consumption of 40–60 kg/ha can yield an additional 30–45 million tonnes of food grains. However, there are certain problems in the use of fertilizers like discrepancies in the use of fertilizers, that is, NPK ratio is 6.7:2.4:1 against their desirable ratio of 4:2:1; low fertilizer consumption; imprudent NBS policy which led to increase in fertilizer prices and decrease in consumption; and higher dependence on imports and hazardous impact on health and environment. The tree major schemes that government is running in fertilizer sector are NBS scheme (2010), city compost scheme (2016), and DBT scheme (2016).
Pesticides: India lags behind many nations in terms of pesticide usage. Despite its advantage in killing harmful insects, pesticide usage can cause various problems like impacting human health due to exposure, contaminating environment, causing severe groundwater pollution, and impacting soil fertility. At the policy level, various schemes are being running: implementation of insecticides Act, 1968; launching of integrated pest management scheme; submission on plant protection and plant quarantine, and establishment of central insecticides laboratory at Faridabad.
Irrigation: In India, gross irrigated area as a percentage of total cropped area is 49% and rest of the country's lands depend upon rainfall. The main three sources of irrigation in India are well and tubewell, canal, and tank and all these three contribute 61.41, 25.6, and 3.13% of total irrigation, respectively. Irrigation is important for Indian agriculture in different ways, viz., positive impact of irrigation on yield; scanty rainfall; increase in crop intensity; HYV seeds needing more water for better productivity; provides stability to agriculture and multiple direct and indirect benefits to the economy. Irrigation in India also suffers from certain problems such as underutilized irrigation potential; inefficiency in the use of irrigation as agriculture consumes 84% of available water; unequal regional spread of irrigation with Punjab being the highest irrigated and Assam being the lowest; and overexploitation of water resources which has resulted in a significant decline in the groundwater table. The Government launched various irrigation schemes like classification of irrigation schemes (1950–1951), CADP (1974–1975), RIDF (1995–1996), AIBP (1996–1997), CADWMP (2004–2005), MI (2006), NMMI (2010), and PMKSY (2015). However, to improvise irrigation efficiency in the country, the country should emphasize on MI, adopt prudent agronomic practices, and learn lessons from Israel which has done remarkable innovations in water management.
2. Green Revolution was introduced in India during the Kharif season of 1966. Norman Borlaug is hailed as the father of Green Revolution and M.S. Swaminathan is called as the father of Green Revolution of India. The major achievements of Green Revolution in India are increase in the production and productivity of food grains (also increase in TFP); increase in input usage (as Green Revolution was a package program); self-reliant agriculture and food security (non-dependence on imports and intensification of food procurement and distribution to the poor and needy); backward and forward linkages; and changes in income and lifestyle of the farmers (by increasing labor productivity/wages) and spread of Green Revolution to other regions of the country (esp. after 1980s which is also hailed as Rainbow Revolution). However, the Green Revolution also had various drawbacks such as increase in regional inequalities (as it benefitted the already irrigated regions of the country); increase in inter-personal inequalities (as only rich farmers with big lands could imbibe new technology inputs); unsustainable agriculture (making lands and ground water addicted with pesticides/chemical fertilizers); and increase in capitalistic farming (adoption of labor displacing technology) and undesirable social consequences (increase in farmer distress and suicides).
3. The second Green Revolution is a transformation in agricultural production/productivity so as to sustain the growing demand by addressing various contemporary issues and inculcates inclusive growth while addressing the problems of small and marginal farmers. The opportunities and challenges associated

with second GR are agro-forestry on degraded land (by promoting drought-tolerant fruit crops and agri-horti-pastures); livestock development (as it provides stable source of income); efficient management of water resources; conserving virtual water (by increasing water import dependence); and thrust on biotechnology (via promotion of new varieties of HYV seeds) and capacity building (by improving the productivity of women and weaker rural households.

Endnotes

1. Pingali, P. (2014). *Green Revolution: Impacts, Limits, and the Path Ahead*, Chapter 4. In W. Falcon (Ed.) Frontiers in Food Policy. Stanford, CA: Stanford University Press.
2. Chandra, B., Mukherjee, M. & Mukherjee, A. *India After Independence (1947–2000)*, Penguin Books India. New Delhi. p.411.
3. Department of Agriculture Cooperation & Farmers Welfare. *Seeds*. Retrieved http://agricoop.nic.in/divisiontype/seeds (Accessed on January 11, 2019).
4. Economic Survey, 2016–2017, p.171.
5. *The Economic Times*, 13 March, 2018.
6. 29th Report of the Standing Committee on Agriculture (2015–2016) tabled in Lok Sabha on the subject "Impact of Chemical Fertilizers and Pesticides on Agriculture and Allied Sectors in the Country."
7. Pocket Book of Agriculture Statistics, Department of Agriculture, Cooperation & Farmers Welfare, GOI, 2017–2018.
8. India's flawed fertilizer policy, Livemint, April 1, 2015.
9. Kinekar, B. (2011). Potassium fertilizer situation in India: Current use and perspectives. *Karnataka Journal of Agricultural Science, 24 (1) : (1-6)*
10. State of Agriculture in India, PRS Legislative research, p.11.
11. Press Information Bureau, Government of India, January 20, 2016.
12. Economic Survey, GOI, 2017–2018.
13. Aktar, W., et al. (2009). Impact of pesticides use in agriculture: Their benefits and hazards. *Interdisciplinary Toxicology*, 2(1), 1–12.
14. Gupta, S.K., Jani, J.P., Saiyed, H.N., & Kashyap, S.K. (1984), Health hazards in pesticide formulators exposed to a combination of pesticides. *Indian Journal of Medicinal Research*, *79*, 666
15. Down to earth, November 27, 2017
16. Aktar, W., et al. (2009). Impact of pesticides use in agriculture: Their benefits and hazards. *Interdisciplinary Toxicology*, 2(1), 1–12.
17. Down to earth, June 27, 2018.
18. Press Information Bureau, Government of India October 8, 2014.
19. Annual Report, Department of Agriculture, Cooperation & Farmers Welfare, Ministry of Agriculture, GOI, p.98.
20. Hanumantha Rao, C.H. Agriculture, food security, poverty and environment, New Delhi.
21. Jin, Y., et al. (2012). The impact of irrigation on agricultural productivity: Evidence from India. In International Association of Agricultural Economists (IAAE) triennial conference.
22. Gandhi, B. (2011). Groundwater irrigation in India. In: IDFC, India Infrastructure Report, New Delhi.
23. FAO. (1999). Poverty reduction and irrigated agriculture, IPTRID Issues Paper No. 1.
24. Bhatia, R., Malik, R.P.S., & Bhatia, M. (2007). Direct and indirect economic impacts of the Bhakra multipurpose dam, India. *Irrigation and drainage*, *56*(2–3), April–July 2007.
25. NITI Aayog, Government of India. (2015). Raising agricultural productivity and making farming remunerative for farmers. Retrieved from (Accessed on March 10. 2019) https://niti.gov.in
26. *Ibid.*
27. Hoekstra, A.Y., Chapagain, A.K. (2008). *Globalization of water: Sharing the planet's freshwater resources*. John Wiley and Sons.
28. Esha Zaveri. India's groundwater future is at stake, *The Hindu Business Line*, May 9, 2017.
29. Chinnasamy, P., & Agoramoorthy, G. (2015). Groundwater storage and depletion trends in Tamil Nadu State, India. *Water Resources Management*, *29*(7):2139–2152.

30. Banerji, A. (2015). Water level going down by 36 cm every year in district, *The Tribune*, March 22, 2015.
31. For details, see the link http://pmksy.gov.in/AboutPMKSY.aspx.
32. Task force on Micro irrigation Accessed from http://pmksy.gov.in/microirrigation/Archive/TaskForce_on_ MicroIrrigation.pdf
33. Huguenard, S. (2017). Time to focus on 'more crop per drop', *The Hindu Business Line*, July 19, 2017.
34. Gulati, A. (2017). Irrigation tips from an arid country, *The Indian Express*, July 3, 2017.
35. Blyn, G. (1966). *Agricultural trends in India, 1891–1947: Output, availability and productivity*. Philadelphia: University of Pennsylvania Press.
36. Fitzgerald-Moore, P., & Parai, B.J. *The green revolution* Accessed from http://people.ucalgary.ca
37. Pingali, P.L. *Green revolution: Impacts, limits, and the path ahead.* Seattle: Bill & Melinda Gates Foundation, Agricultural Development.
38. FAO. (2004). *The state of food and agriculture 2003–2004.* Rome: Food and Agriculture Organization of the United Nations.
39. Rada, N.E. (2013). Agricultural growth in India: Examining the post-green revolution transition. Economic Research Service, US Dept. of Agriculture, retrieved from https://ageconsearch.umn.edu (Accessed on December 5, 2018).
40. Deccan Herald, January 19, 2011.
41. Pingali, P.L. *Green revolution: Impacts, limits, and the path ahead*. Seattle: Bill & Melinda Gates Foundation, Agricultural Development.
42. Yanagisawa, H. (2008). Economic growth and transformation of rural society in contemporary India, *Chiba Daigaku Keizai Kenkyu*, *23*(3), 283–314.
43. Fujita, K. (2010). The Green Revolution and its significance for economic development. Working papers 17, JICA Research Institute.
44. Sawant, S.D., & Achutan, C.V. (1995). Agriculture growth across crops and regions, EPW, March 1995. p. A2–A13.
45. Bhalla, G.S., & Singh, G. (2009). Liberalization and Indian agriculture—A state wise analysis, EPW, December 26, 2009.
46. Fujita, K. (2010). The Green Revolution and its significance for economic development, Working Papers 17, JICA Research Institute.
47. Newman, B. (2007). A bitter harvest: Farmer suicide and the unforeseen social, environmental and economic impacts of the green revolution in Punjab, India. Development Report No. 15. January 2007. Food First: Institute for Food and Development Policy, Web.
48. Srivastava, S.K., et al. (2017). Revisiting groundwater depletion and its implications on farm economics in Punjab, India. *Current Science, 113*(3), August 10, 2017.
49. Shiva, V. (1993). The violence of the green revolution: Third world agriculture, ecology and politics (2nd ed.). London: Zed Books Ltd. Print.
50. For detailed discussion on "farmers' suicides," refer to Chapter 13 "Agriculture Finance in India."
51. Vasavi, A.R. (2009). Suicides and the making of India's agrarian distress. *South African Review of Sociology*, *40*(1), 94–108. Web. August 27.
52. Kaur, B., et al. (2011). Causes and impact of labour migration: A case study of Punjab agriculture, *Agricultural Economics Research Review, 24* (Conference Number), 459–466
53. Singh, G., & Singh, J. (2006). Green revolution and economic plight of agricultural labour in Punjab, *The Indian Journal of Labour Economics, 49*(4).
54. Economic Survey, 2010–2011, p.215.
55. Plant a second Green Revolution—A global food summit is a test of leadership in pushing research on higher crop yields. *The Christian Science Monitor*. June 3, 2008. Retrieved March 7, 2019.
56. Nayak, D., et al. Rehabilitation of degraded lands through agroforestry systems in Rajasthan and Odisha, India", retrieved from http://www.worldagroforestry.org (Accessed on July 5, 2018).
57. *The Tribune*, May 23, 2012.
58. Second Green Revolution for sustainable livelihood of small farmers, Concept Paper, BAIF Development Research Foundation, Pune, p.4.
59. Second Green Revolution for sustainable livelihood of small farmers, Concept Paper, BAIF Development Research Foundation, Pune, p.4.
60. Craswell, E., Bonnell, M., Bossio, D., Demuth, S., & van de Giesen, N. (2007). *Integrated assessment of water resources and global change: A north-south analysis*. Springer Netherlands. p.40.
61. Dey, D. (2009). The 2nd Green Revolution in India: The emerging contradictions, consequences and the need for an alternative initiative, Working Paper, Social Science Research Network, retrieved from https://papers.ssrn.com/ (Accessed on November 6, 2018).
62. Chandrasekhara Rao, N., Pray, C.E., & Herring, R.J. (2015) Biotechnology for a second green

revolution in India: Socioeconomic, political, and public policy issues, *The Journal of Agro-biotechnology Management and Economics*, *18*(2), Article 1.

63. Munshi, S. It's time to recognize and empower India's women farmers, Lecture in India Economic Summit, Accessed from https://www.weforum.org

64. Second Green Revolution for sustainable livelihood of small farmers, Concept Paper, BAIF Development Research Foundation, Pune, p.4.

CHAPTER 12

Agriculture Prices and Food Security

You cannot build a peaceful world on empty stomachs and human misery.

—Norman Borlaug

Introduction

Let us assume that farmers in India reap excellent harvest due to good rains and there is no crop failure because of pest or insect attack. But the food grains due to inelastic demand* will pile up in the stocks and there will be a general glut in the market. Supply being more and demand remaining constant, the prices of food grains will experience a steep fall and hence farmers will end up earning lesser revenue. The inference we can draw from above is that the good harvest is not good for farmers. This problem is called the paradox of plenty in agriculture. The consumers too can suffer in case there is poor harvest (due to any exogenous reason) and prices soar high because of supply shortage. To safeguard the interests of both farmers as well as consumers, government's role and intervention becomes essential. Agriculture prices thus safeguard the interest of both the farmers as well as consumers.

This chapter will focus upon the following significant issues:

- Objectives of agriculture price policy
- Components of agriculture price policy
- Advantages and disadvantages of agriculture price policy
- Food security and its components
- Government measures to promote food security
- Critical appraisal of food security

Agriculture Price Policy and Its Objectives

The history of food price policy can be taken back to the Bengal famine of 1943. Before this, there was no set principle of food price policy but only a sort of ad-hoc arrangement of providing food relief during crisis. After the Bengal famine, the Government established Foodgrains Policy Committee under the Chairmanship of Sir George Gregory. Due to emergence of food shortage, India

* Inelastic demand means despite the price change, the demand for foodgrains remains unaffected.

began to import wheat from the United States under PL-480 in the year 1956.* The Foodgrain Enquiry Committee 1957, headed by Asoka Mehta, further suggested the maintenance of buffer stocks, and setting up of the foodgrains stabilization organization to undertake purchase and sale operàtion of foodgrains. On the recommendation of Committee, the Food Corporation of India (FCI) was set up in 1965 with the aim to procure and facilitate Public Distribution System (PDS). The Foodgrains Price Committee under the chairmanship of L.K. Jha (famously known as Jha committee) in 1964 recommended setting up of Agriculture Price Commission to build a balanced and integrated price structure of the country as a whole. Accordingly, Agriculture Price Commission was established by the Government in 1965, which was later renamed as Commission for Agriculture Cost and Prices (CACP) in 1985. Ever since its inception, the commission is announcing minimum support price (MSP)/procurement price for different agriculture commodities.

The objectives, thrust, and instruments of agricultural price policy have undergone noticeable shifts during the past 50 years. Up to the mid-1960s, when agriculture production was low, the main instruments of price policy were controls/restrictions on foodgrain sales, food imports, and distribution of foodgrains at subsidized price. After the mid-1960s especially after the introduction of green revolution, price policy was assigned a positive role of augmenting the availability of foodgrains by increasing domestic production. Thus, the emphasis of the policy was to achieve remunerative prices for the farmers and providing foodgrains to the consumers at reasonable prices. However, the broader objectives of agriculture price policy of the Government are:

1. to protect or insure the farmer through guaranteed MSP;
2. to induce the desired output of different crops as per growth targets;
3. to provide stability to the agriculture sector in general and farmers' income in particular;
4. to induce farmers to part with a large proportion of foodgrains production as a marketed surplus; and
5. to protect the consumer against excessive rise in prices.

Instruments of Agriculture Price Policy

There are three major instruments of agriculture price policy of the government.[1]

1. MSP/procurement price as assured prices,
2. maintaining buffer stocks, and
3. distributing foodgrains at issue prices through the public distribution system.

Minimum Support Price (MSP)

MSP is the guaranteed price at which government purchases foodgrains from the farmers in case market prices fall below it. The government announces MSP for around 23 crops and in case of wheat and rice there is open-ended policy, that is, there is no limit on the government purchase (Table 12.1). *Procurement price* on the other hand is the price at which government procures

*The United States' president Dwight D. Eisenhower signed into the law Agricultural Trade Development and Assistance Act on July 10, 1954, commonly known as PL-480. In 1961, President John F. Kennedy renamed it as "Food for Peace."

TABLE 12.1 MSP of Wheat and Rice

Marketing Season	MSP of Wheat	MSP of Paddy	
		Common	Grade A
2007–2008	850	745	675
2008–2009	1,000	900	930
2009–2010	1,080	1,000	1,030
2010–2011	1,100	1,000	1,030
2011–2012	1,170	1,080	1,110
2012–2013	1,285	1,250	1,280
2013–2014	1,350	1,310	1,345
2014–2015	1,400	1,360	1,400
2015–2016	1,450	1,410	1,450
2016–2017	1,525	1,470	1,510
2017–2018	1,625	1,550	1,590
2018–2019*	1,840	1,750	1,770
2019–2020	1,840	1,815	1,835
2020–2021	1,925	1,868	1,888
2021–2022	2,015	1,940	1,960
2022–2023	2,125	2,040	2,060
2023–2024	2,275	2,183	2,203

Source: Department of Agriculture Cooperation & Farmers Welfare. Retrieved from http://www.agricoop.nic.in (accessed on April 15, 2024).

* Minimum Support Price of wheat for 2018–2019 season to be marketed in 2019–2020.

foodgrains from the farmers to carry out its PDS operations. Technically it must be higher than MSP as procurement price is not the minimum guaranteed price. In India, government procures plentiful foodgrains through MSP policy and there is no need to separately execute procurement price policy. Hence in India, MSP and procurement price policy are one and the same. The MSP is announced by the Government of India (GOI) at the beginning of the sowing season for certain crops on the basis of the recommendations of the CACP (Box 12.1). CACP recommends MSPs of 23 commodities, which comprise seven cereals, five pulses, seven oilseeds, and four commercial crops.[2] To facilitate procurement of foodgrains, FCI and various State Agencies in consultation with the State Government establish a large number of purchase centers at various mandis and key points.

BOX 12.1 How is MSP Determined by CACP?

CACP determines MSP by taking into consideration cost of production, changes in input prices, input–output price parity, trends in market prices, the emerging demand and supply situation, and intercrop price parity; the effects on cost of living, general price level, and industrial cost structure; international price situation; and parity between prices paid and received by farmers' terms of trade. The CACP's methodology has two major advantages: First, it ensures that producers do not suffer any loss and also get commensurate price on selling their produce. Second, the cost of production also captures the market trend to the extent that it reflects the changes in the wage rate and input prices and current international price situation.

There are three main cost concepts that the CACP considers while recommending MSP of crops:

1. A2 = These are the costs that the farmer incurs for buying various inputs such as seeds, fertilizers, hired/owned labor, hired/owned machinery, and rent paid for leased land.
2. A2 + FL =A2 plus imputed value of family labor in producing a crop (i.e., the opportunity cost of working on the field).
3. C2 =A2 + FL plus interest on value of owned capital assets plus rental value of owned land.

A2 + FL cost measure accounts for only variable cost of farming, while C2 includes both variable and fixed cost. Therefore, C2 can be labeled as most comprehensive measure and approximates full production cost.

Sources:

1. Cuts International (2015). Minimum support price and farmers' income. A case study for wheat production in Chittorgarh, Rajasthan (India). Retrieved from http://www.cuts-ccier.org (accessed on March 18, 2019).
2. Tripathi, A.K. (2012). Agricultural price policy, output, and farm profitability—examining linkages during post-reform pin India, *Asian Journal of Agriculture and Development, 10*(1).
3. Commission for Agriculture Cost and Prices (2018). Retrieved from http://cacp.dacnet.nic.in (accessed on March 19, 2019).

Buffer Stock

Buffer stock refers to a reserve of a commodity that is used to offset price fluctuations and unforeseen emergencies. Buffer stocks serve as shock absorbers in the economy and provide a defense mechanism against widely fluctuating price levels. For example, the Government builds stocks of food, agricultural goods, and other essential commodities either through direct purchase from the domestic market or through imports from outside and releases these stocks for sale in the domestic market in case market prices go up. The concept of buffer stock in India was started during the 4th five-year plan (Table 12.2).

TABLE 12.2 Foodgrain Stocking Norms in India (in Lakh Metric Ton)

	Operational Stock			Strategic Reserves		
As on	**Rice**	**Wheat**	**Total**	**Rice**	**Wheat**	**Grand Total**
April 1	115.80	44.60	160.40	20	30	210.40
July 1	115.40	245.80	361.20	20	30	411.20
October 1	82.50	175.20	257.70	20	30	307.70
December 1	56.10	108.00	164.10	20	30	214.10

Source: Foodgrains Stocking Norms. Retrieved from http://fci.gov.in (accessed on March 2, 2019).

Issue Price

It is the price at which foodgrains are sold to general public through fair price shops (FPS)/ration depots. The GOI has been fixing Central Issue Prices of wheat and rice from time to time, which is uniform throughout the country (Table 12.3).

TABLE 12.3 Central Issue Price of Wheat and Rice Effective From July 1, 2002 (Rate:₹/Quintal)

Commodity	Above Poverty Line	Below Poverty Line	Antyodaya Anna Yojana	National Food Security Act	Other than National Food Security Act
Wheat	610	415	200	200	610
Rice	830	565	300	300	830

Source: Public Distribution System. Retrieved from http://fci.gov.in (accessed on March 19, 2019).

Advantages of MSP Policy

Stabilizing Market Prices of Agriculture Products

The MSP is an important policy of the Union Government to determine floor price of major agricultural produces every year for protecting the farmers from the middlemen and fluctuating market conditions as it provides them an assured market in addition to a minimum assured return. A study titled "Evaluation Study on Efficacy of Minimum Support Prices (MSP) on Farmers" conducted by NitiAayog, found that the MSP has succeeded in providing floor rate for major foodgrains like paddy and wheat and other produces such as gram (black and green), spices, oilseeds (groundnut, mustard, til), sugarcane, jute, and cotton, and it did not allow market prices to fall below the MSP fixed for them.[3] More than 90% of the farmers in almost every state included in the study were unanimous with the view that the MSP should continue as it insulated them from an unfavorable market conditions by assuring them a minimum return for their produce.

Technology Incentive

The MSP system was started in India in the mid-1960s to create a favorable incentive environment for the adoption of high yield varieties (HYVs) of wheat and rice, which were seen to possess a vast potential for raising grain production.[4] Since its introduction, MSP has been playing a critical role in stabilizing market prices in addition to helping the beneficiaries in adoption of modern technologies in farming and by inducing investment in cost-reducing technology.

Food Security

MSP policy has been instrumental in elimination the food shortage in the country and ensuring the self-reliance in foodgrains. By announcing MSP for around 23 crops every year, the Government encourages the farmers to produce certain crops while assuring remunerative returns. Consequently, the foodgrain production has increased and the Government's buffer stock has also burgeoned. The Government is running various welfare schemes viz. Public Distribution System, Antyodaya Ann Yojana, Integrated Child Development Service Programme, Mid-Day Meal (MDM) scheme, etc.

Providing Certainty to Farmers' Income

The farmers' income is highly unstable because of many exogenous factors that affect production and productivity. In India the input usage in agriculture is far below than international standards. Around 50% of gross-cropped area is rainfed and there are huge gaps in per hectare fertilizer and pesticide usage. The HYV seed technology has also not disseminated in all parts of the country. All such factors influence farm production and any surplus or scant production affects agriculture prices causing distress to both farmers and consumers. MSP policy thus provides stability to farmers' income and gives an element of certainty to hitherto vulnerable farm sector.

Problems with Agriculture Price Policy

The MSP Controversy

The National Commission on Farmers headed by M.S. Swaminathan in its report submitted in October 2006 recommended fixing MSP at levels "at least 50% more than the weighted average cost of production." But the Commission did not elaborate on what really constituted "weighted average cost of production."[5] As mentioned earlier, the CACP gives three definitions of production costs: A2, A2 + FL, and C2. The government announced 50% over A2 + FL as a new benchmark for calculating MSP. But according to M.S. Swaminathan, MSP announced was higher in absolute terms but below the recommended level and the Government should have announced MSP, 50% above C2 costs. According to M.S. Swaminathan, the price policy of the Government should have three integrated components, such as MSP based on the formula of C2 + 50%, increasing consumption through the effective implementation of the Food Security Act, and school noon meal programs and a favorable procurement policy to ensure that farmers do receive the MSP promised. But according to eminent agriculture economist Ashok Gulati, the right policy instrument would have been income policy that focuses on the income of the farmers. The price policy has a limit if it goes beyond international prices. This will negatively affect exports, lead to accumulation of stock and hurt farmers even more.[6]

MSP and the Farmers' Distress

Agriculture price policy has been largely successful in playing a major role in providing reasonable margin levels over production costs to farmers of both wheat and paddy. Nonetheless, the margin over total cost and variable cost had declined in the post-reform period in both crops. The net income in real terms had declined also, leading to distress among farmers. The decline in profitability has discouraged farmers from increasing their spending on yield-augmenting technology, resulting in poor yield growth rates and in a decline in production growth rates.[7] It was also found that sometimes, the small and marginal farmers resorted to distress sales due to urgent need for money or to repay the loan taken before the sowing season. For some farmers, the MSP fixed is too low as it did not cover the rising farming costs. The Government needs to look into these issues for their appropriate redressal.[8]

Late Announcement of MSP

The instances of farmers coming to know about the MSP after they have sown their farms, and thus depriving them of any planning for their crops keeping in view the MSP, are quite common in India. The study conducted by Niti Aayog has revealed few shocking facts. For example, in Bihar farmers knew about MSP but the awareness about the time of their announcement was very low. In Gujarat 33% of farmers were aware of MSP at the time of their declaration, whereas none of the farmers in Bellary district of Karnataka knew about MSP before the sowing season.[9]

Problems at the Procurement End

Poor infrastructure facilities such as lack of covered storage/godowns facility for temporary storage of produce make MSP policy unworkable. In many states it has been found that the procurement centers are quite far away from the farmlands resulting into heavy transportation cost. In many cases it is found that procurement centers do not open timely and farmers under the fear of likely wastage of foodgrains (which lies in the open) are forced to sell it in the market. The lack of electronic weighing equipment in some places also discourages farmers. There have also been reports of the authorities insisting for revenue records and delay in payments, etc., which de-motivate farmers not to sell produce in the mandis.

Contribution to Inflationary Trend

There have been two major reasons of increase in MSP in the recent past: one, increases in production cost and second, increase in international prices of agriculture goods. When the international market prices of agriculture commodities increase due to supply shock, domestic prices of the respective commodities also undergo an increase more than the existing MSP. Farmers instead of selling their produce to the Government get diverted to the international market. This forces government to offer higher MSP to the farmers. The pulls and pressures of democracy and farmer lobbies make it impossible to roll back these prices without very high political costs, even if global prices recede considerably. The sharp rise in MSP pushes up the price level in the economy as general price level is very much sensitive to changes in foodgrains' prices. The result of these higher support prices is that it hurts the common man. Higher MSP has an adverse impact on poverty reduction as well. Studies confirm that a 10% increase in MSP of wheat and rice leads to a decline in overall GDP by 0.33%, increase in aggregate price index by 1.5%, reduction in investments by 1.9% and has a minuscule impact on agricultural GDP.[10]

Bias in Favor of Surplus States and Rich Farmers

In India around 20 states grow wheat but the three states of Punjab, Haryana, and Madhya Pradesh account for approximately 85% of wheat procurement with FCI and other state agencies. In the case of rice, Punjab and Haryana accounted for 90% of country's procurement.[11] Consequently, the benefits of MSP accrue to only selected states of the country. Furthermore, most of the benefits have been cornered by the large farmers who were able to implement the new agriculture strategy and obtain credit and other inputs easily. The research has revealed that through MSP the average income transfer to large farmers is approximately 10 or more times greater than those received by marginal farmers. Using the C2 benchmark, the total transfer per household in Punjab amounts to an average of approximately ₹13,000 per year, and ranges from approximately ₹3,000 per marginal farmer to ₹34,000 for large farmers.[12]

Blow to Agriculture Diversification

The main idea of MSP policy is to promote agriculture diversification in the country by announcing MSP for 23 crops. But instead of promoting agriculture diversification, the MSP has proved to be a major bottleneck. The Government offers MSP for all such crops but exercises open-ended policies for only wheat and rice. The open-ended policy has incentivized farmers not to go out of the comfort zone and remain stick to the vicious circle of wheat and rice. Consequently, there is shortage of other agriculture items that causes the nation to depend upon food imports. For example, India is the world's largest importer of pulses and edible oil.

Food Security and Public Distribution System in India

According to Food and Agriculture Organization (FAO), food security exists when all people, at all times, have physical and economic access to sufficient, safe, and nutritious food to meet their dietary needs and food preferences for an active and healthy life. Ensuring food security ought to be an issue of great importance for a country like India where more than one-third of the population is estimated to be absolutely poor and one-half of all children malnourished in one way or another.[13] Over the coming decades, a changing climate, growing global population, rising food prices, and environmental stressors will have significant yet uncertain impacts on food security. Adaptation strategies and policy responses to global change, including options for handling water allocation, land use patterns, food trade, post-harvest food processing, and food prices and safety, are urgently needed.[14]

Components of Food Security

Food security has three aspects: (1) availability of food; 2) access of food; 3) absorption of food. Both availability and access signify quantitative aspect of food security whereas absorption (nutrition) covers the qualitative aspect. Let us have a brief discussion on all these three aspects.

Availability of Food

Availability of sufficient stocks of food to meet domestic demand depends upon either domestic supply or imports. Sufficient availability of foodgrains in the country requires policy intervention in the following areas:

Production and Yield of Foodgrains Attainment of self-sufficiency in foodgrains at the national level is one of the country's major achievements in the post-independence period. The growth rate of production of foodgrains must be higher than that of population growth rate so as to ensure comfortable levels of food security. The total production of foodgrains increased by more than five times, that is, from 51 million tonnes in 1950–1951 to 285 million tonnes in 2017–2018. The country's requirement for foodgrains in order to provide for its population is projected to be 300 million tonnes by 2025, which seems to be easily attainable. This implies that the crop output needs to grow at an annual average of 2%, which is close to the current growth trend.[15] The performance of agriculture is important for availability and access to food as around 50% people in the country are dependent on this sector. India's agricultural yield of foodgrains has increased by more than four times since 1950–1951 but country's yield is low when compared to countries such as China, Brazil, and the United States.

Per Capita Availability of Foodgrains The per capita availability of foodgrains has experienced a fluctuating trend during the past 70 years. It is evident from Table 12.4 that per capita availability has increased in the pre-reform period but decreased during 1991–2001 and again increased during 2001–2015. As compared to 1951, the per capita availability of rice has increased by 20% but in case of wheat the growth is more than 210% (Table 12.4).

TABLE 12.4 Per Capita Availability of Foodgrains (g/day)

Year	Rice	Wheat	Total Foodgrains
1951	158.9	65.7	394.9
1991	221.7	166.8	510.1
2001	190.5	135.8	416.2
2015	186	168	465.1
2017	183	182.7	489
2019	192.1	177.1	494.7
2020	201.2	177.7	512.5
2021	73.3	67	186.8
2022	69.6	68.8	

Source: Department of Agriculture, Cooperation & Farmers Welfare. *Agricultural Statistics at a Glance* 2023.

Changes in Consumption Patterns and Demand for Non-Cereal Food As an economy develops and per capita income rises, the food habits of the people also dramatically change. India's food consumption patterns have spectacularly changed in the post-Green Revolution period. The reduction in average cereal consumption may not be a cause of concern because the decline is mostly driven by reduced consumption among the middle- and high-income groups. Substitution away from cereals to other foods is expected when income increases. In recent years, however, there has been decline in the cereal consumption of poor and this is the cause of concern.[16] Pulse is called poor man's protein and its consumption remained almost stagnant. However, the consumption of edible oil, milk, eggs, and fish has increased significantly.

Food Management Food management consists of three instruments: MSPs/procurement prices, buffer stocks, and the PDS. For more details, please refer to the section 'Instruments of Agriculture Price Policy'.

Access to Food

Access to food signifies people's capability to get food. The goals of food security will remain incomplete if the people do not have access to the food they need, either from their own production, from the market, and/or from the government's transfer mechanism. But for that the poor must have sufficient purchasing power to buy food. Adequate purchasing power for the poor to buy food can be ensured in two ways. One is to have an employment intensive pattern of growth, which can provide remunerative work to the poor and enhance their power to purchase food. Another way is to increase income and subsidize food through social protection programs like PDS and employment programs. The country has made significant progress in reducing the problem of hunger but there is still a long way to go as India has demonstrated dismal performance as per Global Hunger Index rankings (Box 12.2). In poverty front, though absolute number has declined, India is still the home for world's largest number of poor on earth. Further the creation of employment is one way of ensuring the Right to Food. With an increase in purchasing power, the poor would be able to increase their food consumption. Another indicator of purchasing power is agricultural wages as increase in wages has proved to be sufficient condition for significant reduction in poverty in rural areas. However, the growth rate of real wages has not been commensurate with increase in cost of living in the country.

BOX 12.2 The Global Hunger Index (GHI)

The Global Hunger Index (GHI) is a tool designed to comprehensively measure and track hunger at the global, regional, and national levels. The International Food Policy Research Institute (IFPRI) calculates GHI scores each year to assess progress and setbacks in combating hunger. The GHI is designed to raise awareness and understanding of the struggle against hunger, provide a means to compare the levels of hunger between countries and regions, and call attention to the areas of the world in greatest need of additional resources to eliminate hunger.

GHI scores are based on four indicators:

Undernourishment: The share of the population that is undernourished (i.e., whose caloric intake is insufficient);
Child Wasting: The share of children under the age of 5 who are wasted (i.e., who have low weight for their height, reflecting acute undernutrition);
Child Stunting: The share of children under the age of 5 who are stunted (i.e., who have low height for their age, reflecting chronic undernutrition); and
Child Mortality: The mortality rate of children under the age of 5 (in part, a reflection of the fatal mix of inadequate nutrition and unhealthy environments).

The Index ranks countries on a 100-point scale, with 0 being the best score (no hunger) and 100 being the worst, although neither of these extremes is reached in practice. Values less than 10.0 reflect low hunger, values from 10.0 to 19.9 reflect moderate hunger, values from 20.0 to 34.9 indicate serious hunger, values from 35.0 to 49.9 reflect alarming hunger, and values of 50.0 or more reflect extremely alarming hunger levels.

As per 2018 GHI report, India has a serious hunger problem (GHI value = 31.1) and ranks 103rd out of 119 countries on the global hunger index. According to the report, India is among the 45 countries that have "serious levels of hunger". Central African Republic ranks 119 at the bottom end.

Source: Global Hunger Index. Retrieved from http://www.globalhungerindex.org (accessed on December 16, 2019). India ranks 103 on global hunger index. The Economic Times, October 15, 2018.

Absorption

India is the home to world's largest number of poor, hungry, malnourished, and anemic people in the world. Access to food, therefore, requires policy intervention in the areas of hunger management and reduction in poverty and unemployment. Nearly 25% of world's hungry people live in India. A survey of over 6 lakh households by National Family Health Survey during 2015–2016 reveals that 36% of Indian children are underweight, while the proportion of stunted children is 38%.* And in some of the worst-affected districts such as Purulia in West Bengal and Nandurbar in Maharashtra, every second child is undernourished.[17] According to new Global Nutrition Report 2017 for 140 nations, India is at the bottom of the table with maximum number of women impacted with anemia in the world, followed by China, Pakistan, Nigeria, and Indonesia. In India, more than half (51%) of all women of reproductive age have anemia, whereas more than one in five (22%) of adult women are overweight.[18] According to Sudha Narayanan, India faces today the triple burden of malnutrition—the coexistence of inadequate calorie intake and under-nutrition among a large section of the population, excess intake of dietary energy leading to obesity and related health issues among another section of the population, and pervasive micronutrient deficiencies.[19]

* For details, kindly see National Family Health Survey Report-4, 2015–2016.

Government Measures to Ensure Food Security

Public Distribution System

PDS in India was introduced around World War II as a war-time rationing measure. Launched in 1939 in Bombay and subsequently extended to other cities and towns, PDS has evolved as the largest distribution network of its kind in the world. Over the years it has evolved as a system of management of scarcity and for distribution of foodgrains at affordable prices and hence an important tool of Government's food security policy. Before the 1960s, distribution through PDS was generally dependent on imports of foodgrains. To improve domestic procurement and storage of foodgrains for PDS, the Government established FCI in 1964 and Agriculture Price Commission (APC) in 1965.

The Revamped Public Distribution System (RPDS) PDS, till 1992, was a general entitlement scheme for all consumers without any specific target. The Government launched RPDS in June 1992 with a view to strengthen and streamline the PDS as well as to improve its reach in the far-flung, hilly, remote, and inaccessible areas where a substantial section of the poor live. Foodgrains for distribution in RPDS areas were issued to the states at 50 paise below the Central Issue Price. The scale of issue was up to 20 kg per card.

Targeted Public Distribution System (TPDS) TPDS was launched in June 1997 by GOI with special focus on the poor. Under TPDS entire population is divided into below poverty line (BPL) and above poverty line (APL), and foodgrains are provided to BPL population at highly subsidized prices from the PDS and foodgrains to APL population at much higher prices.* Thus, the TPDS maintains the universal character but adds a special focus on the people below the poverty line. The maximum income level for the population to be covered under BPL was kept at ₹15,000 per annum. As on 2017, 6.52 crore families are covered under BPL and AAY. Allocation of foodgrains is made to these families at the rate of 35 kg per family per month. For APL families, allocation varies from 15 kg per month to 35 kg per month in different states.[20] PDS is operated under the joint responsibility of the central and the state governments. The Central Government, through FCI has assumed the responsibility for procurement, storage, transportation, and bulk allocation of foodgrains to the state governments. The operational responsibility including allocation within state, identification of eligible families, issue of ration cards, supervision of the functioning of FPSs, etc., rests with the state governments. The size of BPL population and entitlement for the BPL population under TPDS is decided by the Central Government. The allocation for APL families or additional allocation for BPL and APL families are decided somewhat arbitrarily based on past utilization and demand from states. Under the PDS, presently the commodities, namely wheat, rice, sugar, and kerosene, are being allocated to the states/ union territories (UTs) for distribution. Some states/UTs also distribute additional items of mass consumption through the PDS outlets such as pulses, edible oils, iodized salt, spices, etc.[21]

Antyodaya Anna Yojana (AAY)

Antyodaya Anna Yojana (AAY) is a step in the direction reducing hunger among the poorest segments of the BPL population. A National Sample Survey Exercise during 1990s pointed toward the fact that about 5% of the total population in the country sleeps without two square meals a day. This section of the population could be called as "hungry." In order to make TPDS more focused and targeted toward this category of population, the AAY was launched in December

* For details, please refer to Table 12.3.

2000 for 1 crore poorest of the poor families. It was first launched in the state of Rajasthan and was subsequently extended to other states. Under this scheme the identified poor families will be provided with 35 kg of foodgrains each in a month, where wheat will be provided for ₹2 per kg, and rice for ₹3 per kg. There are approximately 2.5 crore beneficiaries under AAY scheme. The color of AAY ration card is green and will be different from standard ration pass.

The following are the eligibility criteria for being a part of the scheme:

- Aged, disabled, pregnant, widow, single or lactating mothers with no support or fixed income will be eligible for the scheme.
- Tribal families and all other families who do not have an assured means of income due to physical or mental disabilities, and has no one who can involve in profitable employment, will be considered eligible for the scheme.[22]

Integrated Child Development Services (ICDS) Scheme

Launched on October 2, 1975, the Integrated Child Development Services (ICDS) Scheme is one of the flagship programs of the GOI (Ministry of Women and Child Development) and represents one of the world's largest and unique programs for early childhood care and development.

Following are the objectives of the Scheme:

- to improve the nutritional and health status of children in the age group 0–6 years;
- to lay the foundation for proper psychological, physical, and social development of the child;
- to reduce the incidence of mortality, morbidity, malnutrition, and school dropout;
- to achieve effective co-ordination of policy and implementation among the various departments to promote child development; and
- to enhance the capability of the mother to look after the normal health and nutritional needs of the child through proper nutrition and health education.

The ICDS Scheme offers a package of six services, viz. supplementary nutrition, pre-school non-formal education, nutrition and health education, immunization, health check-up, and referral services. All children below 6 years of age, pregnant women, and lactating mothers are eligible for availing of services under the ICDS Scheme. BPL is not a criterion for registration of beneficiaries under ICDS. The Scheme is universal for all categories of beneficiaries and in coverage. Till December 2018 around 13.46 lakh Anganwadi Centers (AWCs) are operational in the country.

Mid-Day Meal Scheme

Mid-day meal in schools has had a long history in India. The program was first launched in 1925 by Madras Municipal Corporation for disadvantaged children. By the mid-1980s three states viz. Gujarat, Kerala, and Tamil Nadu and the UT of Pondicherry had universalized a cooked MDM Programme in primary education. By 1990–1991 the number of states implementing the MDM Programme increased to 12 states. With a view to enhancing enrollment, retention, attendance and simultaneously improving nutritional levels among children, the National Programme of Nutritional Support to Primary Education, commonly known as mid-day meal, was launched as a Centrally Sponsored Scheme on August 15, 1995. The scheme was initially started in 2,408 blocks in the country. By the year 1997–1998 the program was introduced in all blocks of the country. It was further extended in 2002 to cover not only children in classes I–V of government, government–aided, and local body schools, but also children studying in Education Guarantee Scheme (EGS) and Alternative and Innovative Education (AIE) centers.

Following are the salient features of the program[23]:

1. MDM is the world's largest school-feeding program reaching out to about 9.78 crore children in over 11.40 lakh schools across the country.
2. To ensure balanced and nutritious diet to children of upper primary group, the quantity of pulses and vegetables has been increased and that of oil and fat has been decreased.
3. To promote good quantity and quality, the Government enhanced the cooking cost (excluding the labor and administrative charges). Around 26 lakh cook-cum-helpers mainly from SC/ST/OBC communities have been engaged to provide MDM to school children. There is one cook-cum helper for schools up to 25 students. For schools with 26–100 students, there are two cooks cum helpers and one additional cook-cum-helper for every addition of up to 100 students.
4. More than 8 lakh kitchen-cum-stores have been constructed to ensure safety of foodgrains and ensure hygienic meals to the children.

National Food Security Act, 2013 (NFSA)

With a view to make receipt of foodgrains under TPDS a legal right, GOI has enacted NFSA that came into force w.e.f. July 5, 2013. NFSA seeks to "provide for food and nutritional security in human life cycle approach, by ensuring access to adequate quantity of quality food at affordable prices to people to live a life with dignity and for matters connected therewith or incidental thereto".[24] By enacting NFSA, the right to food has been made the fundamental right and the PDS has come under its fold.[25] Following are the salient features of NFSA.

1. The Act provides for coverage of up to 75% of the rural population and up to 50% of the urban population. The covered population will receive subsidized foodgrains under TPDS at ₹1, ₹2, and ₹3 per kg for coarse grains, wheat, rice, respectively, at 35 kg per family per month to households covered under AAY, and at 5 kg per person per month to priority households.
2. Corresponding the all India coverage of 75 and 50% in the rural and urban areas, state-wise coverage will be determined by the Central Government. In case, any state's allocation under the Act is lower than their current allocation, it will be protected up to the level of average offtake during last 3 years, at prices to be determined by the Central Government.
3. Pregnant women and lactating mothers and children in the age group of 6 months to 14 years will be entitled to meals as per prescribed nutritional norms under ICDS and MDM schemes. Higher nutritional norms have been prescribed for malnourished children up to 6 years of age. Pregnant women and lactating mothers will also be entitled to receive maternity benefit of not less than ₹6,000.
4. Eldest woman of the household of age 18 years or above to be the head of the household for the purpose of issuing of ration cards. In Chandigarh, Puducherry, and urban areas of Dadra & Nagar Haveli, the Act is being implemented in the cash transfer mode, under which food subsidy is being transferred into the bank accounts of beneficiaries who then have a choice to buy foodgrains from open market.[26]
5. States will have the flexibility to use the existing machinery or set up separate mechanism.

6. Central Government will provide assistance to states in meeting the expenditure incurred by them on transportation of foodgrains within the state, its handling and fair price shop dealers' margin as per norms to be devised for this purpose.
7. Provisions have been made for disclosure of records relating to PDS, social audits, and setting up of Vigilance Committees in order to ensure transparency and accountability. Provision for penalty on public servant or authority, to be imposed by the State Food Commission, in case of failure to comply with the relief recommended by the District Grievance Redressal Officer.
8. Provision for food security allowance to entitled beneficiaries in case of non-supply of entitled foodgrains or meals.

Critical Appraisal of Food Security Measures in India and Policy Implications

Wrongful Identification of Poor

Many studies have been conducted regarding identification of poor and large-scale inclusion and exclusion errors under TPDS has been verified. Ministry of Rural Development constituted an expert group in 2009 to advice on the methodology for conducting the BPL census. It estimated that about 61% of the eligible population was excluded from the BPL list while 25% of non-poor households were included in the BPL list.[27] Many entitled beneficiaries are not getting foodgrains while those who are ineligible are getting undue benefits. A study by Peter Svedberg reveals that 62% of all BPL and AAY cards were in the hands of non-poor households. A report of planning commission too highlighted the existence of ghost cards* that indicates inaccurate classification of beneficiaries and diversion of grains deserving households into the open market.[28]

Double Disadvantage to the Homeless

The open-ended procurement of foodgrains with the government agencies actually reduces the net quantities available in the open market. Taking advantage of the low supplies in the market, traders indulge in the speculation raising the foodgrain prices in the open market to unusually higher level. Now, to claim food under PDS, one needs to have a registered residential address and must be in the possession of ration card. But the homeless poor and migrant laborers who do not have permanent place to live are excluded from the benefit of PDS. The dual market system—the open market and PDS—operates in the disfavor of poor especially the homeless. It is because they do not have access to the fair price shops due to non-possession of ration cards and secondly, they are compelled to purchase from the open market where prices are already high (or artificially inflated).

PDS Leakages

PDS leakage refers to the proportion of PDS foodgrain (rice and wheat) released by the Food Corporation of India that fails to reach consumers. Ashok Gulati and Shweta Saini in their study

* "Ghost cards" are cards made in the name of non-existent people.

have revealed appalling state of PDS leakages in India. According to their study, in 2011–2012, 25.9 MMTs or 46.7% of the off-taken grain leaked from the PDS. More than 50% of foodgrain off-take by the state/UT did not reflect in the consumption figures of more than 15 states. The extent of PDS leakages in some states are: Delhi (82.6%), Gujarat (72.2%), Haryana (70.3%), West Bengal (69.4%), Bihar (68.7%), and Punjab (60.7%). Corruption in the PDS takes place largely under the APL quota.[29] In some states, the bulk of the APL quota went straight to the black market and APL households, unaware of their foodgrain entitlements, ended up treating their ration card as a "kerosene card." All these went on for years because a powerful mafia had grown around the APL quota and most of the victims were unaware of the situation. According to a study by Dreze and Khera, diversion of APL allocations was 67% (diversion of BPL/AAY allocations was 30%) during 2011–2012 for major states in India.[30] Another study by Daniel Overbeck, for 20 states over 6 years period revealed that one percentage point increase in the APL quota increases leakage by about half a percentage point. The point estimate (as per fixed regression technique) for the effect of the APL quota on leakage came out to be 0.503. Simply stated for every extra ton allocated to APL households in India, 503 k is diverted.[31] Five states that are home to nearly 60% of India's poor (viz. Uttar Pradesh, West Bengal, Bihar, Maharashtra and Madhya Pradesh) accounted for 52% of the total grain leakage in the country in the year 2011–2012.[32]

Despite this, there is a strong evidence of declining leakages in recent years for the states, which have seriously undertaken PDS reforms. Bihar's recent experience suggests that even the worst-governed states are capable of improving their PDS. About 75% of rural households in Bihar today have a new ration card, or an Antyodaya card. For the first time, most people know that they are entitled to 5 kg of foodgrains per person per month from the PDS.[33]

Issues Regarding Procurement and Storage of Foodgrains

To carry out its PDS operations and other welfare schemes and to maintain minimum required buffer stock, the Government needs to store procured foodgrains. FCI is the main government agency entrusted with the storage of foodgrains in the central pool. However, FCI's own storage capacity has been insufficient to accommodate the central pool of stock of foodgrains. Therefore, FCI hires space from various agencies such as the central and state warehousing corporations, state government agencies, and private parties. CAG in its report in 2013 also highlighted sub-optimum utilization of the existing storage capacity available with FCI and states.[34] According to a report by the Times of India, nearly 46,658 tonnes of foodgrains was led to rot in its 1,889 warehouses across the country during 2013–2016, while another 143.74 tonnes was reported stolen. Together, this could have fed nearly 8 lakh people from priority families under the National Food Security Act for an entire year.[35]

The Government has taken few steps for better procurement and storage.

1. The Government introduced Decentralised Procurement Scheme (DCP) during 1997–1998 under which foodgrains procurement and distribution is operationalized by the state governments themselves. Under this scheme, the designated DCP states procure, store, and issue foodgrains under TPDS and other welfare schemes of the GOI. The Central Government undertakes to meet the entire expenditure incurred by the state governments on the procurement operations as per the approved costing.[36] But due to non-cooperative attitude of the state governments and their refusal to accept DCP, the policy could not be implemented in the entire country. Only a few states have come

forward. Even the state where DCP has been introduced the massive diversion of foodgrains has been reported, which again questions the transparency issue even if procurement has been decentralized.

2. The Government keeps a certain amount of buffer to meet the prescribed minimum stocking norms for food security, to ensure monthly releases of foodgrains for the TPDS/Other Welfare Schemes, and to augment supply in eventualities like emergency situations arising out of unexpected crop failure, natural disasters, etc. The Government in the recent past (w.e.f. January 2015) has revised the minimum stocking norms of foodgrains in the Central Pool (Table 12.2). But because of open-ended sale and purchase policy of the Government with regard to wheat and rice, the farmers just dump their produce with the FCI and other procurement agencies. Many a times the foodgrains procured are very much higher than the required minimum norms. For example, FCI held foodgrain stock of 46 million tonnes as on October 1, 2017, which is 53% higher than the buffer norm of 30.77 million tonnes of foodgrain. Many state governments are planning to use silos for safe storage of foodgrains in the coming future. The Silo technique, quite popular in foreign countries, is used for bulk storage of grains. Silos are generally made of metals, mainly steel or fiber.

Rising Food Subsidy Bill

Food subsidy comprises two components, consumer subsidy and cost of maintenance of buffer/strategic buffer. The consumer subsidy is difference between economic cost minus central issue price fixed for TPDS and other welfare schemes. The economic cost consists of two elements: (1) cost of procurement (or MSP), and (2) cost of FCI operations involving handling, storage, administrative, transportation, etc. There are two significant points to note, first, food subsidies have increased significantly in the post-reform period and second, food subsidies as a share of GDP have also increased more during the last two decades compared with the 1990s. For example food subsidy bill of the central government increased from ₹62,930 crore during 2010–11 to ₹287,000 crore during FY 2023. Food subsidy as a percentage of GDP was reported to be nearly 2% during 2022–23 (0.4% during early 1990s) and as a percentage of agriculture GDP to be nearly 9% (2.1% during early 1990s). The share of buffer subsidy has declined while the share of consumer subsidy has increased since 1990s. The major reason for rise in food subsidy bill is rising economic cost, mainly due to increase in procurement prices, high procurement and offtake of foodgrains, and falling central issue price.*

The procurement price, offtake quantity, and procurement quantity are important determinants of amount of food subsidy. While most of factors are beyond the control of FCI, there are few components of food subsidy that are under the control of FCI, for example, administration charges, storage losses, etc., and they have shown some improvement during the last decade and there is still need and scope to improve efficiency in operations of FCI. The Government intervention in the form of procurement should be selective and quantity of procurement should not exceed average annual offtake at procurement price. In addition, proactive steps are needed to encourage more states to participate in procurement and distribution of foodgrains including coarse cereals, private and/or public–private partnership in creating scientific storage facilities to reduce storage losses (both quality and quantity), and reduction in state-level statutory and non-statutory charges.[37]

---

* Due to implementation of NFSA, CIP has further gone down for APL and BPL categories.

Summary

1. There is something called paradox of agriculture when good harvest affects farmers negatively. Bad harvest too affects consumers and in order to save the interest of farmers and consumers, the Government every year announces agriculture price policy (APP). The three popular components of APP are minimum support price (MSP) or procurement price (PP), maintaining buffer stock operations, and issue price. MSP is the minimum guaranteed price that the Government offers to the farmers when market prices go below it. The Commission for Agriculture Cost and Prices (CACP) is an advisory body that measures MSP on the basis of A2, A2+FL, and C2 basis. Buffer stock refers to a reserve of a commodity that the Government maintains through direct purchase from the domestic market or through imports from outside and releases these stocks for sale in the domestic market in case market prices go up. Issue price is the price at which government sells foodgrains to general public through fair price shops.
2. MSP policy has been useful in various respects such as stabilizing market prices of agriculture products; building positive correlation between MSP announcement and technology adoption by farmers; promoting food security through self-reliance and implementation of plethora of food security schemes; and providing certainty to farm income. The shortcoming of APP are: (1) farmers still feel dissatisfied despite the Government announcing major hike in MSP (50% over A2 +FL as a new benchmark for calculating MSP) as there is demand for measuring MSP 50% over C2 cost; (2) MSP announcement seems to be insufficient as income of farmers in real terms had declined leading to distress among farmers; (3) late announcement of MSP that deprives farmers of any planning for their crops; (4) poor infrastructure facilities that discourage the farmers to sell their produce to the Government; (5) hike in MSP also causes inflation in the economy and this has primarily occurred due to rise in production cost and increase in international prices of agriculture goods. Farmers lobbying in political circles too causes hike in MSP; (6) major benefits of MSP accruing to few states that produce wheat and rice and the larger farmers who can part with surplus produce and contribute into government's procurement operations; and (7) the open-ended policy makes famers stick to remain in the vicious circle of wheat and rice and thus discourages agriculture diversification.
3. Food security exists when all people, at all times, have physical and economic access to sufficient, safe, and nutritious food to meet their dietary needs and food preferences for an active and healthy life. The three components of food security are: (1) availability of food; (2) access of food; and (3) absorption of food. Availability of food is determined by production and yield of foodgrains; per capita availability of foodgrains; and changes in consumption patterns and demand for non-cereal food. Access to food signifies people's capability to get food and is mainly determined by their purchasing power. Absorption signifies nutritional intake of the masses.
4. The food security measures adopted by the Government of India are: launching of PDS in 1939, revamping it 1992, and then introducing TPDS in 1997; start of AAY in 2000 for poorest of poor families; enactment of NFSA in 2013, which makes the right to food as the fundamental right; launching of Mid-Day Meal scheme at all India level in 1997–1998 with the aim of ensuring balanced and nutritious diet to school children and increase school enrolment ratio; launching of ICDS in 1975 for early childhood care and development.
5. The food security program in India suffers from various shortcomings such as wrongful identification of poor because of exclusion of eligible population and existence of ghost cards; double disadvantages to the homeless as they do not have access to PDS and are compelled to purchase from the open market where prices are already high; PDS leakages in the form of diversion to open market and corruption; problem of procurement of foodgrains due to inadequate infrastructure and rising food subsidy bill.

Endnotes

1. Tripathi, A.K. (2012). Agricultural price policy, output, and farm profitability—examining linkages during post-reform period in India. *Asian Journal of Agriculture and Development, 10*(1).
2. Commission for Agriculture Cost and Prices (2018). Retrieved from http://cacp.dacnet.nic.in (Accessed on December 17, 2018).
3. Niti Aayog. (2016). Evaluation study on efficacy of minimum support prices (MSP) on farmers, Retrieved from https://niti.gov.in (Accessed on February 2, 2017).
4. Tripathi, A.K. (2012). Agricultural price policy, output, and farm profitability—examining linkages during post-reform period in India. *Asian Journal of Agriculture and Development, 10*(1).
5. Damodaran, H. The Cost+50% Swaminathan formula mirage. *Indian Express.* June 22, 2017.
6. Agriculture Price Policy. *Business Today*, July 6, 2018.
7. Tripathi A.K. (2012). Agricultural price policy, output, and farm profitability—examining linkages during post-reform period in India. *Asian Journal of Agriculture and Development, 10*(1).
8. Niti Aayog. (2016). Evaluation study on efficacy of minimum support prices (MSP) on farmers, Retrieved from https://niti.gov.in (Accessed on February 2, 2017).
9. Niti Aayog. (2016). Evaluation study on efficacy of minimum support prices (MSP) on farmers, Retrieved from https://niti.gov.in (Accessed on February 2, 2017).
10. Dev & Rao. Agricultural price policy, farm profitability and food security. *EPW*, Vol. XLV, no. 26 & 27, June 26, 2010.
11. Wheat Procurement. Retrieved on www. http://fci.gov.in (Accessed on March 14, 2019).
12. World Bank (2004). *India: Re-energizing the agriculture sector to sustain growth and reduce poverty.* Retrieved from http://documents.worldbank.org (Accessed on February 22, 2019).
13. Dev & Sharma (2010). *Food security in India: Performance, challenges and policies*, Oxfam India working papers series.
14. International Food Policy Research Institute., *Food Security*. Retrieved from http://www.ifpri.org (Accessed on December 28, 2018).
15. PRS Legislative Research. *State of Agriculture in India* p.6, 2016–2017.
16. Dev & Sharma (2010). *Food security in India: Performance, challenges and policies*, Oxfam India working papers series.
17. Bhattacharya, P. What explains India's high child malnutrition rates?, *Livemint*. June 08, 2017.
18. Day, S. 51% of Indian women aged 15–49 anaemic, most in world: Study., *Times of India*, November 7, 2017.
19. Sudha Narayanan. (2015). Food security in India: The imperative and its challenges, *Asia and the Pacific Policy Studies*, 2(1), 197–209.
20. Public distribution system. Retrieved from http://dfpd.nic.in (Accessed on March 18, 2019).
21. Department of Food and Public Distribution AAY retrieved from https://dfpd.gov.in (Accessed on January 18, 2019).
22. AAY. Retrieved from http://www.pmawasyojana.co.in (Accessed on February 19, 2019).
23. Mid day meal scheme. Retrieved from http://mdm.nic.in/ (Accessed on May 12, 2019).
24. The Gazette of India, September 10, 2013, p.1.
25. Nayak, N., & Nehra, S. (2017). Accessing the right to food in Delhi. *EPW, 52*(23).
26. Economic Survey, Department of Economic Affairs, Ministry of Finance. GOI, 2016–2017, p.183.
27. Planning commission (2009). *Report of the Expert Group to advise the Ministry of Rural Development on the methodology for conducting the Below Poverty Line (BPL) Census for 11th Five Year Plan*, Retrieved from http://planningcommission.nic.in (Accessed on August 17, 2017).
28. Planning Commission (2005). *Performance evaluation of targeted public distribution system.* Retrieved from http://planningcommission.nic.in (Accessed on August 19, 2017).
29. Gulati, A. Saini, S (2015). *Leakages from Public Distribution System (PDS) and the Way Forward*, ICRIER, Working Paper 294,
30. Dreze, J., & Khera, R. (2015). Understanding leakages in the public distribution system. *Economic & Political Weekly, 50*(7), 39–42.
31. Overbeck, D (2016). Leakage and corruption in India's public distribution system. ISID, Accessed

from https://www.isid.ac.in (Accessed on July 16, 2017).

32. Sharma & Alagh. (2013). Food subsidy in India: Its components, trends, causes and reforms for public policy. *Indian Journal of Agricultural Economics, 68*(2).

33. Dreze, J., & Khera, R. (2015). Understanding leakages in the public distribution system. *Economic & Political Weekly, 50*(7), 39–42.

34. Comptroller and Auditor General of India. (2013). *Performance audit report on storage management and movement of food grains in FC* Retrieved from https://www.cag.gov.in (Accessed on February 16, 2016).

35. Kumar, C. Grains rotting with FCI could have fed 8L for a year. C *Times of India*, May 2, 2016.

36. Economic Survey, Department of Economic Affairs. Ministry of Finance. 2016–2017, GOI.

37. Sharma & Alagh. (2013). Food subsidy in India: Its components, trends, causes and reforms for public policy, *Indian* Journal of Agricultural Economics, 68(2).

CHAPTER **13**

AGRICULTURE FINANCE IN INDIA

A farmer is always going to be rich next year.

—Philemon

INTRODUCTION

Finance is one of the critical inputs for agricultural development. It helps farmers to undertake new investments and adopt new technologies. Further, the success and failure of agriculture is largely dependent upon exogenous factors like rainfall, climate change, and pest or insect attack. Agriculture being the largest employer in the country, any change in farmers' income not only affects their lives but also have a considerable impact on overall gross domestic product. Therefore, the importance of agriculture credit and insurance is reinforced by the unique role of Indian agriculture in the macroeconomic framework along with its significant role in poverty alleviation.

We propose to discuss the following issues in this chapter:

- Sources of Agriculture Finance
- Agriculture Insurance in India
- Debt burden and farmers' suicides
- Credit Subsidy in Indian Agriculture
- Report of M.S. Swaminathan on Farmer Distress

SOURCES OF AGRICULTURE FINANCE IN INDIA

Agriculture credit can be categorized into non-institutional credit and institutional credit (Figure 13.1).

Non-institutional Credit

Non-institutional credit is provided by informal sector that does not come under the ambit of the government or central bank's regulation. The major non-institutional sources are money-lenders, landlords, traders, commission agents, relatives, and friends. Rural indebtedness and dependence on informal source of finance is an age-old problem in India. But certain steps taken by the government have reduced the share of non-institutional finance from 89.8% in 1951 to 36% in 2013.[1]

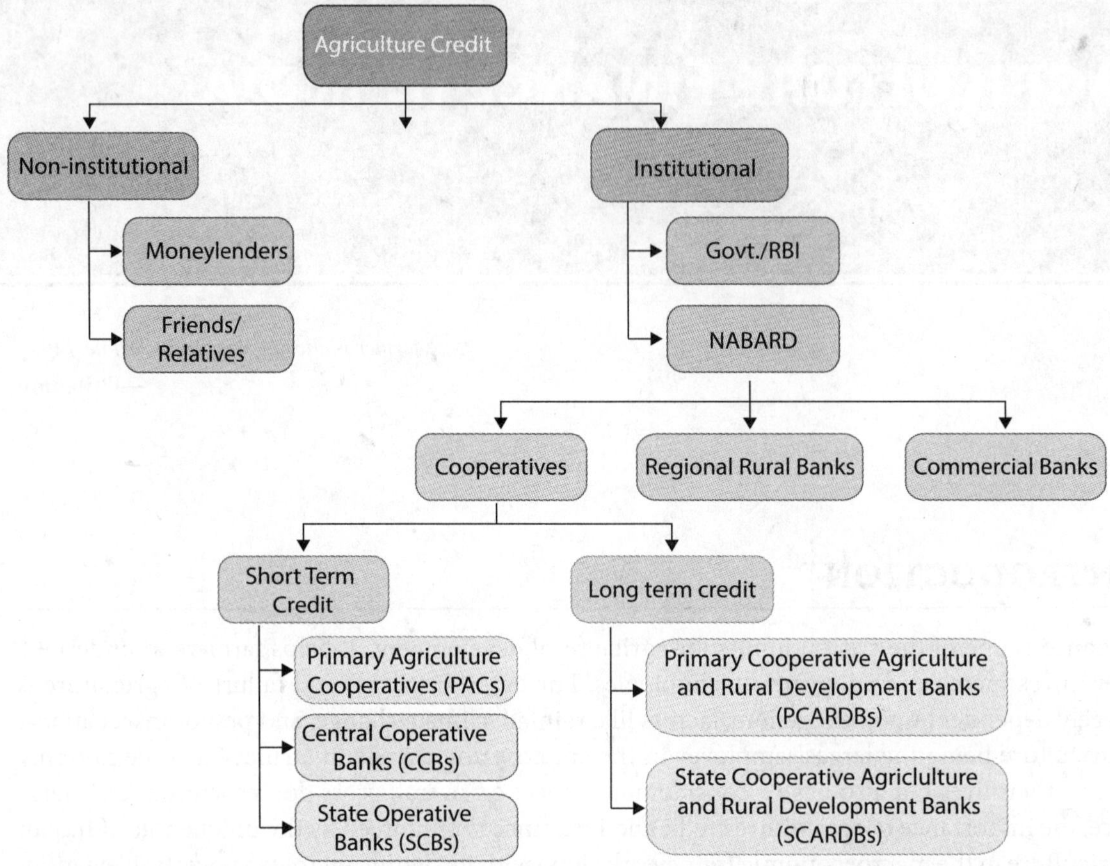

FIGURE 13.1 Agriculture Credit Source: Non-Institutional and Institutional

Institutional Credit

Institutional credit is provided by formal sector and it is regulated by the government to influence the flow of funds in agriculture sector. The major actors in institutional credit are the government, Reserve Bank of India (RBI), NABARD, commercial banks (CBs), cooperatives, and regional rural banks (RRBs). Let us discuss them one by one.

National Bank for Agriculture and Rural Development (NABARD)

National Bank for Agriculture and Rural Development (NABARD) was established on July 12, 1982 on the recommendation of B. Sivaraman Committee. NABARD is fully owned by Government of India and is an apex body for the agriculture credit. The functions/achievements of NABARD can be categorized under three heads: financial functions, developmental functions, and supervisory functions.

Financial Functions

1. *Refinancing facility:* NABARD does not provide direct loans to farmers but finance them through institutional set up. Therefore, refinancing is a way for banks to get funding in respect of term loan for both farm sector and non-farm sector activities for a

period of 18 months to 15 years. The institutions that get such refinancing facilities are SCARDBs, SCBs, RRBs, or scheduled CBs or any other financial institution, approved by RBI.

2. *Rural Infrastructure Development Fund* (*RIDF*): Rural Infrastructure Development Fund (RIDF) was established with NABARD in 1995–1996. Domestic CBs contribute to the fund to the extent of their shortfall in stipulated priority sector lending to agriculture. The major beneficiaries of RIDF are the State Governments, gram panchayats, self-help groups (SHGs), and NGOs. The main objective of the Fund is to help states complete ongoing rural infrastructure projects.[2]
3. *NABARD Infrastructure Development Assistance* (*NIDA*): RIDF discussed above faced two major problems. First, loans cannot exceed the borrowing power of the State Government under Article 293 (1) of the Constitution of India, which limited the states' offtake from RIDF. Second, political influence was noticed in the disbursement of funds. To address such issues, NABARD launched a new line of credit, named NABARD Infrastructure Development Assistance (NIDA). NIDA is a new line of credit support for funding rural infrastructure projects which provides assistance outside of RIDF borrowing. It offers customized terms based on the requirements of the borrower, nature of the project, and risk profile of the borrower on flexible interest rates. NIDA is available for the State Governments and other state-owned organizations, such as corporations.[3]
4. *Long-Term Irrigation Fund* (*LTIF*): The Long-Term Irrigation Fund (LTIF) was established in NABARD during 2017.* The fund aims to bridge the resources gap and facilitate the completion of 99 prioritized irrigation projects as part of Pradhan Mantri Krishi Sinchayee Yojana during 2016–2020 and bringing 76.03 lakh hectares of land under irrigation.[4]
5. *Other programs*: Warehouse Infrastructure Fund was created in the year 2013–2014 with NABARD to meet the requirements for scientific warehousing infrastructure for agricultural commodities in the country. Food Processing Fund was created in NABARD in 2014–2015 to promote food processing industry in the organized sector on a cluster basis. Producers Organization Development Fund was created in 2010 to help farmers transform into agricultural entrepreneurs or agripreneurs.** Apart from all these, NABARD also provides funding to cooperatives, market federations, and other entities.

Developmental Functions

1. *Kisan Credit Card* (*KCC*) *scheme*

   Designed by NABARD in consultation with RBI, Kisan Credit Card (KCC) scheme was introduced by the government in August 1998. Such cards are issued to the farmers on the basis of their land holdings and other criteria such as timely payment of past credits. The scheme helps farmers in multiple ways like production credit, working capital requirements for allied activities, ancillary credit requirements related to crop production contingent needs, and accidental insurance.

---

* LTIF was announced in 2016–2017 Budget.

** A producer organization comprises a group of producers who have joined hands for the purpose of either agricultural or non-agricultural activities.

2. *Microfinance:* Also called as microcredit, it is a type of banking service that is provided to unemployed or low-income individuals or groups so that they can start a small business venture. Generally, the microfinance is routed through SHGs.* NABARD had launched the Self-Help Group-Bank Linkage Programme (SHG-BLP) in 1992. Under this programme, banks are allowed to open savings accounts for SHGs and provide loans to the SHGs against group guarantee. Microfinance movement can be traced back to 1976, when Mohammad Yunus, a Bangladeshi economist and Nobel laureate, started a campaign for microfinance for poor villagers near Chittagong, Bangladesh. His efforts led to the establishment of Grameen Bank in 1983 and soon the movement spread throughout the world.
3. *Eshakti*: Launched on March 15, 2015, the project aims at digitization of all the SHG accounts to bring SHG members under the fold of Financial Inclusion thereby helping them access wider range of financial services together with increasing the bankers' comfort in credit appraisal and linkage.[5]
4. *Other programs*: In order to commercialize innovations and to shape agri-entrepreneurship in the country, NABARD has established incubation centers in different agriculture universities across the country. NABARD also provides marketing opportunities to rural artisans and producers and facilitates their participation in exhibitions across the country. The tribal development programme of NABARD was implemented in the 2003–2004 with a corpus of ₹50 crore.

Supervisory Functions NABARD is empowered to conduct the inspection of cooperative banks and RRBs. In addition, NABARD has also been conducting periodic inspections of state-level cooperative institutions, such as SCARDBs, Apex Weavers Societies, Marketing Federations, on a voluntary basis. Objectives of supervision are protecting the interest of present and future depositors; ensuring that the business conducted by such banks is in conformity with the rules laid down; examining the financial soundness of the banks; and suggesting ways and means for strengthening the institutions so as to enable them to play a more efficient role in purveying rural credit.[6]

Cooperative Credit Societies

The history and evolution of cooperatives can be traced back to 1904 when the British Government passed the Co-operative Credit Societies Act to provide cheaper credit to the farmers. The Maclagan Committee (1915) and the Royal Commission of Agriculture in India (1928) focused on the expansion of co-operatives in the country. The RBI Act, 1934, made provisions to establish an Agriculture Credit Department in the bank and extend refinancing facilities to the co-operative credit system. All India Rural Credit Survey in 1951 recommended the creation of an efficient system of agricultural finance and the development of a sound co-operative credit structure. The All-India Rural Credit Review Committee (1969) recommended the adoption of a multi-agency approach toward agriculture and rural credit, and CBs were expected to complement the efforts of co-operatives to enhance the quantum of credit in the rural economy.

---

*Self-help groups (SHGs) comprise a group of microentrepreneurs who are 10–20 in number and have homogeneous social and economic background. They voluntarily come together, save a regular sum of money, and pool their resources together in the pursuit of self-employment.

The cooperative system in India has been organized into short-term and long-term credit structure. The short-term credit structure is based on a three-tier structure. At the lowest tier are primary agriculture cooperatives (PACs) which are organized at village level. At the second tier are central cooperative banks (CCBs) that are organized at district level. At the third and uppermost tier are the state cooperative banks (SCBs) which are organized at state level. The long-term credit structure is based on a two-tire system: State cooperative agriculture rural development banks (SCARDBs) and primary cooperative agriculture rural development banks (PCARDBs). PCARDBs function at tuluka level or local level, whereas SCARDBs function at state level. In some states, SCARDBs have many branches. SCARDBs supervise and provide financial assistance to PCARDBs. The share of cooperatives in agricultural loans has decreased from 62% in 1980-81 to 7% in 2022–23.

Regional Rural Banks

On the recommendations of the working group on rural banks, the government established RRBs in the year 1975. The RRBs are owned by the Central Government, the State Government, and the Sponsor Bank whose shares are held at the ratios of 50, 15, and 35%, respectively. At present, there are 56 RRBs covering 525 districts with a network of 14,494 branches. The government is planning to consolidate RRBs and bring down their tally from the existing 56 to 36 so as to ensure better scale-efficiency, higher productivity, robust financial health, improved financial inclusion, and greater credit flow to rural areas.[7] The share of RRBs in total institutional credit has increased from 3.4% in 1990-91 to 15.58% in 2022–23.

Commercial Banks

The share of CBs in total institutional credit was just 0.9% during 1951 and decreased to 0.7% during 1961. It simply signifies that rural India in general and agriculture in particular was not in the priority list of commercial banking. To address this problem, the government nationalized 14 banks in 1969 and 6 banks in 1980. The predominance of cooperatives in agriculture credit was termed by many as uni-agency approach which was insufficient to meet the demands of agriculture credit. The All India Rural Credit Review Committee (1969) recommended multi-agency approach to the rural and especially agricultural credit. The multi-agency approach signified the involvement of cooperatives, CBs and RRBs, in financing the productive economic activities in rural area for promoting rural development.[8] The Lead Bank Scheme was introduced in 1969 under which a larger bank in the district is entrusted with the lead responsibility for that district. The lead bank acts as a leader for coordinating the efforts of all credit institutions in the allotted districts to increase the flow of credit to agriculture and other priority sectors. The Service Area Approach (SAA) was a scheme launched by the RBI in 1989 for an orderly development of the rural areas of the country. Under the SAA, all rural and semi-urban branches of banks were allocated specific villages, generally in geographical difficult areas, the overall development and the credit needs of which were to be taken care of by the respective branches. Under priority sector lending norm, the CBs are mandated to achieve certain targets. Under such norms, the banks are required to provide 40% of aggregated net bank credit (ANBC) to certain priority sectors such as agriculture, SSI, and microfinance and the share of agriculture is 18% of ANBC. Apart from all such measures mentioned above, the systematic efforts of CBs in the field of financial inclusion resulted in an increase in the share of CBs in agricultural loans. The share of CBs in total institutional lending has increased from 38% in 1980–81 to 73.39% in 2022–23.

Agriculture Insurance in India

Agriculture insurance is a risk management tool that farmers can use in the eventuality of floods, drought, pests, disease, and a plethora of other natural disasters. In India, there are primarily four agriculture insurance schemes.

Pradhan Mantri Fasal Bima Yojana

The Pradhan Mantri Fasal Bima Yojana (Prime Minister's Crop Insurance Scheme) was launched by Prime Minister of India on February 13, 2016. The new Crop Insurance Scheme is in line with One Nation–One Scheme theme and incorporates the best features of all previous schemes, and at the same time, all previous shortcomings/weaknesses have been removed. The following are the salient features of the scheme:

- There will be a uniform premium of only 2% to be paid by farmers for all Kharif crops and 1.5% for all Rabi crops. In the case of annual commercial and horticultural crops, the premium to be paid by farmers will be only 5%. The premium rates to be paid by farmers are very low, and the balance premium will be paid by the government to provide full insured amount to the farmers against crop loss on account of natural calamities. There is no upper limit on the government subsidy. Even if balance premium is 90%, it will be borne by the government.
- Technology will be used for the better implementation of the program. Smart phones will be used to capture and upload data of crop cutting to reduce the delays in claim payment to farmers. Remote sensing will be used to reduce the number of crop-cutting experiments.

Restructured Weather Based Crop Insurance Scheme (RWBCIS)

The RWBCIS was launched on February 18, 2016 by Prime Minister of India. RWBCIS intends to provide insurance protection to the farmers against adverse weather conditions, such as deficit and excess rainfall, high or low temperature, and humidity, which are deemed to impact adversely the crop production. It has advantage to settle the claims within shortest possible time.[9]

Unified Package Insurance Scheme (UPIS)

Introduced in Kharif 2016 season, the Unified Package Insurance Scheme (UPIS) aims at providing financial protection to citizens associated in agriculture sector, thereby ensuring food security, crop diversification and enhancing growth and competitiveness of agriculture sector besides protecting farmers from financial risks. The Loanee farmers will be covered through banks/financial institutions, whereas non-loanee farmer shall be covered through banks and/or insurance intermediaries. The policy contains seven sections, viz., crop insurance, personal accident insurance, life insurance, building and contents insurance, agriculture pump set insurance, student safety insurance, and agriculture tractor insurance.

Coconut Palm Insurance Scheme (CPIS)

The Coconut Palm Insurance Scheme (CPIS) is implemented since the year 2009–2010. The scheme is administered by Coconut Development Board. The scheme is meant for coconut cultivator who grows at least five healthy nut bearing palms of all varieties.

DEBT BURDEN AND FARMERS' SUICIDES IN INDIA

The phenomenon of suicide by farmers is especially worrisome for India because the majority of the workforce is dependent on agriculture for its livelihood.[10] Between 1995 and 2006, the government official sources indicate that 166,304 farmers died by suicide in India (16,000 per year). A total of 11,290 persons involved in farming sector (consisting of 5,207 farmers/cultivators and 6,083 agricultural labourers) have committed suicides during 2022, accounting for 6.6% of total suicides victims (1,70,924) in the country. Out of 11,290 farmer/cultivator suicides, a total of 10,471 were male and 819 were female. It means on the average three to four farmers commit suicide every day. Majority of victims engaged in farming sector were reported in Maharashtra (37.6%), Karnataka (21.2%), Andhra Pradesh (8.1%), Tamil Nadu (6.4%) and Madhya Pradesh (5.7%). These five states accounted for 80% of farming sector suicides.

Following are the causes of farmer suicides in India.

1. NCRB has classified agriculturists into farmers/cultivators* and agricultural laborers.** Out of total farmer suicides, 47% of the suicides were reported for farmers/cultivators and 53% for agriculture laborers. As per NCRB report published in 2015, the indebtedness- and farming-related issues constitute more than 50% among different causes of farmers' suicides. However, if we consider suicide among agriculture laborers, family problems (40.1%) and illness (19%) are the major causative factors. Certain States/UTs namely, West Bengal, Bihar, Odisha, Uttarakhand, Goa, Manipur, Mizoram, Tripura, Chandigarh, Delhi (UT), Lakshadweep and Puducherry reported zero suicides of Farmers/Cultivators as well as Agricultural Labourers.[11]
2. Against the general perception, the study has also found that there is no clear link between farmer suicides and poverty. Suicide mortality rates are higher in the relatively wealthy states of Maharashtra, Karnataka, and Andhra Pradesh than in poorer states like Bihar and Uttar Pradesh. Further, it is not the poorer farmers who are killing themselves but the richer farmers. Nearly 90% of the farmers who committed suicide in Maharashtra owned more than two acres of land. Six out of 10 owned more than four acres. Farmer suicides are a bigger problem in states with greater access to formal credit such as Maharashtra than the ones like Bihar, where money lenders hold more sway. Therefore, the issue requires an in-depth analysis of the factors behind what is now a systemic crisis in India's farms.[12] For example, a study in Kerala highlighted that farmers' suicide was more

* Farmers/cultivators include persons whose profession is farming and who either cultivates his/her own land or who cultivates lease land with or without the assistance of agricultural laborers.

** Agricultural Laborers are those persons who primarily work in farming sector (agriculture/horticulture) and whose main source of income is from agricultural labor activities.

TABLE 13.1 Major Causes of Suicides Among Farmers/Cultivators

Cause	Percentage share
Bankruptcy or indebtedness	38.7
Farming-related issues	19.5
Family problem	11.7
Illness	10.5
Drug abuse/alcoholic addiction	4.1
Marriage-related issues	2.0
Poverty	1.1
Property dispute	1.1

Source: *Accidental Deaths and Suicides in India (2015)*. National Crime Record Bureau. Ministry of Home Affairs. Govt. of India.

in those districts which are concentrating more on the cultivation of export-oriented commercial crops.[13]

3. While indebtedness has been rising as a cause of farmer/cultivators suicides, the most commonly cited causes of suicide in India for agricultural laborers are "family problem" or "illness." The latter especially has seldom received enough policy attention in the past decades. Access to psychological counseling, healthcare, and better rural infrastructure obviously plays a role in the overall well-being of the farmers. It is not only the male farmers who are committing suicides but female suicide cases have also been reported. The prevalence of suicide rate in the case of female agriculture laborers (12.5% of total suicides) is higher than that of female farmers/cultivators (5.5% of total suicides).
4. The most effective and least distortionary way to support them would be through direct benefit transfers. The new National Health Protection Mission (Ayushman Bharat) should improve rural healthcare. Free LPG connections for poor households should lower their energy burdens while improving the respiratory health of women (smoke from cooking fires is a leading cause of death in many parts of India).[14]
5. Loan waivers are the temporary solutions not the panacea they are made out politically. Loan waivers can help the rich farmers as only the big loans are waived off. Those who want to help India's farmers should be working much harder to figure out what they really need.

CREDIT SUBSIDY IN INDIA

Credit subsidy denotes the difference between interest charged from farmers, and actual cost of providing credit, plus other costs such as write-offs bad loans or loan waivers. Credit subsidy is offered by the government to farmers in order to protect their larger interest. The following are the factors responsible for the credit subsidy in India:

1. crop failure due to exogenous reasons like inadequate rainfall, floods, and pest or insect attack;
2. institutional sources do not fulfill unproductive loan needs, and therefore, farmers are forced to approach to local money lenders;

3. farmers not getting remunerative price of their produce due to glut in the market resulting into decline in their income;
4. massive loan waivers announced by the states from time to time because of farmers lobbying aggressively in political circles especially during election times; and
5. decline in public investment in agriculture over the period of time, which has influenced agrarian economy in multiple ways.

Types of Credit Subsidy

There are generally two popular measures of credit subsidy: interest subvention scheme and farm loan waivers.

Interest Subvention

Interest subvention is the subsidy offered on interest rates. It is a form of waiver of some percentage of interest that promotes some particular industry and general public interest. To promote agriculture credit, the government launched interest subvention scheme in 2006–2007. The government provides interest subvention of 2% per annum to public sector banks, private sector scheduled CBs, cooperative banks, and RRBs for short-term crop loans up to ₹3 lakh per farmer, if the lending institutions provide short-term credit at 7% per annum to farmers. The farmers, who promptly repay their crop loans as per the repayment schedule fixed by the banks, are extended loans up to ₹3 lakh for a maximum period of 1 year at an effective interest rate of 4% per annum (with interest subvention of 3%).[15]

Farm Loan Waiver

A farm loan waiver takes place when the government waives off the part or full amount of loan taken by the farmer from the bank.* Though the government has provided credit subsidy in one form or other in the past, the Agriculture debt waiver was first used as an election strategy in the year 2008, when the then UPA government waived off farm loans worth ₹60,000 crore. Since then, it became a political culture in the country. During 2018–2019, eight State Governments in India gave farm loan waivers worth ₹1.9 trillion. Though, National commission on farmers headed by M.S. Swaminathan in its report suggested farm loan waiver in the distressed districts of the country, for politicians, it has become a regular feature to woo the voters.

The policy of farm loan waiver affects economy in the following manner:

1. It disrupts credit discipline as farmers turn into willful defaulters. They wait for the next loan waiver scheme, which is bad for economy.
2. The honest farmers who had repaid the loans within time feel cheated. It is also a fraud with the tax payers because loans will be waived with taxpayers' money.
3. Farm loan waivers are not a panacea for all problems facing Indian farmers. They provide immediate relief but help little to solve the fundamental problem of rising costs and falling profitability in agriculture.[16]

---

* Sometimes the government also waives off loan taken from money lenders and pays the moneylenders on behalf of farmers.

4. In the anticipation of loan waiver, the borrowers stop repaying the outstanding loan amount. The non-payment of three EMIs turn the loan into non-performing asset (NPA).* Though the State Governments pay banks but payment is staggered in nature which means more NPAs. Higher NPAs cause lending freeze as banks' corpus for next fiscal lending to farmers would go down as banks do not have a financial margin to pump more money and they only circulate the repayments back as fresh loans.
5. Rich farmers too may take loans even if there is no need, with the hope of the next loan waiver scheme. This will impact the farmers who are genuinely in need of loans.
6. Loan waivers increase the fiscal deficit of the states and eventually restrict them from spending money on infrastructure building and welfare schemes, thus impacting employment opportunities and wages.[17]
7. The loan waivers do not cover millions of farmers who lend from sources that are outside the formal economy. According to the NSSO report (2012–2013), approximately 2.5 million agriculture households in Madhya Pradesh borrow from money-lenders. Likewise, about a million farmers in Chhattisgarh are estimated to be outside the formal banking system.[18]

M.S. Swaminathan Report on Farmers' Distress

The National Commission on Farmers, chaired by Prof. M.S. Swaminathan, submitted five reports through the period December 2004 to October 2006. The following are the salient features of the report[19]:

Land Reforms

Land reforms in India signify structural change in land usage, redistribution, and ownership and hence linked with agrarian reforms. The suggestions made by committee in this regard are distributing ceiling-surplus and waste lands; inhibiting diversion of prime agricultural land and forest to corporate sector for non-agricultural purposes; ensuring grazing rights and seasonal access to forests, to tribals and pastoralists, and access to common property resources; setting up a mechanism to regulate the sale of agricultural land, based on quantum of land, nature of proposed use, and category of buyer.

Increasing Irrigation Potential

Irrigation is an indispensable input for Indian Agriculture. The commission recommends sustained and equitable access to water; rainwater harvesting and recharging aquifers; implementation of "million wells recharge program," developing minor irrigation techniques.

Adequate Supply of Funds

For timely and adequate supply of credit, the commission recommends expanding the outreach of the formal credit system to poor and needy; reducing the rate of interest for crop loans to

* If interest and/or installment of principal remains overdue for a period of more than 90 days in the case of a term loan, it automatically becomes an NPA.

4%; moratorium on debt recovery, including loans from non-institutional sources, and waiver of interest on loans in distress hotspots and during calamities, till capability is restored; setting up an "agriculture risk fund" to provide relief to farmers in the aftermath of successive natural calamities; issuing KCCs to women farmers, introducing an integrated credit-cum-crop-live-stock-human health insurance package; setting up a "Rural Insurance Development Fund" to take up development so as to spread rural insurance and forming and strengthening producers' organizations such as SHGs.

Increase in Agriculture Production and Productivity

In India, the productivity level of many crops is below world average. For the long term and sustained increase in agriculture, the commission recommended out of box measures like significant increase in public investment in agriculture-related infrastructure particularly in irrigation, drainage, land development, water conservation, research development, and road connectivity; a national network of advanced soil testing laboratories with facilities for detection of micro-nutrient deficiencies and promotion of conservation farming, which will help farm families to conserve and improve soil health, water quantity and quality, and biodiversity.

Providing Food Security

India is the home for world's largest number of poor and hungry people. Food security has always remained a challenge for policy makers. The commission felt that by raising demand for foodgrains as a result of increased consumption, we will not only help poor by satiating their hunger but the economic conditions essential for further agricultural progress can also be created. The commission recommended universalization of PDS*; reorganizing the delivery of nutrition support programs on a life-cycle basis with the participation of panchayats and local bodies; eliminating micronutrient deficiency induced hidden hunger through an integrated food cum fortification approach; setting up of more "Community Food and Water Banks" operated by Women SHGs, starting a Rural Non-Farm Livelihood Initiative to better the lives of small and marginal farmers; formulating a National Food Guarantee Act.

Arresting Farmers' Suicides

To arrest the incidences of farmers' suicides, the commission recommended providing affordable health insurance and revitalizing primary healthcare centers; setting up State-level Farmers' Commission with representation of farmers for ensuring dynamic government response to farmers' problems; restructuring microfinance policies to serve as Livelihood finance; covering all crops by crop insurance with the village and not block as the unit for assessment; extending the "National Rural Health Mission" to suicide hotspot locations on priority basis providing for a Social Security net with provision for old age support and health insurance; decentralize water use planning and every village should aim at Jal Swaraj with gram sabhas serving as pani panchayats; ensure the availability of quality seed and other inputs at affordable

---

*Commission emphasized that the total subsidy required for this would be one per cent of the gross domestic product.

costs and at the right time and place; recommending low risk and low cost technologies which can help to provide maximum income to farmers because they cannot cope with the shock of crop failure, particularly those associated with high cost technologies like Bt cotton; focused "Market Intervention Schemes" (MIS) in the case of life-saving crops such as "cumin" in arid areas; setting up a price stabilization fund in place to protect the farmers from price fluctuations; setting up Village Knowledge Centers (VKCs) or Gyan Chaupals in the farmers' distress hotspots, and spearheading public awareness campaigns to make people identify early signs of suicidal behavior.

Making Agriculture Competitive and Remunerative

In India, majority of farmers are small and marginal farmers, and for such farmers, agriculture is not a competitive and remunerative profession. To make farming competitive and remunerative, the commission recommends the following:

- promotion of commodity-based farmers' organizations such as "Small Cotton Farmers' Estates" to combine decentralized production with centralized services, such as post-harvest management, value addition, and marketing, for leveraging institutional support and facilitating direct farmer-consumer linkage.
- MSP policy needs to be more inclusive, and for that, MSP needs to be put in place for crops other than wheat and rice also. The commission also recommended millets and other nutritional cereals to be permanently included in PDS.
- MSP should be at least 50% more than the weighted average cost of production.
- The availability of data about spot and future prices of commodities should be available through the Multi-Commodity Exchange (MCD) and the NCDEX and the APMC electronic networks covering 93 commodities through 6,000 terminals and 430 towns and cities.
- APMC Acts relating to marketing, storage, and processing of agriculture produce need to shift to one that promotes grading, branding, packaging, and development of domestic and international markets for local produce, and move toward a Single Indian Market.

Increasing Employment Opportunities of Rural Community

The share of agriculture in country's employment was 75.9% during 1960–1961, and thereafter, came down dramatically. At present, it provides employment to nearly 45% of workforce. The huge dependence on agriculture leads to disguised unemployment and generates lower productivity per capita. Taking stock of such situation, the commission recommends creating productive employment opportunities in industry and services (viz., trade, restaurants and hotels, transport, construction, repairs, and certain services) and improving the "quality" of employment in such sectors so that real wages rise with the increase in productivity. The emphasis should be on relatively more labor-intensive sectors and inducing a faster growth of these sectors; and improving the functioning of labor markets through without eroding the core labor standards. The "net take home income" of farmers should be comparable to those of civil servants.

Preservation of Biosecurity

India has a rich flora and fauna and blessed with bio-resources that are paramount for the nutrition and livelihood of millions of rural Indians. The report recommends preserving traditional rights of access to biodiversity, which include access to non-timber forest products including medicinal plants, gums and resins, oil yielding plants, and beneficial micro-organisms; conserving, enhancing, and improving crops and farm animals as well as fish stocks through breeding; encouraging community-based breed conservation (that is, conservation through use); and, allowing export of indigenous breeds and import of suitable breeds to increase the productivity of ordinary animals.

Summary

1. Finance is a significant input. In India, there are both non-institutional and institutional sources of credit. The non-institutional sources include friends, relatives, and moneylenders, and they remain outside the ambit of RBI regulations.
2. Under institutional source which falls under the government/RBI supervision, NABARD is the apex credit agency. Established in 1982, NABARD exercises financial, developmental, and supervisory functions in the field of agriculture credit. Under financial functions, NABARD provides refinancing facilities and implements certain important schemes like RIDF, NIDA, and LTIF. Through development functions, NABARD executes functioning of KCCs, microfinance, e-shakti, and certain other programs. Under supervisory functions, NABARD conducts periodic inspections of RRBs and cooperative banks.
3. The major sources of institutional finance are cooperatives, RRBs, and CBs. Cooperative movement in India started in 1904. The cooperative system in India has been organized into short-term and long-term credit structure. Under short-term structure, PACs work at village level, CCBs at district level, and SCBs at state level. Under long-term structure, SCARDBs function at state level and PCARDBs function at local level. RRBs were established in 1975 and are sponsored by the Central Government, the State Government, and CB. The share of CBs in institutional lending was bare minimum at the time of independence. However, certain steps like Bank Nationalization, Lead Bank Scheme, Priority Sector Lending norms, and Service Area Approach placed commercial banking in the forefront of agriculture credit.
4. Agriculture insurance provides millions of farmers a safety net in the eventuality of inadequate rainfall, crop failure, or collapse in market prices. In India, the government at present is running four popular agriculture insurance schemes. They are Pradhan Mantri Fasal Bima Yojna, Restructured Weather Based Crop Insurance Scheme, Unified Package Insurance Scheme, and Coconut Palm Insurance Scheme.
5. India reports maximum number of farmer suicide cases every year in the world. Around 12,000 farmers commit suicide every year. NCRB collects nationwide data on farmers and farm laborers. A total of 70% of suicides are reported in the case of farmers/cultivators and 30% of suicides are reported in the case of farm laborers. According to NCRB, indebtedness is the major cause of farmers'/cultivators' suicide, whereas family problem is the major factor of suicide for agriculture laborers.
6. Credit subsidy is offered by the government to farmers in order to protect their larger interest. Major causes of credit subsidy are crop failure, low capital formation in agriculture, and farmers not getting remunerative price of their agriculture produce. In India, major tools of credit subsidy are interest subvention and loan waivers. But over the period of time, loan waivers have become political gimmick to woo the voters that affect the economy in multiple ways, viz., rise in fiscal deficit of the states, increase in NPAs of the banks, promoting credit indiscipline, and making honest farmers resentful who repaid loans in time.

Endnotes

1. *NSSO's 70th round (January–December 2013).* Ministry of Statistics and Program Implementation. Government of India.
2. Rural Infrastructure Development Fund. Retrieved from https://www.nabard.org (Accessed on January 16, 2019).
3. NABARD Infrastructure Development Assistance. Retrieved from https://www.nabard.org (Accessed on January 16, 2019).
4. Long-Term Irrigation Fund. Retrieved from https://www.nabard.org (Accessed on December 11, 2018).
5. E. Shakti. Retrieved from https://www.nabard.org (Accessed on January 22, 2019).
6. NABARD Functions. Retrieved from https://www.nabard.org (Accessed on January 23, 2019).
7. *Govt begins work to consolidate regional rural banks. The Hindu Business Line.*, September 23, 2018.
8. Krishna Kishore, N.T. (2012). Agriculture credit in India: An integrated rural credit approach. *International Journal of Scientific and Research Publications*, 2(3), March 2012, ISSN 2250-3153.

9. *Annual report, 2017–18*. Department of Agriculture, Cooperation & Farmers Welfare. The Ministry of Agriculture and Farmers Welfare. GOI.
10. Basu, D., Das, D., & Misra, K. (2016). Farmer Suicides in India: Trends across major states, 1995–2011. *EPW, I*(21), May 21, 2016.
11. Accidental death and suicides in India. Retrieved from http://ncrb.gov.in/StatPublic (Accessed on April 27, 2024).
12. Kishore R. Why the farmer suicide debate is counter-productive to understanding India's agrarian crisis? *The Hindustan Times*, December 27, 2018.
13. Jeromi, P.D. (2007). Farmers' indebtedness and suicides: Impact of agricultural trade liberalisation in Kerala. *Economic and Political Weekly*, August 4, 2007.
14. Ravi, S. Debt isn't killing India's farmers. *The Livemint*, December 24, 2018.
15. Interest Subvention. Retrieved from http://agricoop.nic.in (Accessed on March 4, 2019).
16. Bera, S. 8 states. ₹1.9 trillion. It's raining farm loan waivers, but are farmers really gaining? *Livemint*, December 21, 2018.
17. Shrivastava, R. Two big reasons why Congress farm loan waiver will add to farmers' woes. *India Today*, December 21, 2018.
18. Farm Loan Waiver. *The Times Now News*, January 11, 2019.
19. *Swaminathan report on farmers' distress*. Retrieved from agricoop.nic.in (Accessed on November 16, 2018).

CHAPTER **14**

AGRICULTURE MARKETING IN INDIA

The farmer is the only man in our economy who buys everything at retail, sells everything at wholesale, and pays the freight both ways.

—John F. Kennedy

INTRODUCTION

Traditionally, agricultural marketing involved essentially the buying and selling of agricultural production. But in modern times the agricultural marketing system is defined in broadest terms, as physical and institutional set up to perform all activities involved in the flow of products and services from the point of initial agricultural production until they are in the hands of ultimate consumers. This includes assembling, handling, storage, transport, processing, wholesaling, retailing, and export of agricultural commodities as well as accompanying supporting services such as market information, establishment of grades and standards, commodity trade, financing and price risk management, and the institutions involved in performing the above functions.[1]

In this chapter we propose to discuss the following issues:

- Types of Agriculture Markets
- Government Measures for the Improvement of Marketing System in India
- Reforms in Agriculture Markets
- Co-operative Agriculture Marketing

TYPES OF AGRICULTURE MARKETS

Rural Primary Markets

There are around 650,000 small and large villages in India. These villages are inhabited by about 850 million consumers making up for about 70% of population and contributing around half of the country's gross domestic product (GDP).[2] Rural primary markets include mainly the periodical markets known as Haats, Shandies, Painthsand Fairs which are estimated to be more than 21,000 to a maximum of 47,000 in the country. Located in rural and interior areas, they serve as focal points to a great majority of the farmers—mostly small and marginal for marketing their farm produce and for purchase of their consumption needs. The commodities collected in these markets find their way to the wholesale assembling markets in the process of movement to consumers. It is estimated that 90% of the total marketable surplus in the remote areas is sold through these markets.[3] According to the report of Marketing and Research Team (MART), New Delhi one Haat caters to approximately 14 villages. It was observed that 50% Haats were organized by the panchayats or town administration.[4] Despite the benefits associated with rural primary markets, very little efforts have been made so far by the government agencies/market authorities to develop the rural primary markets. Only 15% of these markets have been brought under the ambit of regulation.

The Wholesale/Assembling Markets

The Wholesale/Assembling Markets or the secondary markets constitute the basic link in the market structure of the country. They are better organized than the rural primary markets and present divergent picture with regard to facilities offered and services provided. The wholesale markets are located in the district and taluk headquarters, important trade centers, and nearby railway stations, and perform assembling and distribution functions. In most of these markets, a large number of commodities are traded. Specialized single commodity markets are not many except few markets for cotton, jute, oilseeds, fruits, and vegetables. The management of such markets is done by a market committee which has nominees of the state government, local bodies, arhatiyas, brokers, or farmers. Most of the states have already enacted legislations (Agriculture Produce Marketing Committees Act) to provide for regulation of agriculture-produce markets. There are presently 7,246 markets in India. The business is conducted according to market practices established by age old customs, or as per the regulations of Agriculture Produce Marketing Committees (APMC) Act wherever regulated. These markets play an important role in determining the prices of agricultural produce assembled there and as such have a governing impact on terms of trade between agriculture versus other sectors of economy.

Terminal Markets

The scheme of Terminal Markets Complex (TMC) has been conceptualized and introduced as a new model under National Horticulture Mission. It is implemented in a Public–Private Partnership (PPP) mode in a Hub (Main Market) and Spokes (Collection Centers) format by private enterprise. The project aims at helping the farmers in reaping the benefit through better price realization, reducing wastages, and creating opportunities of rural employment in addition to regular supply of agricultural commodities including fruit and vegetables.[5] Terminal markets are quite popular in developed countries and the idea is expected to gain ground in India. The Safal complex of NDDB is one such format, located at Bengaluru. They are expected to be located nearer to big cities and terminal points providing the final link in the market structure. The sellers are usually the traders and not the growers in these markets unlike the primary and secondary markets. The terminal markets provide multiple options to farmers for disposal of produce. Such markets are expected to reduce post-harvest losses and increase farmers' realization.

Retail Markets

Famously called as "MOM and POP" stores, retail markets directly serve the common man and constitute last links in the marketing chain. Generally the small-sized retailers are located in the entire length and breadth of the country and serve the needs of inhabitants in a particular locality. In recent times, there is tremendous interest in setting up of retail chains for food items including fresh produce. Few MNCs and large number of private players have entered in the retail segment and are expected to revolutionize the system of handling of agricultural produce. Modern organized retail can take several forms, from small neighborhood stores (like Mother Dairy outlets) to air-conditioned malls (like Big Bazaar). The modern organized retail offers better prices to both consumers and producers and reduces the gap between the two. Modern retailers are able to offer better prices to consumers and producers because of the economies of scale in procurement, handling, and logistics.[6]

Characteristic Features of Agriculture Marketing in India

After independence, GOI took plethora of steps to promote agriculture marketing in India. Following are the salient features of Agriculture Marketing in India:

Agricultural Produce Market Committee

Agricultural Produce Market Committee (APMC) is a statutory market committee constituted by a State Government in respect of trade in certain notified agricultural or horticultural or livestock products, under the Agricultural Produce Market Committee Act issued by that state government. Under Constitution of India, agricultural marketing is a state subject. While intra-state trades fall under the jurisdiction of state governments, inter-state trading comes under Central or Federal Government. Thus, agricultural markets are established and regulated mostly under the various State APMC Acts. The whole geographical area in the state is divided and each one is declared as a market area which is managed by the APMC constituted by the state government. States also constitute a Market Board which supervises these market committees. APMCs generally consist of representatives of farmers, traders, warehousing entities, registrar of co-operative societies, etc. No person or agency is allowed to freely carry on wholesale marketing activities and the first sale in the notified agricultural commodities produced in the region such as cereals, pulses, edible oilseed, fruits, and vegetables and even chicken, goat, sheep, sugar, fish etc., can be conducted only under the aegis of the APMC, through its licensed commission agents.

Functions of APMCs are ensuring transparency in pricing system and transactions, providing extension services to farmers, ensuring timely payment for agricultural produce to farmers, promoting agricultural processing activities, publicizing data on arrivals and rates of agricultural produce, and promoting PPP in the management of agricultural markets. There are about 2,477 principal regulated markets based on geography (the APMCs) and 4,843 sub-market yards regulated by the respective APMCs in India.[7]

However, with time, such APMCs developed into restrictive agencies which instead of promoting and safeguarding the interest of farmers turned into manipulative and exploiter bodies. Let us understand, how:

- APMC Act restricts the farmer from entering into direct contract with any processor/manufacturer/bulk processor acquiring the status of restrictive and monopolistic markets and thus harming the farmers.

- APMCs charge multiple levies and taxes viz. statutory levies/mandi tax, VAT, a licensing fee from the commissioning agents, a small licensing fees from a whole range of functionaries such as warehousing agents and loading agents which add up to hefty amounts, create market distortions with cascading effects, and strong entry barriers. All this has led to a highly fragmented and high-cost agricultural economy, which prevents economies of scale and unbroken movement of agriculture goods across district and state borders.
- APMC operations are hidden from scrutiny as the fee collected, which are at times exorbitant, is not under State legislature's approval. Agents in an APMC many times form cartel creating monopsony*-like situation. Produce is procured at manipulatively low price (from farmers) and sold at higher price (to consumers), defeating the very purpose of APMCs.
- APMCs play dual role of regulator and market. Consequently, their role as regulator is undermined by vested interest in lucrative trade. Generally, member and chairman are nominated/elected out of the agents operating in that market.
- Exporters, processors, and retail chain operators cannot procure directly from the farmers as the produce is required to be channelized through regulated markets and licensed traders. Monopolistic practices and modalities of the state-controlled markets have prevented private investment in the sector which has further prevented development of a competitive marketing system on a pan-India basis.

Grading and Standardization

Government established the Directorate of Marketing and Inspection (DMI) in 1935 to implement the agricultural marketing policies and programmes for the integrated development of marketing of agricultural and other allied produce in the country. Agricultural Produce (Grading and Marketing) Act was passed in 1937 which was later amended in 1986. Head office of DMI is located at Faridabad, Haryana. It has 11 regional offices at Delhi, Mumbai, Chennai, Kolkata, Hyderabad, Chandigarh, Jaipur, Lucknow, Bhopal, Kochi, and Guwahati, and the Central Agmark Laboratory at Nagpur. Besides, there are 27 sub-offices and 11 Regional Agmark Laboratories (RALs) spread all over the country. Agmark is the acronym for Agriculture Marketing and important commodities are graded for internal trade and export. In total, 222 commodities have been graded so far till date.[8] Apart from Agmark, the Food Safety and Standards Authority of India (FSSAI) also regulates the quality and safety of food business in India.**

*A market situation where there is only one buyer who then exercises control over the price at which he buys.

**The Food Safety and Standards Authority of India (FSSAI) has been established in 2008 under Food Safety and Standard, 2006 which consolidates various acts and orders that have hitherto handled food-related issues in various ministries and departments. FSSAI has been created for laying down science-based standards for articles of food and to regulate their manufacture, storage, distribution, sale, and import to ensure availability of safe and wholesome food for human consumption. It is important to note that AGMARK is an inspection seal provided for quality of agricultural products, whereas, FSSAI Licensing covers every food item whether agricultural or non-agricultural.

Changes in Standard Weights and Measures

The standard weights act was passed by government in 1939 so as to discourage the Arhatiyas and brokers who used to cheat the farmers. The act encouraged many state governments to pass legislations thereafter. In 1958, the Indian government enacted a new legislation and the metric system of measures was adopted. The metric system replaced all the old systems of weight and measures and has introduced uniformity with respect to weight and measures in the country. The Standards of Weights and Measures Act, 1976 provides necessary powers to the government to inspect weighing and measuring instruments during their use to prevent fraudulent practices, regulation of inter-state trade and commerce in weights and measures, and regulation of export and import of weights and measures and commodities in packaged form.[9]

Godown and Storage Facility

According to the working group report, about 30% farm produce is stored under open condition, leading to wastage and distress sales.[10] The godown and storage infrastructure provides safety cushion to farmers as they are not compelled to sell their produce immediately after the harvesting of crops. It increases farmers' bargaining power and save them from the distress sale. Keeping such considerations in view, the Rural Credit Survey Committee (1954) suggested establishment of a three-tire storage system in the country at (1) national level, (2) state and district level, and (3) village and rural level. On the basis of such recommendations, Central Warehousing Corporation (CWC) was set up in 1957 and this was followed by State Warehousing Corporations in a number of states.

Development of Market Information Infrastructure

Agriculture is a highly unorganized sector and farmers remain unaware about the nationwide price trend of agriculture commodities. Government has come out with many measures to overcome such shortcoming. Special talks and programmes are organized by Doordarshan and All India Radio and agriculture market price trends are reviewed regularly. Presently, wholesale price of 300 commodities and about 2,000 varieties are reported on the Agriculture Marketing Information Network (AGMARKNET) portal from more than 1,800 markets covering all major agricultural and horticultural produce.

Agriculture Price Policy

To bring certainty in agriculture and make farming fool proof from the vagaries of marker fluctuations, government announces minimum support price policy every year for around 24 major crops. The prices are fixed in accordance with the recommendation of Commission for Agriculture Cost and Prices (CACP).*

Institutional Support

CCS National Institute of Agricultural Marketing

Chaudhary Charan Singh National Institute of Agricultural Marketing (NIAM) was established by GOI in 1988 with the objective to augment the agricultural marketing infrastructure of the country through programme of teaching, research, and consultancy services.

---

*For detailed discussion, see the chapter 12, Agriculture Prices and Food Security.

Small Farmers' Agribusiness Consortium

Small Farmers' Agribusiness Consortium (SFAC) was set up as a registered society in 1994. It provides a platform for increased accessibility and cheaper availability of agricultural inputs to small and marginal farmers and in establishing forward and backward linkages in supply chain management. This initiative has triggered mobilization of farmers for aggregation across the country with ultimate aim of sustainable business model and augmented incomes. SFAC has pioneered the formation and growth of Farmer Producer Organizations (FPOs)/Farmer Producer Companies (FPCs), which is now being implemented across the length and breadth of the country. SFAC offers schemes such as Equity Grant and Credit Guarantee Fund Scheme to FPCs to improve availability of working capital and development of business activities. SFAC promotes development of small agribusiness through its Venture Capital Assistance (VCA) Scheme for value-added processing and marketing linkages. SFAC is also implementing the National Agriculture Market Electronic Trading (e-Nam) platform. The purpose is to provide single unified market for agricultural products with much higher price discovery for farmers.[11]

Agricultural Marketing Infrastructure

Under the Agricultural Marketing Infrastructure (AMI) sub-scheme, there are two components (1) Storage Infrastructure and (2) Marketing Infrastructure other than Storage. The main objectives of the AMI scheme are promoting innovative and latest technologies, encouraging private and co-operative sector investments, direct marketing, creating scientific storage capacity, and providing training to farmers.

Reforms in Agriculture Marketing

Agriculture Marketing laws have been regulated by the state governments. To remove restrictive provisions in the state marketing laws and monopolistic approach of APMCs, provide better price realization to the farmers through improved and alternative marketing channels, enhance investment in development of post-harvest marketing infrastructure, reforms in the sector are required. Central government has been engaging with the states for more than a decade to implement reforms in the sector.[12] Following reform measures have been taken by the government in the field of agriculture marketing in the country.

Agricultural Produce and Livestock Marketing (Promotion & Facilitation) Act, 2017

Government formulated a Model APMC Act in 2003 and also Model Rules in 2007 which were shared with the states/UTs for their guidance and implementation. Government came out with Agricultural Produce and Livestock Marketing (Promotion & Facilitation) Act, 2017 by replacing the APMC Act, 2003. APMC Act had many limitations. For example, under the former act, farmers were supposed to sell at APMC mandis only. There are 6,746 such mandis and each one is located at a gap of 462 km. They are subjected to different kinds of fees. The new model law seeks to establish a regulated wholesale agri-market at a distance of every 80 km.[13] Following are the salient features of Model APLM Act, 2017:

1. Abolition of fragmentation of market within the state/UT by removing the concept of notified market area.

2. Full democratization of Market Committee and State/UT Marketing Board.
3. Removal of intermediaries in food supply chain by integration of farmers with processors, exporters, bulk retailers, and consumers.
4. Clear demarcation of the powers and functions between Director of Agricultural Marketing and Managing Director of State/UT Agricultural Marketing Board. Former will conduct regulatory functions, while the latter will be mandated with developmental responsibilities.
5. Creation of a conducive environment for setting up and operating private wholesale market yards and farmer consumer market yards, so as to enhance competition among different markets and market players for the farmer's produce, to the advantage of the latter.
6. Promotion of direct interface between farmers and processors/exporters/bulk-buyers/end users so as to reduce the price spread bringing advantage to both the producers and the consumers.
7. Enabling declaration of warehouses/silos/cold storages and other structures/space as market sub-yard to provide better market access/linkages to the farmers.
8. Giving freedom to the agriculturalists to sell their produce to the buyers and at the place and time of their choice, to whom so ever and wherever they get better prices.
9. Promotion of e-trading to enhance transparency in trade operations and integration of markets across geographies.
10. Provisions for single-point levy of market fee across the state and unified single trading licence to realize cost-effective transactions.
11. Promotion of national market for agriculture produce through provisioning of inter-state trading licence, grading and standardization, and quality certification.
12. Rationalization of market fee and commission charges.
13. Provision for Special Commodity Market yard(s) and Market yard(s) of National Importance (MNI).
14. Providing a level playing field to the licensees of private market yard, private market sub-yard, electronic trading, and direct marketing vis-à-vis the APLMCs and removing the conflict of interest that the latter are likely to practise, if both development and regulatory functions are centered in the same authority.

Contract Farming

Under contract farming, the farmer is contracted to plant the contractor's crop on his land, harvest and deliver to the contractor a quantum of produce based on anticipated yield and contracted acreage at a pre-agreed price.

The Indian Agriculture gains in the following ways via contract farming:

- Reducing the load on the central and state level procurement system.
- Promoting private sector investment in agriculture.
- Promoting diversification in Indian agriculture and provide market focus in terms of crop selection by Indian farmers.
- Ensuring consistency of agriculture income.
- Promoting processing and value addition.
- Generating gainful employment in rural areas and reducing migration from rural to urban areas.
- Making agriculture self-reliant.

Contract farming ensures a win–win deal to both farmers as well as firms. The farmers get exposure to world class mechanized agro technology and technical advice free of cost at the doorstep apart from regular crop monitoring. The farmer obtains an assured up-front price (remunerative returns) and market outlet for their produce and thus gets saved from the vagaries of market fluctuations. The firm on the other hand also gets immense benefits like uninterrupted and regular flow of raw material and protection from fluctuation in market pricing. The business model can be developed on the basis of long-term planning and builds long-term commitment that go a long way in the development of farm-firm linkage. Further, the dedicated supplier base helps generating goodwill for the organization. Contract farming by Pepsico for tomato in Punjab, Jain Irrigation's Contract farming for mango, SAB Miller for barley, and McCain for potato in Gujarat are some success stories that created a win–win deal for both the contracting company and the farmers.[14] However, there are two major limitations for which contract farming model has been criticized. First, lack of enforceability of contractual provisions can result in breach of contracts by either party.[15] Second, there is a general criticism of contract farming models for being partial as they favor big business houses while exploiting the unorganized small farmers.

To address such issues and to make contract farming both viable and popular, government enacted Model Agriculture Produce and Livestock Contract Farming and Services (Promotion & Facilitation) Act, 2018. Following are the salient features of the Model Contract Farming Act, 2018[16]:

1. To protect the interest of the farmers, they will be considered as weaker of the two parties entering into a contract.
2. Inclusion of service contracts all along the value chain including pre-production, production, and post-production.
3. For online registration of sponsor and recording of agreement, the Act provides for "Registering and Agreement Recording Committee" or an "officer" at district/block/taluka level.
4. Contracted produce will be covered under crop/livestock insurance in operation.
5. Contract framing will remain outside the ambit of APMC Act.
6. No permanent structure can be developed on farmers' land/premises.
7. No right, title of interest of the land shall vest in the name of sponsor.
8. To popularize contact farming among small and marginal farmers promotion of FPOs/FPCs to mobilize small and marginal farmers has been provided.
9. To ensure buying of entire pre-agreed quantity of agricultural produce, livestock, or its product of contract farming producer as per contract.
10. To promote contract farming and services at village/panchayat level, contract Farming Facilitation Group (CFFG) has been provided.
11. For quick disposal of disputes, accessible and simple dispute settlement mechanism at the lowest level possible has been provided under the Act.

Direct Marketing

Direct marketing involves selling products directly to the consumer in order to allow the producer the possibility of receiving a higher price. This usually involves three critical steps: making a direct connection to consumers, determining the consumer wants or needs, and offering products that meet those needs. Direct marketing may take many forms and usually includes a combination of techniques, such as selling to farmer markets, door-to-door sales, internet marketing, direct sale to restaurants or institutions, and so on.[17] By removing intermediaries, direct marketing offers win–win deal that ensures consumers fresh farm produce at low prices and better returns to farmers. Both the model APMC Act, 2003 and model APLM Act, 2017 have emphasized direct marketing to promote trade. Few states have already taken initiative in this regard viz. "rythu bazars" in Andhra Pradesh, "apni mandi" in Punjab, and "uzhavarsanthai" in Tamil Nadu.

Establishment of e-Markets

Launched by the Prime Minister, Narendra Modi in April 2016, National Agriculture Market (NAM) is a pan-India electronic trading portal which networks the existing APMC mandis to create a unified national market for agricultural commodities. The NAM portal provides a single window service for all APMC-related information and services. As discussed earlier, APMC Act divides the state into several market areas and each area has its own marketing regulation. But this market fragmentation even within the state obstructs free flow of agriculture commodities from one market area to another. Further multiple handling of agri-produce and multiple levels of mandi charges ends up escalating the prices for the consumers without commensurate benefit to the farmer. NAM addresses these challenges by creating a unified market through online trading platform, both at state and national level and promotes uniformity, streamlining of procedures across the integrated markets, removes information asymmetry between buyers and sellers, and promotes real-time price discovery based on actual demand and supply. It promotes transparency in auction process, and access to a nationwide market for the farmer, with prices commensurate with quality of his produce and online payment and availability of better quality produce and at more reasonable prices to the consumer.[18]

Deregulation of Marketing of Fruits and Vegetables

Fruits and vegetables being perishable crops need different set of markets and marketing system with reduced supply chain and adequate marketing infrastructure including cold storages and cold chain. Existing organized system of marketing through network of APMC markets used to be attributed for high post-harvest losses, long intermediation in supply chain, and low return to the farmers. Government is encouraging the states to provide complete freedom to the farmers as well as buyers and investors to invest in development of marketing infrastructure outside the market yard so as to facilitate emergence of various channels of marketing. However, APMCs will remain the alternate choice for the farmers. Till now, 14 states (Madhya Pradesh, Himachal Pradesh, Delhi, West Bengal, Odisha, Rajasthan, Chhattisgarh, Gujarat, Maharashtra, Haryana, Karnataka, Assam, Nagaland, and Meghalaya) have moved in this direction, though in varied forms.[19]

Ranking States in Terms of Marketing Reforms

NITI Aayog has constructed an index to compare the status of reforms in agriculture sector across states and UTs. The index is termed as Agricultural Marketing and Farmer Friendly Reforms Index (AMFFRI). It is based on actions taken by each state and UT to (1) reform the system of agriculture marketing, (2) facilitate and liberalize lease in and lease out of agricultural land, and (3) freedom to fell and sell forest produce grown on private land. Weights were assigned to each of the three dimensions viz. marketing reforms were given a weightage of 74%, liberalization of land lease was assigned weightage of 16%, and freedom to fell and sell forest produce grown on private land was provided weightage of 10% (Table 14.1).

TABLE 14.1 Variables Included in AMFFRI and Their Weight and Score

S. No.	Category	Weightage (%)
1	**Agricultural marketing includes 10 indicators viz.** private mandi, direct marketing, contract farming, e-trading, single-point levy, direct sale to consumers by farmers, single traders license, participation in E NAM, special treatment to fruits and vegetables, taxes/fee/levy in primary market	74
2	**Land lease**	16
3	**Forestry: Liberalized felling and transit of trees**	10

Source: NITI Aayog (2016). *Study Report on Agricultural Marketing and Farmer Friendly Reforms Across Indian States and UTs*. New Delhi.

Agriculture marketing reforms aim to promote competition, efficiency, transparency, and removal of regulatory restrictions having adverse effect on producers, modernization of marketing, and creation of healthy trading environment. These reforms indicate the ease of doing agribusiness and range of choices and options granted to producers to sell their produce. Agriculture marketing is a state subject and all states in the country have not implemented entire set of market reforms. Also, land leasing and harvest and marketing of some trees species on private farm land are subjected to various degrees of restrictions in almost all the states/UTs. Maharashtra earned the top rank in AMFFRI. The state has implemented most of the marketing reforms and it offers best environment for doing agribusiness in the country. Gujarat ranks second followed by Rajasthan and Madhya Pradesh. Agriculture advanced state Punjab ranks 14th because of poor implementation of market reforms. Many states/UTs viz. Uttar Pradesh, Punjab, West Bengal, Assam, Jharkhand, Tamil Nadu, and Jammu and Kashmir could not reach even halfway mark of reforms score. It is because some states/UTs do not have APMC Act, which offers a huge challenge to provide ranking to these states in market reforms (Table 14.2).[20]

TABLE 14.2 Ranking of States in Terms of Implementation of Marketing and Other Farmer-Friendly Reforms, as on October 2016*

State	Score	Rank	State	Score	Rank
Maharashtra	81.7	1	Mizoram	37.0	16
Gujarat	71.5	2	Nagaland	33.3	17
Rajasthan	70.0	3	Sikkim	32.6	18
Madhya Pradesh	69.5	4	West Bengal	32.5	19
Haryana	63.3	5	Tripura	29.1	20
Himachal Pradesh	59.5	6	Odisha	27.9	21
Andhra Pradesh	56.2	7	Uttarakhand	25.2	22
Karnataka	55.5	8	Arunachal Pradesh	21.1	23
Telangana	54.3	9	Chandigarh	20.1	24
Goa	52.8	10	Tamil Nadu	17.7	25
Chhattisgarh	51.4	11	Meghalaya	14.3	26
Jharkhand	49.4	12	Jammu and Kashmir	7.4	27
Uttar Pradesh	47.8	13	Lakshadweep	7.4	28
Punjab	43.9	14	Delhi UT	7.3	29
Assam	37.1	15	Puducherry	4.8	30

Source: NITI Aayog (2016). *Study Report on Agricultural Marketing and Farmer Friendly Reforms Across Indian States and UTs*. New Delhi.

*Some states and UTs either did not adopt APMC Act or revoked it. They include Bihar, Kerala, Manipur, Daman and Diu, Dadra and Nagar Haveli, and Andaman and Nicobar. They are not included in the ranking.

Co-operative Agriculture Marketing

All the measures discussed earlier benefit mostly the big farmers who have adequate marketable surplus, whereas the small and marginal farmers continue to sell major part of their produce to money lenders at very cheaper price to meet their credit needs. Therefore, co-operatives were formed to organize small and marginal farmers so as to enable them to obtain fair price for their produce. The history of co-operative marketing in India can be traced back to 1912, when the Cooperative Marketing Societies Act, 1912 was passed. The first Co-operative Society was formed in Hubli in 1915 to encourage cultivation of improved cotton and to sell it collectively.

Following are the merits of co-operative marketing:

1. Small and marginal farmers are generally illiterate and ignorant and are vulnerable to exploitative plots of intermediaries. By forming co-operatives and selling their produce through one single agency farmers' bargaining strength increases with respect to traders and intermediaries.
2. Co-operatives promote direct marketing as farmers can sell their produce directly to the final consumer. Co-operatives ensure win–win proposition and ensure fair prices to both farmers and consumers.
3. Marketing co-operative societies carry the provision of providing credit to the farmers and thus save them from the exigency of selling their produce immediately after harvest. It helps farmers to get better return as they can search for valuable purchaser of their produce.
4. Co-operative societies also have provision for storage facility and helps farm store their produce and wait for better prices. There is no danger of crop getting damaged from rains, rodents, and theft.
5. Co-operatives ensure subsidized inputs to the farmers such as seeds, manures, fertilizers, and pesticides, and thus help to reduce their cost of production. Co-operatives also undertake processing activities such as crushing oilseeds and ginning and pressing of cotton.

Structure and Progress of Co-operative Marketing in India

The structure of co-operative marketing societies consists of the National Agricultural Cooperative Marketing Federation of India Ltd. (NAFED) at the national level, the state co-operative marketing federations at the state level, and primary marketing co-operative societies at the agricultural market (Mandi) level. The organizational structure of co-operative marketing is not uniform across the country and varies from state to state. It is a two-tier structure consisting of primary marketing co-operatives at the mandi level and state marketing federation at the state level in the states of Assam, Bihar, Kerala, Karnataka, Madhya Pradesh, Odisha, Rajasthan, West Bengal, and North-eastern states. On the other hand, it is a three-tier structure consisting of primary marketing co-operatives at the base, central marketing societies at the district, and state marketing federations at the state levels in the rest of the states. Few state marketing federations are MARKFED in Punjab, HAFED in Haryana, HIMFED in Himachal Pradesh, RAJFED in Rajasthan, MAHAMARKFED in Maharashtra, TANFED in Tamil Nadu. Let us have a brief idea of NAFED. NAFED was established on October 2, 1958 as an apex co-operative marketing body with the objective to promote co-operative marketing of agricultural produce to benefit the farmers. Agricultural farmers are the main members of NAFED, who have the authority to say in the form of members of the General Body in the working of NAFED.

Following are the important objectives of NAFED[21]:

1. To organize, promote, and develop marketing, processing, and storage of agricultural, horticultural, and forest produce.
2. To distribute agricultural machinery, implements, and other inputs.
3. To undertake inter-state, import and export trade, wholesale or retail as the case may be.
4. To organize consultancy work in various fields for the benefit of the co-operative institutions in general and for its members in particular.
5. To act as warehouseman under the Warehousing Act and own and construct its own godowns and cold storages.
6. To maintain transport units of its own or in collaboration with any other organization in India or abroad for movements of goods on land, sea, air, and operate freight station, container depot and undertake other incidental activities.
7. To collaborate with any international agency or a foreign body for development of co-operative marketing, processing, and other activities for mutual advantage in India or abroad.
8. To undertake marketing research and dissemination of market intelligence.

Political Economy of Farm Laws

The 1991 economic reforms initiated by Dr. Manmohan Singh impacted different sectors of the economy but the agricultural reforms were bypassed and it was left to Vajpayee Government who brought APMC Model Act, 2003- aiming at facilitating contract farming model, single market fee, and allowing farmers and private persons to set up their market. The Modi Government passed three Agriculture bills on 27 September 2020— (1) Farmers' Produce Trade and Commerce (Promotion and Facilitation) Act, 2020, (2) Farmers (Empowerment and Protection) Agreement on Price Assurance and Farm Services Act, 2020 and (3) Essential Commodities (Amendment) Act, 2020. The Parliament repealed the three farm laws in November 2021 due to longstanding demands of farm unions. However the bill that attracted the attention of entire world needs to be understood. The three farm laws offered three basic liberties to the farmer- First, he could sell anywhere to anyone, freeing him from having to sell to a monopoly cartel at the APMC mandi; second, freedom to lease unviable lands for a job and a share in profits and also the freedom to make forward contracts and hence transferring their risk to businessmen; and third, the freedom to store inventory which was constrained so far by stocking limits in the Essential Commodities Act. This gives incentive for cold storages to come up, to whom farmers can now sell directly.

The Act was applauded by almost all political parties and stakeholders however, not all the states passed the bill and inter-state barriers continued. The thick-skinned politicians and farmer unions sabotaged the interest of farmers and as a consequence income from farming did not grow as much as income in other sectors. The brave farmers of Punjab and Haryana, the majority of who own marginal landholdings deserve a better lifestyle as that of middleman and powerful farm union leaders with strong political backgrounds.

Points in Favour

1. Indian farmers badly require the infusion of capital and technology to adopt scientific methods in agriculture practices and to grow high-value crops. Neither the farmer has money to pay for it, nor the government. Hence, the new law gives farmers the freedom to lease their lands to agri-professionals with capital and technology, and become in turn shareholders and workers on the same land, setting the stage for the second green revolution.
2. Government has already assured them that the land transfer to private players will not take place, farmers would have the freedom to cancel the contract at any point of time, and payments to the farmers will be made within time. Today the PPP model (public-private participation) has become common in almost every economic and social sphere, and the contract farming model is already existent in many states. PepsiCo presently works with farmers, spread across West Bengal, Maharashtra, Punjab, Gujarat, UP, Karnataka, Bihar, Haryana, and Chhattisgarh and more than 45 percent of these are small and marginal farmers with a landholding of one acre or less. Similarly, many MNCs like Nestle, Hindustan Unilever, Kellogg's, ITC, etc. to name a few have joined hands with farmers. Moreover, it is farmers' call to enter into the contract and they can go for any company which serves their interest in a better way.

To establish an agrarian economy that ensures food and nutrition security to a population of over a billion, the raw material for its expanding industrial base, surpluses for exports, and a fair and equitable rewarding system for the farming community- contract farming provides plenty of opportunities. It is a win-win proposition that provides a paradigm shift to new-age farming, and assures reliable input service to farmers and desired farm produce to the contracting firms.

3. The Essential Commodities (Amendment) Act, 2020 wants to bring changes in the 1955 Act which was legislated at a time when the country was facing a scarcity of foodstuffs due to persistent low levels of foodgrains production. India used to import wheat from the US under PL-480 and the food shortage led to massive hoarding practice by black marketers. The situation has much changed as wheat production has increased 10 times (from less than 10 million tonnes in 1955–56 to about 100 million tonnes in 2020–21), while the production of rice has increased from around 25 million tonnes in mid 1950s to about110 million tonnes during the same period). The production of foodgrains has crossed 300 million tonnes mark and India has become net exporter of many agricultural products. The new Act seeks to liberate agricultural markets from the limitations imposed by permits and mandis that were originally designed for an era of food shortage. The new Act will attract private investment in the value chain of commodities removed from the list of essentials, such as cereals, pulses, oilseeds, edible oils, onions and potatoes. It is because the Essential Commodities Act, 1955 which was originally enacted to protect the interests of consumers by checking illegal trade practices such as hoarding, had become a hurdle for investment in the agriculture sector in general, and in post-harvesting activities in particular. It prevented the private sector to investing in cold chains and storage facilities for perishable items.[22]

Points in Disfavour

1. There is a concern that creation of private mandis will push all agriculture businesses towards private markets. The government markets and commission agents will die their natural death and big traders and giant companies will operate in the markets and procure farm produce at incidental prices. Although the government has proposed that there will be uniform policy of taxes, fee, and cess both for government and private markets. But the governments would deliberately delay procurement as in case of paddy and turn the public markets inefficient and redundant.[23]
2. A few farm unions are apprehensive about grabbing the farmers' land by the large corporations under the contract farming. Although the Government has put a proposal to dispel the fears of farmers by saying that there will be no sale, lease, and transfer of land during the period of contract agreement. But the history of contract farming has many examples of non-payment by the companies making various excuses like substandard produce. For example in the case of sugarcane payments were held for many years. In another case, farmers' produce was not bought by firms making excuses of poor quality. Such instances pushed the farmers into debt trap as they were unable to repay the loans and had no option other than to sell/lose their lands.[24]
3. Another fear in the mind of farm unions is about the Essential Commodities (Amendment) Act, 2020. As per their stand before the government, the new Act will hurt farmers and consumers, and will only benefit hoarders. The chances of hoarding of Essential food items like pulses, onions and edible oil, which are part of a common man's daily essential commodities are quite high. The big MNCs that will enter in the supply chain process, if not regulated, will go deep into villages to buy crops directly leading to both hoarding and price rise.

Summary

1. Agriculture marketing comprises all activities involved in the flow of goods and services from the point of initial agricultural production to ultimate consumption.
2. There are mainly four types of agriculture markets. Rural primary markets located in rural areas are periodical markets. The wholesale market is located in district headquarters or important trade centers, deals in large number of commodities, and helps determining prices of agriculture produce. The terminal market is the new experiment in India and functions in hub and spoke format by private enterprises. Retail markets directly serve the common man and constitute last link in the marketing chain.
3. Agriculture marketing has undergone dramatic changes since independence. Various states have passed APMC Acts so as to regulate the agriculture trade and providing farmers with certain advantages like ensuring transparency in pricing timely payment for their produce and so on. Other features of agriculture marketing are enacting the Agricultural Produce (Grading and Marketing) Act 1937; enacting the standard weights Act 1939; establishment of three-tire storage system in the country and setting up of CWC in 1957; development of market information infrastructure; regular announcement of agriculture price policy; institutional support to agriculture by establishing National Institute of Agriculture Marketing in 1988, setting up Small Farmers' Agribusiness Consortium in 1994 and development of agriculture marketing infrastructure.
4. In the recent past, government has introduced many agriculture marketing reforms. Agricultural Produce and Livestock Marketing (Promotion & Facilitation) Act, 2017 was enacted by replacing the APMC Act, 2003. Model Agriculture Produce and Livestock Contract Farming and Services (Promotion & Facilitation) Act, 2018 has been enacted to promote contract farming in the country. Direct farming which seeks to ensure win–win deal to buyers and sellers is being promoted. National Agriculture Market (NAM) has been launched to create a unified national market for agricultural commodities. Market for fruits and vegetables is being deregulated to facilitate emergence of various channels of marketing. Agricultural Marketing and Farmer Friendly Reforms Index has been introduced by NITI Aayog in 2016 to rank the states on the basis of three indicators.
5. Agriculture co-operative marketing is being promoted to organize small and marginal farmers so as to enable them to obtain fair price of their produce. NAFED is the nodal agency that works at national level.

Endnotes

1. Planning Commission (2007). *Report of the working group on policy required for internal and external trade for the XI five year plan 2007–12*. p.18. Retrieved from http://Planningcommission.nic.in (Accessed on May 22, 2018).
2. Indian Rural Market (2017). Retrieved from https://www.ibef.org (Accessed on December 19, 2017).
3. Planning Commission (2007). *Report of the working group on policy required for internal and external trade for the XI five year plan 2007–12*. p.18. Retrieved from http://Planningcommission.nic.in (Accessed on May 22, 2018).
4. *Traditional Haats and Melas in India*. A research report by Pradeep Kashyap, sponsored by the Ministry of Rural Areas and Employment, Government of India.
5. Terminal markets complex scheme to help farmers get better prices. *Press Information Bureau*. Retrieved from http://pib.nic.in (Accessed on March 21, 2018).
6. Rangarajan, C. (2015). *Modern organised retail and its impacton agriculture*. Springer India; Rao, N.C., Radhakrishna, R., Mishra, R.K., Kata, V.R. (Eds.) (2016)., Organised retailing and agri-business. *India Studies in Business and Economics*, Springer India.
7. Economic Survey (2014–15). *Department of Economic Affairs, Ministry of Finance*, Govt. of India.

8. Grades and Standard. (2019). Retrieved from http://dmi.gov.in (Accessed on April 24, 2019).
9. Department of consumer affairs. Retrieved from http://consumeraffairs.nic.in (Accessed on March 24, 2019).
10. Planning Commission (2007). *Report of the working group on policy required for internal and external trade for the XI five year plan 2007–12*. p.18. Retrieved from http://Planningcommission.nic.in (Accessed on May 22, 2018).
11. *Small Farmers' Agribusiness Consortium*. Retrieved from http://sfacindia.com (Accessed on March 28, 2019).
12. *Brief History of Agricultural Marketing Regulation, its Constraints and Reforms in the Sector*. Retrieved from http://dmi.gov.in (Accessed on March 29, 2019).
13. *Financial Express*, April 24, 2017.
14. Agriculture Marketing Reforms. Retrieved from https://www.ruralmarketing.in (Accessed on March 29, 2019).
15. Gulati, Ashok & K. Joshi, P & Landes, Maurice. (2019). Contract Farming in India: An Introduction. Retrieved from https://www.researchgate.net (Accessed on March 30, 2019).
16. Press Information Bureau, Government of India, May 22, 2018.
17. Clause, Reg. *Direct marketing–Getting started*. Accessed from https://www.agmrc.org (Accessed on March 30, 2019).
18. eNam. Retrieved from http://www.enam.gov.in (Accessed on March 30, 2019).
19. Department of Agriculture (2018). *Annual Report-2016–17*. Ministry of Agriculture.Govt. of India.
20. Niti Aayog. (2016). *Study report on Agricultural Marketing and Farmer Friendly Reforms across Indian States and UTs*. New Delhi.
21. National Agricultural Cooperative Marketing Federation of India Ltd. Retrieved from http://www.nafed-india.com (Accessed on March 30, 2019).
22. Redefining essential items: Why it was needed, and who it will impact. Indian Express, September 26, 2020.
23. Why farmers still oppose the Centre's proposals on farm laws. Indian Express, December 16, 2020.
24. *ibid*

CHAPTER 15

INDUSTRIAL DEVELOPMENT AND POLICIES

The country that is more developed industrially only shows,
to the less developed the image of its own future.
—Karl Marx

INTRODUCTION

Before the advent of British, Indian industry was far more productive, efficient, and advanced as compared to the other nations. The colonial rule systematically destroyed India's unique industrial heritage and as a result we inherited a weak industrial base from British at the time of independence. In the early 1950s, the Indian industry was marked by dilapidated production and productivity levels, fragile infrastructure, lower demand, and poor exports. The policy makers of that time had to provide certain vision to this significant sector of Indian Economy and therefore, the government came out with many proposals that set the stage and pace for industrial growth in the years to come. Since then, the nation had been commutated to a mixed economy, though the balance between the public and private sectors seemed at times to be leaned in favor of the former especially during the first four decades after independence. It was only after the economic reforms of 1991, that, Indian industry underwent a significant paradigm shift.

This chapter will discuss the following key issues:

- Characteristic Features of Indian Industry
- Journey of Indian Industry Since Independence
- Industrial Policies of India
- Impact of New Industrial Policy on Indian Industry
- Why is Manufacturing Sector Important for India?
- New Manufacturing Policy
- Make in India and Its Performance Appraisal

CHARACTERISTIC FEATURES OF INDIAN INDUSTRY

1. *Sectoral Share and Employment:* Industrial sector in India comprises four sub-sectors. They are mining and quarrying; manufacturing; electricity, gas, water supply and other utility services; and construction. Out of these four sub-sectors, manufacturing

TABLE 15.1 Sectoral Composition of the IIP

	Base Year 2011–12	
Sector	**Weights (%)**	**Item Groups**
Mining	14.373	1
Manufacturing	77.633	405
Electricity	7.994	1
Total	100	407

Source: *Annual Survey of Industries, 2017–18.* Ministry of Statistics and Programme Implementation. Govt. of India.

TABLE 15.2 Use-Based Classification

New Series (Base 2011–12)	Item Groups	Weights (%)
Primary goods	15	34.05
Intermediate goods	110	17.22
Capital goods	67	8.22
Infrastructure/construction goods	29	12.34
Consumer durables	86	12.84
Consumer nondurables	100	15.33
Total	407	100

Source: *Annual Survey of Industries, 2017–18.* Ministry of Statistics and Programme Implementation. Govt. of India.

contributes nearly 17% of gross value added (GVA) and construction contributes around 9% of GVA. Mining and quarrying and electricity, gas, water supply, and other utility services contribute around 2 and 2.35%, respectively. The share of industry as a percentage of GVA has increased from nearly 17% in 1950–51 to 30% in 2022–23.[1] The index of industrial production (IIP) constitutes three sectors viz. Mining, Manufacturing and Electricity comprising 407 items.

2. *New Index of Industrial Production (Base 2011–12):* The Index of Industrial Production (IIP) is an index which shows the growth rates in different industry groups of the economy in a stipulated period of time. The IIP is computed and published by the CSO on a monthly basis. The base year for the current series of IIP is 2011–12. The new IIP has 839 items and 407 item groups compared to 682 item and 399 item groups in the old IIP (with base year 2004–05). The new series covers only organized sector whereas the old series also covered unorganized sector. The sectoral composition of IIP constitutes mining, manufacturing and electricity sector and manufacturing with 405 item groups has got maximum weight of 77.6% (Table 15.1). The analytical grouping of IIP data is done on the basis of use-based classification and eight core industries. In the use-based classification, five items are taken. They are primary goods, capital goods, intermediate goods, infrastructure/construction goods, and consumer goods, both durable and non-durable (Table 15.2).[2]
3. *Core Industries:* Industries that are necessary for industrialization of a country are called core industries. In India, the Department of Industrial Policy and Promotion (DIPP), Ministry of Commerce and Industry has classified eight industries as core industries. These industries are coal, crude oil, natural gas, refinery products, fertilizers, steel,

cement, and electricity. The eight core industries comprise nearly 40% of the weight of items included in the IIP with base 2011–12.[3]

4. *Growth Rate of Indian Industry:* The growth rate of Industry in India's GVA has been 7.7, 6.3 and 4.9% during 2016–17, 2017–18 and 2018–19 respectively. In 2019–20 and 2020–21, the growth rate was recorded at 0.9 and –9.6% respectively. Industry sector witnessed modest growth of 4.1% in FY23 compared to the strong growth of 10.3% in FY22. The growth of Indian industry was lower during 12th plan as compared to the period of 10th and 11th 5-year plan. The unsatisfactory performance of industrial sector can be attributed to sharp decline in investment activity, rising cost, and falling demand which led to reduction in corporate profitability and adversely affected the investment decisions of the firms.
5. *Industrial Employment:* As per NSSO 68th round survey and PLFS Quarterly 2021 survey, the share of industrial employment as a percentage of total employment has increased from 10.7% in 1951 to around 25% in 2023. The share of manufacturing, construction, and mining and quarrying in the total employment was 12, 12, and 0.5%, respectively, for the year 2022–23.

JOURNEY OF INDIAN INDUSTRY SINCE INDEPENDENCE: TRENDS IN PRODUCTION AND GROWTH

The journey of Indian industry is quite interesting and can be summed up into four phases including both pre-reform and post-reform period.

Phase I (1951–1965): The period of industrial foundation.
Phase II (1965–1980): The period of industrial fall.
Phase III (1980–1991): The period of industrial recovery.
Phase IV (1991 onwards): The post-reform period.

Phase I (1951–1965): The Period of Industrial Foundation: The story of Indian Industry began from second 5-year plan onward. The country adopted an industrial strategy biased toward capital goods based on the model given by P. C. Mahalanobis, famously called Mahalanobis model.* It was the time when India laid down the foundation of public sector enterprises which were focused on the production of basic and capital goods industries. The industrial growth rate was spectacular during the Phase I as growth rate of Industrial production was 5.7, 7.2, and 9% during the first, second, and third 5-year plan, respectively. Significantly, the growth rate of capital goods industry shot up considerably from 9.8% p.a. in the first plan to 13.1% p.a. in second plan and further to 19.6% p.a. in third plan.

Phase II (1965–1980): The Period of Industrial Fall: The growth phenomenon experienced during the first phase started receding and there was a spectacular fall in the industrial growth during the second phase. This period experienced a growth rate of around 4.2%.[4] The capital goods industry which had demonstrated a terrific growth, registered less than 3% growth rate during this period. Basic goods industries also experienced a steep fall in their growth rate. Many factors can be attributed to this dramatic fall. The two wars with Pakistan during 1965 and 1971, the fall in public investment, oil crisis of 1973, and political uncertainties of 1970s contributed in

*Founder of Indian Statistical Institute, Prof. P.C. Mahalanobis is hailed as father of modern statistics in India. He is best remembered as the architect of India's Industrial policy after independence.

TABLE 15.3 Average Annual Industrial Growth Rate: India and Some Asian Economies

Country	Industry		Manufacturing	
	1965–1980	1980–1990	1965–1980	1980–1990
India	4.2	6.6	4.1	7.1
China	10.0	12.5	8.9	14.4
Pakistan	6.4	7.3	5.7	7.7
Thailand	9.5	9.0	11.2	8.9
South Korea	16.4	12.2	18.7	12.7
Turkey	7.2	6.2	7.5	7.2
Malaysia	–	7.1	–	8.8
Indonesia	11.9	5.6	12.0	12.5

Source: World Bank, World Development Report, 1992. Retrieved from https://www.worldbank.org (Accessed on March 28, 2016).

different ways to bring down the industrial growth rate. Many economists blamed wrong industrial policies viz. controls on output, investment and trade—popularly called the "Permit Licence Raj"—which stifled private initiative and wasted meager public resources.[5]

Phase III (1980–1991): The Period of Industrial Upturn: The rate of industrial growth was 6.6% during 1980–1991. 1980 onward, after the domestic political uncertainty had ended, industrial policy witnessed greater pragmatism with a gradual loosening of controls, and a greater willingness to import technology and foreign private capital to modernize the manufacturing sector.[6] The liberal fiscal regime too helped to expand the demand for manufactured goods in the economy. Higher growth rate in agriculture sector (as during this time the green revolution had started paying dividends) and resultant income effect led to the increase in demand of manufacturing goods in rural India.[7] This was also the time when service sector became forefront of country's growth. The increase in income in service sector changed the consumption pattern of the service class toward consumer durables. The higher growth rate in infrastructure was also the major reason for the growth turnaround during this phase.

Table 15.3 elaborates India's standing in the industrial performance vis-à-vis other Asian economies during 1965–1980 and 1980–1990. India's manufacturing growth rate and industrial growth rate was lower compared to other nations during the pre-reform period. Table 15.3 clearly demonstrates the gap between India and Asian economies during the planning era and reveals why such nations are far ahead to India even today in terms of industrial strength.

Phase IV: (1991 onwards): The Post-Reform Period: The average industrial growth rate during this phase was around 6.2%. The economic crisis of 1991 led to wide scale reforms in Indian economy and the new industrial policy initiated various measures like shrinking the public sector reservation, doing away with licensing and MRTP Act, liberalization of trade and exchange rate policies, and introduction of monetary and fiscal sector reforms. The fourth phase covers five plans comprising 8th plan (1992–1997), 9th plan (1997–2002), 10th plan (2002–2007), 11th plan (2007–2012), and 12th plan (2012–2017). The industrial growth rate during these plans was 7.4, 5.0, 8.2, 6.9, and 3.7%, respectively. The post-reform period also witnessed spectacular increase in FDI. However, the period was marked by slowdown in public investment, infrastructural constraints, and exposure to external competition. The global financial crisis of 2007–08 and the Eurozone crisis thereafter too affected industrial growth up to a large extent. The 12th plan period particularly was marked by twin balance sheet problem that affected industrial investment activities.

INDUSTRIAL POLICY

Industrial Policy of the Government seeks to maintain a sustained growth in productivity, to enhance gainful employment, to achieve optimal utilization of human resources, to attain international competitiveness, and to transform India into a major partner and player in the global arena. The industrial policy of India during the pre-reform period was a continuous process and aimed at promoting the socialistic pattern of growth by guiding and determining the state intervention in the field of industrial development. The government announced various policy steps in the form of following:

- Industrial policies during pre-reform period
- New industrial policy of 1991

Industrial Policies During Pre-reform Period

1. *Industrial Policy Resolution (IPR), 1948:* The IPR 1948 accepted the importance of both public and private sectors. The IPR 1948 had following salient features. It categorized large scale industries into four parts: (1) public sector, (2) mixed sector, (3) controlled private sector, and (4) private and co-operative sector. Rapid development of cottage and small scale industries was emphasized in order to utilize local resources, generating employment avenues and promoting production of consumer goods. The policy lamented that employer–employee relations should be amiable and the workers should get fair wages and social security measures. The role of foreign capital for industrial development was recognized and the arena of foreign capital was completely under government control. Special stress was laid on development of roads, railways, electricity, and irrigation.
2. *Industries (Development and Regulation) Act, 1951:* The Indian Parliament passed Industries (Development and Regulation) Act, 1951 in October 1951, though the Act came into force on May 8, 1952. This act introduced in the country the notorious License Raj through regulation of industrial investment and production. Both public and private sector units included in the schedule of the Industries (Development and Regulation) Act, 1951 were required to be registered and take permission from the government with regard to expansion of their economic activities. The government was empowered to regulate the production, pricing, and distribution of products manufactured by the units included in the schedule of the Act. In extreme circumstances, the government could also take over the activities of such units. It was the industrial policy of 1991 which substantially brought down the number of items under industrial licensing.
3. *Industrial Policy Resolution, 1956:* The IPR 1956 was such a comprehensive document that it is also hailed as the economic constitution of India. Based on Mahalanobis model of growth, it emphasized focus on heavy industries which would lead the economy toward a long-term higher growth path. To achieve this objective, the resolution accorded a predominant role to the state to assume direct responsibility for industrial development. The IPR 1956 classified industries into three categories. The first category comprised 17 industries (included in Schedule A of the Resolution) exclusively under the domain of the government. The second category comprised 12 industries (included in Schedule B of the Resolution), which were envisioned to be progressively state owned but private sector

was expected to supplement the efforts of the state. The third category of industries was left for private sector but the state could enter into this category as well. Another objective spelt out in the IPR 1956 was the removal of regional disparities through development of regions with low industrial base. The policy also recognized the role and importance of small scale and cottage industry the same way as it was done in IPR 1948.

4. *Industrial Policy in the Decades of 1960:* To review various aspects pertaining to concentration of economic power and operations of industrial licensing under the IDR Act, 1951, GOI set up Monopolies Inquiry Commission (MIC) in 1964. The government established two more committees, first under Dr R.K. Hazari (famously known as Hazari Committee) to review the working of the licensing system and second under Mr Subimal Dutt (famously known as Dutt Committee) which is also called the Industrial Licensing Policy Inquiry Committee. Hazari Committee submitted its report in 1967 and Dutt Committee in 1969 and both the committees were highly critical of industrial license system. Hazari Committee observed that Industrial Licensing system failed to achieve the cherished goal of balanced regional development and the Committee termed industrial license as a passport to an entrepreneur to conduct business in India. Dutt Committee also observed that due to the License Raj, a very strong nexus has developed between the industrial houses, politicians, and bureaucrats and there was a need to harmonize the social interest with private interest. It proposed setting up of a monopolies commission with necessary teeth to deal with the problems of concentration of economic power and suggested the classification of industries into sectors such as core sector, non-core sector, and reserved sector. The committee recommended that larger industrial houses should be given licenses only for operating in core and heavy investment sectors, thereby calling for reorientation of License Raj. The government in 1969 came out with monopolies and restrictive Trade Practices (MRTP) Act to effectively control concentration of economic power in the country. The MRTP Act, 1969 defined large business houses as those with assets of ₹200 million and above. Large industries were designated as MRTP companies and were entitled to operate in businesses that were not reserved for the small scale sector or the government.
5. *Industrial Policy Statement of 1973:* The government accepted the recommendations of Dutt Committee and included the term Core Industry. To overcome the foreign exchange crunch, the government came out with new act, that is, foreign exchange regulation act.
6. *Industrial Policy Statement of 1977:* The Industrial Policy statement of 1977 was framed by Janta Government and then Industry Minister George Fernandes tried to do away with many things introduced by Indira Gandhi regime. It was peculiar in many ways. First, the policy aimed to give boost to small scale sector. For the first time, an Industrial Policy defined a "tiny unit" as a unit with investment in machinery and equipment up to ₹1 lakh and situated in towns or villages with a population of less than 50,000 (as per 1971 census). The list of items reserved for SSI was raised from 180 to 504 and 807 in May 1978. The cottage and small scale industries were redefined and the concept of village industries was evolved.
7. *Industrial Policy Statement of 1980:* A number of measures were initiated toward technological and managerial modernization to improve productivity, quality, and to reduce cost of production. The government steadily introduced few liberalization measures as the public sector was freed from a number of constraints and was provided with greater autonomy. The process of deregulation started and in 1988, all industries, except 26

industries specified in the negative list, were exempted from licensing. The exemption was, however, subject to investment and locational limitations. The government modernized and expanded scales of production of automotive industry, cement, cotton spinning, food processing, and polyester filament yarn. In June 1988, the Government of India announced the Growth Centre Scheme under which 71 Growth Centers were proposed to be set up throughout the country to promote industrialization of backward areas. The Growth Centers were to be endowed with basic infrastructure facilities such as power, water, telecommunications, and banking to enable them to attract industries.

New Industrial Policy of 1991

The new industrial policy was announced on July 24, 1991. Through the Industrial Policy of 1991, government decided to take a series of initiatives in respect of the policies relating to the following areas.

1. Industrial Licensing
2. MRTP Act
3. Foreign Investment
4. Foreign Technology Agreements
5. Public Sector Policy

1. *Industrial Licensing Policy:* As discussed earlier, the Industrial Licensing was governed by the Industries (Development & Regulation) Act, 1951. A substantial modification of Industrial Licensing Policy was deemed necessary with a view to enhance capacity creation and productivity of industrial sector. Industrial licensing has, therefore, been abolished for most of the industries and at present there are only four industries related to security, strategic and environmental concerns, where an industrial license is currently required. These are cigars and cigarettes of tobacco and manufactured tobacco substitutes, electronic aerospace and defense equipment, industrial explosives, and specified hazardous chemicals.[8]
2. *MRTP Act:* The MRTP Act was passed by Indian Parliament in 1969 but it came into force in June 1970. Under the Act, all firms with assets above a certain size (₹100 crore since 1985) were classified as MRTP firms. Companies under MRTP Act were normally required to obtain the approval of the government in respect of substantial expansion of production capacity, diversification of existing activities, establishment of inter-connected undertakings and amalgamation, merger or takeover. It had a negative effect on industrialization of Indian economy and especially diversification of large scale private firms. The industrial policy of 1991 amended the MRTP Act and scrapped the threshold limit of assets in respect of MRTP and dominant undertaking. MRTP Act was later repealed and replaced by Competition Act 2002 with effect from September 1, 2009. The MRTP commission was replaced by Competition Commission of India.[9]
3. *Foreign Investment:* Industrial policies prior to 1991 welcomed FDI but emphasized that ownership and control of all enterprises involving foreign equity should be in Indian hands. The Balance of Payments problem during mid-1960s forced the country to adopt a more restrictive approach toward FDI and consequently the number of industries for foreign investment was steadily narrowed down and by 1973 there were only 19 industries where FDI was permitted. The new industrial policy realized that foreign

investment would bring abundant advantages of technology transfer, marketing expertise, introduction of modern managerial techniques, and new possibilities for promotion of exports. This was seemed to be particularly necessary in the changing global scenario of industrial and economic co-operation marked by mobility of capital. The government, therefore, decided to welcome foreign investment which was in the interest of the country's industrial development.[10] Government took series of steps to promote foreign investment viz. relaxing the FDI cap in various industries, repealing the FERA Act, 1973 and replacing it with FEMA Act, 1999, removal of dividend balancing clause,* and so on.

4. *Foreign Technology Agreements:* The industrial policy statement of 1991 realized that there was a great need for promoting an industrial environment where the acquisition of technological capability received priority. Such a relationship became difficult to achieve when the approval process included unnecessary government interference on a case-to-case basis involving endemic delays and fostering uncertainty. It was recognized that "the Indian entrepreneur has now come of age so that he no longer needs such bureaucratic clearance of his commercial technology relationships with foreign technology supplier. Indian industry can scarcely be competitive with the rest of the world if it is to operate within such a regulatory environment." With a view to injecting the desired level of technological dynamism in Indian industry, government provided automatic approval for technology agreements related to high priority industries within specified parameters. FDI up to 100% was allowed under the automatic route in all activities/sectors except the sectors where prior approval of the government was required. Indian companies were allowed to negotiate the terms of technology transfer with their foreign counterparts according to their own commercial judgment.[11]
5. *Public Sector Policy:* The IPR 1956 assigned a pre-eminent position to public sector in Indian industry to enable it to achieve "commanding heights of the economy". But after the initial exuberance of the public sector entering new areas of industrial and technical competence, a number of problems have begun to manifest viz. insufficient growth in productivity, poor project management, overmanning, lack of continuous technological upgradation, inadequate attention to R&D and human resource development, low rate of return on the capital invested, and so on. The industrial policy of 1991 adopted following measures so as to make public sector more growth oriented and technically dynamic.
   - **(a)** The industrial policy of 1956 had reserved 17 industries for public sector. The 1991 industrial policy reduced this number to eight and at present only two industrial sectors are reserved for public sector. They are atomic energy and railways (excluding construction, operation and maintenance of certain works/projects like sub-urban corridor projects through PPP, high-speed train project, dedicated freight lines, mass rapid transport systems, etc.).[12]
   - **(b)** Public enterprises which are chronically sick and which are unlikely to be turned around will, for the formulation of revival/rehabilitation schemes, be referred to the

*Under dividend balancing clause, companies were required to offset the outflow of foreign exchange for dividend payments (in the form of repatriation of profit to their home countries) by export earnings. To put simple, the outflow of foreign exchange on payment of dividend shall not exceed the amount of export earning of the company. It would help India maintain its foreign exchange reserves.

Board for Industrial and financial Reconstruction (BIFR), or other similar high-level institutions created to protect the interests of workers likely to be affected by such rehabilitation packages.

(c) To raise resources and encourage wider public participation, a part of the government's shareholding in the public sector would be offered to mutual funds, financial institutions, general public, and workers. This paved the way for disinvestment policy in India.

(d) There will be a greater thrust on performance improvement through the Memorandum of Understanding (MOU) system through which managements would be granted greater autonomy and will be held accountable. MOUs signified an arm's length relationship between government and public-sector enterprise and the government would not interfere into day-to-day business of the public sector enterprises.

Impact of New Economic Policy on Indian Industry

1. *Erratic Industrial Growth During the Post-Reform Period:* Reforms failed to provide certainty and stability for industrial growth. During 1981–82 to 1990–91, the industry grew at an annual average growth rate of 7.8% and during 1991–92 to 1998–99, the industrial growth moderated to 5.9%. It increased marginally to 6.3% during 1999–2000 to 2004–05 and thereafter it followed the fluctuating trend. The industrial growth crossed 9% during 2007–08 and 2009–10 and dipped down to below 5% during 2009–10 to 2012–13. The growth rate of Indian industry was unsatisfactory during 12th 5-year plan (2012–2017) and the major factors responsible for the lower industrial growth rate during this period were twin balance sheet problem, credit squeeze by banks, falling demand, and major supply bottlenecks faced by core industries.
2. *Contribution to GDP:* The share of industry in country's GDP increased from 16.6% in 1990–91 to around 30% in 2017–18. The reforms have not influenced the industrial sector as much as it was envisaged during the launch of new industrial policy of 1991. The falling share of agriculture was grabbed by service sector, which contributes more than 50% in the economy of India. The new initiatives viz. Make in India, new manufacturing policy and boost to infrastructural reforms will definitely help raising the industrial GVA in the years to come.
3. *Structural Change in Indian Industry:* The pronouncement of new industrial policy altered the structural landscape of Indian industry. The economic reforms in the industrial sector have added new dimensions and enhanced private sector participation. The investment by public sector industry is falling and that of private sector is increasing. The change can be witnessed in the light of many reform measures taken after 1991 viz. removal of industrial licensing, de-reservation of public sector, and disinvestment program. The initiatives like new manufacturing policy, industrial corridors, and Make in India provide a new headway to the private entrepreneurs in India. For the last few years, the country has witnessed huge rise in the number of young and female entrepreneurs. As per NSSO 68th round survey, the public sector employment is shrinking (from 194.66 lakh persons in March 1995 to 175.48 lakh persons in March 2011) and that of private

sector is increasing (80.59 lakh persons to 114.22 lakh persons during the same period). In fact, there is negative growth rate in employment in organized public sector.

4. *Distortion in Industrial Production:* The long-run industrial development of a nation depends mainly on the production and growth of basic and capital goods industries. During the decade of 1980s, such industries recorded huge growth rate of 7.9 and 11.5%, respectively, but in the later years the growth rate dwindled and during 2012–2017, the capital goods industry recorded negative growth rate. The distortion in the production structure does not omen well for the country especially if we want to make gains in industrialization.
5. *Emergence of Strong Manufacturing Sector:* Manufacturing has emerged as one of the high growth sectors in India. It contributes nearly 17% of GDP. The GVA at basic current prices from the manufacturing sector in India grew at a CAGR of 4.34% during 2012–2018. With the help of Make in India drive, India is on the path of becoming the hub for hi-tech manufacturing global MNCs attracted by India's market of 1.3 billion consumers and increasing purchasing power. Cumulative FDI in India's manufacturing sector reached US$ 76.82 billion during April 2000 to June 2018.[13]

WHY IS MANUFACTURING SECTOR SIGNIFICANT FOR INDIA?

Manufacturing contributes in the economic development of a nation in different ways. It contributes into nation's GDP, increases exports, generates abundant employment opportunities, and saves valuable foreign exchange due to reduction in imports. In 1990, India's GDP per capita ($385) was higher than that of China's ($318) and total GDP was almost equal to that of China. Since then, China has outgrown India in terms of economic size, with its GDP almost five times that of India's. The spectacular growth story of China can be attributed to careful planning, huge investment in infrastructure, incentives and subsidies, progressive decentralization, and market-oriented reforms that led to its manufacturing revolution. Manufacturing contributes 17% of India's GDP, whereas, in China, South Korea, and Thailand, it contributes 29, 29, and 27%, respectively. Manufacturing leads to sustainable economic growth and according to some estimates, every job created in manufacturing has a multiplier effect of three additional jobs in other sectors.

Problems of Manufacturing Sector

1. In terms of quality of power, India ranks 80 out of 137 countries as per World Economic Forum. According to the World Bank, access to electricity is the second-most important obstacle for manufacturing firms and is holding back corporate investment. India also faces the highest transmission and distribution losses in electric power in emerging Asia due to low technological investment in innovations.
2. In developed nations, logistic costs are around 7–8% of GDP, whereas in India, logistics costs are almost double, around 14–15% of GDP. Around 60% of the country's cargo travels by road thanks to over-saturated railway networks, high-rail freights, long transit times, inadequate port depths, high turnaround time at ports, and poor warehousing

facility. The distance from Guangzhou in China to Mumbai is five times greater than that between Delhi and Mumbai, but the cargo cost is almost comparable.

3. India's demographic and low labor cost advantage is eroded by growing skill mismatch and low productivity of labor. Today, 62% of India's population is in the working age group and more than 54% of the total population is below 25 years of age. However, it is estimated that only 4.7% of India's workforce is formally skilled, as against 52% in the United States, 68% in the United Kingdom, 75% in Germany, 80% in Japan, 96% in South Korea, and 24% in China. As per official estimates, India needs to train 126 million people across 34 sectors. Aspiring Minds, an Indian employability assessment firm, estimates that more than 80% of engineers in India are "unemployable." This has an impact on productivity. As per OECD estimates, manufacturing productivity in value added per hour worked terms for China and Brazil is 1.6 and 2.9 times higher, respectively, than in India.[14]
4. India's record of R&D spending is abysmal. For the last two decades, India's spending on R&D has become stagnant around 0.6–0.7%. This is much lower than the United States (2.8%), China (2.1%), South Korea (4.2%), and Israel (4.3%). Higher R&D spending builds a nation's technological and innovative strength, which creates a highly competitive manufacturing sector. In most countries, the private sector carries out the bulk of research and development even if government must play an import funding role. However, in India, the government is not just the primary source of R&D funding but also it is the primary user of these funds. In private sector, there are 26 Indian companies in the list of the top 2,500 global R&D spenders compared to 301 Chinese companies. A total of 19 of these firms are in just three sectors: pharmaceuticals, automobiles, and software.[15]
5. MSMEs are the future of India's manufacturing sector. MSMEs contribute nearly 32% of the GDP but get only 17% of total credit disbursed to industry, whereas 83% of total credit goes to large scale and big corporates. The average loan granted to MSMEs under the Pradhan Mantri Mudra Yojana has been low of the size of ₹50,000, despite low levels of NPAs for this sector. If we want our MSMEs to innovate, export, and prosper, we must create suitable conditions for them in terms of cost and provision of capital.[16]

Recent Policy Initiatives in Manufacturing Sector[17]

1. New manufacturing policy announced in 2011 and Make in India in 2014 will usher in new era of manufacturing growth.
2. To provide boost to manufacturing, government has also started various schemes such as Start up India, Stand up India, Skill India, Digital India, Mudra Scheme, Smart City, and Atal Innovation Scheme.
3. The draft National Policy on Electronics (NPE) released by government envisages creation of a US$ 400 billion electronics manufacturing industry in the country by 2025.
4. Exempted 35 machine parts from basic custom duty in September 2018, so as to boost mobile handset production in the country.
5. Income tax rate reduced to 25% for all companies having a turnover of up to ₹250 crore. Budget 2019–20 extended this incentive to companies with turnover up to ₹400 crore.

6. Launching of phased manufacturing program aimed at adding more smartphone components under the Make in India initiative, thereby giving a push to the domestic manufacturing of mobile handsets.
7. The Government of India is in talks with stakeholders to further ease FDI in defense under the automatic route to 51% from the current 49%, in order to give a boost to the Make in India initiative and to generate employment.
8. Approval of "Strategic Partnership" model by government will enable private companies to tie up with foreign players for manufacturing submarines, fighter jets, helicopters, and armored vehicles.
9. The Union Cabinet has approved the Modified Special Incentive Package Scheme (M-SIPS) to encourage investment and production in the electronic goods sector.

National Manufacturing Policy, 2011

Government announced National Manufacturing Policy (NMP) in 2011 to bring about a quantitative and qualitative change and to give necessary impetus to the manufacturing sector.

Objectives of NMP[20]

1. Increase manufacturing sector growth to 12–14% over the medium term to make it the engine of growth for the economy and enable it to contribute at least 25% of the National GDP by 2022.
2. Create 100 million additional jobs by 2022.
3. Create appropriate skill sets among the rural migrant and urban poor to make growth inclusive.
4. Increase domestic value addition and technological depth in manufacturing.
5. Enhance global competitiveness of Indian manufacturing through appropriate policy support.
6. Ensure sustainability of growth, particularly with regard to the environment including energy efficiency, optimal utilization of natural resources, and restoration of damaged/degraded eco-systems.

Policy Instruments

Specific policy instruments have been conceptualized to achieve the objectives stated earlier. These policy interventions are[21] (1) rationalization and simplification of business regulations; (2) simple and expeditious exit mechanism for closure of sick units while protecting labor interests; (3) financial and institutional mechanisms for technology development, including green technologies; (4) industrial training and skill upgradation measures; (5) incentives for SMEs; (6) special focus sectors; (7) leveraging infrastructure deficit and government procurement, including defense; (8) trade policy; and (9) clustering and aggregation, that is, establishment of National Investment and Manufacturing Zones (NIMZs). (Box 15.1).

BOX 15.1 What are National Investment and Manufacturing Zones?

National Investment and Manufacturing Zones (NIMZs) as envisaged by National Manufacturing Policy, 2011 are integrated industrial townships with state-of-the-art infrastructure and land use on the basis of zoning; clean and energy-efficient technology; necessary social infrastructure; and skill development facilities to provide a productive environment to persons transiting from the primary sector to the secondary and tertiary sectors. The government has announced 8 investment regions along the Delhi Mumbai Industrial Corridor (DMIC) and 14 NIMZs outside the DMIC region have also been given in-principle approval.

Key features of the proposed NIMZs are as follows:

- The state government will provide suitable land having an area of 5,000 ha in size.
- At least 30% of NIMZs area will be utilized for location of manufacturing units.
- A special purpose vehicle will be constituted to take care of functioning of the NIMZ.
- The state government will provide water, power connectivity, and other infrastructure and utility linkages.
- The external physical infrastructure like rail, road (national highways), airports, and telecommunications will be provided by central government.
- Viability gap funding not exceeding 20% of project costs will be provided by central government.
- Soft loans from multilateral financial institutions will be explored and the developers of NIMZs will be allowed to raise external commercial borrowings for developing internal infrastructure of the NIMZs.

Sources:

1. Economic Survey, Department of Economic Affairs, Ministry of Finance. 2011–12, p.216.
2. Point of view, National Manufacturing Policy, PricewaterhouseCoopers. Retrieved from https://www.pwc.in (accessed on March 14, 2019).
3. National Investment and Manufacturing Zones (NIMZs). March 11, 2016. Press Information Bureau. Government of India. Ministry of Finance

Make in India

The Make in India initiative was launched by the Government of India on September 25, 2014, with the primary goal of making India a global manufacturing hub, by encouraging both multinational as well as domestic companies to manufacture their products within the country. The DIPP, in consultation with various central ministries, state governments, industry leaders, and other stakeholders, has formulated a strategy for increasing the contribution of the manufacturing sector to 25% of the GDP by 2020. As envisaged by the NMP 2011, Make in India seeks to create 100 million additional jobs in manufacturing by 2022. The logo of "Make in India"—a lion made of gear wheels—itself reflects the integral role of manufacturing in government's vision and national development. The initiative is built on four pillars which are as follows:[20]

New Processes

The new processes under Make in India involves following steps. The reform process is aligned with parameters of World Bank's "Ease of Doing Business" index to improve India's ranking so as to create possibilities for getting FDI and foster business partnerships.

(a) The India Aspiration Fund has also been set up under SIDBI for venture capital financing of newly set-up or expanding units in the MSME sector.
(b) SIDBI Make in India Loan for Small Enterprises (SMILE) has been launched to offer loans to Indian SMEs with less stringent rules.
(c) Micro Units Development Refinance Agency (MUDRA) Bank has been set up to provide development and refinance to commercial banks/NBFCs/cooperative banks for loans given to micro-units.

New Infrastructure

Infrastructure is integral to the growth of any industry. Various steps have been taken by the government to promote infrastructure.

(a) Efforts are already being made to develop industrial corridors, smart cities with state-of-the-art technology, and high-speed communication.* Innovation and research activities are supported by a fast-paced registration system and improved infrastructure for Intellectual Property Rights (IPR) registrations.
(b) Training for the skilled workforce for the sectors is also being addressed.
(c) Schemes such as Start-up India and Stand-up India for boosting entrepreneurship.
(d) An innovation promotion platform called Atal Innovation Mission (AIM) and a techno-financial, incubation and facilitation program called Self-Employment and Talent Utilization (SETU) are being implemented to encourage innovation and start-ups in India.

New Sectors

A total of 25 sectors have been identified to promote under Make in India campaign. The government has eased FDI norms for railways, defense, and pharmaceutical. With the objective of promoting investment in the country, a full-fledged investment facilitation cell has been set-up under the Make in India initiative, primarily to support all investment queries as well as to handhold and liaison with various agencies on behalf of potential investors.** The 25 sectors identified under "Make in India" are automobiles, automobile components, aviation, biotechnology, chemicals, construction, defense manufacturing, electrical machinery, electronic systems, food processing, information technology and business process management, leather, media and entertainment, mining, oil and gas, pharmaceuticals, ports and shipping, railways, renewable energy, roads and highways, space and astronomy, textiles and garments, thermal power, tourism and hospitality, and wellness.[21]

New Mindset

Indian Government has always been seen as a regulator and not a facilitator. This initiative intends to change this by bringing a paradigm shift in the way Government interacts with

---

*Six industrial corridors are being developed across various regions of the country. Industrial cities will also come up along these corridors.

**DIPP has set up a special management team to facilitate and fast track investment proposals from Japan, the team known as "Japan Plus" has been operationalized w.e.f. October 2014. Similarly, "Korea Plus," launched in June 2016, facilitates fast track investment proposals from South Korea and offers holistic support to Korean companies wishing to enter the Indian market.

BOX 15.2 Ease of Doing Business

Ease of doing business (EODB) is an index published by the World Bank. The index advocates for both regulatory quality and efficiency. A nation's ranking on the index is based on the average of 10 sub-indices: (1) starting a business, (2) dealing with construction permits, (3) getting electricity, (4) registering property, (5) getting credit, (6) protecting investors, (7) paying taxes, (8) trading across borders, (9) enforcing contracts, and (10) resolving insolvency. In the EODB index, "higher rankings" (a lower numerical value) indicate better, usually simpler, regulations for businesses and stronger protections of property rights. New Zealand has topped the Ease of Doing Business rankings in 2017, 2018, and 2019. India's ranking has improved from 134 in 2015 to 77 in 2019. The World Bank Group since 2021 has discontinued the publication of EODB ranking of the countries after findings of data irregularities and ethical concerns in the 2018 and 2020 reports.

Source: Doing Business 2019—Training for Reform, World Bank, 16th edition, Indian Express, 18 September, 2021.

various industries. It will focus on acting as a partner in the economic development of the country alongside the corporate sector. An interactive portal http://makeinindia.com for dissemination of information and interaction with investors has been created with the objective of generating awareness about the investment opportunities and prospects of the country, to promote India as a preferred investment destination in markets overseas and to increase Indian share of global FDI.[22]

New Industrial Initiatives

Startup India

The Startup* India campaign was launched by Prime Minister on August 15, 2015 to build a strong eco-system for nurturing innovation and startups in the country which will drive economic growth and generate large-scale employment opportunities. The government through this initiative aims to empower startups to grow through innovation and design.[23]

The action plan of this initiative is based on the following three pillars:

- Simplification and handholding
- Funding support and incentives
- Industry-academia partnership and incubation

Standup India

Launched on August 15, 2015, the aim of the scheme is to facilitate loans between ₹10 lakh and ₹1 crore to at least one SC/ST borrower and one woman borrower per bank branch of all

*A startup is an entity, private, partnership or limited liability partnership firm that is headquartered in India, which was opened less than 5 years ago and have an annual turnover less than ₹25 crore. To be eligible for considering as startup, the entity should not be formed by splitting up or reconstruction and its turnover should not have crossed ₹25 crore during its existence.

scheduled commercial banks for setting up a green field enterprise. The enterprise may be in manufacturing, trading, or service sector.[24]

Skill India

It is a campaign launched by government on July 15, 2015 with an aim to train 400 million people in India in different skills by 2022.

Digital India

Launched by Prime Minister on July 1, 2015, the scheme aims at ensuring accessibility of government services electronically by improving online infrastructure and by increasing Internet connectivity.

Mudra Scheme

Micro Units Development and Refinance Agency (MUDRA) Limited bank was formed in April 2015 by the Government of India. The scheme aims at providing integrated financial support to the micro-enterprises sector, which includes small manufacturing units, food service units, and small industries to name a few. The basic motive of establishing Mudra is to extend the facility of institutional finance to small business entities involved in various trading, manufacturing, and service activities.

Smart City

Launched by Prime Minister on June 25, 2016, the Smart City Mission is an urban renewal and development program with the mission to develop 100 cities across the country making them citizen friendly and sustainable with a capital outlay of US$ 7 billion.

Atal Innovation Mission (AIM)

It is a flagship initiative set up by the NITI Aayog to promote innovation and entrepreneurship across the length and breadth of the country, based on a detailed study and deliberations on innovation and entrepreneurial needs of India in the years ahead.

The Atal innovation mission has two core functions. They are as follows:

- Entrepreneurship promotion: Through SETU, wherein innovators would be supported and mentored to become successful entrepreneurs.
- Innovation promotion: To provide a platform where innovative ideas are generated.[25]

Summary

1. Indian industry comprises four sub-sectors: mining and quarrying; manufacturing; electricity, gas, water supply and other utility services; and construction and out of these, manufacturing contributes maximum to GDP (18%). The eight core industries in India are coal, crude oil, natural gas, refinery products, fertilizers, steel, cement and electricity. The growth rate in different industry groups of the economy is reflected by IIP on the basis of use-based classification and eight core industries. The base year for the current series of IIP is 2011–12. The industrial growth rate for the years 2016–17 and 2017–18 was 4.8 and 4.5%, respectively. The share of industry in total employment increased from 10.7% in 1951 to 25% in 2011. The journey of Indian industry can be summed up in four different phases. The phase I (1951–1965) was marked by higher industrial growth rate as industry grew at 5.7, 7.2, and 9%, respectively, during the first, second and third 5-year plan period. The Phase II (1965–1980) experienced dramatic fall in growth rate to 4.2%. Industry in Phase III experienced an upturn as growth rate of 6.6% was recorded. The Phase IV which is also the post-reform phase experienced an industrial growth rate of 6.2%.
2. Industrial policies of India can be categorized into two phases: pre-reform policies and new industrial policy of 1991. The industrial policy of 1948 recognized the role of both public and private sectors and emphasized development of cottage and small scale industries. Industries (Development and Regulation) Act, 1951 introduced industrial licensing to regulate industrial investment and production. The IPR 1956 hailed as the economic constitution of India was based on Mahalanobis model and categorized industries into three parts. The industrial policy during the decade of 1960s was characterized by setting up of MRTP commission, establishment of Hazari Committee & Dutt Committee, and enactment of MRTP Act 1969. The 1973 policy introduced the concept of Core Industry and the 1977 IPR suggested steps to promote small-scale sector. The IPR 1980 was characterized by adoption of liberalization measures, deregulation and announcement of growth center scheme. New industrial policy was announced in July 1991 and focused on five parameters: (1) Industrial licensing was abolished for most of the industries and at present there are only four industries at present; (2) MRTP Act which came into being in 1969 was repealed and replaced by Competition Act 2002; (3) Foreign investment was promoted by taking certain decisions like relaxing the FDI cap in various industries, repealing the FERA Act, 1973 and replacing it with FEMA Act, 1999, removal of dividend balancing clause; (4) Under foreign technology agreements, FDI up to 100% was allowed under the automatic route and companies were allowed to negotiate the terms of technology transfer with their foreign counterparts; and (5) Public sector policy changes include de-reservation of items reserved for public sector, rehabilitation of sick units, wider participation in public sector shareholding, and signing of MOUs. The impact of industrial policy was erratic industrial growth, marginal increase in industrial GDP, structural changes in Indian industry, distortion in industrial production, and emergence of strong manufacturing sector.
3. Manufacturing sector is paramount in placing the economy into the trajectory of higher growth. The chinese growth phenomenon occurred due to manufacturing revolution. The problems faced by Indian manufacturing sector are unsustainable power supply, higher logistic costs, vast proportion of unskilled labor, abysmal R&D spending, and backwardness of MSMEs. Apart from the announcement of NMP, 2011 and Make in India campaign, government has announced plethora of schemes for the development of manufacturing sector during the recent past.
4. Government announced NMP in 2011 to bring about a quantitative and qualitative change in India's manufacturing sector by targeting the growth rate of 12–14% over the medium term, raising its share to 25% of the GDP by 2022, and creating 100 million additional jobs by 2022.
5. Make in India was announced by government in 2014. It aims at making India a global manufacturing hub, increasing the contribution of the manufacturing sector to 25% of the GDP by 2020, and creating 100 million additional jobs in manufacturing by 2022. The initiative is based on four pillars which are new processes, new infrastructure, new sectors, and new mindset.
6. To provide boost to manufacturing, government has also started various schemes such as Start up India, Stand up India, Skill India, Digital India, Mudra Scheme, Smart City, and Atal Innovation Scheme.

Endnotes

1. National Statistics Office, MOSPI, retrieved from https://static.pib.gov.in on 28 April, 2024.
2. *Economic survey*. Department of Economic Affairs, Ministry of Finance. 2017–2018, p.121.
3. *Economic survey*. Department of Economic Affairs, Ministry of Finance. 2017–2018, p.122.
4. Shetty, S.L. (1978). *Structural retrogression in the Indian Economy since the mid-sixties*. EPW, p.8.
5. Nagaraj, R. (2003). *Industrial policy and performance since 1980: Which way now?* EPW.
6. Nagaraj, R. (2003). *Industrial policy and performance since 1980: Which way now?* EPW.
7. Tharmarajakshi, R. (1990). *Inter-sectoral terms of trade revisited*. EPW.
8. Industrial Policy. Retrieved from https://dipp.gov.in (Accessed on March 29, 2016).
9. Chakravarthy, S. *MRTP ACT metamorphoses into competition act*. Retrieved from https://cuts-international.org (Accessed on March 28, 2016).
10. *Statement of Industrial Policy*, New Delhi, July 24, 1991. Retrieved from http://dcmsme.gov.in (Accessed on March 27, 2016).
11. *Statement of Industrial Policy*, New Delhi, July 24, 1991. Retrieved from http://dcmsme.gov.in (Accessed on March 27, 2016).
12. India 2018, A Reference Annual. Publication division. Ministry of information and broadcasting. GOI, New Delhi, Chapter 9.
13. *Manufacturing sector in India*. IBEF (2018). Retrieved from https://www.ibef.org (Accessed on March 18, 2019).
14. Priya, P., & Ghosh, A. (2018). *Why India's manufacturing sector needs a big push*. Financial Express.
15. *Economic Survey*. Department of Economic Affairs, Ministry of Finance. 2017–2018, pp.121–122.
16. *Annual report*, 2017–2018, Ministry of MSMEs, Government of India.
17. *Economic Survey*. Department of Economic Affairs, Ministry of Finance. 2015–2016, 2016–2017, 2017–2018.
18. *DIPP, Press Note 2, 2011 series*. Government of India, Ministry of commerce and industry.
19. Government of India, Ministry of commerce and industry, DIPP, Press Note 2, 2011 series.
20. Make in India. Retrieved from http://www.makeinindia.com (Accessed on April 9, 2018).
21. Make in India. Retrieved from http://www.makeinindia.com (Accessed on April 9, 2018).
22. *Economic survey*, Department of Economic Affairs, Ministry of Finance. 2015–2016, p.135.
23. Startup India. Retrieved from https://www.startupindia.gov.in (Accessed on November 22, 2018).
24. *Standup India*. Retrieved from https://www.standupmitra.in (Accessed on December 14, 2018).
25. *Atal Innovation Mission*. Retrieved from http://www.niti.gov.in (Accessed on November 23, 2018).

CHAPTER **16**

PUBLIC, PRIVATE, AND SMALL SECTOR IN INDIAN ECONOMY

The only constant in the technology industry is change.

—**Marc Benioff**

INTRODUCTION

Immediately after independence, India opted for a mixed economy. In a mixed economy, both public and private sectors coexist. The respective spheres of public and private sectors are well defined and the two sectors function in a manner that is conducive to the achievement of overall development of the national economy. The Industrial Policy Resolution of 1956, which has assigned a dominant role to the public sector in a number of vital industries, also made it very clear that as an agency for planned national development in the context of the country's expanding economy, the private sector will have the opportunity to develop and expand. However, the public sector remained dominant until 1991 and it was only after the introduction of economic reforms, that private sector registered a spectacular growth.

In this chapter, we will discuss the following topics:

- Public sector enterprises and their objectives
- Central public sector enterprises and their performance appraisal
- The policy of disinvestment and privatization
- Private sector in Indian economy and its performance appraisal
- Twin balance sheet problem
- The insolvency and bankruptcy code
- Micro, small, and medium enterprises: Achievements, problems, and policies

PUBLIC SECTOR ENTERPRISES

Before 1947, public sector was almost absent in the Indian economy. The only instances worthy of mention were the Railways, the Posts and Telegraphs, the Port Trust, the Ordnance and the Aircraft factories and few government managed undertakings like the Government salt factories, quinine factories, etc. The Indian policy makers firmly believed that political independence without economic self-reliance will have no meaning and therefore, Industrial Policy

Resolution (IPR) 1956 clearly made a roadmap for the deliberate enlargement of our public sector. The second 5-year plan also emphasized the adoption of socialist pattern of society as the national objective, and stated that all industries of basic and strategic importance, or in the nature of public utility services, should be in the public sector. It was further emphasized that the public sector has to expand rapidly and has to come forward in the areas where the private sector is either unwilling or unable to invest. Public sector enterprises offer a wide range of products and services which include (1) manufacturing of steel, heavy machinery, machine tools, instruments, heavy machine building equipment, heavy electrical equipment for thermal and hydel stations, transportation equipment, telecommunication equipment, ships and submarines, fertilizers, drugs and pharmaceuticals, petrochemicals, cement, and textile; (2) mining of coal and minerals; (3) extraction and refining of crude oil; (4) operation of air, sea, river, and road transport; (5) national and international trade; (6) Consultancy; (7) contract and construction services; (8) inland and overseas telecommunication services; (9) financial services; (10) consumer items such as newsprint, paper, and contraceptives, and (11) hotel and tourism services.

As per IPR 1956, the main objectives for setting up the Public Sector Enterprises were to help in the rapid economic growth and industrialization of the country and create the necessary infrastructure for economic development; to earn return on investment and thus generate resources for development; to promote redistribution of income and wealth; to generate employment opportunities; to promote balanced regional development; to assist the development of small-scale and ancillary industries; and to promote import substitutions, save and earn foreign exchange for the economy.

The public sector can be classified into three types:

1. CPSEs (Central Public Sector Enterprises)—Companies where the direct holding of the Central Government or of other CPSEs is 51% or more;
2. PSBs (Public Sector Banks)—Banks where the direct holding of the Central/State Government or other PSBs is 51% or more;
3. SLPEs (State Level Public Enterprises)—Companies where the direct holding of the State Government or other SLPEs is 51% or more.

Central Public Sector Enterprises (CPSEs)

CPSEs are companies owned by the union government of India with more than 51% stake. The Department of Public Enterprises is the nodal department for all the CPSEs and formulates policy pertaining to CPSEs. It lays down, in particular, policy guidelines on performance improvement and evaluation, autonomy and financial delegation, and personnel management in CPSEs. There are totally 339 CPSEs under the administrative control of various ministries/departments and out of these 255 were operational and rest was under construction. In 2017–18, there were 184 profit-making CPSEs with net profit of ₹1,59,635 crore and 71 loss-making CPSEs with net loss of ₹31,261 crore. Indian Oil, ONGC, NTPC, Coal India Ltd., and Power Grid Corporation are the top five PSUs in India. BSNL, Air India Ltd, MTNL, Hindustan Photo Films Manufacturing Co. Ltd., and Western Coalfield Ltd. are the top five loss-making CPSEs in 2017–18.[1]

BOX 16.1 Classification of CPSEs: Maharatnas, Navratnas, and Miniratnas

Government has classified certain CPSEs as Maharatnas, Navratnas, and Miniratnas.

Maharatnas: Maharatna Scheme was introduced for CPSEs with effect from 19th May, 2010, in order to empower mega CPSEs to expand their operations and emerge as global giants. The objective of the scheme is to delegate functional autonomy and powers to the boards of identified large-sized Navratna CPSEs so as to facilitate expansion of their operations, both in domestic as well as global markets.

As on December 2023, 13 CPSEs have been identified as Maharatnas. These are Bharat Heavy Electricals Ltd., Bharat Petroleum Corp. Ltd., Hindustan Petroleum Corporation Limited, Power Grid Corporation of India Limited Coal India Ltd., Gail (India) Ltd., Indian Oil Corp. Ltd., NTPC Ltd., Oil & Natural Gas Corp. Ltd., Steel Authority of India Ltd., Power Finance Corporation, Rural Electrification Corporation Limited, and Oil India Ltd.

The CPSE eligible for becoming Maharatna should fulfil certain conditions, viz. have Navratna status; listed on the Indian stock exchange, an average annual turnover of more than ₹25,000 crore during the last three years; earn an average annual net worth of more than ₹15,000 crore during the last 3 years; earn average annual net profit of more than ₹5,000 crore during the last 3 years; and should have significant global presence or international operations.

Navratnas: Navratna Scheme was introduced in the year 1997 for CPSEs, which have comparative advantage and provided them with greater autonomy to compete in the global market so as to support them in their drive to become global giants. As on December 2023, Government has identified 16 public sector enterprises as Navratnas. The eligibility criteria for a CPSE is that it must be a Miniratna Category—I and must have obtained "excellent" or "very good" rating under the Memorandum of Understanding system in 3 of the last 5 years, and have composite score of 60 or above in the six selected performance parameters, namely, (1) net profit to net worth, (2) manpower cost to total cost of production/services, (3) profit before depreciation, interest and taxes to capital employed, (4) profit before interest and taxes to turnover, (5) earnings per share, and (6) inter-sectoral performance.

Miniratnas: The scheme of Miniratnas was launched in October 1997. Under this scheme, the government decided to grant enhanced autonomy and delegation of financial powers to some other profit making companies with an objective to make them efficient and competitive.

Only those CPSEs will be eligible for Miniratna status, which have not defaulted in the repayment of loans/interest payment; do not depend on budgetary support of the government; have at least three non-official directors in their board.

Miniratnas have two categories.

Miniratna Category I: Such CPSEs should have made profit in the last 3 years continuously, the pre-tax profit should have been ₹30 crore or more in at least 1 of the 3 years and should have a positive net worth. As on December 2023, there are 57 Miniratna category-I CPSEs.

Miniratna Category II: Such CPSEs should have made profit for the last 3 years continuously and should have a positive net worth. As on December 2023, there are 11 Miniratna category-II CPSEs.

Source: Press Information Bureau, Ministry of Heavy Industries & Public Enterprises, Government of India, July 21, 2014. http://www.bsepsu.com/miniratnas.asp and data accessed from https://dpe.gov.in/ac as on 28 April, 2024

Performance of Public Sector

1. **Capital Formation and Development of Infrastructure:** After independence, the private sector did not show its inclination for investment in physical and social infrastructure as such industries did not promise quick profits and were characterized by long gestation period. The areas like irrigation, power, communication, transportation, roads, railways, shipping, etc. were need of the hour and government had to make proactive effort to invest into such industries and to lay a future roadmap for growth and development. As a result of policy backup, public sector laid down the foundation for capital development of the nation as a number of heavy and capital goods industries were established during second and third 5-year plan. Much of the investment via PSUs came through government budget allocation as the public sector savings were miniscule as compared to private sector and householder's savings. The share of public sector investment has come down from 60% during the third 5-year plan to 24% during the 11th 5-year plan and 7.5% during 2016–17.[2] The decline in the share of public sector investment can be attributed to fall in public sector savings over the period of time and increasing role of private sector in nation building for the three decades. Despite the decline in public sector investments, there is an impressive record of productivity growth of public sector enterprises that can be corroborated by declining average capital-output ratio* from 7.0 in 1981–82 to near 4% at present. It is arguable that the decline in capital-output ratio could mean a shift in public investment to less capital-intensive activities. The decline in the capital-output ratio is due to shift in the investment composition from manufacturing to infrastructure that is capital intensive.[3]
2. **Strong Industrial Base:** The spectacular growth of East Asian tigers and China suggests that a strong industrial sector is the prerequisite for overall higher growth of the economy. Besides general public, as a beneficiary of PSUs, the private sector too needs "basic services" from PSUs (e.g., power, transport and communications) and it is likely to suffer if a state does not invest in heavy and basic capital goods industries. During the initial years of planning, the government embarked upon setting up of basic and capital goods industries to strengthen the capital base of the economy. The share of Industrial Sector in GDP at FC was 16.6% during 1950–51 and rose to around 32% during 2017–18. The share is projected to increase further in the likelihood of manufacturing and construction sector expansion.
3. **Removal of Regional Disparities:** In the pre-independent India, the industry was mainly concentrated in the three presidency regions namely Kolkata, Chennai, and Mumbai. Polices of British India, large market and port connectivity were the main reasons of industry being settled around these princely states. However, after independence government charted out a development strategy and deliberately established industrial units in the impoverished states of Bihar, West Bengal, Madhya Pradesh, and Odisha. Around 50% of PSUs were set up in these four states only as this region comprised nearly half of

*Capital output ratio also called incremental output ratio (ICOR) signifies how much additional capital is required to generate additional output or income. For example, if the 5% additional capital is required to push the overall output or GDP by 1%, the ICOR will be 5. Lower the ICOR, the better it is. ICOR reflects how efficiently capital is being used to generate additional output. So, a country with ICOR of 2 or 3 or 4 is always better than a country with ICOR of 5.

BPL families of the country. It was believed that such industrial units will create the necessary ripple effect and the hitherto neglected hinterlands will emerge as "growth centers" that will unleash high economic opportunities for the residents of such regions.

4. **Earner and saver of Foreign Exchange:** Like any underdeveloped country, India during the initial years of planning was characterized by negligible exports, higher import requirements and low level of foreign exchange reserves. The policy of import substitution was adopted with two motives in the mind (1) to promote the indigenous industry and (2) to save the valuable foreign exchange reserves. The PSUs like Bharat Heavy Electrical Limited (BHEL), Bharat Electronics Limited (BEL), Hindustan Antibiotics Limited (HAL), Indian Drugs and Pharmaceutical Limited (IDPL), Indian Oil Corporation (IOC), Oil and Natural Gas Commission (ONGC), and many more were established to augment the indigenous production and substitute nation's imports. These units not only produced the capital goods, industrial machinery, essential consumer goods, and other equipment and saved the valuable foreign exchange but also helped reducing the dominance of foreign players in this field. There are other PSUs that played a prominent role in boosting the country's exports in many parts of the world. Hindustan Steel Limited (HSL), Hindustan Machine tools Limited (HMT), Metals and Mineral Trading Corporation Limited (MMTC), and State Trading Corporations (STCs), etc. played a pivotal role in expanding country's exports over many decades. The public sector has contributed in the augmentation of FERs in the following ways: (1) through direct exports of the goods produced in PSUs; (2) by rendering of services for other public and private entities; and (3) through trading and marketing services of the units through which exports are channelized.
5. **Check over economic concentration and promoting public welfare:** New research has shown the positive impact of public services such as health care and education for improving or maintaining equality and improvising people's lives.[4] Public sector can help removing inequalities through various welfare programs (also through corporate social responsibility) like spending profits directly for welfare programs, adopting discriminatory policies by supplying material to small-scale industries at low price and large-scale industries at high price; providing better wages to laborers, and social security programs like construction of colonies, townships and schools for the workers and their families; and producing mass consumption goods and supplying them at subsidized prices.

Problems of Public Sector

1. **Wrong Price Policy:** Private sector is profit driven but it is not the case with the public sector. The purpose of setting up and operating the public sector is varied and price policy is determined by the objective, which it is expected to serve. The real culprit of poor public sector saving is not the public sector enterprises (that have been the subject of much of reforms) but inadequate pricing of the utilities and infrastructure services, and lack of recovery of user charges for the services rendered. The public sector prices have risen at a slower rate than the overall prices in the economy over the long run, adversely affecting its financial position.[5] As PSEs serve in social sector, the prices of their products are deliberately kept low, that yield a no profit no loss situation as profit maximization is not the goal of PSEs. For example, Hindustan Machine Tools, Hindustan Shipyard, and many public sector manufacturers kept the prices of their products low during many

years since the beginning of 5-year planning. Indian Railways, Indian Airlines and state electricity boards charged lesser prices against the utility offered notwithstanding their being the monopolies. The units dealing with steel manufacturing, fertilizer production, and electricity generation (to name the few) also suffered losses for many years because of the fulfillment of their social objectives. Therefore, in some cases the PSEs tried to equate total revenue with total cost and in some cases, they opted for losses. Keeping this in view, the government is shifting away from administered/command or control-type price mechanism to market-based instrument of regulation. Petroleum products, cement, steel, and fertilizers (except urea) and many consumer goods have already been decontrolled. The railways and power, etc. are also undergoing a change as well but being politically sensitive the reform process is quite slow in such areas.

2. **Inefficiency:** Another criticism against public sector enterprises is that they are inefficient and do not make higher profits as compared to the private sector. The private sector is considered far more efficient and profitable due to optimal pricing, cost cuts, and professional management. However, the rate of profit can be good but not sufficient criterion to judge public sector's efficiency. The correct measure of profitability should be based on purpose. From the viewpoint of a private individual, the ratio of net profits to equity capital (or net worth) may be appropriate, but it may be unsuitable to measure a PSE's contribution to the economy, for many reasons. One, PSEs usually have a high depreciation cost since they have to invest not only in plant and machinery but also in social infrastructure like schools, hospitals, roads, irrigation, etc. for which budgetary provisions are made. Second, a PSE's capital structure is not aimed to maximize return on shareholders' investment, but provision of goods and services that the market (private sector) fails to supply—the argument of "missing market."[6] However, one cannot deny the fact that the Indian development strategy since 1950s also contributed to the stifled growth and efficiency of PSEs. There was gross mismanagement with regard to the functioning of PSEs. For example, there was extensive bureaucratic control over production, investment, and trade; trade and foreign investment policies were inward looking, and the public sector was deliberately allowed to go well beyond the conventional confines of public utilities and infrastructure.[7] India's control system was not only microeconomically inefficient but macroeconomically perverse, and in fact greatly responsible for persistent fiscal deficits and periodic balance of payment crises.[8]
3. **Underutilization of capacity:** Underutilization of capacity signifies a condition when the resources available are not being used to their fullest potential. For a number of years, most of the PSEs operated at less than 50% of their capacity thanks to lack of foresightedness on the part of the government. In the initial years of planning, the PSE investment and production patterns were based on plan priorities. But during the later years, the public sector became an instrument for meeting immediate or ad hoc demands such as producing mass consumption goods, stimulating growth in economically backward areas or using locally available raw materials even if it was of poor quality. The public sector units were assigned another task of taking over private sector sick units with a view to maintaining production and protecting employment. Poor decision-making, labor disputes, and political interference also led to the generation of inefficiencies in the production process of Indian public sector.
4. **Failures during planning and construction stage:** The PSEs were not led by able administration get manifest from the failures at planning and construction stage. For example,

for the setting up of production plants, selection of site was not based on detailed soil investigation. The actual costs of projects far exceeded the original estimates and the projects took much longer time to complete than originally envisaged. Further, the projects often embodied inappropriate technology or product mix. For instance, the site for Heavy Electricals Limited was selected without any explicit calculation of, the cost of alternative locations and later was changed, when found unsuitable. There was a deliberate policy on the part of government to establish public sector enterprises in the backward regions so as to provide spread effect to the region. It took a great toll on resources so as to build basic facilities and required infrastructure in the region.

DISINVESTMENT

Disinvestment means withdrawal of government equity from public sector enterprises. Also called "divestment" or "divestiture," it envisages the action of an organization (or government) to sell or liquidate its assets in favor of private player. If the government sells shares but retains more than 50% of equity with itself, the company continues to be a public sector company. But if government sells more than 50% of its shares to private sector, then the company ceases to be a PSE and will become a private concern. Therefore, disinvestment is a way toward privatization. As discussed earlier, PSEs which were once called "temples of modern India"* by Pundit Nehru were conceived as instruments to bring socioeconomic transformation of the country. But most of them could not provide reasonable return even after few decades of operation. The poor industrial growth and performance along with large number of sick PSUs forced the government in the early1990s to rethink its strategy toward PSUs. The structure adjustment programs (SAP)** that were introduced as a condition to take loan from IMF and World Bank also emphasized disinvestment and privatization of Indian Industry.

Types of Disinvestment

1. **Minority Disinvestment:** A minority disinvestment is one such that, at the end of it, the government retains a majority stake in the company, typically greater than 51%, thus ensuring management control. Currently, the government's disinvestment policy constitutes minority disinvestment in PSUs. The minority disinvestment can be done by either auctioning to institutions or by an offer for sale. Under the first category, the examples are Andrew Yule & Co. Ltd., CMC Ltd., etc. Examples of minority sales via offer for sale include recent issues of Power Grid Corp. of India Ltd., Rural Electrification Corp. Ltd., NTPC Ltd., NHPC Ltd., etc.

*The term "temples of modern India" was coined by India's first Prime Minister Pundit Jawaharlal Nehru while inaugurating Bhakhra Nangal Dam to describe scientific research institutes, steel plants, power plants, and dams being established in India after 1947 to provide big push to Indian economy.

**Structural adjustment programs (SAPs) consist of loans provided by the IMF and the World Bank to nations undergoing economic crises. The borrowing from IMF and World Bank required such countries to implement certain policies in order to obtain new loans at lower interest rates. However, the conditionality clauses attached to the loans have been criticized because it not only takes away the autonomy of the nation's adopting such policies but also have bearing on their social sector.

2. **Majority Disinvestment:** Under this even after disinvestment, the government retains a minority stake in the company, that is, it sells off a majority stake. Government sold certain sick units to profit-making PSUs like BRPL to IOC, MRL to IOC, and KRL to BPCL. There are certain examples where the government made majority disinvestment in favor of private sector. For example, Modern Foods was sold to Hindustan Lever, BALCO to Sterlite, and CMC to TCS.
3. **Complete Privatization:** Under this 100% control of the company is passed on to a buyer. For example, the government sold 100% control in case of 18 hotel properties of ITDC and 3 hotel properties of HCI. Disinvestment and Privatization are often loosely used interchangeably. There is, however, a vital difference between the two. Disinvestment may or may not result in privatization. When the government retains 26% of the shares carrying voting powers while selling the remaining to a strategic buyer, it would have disinvested, but would not have "privatized," because with 26%, it can still stall vital decisions for which generally a special resolution (three-fourths majority) is required.[9]

Methods of Privatization

The following six different methods of disinvestment are practiced worldwide:

1. **Initial Public Offering (IPO)**: In this case, the shares are offered to public for subscription for the first time by an unlisted public enterprise or the government out of its shareholding or a combination of both.
2. **Further Public Offering (FPO):** In this case, the PSE is listed with the stock market and the shares are offered by PSE or the government out of its shareholding or a combination of both to the public for subscription.
3. **Offer for sale (OFS):** This method is being used extensively by the government since 2012. It involves offer of shares by promoters through Stock Exchange mechanism. Shares are auctioned on the platform provided by the stock exchange.
4. **Strategic sale**: Under this method, the government sells shares to a private player or strategic partner along with management. The government sold a large number of CPSEs during 2001–02 to 2003–04 under strategic sales method.
5. **Institutional Placement Program (IPP)**: Under this method, only institutions are allowed to participate in the offering.
6. **CPSE Exchange Traded Fund (ETF)**: It is the method that allows the simultaneous sale of government stake in various CPSEs across different sectors through single offering. This method provides a mechanism for the government to monetize its shareholding in those CPSEs that form part of the ETF basket.

Objectives/Merits of Disinvestment in India

The new economic policy initiated in July 1991 clearly indicated that PSUs had shown a very negative rate of return on capital employed. Inefficient PSUs proved to be a drag on the government's resources turning to be more of liabilities to the government than being assets. Many undertakings traditionally established as pillars of growth had become a burden on the economy. The national gross domestic product and gross national savings were also getting adversely affected by low returns from PSUs. About 10–15% of the total gross domestic savings were getting reduced on account of low savings from PSUs. In relation to the capital employed, the levels of profits were too low.[10] Because of the various problems that PSUs suffered during the pre-reform era, the government felt the need to get rid of these units and to concentrate on core activities. The government also took a view that it should move out of non-core businesses, especially the ones where the private sector had now entered in a significant way. The disinvestment was also seen by the government as a tool to reduce burden of financing the PSUs and raise funds for meeting general/specific needs.

The following are the main objectives/merits of disinvestment in Indian context:

1. **To promote efficiency and market discipline:** Research now supports the proposition that privately owned firms are more efficient and more profitable than otherwise comparable state owned firms. The private sector firms are subject to capital market discipline as their ability to raise funds from capital market depends on their performance and goodwill. The profit motive criterion guides the policy framework of private management, which instills productivity and efficiency in its working and attitude. The decision-making is transparent and fast and the response time is not large as in the case of PSEs.[11] Privatization increases labor productivity, as firms retrench labor and invest in capital after privatization. In the case of Indian PSUs, retrenchment is not so easy so the result is largely due to more efficient use of labor through restructuring and also possibly due to new investment in equipment from the proceeds of the disinvestment: some of which are retained by the PSU and some passed back to the budget.[12]
2. **To improve public finances:** Modern governments are welfare government. Compared to advanced nations, India spends very little on health, education, and other social areas. According to some estimates, the government has about ₹2 lakh crore locked up in public sector enterprises. The disinvestment receipts are capital receipts and constitute non-inflationary resources for the budget, which can help the government to plan its resource allocation in a better and efficient way.[13] The importance of disinvestment lies in utilization of funds for financing the increasing fiscal deficit, financing large-scale infrastructure development, investing in the economy to encourage spending, retiring government debt (almost 40–45% of the center's revenue receipts go toward repaying public debt/interest) and for social programs like health and education. Privatization will reduce government's commitment and involvement in enterprise decision making and thereby it will be in a better position to provide infrastructure and welfare goods to the public, which at present it is unable to do adequately on account of its pre-occupation with production activities.
3. **To depoliticize non-essential services:** Indian PSEs are highly centralized and there is a big power difference that exists even now. The lower and middle management are rarely involved in decision-making and there are also problems of coordination between different departments and agencies. A study conducted by IIM Ahmedabad reveals that challenges of leading public sector undertakings are political interference and lack of autonomy, rigid rules, and HR practices, lack of employee motivation.[14] Such political decision-making is unavoidable in PSEs and is a major cause of decline in operational efficiency. Empirical evidences from many countries such as Italy, France, Pakistan, and South Korea has proved that efforts to improve managerial efficiency in PSEs by administrative measures are short-lived and unsustainable. All these factors make disinvestment a panacea for the overhauling of PSEs.[15]

Disadvantages of Disinvestment

1. **Impact on employment:** The major reason why trade unions' general stance toward divestiture is largely defensive and uncompromising is because of the fact that privatization usually results in a decline in the number of employees, as well as changes in organization, pay and other working conditions. Private sector in order to infuse efficiency goes for cost cuts and layoff of surplus labor. Therefore, with disinvestment, as far as the workers are concerned, initial apprehensions regarding employment are justified. Further, the change of ownership from public to private usually means losing a status resembling that of a civil servant to becoming a private sector employee with no guaranteed job security. Nevertheless, it is also interesting to note that there have also been instances whereby employment has been protected through guarantees given by governments, or by agreements signed between trade unions and governments and/or the new employing body.[16]
2. **Inefficient use of disinvestment receipts:** G.V. Ramakrishna commission in 1997 had suggested that the proceeds of disinvestment should be utilized for four purposes, that is, for retiring public debt, restructuring PSEs, developing social infrastructure, and voluntary retirement schemes. However, the government used the disinvestment proceeds to offset the shortfalls in revenue receipts so as to reduce the fiscal deficit.[17] Using capital receipts (from disinvestment) to meet current consumption needs (revenue expenditure) was equivalent to frittering away of valuable public assets or selling family silver to support an extravagant lifestyle. Using disinvestment proceeds to finance the recurrent budget is a questionable practice. Instead, disinvestment proceeds should be allocated to the recently created National Infrastructure Strategic Fund (NISF), which can then be used to finance infrastructure projects.
3. **Question on performance after disinvestment:** Sudhir Naib in his study of 38 partly disinvested enterprises found that there was fall in profitability, decline in asset—turnover ratio (sales/total assets) and drop in employment level. In case of partial divestiture with majority shareholding with the government, and the divested equity being thinly spread, there has been no change in the management. As a result, no qualitative change in monitoring mechanism of the PSEs has taken place and thus no improvement has been seen in terms of profitability and operational efficiency. The study also suggests that instead of partial divestiture government can think of strategic sale, as the management control passes to the strategic partner. This will free the enterprises from political/bureaucratic controls, enabling them to take decisions in line with market demands.[18] Further, privatization is seen to work best when allied with competition or deregulation in the economic system, stronger institutional and regulatory framework, effective law enforcement and swift judicial processes, developed capital markets, and strong mechanisms of corporate governance.[19]
4. **Loss of income by the government:** Disinvestment makes government forego dividends on the equity holdings by selling off its stakes, that is, the future streams of income from dividends are forgone against a one-time receipt from the sale of stakes. Considerable disinvestment of by the government would squeeze this important source of revenue. Further, the effective tax rate for the CPSEs taken together is far greater than that of private sector companies which means that while not only a major tax revenue source will be

lost, the private sector which ideally should be paying an equivalent tax rate is exempted due to tax concessions.*

5. **Fails to widen the investor base:** One argument in favor of disinvestment is that it promotes capital widening in the country as retail investors become shareholders after equity sale by the government. But it depends how developed a capital market is in country. In LDCs, capital markets are underdeveloped and the ownership of disinvestment goes to big corporate houses. A nationwide survey conducted by the NCAER revealed that only 0.5% of Indian households invest in equities. Thus, in any case disinvestment is going to benefit this miniscule portion of Indian households. In short, the benefits of disinvestment accrue to big corporate rather than a common man.
6. **Question of disinvestment of profitable PSEs:** Since the beginning of disinvestment process in the country, there had been a precocious debate on whether profitable PSEs must be disinvested or not. Two different schools of thought have emerged in this regard. The opponents maintain that PSEs are not mere profit-making machines but instruments used by the governments to achieve a range of objectives. The PSEs who are already profit earning provide a permanent source of income through dividend income and taxes besides supplying the essential services to common man. The proponents, however, argue that to remain in business is not government's business and the government should rather focus on the development of social infrastructure. We propose the following two viewpoints in this regard:
   - **(a)** Profitability and efficiency are two different parameters. A unit is profitable does not mean it is efficient. But a unit is efficient always mean it is profitable. The PSEs who are profitable have enjoyed monopolies over a longer period of time. Transferring such PSEs' assets with generally low return toward public social infrastructure is a win–win idea, because the private sector will improve efficiency. The business of the government is public infrastructure, not public companies. Transforming public assets into public infrastructure would be a lasting reform.[20] Privatization will reduce government's commitment and involvement in enterprise decision making and thereby it (government) will be in a better position to provide infrastructure and welfare goods to the public.
   - **(b)** Privatization is appropriate where market failures are less serious than state failures. Therefore, the privatization of firms by the central government in reasonably competitive industries, such as 19 hotels of ITDC, Modern Foods—a bakery, BALCO—an aluminum company, Maruti—a car manufacturing company, is fine. But in key essential services and strategic and defense-related sectors, public sector should continue to operate.[21]
   - **(c)** It is not necessary that government will lose income after disinvestment. For example, BALCO which was giving government an average dividend of ₹5.69 crore every year on the equity sold, started giving ₹82.65 crore every year after disinvestment. Similarly, CMC a profitable company was giving an average dividend of only ₹0.80 crore started giving ₹15.2 crore annually. Similarly, Maruti gave average returns of ₹13 crore annually started giving ₹242 crore annually post-disinvestment.

---

*Many benefits are extended to private players operating in special economic zones. Furthermore, the government provides tax sops or exemptions to private players during recession and other times.

Journey of Disinvestment in India

The journey of disinvestment in India is marked by many crests and troughs and can be discussed in four parts.

1. **Period from 1991–92 to 2000–01:** The disinvestment in India began at large scale in the year 1991–92, when 31 PSEs were disinvested for ₹3,038 crore. The Narasimha Rao Government established Rangarajan Committee on "disinvestment of shares" which submitted its report in April 1993. The committee suggested disinvestment up to 49% for industries explicitly reserved for the public sector, 74% for strategic industries and 100% for all other industries.[22] In 1996, the government set up "disinvestment commission" headed by G.V. Ramakrishna to advice, supervise, monitor, and publicize gradual disinvestment of Indian PSUs. The commission made recommendations in the year 1999 on 58 PSUs and indicated a shift from public offerings to strategic/trade sales with the transfer of management. Dr R.H. Patil subsequently took up the chairmanship of this commission in July 2001 but the commission ceased to exist in May 2004. Earlier in 1999, Government had established Department of Disinvestment to provide impetus to disinvestment process. During 1991–92 to 2000–01, the government realized less than 50% of disinvestment receipts against the laid down targets. The reasons for the poor performance of disinvestment policy and lower realization of receipts during this period were unfavorable market conditions, unattractive offers by the government to private sector investors, lack of transparency, and opposition on the valuation process, resistance from employee and trade unions, and poor political will. This was the period when the government opted for minority disinvestment route by selling shares of PSUs like IOC, BPCL, HPCL, GAIL, VSNL, etc. to private players or institutional investors like UTI.
2. **Period from 2001–02 to 2003–04:** Government established ministry of disinvestment in September 2001. During this time a maximum number of disinvestments took place either in the form of strategic sales (involving an effective transfer of control and management to a private entity) or an offer for sale to the public with the government still retaining control of the management. Many companies which were disinvested through strategic sales during this period comprised BALCO, CMC Ltd., Hindustan Zinc Ltd., Hotel Corp. of India Ltd., HTL Ltd., IBP co. Ltd., ITDC (18 hotel properties), IPCL, Jessop & co. Ltd., Lagan Jute Machinery Co. Ltd., Maruti Suzuki India Ltd., Modern Food Industries (India) Ltd., Paradeep Phosphates Ltd., and Tata Communications Ltd. The strategic sales route fetched better revenue to the government than that of minority sales route. During this period, against an aggregate target of ₹38,500 crore to be raised from PSU disinvestment, the government managed to raise only ₹21,163.68 crore.
3. **Period from 2004–05 to 2008–09:** The new UPA-I government converted the ministry of disinvestment into department under the ministry of finance in May, 2004. With coalition government at the center the issue of disinvestment remained a contentious subject due to different political perspectives. The disinvestment remained in the state of slumber during this period and hence during 2003–04 to 2008–09, the total receipts from disinvestments were only ₹8,515.93 crore.
4. **Period from 2009–10 onwards:** A stable government under both UPA and NDA led to a renewed thrust on disinvestments. The government started the process by selling minority stakes in listed and unlisted (profit making) PSUs. Many companies were disinvested,

TABLE 16.1 Performance of Disinvestment

Year	Target	Achievements
1991–92	2,500	3,038
1991–92 to 2000–01	54,300	20,079
2001–02 to 2003–04	38,500	21,164
1991–2005	96,800	47,832
2004–05 to 2008–09	–	8,516
2010–11 to 2013–14	1,50,000	75,814
2014–15	43,425	24,349
2015–16	41,000	23,997
2016–17	56,500	46,246.58
2017–18	72,500	1,00,942
2018–19	80,000	85,314.17
2014–15 to 2018–19	3,20,925	2,79,963.7
2019–20	65,000	50,294
2020–21	32,000	32,742
2021–22	78,000	13,534
2022–23	50,000	31,059
2023–24	51,000	14,564

Source: Economic survey 2015–16, 2016–17, 2017–18, 2019–20, 2020–21. Department of Economic Affairs. Ministry of Finance. Govt. of India, Budget Document 2021–22, 2022–23, 2023–24 and 2024–25.

like NHPC Ltd., Oil India Ltd., NTPC Ltd., REC, NMDC, SJVN, EIL, CIL, MOIL, etc. through public offers. However, from 2011 onwards, disinvestment activity slowed down considerably. During 2010–11 to 2013–14, the government realized the disinvestment of ₹75,814 crore against the target of ₹1,50,000 crore. Disinvestment could not be realized fully during subsequent years of 2014–2017. However, some improvement was seen during 2017–18 and 2018–19. The NDA Government set disinvestment target of ₹50,000 crore and realized the sales of ₹51,000 crore during 2022–23 and 2023–24 but managed to realise lesser amount of capital receipts.. Table 16.1 summarizes the figurative achievement of government disinvestment efforts over the years.

Private Sector in Indian Economy

The private sector refers to all types of firms or organizations, which are owned, controlled, and managed exclusively by private individuals or entities with the intention of making a profit. Private sector businesses can be individually owned or collectively owned. The examples of collectively owned firms are partnership firms, joint-Hindu family, joint-stock companies, and cooperatives. The most important of these four categories is the joint-stock organization, which is otherwise popularly known as the corporate sector. If joint-stock companies or firms are created under the statutes of parliament or state legislatures, then they are called statutory companies or corporations. Examples are Life Insurance Corporation, Oil and Natural gas Corporation, and Indian Oil. If joint stock companies are registered under Companies Act, 1956, then they are called registered companies. Examples are Reliance Industries, Infosys, Hindustan Unilever, and Nestle.

Role of Private Sector in Indian Economy

The private sector has played a significant role in the development of the country. Let us discuss briefly.

1. As on June end 2020 a total of over 20 Lakh companies were registered in the country. Out of them 12.15 Lakh companies were active (comprising 10,70,383 private companies and 73,389 public companies.[23] The pace of company formation in the private sector has speeded up since around the mid-1980s and the paid-up capital rose sharply since the late 1990s. To quantify the trends, between 1991 and 2014, while the number of companies multiplied more than three times, their paid-up capital ballooned nearly eight times. The boom in company registration has, expectedly, coincided with the liberal economic reforms.[24]
2. Private corporate sector contributes nearly 35% of country's GDP and around 12% of gross national savings. The organized private sector employed about 13 million persons as on 2015–16.[25]
3. In 1991, a majority of the companies in the private corporate sector were in the manufacturing sector; but since 2013 the corporate financial sector had overtaken it. At present the financial sector dominates the private corporate sector with 60% of the number of companies.
4. Agriculture and allied activities that accounted for nearly 17% of GDP and nearly 45% of employment are completely in the private sector. Small scale and cottage industries, trading, consumer goods industries, construction, etc. are some of the other areas in which the private sector has been playing a major part. Such private enterprises play a pivotal role in meeting the demand and supply problems of millions of Indians on a daily basis.
5. The private sector comprises both organized and unorganized/informal sector. In the organized sector corporate sector dominates. But it is the large informal sector that plays a predominant role in the national income and employment. More than 90% of India's workforce is engaged in this informal sector.

TABLE 16.2 Top 10 Companies as per ET 500 Companies List

Rank	Company	Turnover ₹Crore
1	Life Insurance Corporation of India	724,744
2	Reliance Industries Ltd.	718,061
3	Indian Oil Corporation Ltd.	593,653
4	ONGC Ltd.	500,171
5	State Bank of India	406,973
6	Hindustan Petroleum Corporation Ltd.	353,810
7	BPCL Ltd.	351,730
8	Tata Motors Ltd.	281,617
9	Tata Steel Ltd.	246,198
10	Rajesh Exports Ltd.	243,168

Source: ET 500 companies. *The Economic Times*. 28 April, 2024

Problems of Private Sector

1. **Low growth rate of credit:** The major problem of private corporate sector is lower credit supply which can be attributed to poor balance sheets of public sector banks due to higher non-performing assets. But there is also weak demand for credit. For example, nominal credit growth to industry during 2017–18 (April–December) was −1.5%. The government in order to correct this anomaly announced bank recapitalization to the tune of ₹2.11 lakh crore. The move is aimed at easing the balance sheets of the public sector banks, conditional on cleaning up their balance sheets, thereby helping banks to accelerate the pace of credit disbursement. In the wake of the credit slowdown, the private sector has tried to raise funds through alternative sources such as corporate bonds and commercial papers.[26]
2. **Growing distrust:** India is affected by the problem of stigmatized capitalism. There is a growing distrust for private sector and consequently, if the government goes for big reforms like privatization, it would be seen as being pro-business and anti-poor.[27] Since this can prove to be a serious bottleneck, it is important to examine why—despite visible gains from economic reforms—India is still not certain about the role of the private sector.[28] There could be three broad reasons.[29] First is the legacy of the pre-reform era when the private sector was seen with suspicion and profit and wealth were bad words. Businesses close to the ruling establishment are still seen to be gaining. This has put speed-breakers on India's speed of reforms, a phenomenon that can be aptly described as "a strong consensus for weak reforms." Second, the private sector is seen by many as excessively driven by self-interest. There are also governance issues which have dented confidence. Third, the government has not been able to create stronger regulations. Certain areas are marked by regulatory gaps and lack of clarity in rules, while others require an excessive compliance burden, which jeopardize the smooth functioning of the private sector.[30]
3. **The burden of corporate debt:** The ever-increasing corporate debt has become the cause of much concern during recent times. The NPAs of the banks have recently increased due to inability of corporate houses to repay the loans and even honor the interest obligations.

BOX 16.2 Corporate Social Responsibility (CSR)

As per section 135 of companies Act, 2013, all profit making corporates, including CPSEs, exceeding threshold limits prescribed in the act, are mandated to spend at least 2% of average net profits of the company made during the three immediately preceding years on CSR. CSR is good both for companies and societies around them and brings many benefits to both sides. The corporations can gain financial benefits through working for the good of the people, and at the same time, create a positive reputation and respect, securing their position on the market. The society in which such companies function can observe an increase of quality of education, technology, and infrastructure, as well as better health and security of people. Overall, following the rules of CSR may lead to a higher standard of living of people surrounding the socially responsible business.

Source: Księżak, P. (2016). The benefits from CSR for a company and society. *Journal of Corporate Responsibility and Leadership, 3* (4).

BOX 16.3 Electoral Bond

An electoral bond is a bearer instrument like a promissory note or like a bank note whereby a citizen, or a corporate body, in India is eligible to purchase (through cheque or digital payments only) the bond from notified branches of the public sector bank. The electoral bonds will not bear the name of the donor. In essence, the donor and the party details will be available with the bank, but the political party might not be aware of who the donor is. The intention is to ensure that all the donations made to a party will be accounted for in the balance sheets without exposing the donor details to the public.

The electoral bond system (EBS) is surrounded with controversy based on three main grounds: First, anonymity clause for the individuals or corporates buying electoral bonds defeats the fundamental principle of transparency. Anonymous donations would make it a convenient channel for black money. To extend this further, EBS could be an easy way out for businesses to round-trip their cash parked in tax havens to political parties in exchange for benefits showered by later. Further, there is removal of 7.5% cap on corporate donations (by amending the Companies Bill 2013). This allows for unlimited corporate donations even from the loss making companies as well. Finally, given the fact that a public sector bank (SBI) will be sole repository of donor details, in effect the ruling party at the center (given the proximity with the bank) will have an upper hand on this new mode of donations. The electoral bond scheme was struck down by the Supreme Court on February 2024 on the ground that it violates the right to information under Article 19(1)(a) of the Constitution.

Source: The Hindu, March 27, 2019; India matters: Observer Research Foundation, March 28, 2019; The Economic Times, April 13, 2019. The Hindu, Feb 15, 2024.

The problem was referred as "twin balance sheet problem" by economic survey 2016–17 that signifies the coexistence of over leveraged companies and bad loan encumbered banks. For the financial year 2017–18, the NPAs of banking sector stood at 9.3% and that of public sector banks stood at 11.7%.[31]

4. **Concentration of economic power:** One of the major criticisms leveled against private corporate houses is concentration of economic power. Though the number of companies in private corporate sector has grown exponentially in recent times, the distribution of their output is highly skewed with the top 100 companies and the top 500 companies accounting for nearly 50% and 75% of the gross value added.
5. **Threat to electoral democracy:** The private sector is also criticized for affecting the sovereign decision-making process through big financial findings to political parties. The corporates have devised many ways to please their political masters and the very recent tactic is the issuance of electoral bonds. Such bonds undermine India's electoral democracy by inviting unbridled corporate influence. (see Box 16.3).

The Twin Balance Sheet Problem

The twin balance sheet problem refers to the stress on balance sheets of banks due to non-performing assets (NPAs) or bad loans on the one hand, and heavily indebted corporates on the other.[32] In early 2016, banks in India reported that non-performing assets had soared, to such an extent that provisioning had overwhelmed operating earnings. Non-performing assets of banks increased to 9% and four-fifths of the non-performing assets were in the public sector banks.* Further, around 40% of the corporate debt was owed by companies that had an interest coverage ratio less than 1, meaning they did not earn enough to pay the interest obligations on their loans. What added to the worries of policy makers was that India's NPA ratio is higher than any other major emerging market (with the exception of Russia), higher even than the peak levels seen in Korea during the East Asian crisis of 1997. Typically, countries with a twin balance sheet (TBS) problem follow a standard path. Their corporations overexpand during a boom, leaving them with obligations that they cannot repay. So, they default on their debts, leaving bank balance sheets impaired, as well. This combination then proves devastating for growth, since the indebted corporations are reluctant to invest, while those that remain sound cannot invest much either, since fragile banks are not really in a position to lend to them.[33]

Causes of Twin Balancesheet Problem

1. **Overheating of economy:** During the mid-2000s economies all over the world were booming and almost no country was growing as rapidly as India. Indian GDP had surged to 9–10% per annum making many to predict that India would soon enter into double-digit growth. The corporate profitability was amongst the highest in the world, encouraging firms to hire more workers, which also caused wages to soar high. It seemed that India had finally "arrived," earning the long-awaited reward for the economic reforms that were started during 1991.[34] Firms made fresh plans, launched new projects worth lakhs of crores, particularly in infrastructure-related areas such as power generation, steel, and telecoms, setting off the biggest investment boom in the country's history. The investment-GDP ratio had soared by 11% points, reaching over 38% by 2007–08. This investment was financed by an astonishing credit boom and in the span of just 3 years, running from 2004–05 to 2008–09, the amount of non-food bank credit doubled. In addition to this, there were also large inflows of funding from overseas, with capital inflows in 2007–08 reaching 9% of GDP. It increased the debt of non-financial corporations. Firms abandoned their conservative debt/equity ratios and leveraged themselves up to take advantage of the perceived opportunities. This was the time when things started to go wrong. Costs soared far above budgeted levels, as securing land and environmental clearances proved much more difficult and time consuming than expected.
2. **Increase in the cost of debt:** Due to overheating of economy the financing costs in the country increased rapidly. RBI increased interest rates to arrest double-digit inflation that affected the domestic borrowers. Firms that had borrowed abroad when the rupee was trading around ₹40/dollar were hit hard when the rupee depreciated, forcing them to repay their debts at exchange rates closer to ₹60–70/dollar. Higher costs, lower revenues, greater financing costs—all squeezed corporate cash flow, quickly leading to debt servicing problems. By 2013, nearly one-third of corporate debt was owed by companies with an interest coverage ratio less than 1 (IC1 companies), many of them in the infrastructure (especially power generation) and metals sectors. By 2015, the share of IC1 companies reached nearly 40%, as slowing growth in China caused international steel prices to collapse, causing nearly every Indian steel company to record large losses.

*Non-performing assets of banks rose to 11.2% or at ₹10.39 trillion during 2017–18.

Why TBS Did Not Cause Economic Crisis in India?

In the recent past, TBS had occurred in Japan after its bubble burst in the 1990s, and in the United States during 2007–08 global financial crisis and in Europe during Euro zone crisis 2009 onwards. In all these nations, TBS led to economic crisis. But in India, TBS coexisted with strong levels of aggregate domestic demand, as reflected in high levels of growth despite very weak exports and moderate, at times high, levels of inflation. In other words, India developed its own unique version of TBS and Economic survey 2016–17 called it a "Balance Sheet Syndrome with Indian Characteristics."

(a) During boom, India invested heavily on the diverse construction sector. For example, new power plants were installed, and new roads, airports, and ports built. As a result, aggregate demand did not dip and there was ample room for the economy to grow despite the occurrence of global financial crisis even as the infrastructure investments themselves did not prove financially viable. So, the legacy of the historic mid-2000s investment boom was a curious combination of both TBS and growth. In comparison, the US boom was based on housing construction, which proved far less useful after the crisis.

(b) The most important difference between India and other countries, however, was the way in which the financial system handled intense stress on corporations. In other countries, creditors would have triggered bankruptcies, affecting stock markets and growth. But in India the strategy was to "give time to time," meaning to allow time for the corporate wounds to heal. That is, companies sought financial accommodation from their creditors, asking for principal payments to be postponed, on the grounds that if the projects were given sufficient time they would eventually prove viable. The same strategy had worked well in the previous business cycle, during the early 2000s. At that time, non-performing loans had also reached high levels, but they then subsided a few years later when demand picked up and commodity prices recovered. Accordingly, banks decided to give stressed enterprises more time by postponing loan repayments. They also extended fresh funding to the stressed firms to tide them over until demand recovered. As a result, total stressed assets have far exceeded the headline figure of NPAs. In many ways, then, India's path has resembled that of China, albeit on a much smaller scale, since India's estimated bad loans are just one-seventh the amount assessed for China. Both countries provided generous amounts of bank financing to allow highly levered corporations to survive. And in both countries, this strategy has proved successful so far in allowing rapid growth to continue. But there remains a question of whether the model is truly sustainable.

Solution to TBS Problem

To address the TBS challenge, Economic Survey 2016–17 recommends four R's strategy:[35] Recognition, Recapitalization, Resolution, and Reform. According to survey, banks must value their assets as far as possible close to true value (recognition) as the RBI has been emphasizing; once they do so; their capital position must be safeguarded via infusions of equity (recapitalization) as the banks have been demanding; underlying stressed assets in the corporate sector must be sold or rehabilitated (resolution) as the government has been desiring, and future incentives for the private sector and corporate must be set-right (reform) to avoid a repetition of TBS-like problems.[36] The government has followed a two-pronged policy to tackle the TBS problem. First, it has introduced the Insolvency and Bankruptcy Code (IBC) for time-bound resolution of insolvency proceedings of firms. Second, it plans to recapitalize the banks to improve its provisioning for NPAs. The government has announced to pump in ₹48,239 crore in 12 public sector banks during 2018–19 to help banks maintain regulatory capital requirements and finance growth plans. But many experts want more reforms, such as the privatization of PSBs to improve its governance and align incentives of bankers with that of the bank.

Insolvency and Bankruptcy Code (IBC), 2016

Insolvency takes place where the debtor is not in a position to repay its loans to creditors. On the other hand, bankruptcy is the legal declaration of insolvency. So, the former is a financial condition and the latter is a legal position. All insolvencies need not lead to bankruptcy. The IBC code was enacted by Indian Parliament in the year 2016. The IBC has a sequential procedure of Insolvency resolution, failing which, it leads to bankruptcy. The broader objectives of IBC are solving the twin balance problem, developing a robust corporate bond market, improving the credit environment, streamlining the corporate insolvency resolution process, preventing value destruction if there is corporate distress, and consequently providing a fillip to India's competitiveness as a business destination.[37] The IBC code was amended by the government and the Insolvency and Bankruptcy code (amendment) act, 2017 got presidential accent on January 18, 2018.

Why Was IBC Needed?

Before IBC, the bankruptcy was being handled under at least 13 different laws. The IBC repealed two older laws, for example, the Presidency Towns Insolvency Act, 1909 and Provincial Insolvency Act, 1920. In addition, it amended 11 laws, including the Companies Act, 2013, Recovery of Debts Due to Banks and Financial Institutions Act, 1993 and Sick Industrial Companies (Special Provisions) Act, 1985, among others. Earlier, if a company defaults, there were at least four different legal routes available to the debtors and creditors, viz. the high courts, the Company Law Board, the Board for Industrial and Financial Reconstruction (BIFR), and the Debt Recovery Tribunals (DRTs). It led to overlapping jurisdiction giving rise to the potential of systemic delays and complexities in the process. Such delays led to the devaluation of the assets involved, thus making the insolvency negotiations redundant. The consequence was rising NPAs and mounting stressed assets of the banking system.

The IBC Ecosystem and Its Functioning

National Company Law Tribunal (NCLT) is the adjudicating authority and has jurisdiction over companies and other limited liability entities. Debt Recovery Tribunal (DRT) has jurisdiction over individuals and partnership firms other than Limited Liability Partnerships. The Insolvency and Bankruptcy Board of India (IBBI) is an apex body for promoting transparency and governance in the administration of the IBC; will be involved in setting up the infrastructure and accrediting Insolvency Professionals (IPs)* and Information Utilities (IUs).** IBBI has 10 members from Ministry of Finance, Law, and RBI.

Now, let us understand the process under IBC. Let us suppose, a corporate debtor has committed a default. Now as per IBC, the amount of default should be ₹1 lakh or more. If the application is admitted, the corporate insolvency resolution process will start and NCLT will declare a moratorium period during where no legal proceedings may be instituted or continued against the corporate debtor. Further, an "interim resolution professional" will be appointed and a public announcement of the initiation of the corporate insolvency process issued. The IBC prescribes detailed manner in which the corporate insolvency process is to be carried out, which includes the formation of a resolution plan to attempt to revive and rehabilitate the business of the company. However, if no resolution plan is agreed upon or approved by the NCLT within 180 days of the admission of the application, the company will be wound up as per the provisions of the bankruptcy Code. The IBC code moves beyond the concept of a "sick" company and consolidates the revival process for all companies under one law, before a single tribunal. This should make the process more speedy and efficient. The success of such a move will, however, depend on the NCLT being provided with the necessary infrastructural and legal support to handle the potential volume of matters. It remains to be seen whether a qualified pool of insolvency resolution professionals who will help with the implementation of the law will be efficiently formed. The new regime can also aid corporates to achieve greater efficiency in functioning by promoting an environment that supports commercial prudence and people who want to do business. Banks and lenders may approve of the new regime as it allows for a speedy resolution of matters where large amounts of funds may be tied up, while simultaneously allowing such creditors to be an active part of the resolution process of a corporate debtor.

Key Advantages of IBC

1. The IBC code has changed the debtor–creditor relationship. The creditor no longer chases the debtor. In fact, it is otherwise. It will help to resolve the balance sheet problem in an effective manner.
2. The IBC is modeled toward maximization of value of assets, striking a balance between liquidation and reorganization, ensuring equitable treatment of similarly situated creditors, provision of timely, efficient and impartial resolution, and ensuring a transparent and predictable insolvency law with incentives to gather and dispense information.[38]
3. The code aims to resolve insolvencies in a strict time-bound manner—that is, within 180 days (extendable up to 270 days). For small ventures and startups, the resolution time period is 90 days which can be extended by 45 days.
4. The IBC has helped address stressed assets worth approximately ₹3 trillion directly or indirectly—since the new law came into force in December 2016. In 2018, over ₹80,000 crore was recovered from various corporate debtors, which had defaulted payments,

*Persons enrolled with IPA (insolvency professional agency) and regulated by Board and IPA will conduct resolution process; it will act as liquidator/bankruptcy trustee; they are appointed by creditors and override the powers of the board of directors.

**A centralized repository of financial and credit information of borrowers; would accept, store, authenticate, and provide access to financial data provided by creditors.

under the IBC through various insolvency proceeding at the NCLT and the NCLAT (National Company Law Appellate Tribunal).[39]

5. The IBC code helped India to gain the confidence of international rating agencies and improve World Bank's ease of doing business rankings.

Challenges for IBC

1. There are delay tactics being played by companies. For example, the resolution process for Essar Steel extended beyond the 270-day deadline of April 29, 2018. Several cases are getting delayed mainly due to recalcitrant promoters who are using legal shields to drag on the resolution process.[40] Defaulted promoters are challenging, in the Supreme Court, the validity of Section 29A, which bars them from bidding for their own stressed assets.
2. Finding buyers for stressed assets is a difficult task. The endless litigation has kept foreign investors away from bidding for stressed assets, leaving domestic companies to hold sway.[41]
3. There is a lack of infrastructure and absence of specific provisions under the Code. There are around 10,000 cases pending before the NCLT and the NCLAT at different stages and without infrastructure expansion, there is little chance of all the cases being cleared soon.[42] The success of IBC will depend on the NCLT being provided with the necessary infrastructural and legal support to handle the potential volume of matters. It remains to be seen whether a qualified pool of insolvency resolution professionals who will help with the implementation of the law will be efficiently formed.

Micro, Small, and Medium Enterprises (MSMEs)

The micro, small, and medium enterprises Development Act, 2006 defines MSMEs on investment basis for both manufacturing and service enterprises. In the case of manufacturing enterprises, the microenterprise was defined as an enterprise where the investment in plant and machinery did not exceed ₹25 Lakh; a small enterprise was defined as an enterprise where the investment in plant and machinery was more than ₹25 lakh but did not exceed ₹5 crore; and a medium enterprise was defined as an enterprise where the investment in plant and machinery was more than ₹5 crores but did not exceed ₹10 crores. In the case of service enterprises, the microenterprises were defined as an enterprise where the investment in plant and machinery did not exceed ₹10 lakh; a small enterprise was defined as an enterprise where the investment in plant and machinery was more than ₹10 lakh but did not exceed ₹2 crore; and a medium enterprise was defined as an enterprise where the investment in plant and machinery was more than ₹2 crores but did not exceed ₹5 crores.[43]

New Definition of MSMEs

The Ministry of Micro, Small and Medium Enterprises, vide its notification dated June 1, 2020, revised MSME classification by inserting a composite criterion for both investment in plant and machinery and annual turnover of enterprises. Also, the distinction between the manufacturing and the services sectors under erstwhile MSME definition has been done away with. This removal will create parity between the sectors. According to new definition, the Micro enterprise will be one where investment in Plant & Machinery/Equipment is not more than ₹1 crore and Annual Turnover not more than ₹5 crores. A small enterprise will be one where Investment in Plant & Machinery/Equipment is not more than ₹10 crores and Annual Turnover not more than ₹50 crores. In case of medium enterprise Investment in Plant & Machinery/Equipment is not more than ₹50 crores & Annual Turnover not more than ₹250 crores.

Performance of MSMEs in Indian Economy

1. **Contribution to GDP:** The micro, small, and medium enterprises (MSME) sector has emerged as a highly vibrant and dynamic sector of the Indian economy over the last five decades. There are 633.88 lakh MSMEs in India. On the basis of nature of activity, MSMEs are categorized as manufacturing, trade, other services, and electricity. The total number of units in these four categories is 31, 36, 33, and 0.03%, respectively. The MSMEs are widening their domain across sectors of the economy, producing a diverse range of products and services to meet demands of domestic as well as global markets. The MSME sector accounts for 29% of total GDP and 45% of industrial output of the country.[44]
2. **Employment generation:** India is a labor surplus nation. The country needs to focus on those industries which are labor absorbing rather than labor displacing. The importance of MSMEs can be established from the fact that the labor intensity in micro and small enterprises is four times higher than that of large enterprises. MSME sector has been generating 11.10 crore jobs in the rural and the urban areas across the country. Manufacturing, trade, and other services constitute 32, 35, and 33% of employment share, respectively. Micro sector alone provides employment to 1076.19 lakh persons, which accounts for around 97% of total employment in the sector. Small sector and medium enterprises contribute 2.88% and 0.16% of total employment, respectively in MSMEs. In gender wise employment, 24% of workers are females and 76% of workers are males.[45]
3. **Regional equality:** Large-scale industries are located near the source of raw material. The iron and steel industry, paper industry, coal industry, cement industry, etc. are concentrated in very few states of the country, which are rich in respective minerals. However, the MSMEs are market centric and are concentrated around the region where there is sufficient purchasing power for their products. This is the reason why MSMEs are located throughout the length and breadth of the country and promote regional equality. There are around 634 lakh MSMEs located in all the states of the country. Uttar Pradesh with maximum number of the units (14%) leads among the states followed by West Bengal (13.9%), Tamil Nadu (8%), Maharashtra (8%), and Karnataka (6%), respectively.
4. **Equitable distribution of income and inclusive growth:** In India, out of 633.88 lakh MSME units, 51% are located in rural areas providing employment to 45% of the workforce engaged in MSME sector. The presence of MSMEs in the rural segment is significant keeping in view the 70% of population that lives in villages and the large disguised workforce engaged in agriculture. Further, the ownership of MSMEs is more widespread than that of large-scale units. Overall, around 66.5% of micro units are owned by the socially backward group (SC, ST, and OBC). In rural areas, almost 73.67% of MSMEs are owned by socially backward groups. The number is significant because microenterprises

constitute 99% of total number of MSMEs. Further, gender wise 80% of MSMEs are owned by males and 20% by females.[46]

5. **Exports:** The MSMEs play an important role in export promotion of the country and contribute around 40% of the total exports of the country. More than 93% of MSME exports consist of non-traditional items such as readymade garments, processed food, leather products, sports, gems, and jewelery. In traditional exports, the coir industry is an agro-based industry, which has created a niche in the international market. To maintain its slot in the international and global markets, MSMEs are required to remain globally competitive. They have to continuously update themselves to meet the challenges emerging out of changes in technology, changes in demands, emergence of new markets, etc.[47]

Problems of MSMEs in India

1. **Inadequacy of finance:** India's MSME sector faces a major problem in terms of getting adequate credit for expansion of business activities. Out of the total credit disbursed to the industry by banking sector, MSME sector receives only 17% and large-scale industry receives around 83%.[48] Banks have also been mandated to provide 40% of aggregated net bank credit to priority sector comprising agriculture, small-scale industry, microfinance, etc. Though priority sector targets are accomplished by banks on paper, banks are reluctant to lend to small-scale sector because of low recovery rates. And whenever they lend to MSMEs, banks insist against the spirit of RBI guidelines. The government in order to meet the structural adjustment program conditionality imposed credit restrictions on small-scale industries during the post-reform phase, which placed the small-scale firms in triple bind. The first bind was credit squeeze, second bind was bias against lending the small firms, and the third bind was large firms buying intermediate goods and other inputs from small firms delayed payments to small firms because of credit squeeze.[49]
2. **Industrial sickness:** In India, there were 4,80,280 sick MSMEs with outstanding loan of ₹32,674 crore. Among the various reasons for industrial sickness, the three major reasons were lack of demand, shortage of working capital, and marketing problems. Among all the registered units declared sick, lack of demand accounted for sickness in 72% of MSMEs, whereas shortage of working capital and marketing problems accounted for sickness in 48% and 45% of MSMEs, respectively. For unregistered units, these figures are 84, 47, and 41%, respectively.[50]
3. **External competition:** In India, the small-scale sector was provided with special protection and patronage through reservation policy in 1967. The number of reserved items stood at 836 during 1989. The de-reservation during post-reform period and dumping by China created a non-level playing field causing loss and closure of small-scale units in India. Removal of quantitative restrictions and lowering of tariff turned tides against Indian firms and they lost market because of cheaper imports. The MSMEs characterized as they are by unviable scale, obsolete technology, supply chain inefficiencies, and unskilled workers are urged by the new policy paradigm to transform to innovative and globally competitive businesses. Least they miss this moment—the moment that promises a great leap forward. What is perhaps forgotten is that the plight of Indian MSMEs is a sheer reflection of the informal and fragmented economic and social framework within which they function. Reforming MSMEs, hence, becomes part of the fundamental

project of redrawing political strategies to address the structural infirmities in resource distribution and use.[51]

4. **Infrastructural constraints:** A SIDBI report in 2010 conducted a survey on 200 MSMEs across the country and found that the major concern to MSMEs from the point of view of their growth and development is non-availability of infrastructure support. Lack of proper infrastructural facilities can cause serious damages to an enterprise's value chain process, like production, consumption, and distribution of the products. There is a need for common infrastructure projects for MSMEs. MSMEs, through coming together and sharing the costs of infrastructure, which are otherwise prohibitive for individual MSMEs, could benefit from economies of scale, synergy, and collective bargaining by collaborating with each other particularly on aspects of common infrastructure, common facilities, raw material procurement, marketing and transportation of finished goods, testing laboratory, common tooling/machining, research and development, etc.[52]
5. **Technological constraints:** Technology plays a vital role in an economy, particularly in its developmental phase. In this era of globalization, the MSME sector needs to compete not just at the local or the national level but also at the global level. Access to modern technology is acting as a serious threat to the growth of the sector. Unless the sector equips itself with the latest technologies, processes, and machinery, it will not be in a position to meet the stringent quality standards set by the international buyers. Though India has a vast pool of technical talent with a well-developed intellectual infrastructure, the country still scores low in the matter of developing and adopting new technologies in the MSME sector. The MSME sector today needs an effective information system to support and deliver information to different users. Such information systems will be used to provide an effective interface between users and computer technology and will also provide information for managers on the day-to-day operations of the enterprises.
6. **Marketing problems:** To withstand the onslaught of competition from large enterprises within and outside, MSMEs need to respond promptly to the evolving marketing needs and innovations. The sector needs to be provided better market access facilities in order to sustain and further enhance its contribution toward output, employment generation, and exports. Even today, most small businesses in India are set up by first generation entrepreneurs. They often have a product or service idea and some fervor to work hard. However, the limited market access namely capital access, brand promotion solutions, marketing support, logistics and sales support, and information and communication technology (ICT) support stalls the fervor to take the enterprise to next level. MSMEs in India are broadly unaware of technology solutions as less than 6% of Indian MSMEs have access to personal computers and advertise online.[53]

Government Schemes for the Development of MSMEs

1. **Prime Minister's Employment Generation Programme (PMEGP):** The scheme was launched on August 15, 2008 and aims at generating employment opportunities in rural as well as urban areas of the country through setting up of new self-employment ventures or microenterprises. The scheme also aims to help arrest the migration of rural youth to urban areas and increasing the wage-earning capacity of artisans.

2. **Credit Linked Capital Subsidy Scheme (CLCSS):** Launched on October 01, 2000, the objective of the Scheme is to facilitate technology upgradation in Micro and Small Enterprises (MSEs) by providing capital subsidy of 15% (limited to maximum of ₹15.00 lakhs) on institutional finance availed by them for induction of well-established and improved technology. Maximum limit of eligible loan for calculation of subsidy under the scheme is investment in approved plant and machinery up to ₹1.00 crore for induction of well-established and improved technologies.[54]
3. **Credit Guarantee Trust Fund For MSEs (CGTMSE)—Provision of collateral free credit for MSMEs:** Guarantees are provided for extending collateral-free lending to micro and small enterprises through banks and financial institutions (including NBFCs). The scheme covers collateral free credit facility to new and existing MSMEs up to ₹200 lakh per borrowing unit. The guarantee cover provided is up to 75% of the credit facility up to ₹50 lakh (85% for loans up to ₹5 lakh provided to microenterprises, 80% for MSEs owned/operated by women and all loans to NER) with a uniform guarantee at 50% of the credit exposure above ₹50 lakh and up to ₹200 lakh. A composite all in annual guarantee fee of 1.0% per annum of the credit facility sanctioned (0.75% for credit facility up to ₹5 lakh and 0.85% for above ₹5 lakh and up to 200 lakh for women, micro enterprises and units in NER including Sikkim) is charged.
4. **A Scheme for Promotion of Innovation, Rural Industry, and Entrepreneurship (ASPIRE):** ASPIRE was launched by Government of India in 2015 with an objective to set up a network of technology centers, incubation centers to accelerate entrepreneurship and also to promote start-ups for innovation and entrepreneurship in rural and agriculture-based industry.
5. **Scheme of Fund for Regeneration of Traditional Industries (SFURTI):** SFURTI scheme was launched in the year 2005 for making traditional industries more productive and competitive by organizing the traditional industries and artisans into clusters. Government revamped SFURTI in the year 2015 and under the revamped scheme there will be three types of clusters and the clusters are (1) heritage clusters (1,000–2,500 artisans), (2) major clusters (500–1000 artisans), and (3) mini clusters (up to 500 artisans).[55]
6. **Financial support to MSMEs in ZED certification:** Launched in 2016, the scheme will be implemented in 22,222 MSMEs with the total project cost of ₹491 crore. The scheme envisages promotion of Zero Defect and Zero Effect (ZED) manufacturing amongst MSMEs. The objective will be achieved by developing an ecosystem for Zero Defect manufacturing in MSMEs, promoting adaption of quality tools/systems and energy efficient manufacturing, enabling MSMEs to manufacture of quality products and to encourage MSMEs to upgrade their quality standards in products and processes with adoption of Zero Defect production processes and without impacting the environment, etc.[56]

Summary

1. There are total of 339 CPSEs, out of which 255 are operational, 184 are profit making 71 are loss making. The public sector in India has performed wonderfully and has contributed to the capital formation and development of infrastructure; building up of strong industrial base; removal of regional disparities; earner and saver of foreign exchange; checking the economic concentration; and promoting public welfare. However, the PSEs also suffer from certain shortcomings. They are wrong price policy; inefficiency; underutilization of capacity; and, failures during planning and construction stage.
2. Disinvestment means withdrawal of government equity from public sector enterprises. Disinvestment is of three types (1) minority disinvestment, where the government sells minority stake; (2) majority disinvestment, where the government sells majority stake; and (3) complete privatization, where the government sells 100% stake. There are six different methods of disinvestment. They are initial public offering, further public offering, offer for sale, strategic sale, institutional placement program, and CPSE exchange traded fund. The objectives of disinvestment include promoting efficiency and market discipline, improving public finances, and depoliticizing non-essential services. The disadvantages of disinvestment include reduction in employment as private sector may go for cost cuts and layoff of surplus labor; imprudent use of disinvestment receipts as much of the receipts are spent on revenue expenditure; no change in the performance of PSEs after disinvestment as highlighted by few studies; loss of income to the government due to forgoing of dividend income and effective tax earnings; failure of disinvestment process to widen the investor's base, and debate with regard to sale of profitable PSEs.
3. The private sector refers to all types of firms or organizations, which are owned, controlled, and managed exclusively by private individuals or entities with the intention of making a profit. Private corporate sector contributes nearly 35% of the country's GDP and around 12% of gross national savings. The organized private sector employed about 13 million persons as on 2015–16. Reliance Industries Ltd. is the largest private company in the country on a turnover basis. Private sector is also criticized on several grounds like low growth rate of credit, growing distrust, the burden of corporate debt and consequent growth of NPAs, concentration of economic power in the hands of few, and threat to electoral democracy through interference in decision-making.
4. The twin balance sheet (TBS) problem refers to the stress on balance sheets of banks due to non-performing assets (NPAs) or bad loans on the one hand, and heavily indebted corporates on the other. In India, twin balance sheet problem was caused by overheating of the economy and rise in the cost of debt. But the TBS in India did not prove to be fatal to the economy mainly due to two reasons, one, the construction boom in the country did not let the aggregate demand fall and second, matured handling of debts by creditors. Government, in order to resolve the TBS problem adopted two-pronged strategy: enactment of IBS code and recapitalization of banks.
5. The IBC code was enacted by the Indian Parliament in the year 2016. The objectives of IBC are solving the twin balance problem, developing a robust corporate bond market, improving the credit environment, streamlining the corporate insolvency resolution process, preventing value destruction if there is corporate distress, and consequently providing a fillip to India's competitiveness as a business destination. The code has certain advantages like, changing the debtor–creditor relationship, maximization of value of assets, resolving insolvencies within 180 day, and helping the country gaining good rankings by foreign credit rating agencies.
6. According to new definition, the Micro enterprise will be one where investment in Plant & Machinery/Equipment is not more than ₹1 crore and Annual Turnover not more than ₹5 crores. A small enterprise will be one where Investment in Plant & Machinery/Equipment is not more than ₹10 crores and Annual Turnover not more than ₹50 crores. In case of medium enterprise Investment in Plant & Machinery/Equipment is not more than ₹50 crores & Annual Turnover not more than ₹250 crores. The MSME sector accounts for 29% of total GDP, 45% of industrial output of the country, 40% of total exports, generates 11.10 crore jobs, lead to regional equality due to decentralized expansion, equitable distribution of income and inclusive growth. The problem of MSMEs

includes inadequacy of finance, industrial sickness, external competition, infrastructural constraints, technological constraints, marketing problems. To promote MSMEs government has introduced a number of schemes like PMEGP, CLCSS, CGTMSE, ASPIRE, SFURTI, and ZED certification.

Endnotes

1. *Public Enterprise Survey, 2017–18*, Vol-1, Department of Public Enterprises, Ministry of Commerece and Industry. Government of India.
2. Economic survey. Department of Economic Affairs. Ministry of Finance. Govt. of India. 2017–18, p.12.
3. Nagraj, R. (2006). Public sector performance since 1950, a fresh look. *EPW*, p.2552.
4. Hermann, C. (2016). The public sector and equality. *Global social policy 16*(1).
5. Nagraj, R. (June 24, 2006). Public sector performance since 1950 a fresh look. *EPW*, p.2553.
6. Nagraj, R. (June 24, 2006). Public sector performance since 1950 a fresh look. *EPW*, p.2553.
7. Jagdish, B. (1993). *India's economy: The shackled giant*. Clarendon Press
8. Joshi, V., & Little, I M D. (1994). *India: Macroeconomics and political economy*, 1961–1991. Delhi: Oxford University Press.
9. *Disinvestment*. Retrieved from http://www.bsepsu.com (Accessed on January 18, 2019).
10. *Disinvestment*. Retrieved from http://www.bsepsu.com (Accessed on January 18, 2019.
11. Megginson, W. & Netter, J. (2001). From state to market: A survey of empirical studies on privatization. *Journal of Economic Literature, 39*, 321–89.
12. Chhibber, A., & Gupta, S. (2017). Bolder disinvestment or better performance contracts? Which way forward for India's state-owned enterprises, *NIPFP working paper series,* Working Paper No. 205. New Delhi, pp.21–22.
13. Kaur, S. (2005). Privatization and public enterprise reform: a suggestive action plan. ASARC Working Paper. Retrieved from https://crawford.anu.edu.au (Accessed on January 19, 2016).
14. Gupta, V., Kulkarni, S., Khatri, N. (2018). Leadership and Management of Public Sector Undertakings in an Emerging Economy, IIM Ahmedabad. W. P. No. 2018–01–04, January 2018.
15. Jalan, B. (1996). *India's economic policy*. Penguin. New Delhi.
16. Kaur, S. (2005). Privatization and public enterprise reform: a suggestive action plan, ASARC Working Paper 2004–08. Retrieved from https://crawford.anu.edu.au (Accessed on February 24, 2019).
17. Chandrasekhar, C. P., & Ghosh, J. (2002). *The market that failed: A decade of neoliberal economic reforms in India*. New Delhi: LeftWord.
18. Naib, S. (July 19, 2003). *Partial divestiture and performance of Indian public sector enterprises*. EPW, p.3092–3093.
19. Ram Mohan, T. T. (December 29, 2001). *Privatisation: Theory and evidence*. EPW, p.4871.
20. Chhibber, A., & Gupta, S. (2017). Bolder disinvestment or better performance contracts? Which way forward for India's state-owned enterprises, NIPFP working paper series, Working Paper No. 205. New Delhi, pp.21–22.
21. Kaur, S. (2005). Privatization and public enterprise reform: A suggestive action plan, ASARC Working Paper 2004–08. Retrieved from https://crawford.anu.edu.au (Accessed on February 24, 2019).
22. The Oxford companion to Indian Economy, *OUP*, New Delhi, pp.438–442.
23. *Annual Report, 2017–18*. Ministry of corporate affairs. p.22.
24. Nagraj, R. (November 7, 2015). Size and structure of India's private corporate sector: Implications for the new GDP series. *EPW 45*, 42.
25. Economic Survey 2017–18. Department of Economic Affairs. Ministry of Finance. Govt. of India. p.10.
26. Economic Survey, 2017–18. Department of Economic Affairs. Ministry of Finance. Govt. of India. p.123.
27. India needs to build trust in the private sector. *Livemint*, July 31, 2018.
28. Why India doesn't trust its private sector? Livemint, Feb 7, 2017.

29. Economic Survey, 2016–17. Department of Economic Affairs. Ministry of Finance. Govt. of India. p.39.

30. Gross NPAs jump to 11.2% in FY 18: RBI Report. *The Hindu Business Line*. December 28, 2018.

31. Nagraj, R. (November 7, 2015). Size and structure of India's private corporate sector: Implications for the New GDP Series. *EPW*, 1 (45) 47. *The Hindu*, April 15, 2018.

32. Resolution of twin balance sheet problem to take upto nine months. *The Hindu*, April 15, 2018.

33. Economic Survey, 2016–17, Department of Economic Affairs. Ministry of Finance. Govt. of India pp.82–83.

34. Economic Survey, 2016–17, Department of Economic Affairs. Ministry of Finance. Govt. of India pp.82–83.

35. Economic Survey, 2015–16, Department of Economic Affairs. Ministry of Finance. Govt. of India. p.19.

36. Economic Survey prescribes 4 R's to address problems at public sector banks. *The Economic Times*, February 27, 2016.

37. Decoding the Code: Survey on Twenty One Months of IBC in India, *CII*. Retrieved from https://www.pwc.in (Accessed on February 24, 2019).

38. Decoding the Code: Survey on Twenty One Months of IBC in India, *CII*. Retrieved from https://www.pwc.in (Accessed on February 24, 2019).

39. Livemint, December 25, 2018.

40. Business standard, December 28, 2018.

41. The Hindu Business Line, December 31, 2018.

42. The Economic Times, September 23, 2018.

43. The Gazette of India, September 30, 2006, New Delhi, p.1–2.

44. Annual Report, 2017–18, Ministry of micro, small and medium enterprises, New Delhi.

45. National Sample Survey (NSS) 73rd round on MSMEs. The Ministry of Statistics and Programme Implementation. Govt. of India.

46. National Sample Survey (NSS) 73rd round on MSMEs. The Ministry of Statistics and Programme Implementation. Govt. of India.

47. Annual Report, 2017–18, Ministry of micro, small, and medium enterprises, New Delhi.

48. Economic Survey, Department of Economic Affairs. Ministry of Finance. 2017–18, p.127.

49. Morris, S. (2001). *"Finance and small firms"*, in the growth and transformation of small firms in India. New Delhi.

50. Sickness in SSI Sector, Chapter 5, 5th All India Census of MSMEs. Retrieved from http://dcmsme.gov.in (Accessed on April 19, 2019).

51. Nair, T. & Das, K. (2015). Financing the MSME sector in India: Approaches, challenges and options, Gujarat Institute of Development Research Ahmedabad, Working Paper No. 230. p.23.

52. Vision 2020: Implications for MSMEs, Report by FICCI & Grant Thornton Retrieved from www.ficci.in (Accessed on May 14, 2019). p.38.

53. Vision 2020: Implications for MSMEs, Report by FICCI & Grant Thornton, Retrieved from www.ficci.in (Accessed on May 14, 2019). p.31.

54. Credit linked Capital Subsidy Scheme under Ministry of MSME. *Business Standard*, December 7, 2016.

55. Press Information Bureau, Government of India, Ministry of Micro, Small & Medium Enterprise, August 01, 2014.

56. Annual Report, 2017–18, Ministry of micro, small and medium enterprises, New Delhi.

CHAPTER **17**

Service Sector in India—Characteristics, Growth, and Sustainability

With the continuously stronger move of society into the information age, we're becoming more and more globally connected. Future society has to be prepared for the flexibility and agility of the specialized work force.

—Martin Gaedke

Introduction

Perception of the world changes with time. For more than 200 years, it was argued that economic development, growth, and structural transformation out of agriculture were best achieved through developing a labor-intensive manufacturing sector. Expansion of the service sector was seen as giving rise to stagnant growth.[1] Services were considered as menial, low skilled, low wage, low productivity sectors-, with low innovation, low learning, and low spillovers. Today, services can be among the most dynamic sectors in an economy, even in poor countries.[2] Service sector is much diversified sector today ranging from housemaids to neurosurgeons. Around 70% of the global economy is now accounted for by services. Services are the fastest growing sector in global trade. The share of developing countries in world service exports is increasing consistently and the average growth of service exports from developing nations has exceeded that of rich countries during the last two decades. The robust performance of service sector during the last three decades is a striking feature of India's growth performance. In this chapter, we propose to discuss the following:

- Characteristic features of India's service sector
- Reasons for rise in service sector of India
- Sustainability of service sector growth.

Characteristic Features of India's Service Sector

The service sector of India has witnessed a remarkable change during last few years. Following are the characteristic features of Indian service sector.

Increasing Share of Services in GDP

Agriculture remained the largest contributor to gross domestic product (GDP) during the decades of 1950s, 1960s, and 1970s. The share of Industry in overall GDP increased during the first four decades after independence but turned stagnant thereafter. The service sector that was number two since independence in terms of share in GDP emerged as the leading contributor in the decade of 1980s. In fact the declining share of agriculture has been usurped by service sector. Agriculture's shares of GDP and employment declined because of two reasons: first, the income elasticity of demand for food is less than 1 and second, price of food items relative to non-food items is likely to decline with global economic growth.[3] The share of service sector in country's GDP has increased from 30.3% in 1950–1951 to 42.7% in 1990–1991 and 54.2% in 2017–2018. The major reasons for rise in the share and higher growth of service sectors have been discussed in the next section.

Higher Growth Rate as Compared to Other Sectors

Among the three sectors, the industrial growth rate was highest during first four decades after independence. The growth rate of services out surpassed all other sectors during the decade of 1990s and there was no looking back. Moreover, the growth in services was also less cyclical and more stable than that of agriculture and industry. The major reasons cited for the higher growth rate of service sectors are splintering, higher domestic demand, and exports. Notwithstanding the lower agriculture growth rate and inconsistent industrial growth rate, India emerged as the fastest growing nation in the world and this feat can be attributed primarily to higher growth rate of service sector (Table 17.1).

TABLE 17.1 Growth Rate at Basic Price by Economic Activity

Sector	2017–2018	2020–21	2022–23	2023–24
I. *Agriculture, Forestry, & Fishing*	5.0	3.0	4.7	0.7
II. *Industry*				
Mining & Quarrying	5.1	–9.2	1.9	8.5
Manufacturing	5.9	–8.4	–2.2	7.5
Electricity, Gas, Water Supply, & other Utility Services	8.6	1.8	9.4	10.7
III. *Services*				
Construction	5.6	–10.3	9.4	6.5
Trade, Hotels, Transport, Communication, and Services related to Broadcasting	7.8	–18.0	12.0	8.2
Financial, Real Estate & Professional Services	6.2	–1.4	9.1	–1.4
Public Administration, Defence, and other Services	11.9	–4.1	8.9	7.7
GVA at Basic Price	6.9	–6.5	6.7	6.9

Source: Growth Rate at Basic Price. *Ministry of Statistics & Programme Implementation. Govt. of India.*

FDI Inflows in Service Sector

India's top 10 services constitute nearly two-third of total FDI inflows and top 5 services constitute 47% of total FDI inflows (Table 17.2). FDI is crucial for promoting production and

TABLE 17.2 FDI in Service Sector (2000–2023)

Sector	Percentage to Total
Service sector*	16%
Computer Software & Hardware	15%
Telecommunications	6%
Trading	6%
Construction	5%
Top 5 services	47% of total FDI

***Services** include Financial, Banking, Insurance, Non-Financial/Business, Outsourcing, R&D, Courier, and Tech. Testing and Analysis.

Source: DIPP, FDI statistics. *Ministry of Commerce and Industry. Govt. of India.*

dissemination of fresh technology and R&D. Taking the case of transportation alone, India needs around $1 trillion for overhauling its infrastructure sector such as ports, airports, and highways to boost growth. In the recent times, the government has taken several measures such as fixing timeliness for approvals and streamlining procedures to improve ease of doing business in the country and attract foreign investments. The other sectors that are in the priority list of the government include single-brand retail, multi-brand retail, print media, and construction.[4]

Trade in Services

India's services exports stood at US$ 254.5 billion in FY22 recording a growth of 23.5% over FY21. Software and business services together constitute more than 60% of India's total services exports and exhibited strong growth during FY23. While strong revenues in major information technology (IT) companies from various segments such as retail and consumer business; communications and media; healthcare; and banking, financial and insurance services drove the growth in software exports, a significant pick-up in engineering, and research and development related services boosted the growth in business services exports during the quarter.[5] Services imports rose by 25.1% between FY22 and FY21 to reach US$ 147.0 billion. The increase in services imports is mainly on account of payments for transport services, travel and other business services.

Indian Service Sector and Global Comparisons

Globally India's overall rank in terms of gross value added (GVA) is better than that of services GVA. In developed nations service sector contributes more than three-fourth of their GVA and share of service sector employment in total employment is also high. For example, services contribute nearly 80% of GVA and employment, respectively, in both the United States and United Kingdom. India's global standing in service sector is distinct in three respects. First, the growth rate of services is fastest in the world and indeed the higher services growth has placed India in the higher trajectory of overall growth. Second, despite the higher share of services, the share of employment is lower, which is not the case with many advanced nations. Third, share of services in total exports is very high and matches with that of developed nations.

Reasons for Growth in Service Sector

The phenomenal growth of service sector can be attributed to following factors:

Splintering

Splintering means breaking into small parts. Few economists also call it as "fragmentation" process. For example, painting a car is done by contracting it out (outsourcing) to a separate painting firm and the painting value addition then becomes part of the service sector, with little change in the overall real situation. Outsourcing (via services) leads to gains from trade and increases in national income.[6] As an economy matures agriculture and manufacturing requires increasing services of specialized set of institutions or people in the field of banking, accounting, R&D, marketing, transportation, communication, consultancy, etc. Further technological changes have further led to splintering and disembodiment of services and made many services tradable, just like manufactured goods.[7]

Spurt in Domestic Demand

During the pre-reform period, the share of services in total consumption basket increased from 8% in 1950–1951 to 20% in 1990–1991. However, the post-reform period has led to huge increase in the private final consumption expenditure with regard to services as its share has increased to nearly 50%. There is a popular perception that service sector growth phenomenon is attributed to outsourcing and disguised manufacturing activities. However, recent research has tried to over shed this myth and found that due to higher increase in income per capita (income effect) demand for education, communication, IT-related services, medical care, and health services has increased manifold.[8] The service sector remains the key driver of India's economic growth, contributing almost two-third of its GVA growth.[9]

Technology, Transportability, and Tradability

The Technology, Transportability, and Tradability (the 3Ts) are driving the service revolution. The world has witnessed a dramatic revolution in information *technology* during the last three decades and it has given services a physical presence. A medical check-up may still require a meeting with a doctor, but the results of an X-ray may be reviewed by a radiologist in a different country, the details of the examination may be transcribed by a person working in a different time zone, and medical records may be stored and updated on a remote server. Because of *Transportability*, service information is no longer restricted by time and space and can be easily transported over long distance with little or no degradation in quality. The worldwide decrease in the price of telephone tariffs and Internet services has exacerbated this process. Notwithstanding the decrease in prices in the cost of services, speed, clarity, and reliability of transportation of services has increased manifold. *Tradability*, refers to the fact that many modern services, which are transported digitally, face few government barriers when they are moved from one country to another. There are no borders, customs, or tariffs on the international exchange of most modern impersonal services.[10]

Globalization of Services

The range of business processes that can be globalized and digitized is constantly expanding: processing insurance claims; desktop publishing; the remote management and maintenance of IT networks; compiling audits; completing tax returns; transcribing medical records; and financial research and analysis. The list of possible activities is almost endless. World exports of commercial services are almost doubled as compared to that in 2006.[11] The globalization of services will continue to be a strong force for two reasons. First, services account for more than 70% of global GDP, more than double in size compared to the manufacturing sector. Second, the cost differential in the production of services across the world is enormous. In the past, the only option to narrowing such cost differentials was through migration, but migration has been heavily regulated and global international migration has remained steady at about 3% for decades. Now that service providers can sell services without crossing national borders by making use of the Internet (outsourcing), the scope for exploiting cost differentials is much higher. What is more, it is very hard for governments to regulate modern impersonal services, so prospects for rapid expansion in service exports are good.

Is Service-led Growth Sustainable?

During the recent years, acceleration in country's GDP has been due to dynamism of service sector while the contribution of industry has tended to stagnate over the last four decades. This has led to the speculation whether India would leapfrog from a predominantly agricultural to a directly service-dominated economy by skipping the intermediate stage of rising share of industrial sector that was experienced by all existing advanced nations. Every economy passes through a three-stage process in its evolutionary growth journey. Many economists like Fisher (1939), Clark (1940), Rostow (1960), and Kuznets (1971) developed their models and suggested that development is a three-stage process. In the first phase, agriculture sector dominates with largest contribution in GDP and employment. During second stage, the share of industrial sector in economic activities increases, which, in turn, promotes wide range of activities in service sector. The dominance of service sector in the growth process is associated with the third stage of development. India's growth pattern in the 21st century is remarkable because it contradicts a seemingly iron law of development. This law—which is now conventional wisdom—says that industrialization is the only route to rapid economic development for developing countries. It goes further to say that as a result of globalization the pace of development can be explosive. But the potential for explosive growth is distinctive to manufacturing only. This is no longer the case.[12]

The Case for Service-led Growth

Service Growth and Poverty Reduction

In general perception poverty reduction is associated with agriculture sector growth. But the recent research has documented that agriculture growth has little impact on poverty reduction especially when a major chunk of workforce is engaged in this very sector. A study while taking a sample of 50 countries has revealed that growth in the service sector is more correlated with poverty reduction than growth in agriculture.[13] While using a panel of Indian state data from 1994–2005, it was found that the trend growth in the service sector among Indian states is associated with a decrease in the trend of the headcount poverty rate of almost 1.5 points during the sample period. Furthermore, the service sector growth is strongly associated with a reduction in both urban and rural poverty rates. Some states like Andhra Pradesh, Kerala, and Tamil Nadu have experienced a significant decrease in urban poverty that is associated with an increase in their service sector share.

Services Growth and Job Creation

There has been a lot of debate about the capacity of the service sector to generate employment. Critics have lamented that service sector growth has been jobless growth. It has been argued that employment growth has not kept pace with income growth in the sector or with the rise in its share of GDP. Furthermore, the change in the production structure from agriculture to services has not been reflected by a proportionate change in the occupational structure. However, following observation can be made with regard to service sector growth and employability. First, the service sector has created maximum number of jobs in South Asia in recent years. For example, in India and Pakistan, the service sector has created jobs at a faster pace than agriculture or industry in the past 20 years. Second, services contribute to poverty reduction via two channels, direct and indirect. According to few estimates, indirect effect of a growing service sector can be larger than the direct effect. As per NASSCOM estimates, for every job created in the IT sector, four additional jobs are created in the rest of the economy. Third, wage growth has been higher in the service sector than in manufacturing and agriculture. While manufacturing wages fell in the early 2000s in both rural and urban India despite rapid economic growth, service sector wages in utilities, trade, transport, and even rural finance improved.[14] Fourth, countries with high employment in services tend to have the highest participation of women in the labor market. The development of service industries, therefore, brings new workers into the labor force, making the contribution to aggregate growth even larger. Higher household incomes and enhanced economic status for women in turn reduce the number of children per household, drive higher levels of education and health care for those children, and increase household savings and the ability to accumulate assets that generate additional income.

Trading in Services

There are four different ways in which services trade can be done as per general agreements on trade in services (GATS) of WTO.* In Mode I of GATS, trade in services involves arm's length supply of services, with the supplier and buyer remaining in their respective locations. For example, accounting of a firm in London can be done in Hyderabad and records can be shared via Internet. Mode I services are generally as IT and IT-enabled service exports, and it accounts for some 28% of global trade in services. Mode 2 services are provided by moving the service recipient to the location of the service provider. Travel by foreign residents including tourists is the dominant form of Mode 2 exports.[15] It accounts for nearly 14% of services exports. Mode 3 services that constitute nearly 57% of service trade involve commercial presence of service provider and takes place through FDI. Mode 4 services involve movement of natural persons, which

*GATS has been discussed in detail in the chapter 20 WTO, International Economic Institutions and Regional Trade Blocks.

brings in remittances and constitutes nearly 1% of total service trade. According to World Bank, there is a stronger correlation between service sector value-added growth and service sector exports. It also verifies that service-led growth is not only due to spurt in domestic demand but also due to exports. The recent research has also verified that the ratio of service trade in service output for developing countries has increased much faster than it has for developed countries. It means that developing countries are more concentrated on production of services that can be traded, rather than for domestic consumption. Indian IT firms have carved a niche in service sector exports; in FDI, service sector is the major recipient of FDI and India is also the world's largest recipient of remittances. India is an emerging economy and service sector is still in the expansionary phase. The service-led growth, therefore, is both enduring and sustainable.

The Case Against Service-led Growth

Despite the benefits of service-led growth, there are certain set of economists who emphasize that services are hugely important, but they cannot, by themselves, assure rapid and sustained growth of economy. Following points can be put forward in this regard.

1. Employment in manufacturing requires learning of a particular skill set, whereas employment in services requires at least a college degree. A strategy that relies exclusively on services as the engine of growth must provide a minimum of 15 years of education before workers are transferred out of agriculture. This is not feasible for a country like India where major chunk of adults are engaged in agriculture. If India is to transition to a modern economy in less than two decades, it cannot escape the industrialization stage. Each leg needs to be strengthened through a set of policy initiatives.[16]
2. The employment elasticity of service sector is lower than that of industry. Overemphasizing service-led growth is not justifiable in a labor surplus country like India.
3. The long-term development record of seven fastest growing economies of Botswana, Singapore, China, South Korea, Thailand, Indonesia, and Malaysia for the period 1965–1999 revealed that there was not a single instance of service growth exceeding industrial growth.[17] The lower growth rate of GDP in 12th plan period (2012–2017) also proves that even when services are growing at decent pace, they alone cannot compensate for slow expansion of the overall economy. India must walk on two legs, that is, services and industry must grow together.

Summary

1. Around 70% of the global economy is now accounted for by services. In India service sector is characterized by its increasing share in GDP from 30.3% in 1950 –1951 to 54.2% in 2017–2018; higher and stable growth rate as compared to other sectors; higher FDI inflows—the top five services account for 45% of total FDI inflows; increase in service sector exports—software services being the largest export item; and fastest growth of services in the world despite its share in employment is lower in comparison to the other advanced nations.
2. The reasons for growth of service sector in India are: (1) splintering, which means fragmentation of tasks into specialized set of services; (2) spurt in domestic demand and export for services, due to higher increase in income per capita and ever increasing demand for education, communication, IT-related services, medical care, health services, etc.; (3) Technology, Transportability, and Tradability (the 3Ts), technology gives services the physical presence, transportability eliminates time and space barrier, and tradability makes borders immaterial; and (4) finally globalization of services due to services trade and vast cost differences.
3. Two different schools of thought have emerged with regard to sustainability of service sector growth. The proponents of service sector sustainability maintain that growth in the service sector is more correlated with poverty reduction than growth in agriculture. Employment creation in service sector is higher and fast during past two decades as suggested by empirical research, with additional advantages of higher wage growth rate in services as compared to other sectors and vast potential of absorbing women labor force. Furthermore, the tradability of services too has undergone a paradigm shift due to general agreement on trade in services. But contrary views also have some merit. Employment in manufacturing requires learning of a particular skill set, whereas employment in services requires at least a college degree, the reason why services in India are not providing employment as in the case of developed nations. Services are characterized by low employment elasticity and empirical evidences too suggest that services alone cannot place the economy on higher growth trajectory. Industrialization and service revolution must go side by side.

Endnotes

1. Baumol, W.J. (1967). Macroeconomics of unbalanced growth: the anatomy of urban crisis. *American Economic Review, 57*(3), 415–426. Kaldor, N. (1966). *Causes of the slow rate of economic growth of the United Kingdom*. Cambridge: Cambridge University Press.
2. Ghanii, E. (2011). The services revolution, Paper presented at ILO Conference, Geneva, Retrieved from https://www.ilo.org (Accessed on February 14, 2016).
3. Anderson. (1987). On why agriculture declines with economic growth. *Agricultural Economics, 1,* 195–207.
4. FDI in services sector up 26% to 868-billion in FY17. *Livemint*. June 4, 2017.
5. *Economic Survey*. Department of Economic Affairs. Ministry of Finance. Govt. of India. 2022–23, pp.318–319.
6. Bhagwati, Panagariya, and Srinivasan. (Fall 2004). The muddle over outsourcing. *The Journal of Economic Perspectives*. Vol 18, Number 4, pp.93–114.
7. Bhagwati, J. (1984). Splintering and disembodiment of services. Retrieved from onlinelibrary.wiley.com (Accessed on February 16, 2016).
8. Eichengreen & Gupta. (2010). The service sector as India's road to economic growth. *ICRIER*, Working Paper.
9. *Economic Survey*. Department of Economic Affairs. Ministry of Finance. Govt. of India Chapter 7, p.106.
10. Ghanii, E. (2011). *The services revolution* (pp.4–5). New Delhi: *OUP*.
11. *World TRADE Statistical review, 2017*. Retrieved from https://www.wto.org. (Accessed on February 16, 2016). p.11.
12. Ghanii, E. (2011). *The services revolution* (pp.4–5). New Delhi: *OUP*.

13. Ghanii, E. (2011). *The services revolution* (pp.4–5). New Delhi: *OUP*.
14. Ghanii, E. (2011). *The services revolution* (pp.4–5). New Delhi: *OUP*.
15. Bhagwati, Panagariya, and Srinivasan. (Fall 2004) The muddle over outsourcing. *The Journal of Economic Perspectives*. Vol 18, Number 4, pp.93–114.
16. Panagariya, A. (2008). *The emerging giant*. New Delhi: OUP.
17. Acharya, S. Services not the real savior. *The Economic Times*, September 5, 2002.

CHAPTER 18

FOREIGN TRADE AND POLICY

Ships are my arrows, the sea my bow, the world my target.
—Robert Their

INTRODUCTION

Adam Smith in his book *Wealth of the Nations* asserted that the 'Trade is the engine of growth.' Trade helps nations to increase their GDP, employment, production, and consumption levels along with many other qualitative aspects related to growth and development of the nations. Foreign trade has indeed worked as an "engine of growth" in the past for example in case of Great Britain in the nineteenth century and Japan in the twentieth century, besides others. In recent times, the "outward-oriented growth strategy" adopted by the Newly Industrializing Economies of Asia, viz. Hong Kong, Singapore, Taiwan, Malaysia, Thailand, and South Korea, has enabled them to overcome the constraints of small resource-poor underdeveloped economies. In recent times, India, China, Brazil, Argentina, and Mexico are also following the same strategy.

This chapter addresses the following key issues:

- Advantages of Foreign Trade
- Analysis of India's Foreign Trade
- Foreign Trade Policy During Pre-Reform and Post-Reform Period
- Special Economic Zones

WHY NATIONS' TRADE?

Foreign trade contributes to economic development of a nation in a number of ways.

First, the foreign trade if allowed freely works on the principle of comparative advantage, an unchallenged and a fundamental law given by classical economists.* The law states that a nation will produce and export the commodity of its comparative advantage (in which it has greater specialization) and will import the commodity of its comparative disadvantage (in which it has lesser specialization). Comparative advantage acts as a stimulus to trade which leads to better

*The theory was given by David Ricardo in his celebrated work *The Principles of Political Economy and Taxation*, published in the year 1817.

specialization, optimal factor allocations, higher production, and consumption levels than previously enjoyed.

Secondly, difference in resource or factor endowments is an important reason and such demand and supply gaps lead to trade among nations. For example, India does not have sufficient petroleum oil resources and therefore, imports heavily from Arab nations.

Thirdly, taste preferences too affect trade largely across the nations. Some people prefer to buy German made homeopathy medicines or other allopathic medicines that belong to a particular foreign brand.

Fourthly, the underdeveloped nations do not have access to state-of-art technology that causes low efficiency and poor productivity levels. The import of foreign technology helps in filling this technology gap that leads to increase in total factor productivity, which ultimately unleashes the forces of higher growth.

Fifthly, trade inculcates the spirit of competition and dynamic change through competition from imports, pressure of competing for export markets, and hence a better allocation of resources in markets meeting domestic demand and foreign demand.

Finally, the history is full of evidence that the nations which were more open and vigorously engaged in trade are more developed, rich, and competitive. On the contrary, the nations which were less open or relatively more closed remained underdeveloped, impoverished, and uncompetitive in many respects. As discussed earlier, the newly industrialized countries of South East Asia found their GDP rising multifold after adopting pro-trade or trade-led growth policies. Furthermore, the new research has also validated that increased openness to trade has strongly been associated with the reduction of poverty in most developing countries.

Characteristics of India's Foreign Trade

A proper analysis of a country's foreign trade can be attempted in three component parts, viz. (1) value of trade, (2) composition of trade, and (3) direction of trade.

Value of Trade

Value of trade signifies two things:

1. Share of exports/imports in GDP
2. Share of exports/imports in world trade

Share of Exports/Imports in GDP

The share of exports/imports in GDP reflects the extent of outward orientation or openness of the economy in regard to the trade activity. The ratio of exports to GDP also signifies the supply capability of the economy vis-à-vis its exports. It is also called average propensity to export. Similarly, ratio between imports and GDP gives the average propensity to import. India's total exports have increased by more than 3,200 times during the last seven decades, from ₹606 crore in 1950–51 to over ₹15,182,371 crore in 2017–18. The export performance had not been uniform since 1951. Exports constituted 6% of GDP during 1951 and increased to nearly 13% during 2017.[1] Over the last 30 years, the upward trend has been maintained, although there might have been some occasional dips. Currently, the export sector is poised for a major breakthrough, looking at the government's efforts to boost manufacturing and service sector exports through schemes like Make in India. This will help exporters to successfully exploit the scope of productivity gains that exist today. Increased availability of infrastructure and credit has also helped considerably to maintain competitiveness.

India's total imports have increased nearly 5,000 times during the last seven decades from ₹608 crore in 1950–51 to an estimated amount of ₹3,001,016 crore in 2017–18. According to an estimate, 1% increase in national income requires imports to grow by 1.2%. This would mean that import bill of the country is expected to rise by about 11% per annum if India aims at achieving 9% consistent growth rate. Overall imports have increased right since 1954–55, with some blips now and then. In 2017–18, India's imports constituted around 20% of the total GDP.[2]

Share of Exports/Imports in World Trade

The share of exports in the world trade indicates the importance of a nation in the world economy. It reflects the market thrust that the country is able to realize in presence of the various competitors in the world market. Changes in this ratio, thus, indicate the shift in the position of the comparative advantage of the country. India's share in the total world exports was as much as 2.2% in 1951. Because of inward looking strategies, it came down steeply to 1.3% in 1958, 1.1% in 1965, and further 0.42% in 1980–81. It was in spite of the country's natural comparative advantages: low wages, and intelligent and educated workforce, raw cotton and, of course, preferential access to OECD markets.

During the 1980s and the 1990s in wake of picking up by India's exports, there has been some improvement in the ratio which has varied between 0.50 and 0.80%, indicating the vast possibilities of growth available in the export sector. However, India's export share in the world increased from 0.7% in 2000 to nearly 1.7% in 2017–18. Comparatively, the share of China has more than doubled from 3.9% to 13% during the same period.[3] In short, India's exports during the last six decades have shown a mixed trend. Whereas the rate of growth as measured in terms of past performance or in terms of its share of national income shows an appreciable rise, it presents a picture of poor performance when measured in terms of the share in world.

Furthermore, changes in the value of exports may be compared to the changes in the value of imports. The relationship between these two variables is known as the export/import ratio or terms of trade (TOT), that is, the terms at which exports exchange for imports, or in simple words, it is the capacity of exports to buy imports. If the exports value in terms of imports value shows an increase, the TOT are said to be favorable. Favorable TOT implies that for a given value of exports, the country can import more products from its trade partner. Conversely, if the TOT are unfavorable, a country has to give up more exports to make a given volume of imports. India's TOT with China was 0.3% in 2007–08 but deteriorated to 0.17 in 2017–18. It is because India's trade deficit with China has increased from $30 billion in 2008–09 to $53.5 billion in 2018–19, and the trade deficit has increased because of Beijing's policies that ensured technical advancement, state support, and selective de-linking of cost and price.*

Composition of Trade

By composition of foreign trade, we mean the kind of commodities a nation trades with foreign countries. It is a typical basket of exports and imports of a country with the rest of the world. Like many other parameters, the composition of trade too reflects a nation's development plans. For

*In 2018–19, India's exports to China were US $16.75 billion; India's imports from China were US $70.32 billion.

TABLE 18.1 Group-wise Composition of Exports (% of total)

Commodity Groups	1960–61	1990–91	2019–20	2020–21
Agriculture and allied products	44.2	19.4	11.2	14.3
Ores and minerals	8.1	4.6	2.2	3.2
Manufactured goods	45.3	72.9	71.3	71.2
Crude & Petroleum Products (incl. Coal)	1.1	2.9	13.6	9.2
Other	1.3	0.2	1.8	2.1

Source: *Economic Survey, 2021–22,* Statistical Appendix.
Department of Economic Affairs. Ministry of Finance. Govt. of India.

TABLE 18.2 Item-wise Leading Exports of India (2022–23)

Rank	Item	% of Total
1	Engineering Goods	23.73
2	Petroleum Products	21.59
3	Gems & Jewellery	8.41
4	Organic & Inorganic Chemicals	6.72
5	Drugs & Pharmaceuticals	5.63
6	Electronic Goods	5.24

Source: Handbook of Statistics, RBI, 2023, p.188.

example, more a nation trades industrial and tertiary sector products, more developed it is. Furthermore, the research verifies that there is a great degree of possibility of specialization leading to competitive trade practices in the countries involved in export and import of such products. The United States, the United Kingdom, Australia, Canada, Japan, and many countries of the Western Europe can be placed in this category.

At the time of independence, India's composition of foreign trade was highly tilted toward primary articles reflecting uncompetitive trade pattern and an underdeveloped nature of Indian economy. However, much has changed since independence, and today, agriculture exports constitute around 12% of total exports and agricultural imports constitute around 3% of total imports. It is not that country's potential of agricultural trade has decreased but that of industrial and tertiary products has increased. Table 18.1 reveals the shrinking share of primary products consisting agriculture and allied products and ores and minerals, and expanding share of manufactured goods and petroleum products over the period of time. The petroleum products and mineral fuels have shown a marvelous jump because of the increase in domestic production capacities by both government and private companies and cost-effective refining of crude petroleum.

As manufacturing exports constitute three-fourth of India's total exports, the top items of exports are from manufacturing exports only. Table 18.2 depicts the leading items wise export composition. The Gems and Jewellery scores first position in commodity composition of exports mainly because India imports raw metal and exports the finished metal due to low processing costs. Machinery & instruments, Transport equipment, Manufacturers of metals hold second, third and fourth position respectively and verifies country's increasing efficiency in the production of engineering goods. The Readymade garments takes fifth position mainly because of the comparative advantage India enjoys in the production of textiles.

Table 18.3 includes the broader composition of India's imports. The food and allied products constituted 19.1 of total imports in 1960–61, and its share in total imports has come down to

TABLE 18.3 Group-wise Composition of Major Imports (2020–21)

Commodity Group	% of total
Food and allied products	4.5
Fuel	25.1
Fertilizers	1.9
Capital goods	12.7
Paper board manufacturer and newsprint	0.8
Others	41.6
Unclassified	13.3

Source: Computed from *Economic Survey, 2020–21*. Statistical Appendix. Department of Economic Affairs. Ministry of Finance. Govt. of India.

TABLE 18.4 Itemwise Leading Imports of India (2022–23)

Rank	Item	% of total
1	Petroleum, Oil and Lubricants (POL)	29.34
2	Electronic goods	10.82
3	Coal, Coke & Briquettes, etc.	6.93
4	Gold & Silver	4.5
5	Organic & Inorganic Chemicals	4.67
6	Pearls, precious, semi- precious stones	4.29

Source: Handbook of Statistics, RBI, 2023, p.190.

around 4.5% in 2020–21, reflecting India's self-sufficiency in food products. The share of capital goods has also come down from 31.73% to 12.7% during the same period, indicating India's growing expertise in machines.

Table 18.4 contains the leading items of India's imports. The Petroleum, Oil and Lubricants (POL) constitutes nearly 21% of total imports and has been leading importable item over the last seven decades. The electronic goods were at second position in 2020–21 with 13.8% share and major sources of such imports were China, Singapore and other East Asian countries besides the United States and few countries of EU. However the share of electronic goods came down during 2019–20 due to impact of covid world wide. China was major supplier of electronic goods and the shutting down of factories in China due to spread of covid 19 was provided major setback to Indian imports. Chemicals are ranked second and comprise organic chemical, inorganic chemical, chemical materials & products and dyeing, tanning & colouring material. India is one of the world's largest importers of gold, which is widely considered a "safe haven" asset.[4] It occupies third position in the overall item-wise imports. Chemicals are ranked second and comprise organic chemical, inorganic chemical, chemical materials & products and dyeing, tanning & colouring material. Transport equipment hold fourth position in India's total imports. India specializes in the processing and finishing of the pearls, precious, and semi-precious stones which occupy fifth position in country's total imports.

Direction of Trade

The Direction of trade signifies the destination of India's exports and sources of India's imports. It is indicative of the structure and level of economic development.

Direction of Exports

Continent wise, Asia is the largest export destination of India followed by America and Europe. In more recent times, India's exports to Asia and Oceania markets, with whom

TABLE 18.5 Direction of India's Trade—Region Wise (2022–23)

Region	Exports (%)	Imports (%)
Europe	21.83	12.58
Africa	11.37	6.53
America	23.44	11.22
Asia	41.50	62.91
CIS and Baltics	1.04	6.73
Unspecified region	0.83	0.04

Source: *Monthly Bulletin on Foreign Trade Statistics April 2023, Ministry of Commerce.*

TABLE 18.6 Country-wise Top Ten Export Destinations of India (2022–23)

Country	US$ million	Exports (%) 2020–21
The United States	78,548.60	17.44
The UAE	31,608.82	7.02
Netherland	21,620.73	4.80
China P Rp	15,331.94	3.40
Singapore	11,992.96	2.66
Bangladesh	11,672.60	2.59
UK	11,458.52	2.54
Saudi Arab	10,727.67	2.38
Germany	10,136.69	2.25
Indonesia	10,026.25	2.23

Source: *Monthly Bulletin on Foreign Trade Statistics April 2023, Ministry of Commerce.*

ethnically, culturally, and economically India is closer, have revealed a sharp jump. In fact, the current boom in exports is sustained largely by what officials see as an unexpected and healthy rise in exports to the Asia and Oceania countries, which include the ESCAP countries like Australia, Iran, Japan, Korea, Malaysia, Singapore, Thailand, Hong Kong, Bangladesh, and Nepal. The shift in favor of these countries implies that Indian exporters have concentrated at last in markets closer home to capitalize on the advantages from lower freight cost[5] (Table 18.5).

In country-wise exports, the relative importance of the United Kingdom and the United States as outlets for our exports has declined over the years. Whereas in 1950–51 these countries together accounted for more than 40% of India's exports, this share has come down presently to around 25%. The United States, all the same, continues to be our principal buyer. The UAE is the second largest export destination followed by China, Hong Kong and Singapore (Table 18.6).

Direction of Imports

The direction of imports has largely been influenced by the development of the economy. In the initial stages of growth, a large part of the development process was financed through foreign aid

TABLE 18.7 Top 10 Source Nations of India's Imports, 2020–21

Country	US$ million	Imports (%)
China	98,505.79	13.80
The UAE	53,232.54	7.46
The United States	50,240.10	7.04
Russia	46,212.71	6.47
Saudi Arab	42,035.27	5.89
Iraq	34,385.50	4.82
Indonesia	28,820.41	4.04
Singapore	13,305.00	3.30
Korea Rp	21,227.32	2.97
Australia	16,756.17	2.66

Source: Computed from *Monthly Bulletin on Foreign Trade Statistics April 2023, Ministry of Commerce.*

which was primarily in the form of tied aid. As a result, a large part of imports originated from the aid-giving countries. However, much has changed since then. Region wise, India imports maximum imports from Asia (62%), Europe (15%), and America (13%) (Table 18.5). A more significant development has been the emergence of oil-producing countries as a significant purchasing center for us. This has been caused largely by sharp increase in the unit value of petroleum and its products. The OPEC alone accounts for about 16% of our total imports. The EU as a group accounts for about 11% of our imports.

In country-wise imports, China is the India's largest source contributing to nearly 14% of total imports (Table 18.7). In 1965–66, more than 35% of India's total imports came from the United States. Since then, the share of the United States has declined to number two. The UAE, Saudi Arab, and Iraq are the third, fourth, and fifth suppliers, respectively, of our imports. The relative share of the Switzerland and Hong Kong in India's imports has also declined, although both nations continue to be principal supplier. Among the centrally planned economies, the former USSR was an important purchasing center for us. But in the recent years, the importance of these countries is on the decline. Russia along with other East European countries presently accounts for not more than 2% of India's total imports.

Diversification or Concentration?

As a country develops and its trade gets diversified, it has to seek new outlets for its exports. Its horizon of choice in terms of imports also gets widened. The country begins to trade with an increasingly large number of countries. In this regard, one could ask whether there has been a concentration or dispersion of the markets for exports and sources of supply for imports. Just the two continents Asia and Europe account for 70% of India's exports and just seven nations, viz. the United States, China, the UAE, Hong Kong, Singapore, Saudi Arab, and Switzerland contribute to one-third of India's foreign trade. It signifies that India's foreign trade is not diversified. India would have to explore new sources of imports and new markets for its products in the fast globalizing world. For example the share of American continent in India's overall exports is 21%, whereas that of Latin America is just 3%. Africa constitutes around 9% of country's exports. India needs to tap central and Northern Africa, while intensifying efforts in western African countries.

Foreign Trade Policy (FTP) of India

The exports and imports of a nation are an important ingredient of its Balance of Payment schedule and solutions to the problems of Balance of Payments depend considerably on the policies we adopt in our export and import sectors. In India, Ministry of commerce announces annual or perspective (5 yearly) export–import policy (EXIM Policy) or foreign trade policy (FTP). Let us have a brief idea about FTP during pre-reform and post-reform period.

FTP in Pre-reform Period

India's trade policy in the post-independence years was influenced by certain factors. During 1950s, the economic models of few noted economists of the world, such as those of Ragnar Nurkse (Balanced Growth Theory), Rosenstein Rodan (Big Push Theory), Prebisch-Singer (Secular Deterioration), and Feldman-Mahalanobis (Capital Goods and Heavy Industry), were dominant, and they minimized the classical notion of trade as an "engine of growth." The studies highlighted that since the less developed countries are the producer and exporter of primary goods, they are competed out by the manufactured goods of developed countries, and hence, terms of trade work in favor of developed countries, and there are secular deterioration in the terms of trade of the less developed nations. It created two strong beliefs in the mind of Indian policymakers of that time. One was the fatalistic view that the raising export earnings were impossible (few economists call this notion as export pessimism), and the other was that the import substitution by itself will be able to solve India's Balance of Payment difficulties.

Following are the salient features of FTP during pre-reform period.

Policy of Import Restriction

The government strategy of development placed much emphasis on heavy industrialization in order to reduce external dependence. It resulted in heavy demand for the import of intermediate and capital goods that led to exhaustion of limited foreign exchange reserves (sterling balances) and caused balance of payment crisis of 1956–57. The Government quickly responded by raising tariffs and introducing comprehensive licensing on a variety of imports.[6] The average tariff for agriculture, mining, and manufacturing was 125% during 1990.[7] However, it was brought down during post-crisis period. Import licensing*was highly restrictive: the intent was virtually to eliminate "consumer goods imports" and replace them with domestically produced goods (or to prevent their consumption in the case of items classified as luxury goods).[8] Imports were classified into different categories, viz. non-permissible (banned), limited permissible (mandatory certification and clearance is required), and open general license (no certification or clearance is required).

Policy of Import Substitution

The policy of import substitution advocates replacing the imports of a nation with indigenous production. The policy of import substitution can be justified on the following grounds. First, it

*An import license is a document issued by the government that allows a specific amount of a specific item to be imported by a specific user for specified purpose, sometimes even from a specified source of supply.

BOX 18.1 Import Substitution Versus Export Promotion

The policy of import substitution signifies replacing imports with indigenous production. It can be done by imposing quantitative restrictions, tariffs, or other trade barriers. The major advantage of import substitution is that it helps a nation to achieve self-reliance and save its valuable foreign exchange reserves. It benefits producers as there is no competition (from importers), but consumers suffer because their consumption choice becomes limited. Further, the policy of import substitution harbours inefficiencies, increases costs, and makes the indigenous industry uncompetitive. India embarked upon the policy of import substitution under Mahalanobis's strategy of public sector development.

The policy of export promotion, however, is based on the principal of comparative advantage, and the country concentrates on the production and exports of products in which it is relatively more efficient. It leads to optimum allocation of resources, enhances total factor productivity, promotes competitive environment, and leads to specialization. The export promotion as a policy tool was introduced in 1980s, but it was enforced with vigour only after the new economic policy of 1991.

Source: Bruton, H. (1998). A Reconsideration of Import Substitution. *Journal of Economic Literature, 36(2)*, 903–936.

helps a nation to save its valuable foreign exchange reserves which could have been spent in the payment of imports; second, it helps a country to achieve self-reliance, and third, it promotes the indigenous industry and prepares it to become exporter as well. The policy has been criticized by a number of economists on various grounds. First, the luxury goods import was restricted due to huge tariff rates, and this led to the increase in the indigenous production of such goods. The policy of promoting the production of luxury goods was totally out of line with the average per capita income in the country, and the demand tended to fall after certain point because of massive poverty and resultant less demand. It led to the generation of unutilized capacity and higher average cost in such firms. Second, the much homework was not done before implementing the policy of import substitution. Valuable resources could have been saved if the process of import substitution had been more selective with a limited number of strategically chosen sectors and industries, where a concentration of effort and resources could have maximized the gains in efficiency.[9] Third, the import substitution strategy produced supply-side constraints and led to administrative burdens in a system of physical control, adverse effect on entrepreneurship by providing incentives for rent-seeking rather than long-term corporate planning, little or no incentive for technological up gradation, and so on. According to Bhagwati, Desai, Srinivasan, and Ahluwalia, the supply-side constraints caused low long-run growth of the Indian economy. Finally, G.M. Meier too argues that the import substitution policy was not targeted according to systematic economic criteria but instead was pursued in a chaotic, inefficient manner and for too a long time. The policy proved to be fatal for Indian economy as it led to massive misallocation of resources and generated inefficient and unproductive industrial structure (Box 18.1).

Export Policy During the Pre-reform Period

The Export policy in the pre-reform period can be classified into three distinct phases: Phase I (1952–1973); Phase II (1973–1980), and Phase III (1980–1990).[10] During the *first phase* of export policy, the export pessimism gripped the Indian policymakers of that time to such an extent that the whole FTP became restrictive and inward looking. The policies of import substitution and protectionism damaged the export capacity of developing world. India too was not an exception. From 1952–1966, India witnessed fall in the share of its traditional exports and insufficient expansion of non-traditional exports. In June 1965, India devalued its currency by 36.5%, which was followed by few liberal steps like reduction in tariffs. During 1966 and 1967, export subsidies were provided to many non-traditional export goods like engineering goods, chemicals, paper products, textile, and iron and steel.

Many economists like Vasilis Panoutsopoulos, Gunasekera, Rodney Falvey, Gan Wee Beng, and Ashok Desai examined the growth of exports from developing countries, to test the validity of export pessimism and found the contrary. Examining the pattern of trade for Hong Kong, Taiwan, the Republic of Korea, and Singapore, Vasilis Panoutsopoulos found that export pessimism was unwarranted in the 1950s and 1960s and that industrial country markets were able to adjust to greater market penetration by developing countries in the 1970s. He found that in the 1980s developing countries increased their exports of textiles and clothing, machinery, and production components to industrial countries. The newly industrializing countries were leaders of market penetration in both traditional products such as toys and new products such as machinery.[11] In India too, during the *second phase*, it was implicitly recognized that import substitution policies by themselves could not bring about viability in India's balance of payments. The Government therefore, started giving high priority to exports. The growth and profitability of Indian exports picked up but could not last long as export promotion policies continued to be pursued as "exceptions" to normal development policies. The *third phase* witnessed an explicit positive approach toward exports, and exports were now being seen as an integral part of industrial and development policies. Phase III drew a sharp contrast as compared to the previous two phases, and the Government emphasized technological upgradation and freer export and import policies to boost India's trade with rest of the world.

FTP in Post-reform Period

Liberal Imports and Exports

As discussed earlier, the FTP of India in the pre-reform period was restrictive and cumbersome. The system was so complex that there was different type of import licenses, different categories of importers, and alternate ways of importing. The quantitative restrictions (QRs) were removed on import of capital goods, intermediate goods, and raw materials, but retained for consumer goods. However, as per the directions of WTO, India also dismantled the remaining QRs in 2001.[12] During early 1990s, the rupee had depreciated considerably making imports costly and exports competitive in the international markets. Consequently, it encouraged the Government to reduce the maximum rate of import duty from 100 to 85% during the 1993–94 annual budget. The successive budgets reduced it further, and now, the peak rate of custom duty for non-agricultural goods is 10%.

Decanalization of Trade

Before 1991, the extent of canalization of exports and imports was very high and the trade was canalized through some public sector agencies in India. The Exim Policy, 1991, made an attempt of progressive reduction in the extent of canalization. Accordingly, 16 export items and 20 import items were decanalized. Later on, Exim Policy 1992–1997 also decanalized number of imported items including non-ferrous metals, natural rubber, news print, and raw materials for fertilizers.

The Managed Float System of Exchange Rate

By end-June 1991, India's reserves of foreign currency had plunged to $1,124 million, adequate to cover just about 2 weeks of imports.[13] The Government devalued its currency in two steps, that is, in July 1 and July 3, 1991 by 18.5% against the US dollar. It was followed by partial convertibility of rupee in 1992–93 and full convertibility in trade account in 1993–94, and in August 1994, the country achieved full convertibility in current account. The present system of exchange rate which is called managed float has facilitated the trade by virtue of removing government control on exchange rate management. However, the RBI does intervene in the foreign exchange market (through market stabilization scheme) in case of steep rise and fall in exchange rates.

Establishment of Special Economic Zones

The FTP of 2000 announced setting up of Special Economic Zones (SEZs) to promote FDI and exports. The Government later came out with SEZ Act 2005, supported by SEZ rules 2006 and the Act came into force on February 10, 2006. The major purpose of SEZs is to promote FDI, Exports, Employment, and GDP of the country. The SEZs are provided various sorts of exemptions and incentives so as to promote both indigenous and foreign investment.

Establishment of Agriculture Export Zones

The Government announced setting up of Agriculture Export Zones (AEZs) in 2001 FTP policy to promote agricultural exports of the country. The concept of AEZs takes a comprehensive look at a particular produce/product located in a contiguous area for the purpose of developing and sourcing the raw materials, their processing/packaging, leading to final exports. The entire effort is centered around the cluster approach of identifying the potential products, the geographical region in which these products are grown, and adopting an end-to-end approach of integrating the entire process right from the stage of production till it reaches the market.[14] At present, there are 60 AEZs located in 20 different states of the country.

Establishment of Export-Oriented Units

The Establishment of Export-Oriented Units (EOUs) scheme introduced in early 1981 is complementary to the SEZ scheme (erstwhile EPZ scheme). It adopts the same production regime but offers a wider option in location with reference to factors like source of raw materials, port of export, hinterland facilities, availability of technological skills, existence of an industrial base, and the need for a large area of land for the project. Over the last few years, EOUs have evolved as a major player in the country's export effort. They have become dominant players in our export strategy, and their share in the country's export performance is about 10%.[15]

Export Houses and Trading Houses

Before 1991, the export units were categorized as Export Houses, Trading Houses, and Star Trading Houses. The new policy permitted such units to import a wide range of items, to make duty-free imports for exports and invite 51% foreign equity for the promotion of exports. In April

2007, the Government broadly divided export houses into five categories: (1) Export House, (2) Star Export House, (3) Trading House, (4) Star Trading House, and (5) Premium Trading House. The exporters were granted such status on achieving the volume of exports to the tune of ₹20, ₹100, ₹500, ₹2500, and ₹10,000 crore, respectively. The subsequent policies also extended different benefits and concessions to such houses.

Market Access Initiative Scheme

The scheme was launched in 2001–02 to undertake marketing promotion efforts abroad. The scheme arranges in-depth market studies for selecting products in some chosen countries in order to generate date for the promotion of exports from India. This scheme also helps in displaying Indian brands or products in the international market. The scheme is formulated on focus product–focus country approach to evolve specific strategy for specific market and specific product through market studies/survey. Assistance is provided to exporters for the enhancement of export through accessing new markets or through increasing the share in the existing markets. The scheme also assists in upgrading the quality of products as per the requirement of overseas market and also in making publicity, campaigns, etc.[16]

Foreign Trade Policy (2015–2020)

The Government announced the 5-year FTP for the period 2015–2020 on April 1, 2015. The Government also aims at increasing the exports of goods and services from $465.9 billion in 2013–14 to $900 billion and increasing India's share in world exports from 2 to 3.5% by 2019–20. The characteristic features of FTP 2015–2020 can be discussed under four heads. First, "Simplification & Merger of Reward Schemes"; second, "Boost to 'Make in India'"; third, "Trade Facilitation & Ease of Doing Business"; and fourth, "Other measures." Following are the salient features of FTP 2015–20.[17]

Simplification & Merger of Reward Schemes

1. Earlier there were five different schemes (Focus Product Scheme, Market Linked Focus Product Scheme, Focus Market Scheme, Agricultural Infrastructure Incentive Scrip, VKGUY) for rewarding merchandise exports with different kinds of duty scrips with varying conditions attached to their use. Now all these schemes have been merged into a single scheme, namely Merchandise Export from India Scheme (MEIS), and there would be no conditionality attached to the scrips issued under the scheme.
2. Served from India Scheme (SFIS) has been replaced with Service Exports from India Scheme (SEIS). SEIS shall apply to "Service Providers located in India" instead of "Indian Service Providers" regardless of the constitution or profile of the service provider.
3. Incentives of MEIS & SEIS will be available to the units located in SEZs also.
4. All scrips issued under MEIS and SEIS and the goods imported against these scrips would be fully transferable. Scrips issued under Exports from India Schemes can be used for payment of customs duty for import of inputs/goods, payment of excise duty on domestic procurement of inputs or goods, payment of service tax on procurement of services, basic Customs Duty paid in cash or through debit under Duty Credit Scrip can be taken back as Duty Drawback, if inputs so imported are used for exports.

5. Business leaders who have excelled in international trade and have successfully contributed to country's foreign trade are proposed to be recognized as status holders and given special treatment and privileges to facilitate their trade transactions, in order to reduce their transaction costs and time. The nomenclature of Export House, Star Export House, Trading House, Star Trading House, and Premier Trading House certificate has been changed to one, two, three, four, five-star Export House respectively. The criteria for export performance for recognition of status holder have been changed from rupees to the US dollar earnings. Manufacturers who are also status holders will be enabled to self-certify their manufactured goods as originating from India with a view to qualify for preferential treatment under different Preferential Trading Agreements (PTAs), Free Trade Agreements (FTAs), Comprehensive Economic Cooperation Agreements (CECAs) and Comprehensive Economic Partnerships Agreements (CEPAs) which are in operation.

Boost to "Make in India"

1. In order to boost the Make in India campaign, special steps have been taken to help the indigenous capital goods manufacturing industry. Under the Export Promotion Capital Goods (EPCG) scheme, in case capital goods are procured from indigenous manufacturers, specific export obligation has been reduced to 75%. Under the MEIS, export items with high domestic content and value addition have generally been provided higher levels of incentives.

Trade Facilitation & Ease of Doing Business

1. Hard copies of applications and specified documents which were required to be submitted earlier for incentive schemes and duty exemption schemes have now been dispensed with.
2. Landing documents of export consignments as proof for notified market can now be digitally uploaded as specified. There will be no need to submit copies of permanent records/documents repeatedly with each application, once the same are uploaded in the exporter/importer profile.
3. Dedicated e-mail addresses have been provided for faster and paperless communication with various committees of the Directorate General of Foreign Trade (DGFT), for example, Norms Committee and Exim Facilitation Committee.

Other New Initiatives

1. Export Oriented Units (EOUs), Electronic Hardware Technology Park (EHTPs) and Software Technology Parks (STPs) have been allowed to share infrastructural facilities among themselves. This will enable units to utilize their infrastructural facilities in an optimum way and avoid duplication of efforts and cost to create separate infrastructural facilities in different units.
2. Calicut Airport, Kerala and Arakonam Inland Container Depot (ICD), Tamil Nadu have been notified as registered ports for import and export.
3. In an endeavor to resolve quality complaints and trade disputes, between exporters and importers, a new chapter, namely "Quality Complaints and Trade Disputes" has been incorporated in the FTP. For resolving such disputes at a faster pace, a Committee on

Quality Complaints and Trade Disputes (CQCTD) will be constituted in 22 offices and will have members from EPCs/FIEOs/APEDA/EICs.

4. The Government has already recognized 33 towns as export excellence towns. It has been decided to add Visakhapatnam and Bhimavaram in Andhra Pradesh as towns of export excellence (Product Category—Seafood).

SPECIAL ECONOMIC ZONES (SEZs) IN INDIA

Asia's first Export Processing Zone (EPZ) was set up in Kandla in 1965. Seven more zones were set up thereafter. However, the zones were not able to emerge as effective instruments for export promotion on account of the multiplicity of controls and clearances, the absence of world-class infrastructure, and an unstable fiscal regime.[18] The Government announced the SEZ policy on April 1, 2000. The prime objective was to enhance foreign investment and provide an internationally competitive and hassle-free environment for exports. Furthermore, to instill confidence into investors and signal the Government's commitment to a stable SEZ policy regime, a comprehensive SEZs Act 2005, was enacted by the parliament. The SEZ Act 2005, supported by SEZ Rules, came into effect on February 10, 2006.

SEZ is a specifically delineated duty-free enclave and shall be deemed to be foreign territory for the purposes of trade operations and duties and tariffs. In other words, SEZ is a geographical region that has economic laws different from a country's typical economic laws. Usually the goal is to increase foreign investments. SEZs have been established in several countries, including China, India, Jordan, Poland, Kazakhstan, Philippines, and Russia (Table 18.8).[19]

Facilities and Incentives Extended to SEZs[20]

1. Duty-free import/domestic procurement of goods for development, operation, and maintenance of SEZ units.
2. Hundred percent Income Tax exemption on export income for SEZ units under Section 10AA of the Income Tax Act for first the 5 years, 50% for the next 5 years thereafter, and 50% of the ploughed back export profit for the next 5 years.
3. Exemption from GST.
4. Exemption from other levies as imposed by the respective state governments.
5. Single window clearance for central and state-level approvals.
6. Exemption from customs duties for development of SEZs.

TABLE 18.8 Special Economic Zones: Factsheet (As on 19.02.2024)

Approved SEZs	424
Operational SEZs	278
Approved companies/units	5,713
Employment as on 30th September, 2023	1,95,984 persons
Exports in 2022–23	₹12,63,578 crore
Investment as on 30th September, 2023	₹6,69,980 crore

Source: Special Economic Zones: Factsheet. Retrieved from http://sezindia.nic.in/ (accessed on April 15, 2024).

Objectives/Benefits of SEZs

The main objectives of the SEZ Act are the following:[21]

Contribution to GDP

SEZs lead to generation of additional economic activity and, hence, contribute to GDP of the country. In India, there are more than 400 approved SEZs and more than 200 operational SEZs, and the number of approved units in such zones is 5,481.

Contribution to Exports

SEZs have long been touted as a method of increasing exports and, as a result, improving the level of development in a region. In an open economy, SEZs increase the likelihood of exporting by as much as 25%.[22] In India, the exports from SEZs have increased from ₹22,800 crore in 2005–06 to ₹7,59,524 crore in 2019–20.

Increase in Investment

Further SEZs offer numerous benefits to investors like tax incentives, provision for infrastructure and utilities, single window clearance, simplified procedures, exemptions from various restrictions, and so on. Such measures foster a conducive business climate to attract both indigenous and foreign investment. Total investment in SEZs, both domestic and foreign, increased from ₹4,035 crore in 2005–06 to ₹6,38,235 crore in December 31, 2022.

Creation of Employment Opportunities

Employment generation, both direct and indirect, has been an important channel, through which SEZs have impacted on human capital enrichment.[23] The total number of employed persons has increased from 1.3 lakh in 2005 to around 26.16 lakh in 2020.

Development of Infrastructure Facilities

The creation of infrastructure is a necessary pre-condition to promote industrialization in the country. SEZs attract both indigenous and foreign investment by providing world-class and state-of-art infrastructure facilities.

Demerits of SEZs

Usurping the Prime Agricultural Lands

In India, the land available for agriculture is shrinking at a fast pace. An average size of SEZ is around 5,000 ha. With more SEZs in pipeline, the transfer of excessive lands from agriculture to SEZs will have an appalling effect on agriculture production in the country. Furthermore, there is a nexus between SEZ builder, politicians, and bureaucrats. Lands are grabbed at meager prices, and farmers are not adequately compensated. For example, India Today in 2006 reported one shocking instance in Maharashtra. The Government bought land from farmers at around ₹50,000 per ha. After holding on to it for years, it sold it to a corporate for ₹62 lakh per ha. While the profiteering of the Government was bad, the corporate in turn parceled the land at ₹10 crore per ha to co-developers of its SEZ.[24]

The Problem of Displacement of Local Population

Special Economic Zones acquire land from the farmers but such acquisition leads to displacement, meager compensation, and no alternative livelihood to the displaced families. For example, in Nandigram (West Bengal), the proposed SEZ acquired not only large tracts of agricultural land, but also residential areas displacing the entire population of 27 villages.[25] In Singur (West Bengal), around 1,000 acres of prime agricultural land was acquired for the now-famous Nano plant of the Tata Motors. Though it was not a SEZ project but led to a major controversy and agitations by farmers. According to some estimates, one million people who primarily depend upon agriculture face eviction due to the establishment of SEZs and the loss of income to evicted families is more than ₹200 crore a year.

Tax Exemptions and Revenue Foregone

The SEZs are exempted from various taxes like GST, custom duty, and so on, and also provide with numerous incentives. According to CAG report released in November 2014 on the performance of the SEZs and tabled in Parliament, the SEZs have availed of various concessions/exemptions of central as well as of state taxes. The annual statement of revenue forgone under the central tax system for the period from 2006–2013 works out to ₹83,104 crore on account of direct taxes and customs. Furthermore, the Ministry of Finance, in a study, pegged the loss at ₹175,487 crore from tax holidays granted to SEZs between 2004 and 2010. So, there is loss to the exchequer in terms of "tax forgone" without commensurate outcomes but not in terms of "sum lost," as some would like to interpret.[26]

Generation of Inequity

The special economic zones have miserably failed to promote balanced regional development in the country. Of the total SEZs approved, 75% are concentrated in six developed states—Maharashtra, Andhra Pradesh, Tamil Nadu, Karnataka, Haryana, and Gujarat. Except Haryana (mainly the NCR belt), all are peninsular states meaning thereby the SEZs have not gone into North, East, or middle Indian states. In India, 56.64% of SEZs cater to the IT/ITES though they occupy less than 20% of area. It has also been seen that most of SEZs are concentrated in just 20 states of the country. The manufacturing sector which is being seen as the sine qua nun for India's future growth miracle has very less presence in SEZs.

Underperformance

The units in SEZs have failed to perform as per nation's expectations and target achievements of investment, exports and employment are far from realization. The CAG report found non-performance on targets in employment (ranging from 65 to 96%), investment (ranging from 24 to 75%), and exports (ranging from 46 to 93%). In case of employment, the CAG reports that in 117 developers/units in 12 states, the actual employment (284,785 persons) vis-à-vis the projections (3,917,677 persons) made by the developers/units had fallen short by nearly 93% (3,632,892 persons). There are cases of breach of conditions relating to the memorandum of understanding (MOU) reached between developers and the Government on employment.[27]

Summary

1. The classical economists emphasized trade as an engine of growth. There are various benefits of trade: law of comparative advantage, filling of demand and supply gap, technology benefits, competition and dynamic change, and correlation between exports and growth.
2. A country's foreign trade analysis can be attempted in its three-component parts: (1) Value of trade, (2) Composition of trade, and (3) Direction of trade. The value of trade signifies two things: share of exports/imports in GDP and share of exports/imports in world trade. Exports constituted 6% of GDP during 1951 and increased to nearly 13% during 2017. Imports constituted 6% of GDP during 1951 and increased to nearly 20% during 2017. India's share in world exports has come down from 2.2% in 1951 to 1.7% in 2017.
3. At the time of independence, India's composition of foreign trade was highly tilted toward primary articles reflecting uncompetitive trade pattern and an underdeveloped nature of Indian economy. Over the period of time, the share of primary products has decreased and that of manufactured goods has increased. The share of manufacturing exports has increased from 45–70% from 1960–61 to 2018–19 and that of agriculture & allied has decreased from 44 to 12 percent during the same period. In manufacturing, the leading export items are Gems and jewellery, machinery & instruments and transport equipment. POL is the largest import item in the country comprising more than one-fourth of import expenditure. In imports, the food and allied products constituted 19.1 of total imports in 1960–61, and its share has come down to around 3% in 2018–19 reflecting India's self-sufficiency in food products. The share of capital goods has also come down from 31.73% to around 13% during the same period, indicating India's growing expertise in machines. However, in group-wise imports, fuel and capital goods dominate with 40% of total imports. The largest import items of India are POL, electronic goods, and gold and silver. Continent wise, Asia is the largest export destination of India followed by America and Europe. The major export destination nations of India are the United States, the UAE, China, Hong Kong, and Singapore. Similarly, continent wise, Asia, Europe, and America are the major sources of India's imports. However, in country-wise ranking, China is India's largest source of imports followed by the United States, the UAE, Saudi Arab, and Iraq.
4. The import policy of pre-reform India was inward-looking and guided by import restrictions and import substitution. Export policy too suffered from pessimism in the early years of planning but got outward orientation after 1980s. Many steps were taken to correct the course of FTP during post-reform period. These are liberal import and export policies; decanalization of trade; adoption of managed float system of exchange rate; establishment of SEZs; establishment of agriculture export zones; establishment of export-oriented units; export houses and trading houses; and market access initiative scheme.
5. The Government announced the 5-year FTP for the period 2015–2020 on April 1, 2015 and aimed at increasing the exports of goods and services from \$465.9 billion in 2013–14 to \$900 billion by 2019–20 and to increase India's share in world exports from 2 to 3.5%. The Characteristic features of FTP 2015–2020 can be summed up in four heads: First, Simplification & Merger of Reward Schemes; second, Boost to"Make in India"; third, Trade Facilitation & Ease of Doing Business and Fourth, other measures.
6. SEZ is a geographical region that has economic laws different from a country's typical economic laws. Usually the goal is to increase foreign investments. The Government announced the Special Economic Zone (SEZ) policy on April 1, 2000. The Special Economic Zones Act, 2005, was enacted by the Parliament. The SEZ Act, 2005, supported by SEZ Rules, came into effect on February 10, 2006. The Government provides multiple facilities and incentives to SEZs to promote FDI and indigenous investment. The main advantages/objectives of SEZs are increase in investment, both indigenous and foreign; increase in exports because of cost-effective world-class manufacturing, creation of employment opportunities—which also leads to human capital enrichment; contribution to GDP because of increased economic activity and development of infrastructure facilities. The disadvantages of SEZs are usurping the prime agricultural lands, which may affect agriculture production; the problem of displacement of local population, which take place because of nexus between politicians and SEZ developers; tax exemptions and revenue foregone because of various exemptions; generation of inequity and underperformance as most of the SEZs are concentrated.

Endnotes

1. *Handbook of Statistics, RBI. 2017–2018* (p.300)
2. *Handbook of Statistics, RBI. 2017–2018*. p.300.
3. WTO Statistics database. Retrieved from http://stat.wto.org (Accessed on April 16, 2019).
4. The value of India's gold imports are declining but that's a good thing. (July 16, 2018). *Business Insider*.
5. Mustafa. (2010). *Foreign Trade Finance and Documentation* (p.18). New Delhi: Laxmi Publications.
6. Bhagwati & Srinivasan. (1975). "Foreign trade regimes and economic development: India"
7. GATT. (1993) *Trade policy review: India*, Vol.1. Geneva: WTO.
8. Acharya, S. & Mohan, R. (2011). India's economy: Performance and challenges. *Essays in honour of Montek Singh Ahluwalia*. New Delhi: OUP.
9. Ahmed, J. (1987). Foreign trade and balance of payments, in J.S. Uppal (Ed.), *India's economic problems*. New Delhi.
10. Jalan, B. (1992). *The Indian economy: Problems and prospects* (p.178). Penguin. New Delhi.
11. Panoutsopoulos, V. (1992). The growth of exports from developing countries: Export pessimism and reality, in H. Hughes (Ed.) *The dangers of export pessimism*. San Francisco, CA: International Center For Economic Growth.
12. Krueger, A.O., India's trade with the world-retrospect and prospect, in S. Acharya and R. Mohan (Ed.), Indian economy: Performance and challenges New Delhi: OUP.
13. On this day 25 years ago: An invaluable devaluation. (July 6, 2016). *Indian Express*.
14. *Agriculture Export Zones*. Retrieved from http://farmer.gov.in (Accessed on November 11, 2018).
15. *Export-Oriented Units*. Retrieved from http://eouindia.gov.in (Accessed on November 11, 2018).
16. *Market Access Initiative Scheme*. Retrieved from http://www.fisme.org.in (Accessed on November 12, 2018).
17. *Foreign Trade Policy 2015–20*. Department of Commerce, Ministry of Commerce and Industry. Govt. of India.
18. *Department of Commerce, Annual Report, 2011–12* Ministry of Commerce and Industry. (p.81).
19. What is Special Economic Zone? (July 8, 2005). *The Economic Times*.
20. Special Economic Zones. Retrieved from http://sezindia.nic.in (Accessed on March 12, 2019).
21. Department of Commerce, *Annual Report, 2011–12* Ministry of Commerce and Industry. Govt. of India. (p.81).
22. Davies & Mazhikeyev. (February 5, 2016). The impact of special economic zones on exporting behavior. *Working Paper*. Retrieved from https://cepr.org (Accessed on November 14, 2018).
23. Aggarwal, A. (May 2007). Impact of special economic zones on employment, poverty and human development. Working Paper No. 194. Indian Council for Research on International Economic Relations.
24. Some praise it, some condemn it, but there's something special about SEZs. (October, 9, 2006). *India Today*.
25. Banerjee, P.S. (2019). *Politics and conflicts behind SEZS in West Bengal* Retrieved from https://www. cetri.be (Accessed on April 4, 2019).
26. Sahoo, P. (April 4, 2015). Time to review the Special Economic Zones Act. *EPW, 1*(14), 24–25.
27. Sahoo, P. (April 4, 2015). Time to review the Special Economic Zones Act. *EPW, 1*(14), 24–25.

CHAPTER 19

Balance of Payments, Foreign Exchange, and Investment

FDI is a responsibility for Indians and an opportunity for the World. My definition of FDI for the people of India is 'First Develop India'.

—**Narendra Modi**

Introduction

The study of Balance of Payments (BOPs) has become a matter of great interest to all concerned. It is considered as an economic barometer of a country's health because it not only reflects a country's strength in trading goods and services but also demonstrates the size of capital inflow and outflow. Further, it sheds light on the size of foreign exchange reserves a country has possessed over the period of time. The position of BOP also helps in determining the overall trade, monetary and fiscal policies of the country.

The present chapter will focus on the following issues:

- BOP and its trends
- Foreign exchange rate system in India
- Foreign exchange reserves and its management
- Foreign Direct Investment (FDI), its advantages and disadvantages
- Capital account convertibility and its advantages and disadvantages

Balance of Payment

The BOPs is the systematic record of economic transactions of a nation with the rest of the world in a single accounting year. The main purpose of the BOP is to inform the government of the international position of the nation and to help it in its formulation of monetary, fiscal, and trade policies. Governments also regularly consult the BOP of important trade partners in making policy decisions.

Table 19.1 shows the schedule of BOP that will help to understand the concept profoundly.

The BOP can be classified into two major accounts, that is, *the Current Account and Capital Account*. *The current account* comprises export and import of goods/merchandise and balance in the invisible account. *Goods Account or Trade Balance* constitutes export and import of goods/merchandise, and because goods are tangible or visible, this account is also called as *Visible Trade Balance or Balance of Trade.* If exports of goods are greater than imports of goods we get trade surplus; and if exports of goods are less than imports of goods we get trade deficit.

The invisible account is further divided into (1) Non-Factor Services, (2) Income, and (3) Private Transfers. As the name suggests the invisible account contains invisible or intangible

TABLE 19.1 Balance of Payments Schedule

Items	Receipts	Payments
1. Current account (a+b)		
a. Goods export and import (goods account)		
b. Services/invisibles export and import (invisibles account) (i)+(ii)+(iii)		
i. Non-factor services		
ii. Income		
iii. Private transfers/foreign remittances		
2. Capital account (c)+(d)+(e)+(f)+(g)+(h)		
c. External assistance		
d. External commercial borrowing		
e. NRI deposits		
f. Banking capital		
g. FII		
h. FDI		
3. Overall Balance of Payment Account (1+2)		

items. *Non-Factor Services* include export and import of travel, transportation, insurance, Government not included elsewhere (GNIE), and miscellaneous. Miscellaneous includes communication, construction, financial, software, news agency, royalties, management, and business services. *Income* includes interests, profits, and dividends received from foreign countries and paid out to foreign countries. *Private Transfers* (*also foreign remittances, unilateral transfer, or unrequited transfer*) are the flow in one direction with no automatic reverse flow in other direction. For example, an Indian settled in Australia remitting $100 to his aged parents in Chandigarh is a private transfer inflow item in India's BOP.

The Capital account can be classified by instrument (debt or equity) and maturity (short or long term). The *external assistance* is of two types: the first is borrowings from/to other countries called as bilateral debt; and the second is borrowing from international financial institutions, also called as multilateral debt. *External Commercial Borrowings* (*ECBs*) comprise funds raised by Indian companies from markets abroad via Global depository receipts/American depository receipts. *Non-Resident Indian* (*NRI*) *deposits* in banks, bonds, or other financial instruments also constitute debt component of India's BOP. However, *Foreign Direct Investment FDI and Foreign Portfolio Investment* (*FPI*) constitutes non-debt component of India's BOP. FDI is long-term investment that goes into production of goods and services whereas FPI is short-term capital, which goes into hedge funds, shares, mutual funds, etc. The current account and capital account together constitute the overall BOP of the country. The increase in reserves indicates an overall surplus in BOP and decrease in reserves indicate overall deficit of BOP.

Trends in India's BOP

India's Balance of Trade

Indian exports have come a long way from the time of independence in terms of value. The total value of India's merchandise exports increased from US$ 1.3 billion in 1950–51 to US$ 303 billion in 2107–18, a compound rate of 8.5%. Indian economy and foreign trade have shown progress post liberalization. In contrast to the pre-reform period (1950–1990), the actual growth of exports in the post-reform period has been above the potential offered by the growth of world demand. The gap between the actual and potential is mainly explained by an improvement in the overall competitiveness of India's exports.[1]

However, India's trade deficit has widened since independence. During 1950–51, India's trade deficit was ₹2 crore. It increased to US$ 180.3 billion in 2018–19.[2] Higher trade deficit of India demonstrates India's burgeoning imports and lower growth rate of exports as compared to that of imports. Trade deficit as a proportion of GDP increased from 4.9% in 2016–17 to 6.0% in 2017–18 and further to 6.7% in 2018–19. The merchandise trade deficit for FY 2022–23 was estimated at $266.78 Billion as against $191.05 Billion during FY 2021–22.

India's Current Account

The period from 1956–1976 was marked by severe current account deficit (CAD), however, the country experienced minor current account surplus during three consecutive years 1976–77, 1977–78, and 1978–79. The major reasons for current account surplus during this phase were increase in remittances from Middle East, strong growth of exports, and decline in oil imports because of increase in indigenous oil production.[3] The period from 1980–1991 was also marked by a severe BOP difficulties and in late 1980s and early 1990s, the CAD surged all time high. The economic crisis of 1990 and the reforms introduced thereafter strengthened India's current account. India experienced current account surplus consecutively for 3 years during 2001–02, 2002–03, and 2003–04. The reason for the current account surplus was burgeoning service sector exports and increase in invisible receipts. But 2004 onward, there was deterioration in current account due to increase in oil prices. The country experienced a historical high CAD (5.01% of GDP) during 2012–13 due to the onslaught of global financial crisis which resulted into decline of exports of goods and services and private transfers. Since then, there is a turnaround in the current account balance and for 2017–18 and 2018–19, India's current account deficit was 1.8 and 2.1% of GDP respectively.[4] For the year 2019-20 the current account deficit narrowed down to 0.9% of GDP. As per advance estimates India is expected to experience the current account surplus in the financial year 2020–21 due to covid 19 impact which has resulted into the huge contraction of import demand. For 2022–23 as a whole, India's current account deficit stood at $67.0 billion or 2.0% of GDP.

India received most of the remittances from Gulf countries during pre-reform period and senders were generally unskilled workers employed in various activities in such countries. The post-reform period witnessed a structural change in India's foreign remittances. During this time most of the remittances accrued from developed world comprising nations such as the United States, Canada, the United Kingdom, Australia, New Zealand, and many East Asian countries like Hong Kong, Malaysia, Singapore, etc. The persons who remitted most of such transfers were high-end workers, scientists, academicians, IT professionals, and doctors. The inward remittances to India in 2023 rose 12.3% to $125 billion, accounting for 3.4% of its gross domestic product (GDP), according to estimates released by the World Bank. In 2022, India's inward remittances stood at $111.22 billion. India continues to be the highest recipient of remittances globally, followed by Mexico ($67 billion) and China ($50 billion).

India's Capital Account

India enjoys surplus in its capital account because capital inflows are greater than capital outflows. India's current account deficit since 1950s was financed by external assistance in the form of multilateral debt. But over the period of time, the capital account has undergone a structural paradigm shift. India's dependence upon external assistance both from bilateral and multilateral sources has decreased. Foreign direct investment has emerged as the largest component of capital account followed by foreign institutional investment, NRI deposits and external commercial borrowings. Net FDI inflows at US$ 71 billion in 2022–23 were lower than US$ 85 billion in 2021–22.

Overall Balance of Payment

India enjoys overall surplus in its BOP because the capital account is not only in surplus but it also overcompensates India's current account deficit. India's overall BOP surplus was ₹423,206 crore during 2019–20.

India's Foreign Exchange Rate System

Types of Exchange Rate System

Exchange rate is the price of one currency in terms of another currency. It is the rate at which one currency is exchanged for other. Exchange rate regime is the way the central bank of a country manages its currency vis-à-vis other foreign currencies in the foreign exchange market.* Such regimes are mainly fixed exchange rate system, flexible or floating exchange rate system, and system of managed float. In case of *Fixed Exchange Rate System*, the currency value is fixed vis-à-vis other currency or to a basket of currencies or with some metal like gold. It is also called *Pegged Exchange Rate System*. The major advantage of fixed exchange rate system is that it reduces volatility in foreign exchange markets and makes trade and investment predictable. The classic example of a fixed exchange rate system is the period between 1880 and 1914, which is also called the "classical" gold standard period. During the two world wars was the phase of transition when countries intermittently adopted, abandoned, and again adopted the gold standard. After the second world war, the US$ emerged very strong and *Bretton Woods system* (1944–1973) replaced the gold standard with US$ as the official reserve asset.

Under the Bretton Woods system, there was an obligation for each country to maintain the exchange rate (±1%) by tying its currency to gold and the ability of the IMF to bridge temporary imbalances of payments. The American dollar was the only currency strong enough to meet the rising demands for international currency transactions at that time, and therefore, the United States agreed both to link the dollar to gold at the rate of $35 per ounce of gold and to convert dollars into gold at that price. The Bretton Woods system continued for more than two decades and on August 15, 1971, President Richard Nixon of the United States suspended conversion of US$ into gold because of deteriorating BOP situation and massive flight of US$ from America. In March 1973, the Bretton Woods system collapsed and it saw the emergence of floating exchange rate system.

Under the *Flexible or Floating System*, the exchange rate is determined by the interaction of demand and supply forces. The major advantage of this exchange rate system is that it allows the domestic currency to depreciate or appreciate freely and hence guides it to attain automatic equilibrium. But since the flexible exchange rate system makes the exchange rate unpredictable and unstable, the countries world over have switched to a *Hybrid Exchange Rate System or the System of Managed Float*. Under this, the currencies are allowed to float freely within a band and in case of any exigency the central bank intervenes in the foreign exchange market. Central bank's intervention in the foreign exchange market is called sterilization.** The system of managed float is also called "Snake in a tunnel policy" (Box 19.1).

---

*Foreign exchange market is the market where the participants buy, sell, or speculate the international currencies. The participants include banks, commercial companies, central banks, investment management firms, hedge funds, traders and retail forex brokers, and investors.

**Sterilization is a method through which RBI intervenes in the foreign exchange market to offset the impacts of change in money supply caused by changes in foreign exchange inflow and outflow. RBI squeezes or releases foreign currency so as to stabilize foreign exchange market.

BOX 19.1 How does Currency Depreciate/Devalue and Appreciate/Revalue?

Let us suppose India trades only with the United States and currencies involved in trade are dollar and rupee. There are certain set of people who demand dollars. Such people are importers, tourists going abroad, people who send remittances abroad, FDI outflow, FII outflow, etc. Supply of dollars is generated by exporters, tourists coming from other countries, foreign remittances, capital inflow in the form of FDI, FII, NRI deposits, ECBs, etc. The forces of demand and supply will generate a price at which both currencies will be traded. If $1 is exchanged for ₹60, then it will be exchange rate as per flexible exchange rate policy. This will be the price at which all transactions (in current and capital account) between India and the United States will take place. Now, under flexible exchange rate regime, the forces of demand and supply will keep exchange rate volatile. If demand for dollars is more, dollar will become expensive (let us assume $1 = ₹65), called appreciation of dollar or depreciation of rupee. If supply of dollars is more, dollar will become cheaper (let us assume $1 = ₹55), called depreciation of dollar or appreciation of rupee. Rupee depreciation provides boost to exports because for $1 exports, exporter will be earning more rupees than previously. It will encourage exporter to raise supply of exports and will also encourage new entrants into export business. But depreciation of currency will also affect imports, because for every unit of import, the importer needs to pay more in terms of rupee than previously. On the other hand, rupee appreciation will make imports cheaper and discourage exports.

Government can also lower or raise the value of currency vis-à-vis foreign currency, through the method of devaluation and revaluation depending on the macroeconomic condition of the economy. "Devaluation" means official lowering of the value of a country's currency vis-a-vis foreign currency. "Revaluation" means official raising of the value of a country's currency vis-a-vis foreign currency. Impact of devaluation and revaluation are same as depreciation and appreciation with the difference that devaluation/revaluation is government induced and depreciation/appreciation is automatic.

Evolution of Indian Exchange Rate System

Phase I: The Par value System (1947–1971)

Immediately after independence, India adopted the Bretton Woods system (or par value system of IMF) whereby the rupee's external value was fixed at 4.15 grains of fine gold with pound sterling as the intervention currency. Indian currency was pegged at ₹4.76 per US$ and ₹13.33 per pound sterling in September 1949. It remained unchanged up to June 1966 when the rupee was devalued by 36.5% to ₹7.50 per US$ and ₹21 per pound sterling.* Since 1966, the exchange rate of rupee remained fixed till 1971.

Phase II: The Pegged Regime (1971–1992)

With the breakdown of the Bretton Woods System, in December 1971, the rupee was linked with pound sterling (from December 1971 to September 1975). There was downward pressure on the pound sterling vis-à-vis other major international currencies and rupee being linked to it also

*Huge budgetary deficit, trade deficit, and cut in foreign aid after the 1965 war with Pakistan forced Indira Gandhi Government to go for rupee devaluation.

BOX 19.2 What is Purchasing Power Parity (PPP)?

The theory of PPP was developed by Gustav Cassel in 1918. It is the rate at which the currency of one country would have to be converted into that of another country to buy the same amount of goods and services in each country.

According to theory: $E = P_1/P_2$, where "E" represents exchange rate of currency 1 to currency 2; P_1 represents the prices of good "x" in currency 1 and P_2 represents the prices of good "x" in currency 2. For example, a cup of tea that sells for ₹10 in Indian city should cost US$ 5.00 in a US city when the exchange rate between India and the United States is ₹2/1$. To facilitate price comparisons across countries, the International Comparisons Program (ICP) was established by the United Nations and the University of Pennsylvania in 1968. PPPs generated by the ICP are based on a global survey of prices. The most recent ICP results covering 199 economies were released in April 2014 for the reference year of 2011.

The PPP exchange rate are different than the market exchange rate because the latter includes transportation costs, tariffs, and other frictions. Market rates are more volatile, and using them could produce quite large swings in aggregate measures of growth even when growth rates in individual countries are stable. On the other hand, PPP exchange rates are more stable and are widely used when comparing GDP from different countries.

Sources:

1. World economic outlook (2018). Retrieved from https://www.imf.org (accessed on November 19, 2018).
2. International Comparison Program (ICP). Retrieved from https://www.worldbank.org (accessed on November 19, 2019).

caused rupee's misalignment vis-à-vis other currencies. In order to overcome the weaknesses associated with a single currency peg and to ensure stability of the exchange rate, the rupee, with effect from September 1975, was pegged to a basket of currencies. The currencies included in the basket as well as their relative weights were kept confidential by the Reserve Bank to discourage speculation.[5] During this period (1975–1992), RBI officially determined the exchange rate of rupee within a nominal band of ±5% of the weighted basket of currencies.

During this period both macroeconomic policies and structural factors contributed to misalignment in foreign exchange rate system. Many countries like China and Indonesia devalued their currencies despite the low inflation rates during 1980s which aggravated this misalignment. Comparatively, Indian exchange rate was overvalued that killed export competitiveness while boosted demand for imports.[6] Foreign exchange transactions too were controlled through the Foreign Exchange Regulations Act (FERA), 1973 and such restrictions resulted in an extremely efficient unofficial parallel (Hawala) market for foreign exchange. During phase I and II, exchange rate was never used as a tool of macroeconomic management except for occasional and dramatic episodes of devaluation as in 1949 and in 1966.

Phase III: Post-Reform Period (1991 Onward)

During 1990–91, the country went through the times of economic crisis. By now, it was recognized that both macroeconomic policy and structural factors had contributed to BOP problem. The current account deficit (CAD) increased to 3.0% of GDP in 1990–91 and the foreign exchange reserves shrunk to less than a billion dollar by July 1991. The High Level Committee on Balance of Payments (Chairman Dr. C. Rangarajan) recommended corrections and proactive measures, viz. (1) adoption of market determined exchange rate system, (2) avoiding use of exchange mechanisms for subsidization, (3) maintaining adequate level reserves to take care of short-term fluctuations, (4) continuing the process of liberalization on current account, and (5) reinforcing effective control over capital transactions. The committee also recommended to unify the exchange rate, as an important step toward full convertibility. The government devalued rupee by 9% and 11% between July 1 and 3, 1991, respectively, to offset the massive downfall in the foreign exchange reserves, to instill confidence in the investors and to improve domestic competitiveness. It effectively brought to a close the period of pegged exchange rate and adoption of Liberalised Exchange Rate Management System (LERMS).

Liberalized Exchange Rate Management System (1992–93)

Following the recommendations of Rangarajan Committee to move toward the market determined exchange rate, the government in the budget for 1992–93, announced LERMS. The LERMS introduced partial convertibility of rupee by involving dual exchange rate system. Under this 40% of the foreign exchange earnings were to be surrendered at the official exchange rate while the remaining 60% were to be converted at a market determined rate. The foreign exchange surrendered at official rate was used by government to make essential imports like crude oil, lifesaving drugs, fertilizers, etc. As the official foreign exchange was higher (revalued) than the market determined exchange rate, it was just like taxing the exporters to subsidize the government's essential imports.

Managed Float System (1993 Onward)

The LERMS was a transitional mechanism which not only provided stability to exchange rate but also led to build up of foreign exchange reserves. The dual exchange rate system was replaced by unified exchange rate system in March 1, 1993. The 60:40 ratio was extended to 100% conversion for almost the entire merchandise trade transactions (export or import of goods) and all receipts, whether on current or capital account of BOPs, but not all payments. However, the official rate of exchange of RBI stayed on for conversion of items not permitted under market determined rate, various exchange control norms of RBI remained in operation all along, and even restrictions for a number of invisible transactions continued. India finally achieved full convertibility on current account when RBI further liberalized payments and accepted obligations under Article VIII of the IMF.[7] India has not yet achieved full convertibility in capital account. It is to be noted that

BOX 19.3 What are NEER and REER?

Nominal Effective Exchange Rate (NEER) is the weighted average of bilateral nominal exchange rates of the home currency in terms of foreign currencies. It is the exchange rate of one currency against a basket of currencies, weighted according to trade with each country (not adjusted for inflation).

Real Effective Exchange Rate (REER) is the weighted average of nominal exchange rates, adjusted for inflation. REER is calculated on the basis of NEER. REER captures inflation differentials between India and its major trading partners and reflects the degree of external competitiveness of Indian products. It captures movements in cross-currency exchange rates.

Source: NEER and REER. *RBI Bulletin*, December 16, 2005.

India did not adopt free float system as it will take away autonomy of RBI to intervene in case any exigency arise. The experience with managed float is satisfactory as the foreign exchange market was characterized by orderly conditions except a few incidents of instability.

FOREIGN EXCHANGE RESERVES AND ITS MANAGEMENT

Foreign exchange reserves are the international reserve assets held by the central bank in foreign currencies. Such reserve assets are in the form of foreign bank notes (like US$, Euro, Pound Sterling, Yen, etc.), marketable securities/bonds, government securities, gold, Special Drawing Rights (SDRs), and reserve position in the IMF.

Objectives of Holding Foreign Exchange Reserves

IMF has laid down certain objectives for holding the foreign exchange reserves.[8] They are as follows:

1. Support and maintain confidence in the policies for monetary and exchange rate management including the capacity to intervene in support of the national currency;
2. Limit external vulnerability by maintaining foreign currency liquidity to absorb shocks during times of crisis or when access to borrowing is curtailed and in doing so;
3. Provide a level of confidence to markets that a country can meet its external obligations;
4. Demonstrate the backing of domestic currency by external assets;
5. Assist the government in meeting its foreign exchange needs and external debt obligations; and
6. Maintain a reserve for national disasters or emergencies.

What Should be Ideal Size of FERs?

During the Bretton Woods system the central banks of nations held foreign exchange reserves to maintain the external value of their respective currencies at a fixed level. But when countries adopted a system of managed float, it required intervention of central banks in the foreign exchange market from time to time. But the question that requires immediate attention is: What should be the ideal size of foreign exchange reserves a central bank needs to hold at any point of time? Traditionally, the adequacy of foreign exchange reserves was determined on the basis of a simple logic: that is, the stock of foreign exchange reserves (FERs) should be equivalent of few months of imports. However, the East Asian crisis of 1997 proved this approach wrong. The increase in the pace of globalization and the emergence of stronger short-term capital movements across the borders, the reserve adequacy also needs to be addressed wisely. The Guidotti–Greenspan rule* states that a country's reserves should equal short-term external debt (1 year or less maturity), implying a ratio of reserves-to-short-term debt of 1. The idea was supported by empirical research showing that short-term external debt appears to be a potent predictor of currency crises.[9] Many

*The Guidotti–Greenspan rule is named after Pablo Guidotti—Argentine former deputy minister of finance and Alan Greenspan—former chairman of the Federal Reserve Board of the United States. Guidotti first stated the rule in a G-33 seminar in 1999, while Greenspan widely publicized it in a speech at the World Bank.

economists have done a valuable research on this theme and there is a wider acceptable view that the appropriate size of foreign exchange reserve depends upon following key factors—size of the economy (whether it is advanced market economy, emerging market economy, or a low-income country); current account convertibility; capital account convertibility; degree of exchange rate flexibility, and the opportunity cost of holding foreign exchange reserves.[10]

The Indian Case

India's foreign exchange reserves have increased considerably during the post-reform period from US$ 5.8 billion at end-March 1991 to US$ 424.5 billion in 2017–18. The major reasons for increase in foreign exchange reserves are, huge inflow of foreign remittances and other invisible receipts, increase in foreign investment, commercial borrowings, and NRI deposits over the years. The FERs build up showed its ascendance at the beginning of twenty-first century and in the year 2007–08, the figure crossed US$ 300 billion. It again dipped in 2008–09 to $251 billion due to the impact of the global financial crisis and Eurozone crisis, fluctuated for few years and started rising steadily after 2012–13. The adequacy of India FERs can be revealed by the fact that by the end of March 2018 the import cover increased to 10.9 months and the ratio of short-term debt to the foreign exchange reserves was also reported 24.1% during the same period (Table 19.2).

What Is RBI Doing With Its Foreign Exchange Reserves?

The guiding objectives of foreign exchange reserve management in India are similar to those of many central banks in the world. The demand placed on the foreign exchange reserves may vary widely depending upon a variety of factors including the exchange rate regime adopted by the country, the extent of openness of the economy, the size of the external sector in a country's GDP and the nature of markets operating in the country. While liquidity and safety constitute the twin objectives of reserve management in India, return optimization is kept in view within this framework.[11] RBI does not keep its stock of FERs idle but make ideal uses of it. Let us have a brief look on what RBI does with country's valuable FERs.[12]

1. *Gold:* The Reserve Bank held 586.44 tonnes of gold as on September 2018; of which, almost 50% is held overseas in safe custody with the Bank of England and the Bank for International Settlements (BIS).

TABLE 19.2 India's Foreign Exchange Reserves

Year	Foreign Exchange Reserves (US$ billion)
1960–61	0.637
1990–91	5.8
2000–01	42.3
2004–05	141.5
2007–08	309.7
2010–11	304.8
2015–16	360.2
Feb 11, 2022	630.19
March 29, 2024	645.6

Source: Report on Currency and Finance, 2017–18. RBI, The Times of India, Feb 12, 2022, The Economics Times, April 5, 2024.

2. *Foreign currency assets invested overseas:* The foreign currency assets comprising multi-currency assets are held in multi-asset portfolios as per the best international practices. As at end-March 2018, out of the total foreign currency assets 66% was invested in securities, 27% was deposited with other central banks, the BIS, and the International Monetary Fund (IMF), and remaining 7% comprised deposits with overseas branches of commercial banks.
3. *New arrangement to borrow (NAB):* Established following the Mexican economic crisis, NAB is a collective arrangement between IMF, 26 nations and International financial institutions (IFIs) under which the countries and IFIs lend a certain amount of capital to IMF. The IMF uses such funds in case its lending falls short of borrowers' needs. RBI has subscribed to Notes equivalent to SDR 800.69 million under NAB till end-March, 2016, as part of GOI's contribution.
4. *Note Purchase Agreement (NPA):* Under the NPA 2016, entered between RBI and IMF, RBI has agreed to invest an amount equivalent to USD 10 billion in SDR denominated notes issued by IMF.
5. *Increase in quota share of India in IMF:* Under IMF's New Arrangements to Borrow (NAB) and quota increase to the IMF, India's commitment to IMF is SDR 4,440.91 million.*
6. *Investment in bonds issued by IIFC (UK):* The Reserve Bank has the mandate to invest up to USD 5 billion, in the bonds issued by the India Infrastructure Finance Company (UK) Limited. As at end-September 2018, the amount invested in such bonds stood at USD 2,100 million.
7. *SAARC Swap Arrangement between India and Bhutan:* Bhutan had availed USD 100 million on May 10, 2018 for 3 months which was rolled over for a period of 3 months on August 10, 2018.

FOREIGN DIRECT INVESTMENT

Foreign Direct Investment (FDI) is investment made in a country by a foreign investor (generally by a MNC) in order to control the ownership of an entity or business enterprise. As per OECD benchmark definition of FDI, FDI inflows should be counted from 10% stock or asset ownership in a company.[13] Based on Arvind Mayaram committee recommendations, India too accepted this definition in June, 2014. An investor may be allowed to invest below 10% and this can be treated as FDI subject to the condition that the FDI stake is raised to 10% or beyond within 1 year from the date of the first purchase. Any investment by way of equity shares, compulsorily convertible preference shares/debentures less than 10% is treated as foreign institutional investment (FII) or foreign portfolio investment (FPI).[14] So, broadly foreign investment is categorized as FDI and FII (Table 19.3).

Types of FDI

There are three types of FDI.

Greenfield FDI

It is a type of investment in which a parent company creates a subsidiary in the host country, builds its operations from very beginning or scratch. Example of greenfield FDI are McDonald's, Hyundai India, Pepsi India, etc.

*For detailed discussion on IMF Quota, please refer to Chapter 20 WTO, International Economic Institutions and Regional Trade Blocks.

TABLE 19.3 Difference Between FDI and FII

Sr. No.	Foreign Direct Investment	Foreign Institutional Investment
1	It goes directly into machines, i.e., in the production of goods and services.	It goes into hedge funds, short-term equities, and securities, etc.
2	It has long-term perspective.	It has short-term perspective.
3	It contributes into GDP of the country by way of production of goods and services.	The GDP of a nation rises because of economic activity or increase in production. The FII does not go into production activities but in short-term equities and can be recalled by the investor at any time. However, the profit and losses and the taxes imposed on such investments (e.g., capital gain tax) may add or subtract from a country's GDP. But the amount will be too small as compared to the contributions made by FDI.
4	It is stable in nature and there is hardly any threat of capital flight.	It is generally volatile in nature and threat of capital flight is always there in the eventuality of economic slowdown or political instability or because of herd behavior of short-term capital. Tobin Tax was suggested by James Tobin to discourage capital flight.
5	It depends upon the macroeconomic profile of the host nation and economic and political stability.	It depends upon the arbitrage and hedging variations across different parts of the world. It also depends upon the capital liberalization measures adopted by a nation to attract such capital.
6	It is of different types like Greenfield investment, Brownfield investment, and Joint ventures.	It is also called hot money and takes the form of hedge funds.

Brownfield FDI

It is the investment in which the MNC acquires the shares of an existing company in the host country. For example, Ranbaxy in India was acquired by Daiichi Sankyo of Japan in 2008.

Joint Venture

In this model of FDI, the foreign company and local company join hands to share investment, technology, profits, etc., on the basis of an agreement. For example, Hero Honda.

Routes of FDI in India

There are two routes of FDI in India.

Automatic Route of RBI

FDI is allowed under the automatic route without prior approval either of the Government or the Reserve Bank of India (RBI) in all activities/sectors as specified in the consolidated FDI Policy, issued by the Government of India from time to time.[15] The Indian company receiving FDI under either the automatic route or the government route is required to comply with provisions of the FDI policy including reporting the FDI and issue of shares to the RBI. Investor needs to follow a two-stage reporting procedure. First, within 30 days of receipt of share application money/amount of consideration from the non-resident investor, the Indian company is required to report to the foreign exchange department, regional office concerned of the RBI, under whose jurisdiction its Registered Office is located; and second, upon issue of shares to non-resident investors the company is required to submit required documentation with foreign exchange department, regional office concerned of the RBI. There are many sectors in India where foreign investors are allowed to invest up to 100%, for example, Food Product Retail Trading, Broadcasting Carriage Services, Construction Development, Industrial Parks—new and existing, Trading-Wholesale, Trading-E-commerce, etc.

Government Route

Foreign investment in activities not covered under the automatic route requires prior approval of the government. Proposals for foreign investment under government route are considered by respective administrative ministry/department. In case of proposals involving total foreign equity inflow of more than ₹5,000 crore, approval of Cabinet Committee on Economic Affairs is required. FDI from Pakistan is also placed under government route. Investment in defense up to 49% is allowed under automatic route and beyond 49% is through government route.

Characteristic Features of FDI in India

1. India has emerged as one of the largest and most sought after FDI destinations in the world. The FDI receipts in India have increased by around 18 times from $2463 million in 2000–01 to $46,034 million in 2022–23.*
2. In sector-wise classification, Computer Software and Hardware in India attracts maximum FDI, followed by service sector and trading. The top five sectors get nearly 60% of FDI in the country (Table 19.4).
3. Singapore and Mauritius have emerged as the largest FDI donor to the country. These two nations constitute around two-third of FDI in the country. The United States, the United States, and Cayman Islands occupy third, fourth, and fifth position, respectively.

TABLE 19.4 Sectors Attracting Highest FDI Equity Inflows (In US$ Million) 2022–23

Ranks	Sector	2022–23 (April – March)	Percentage Share
1	Computer Software & Hardware	9,394	20.41
2	Services Sector*	8,707	18.91
3	Trading	4,792	10.41
4	Drugs & Pharmaceuticals	2,058	4.47
5	Automobile Industry	1,902	4.13
	Total FDI Equity Inflows	46,034	100%

Source: FDI DIPP Statistics accessed from https://dipp.gov.in/publications/fdi-statistics as on 15 April, 2024.

*Services sector includes Financial, Banking, Insurance, Non-Financial / Business, Outsourcing, R&D, Courier, Tech. Testing and Analysis, Other

TABLE 19.5 Top FDI donors to India 2022–23 (in US$ Million)

Country	2022–23 (April – March)	Percentage Share
Singapore	17,203	37.37
Mauritius	6,134	13.32
The USA	6,044	13.13
UAE	3,353	7.28
Netherland	2,498	5.43
Total FDI Equity Inflows from all Countries	46,034	100

Source: FDI DIPP Statistics accessed from https://dipp.gov.in/publications/fdi-statistics as on 15 April, 2024.

UAE and Netherlands have emerged biggest donors because of round tripping or treaty shopping. The investment belongs to other developed regions like the United States and Europe but routed through tax havens* (like Mauritius, Singapore, the Netherlands, etc.) because such nations have signed double tax avoidance agreement (DTAA) with India (Table 19.5).

4. In India, peninsular India receives around 50% of FDI. The top FDI receiver states (in terms of receipts of FDI in RBI's regional office) in the country are Maharashtra, Karnataka, Gujarat, Delhi and Tamil Nadu.

Advantages of Foreign Direct Investment

FDI Fills the Three Gaps

Economists in the decades of 1960s and 1970s developed a two-gap model wherein they explained the saving constraints and foreign exchange constraints for the underdevelopment of less developed nations.** In 1990s, there has been increasing interest in the three-gap model introducing the fiscal constraint as the third gap that limits the growth prospects of developing nations.*** The two-gap model explains the saving gap and foreign exchange gap. In a country like India, the *saving gap* emanates from the low per capita income level of the masses. Unlike in the west where more than 80% of savings are done by the corporate sector and remaining is done by household and government sector, the situation is reverse in India as around 60% of national savings are done by household sector. Low income level and savings transform into low investment in the economy that leads to lower than potential growth.

---

*A tax haven is a country with very minimal, almost zero tax regime.

**Chenery & Bruno (1962), Chenery & Strout (1966), Mckinnon (1964), and Weisskopf (1972) made important contributions in the development of two-gap model.

***Bacha (1990), Solimano (1990), and Taylor (1993) have done a significant research in the development of three-gap model.

The foreign exchange gap occurs due to persistent trade deficit. It is the gap between import requirements for a given level of production and foreign exchange earnings. With scarce or limited foreign exchange resources, a country is not in a position to make essential imports or buy significant technology or capital imports. The larger trade gap undermines productive investment due to limited imports of capital goods needed for investment.[16] The developing countries because of their perennial nature of trade deficit generally face such type of situation and it is where the role of FDI comes into picture. The capital inflows constitute net additions to a less developing country's productive resources thus increasing its growth rate. *The fiscal gap* reflects the inability of a developing country's government to finance the public investment required to support a given level of financial output. Higher fiscal deficit also leads to inflation and adversely affects the BOPs. The developing country governments can guide the FDI to go into such channels, thereby plugging the fiscal gap, which will ultimately ensure better growth returns.

FDI and the Technology Transfer

Posner in 1961, developed the technology gap theory wherein he describes an advantage enjoyed by the country that introduces new goods in a market.[17] As a consequence of research activity and entrepreneurship, new goods are produced and the innovating country enjoys a monopoly until the other countries learn to produce these goods, in the meantime they have to import them.[18] There are further two lags, one is demand lag that is time taken by the local market (of importing nation) to accept the goods and the second is imitation, which is nothing but time taken by indigenous entrepreneurs (of importing nation) to manufacture or copy the same product. Consequently, a technology gap emerges between developed and less developed nations. The MNCs fill such gap via technology transfers. During the post WTO phase, the nations have witnessed a mass movement of FDI from developed nations into developing economies either in the form of establishing R&D plants or via contract R&D and contract manufacturing. The main reason for migration of FDI is intense competition among MNCs to provide innovative products to the emerging markets so as to take advantage of capturing the market early. Another important reason is the cost advantage in emerging markets where the producer is able to get cost effective, highly efficient manpower. In the post 1990 period, the huge FDI inflows in China, Thailand, Indonesia, Brazil, and India can be attributed to such factors. In India, the pharmaceutical and IT sectors have witnessed many contract agreements between MNCs and indigenous manufacturers in the field of R&D and manufacturing.

Efficiency-Seeking FDI

FDI can help create higher skilled and better-paid jobs, promote the transfer of knowledge, raise productivity, and diversify and upgrade the value-added component of exports—all of which affect a country's ability to integrate with global value chains.[19] According to British economist John Dunning, FDI that comes into a country has different motivations, for example, natural resource-seeking investment, market-seeking investment, strategic asset-seeking investment, and finally efficiency-seeking investment.[20] This last category—efficiency-seeking FDI—is particularly important for countries looking to integrate into the global economy and move up the value chain. This type of FDI has many advantages—it is not only export oriented, but also leads to export diversification. It can become more than a source of capital, creating new jobs that are more diversified and with greater productivity and value. The efficiency-seeking FDI can also lead to expertise and technology transfers, thus filling the technology gap in the host nations and leading to R&D and knowledge spillovers.

In India too FDI in automobile sectors has helped channel technical and material know-how into production processes and facilitated the growth of this very industry in the last two decades. The industry has attracted FDI worth US$ 21.38 billion during the period April 2000 to March 2019 and accounts for around 6% of the country's GDP. Indian auto industry is fourth largest in the world. It has the potential to generate up to US$ 300 billion in annual revenue by 2026, create 65 million additional jobs and contribute over 12% to India's gross domestic product.[21]

FDI Leads to Human Capital Enrichment

A number of studies suggest that human capital levels and spillovers are closely interrelated with technology transfers. Empirical evidences too indicate that MNCs tend to provide more training and other upgrading of human capital than do domestic enterprises. Such improvement in the workforce can have extra effects as the trained labor moves to other firms or they become entrepreneurs. In a country like India, where we have a significant number of young workforce, the efforts in human capital enrichment may unleash the potential to garner the benefits of demographic dividend. However, it is to be noted that the beneficial effects of training provided by FDI can supplement, but not replace, a generic increase in skill levels. The spillover effect of human capital will be smooth and soaring if government invest much in the education of the masses. Indeed the benefits of technology and human capital spillover could gain effectiveness when policies of technological and educational improvement are undertaken conjointly.[22]

FDI and Competition Enhancement

The presence of MNCs stimulates domestic competition and thereby leading eventually to higher productivity, lower prices, and more efficient resource allocation. It is not essential that more competition always leads to lesser prices. The competitive prices mean product price tagged with quality which was earlier not available to the consumers of the host country. In the race of survival of fittest, the firms will either perform or perish. So, in order to remain in the market, they will practice cost cutting through minimal wastage and optimal utilization of resources. Such competitive environment also keeps a check on the producers not to charge exorbitant prices. In India many consumer durables are sold at competitive prices because of the intense price war among the multinationals on one side and between MNCs and domestic players on the other. Electronics, computer hardware and software parts, and auto components offer competitive prices to the consumers in India.

FDI Ensures Consumer Sovereignty

The term 'consumer sovereignty' was coined by William Harold Hutt in his book *Economists and the Public in the year 1936*. The theory elaborates that firms must keep track of what consumers want in order to stay in business.[23] The globalization has changed the paradigms of production and consumption. Goods are produced as per the tastes of the customer. The product differentiation has widened the customer basket of choices. A survey by Indian Council for Research on International Economic Relations (ICRIER) reveals that a majority of the respondents in India are willing to experiment with different brands and want more foreign brands to enter the Indian market.[24] The study revealed that FDI will promote the development of more efficient and lower cost supply chains, resulting in better quality as well as lower-priced products for consumers in India. This will increase consumer spending, which in turn, will drive growth in all sectors of the economy in a virtuous cycle.

Disadvantages of Foreign Direct Investment

The March of Oligopolies

The oligopoly is a market structure where there is a small number of big sized firms producing homogeneous but differentiated products. The large financial and technical size of the firms inhibits the entry of new players and generates a market structure where few big MNCs dominate the market and even influence the consumption patterns in the host country through vigorous marketing campaign. Such companies have a dominant market share in almost every arena of consumer segment, viz. FMCG products, computer and electrical products, automobiles, and different financial and business services. In the absence of effective regulations, they attempt to distort the market competition in their favor. For example, in the 1990s "Microsoft" was charged in the United States with malpractice as the company would make the sale of its operating systems conditional on the purchase of any other Microsoft product. In early 2000, the company was also charged by European commission with the bundling of Windows Media Player into Windows, a practice which rivals complained was destroying the market for their own products. Microsoft was penalized for millions of dollars for destroying the competition in its own favor. It has been also found that in the absence of effective regulations such companies form "cartel" and adopt discretionary measures with regard to both output and prices. The cement cartel in India is the example of such malpractices.

Capturing the Host Country's Market

MNCs also make another tactic of capturing the host country's market by acquisition of shares through Brownfield FDI. Brownfield FDI does not make additions to investments but substitutes local investment by foreign investment thus threatening the local production patterns. For example, the Indian pharmaceutical industry is known in the world for cost-effective generic manufacturing. In 2008, Ranbaxy Laboratories was acquired by Daiichi-Sankyo of Japan. It was followed by Germany's Fresenius Kabi acquiring Dabur Pharma, French drug major Sanofi Aventis buying Shanta Biotech, US-based Mylan acquiring Matrix Lab, and Agila, US-based Hospira acquiring Orchid Chemicals and US-based Abbott Laboratories acquiring Piramal Healthcare. Within the span of 3–4 years, seven Indian well-known pharmaceutical companies were acquired by MNCs in order to benefit from vast Indian market size. There is also an apprehension that once Indian companies are taken over by foreign companies, there will not be any effort to develop new low-cost medicines for the poor. Global pharma companies invest a negligible amount on R&D, often lesser than the domestic pharma companies and even lower than the public sector firms in India.[25] Further, their intention is to gain control over the local market and not to cater the objective or the purpose for which FDI is allowed.[26] Keeping in view such ill effects, the government removed Brownfield FDI in pharmaceuticals from the automatic route and placed it under government route.

The Question of Access to Technology

The technology transfer is often cited as the prominent advantage of FDI to the host country. The National Manufacturing Competitiveness Council of India had made some observations in its "Report of the Prime Minister's Group" (NMCC 2008) regarding the excessively high cost of technology, old technology being transferred through FDI, and the negligible emphasis on whether technology transfer is taking place or on its appropriateness in the Indian context. Nothing has changed since then. It has been found that the technology, while continually being an exclusive asset of the licensor (MNC), is allowed to be used by the licensee for a limited period of time for a specific purpose under various restrictive conditions related to its use and dissemination. The "pricing" and "contract termination" is decided as per the licensor's choice. The technology has to be completely returned on the expiry or termination of the contract. Unfortunately, the questions of absorption or acquisition of technology by the local party is not recognized as a necessary issue either by the licensee, that is, the related Indian subsidiary or by Indian Government. The government is indeed keener on the financial gains related to foreign investments. The real "absorption" of technology in the economy calls for conscious policy efforts and directives.[27]

The Threat to Sovereignty

One of the most important issues states face is the growing power of the multinational corporation at the expense of state sovereignty. The big financial size of MNCs makes them accessible to political circles and maneuver policies in their favor, a concept called crony capitalism.* In India, Dabhol fiasco[28] in the 1990s and infamous absconding of Warren Andeson, the chief of Union Carbide in India after the infamous Bhopal gas tragedy[29] during 1980s are few of many incidents that remind us how unabashedly politicians and MNCs build nexus of plunder and loot. Not only that the political sovereignty is under threat but the consumer sovereignty also gets confiscated. The vigorous marketing tactics and advertisements through brand ambassadors affect consumer behavior in buying a particular product. Man is a social animal and his consumption behavior is not absolute but relative. Bandwagon effect** plays a dominant role in the choices a consumer makes while buying a particular product. MNCs thus promote a culture of consumerism that emphasizes exploitation, not utilization of resources, and leads to unsustainable development of societies.***

---

*Crony capitalism is an economy in which big private corporates and multinationals thrive as a return of money amassed through a nexus (based on quid pro quo) between the business class and the political class.

**It is a psychological phenomenon in which people do something primarily because other people are doing it, regardless of their own beliefs. The consumption behavior thus becomes a relative phenomenon rather than absolute.

***Charlotte McDonald in his famous article 'How many Earths do we need?' published in BBC News Magazine on 16 June 2015 stated that 'If everyone on earth lived like the average American, we would need around 4.6 planets to support us.'

Capital Account Convertibility

In international economic literature, we generally talk about current account convertibility and capital account convertibility. The current account convertibility is the freedom to convert domestic currency into foreign currency and vice versa for the *current account transactions* (i.e., both goods account and services account) at market-determined rates without any restrictions. The capital account convertibility on the other hand is the freedom to convert domestic currency into foreign currency and vice versa for the *capital account transactions* (i.e., investments, debts, banking capital, NRI deposits, etc.) at market-determined rates and that also without any restrictions. India achieved convertibility on current account way back in 1994. But the fuller convertibility on capital account remained pending. What if, the country goes for fuller capital account convertibility regime? Before going into the detail of India's stance on capital account convertibility, let us have a brief discussion on the merits and demerits of capital account convertibility.

Case for Capital Account Convertibility

1. India is a capital-deficit nation. Free access to global capital markets increases available investible resources especially FDI which augments investment and growth. Such capital flows generate positive spillover effects in the form of technology, skills, and knowledge.
2. It also helps developing international linkages and ensures better and more efficient allocation of the global pool of savings to the more productive uses. From the individual country's perspective, the benefits take the form of increase in both the potential pool of investable funds and the access of domestic residents to foreign capital markets. From the viewpoint of the international economy, open capital accounts support the multilateral trading system by broadening the channels through which developed and developing countries alike can finance trade and investment and attain higher levels of income.[30]
3. Open capital accounts facilitate portfolio diversification by investors in developed as well as developing countries.[31] It enhances capital widening and make capital market more efficient.
4. Capital account convertibility ensures fiscal, monetary, and capital market discipline in the host country. It is because the success of capital account convertibility rests on sound macroeconomic policy, it creates a sort of commitment for the country concerned to ensure better macroeconomic management, lest it is punished by the investors. The capital market fulfills an important supervisory function over economic policy.[32]

Case Against Capital Account Convertibility

1. The empirical evidence from certain nations suggests that there is no necessary link between increased capital inflows and full convertibility on capital account. China is the classic example in this regard as it has managed to attract huge capital inflows because of conducive investment policies, huge infrastructure, and domestic demand and as Rajwade puts in … "incidentally, China's success in exports owes a lot to FDI in special economic zones".[33] Jagdish Bhagwati, the celebrated international economist also stated that "after all, China and Japan, different in politics and sociology as well as historical

BOX 19.4 The Impossible Trinity

The "impossible trinity" or the Trilemma is a fundamental contribution of the Mundell-Fleming framework. It states that policy makers in open economies often face a three-way trade-off between the contradictory policy objectives namely, a stable exchange rate, an independent monetary policy designed to target domestic inflation, and open capital markets. A central bank can pursue only two of the policy objectives and achieving the three policy goals simultaneously is impossible. For example, a country with fixed exchange rate system raises the interest rate (through tight monetary policy) to control domestic inflation. High interest rates will attract foreign capital (through arbitrage), which will consequently lead to appreciation of currency which may hurt the exports in the short run. RBI will now intervene in foreign exchange market by buying foreign reserves (may be dollars) and selling rupee (a move called sterilization) to control appreciation of rupee. But releasing the rupee will defeat the very purpose of controlling inflation.

Source: Sengupta, R. (March 2015). The impossible trinity: Where does India stand? WP-2015–05, *IGIDR*. and Obstfeld, M., Shambaugh, J.C., & Taylor, A.M. (2005). The Trilemma in history: Tradeoffs among exchange rates, monetary policies, and capital mobility. *Review of Economics and Statistics, 87* (3), pp.423–438.

experience, have registered remarkable growth rates. Western Europe's return to prosperity was also achieved without capital account convertibility." According to him, it is a nation's policy regarding FDI rather than capital account convertibility, which can be a game changer.[34]

2. Short-term capital flows also termed as hot money are sensitive to macroeconomic conditions like fiscal conditions, inflation management, BOPs, etc. Any macroeconomic shock may cause a cessation or reversal of capital flows. Further capital flows are prone to volatilities derived from information asymmetries, herd behavior, panics, etc., which may be far divested from the fundamental macroeconomic strengths. The experience of Mexico in 1994, East Asian crisis in 1997, Russia in 1998, Brazil in 1999, Argentina in 2001, Iceland in 2008, and very recently the Eurozone crisis have demonstrated the risk of capital account liberalization. As a result of "Impossible Trinity" the full-fledged capital account convertibility demands adoption of flexible exchange rate system, which along with volatile capital flows may prove to be disastrous for the economy (see Box 19.4). But an economy like India which is vulnerable in many fronts cannot take such risks. Even the IMF which was strong votary for capital account convertibility has taken a new institution view after the global financial crisis and Eurozone crisis. In December 2012, the new institutional view of IMF was that—full capital account liberalization may not be an appropriate goal for a nation all the time and capital flow management measures must be in the macroeconomic policy toolkit. The IMF now recognizes that capital flows carry risks and that the liberalization of capital flows before nations reach a certain threshold of financial and institutional development can accentuate those risks. It also acknowledges that under certain circumstances, cross-border capital flows should be regulated to avoid the worst effects of capital flow surges and sudden stops. Very recently, the World Bank has also advocated the use of capital control measures as a last resort to help mitigate a financial crisis and stabilize macroeconomic developments.[35]

India's Approach Toward Capital Account Convertibility

After the economic setback of 1991, the country went for convertibility on current account. The move was in line with Article VIII of the Articles of Agreement of IMF. Subsequently, capital account transactions were also relaxed gradually. The capital control measures were relaxed for foreign investors, both direct and portfolio, non-resident depositors, and Indian corporates which accepted external commercial borrowings (ECB). However, there were restrictions on Indian citizens and corporates to send capital abroad and also on the transfer of capital associated with banks and non-banking financial companies. Meanwhile, RBI established a *committee on capital account convertibility headed by S.S. Tarapore* which submitted its report in May 1997. The committee was of the view that implementing capital account convertibility would increase capital inflows but it would make it difficult to implement an effective domestic monetary policy (See 'Impossibe Trinity in Box 19.4). Therefore, India should not go for fuller capital account convertibility until weaknesses in the economy are completely eliminated. The report suggested a steady approach toward full capital account convertibility, that is, in three phases: Phase I (1997–98), Phase II (1998–99), and Phase III (1999–2000). The transition from one phase to the next should be made, only if certain preconditions are met. The preconditions were reduction of fiscal deficit (fiscal discipline), keeping the inflation in a 3–5% range (price discipline) and reforming the financial sector, including reduction of non-performing assets (financial market discipline). However, in July 1997, the East Asian crisis erupted which subsided the enthusiasm for capital account convertibility in the country.

On March 20, 2006, RBI established a committee on Fuller Capital Account Convertibility headed by S.S. Tarapore or *Tarapore Committee II*, to study the status of capital account convertibility in India and further recommendations. The committee submitted its report on July 31, 2006. After reviewing the existing capital controls, the committee detailed a broad 5-year time frame for movement toward fuller convertibility in three phases: Phase I (2006–07); Phase II (2007–08 to 2008–09); and Phase III (2009–10 to 2010–11). It recommended the meeting of certain indicators/targets as a concomitant to the movement in meeting FRBM targets; shifting from the present measure of fiscal deficit to a measure of the Public Sector Borrowing Requirement (PSBR); segregating government debt management and monetary policy operations through the setting up of the Office of Public Debt independent of the RBI; imparting greater autonomy and transparency in the conduct of monetary policy; and slew of reforms in banking sector including a single banking legislation and reduction in the share of government/RBI in the capital of public sector banks; keeping the current account deficit to GDP ratio under 3%; and evolving appropriate indicators of adequacy of reserves to cover not only import requirements, but also liquidity risks associated with present types of capital flows, short-term debt obligations; and broader measures including solvency.[36,37]

Summary

1. The BOPs is the systematic record of economic transactions of a nation with the rest of the world in a single accounting year. India's BOP can be classified into two major accounts, that is, the current account and capital account. The current account comprises export and import of goods/merchandise and balance in invisible account. The capital account comprises debt or equity of short and long-term nature. India's trade deficit has experienced a huge rise since independence. India's current account has also mostly remained under deficit since independence. The country's capital account is not only in surplus but also overcompensates its current account generating overall surplus.
2. Exchange rate is the price of one currency in terms of another currency. There are broadly three methods of determining the exchange rate. Fixed exchange rate, flexible exchange rate, and system of managed float. In case of fixed exchange rate system, the currency value is fixed vis-à-vis other currency or to a basket of currencies or with some metal like gold. Under the flexible or floating system, the exchange rate is determined by the interaction of demand and supply forces. Under the system of managed float, the currencies are allowed to float freely within a band and in case of any exigency the central bank intervenes in the foreign exchange market. Under flexible exchange rate and managed float system currency depreciates and appreciates depending on the strength of demand and supply forces. When demand for foreign currency is more (or supply of foreign currency is less), the home currency depreciates. When demand for foreign currency is less (or supply of foreign currency is more), the home currency appreciates. India has four different types of exchange rate system since independence: Phase I: The Par value System (1947–1971); Phase II: The Pegged Regime (1971–1992); Liberalized exchange rate management system (1992–93); and Managed float system (1993 onward).
3. Foreign exchange reserves (FERs) are the international reserve assets held by the central bank in foreign currencies. The plentiful of FERs instill confidence in RBI's intervention in the foreign exchange market apart from other benefits. India's foreign exchange reserves have increased from US$ 0.637 billion in 1960–61 to US$ 424.5 billion in 2017–18. The utilization of FERs by RBI is guided by liquidity, safety, and return optimization.
4. FDI is investment made in a country by a foreign investor (generally by MNC) in order to control the ownership of an entity or business enterprise. FDI is different from FII as the former leads to production of goods and services and is of long term nature whereas the later goes into short-term equities and hedge funds. FDI can be in the form of Greenfield FDI, Brownfield FDI, and Joint venture. It can enter India either through automatic route of RBI or government route. For last many years, India has become one of the most attractive FDI destinations in the world. Service sector is the largest recipient of FDI in the country and Singapore is the largest donor of FDI to India. There are many benefits of FDI. First, FDI fills three gaps, saving gap, foreign exchange gap, and fiscal gap. Second, FDI leads to technology transfer to the host nations. Third, it promotes efficiency in economic activities of the host country. Fourth, it enriches human capital through professional work profile and training. Fifth, it increases competition. Sixth, it ensures consumer sovereignty through price competition and widening of markets. The limitations of FDI include, the march of oligopolies which distort market in their own favor in the absence of effective regulations; capturing the host country's market mainly through acquisitions and takeover; improper access to technology to Indian players by foreign MNCs and threat to political sovereignty due to nexus between MNCs and policy makers; and erosion of consumer sovereignty due to vigorous marketing tactics by MNCs or bandwagon effect.
5. The capital account convertibility (CAC) is the freedom to convert domestic currency into foreign currency and vice versa for the capital account transactions (i.e., investments, debts, banking capital, NRI deposits, etc.) at market-determined rates and that also without any restrictions. The benefits of CAC include inflow of foreign capital, effective linkage with other nations, portfolio diversification, and financial market discipline. However, it is not necessary that CAC promotes capital inflows. For example, in China it was government policies toward

investment that made it an attractive FDI destination. Short-term capital may lead to capital flight and make an economy vulnerable. Finally, because of "Impossible Trinity" the full-fledged capital account convertibility demands adoption of flexible exchange rate system which along with volatile capital flows may prove to be disastrous for the economy. The government constituted S.S. Tarapore Committee I and II in 1997 and 2006, respectively, with regard to India's readiness to pursue fuller capital account convertibility regime.

Endnotes

1. Pillania, R.K. (2008). An exploratory study of Indian foreign trade. *Journal of Applied Economic Sciences*.Vol. III, Issue 3, No. 5, pp.281–292.
2. Economic Survey, 2018–19. Department of Economic Affairs. Ministry of Finance. Govt. of India. p. 184.
3. Jalan, B. (1992). Indian Economy-Problems and Prospects. *Penguin*. New Delhi.
4. *World Bank Database*. Retrieved from https://data.worldbank.org (Accessed on March 16, 2019).
5. Dua & Ranjan (2010). Exchange Rate Policy and Modelling in India, RBI. Accessed from https://www.rbi.org.in (November 22, 2018).
6. Tendulkar, S.D. & Srinivasan, T.N. (2003 Reintegrating India with the world economy. *Institute for International Economics*. p.16.
7. *IMF and current account convertibility*. Retrieved from https://www.imf.org (Accessed on December 1, 2018).
8. *Guidelines for foreign exchange reserve management*. Accessed from https://www.imf.org (Accessed on December 1, 2018).
9. Obstfeld, Shambaugh, and Taylor (2008). Financial stability, the trilemma, and international reserves. CEPR. Accessed from http://eml.berkeley.edu (Accessed on December 1, 2018).
10. *IMF: Assessing reserve adequacy*, accessed from https://www.imf.org (Accessed on December 1, 2018).
11. RBI: *Half Yearly Report on Management of Foreign Exchange Reserves*, Oct-Mar, 2016.
12. RBI: *Half Yearly Report on Management of Foreign Exchange Reserves*, April-September 2018.
13. OECD Benchmark Definition of Foreign Direct Investment FOURTH EDITION 2008, accessed from https://www.oecd.org on March 19, 2020.
14. Recommendations of the Arvind Mayaram committee on rationalizing the FDI/FII definition accessed from http://dea.gov.in (Accessed on March 4, 2019).
15. Automatic Route. Retrieved from https://www.rbi.org.in (Accessed on March 4, 2016).
16. Chenery, B.H., & Strout, A.M. (1966). Foreign assistance and economic development. *The American Economic Review 56* (4), 679–733.
17. Posner, M.V. (1961). International trade and technical change. *Oxford Economic Papers 13* (3), 323–341.
18. Gandolfo, G. (2014). *International trade theory and policy*. New York: Springer, p.166.
19. World Economic Forum. (2015). *How can we maximize the benefits of FDI?* Retrieved from https://www.weforum.org (Accessed on March 5, 2016).
20. Dunning, J. (1980). Toward an eclectic theory of international production: Some empirical tests. *Journal of International Business Studies 11* (1), 9–31.
21. Indian Automobiles Industry. Retrieved from http://indiainbusiness.nic.in (Accessed on March 14, 2019).
22. OECD. (2002). *Foreign Direct Investment for Development- Maximising Benefits, Minimising Costs*. Retrieved from https://www.oecd.org (Accessed on October 16, 2016).
23. Hutt, William (1940). The Concept of Consumers' Sovereignty". *The Economic Journal*. Wiley. 50 (197): 66–77.
24. Mukherjee et al. (2011). Impact of Retail FDI Policy on Indian Consumers and way forward", ICRIER Policy Series, No. 5.
25. DIPP seeks to restrict FDI in brownfield pharma projects. *The Hindu Business Line*. September 11, 2013.
26. Foreign direct investment in Indian pharma sector causing concern. *The Pharma Letter*. April 19, 2018.
27. Verma, S. (2018). Pursuing FDI for technology is 'Access' enough?. *EPW* liii (29), pp.17–19.
28. The Real Story of Dabhol, *Outlook*, 30 April, 2001.
29. Bhopal gas tragedy: How Warren Anderson got away from our grasp, *India Today*, November 1, 2014.

30. Fischer, S. (1997). Capital account liberalization and the role of the IMF. In IMF Seminar, "Asia and the IMF" Retrieved from https://www.imf.org (Accessed on October 6, 2016).
31. Padmanabhan, G. (2015). Is India ready for full Capital Account Convertibility? Retrieved from https://rbi.org.in (Accessed on July 5, 2016).
32. Fischer, Cooper, Dornbusch and others. (2007). *Should the IMF pursue capital account convertibility, essays in international finance.* No. 207. Retrieved from ies.princeton.edu (Accessed on October 6, 2016).
33. Rajwade AV (2007). Risks and Rewards of Capital Account Convertibility. *EPW*, Vol. 42 (1).
34. Bhagwati, J. (1998). The Capital Myth: The Difference between Trade in Widgets and Dollars", Foreign affairs, vol. 77, No. 3.
35. Padmanabhan, G. (2015). Is India ready for full Capital Account Convertibility? Retrieved from https://rbi.org.in (Accessed on July 5, 2016).
36. *Economic Survey. 2006–07.* Department of Economic Affairs. Ministry of Finance. p.110.
37. *Report of the Committee on Fuller Capital Account Convertibility*, Retrieved from https://rbidocs.rbi.org.in (Accesed on May 2, 2019).

CHAPTER **20**

WTO, International Economic Institutions and Regional Trade Blocks

ayaṃ nijaḥ paro veti gaṇanā laghucetasām
udāracaritānāṃ tu vasudhaiva kuṭumbakam

This is mine, that is his, say the small minded,
The wise believe that the entire world is a family.

—Maha Upanishad

Introduction

In today's modern world, no nation exists in economic isolation. Different aspects of a country's economy-its agriculture, industry, trade, monetary, and developmental policies are linked with that of other trading partners. This linkage has been strengthened with increased flow of merchandise, services, and capital transfers. Such strong is the bond of a nation with other economies that it is not possible to formulate economic policies without keeping in mind the policies of other nations. The high degree of economic interdependence among nations reflects the historical evolution of world's economic and political order, especially after World War II. The three major international economic organizations that have shaped the modern economic system of the world for the past several decades are the World Trade Organization, World Bank and the International Monetary Fund. In this chapter, an attempt has been made to discuss the following pertinent topics in detail:

- World Trade Organization, its working and agreements
- World Bank Group, its functions and relationship with India
- International Monetary Fund, its functions and relationship with India
- Regional Trade Blocs

World Trade Organization

The World War I, the great depression and the World War II had weakened the international trading system. During the post–World War II period, few nations came together to discuss measures to foster economic ties across the globe. On October 30, 1947, the General Agreement on Tariffs and Trade (GATT) was signed by 23 nations at Geneva. On January 01, 1948, GATT entered into force.[1] India was a founding member of GATT. From 1948–1994, GATT provided the rules for much of world trade and presided over periods that saw some of the highest growth rates in international commerce.[2] Eight rounds of GATT were concluded from 1948–1994 and finally on January 01, 1995, WTO was formed. The WTO's creation marked the biggest reform

BOX 20.1 Ministerial Conference

Ministerial conference is the topmost decision-making body of the WTO, which usually meets after every two years. It brings together all members of the WTO and takes decisions on all matters under any of the multilateral trade agreements. So far, 11 ministerial conference meetings have taken place in different parts of the world.

Sr. No.	Year	Venue
1	9–13 Dec 1996	Singapore
2	18–20 May 1998	Geneva
3	Nov 30–Dec 3, 1999	Seattle
4	9–13 Nov 2001	Doha
5	10–14 Sept 2003	Cancun
6	13–18 Dec 2005	Hong Kong
7	30 Nov–2 Dec 2009	Geneva
8	15–17 Dec 2011	Geneva
9	3–6 Dec 2013	Bali
10	15–19 Dec 2015	Nairobi
11	10–13 Dec 2017	Buenos Aires
12	12 June–17 June 2022	Geneva
13	26 Feb–2 March 2023	Abu Dhabi

Source: Compiled by author

of International Trade since after the World War II. It also brought to reality in an updated form the failed attempt in 1948 to create an International Trade Organization (ITO).*

WTO was the brainchild of eighth GATT round (1986–1994) which started at Uruguay and ended at Geneva (popularly called as Uruguay round). Essentially, the WTO is a place where member country's governments go to try to sort out the trade problems they face with each other. The WTO was born out of negotiations, and everything the WTO does is the result of negotiations. There are 164 members of WTO since 29 July 2016. WTO is headquartered at Geneva and Roberto Azevado is the director general of WTO. The ministerial conference comprising trade/commerce ministers is the highest decision-making body of WTO, which meets generally after every 2 years (Box 20.1). WTO is hailed as a watchdog of international trade, which facilitates smooth and swift flow of merchandise across borders and promotes multilateralism.

Difference Between GATT and WTO

1. The GATT was the result of post-war efforts to reconstruct a smooth and healthy trade and the GATT treaty came into force in 1948 with the signature of 23 members. The WTO was the result of Uruguay round negotiations and was born on January 01, 1995 with the signature of 123 nations.
2. The GATT was an ad hoc agreement, whereas WTO is a perpetual body with a permanent headquarter at Geneva.

*During the Bretton Woods conference held at New Hampshire, United States in 1944, the participant nations delved upon creating the troika of IMF, World Bank and ITO. But the attempt turned abortive and idea was postponed to establish the third organ and instead only IMF and World Bank were established in 1945. IMF and World Bank are also called Bretton Woods twins. Two years later, GATT was signed.

3. GATT was restricted to only free trade among goods whereas WTO encompasses a galaxy of items covering goods, services, investment, intellectual property, dispute settlement, and so on.

Functions of WTO

The following are the six broader functions of WTO:[3]

1. Administering WTO trade agreements;
2. Providing forum for trade negotiations;
3. Handling trade disputes;
4. Monitoring national trade policies;
5. Technical assistance and training for developing countries;
6. Cooperation with other international organization.

The WTO Agreements

The WTO's rules—the agreements—are the result of negotiations between the members. Through these agreements, WTO members operate a non-discriminatory trading system that spells out their rights and their obligations (Box 20.2).

BOX 20.2 What Is Most Favoured Nation (MFN) Status?

Under the WTO agreements, countries cannot normally discriminate between their trading partners. If one country is granted a trade concession such as, for example, lower import duties, then all WTO members must be extended the same concessions. The WTO says that if a country extends favor to another country, the country must return the favor. Though MFN sounds like special treatment, it actually means non-discrimination—treating virtually everyone equally. This principle is known as the Most Favoured Nation treatment. India has accorded "Most Favoured Nation" status to all WTO members, including Pakistan, in accordance with provisions of Article I of GATT in 1996. Despite repeated promises, Pakistan has never granted MFN status to India.

India in February 15, 2019 revoked MFN status after Pulwama attack. India's move is in accordance with its domestic Foreign Trade (Development and Regulation) Act that allows it to prohibit, restrict, or regulate the import or export of goods. It also conforms to the global trade norms, which allows countries any action that they consider necessary for the protection of their essential security interests. Revoking the MFN status to India means India can levy whatever import tariffs it wants, as India has done by hiking custom duty on all imports from Pakistan to 200 pe cent. India's total trade with Pakistan stood at $2.4 billion in 2017–18, with just $488.56 million of this being imports from Pakistan. Pakistan's exports to India made up only 2.1% of its total exports in 2017–18. India's major imports are fruits and nuts, gypsum, sulfur, finished leather, ores, mineral oils, and cement. Revoking Pakistan's MFN status seems to be more of a symbolic move, aimed at signalling to the world the change in India's stance regarding Pakistan, rather than one aimed at doing economic damage.

Sources:

1. Understanding WTO. (2007). The GATT Years: From Havana To Marrakesh, WTO Publication, pp. 10–11.
2. What is Most Favoured Nation status? *The Hindu*, February 16, 2019.
3. What is the "Most Favoured Nation" status that India just revoked from Pakistan? India Today, February 15, 2019.

Let us have a detailed discussion on such agreements:

- General Agreement on Tariff and Trade (GATT)
- Agreements on Agriculture (AOA)
- Trade-related Aspects of Intellectual Property Rights System (TRIPS)
- General Agreement on Trade in Services (GATS)
- Standards and safety
- Agreement on Textile and Clothing (ATC)
- Anti-dumping, Countervailing duties and safeguards
- Non-tariff Barriers
- Trade-related investment measures (TRIMs)
- Plurilateral agreements
- Trade policy reviews: ensuring transparency

General Agreement on Tariff and Trade

Tariffs not only hinder international trade but also lead to its distortion. Accordingly, the individual countries are committed on specific categories of goods and services, which include commitments to "cut and bind" their customs duty rates on imports of goods. In some cases, tariffs are being cut to zero. There is also a significant increase in the number of "bound" tariffs by both developed and developing countries. Bound tariffs are duty rates that are committed in the WTO and are difficult to be increased beyond a committed rate.[4] Tariffs on all agricultural products can be termed as bound tariffs. Developed nations reduced tariffs in a phased manner. Countries also agreed to eliminate import duties and other charges on the trade of IT related products.

Agreement on Agriculture

The objective of the Agreement on Agriculture (AOA) is to reform trade in the sector and to make policies more market oriented. The AOA covers the following three aspects:

1. Market access
2. Domestic support
3. Export subsidies

1. *Market access*: The AOA calls for removal of quota and other non-tariff barriers (NTBs) and replacing them with tariffs and progressively reducing tariffs by a simple average of 36% by the developed countries over 6 years (year ending 2000) and by 24% by developing countries over 10 years (year ending 2004). (The newly committed tariffs and tariff quotas, covering all agricultural products, took effect in 1995.)
2. *Domestic support*: The main complaint about policies that support domestic prices, or subsidize production in some other way, is that they encourage over production. The AOA distinguishes between support programs that stimulate production directly (trade distorting), and those that are considered to have no direct effect (non-trade distorting). All trade-distorting domestic support is placed in "amber box," a reference to the amber color of traffic lights, which means "slow down." Amber box subsidies distort international trade by making products of a particular country cheaper in comparison to the same product in another country. Examples are input subsidies such as electricity, seeds,

fertilizers, irrigation, and minimum support prices. As per WTO rules, the Amber box subsidies are quantified in accordance with the Aggregate Measure of Support (AMS) and removed. Developed countries were required to reduce AMS by 20% over 6 years starting in 1995 and developing countries were required to make 13% cuts over 10 years. Least developed countries were not required to make any cuts. Further, the developed countries are allowed to provide subsidies under AMS up to 5% of agriculture GDP, while the developing countries are allowed to provide such subsidies not more than 10% of agriculture GDP. This concept is called as "*de-minimis*" subsidies.

The non-trade distorting or minimal trade distorting measures are categorized as (1) Green box subsidies and (2) Blue box subsidies. Measures with minimal impact on trade can be used freely—they are in a "green box" ("green" as in traffic lights). Green box measures include government services such as research, disease control, infrastructure, environmental assistance programs, food security, and also include payments made directly to farmers that do not stimulate production, such as certain forms of direct income support. The green box subsidies do not have reduction requirements and upper ceiling. Support under *blue box* includes direct payments made to farmers in the form minimum support price (MSP) and direct payments made to farmers under production-limiting program. These subsidies have an upper ceiling but no reduction requirements.

3. *Export subsidies*: Export subsidies signify the payments made by governments of exporter nations to its exporters to make their product competitive (cheaper) in the international market. The export subsidies distort international trade in the favor of developed nations and in the disfavor of developing nations. In 2005, OECD nations were providing export subsidy worth US$1 billion to their farmers every day that affected the international market prices of agricultural goods causing direct harm to poor nations. Taking averages for 1986–1990 as the base level, developed countries agreed to cut the value of export subsidies by 36% over the 6 years starting in 1995 (24% over 10 years for developing countries). Developed countries also agreed to reduce the quantities of subsidized exports by 21% over the 6 years (14% over 10 years for developing countries). Least-developed countries do not need to make any cuts. The Hong Kong conference (2005) asked for phasing out of all export subsidies by 2013.

The Case for AOA

1. *Increase in exports*: The AOA providing for tarrification by dismantling quotas and other NTBs and further asking for a progressive reduction in tariff rates will benefit Indian agriculture traders. India has huge potential in the export of food grains, fruits, vegetables, flowers, tea, coffee, spices, and other cash crops. Though the government is promoting agriculture export infrastructure in the form of Agriculture Export Zones (AEZs), food parks and various schemes, the need is to create a post-harvesting extension mechanism that minimizes waste and maximizes returns to the farmers.
2. *Diversification of agriculture*: The competitive exports diversify the agriculture sector by stimulating the cultivation of non-food grain cash crops such as floriculture, horticulture, and plantation crops, which enjoy elastic demand in the international market and fetch better prices as compared to food grains. In India where farmers are psychologically trapped in stereotype wheat–rice cycle, diversification is the key whose time has come. Diversification inculcates among the farmers the habit of risk taking, infuses the spirit of farm entrepreneurship, and increases their overall income and lifestyle.

3. *Wider access to domestic consumers*: The free access to agricultural items promotes consumer welfare in terms of wider choice. The steep growth in per capita income of Indians in the past few years has provided them with an option of diversifying their consumption portfolio both in quantity and in quality. Indians nowadays enjoy the apples of the United States, kiwi of New Zealand; vegetables and fruits of China and many more items from the foreign lands. Imports also help to arrest domestic prices by streamlining the supply side.
4. *Reduction in export subsidies*: Export subsidy has a high-trade distortion impact and developed nations have used it to their maximum advantage in the past. The Hong Kong conference of WTO pledged elimination of export subsidies by the end of 2013. As per World Trade Report (2018) of WTO, the export subsidies have been reduced for more than 90% of the items exported by developed nations, which can be considered as a greater step toward level playing field among developed and developing countries. As per WTO norms specified, developing countries may continue to provide export subsidies temporarily until they reach a defined economic benchmark of a US$1,000 per capita income. India was initially within this group but was informed by the WTO Secretariat that it had crossed the threshold back in 2015. The 11 major economies along with the United States had challenged India's export subsidy program in 2018 in the WTO.[5]

The Case Against AOA

1. *WTO and food security issues*: Food security is an important welfare tool in the country because a large chunk of the population is below poverty line and deprived. Government's MSP policy is considered to be subsidy by WTO and counted toward the country's overall ceiling on trade-distorting support (fixed at 10% of the value of produce for developing countries).[6] WTO on the demand of developing countries provided for Peace Clause. According to Article 13 of Agreement on Agriculture that mentions "Peace Clause," the domestic support measures and export subsidies of a WTO member will be allowed even if the subsidy breached the limits specified in the WTO agreement on agriculture and cannot be challenged by other WTO members on grounds of being illegal. The Peace Clause expired by the end of 2003. However, Peace Clause was reintroduced in 2013 as an interim measure to provide respite to developing countries until a permanent solution is arrived. India, as part of the G-33 group of developing countries, has demanded that public procurement subsidies in the form of minimum support price programs should not be treated as trade distorting and be allowed without limits.[7] Countries like the United States, EU, Brazil, and Russia are pressing for removal of such subsidies and making the obligations more onerous by introducing conditions such as prohibition to export from the procured stocks.
2. *Threat to domestic farmers*: In India, food prices are subject to exogenous factors like weather-related uncertainties and pest/insect attack along with changes in demand and supply patterns. Dismantling of trade barriers is likely to increase the volatility of domestic prices and farm income. In case of bumper harvest in the exporter nations, developed nations may resort to dumping that will distort trade in their own favor. The farmers in India are not that much economically sound as that of developed countries. For example, in the United States only 4% of the population is engaged in agriculture as compared to nearly 45% in India. The agriculture is practiced in the west with state-of-art technology whereas in India conventional methods are still in vogue. WTO is likely to create a non-level playing field for which the country needs to be prepared well in advance.

3. *Frequent use of standard and safety measures*: The WTO prescribes for the food safety standards under Sanitary and Phytosanitary (SPS) measures but there is no uniform food safety and standard measure across the globe. For example, in the United States, the food and health safety regulations are governed by Food and Drug Administration (FDA), in India by FSSAI, and few countries have also adopted WHO norm of Good Manufacturing Practices (GMP). The lack of uniform standard has led to discriminate use of SPS measures by WTO member nations. For example, in 2014, the 28 nations European Union banned Alphonso mangoes and four vegetables like eggplant, taro plant, bitter gourd, and snake gourd on the ground that such items were found to be contaminated by pests.[8] Earlier too sanctions have been imposed on flower exports and wheat exports from India on the basis of such measures.
4. *Loopholes in market access*: The developed countries found loopholes in the AOA to benefit most by manipulating tariff cut provisions. The AOA did not specify the process for conversion of non-tariff barriers to tariff barriers. This resulted in high equivalent tariff conversions and distorted the very level playing field intention of AOA. Though the developed countries were required to make steeper cuts, the levels of tariffs imposed by them were significantly higher than the developing counterparts. So, even though they reduced the tariffs, it resulted in an average a higher deduction in tariffs from developing nations than developed countries. The tariff cut imposed on the member nations were applicable on overall tariff levels and thus varied significantly with each product. Developed nations exploited this by reducing tariffs marginally on key products and significantly on products that availed no benefits to their economy. At an aggregate level, they were able to meet their tariff cut obligations. Exports from India also suffered a setback due to high import tariffs.
5. *Over usage of Green Box measures by developed countries*: Once AOA was implemented, developed countries were obligated to reduce their domestic support under Amber box category. However, most of the developed countries resorted to manipulate subsidies and progressively shifted them from Amber box to Green/Blue box, which was allowed under WTO norms. On the contrary, the developing nations are resource poor and failed to match the generosity shown by the developed country counterparts toward their respective agriculture sector.

Trade-Related Aspects of Intellectual Property Rights System (TRIPS)

TRIPS agreements, negotiated in the 1986–1994 Uruguay Round, introduced intellectual property rules into the multilateral trading system for the first time. Ideas and knowledge are an increasingly important part of trade and creators can be given the right to prevent others from using their inventions, designs or other creations—and to use that right to negotiate payment in return for others using them. These are "intellectual property rights (IPRs)." Governments and parliaments have given creators these rights as an incentive to produce ideas that will benefit society as a whole. The extent of protection and enforcement of these rights varied widely around the world and the WTO's TRIPS Agreement is an attempt to narrow the gaps in the way these rights are protected around the world, and to bring them under common international rules. There are seven types of IPRs included under TRIPS Agreement: (1) Copyright and related rights, (2)Trademarks, including service marks, (3) Geographical indications,

(4) Industrial designs, (5) Patents, (6) Layout designs (topographies) of integrated circuits, and (7) Undisclosed information, including trade secrets. Let us discuss each component in detail.

1. *Copyright*: Copyright is a right given by the law to creators of literary, dramatic, musical and artistic works, and producers of cinematograph films and sound recordings. The general rule is that copyright lasts for 60 years. In the case of original literary, dramatic, musical, and artistic works, the 60-year period is counted from the year following the death of the author.[9]
2. *Trademarks*: The agreement defines what types of signs must be eligible for protection as trademarks, and what the minimum rights conferred on their owners must be. It says that service marks must be protected in the same way as trademarks used for goods.
3. *Geographical indications*: A geographical indication (GI) is a sign used on products that have a specific geographical origin and possess qualities or a reputation that are due to that origin.[10] Examples are Basmati rice, Darjeeling tea, and Champagne (a French wine).
4. *Industrial designs*: Under the TRIPS Agreement, industrial designs must be protected for at least 10 years. Owners of protected designs must be able to prevent the manufacture, sale, or importation of articles bearing or embodying a design, which is a copy of the protected design.
5. *Patents*: A patent is an exclusive right granted for an invention, which is a product or a process that provides, in general, a new way of doing something, or offers a new technical solution to a problem. To get a patent, technical information about the invention must be disclosed to the public in a patent application.[11]
6. *Layout designs (topographies) of integrated circuits*: Integrated circuits—commonly known as "chips" or "microchips"—are the electronic circuits in which all the components (transistors, diodes, and resistors) have been assembled in a certain order on the surface of a thin semiconductor material (usually silicon). Companies invest heavily in the creation of a new layout design but the copying of such a layout design may cost only a fraction of the original investment. The layout design (topography) of integrated circuits is protected under a sui generis intellectual property system.[12]
7. *Undisclosed information, including trade secrets*: Certain confidential business information may provide an enterprise with a competitive edge and may be protected as a trade secret. Trade secrets are essentially the internal instruments, the responsibility for their protection remaining with the owner of the secrets. They are not disclosed to anyone including the government and are kept confidential. For example, Coca Cola trade secret is kept locked in a bank vault in Atlanta, can be opened only by a resolution of the company's board and is known to only two employees at the same time.[13]

Case for TRIPS

TRIPS agreements have far-reaching impact on the Indian economy in general and Indian pharmaceutical/health sector in particular. In this section, our effort will be to understand the impact of TRIPS on Indian pharma/health sector.

1. *Increase in R&D*: The TRIPS has facilitated the swift and secured movement of innovated products worldwide. The firms in the developing regions have got an awakening call to perform and speed up their research efforts. In Mexico, R&D tripled after adoption of full intellectual property protection in 1991. Italy has experienced a fourfold increase in

R&D investment since instituting strong IP protection in 1978. In India, the top 20 pharmaceutical firms spent around 1% of their turnover on R&D during 1991 and around 10% in 2018. The increase in R&D behavior of Indian firms will not only help them boost product quality and brand but will also help consumers in terms of superior worth of their money.

2. *From Reverse engineering to Forward engineering*: The TRIPS agreements have not only augmented the R&D budgets of Indian companies but also altered their R&D paradigms. The R&D can be categorized into product R&D (Forward engineering) and process R&D (Reverse engineering). The former signifies R&D efforts in novel discoveries whereas latter means R&D efforts in improvising already existing products. As discussed in the box 20.3, the Patent Act of 1970 facilitated the growth of reverse/backward engineering in India.[14] Before the creation of WTO in 1995, not a single pharmaceutical firm was engaged in the development of new molecular drug discovery but in 2018 around 20 companies in India were developing around 200 new molecular drugs.
3. *TRIPS flexibilities*: It was anticipated that with the introduction of full product patent protection in pharmaceuticals from January 01, 2005, the generic manufacturers will be prevented from introducing new drugs and the lack of competition will result in high prices. But TRIPS provides for some flexibilities to member countries of WTO to take action to tackle such negative consequences of product patent protection. Some of such flexibilities are compulsory licensing, parallel imports, and bolar provisions. If a patentee does not make sufficient production of his product in the country or charges exorbitant prices, then the government can issue *Compulsory Licence* in the favor of non-patentee if the latter is ready to make sufficient supply at affordable prices. In India, the only incidence of compulsory license was reported in March 2012, when Natco Pharmaceutical of Hyderabad was issued a compulsory license by Director General of Indian Patents to produce an anti-cancer drug

BOX 20.3 Patent Act 1970 vs. Patent Act 2005

During 1969, the Indian Pharmaceutical market was tilted toward foreign manufacturers as 68% of the market was captured by MNCs. To correct this imbalance, government enacted Patent Act 1970 that came into force in 1972 wherein it followed a policy of positive discrimination toward the indigenous companies. The Patent Act 1970 provided for process patent only for the period of 7 years. In case of infringement of Patent rights, the burden of proof lied with Patentee. The act gave impetus to the indigenous industry and from over 2,200 units in 1969–70, the size of Indian pharmaceutical industry increased to nearly 24,000 units in 1995–96. The result was that the MNCs lost their market domination. From around 68% market share in the late 1960s, their share declined to 40% by the early 1990s. With the establishment of WTO in 1995, Indian government was under obligation to make Indian Patent Act, TRIPS compliant. Accordingly, Patent Act 1970 was amended three times (in 1999, 2002, and 2005) and the new Patent Act came into force on Jan 01, 2005. The Patent Act 2005 provides for product as well as process patent and the term of patent is 20 years. In case of infringement of Patent rights, the burden of proof lies with the infringer. The new Patent Act is seen as guardian of interest of companies (both foreign and domestic) who invest heavily on R&D. It is believed that Patent Act 2005 will lead to inflow of FDI, promote innovation, and competition in the Indian Pharmaceutical market.

Source: Mahajan, Madhur M. (2011). The emergence of new R&D paradigms in the Indian Pharmaceutical Industry-Post TRIPS Period. *JIPR 16* 321–329.

Nexavar, which was the patented drug of Bayer Pharmaceuticals of Germany.[15] If a patentee is selling certain products at higher prices or making insufficient production in a host country, then the country is allowed under TRIPS agreements to import the same product from another country, termed as *Parallel Imports*. Under *Bolar Provisions* TRIPS agreements permit the manufacturers of generic pharmaceuticals to use the technology of a patented pharmaceutical to perform research work that would assist in the marketing or regulatory approval of the generic product, while the patent is in force. After the expiry of the patents, such generic manufacturers can also produce and market the products.

4. *New Vistas in knowledge sharing*: The new drug development is a costly, time-consuming and risky business. It takes billions of dollars to produce a novel drug. New drug discovery process is a tricky business as of every 10,000 compounds synthesized, only one gets marketing approval. Further, it takes more than 15 years to develop a novel drug.[16] R&D costs in India are much lower and the different economists and international agencies have estimated R&D costs in India just 10 to 30% of costs in the United States.[17] Partnerships, collaborations, and alliances have become increasingly common in the pharmaceutical industry. The MNCs are entering into contract R&D and contract manufacturing agreements with Indian generic players. It is a win-win situation for both. The MNCs cost is reduced, time is saved and through collaboration with Indian company they can penetrate in Indian markets very smoothly. On the other hand, Indian companies receive huge royalty/revenue, get access to state-of-art technology and earn international name and fame.

Case Against TRIPS

1. *Monopoly and prices*: Under the new patent act, monopoly rights of 20 years are provided to the patentee. The monopoly rights are not only absolute but also lead to charging of higher prices by MNCs. It happened in South Africa in the early 2000s when anti-AIDS drugs were sold at very high prices by MNCs. Many African governments issued compulsory licensing in favor of Indian company Cipla and the company was required to sell anti-AIDS drugs in African countries.[18] Cipla supplied anti-AIDS drugs to more than 35 countries, mainly in Africa. The continent had the largest number of HIV cases in the world, with South Africa leading the list.[19] Evergreeing of Patent is another strategy under which the MNCs make trivial/insignificant variations to the existing patented invention and file new patent, thus extending their monopoly.*

---

*Novartis, a Swiss pharmaceutical MNC filed an application in India for patent for Glivec, the blood cancer drug. In January 2006, the Indian patent office ruled that the medicine was not substantially different from one for which patents had already been given in the US and Europe. Thus, it did not pass the novelty test. The section 3(d) of Patent Act 2005 provides for check against 'evergreening' of Patent. This helps them retain monopoly rights for a longer period. Many NGOs of the country including Swadeshi Jagran Manch pressurized the government to pursue the case wholeheartedly and fight it legally. The patent office's ruling was upheld by both the Intellectual Property Appellate Board (IPAB) and the Supreme Court in April 2013. If Novartis had won the case, it would have been granted a monopoly on Glivec, and denied Indian companies the right to make the drug. This would obviously have allowed Novartis to sell the medicine at a much higher price. Already, there was a huge differential with generic versions by Indian companies costing ₹5,000–9,000 for a month's treatment, compared to Glivec's cost of around ₹1.2 lakh a month.

2. *Issues related to health security*: Only 44% of the 1.3 billion people in India have a health insurance policy as of 2017. Healthcare expenditure as a percentage of GDP is just 4.7% in India, while the United States spends about 18% of its GDP. Of the total expenditure on healthcare in India, 70% comes from the private sector, whereas the government spends only 30%.[20] Higher prices charged by patent holder companies will seriously affect affordability and accessibility of Indian lower middle class and poor people. Though the schemes like Ayushman Bharat will help increase health insurance penetration across the country, the section not covered by the scheme will bear the brunt in the eventuality of price hike by patentee.
3. *Brownfield FDI and acquisitions of Indian pharmaceutical units*: Pharmaceutical sector of the country has emerged very competitive during pre-TRIPS period. The country has produced many well-known generic pharma firms, which have made India as one of the lowest drug priced country in the world. But after 2005, with product patent regime under TRIPS, many domestic firms find the going tough. For pharma MNCs, Indian companies provide a diverse strategic value and entry to lucrative emerging markets. During 2005–2013, around eight Indian pharmaceutical companies were acquired by the foreign MNCs prompting government to change the route of Brownfield FDI (under which local firms are acquired by foreign MNCs) from automatic route to government route. Some of the high profile acquisitions include the acquisition of Ranbaxy, Shantha biotech, and Nicholas Piramal by Daiichi Sankyo, Sanofi-Aventis, and Abbott, respectively. These acquisitions have raised concerns with regard to the future availability of affordable medicines as well as the effective use of the WTO TRIPS flexibilities including pre-grant opposition and compulsory license. Today, three of the country's top five drug firms are foreign MNCs and if MNC continued in the same vein, soon they will control nearly 50% of the domestic retail drug market.[21]

General Agreement on Trade in Services (GATS)

The creation of the GATS was one of the landmark achievements of the Uruguay round, whose results entered into force in January 1995. The GATS aims at creating a credible and reliable system of international trade rules; ensuring fair and equitable treatment of all participants (principle of non-discrimination); stimulating economic activity through guaranteed policy bindings; and promoting trade and development through progressive liberalization.[22] GATS agreements are the first and only set of international rules governing international trade in services, which have been developed in response to huge growth in service sector. The GATS distinguishes between four modes of supplying services (1) cross-border trade, (2) consumption abroad, (3) commercial presence, and (4) presence of natural persons (Table 20.1).

There are two obligations under GATS, one the general obligations and the second the specific commitments. The general obligations constitute extending *MFN treatment* by member nations to each other and *transparency* that includes the establishment of administrative procedures for smooth conduct of services trade and sound regulatory mechanism. The special commitments include *market access* by member nations to each other's services trade and extending *national treatment* whereby the member nations do not operate discriminatory measures benefiting domestic services or service suppliers.

TABLE 20.1 Four Modes of GATS

<table>
<tr><th>Modes</th><th>Criteria</th><th>Example</th><th>Supplier Presence</th></tr>
<tr><td>Mode I
Cross-border supply</td><td>Service delivered within the territory of the member from the territory of another member</td><td>International telephone calls, mails, services incorporated in goods</td><td rowspan="2">Service supplier not present within the territory of the member</td></tr>
<tr><td>Mode II
Consumption abroad</td><td>Service delivered outside the territory of the member, in the territory of another Member, to a service consumer of the member</td><td>Tourism, ship repair</td></tr>
<tr><td>Mode III
Commercial presence</td><td>Service delivered within the territory of the member through the commercial presence of the supplier</td><td>Foreign MNCs operating in India or Indian companies operating abroad</td><td rowspan="2">Service supplier present within the territory of the member</td></tr>
<tr><td>Mode IV
Presence of a natural person</td><td>Service delivered within the territory of the member with supplier present as a natural person</td><td>Indians providing services abroad like, fashion models, consultants, doctors, lawyers, university professors</td></tr>
</table>

Source: Compiled by author.

Case for GATS

Developed countries must rise to the challenge of eliminating the barriers they maintain to exports from developing countries, so that we may witness a virtuous cycle of mutually beneficial liberalization. Following are the benefits associated with GATS agreements:

1. GATS will ensure enhanced efficiency as the resources will be deployed where they have the highest returns and thus will generate economy-wide benefits.
2. GATS will help India augment its stock of capital (through increased FDI) and crucially the stock of human capital and technology that is embodied in or associated with such FDI indicating the presence of positive technology spillovers.[23]
3. India has a vast pool of skilled and cost-effective manpower and like software exports can emerge as a significant supplier to developed country markets. For example, health service is a potential area in which India could become a major exporter, either by attracting foreign patients to domestic hospitals and doctors or by temporarily sending its health personnel abroad.
4. GATS will enhance competition and thus lead to better provisioning of services to the domestic consumers.

Case Against GATS

There are several criticisms that have been levelled at the GATS, mostly by non-governmental organizations, consumers, and public interest groups. Following points can be mentioned in this regard:

1. GATS may force countries to open up their services to trade and investment due to pressures from lobbies in developed countries, which would result in a "corporate takeover" of their services by MNCs and forced privatization of their service sector.

2. GATS applies to governments at all levels, including central, state, provincial, local, and municipal. It raises questions about the extent to which governments at all levels would be able to retain sovereignty over domestic regulations.[24]
3. There is ambiguity with regard to GATS' coverage as there is coexistence of government and private suppliers in many services and the agreement does not clarify the conditions, which would make this coexistence "non-commercial" and "not in competition."
4. Critics argue that GATS is a mean to further the commercial interests of MNCs (of developed countries) to access developing country service markets in areas such as insurance, banking, and telecommunications through FDI since one of the modes of supply is commercial presence.

Standard and Safety

WTO agreements on Standard and Safety comprises two components: Sanitary and Phytosanitary Measures (SPS) and Technical Barriers to Trade (TBT). SPS measures are quarantine and biosecurity measures, which applied to protect human, animal, or plant life or health, from risks arising from pests and diseases and from risks arising from additives, toxins, and contaminants in food and feed. It allows countries to set their own standards. If an exporter nation does not prescribe to the standards laid down by importer nation then SPS measures empower the importer nation to impose sanctions on imports.[25] The TBT agreement establishes rules and procedures regarding the development, adoption, and application of voluntary product standards, mandatory technical regulations, and the procedures (such as testing or certification) used to determine whether a particular product meets such standards or regulations. The aim of the TBT agreement is to prevent the use of technical requirements as unnecessary barriers to trade. Both SPS and TBT have been classified as non-tariff measures.[26]

Agreement on Textile and Clothing (ATC)

From 1974 until the end of the Uruguay Round, the trade was governed by the Multi-fiber Arrangement (MFA), under which developed nations had applied huge quota restrictions on developing countries exports. ATC came into force with the establishment of WTO and signifies integration of trade in textile and clothing into the normal rules of the GATT, through gradual phaseout of quota restrictions over the 10-year transition time from 1995–2004. Since January 01, 2005, all quota restrictions on textiles have been removed and ATC has expired.[27] Now, trade in textile and clothing products is no longer subject to quotas under a special regime outside normal WTO/GATT rules but is governed by the general rules and disciplines embodied in the multilateral trading system.*

Anti-Dumping, Countervailing Duties, and Safeguards

Anti-dumping measures: If a company exports a product in host country's market at a price lower than the price it normally charges on its own home market, it is said to be "dumping" the product.

---

*The Agreement on Textiles and Clothing no longer exists: it's the only WTO agreement that had self-destruction built in.

Under WTO rules, if the government is able to show that dumping is taking place, calculate the extent of dumping and prove the injury it is causing to the indigenous industry, the government can impose anti-dumping duties.

Countervailing duty: Subsidies by an exporter nation to its exports can distort international trade in its own favor. An importer nation can use the WTO's dispute settlement procedure to seek the withdrawal of the subsidy or the removal of its adverse effects. It can also launch its own investigation and ultimately charge extra duty known as countervailing duty on subsidized exports of the exporter nation that are found to be hurting domestic producers of importer nation.

Safeguard measures: A WTO member may restrict imports (by applying import duties, etc.) of a product temporarily and take safeguard actions if its domestic industry is seriously injured or threatened with the injury caused by a surge in imports. In such a case, WTO rules provides for safeguard measures.

Non-Tariff Barriers (NTBs)

NTBs are trade barriers that restrict imports (or exports) of goods or services through measures other than tariffs. Non-tariff barriers comprise bureaucratic or legal issues that could involve hindrances to trade. Few examples of NTBs are import licensing, rules for the valuation of goods at customs, pre-shipment inspection: further checks on imports, rules of origin, etc.

Trade-Related Investment Measures

TRIMs measures call for introducing national treatment of foreign investment and removal of all such measures that discriminate foreign investment in favor of domestic investment. For example, it discourages measures that limit a company's imports or set targets for the company to export (trade balancing requirements) or require particular levels of local procurement by MNCs (local content requirements).[28]

Plurilateral Agreements

Plurilateral Agreement is an agreement between more than two countries but not a great many, which would be multilateral agreement. At present, there are two plurilateral agreements (1) trade in civil aircraft and (2) government procurement. *The Agreement on Trade in Civil Aircraft* entered into force on January 01, 1980. The agreement eliminates import duties on all aircrafts, other than military aircraft, as well as on all other products covered by the agreement—such as aircraft engines and other parts and components. *An Agreement on Government Procurement* entered into force on January 01, 1981. Its purpose is to open up as much of this business as possible to international competition. It is designed to make laws, regulations, procedures, and practices regarding government procurement more transparent and to ensure they do not protect domestic products or suppliers, or discriminate against foreign products or suppliers.[29]

Trade Policy Review Mechanism

All WTO member nations need to inform the WTO and fellow members of specific measures, policies, or laws through regular notifications; and the WTO has to conduct regular reviews of individual countries' trade policies. This agreement is termed as trade policy reviews. The objectives of Trade Policy Review Mechanism are to increase the transparency and understanding of countries' trade policies and practices, through regular monitoring; improve the quality of public and intergovernmental debate on the issues; and to enable a multilateral assessment of the effects of policies on the world trading system.[30]

International Monetary Fund

International Monetary Fund (IMF) was established in the year 1944 at the Bretton Woods conference and is headquartered at Washington DC. The IMF's primary purpose is to ensure the stability of the international monetary system—the system of exchange rates and international payments that enables countries (and their citizens) to transact with each other.[31] IMF has 189 members and Christine Lagarde is the Managing Director of IMF.

Functions of IMF

1. *Surveillance over members' economic policies*: IMF members countries are required to pursue economic policies that are consistent with the objectives of the IMF. IMF has the legal authority to oversee compliance by members and has the mandate to examine on a regular basis the economic circumstances of virtually every country in the world.
2. *Financing temporary balance of payments needs*: IMF lends member countries during the temporary balance of payment crisis to put in place orderly corrective measures and avoid a disorderly adjustment of the external imbalance. IMF also plays an important catalytic role in helping member countries to mobilize external financing for their balance of payments needs.
3. *Combating poverty in low-income countries*: The IMF provides concessional loans to poor nations to help support these countries' efforts to eradicate poverty. To fulfill this objective, the IMF works closely with the World Bank and other international economic institutions. IMF mobilizes external financing and donor support for such countries and participates in two international initiatives to provide debt relief: the Heavily Indebted Poor Countries (HIPC) Initiative and the Multilateral Debt Relief Initiative (MDRI).
4. *Mobilizing external financing*: The bilateral and multilateral lenders and donors rely on an IMF endorsement of a country's economic policies or might even require a formal IMF supported economic program before committing or disbursing their own resources to that country or granting debt relief. IMF policy assessments and recommendations also provide important signals to investors and financial markets regarding a country's economic future, and impact on investor and market confidence in the economy.
5. *Strengthening the International Monetary System*: The IMF is the central institution in the international monetary system. It serves as a forum for consultation and collaboration by members on international monetary and financial matters, and works with other multilateral institutions to devise international rules that would facilitate the prevention and orderly resolution of international economic problems.

BOX 20.4 IMF Quotas and SDRs

IMF Quotas: Each member country of the IMF is assigned a quota, broadly based on its relative position in the world economy. A member country's quota determines its maximum financial commitment to the IMF, its voting power, and has a bearing on its access to IMF financing. The current quota formula is a weighted average of GDP (weight of 50 %), openness (30 %), economic variability (15 %), and international reserves (5 %). India is among the top 10 quota holding countries at the IMF. India has SDRs 13,114 million (2.76% of total) quota with IMF. The United States has the largest share (17.7%). A member can borrow up to 200 % of its quota annually and 600 % cumulatively. However, access may be higher in exceptional circumstances. A member must pay its subscription in full upon joining the fund: up to 25 % must be paid in SDRs or widely accepted currencies (such as the US dollar, the euro, the yen, or the pound sterling), while the rest is paid in the member's own currency.

Special drawing rights (SDRs): The SDR is an international reserve asset, created by the IMF in 1969 to supplement the existing official reserves of member countries. SDRs are allocated to member countries in proportion to their IMF quotas. The SDR also serves as the unit of account of the IMF and some other international organizations. The SDR is neither a currency nor a claim on the IMF. Rather, it is a potential claim on the freely usable currencies of IMF members. Its value is based on a basket of five international currencies: US Dollar, Euro, Chinese Yuan, Japanese Yen, and Pound Sterling. SDR is also called paper gold.

Source: World Economic Outlook. IMF. April 2, 2019.

6. *Increasing the global supply of international reserves*: To supplement the international liquidity, IMF introduced an international reserve asset called the Special Drawing Rights (SDRs) way back in 1969. SDRs are hard currency assets and can be exchanged for convertible currencies (Box 20.4).
7. *Building capacity through technical assistance and training*: IMF provides technical assistance and training to help member countries design economic policies and improve economic management capabilities. It helps member nations reduce the risk of policy failures and the countries' resilience to shocks, and facilitating program design and implementation.
8. *Dissemination of information and research*: The IMF makes economic analysis of its member countries, prepares statistical information, and makes projections. It publishes such information in its numerous economic reports and research studies as well as academic journals and working papers, occasional papers, and the Internet. The IMF also conducts research in areas relevant to its mandate and operations, mainly to improve its economic analysis and its advice to member countries.

India's Economic Relationships with IMF

1. India is the founding member of IMF. India's finance minister is the ex-officio governor of IMF. Until 1970, India was among the five nations having the highest quota with IMF and due to this status India was allotted a permanent place in executive board of directors.

2. IMF has extended India financial help from time to time. During 1970s and 1980s, India was one of the largest borrowers of the bank. IMF played a significant role in shaping the macroeconomic reforms of 1990s by extending conditional loan assistance.[32]
3. IMF acts as crisis manager and crisis lender for its member nations from time to time.[33] During the global financial crisis of 2008, India has received about US$4.5 billion from the IMF's SDR to battle economic slowdown. This was part of the about US$ 250 billion allocation of SDR by the IMF to provide liquidity to the global economic system by supplementing IMF's 186 (earlier) member countries' foreign exchange reserves.[34]
4. India's current quota in the IMF is SDR 13,114 million, making it among the top ten largest quota holding countries at IMF and giving it shareholdings of 2.76%.
5. India has availed the services of specialists of the IMF for the purpose of assessing the state of the Indian economy. Teams of experts have often been coming to India and submitting reports. In this way India has had the benefit of independent scrutiny and advice. IMF's projections about the country are tenable and taken very seriously at the policy level and in the academic circles.

World Bank Group

Five institutions together make up the World Bank group. These institutions are International Bank for Reconstruction and Development (IBRD), International Development Association (IDA), International Finance Corporation (IFC), Multilateral Investment Guarantee Agency (MIGA), and International Centre for Settlement of Investment Disputes (ICSID). Out of these, the first two institutions IBRD and IDA are collectively called World Bank. David Malpass is the president of the World Bank group. All the constituents of World Bank group are headquartered at Washington DC.

Let us discuss the constituents of World Bank group one by one:

1. *International Bank for Reconstruction and Development*: The International Bank for Reconstruction and Development (IBRD) was created in 1944 to help Europe rebuild after World War II. The objective once finished, now it lends to governments of middle-income and creditworthy low-income countries. IBRD and IMF are together called Bretton Woods twins. It has 189 members.[35]
2. *The International Development Association*: The International Development Association (IDA) was established in 1960. IDA aims to reduce poverty by providing loans (called "credits") and grants to the world's poorest nations for programs that boost economic growth, reduce inequalities, and improve people's living conditions.[36]
3. *The International Finance Corporation*: Established in 1956, the International Finance Corporation (IFC) is the largest global development institution focused exclusively on the private sector. It helps developing countries achieve sustainable growth by financing investment, mobilizing capital in international financial markets, and providing advisory services to businesses and governments. It has 184 members.[37]
4. *The Multilateral Investment Guarantee Agency*: The Multilateral Investment Guarantee Agency (MIGA) was created in 1988 to promote foreign direct investment into developing

countries to support economic growth, reduce poverty, and improve people's lives. MIGA fulfills this mandate by offering political risk insurance (guarantees) to investors and lenders. MIGA has 181 members.[38]

5. *The International Centre for Settlement of Investment Disputes*: Established in 1966, the International Centre for Settlement of Investment Disputes (ICSID) provides international facilities for conciliation and arbitration of investment disputes. There are 153 members of ICSID. India is not a member of ICSID.[39]

India and Its Relationship with World Bank

1. *Older and sustainable ties*: India is a founding member of World Bank. In fact, the name IBRD was suggested by Indian delegation present at Bretton Woods conference. Established in 1957, the New Delhi office of the World Bank is today the oldest, continuously functioning resident mission.
2. *Largest borrower*: India had been World Bank's largest borrower for a longer period of time. India has borrowed US$ 111,717 million (US $60,786 from IBRD and US $50,932 from IDA) during the period 1954–2018 which is around 10.4% of total lending by World Bank. India no longer borrows from the World Bank's IDA arm that gives highly concessional loans to poor countries; however, it still makes use of the fund from World Bank's IBRD unit to fund schemes for rural roads, cheap LED light, etc. However, in 2022–23 too, India was the largest borrower of World Bank followed by Turkey and Indonesia (Table 20.2).[40] In 2022–23, India borrowed worth US$4,321 million from the World Bank.
3. *Benefits different stakeholders*: In India, the World Bank works in close partnership with the Central and State Governments. It also works with other development partners: bilateral and multilateral donor organizations, non-governmental organizations (NGOs), the private sector, and the general public—including academics, scientists, economists, journalists, teachers, and local people involved in development projects[41] World Bank has funded proactively India's social development programs reducing poverty, hunger, disease, and illiteracy, which directly affect the quality of life, apart from development of renewable energy, construction of roads, sewerage, anti-AIDS campaign, and many more. The World Bank and the Government of India in March 2019 signed a $250 million agreement for the National Rural Economic Transformation Project (NRETP), which will help women in rural households shift to a new

TABLE 20.2 World Bank Top Country Borrowers, Fiscal 2023 (US $ Million)

Country	Commitments from IBRD	Country	Commitments from IDA
India	4,321	Morocco	1,850
Türkiye	3,881	Argentina	1,800
Indonesia	3,250	Colombia	1,750
Ukraine	3,133	Romania	1,327
Philippines	2,336	Angola	1,250

Source: World Bank Annual Report, 2023

generation of economic initiatives by developing viable enterprises for farm and non-farm products.[42]

4. *India's voting power in World Bank*: The World Bank is like a cooperative, made up of 189 member countries. These member countries, or shareholders, are represented by a Board of Governors, who are the ultimate policymakers at the World Bank. Generally, the governors are member countries' ministers of finance or ministers of development. They meet once a year at the Annual Meetings of the Boards of Governors of the World Bank Group and the International Monetary Fund. On the basis of shareholding and voting power, India ranks seventh in IBRD subscriptions (3.15%) and voting power (3%). The United States ranks first with voting share of 15.68%.[43]
5. *World Banks's India Country Partnership Framework*: The World Bank Group in 2018 endorsed a new Country Partnership Framework (CPF) for India for 2018–2022. The CPF aims to support India's transition to a higher middle-income country by the year 2030 and expects to deliver US$25 to 30 billion during this CPF period, ending in FY 2022.[44] The CPF will focus on three broader areas: promoting a resource-efficient growth path, particularly in the use of land and water, to remain sustainable; enhancing competitiveness and enabling job creation; and investing in human capital—in health, education, skills—to improve quality and efficiency of service delivery.[45]

Regional Trade Blocs

Regional trade bloc is an inter-governmental agreement of economic integration among participating nations where regional barriers to trade (tariffs and non-tariff barriers) are reduced or eliminated. Regional trade blocs evolve over the period of time and there are different stages of economic integration. Let us discuss them briefly in the following:

- *Preferential Trade Area*: Preferential Trade Areas (PTAs) exists when member nations extend each other preferential access to selected goods and services by agreeing to reduce tariff barriers (not eliminating them completely) on them. This is the first step toward the creation of a trading bloc.
- *Free trade area*: Free trade areas (FTAs) is an association of trading nations in which member nations agree to remove all tariff and non-tariff barriers among themselves. It is the second step in economic integration. For example, North American Free Trade Agreement (NAFTA).
- *Customs union*: The customs union involves the removal of the tariff barriers among the members, and imposition of uniform tariff rates against non-members. That is, custom union is FTA plus common tariff wall against non-members. For example, Benelux, a custom union of Belgium, Netherlands and Luxemburg, formed in 1948.
- *Common market*: Common market is a custom union plus the free movement of Labor and Capital. It is the fourth stage of economic integration. European Union founded in 1993 is an example of a common market.
- *Economic union*: This is the fifth stage of economic integration. Economic union is a common market plus common monetary, fiscal, trade, and exchange rate policies. Euro Zone founded in 1999 is an example of the Economic Union.

BOX 20.5 Few Important Regional Trade Blocks and Economic Cooperations

European Union: European Union (EU) was formed in 1993 after the signing of Maastricht Treaty. It is a group of 28 countries that operates as a cohesive economic and political bloc. In 2012, the EU was awarded the Nobel Peace Prize for advancing the causes of peace, reconciliation, democracy, and human rights in Europe.

Euro Zone: Formed in 1999, Euro is an economic union of 19 of the 28 EU member states that have adopted the euro (€) as their common currency and sole legal tender. The European Central Bank is the central bank for the euro and administers monetary policy within the Eurozone and is located at Frankfurt, Germany.

SAARC: Established in 1985, the South Asian Association for Regional Cooperation (SAARC) is a regional trade bloc and is headquartered at Kathmandu. There are 8 members of SAARC comprising India, Maldives, Pakistan, Bangladesh, Sri Lanka, Bhutan, Nepal, and Afghanistan. To promote free trade among member nations, South Asian Free Trade Area (SAFTA) was formed on January 01, 2006.

ASEAN: Association of South East Asian Nations (ASEAN) is a regional trade bloc, founded in 1967 and is headquartered at Jakarta, Indonesia. ASEAN has 10 members comprising Indonesia, Philippines, Malaysia, Thailand, Singapore, Brunei, Vietnam, Laos, Cambodia, and Myanmar. The 33rd ASEAN summit was organized at Singapore during November 11–15, 2018.

OPEC: Founded in 1960, the Organization of Petroleum Exporting Countries (OPEC) is a permanent intergovernmental organization of 14 oil-exporting developing nations that coordinates and unifies the petroleum policies of its member countries. The members of OPEC comprise Iran, Iraq, Kuwait, Saudi Arabia, Venezuela, Libya, the UAE, Algeria, Nigeria, Ecuador, Gabon, Angola, Equatorial Guinea, and Congo. Headquarter of OPEC is located at Vienna.

G-7: The group of seven (G-7) was founded in 1975. The Group of Seven (G7) is a group consisting of Canada, France, Germany, Italy, Japan, the United Kingdom, and the United States. The major purpose of the G-7 is to discuss, and sometimes act in concert to help resolve, global problems with a special focus on economic issues.

G-20: The group of twenty (G-20) was founded in 1999 to bring together governments of industrialized and developing economies to discuss key issues related to global economy and financial stability. The G-20 membership comprises a mix of the world's largest advanced and emerging economies, representing about two-thirds of the world's population, 85% of global gross domestic product and over 75% of global trade. The members of the G20 are Argentina, Australia, Brazil, Canada, China, France, Germany, India, Indonesia, Italy, Japan, Republic of Korea, Mexico, Russia, Saudi Arabia, South Africa, Turkey, the United Kingdom, the United States, and the European Union.

OECD: Founded in 1961, organization for economic cooperation and development (OECD) is an intergovernmental economic organisation with around 36 member countries to stimulate economic progress and world trade. It is headquartered at Paris.

NAFTA: Founded in 1994, North American Free Trade Agreement (NAFTA) is a regional trade block, comprising Canada, the United States, and Mexico. NAFTA is one of the largest trade blocks in the world in terms of GDP.

APEC: The Asia-Pacific Economic Cooperation (APEC) is a regional economic forum established in 1989 to leverage the growing interdependence of the Asia-Pacific. APEC's 21 members aim to create greater prosperity for the people of the region by promoting balanced, inclusive, sustainable, innovative and secure growth, and by accelerating regional economic integration.

Mercosur: Mercosur is a regional trade bloc of five Latin American countries namely Brazil, Argentina, Paraguay, Uruguay, and Venezuela. Founded in 1995, its main objective has been to promote a common space that generates business and investment opportunities through the competitive integration of national economies into the international market.

IORARC: Founded in 1997, Indian Ocean Rim Association for regional cooperation (IORARC) is a dynamic inter-governmental organisation aimed at strengthening regional cooperation and sustainable development within the Indian Ocean region through its 22 member states and 9 dialogue partners.

RCEP: The Regional Comprehensive Economic Partnership (RCEP) is a proposed mega free trade agreement (FTA) that is presently being negotiated between 10 ASEAN (Association of Southeast Asian Nations) members — Brunei Darussalam, Cambodia, Indonesia, Lao PDR, Malaysia, Myanmar, Philippines, Singapore, Thailand and Vietnam — and their six trading partners India, China, Australia, New Zealand, Japan and South Korea. If formed, RCEP will be the world's largest economic bloc, covering nearly half of the global economy.

Source: Compiled by author.

- *Political union*: Political union is a final stage in the economic integration with more formal political links among the countries. The unification of West and East Germany in 1990 is an example of the total political union.

Trade blocs have certain advantages and disadvantages. The trade bloc structure interacts in such a way that can increase domestic production capacity, promote upward harmonization of standards, improve institutions, introduce technical know-how into the domestic market and increase preferential access to desirable markets.[46] An expanded regional market can allow economies of large-scale production, foster specialization and learning by doing, and attract foreign investment. Enhanced production and consumption effects in the member nations due to the formation of trade blocs are termed as trade creation effect. Trade creation takes place when some domestic production of one union member is replaced by another member's lower cost imports.

Regional initiatives can also foster a variety of non-economic objectives, such as management of immigration flows, promotion of regional security, and increase in bargaining strength vis-à-vis powerful nations of the world. However, regional trade bloc may also lead to trade diversion if low-cost imports of non-members are replaced by purchases from higher cost member nations. Although regional trade blocs can complement the multilateral trading system, by their very nature, regional trade blocs are discriminatory as they are a departure from the principle of normal trading relations, a cornerstone of the WTO.[47]

There are plenty of examples of both successful and unsuccessful regional trade blocs. It is pertinent to mention here the pre-requisites of a successful regional trade bloc.

Pre-requisites of a Successful Regional Trade Block

1. Similar economic size of the member nations (for example, to become a member of Euro zone, the non-member requires to attain a minimum possible level of economic maturity and needs to strengthen its economic fundamentals);
2. Similar past or cultural homogeneity (almost all the successful trade blocs exhibit a homogeneous or less heterogeneous cultural past);

BOX 20.6 Few Important International Economic Organizations

UNCTAD: United Nations Conference on Trade and Development (UNCTAD) is a permanent intergovernmental body established by the United Nations General Assembly in 1964 and headquartered at Geneva, Switzerland. The goal of UNCTAD is promoting development-friendly integration of developing countries through three key functions (1) providing a forum for intergovernmental deliberations; (2) undertaking research, policy analysis, and data collection to inform these deliberations; and, (3) providing technical assistance to developing countries. UNCTAD has 195 members.

FAO: The Food and Agriculture Organization (FAO) is a specialized agency of the United Nations that leads international efforts to defeat hunger. The goal is to achieve food security for all and make sure that people have regular access to enough high-quality food to lead active, healthy lives. Founded in 1945, FAO has 194 member states and works in over 130 countries. It is headquartered at Rome.

Asian Development Bank: Asian Development Bank (ADB) was established in 1966 to accelerate economic and social development in Asia and Pacific regions. ADB has 68 members and its headquarter is located at Manila, Philippines.

Asian Infrastructure Investment Bank: The Asian Infrastructure Investment Bank (AIIB) is a multilateral development bank with a mission to improve social and economic outcomes in Asia. Headquartered in Beijing, it began operations in January 2016 and has now grown to 97 approved members worldwide. By investing in sustainable infrastructure and other productive sectors in Asia and beyond, the bank aims at better-connecting people, services, and markets that over time will impact the lives of billions and build a better future.

International Fund for Agriculture Development: International Fund for Agriculture Development (IFAD) is an international financial institution and specialized United Nations agency headquartered at Rome. IFDA aims at investing in rural people, empowering them to increase their food security, improving the nutrition of their families and increasing their incomes. IFDA provides grants and low-interest loans to needy nations. India is IFDA's largest borrower.

Source: Compiled by author.

3. Competitive not complementary trade; (e.g., trade among industrialized nations will be competitive and will lead to greater specialization. On the contrary trade by an industrialized and an agricultural nation will be called complementary trade and there will be no trade creation).
4. Congenial political ties among member nations (disturbed Indo-Pak relations that have become detrimental for the success of SAARC);
5. Geographical proximity (it is very absurd to think India forming trade union with Australia as transportation costs will overshadow all other benefits).

If we go deep into the failure of SAARC, we can notice that point 2 and 5 are in favor of SAARC countries but other points are not in favor. Despite geographical proximity and similar past, the unfriendly political ties of India and Pakistan have become a major stumbling block in the process of economic integration. Unequal size of the countries is another factor as India is the only giant figure among all the eight members. Further, the SAARC nations deal in complementary rather competitive trade which undermines the trade creation effect.

Summary

1. There are three major international economic organizations: World Trade Organization, International Monetary Fund, and World Bank Group. WTO was established on Jan 01, 1995. WTO is the watchdog of international trade, which facilitates smooth and swift flow of merchandise across borders and promotes multilateralism. It has 164 members and is headquartered at Geneva. Ministerial conference is the topmost decision-making body of the WTO, which usually meets after every 2 years.
2. WTO agreements are the result of negotiations among members. There are different agreements of WTO. Under GATT, individual countries are committed to specific categories of goods and services, which include commitments to cut and "bind" their customs duty rates on imports of goods. Agreement on Agriculture is to reform trade in the agriculture sector and to make policies more market oriented. It covers three aspects: Market access, domestic support, and export subsidies. TRIPS agreements introduced intellectual property rules into the multilateral trading system and includes seven types of IPRs (1) Copyright and related rights, (2) Trademarks, including service marks, (3) Geographical indications, (4) Industrial designs, (5) Patents, (6) Layout-designs (topographies) of integrated circuits, (7) Undisclosed information, including trade secrets. GATS agreements are the international rules governing international trade in services and include four modes of supplying services: cross-border trade, consumption abroad, commercial presence, and presence of natural persons. WTO agreements on Standard and Safety comprises two components (1) Sanitary and Phytosanitary Measures (SPS) and (2) Technical Barriers to Trade (TBT). Under this member nations can devise their own food safety and technical standards. Agreement on textile and clothing calls for the removal of all quota restrictions on textiles with effect from January 01, 2005. Anti-dumping measures are used to withstand the impact of dumping, countervailing duties are levied to nullify export subsidies and safeguards are implemented if domestic industry is seriously injured. Non-tariff barriers restrict imports (or exports) of goods or services through measures other than tariffs. TRIMs measures call for non-discriminatory treatment of foreign investment. Plurilateral Agreements have been signed by few nations and comprises (1) trade in civil aircraft and (2) government procurement. WTO conducts regular reviews of individual countries' trade policies, under trade review agreements.
3. International Monetary Fund (IMF) was established in the year 1944 at the Bretton Woods conference and is headquartered at Washington DC. The main functions of IMF are Surveillance over Members' Economic Policies, Financing Temporary Balance of Payments Needs, Combating Poverty in Low-Income Countries, Mobilizing External Financing, Strengthening the International Monetary System, Increasing the Global Supply of International Reserves, Building Capacity through Technical Assistance and Training, and Dissemination of Information and Research. India is the founding member of the IMF. During 1970s and 1980s, India was one of the largest borrowers of the bank. India has received aid from the IMF during economic crisis 1991 and even during the global financial crisis of 2007–08. India has availed the services of specialists of the IMF for the purpose of assessing the state of the Indian economy from time to time.
4. Five institutions together make up the World Bank group. IBRD founded in 1944 provides loan to middle income and creditworthy poorer countries. IDA established in 1960 aims to reduce poverty by providing interest-free credits and grants to the world's poorest nations. IFC established in 1956 provides assistance to the private sector. MIGA was created in 1988 to promote foreign direct investment into developing countries. ICSID established in 1966 provides international facilities for conciliation and arbitration of investment disputes. IBRD and IDA are collectively called World Bank, whereas World Bank group constitutes all the five institutions. India is the founding member of World Bank. India had been World Bank's largest borrower for a longer period of time. In India, the World Bank works in close partnership with the Central and State Governments. On the basis of shareholding and voting power, India ranks seventh in IBRD subscriptions. The World Bank Group in 2018 endorsed a new Country Partnership Framework (CPF) for India for 2018–2022, which aims to support India's transition to a higher middle-income country by the year 2030.

5. Regional trade bloc (RTB) is an intergovernmental agreement of economic integration among participating nations where regional barriers to trade are reduced or eliminated. Different stages of RTB are Preferential Trade Area, Free trade area, Customs union, Common market, Economic union, and Political union. The pre-requisites of a successful regional trade bloc are similar size, cultural homogeneity, competitive trade, congenial political ties, and geographical proximity.

Endnotes

1. WTO Press Release on October 27, 1997.
2. Understanding WTO. (2007). *The GATT Years: From Havana To Marrakesh*, WTO Publication, p.15.
3. Functions of WTO. Retrieved from https://www.wto.org (Accessed on June 16, 2015).
4. Understanding WTO (2007). *The GATT Years: From Havana To Marrakesh*, WTO Publication, p.25.
5. Chakraborty, S. (August 20, 2018). Several nations support US charges against Indian export subsidies at WTO. *Business Standard*.
6. Sen, A. (January 9, 2018). India faces food security hurdle in WTO. *The Hindu Business Line*.
7. Sen, A. (December 6, 2018).WTO: We cannot yield on food security. *The Hindu Business Line*.
8. EU bans Indian Alphonso mangoes, 4 vegetables from May 1. (April 28, 2014). *The Hindu*.
9. A Hand Book of copyright law (2018). Ministry of Human Resource Development. Govt. of India.
10. Geographical Indications. Retrieved from https://www.wipo.int (Accessed on March 4, 2017).
11. Patents. Retrieved from https://www.wipo.int (Accessed on March 4, 2017).
12. Layout designs (topographies) of integrated circuits. Retrieved from https://www.wipo.int (Accessed on March 4, 2017).
13. Nair, M.D. (2002). Protection of trade secrets/undisclosed information. *JIPR 7*, 526–529.
14. Mahajan, Madhur M. (2011). The emergence of new R&D paradigms in the Indian Pharmaceutical Industry-Post TRIPS Period. *JIPR 16*, 321–329.
15. Mahajan, Madhur M. (2013). Compulsory Licensing under TRIPS: Issues and prospects, Punjab University. *Law Review 52* & 53, ISSN 0971–5541.
16. Chaudhary, S. (2005). WTO and Indian pharmaceutical industry. *OUP*. New Delhi.
17. Mckinsey & Company Report. (2008). Indian Pharma 2015-Unlocking the potential of Indian Pharmaceutical Market, p.13 and Acharya, S. (2006). The productivity tiger-time and cost benefits of clinical drug development in India. *A White Paper written for Deloitte Consulting, Zurich*.
18. Fisher & Rigamonti. (February 2005). The South Africa AIDS controversy. A Case Study in Patent Law and Policy", The Law and Business of Patents. Harvard Law School.
19. Cipla registers five anti-AIDS drugs in South Africa. *The Economic Times*, September 22, 2003.
20. 56% Indians still don't have a health cover, *Livemint*, 4 December, 2018.
21. MNCs back in control of 50% of Indian pharma market. *The Economic Times*, 24 March, 2010.
22. GATS. Retrieved from https://www.wto.org (Accessed on March 29, 2017).
23. Mattoo, A. (2000). Developing countries in the new round of GATS negotiations: Towards a pro-active role. *World Economy 23* (4), 471–489.
24. Chanda, R. (2002). GATS and its implications for developing countries: Key issues and concerns. DESA Discussion Paper No. 25, United Nations.
25. Orden, D. & Robert, D. (2007). Food regulation and trade under the WTO: Ten years in perspective. Agricultural Economics, International Association of Agricultural Economists, vol. 37(s1), pp.103–118, December.
26. McDaniels, D. & Karttunen, M. (2016). Trade, testing and toasters: Conformity assessment procedures and the TBT committee. WTO Working Paper ERSD-2016–09.
27. Malaga, J. (2003). The agreement on textiles and clothing: Is it a WTO failure? *The Estey Centre Journal of International Law and Trade Policy* 4 (1) 75–85.

28. Understanding WTO (2007). The GATT Years: From Havana To Marrakesh. WTO Publication, p.51.
29. Rudolf, A. & Hamid, M. (2017). Plurilateral trade agreements: An escape route for the WTO? WTO Staff Working Papers ERSD-2017–03.
30. Understanding WTO(2007). The GATT years: From Havana To Marrakesh. WTO Publication, p.53.
31. IMF. Retrieved from https://www.imf.org (Accessed on May 4, 2018).
32. India and the International Monetary Fund. (Retrieved from https://dea.gov.in (Accessed on July 24, 2018).
33. Chandavarkar, A. (2002). Is the IMF a Lender of First or Last Resort? EPW. Vol. 37, Issue No. 36.
34. IMF to Make $250 Billion SDR Allocation on (August 13, 2015). Retrieved from https://www.imf.org/ (Accessed on July 4, 2016).
35. IBRD. Retrieved from https://www.worldbank.org (Accessed on July 5, 2016).
36. IDA. Retrieved from http://ida.worldbank.org (Accessed on July 5, 2016).
37. IFC. Retrieved from https://www.ifc.org (Accessed on July 5, 2016).
38. Multilateral Investment Guarantee Agency. Retrieved from http://www.worldbank.org (Accessed on July 5, 2016).
39. Retrieved from https://icsid.worldbank.org/en/Pages/about/default.aspx
40. Annual report lending data, World Bank, 2018.
41. The World Bank in India. Retrieved from http://web.worldbank.org (Accessed on May 12, 2018).
42. World Bank, Press Release, 5 March, 2019.
43. World bank Group Finances. Retrieved from https://finances.worldbank.org (Accessed on May 12, 2018).
44. The World Bank in India, Newsletter, Vol. 17, No. 4, January 2019.
45. World Bank Partnership Framework for India. The Hindu Business Line, September 21, 2018.
46. DiCaprio, A., et al. (July 2017). Regional trade agreements, integration and development. UNCTAD/SER.RP/2017/1.
47. Carbaugh, "International Economics", 11th Edition, CENGAGE Learning, New Delhi, 2008.

CHAPTER **21**

Indian Monetary System: Banking, RBI, and Money Market

If you owe the bank $100 that's your problem. If you owe the bank $100 million, that's the bank's problem.

—J. Paul Getty

Introduction

In the ancient times, the banking had become full-fledged business activity, and during the Manu Smriti period which followed the Vedic period and epic age, the business of banking was carried on by the members of Vaish community. The famous Kautilya Arthashastra, which is ascribed to be dating back to the 4th century BC, contains references to creditors and lending. During the medieval times, the banking flourished under the patronage of Muslim rulers and experiments were made by issuing metallic money. The English traders, who came to India in the 17th century, established some contacts with the indigenous bankers by borrowing funds from them. The evolution of modern banking practices in India can be ascribed to the British period and it got systematized after independence.

The present chapter attempts to focus on the following topics:

- Evolution and Structure of Commercial Banking in India
- Non-Performing Assets
- Banking Sector Reforms
- RBI, Its Functions and Monetary Policy
- Money Market, Characteristics, and Reforms
- Non-Banking Financial Intermediaries
- Financial Inclusion

Evolution of Indian Banking

We analyze the evolution of modern Indian Banking in three phases: Phase I (1786–1947), Phase II (1947–1991), and Phase III (1991 onwards).

Phase I (1786–1947): The Colonial Period

The foundation of modern Indian Banking was laid down in the eighteenth century with the establishment of the General Bank of India in 1786 and the Bank of Hindustan in 1790. The East India Company established the Bank of Bengal in 1806, the Bank of Madras in 1843, and the

Bank of Bombay in 1868, also called as presidency banks. The Allahabad Bank, established in 1865 and still functioning today, is the oldest Joint Stock bank in India. The first entirely Indian joint stock bank was the Oudh Commercial Bank, established in 1881 in Faizabad followed by Punjab National Bank (PNB) in Lahore in 1895. The three presidency banks were amalgamated in January 1921 and Imperial Bank of India was established, which acquired the threefold role of a commercial bank, of a banker's bank, and of a banker to the government.

It started as private shareholders bank with mostly European shareholders. With the formation of the Reserve Bank of India in 1935, some of the central banking functions of the Imperial Bank were taken over by the RBI. In the very early phase of commercial banking, the regulatory framework was somewhat diffused and the Presidency Banks were regulated and governed by their Royal Charter, the East India Company, and the Government of India of that time. Between 1913 and 1949, banks were governed by Indian Companies Act, 1913. During the first phase, the growth was very slow and banks also experienced periodic failures between 1913 and 1948. There were approximately 1,100 banks, mostly small. Banks were characterized by low deposit mobilization, lesser public confidence, and arbitrary and unequal lending patterns ignoring the pressing needs of masses and weak money market instruments.

Phase II (1947–1991): The Period of Nationalization and Social Control

To streamline the functioning and activities of commercial banks, the Government of India came up with the Banking Companies Act, 1949, which was renamed as the Banking Regulation Act from March 1966. The Reserve Bank of India was nationalized in 1949 and was vested with extensive powers for the supervision of banking in India as the Central Banking Authority. On the recommendations of the All India Rural Credit Survey Committee, the government nationalized Imperial Bank of India in 1955 and in its place constituted State Bank of India (SBI). In 1959, the SBI (subsidiary bank) Act was passed, enabling the SBI to take over eight former state-associate banks as its subsidiaries.

Between 1947 and 1955, 361 banks "failed" in India, at the rate of 40-plus banks a year. All were privately owned. There was no deposit insurance, so savers lost everything when crooked bankers ran off with their cash. Agriculture was neglected area in total agriculture credit during the pre-bank nationalization period. In 1950, farmers got a measly 2.3% share of all bank loans. By 1967, bank lending to farms dropped to 2.2% of the total.[1]

To better align the banking system to the needs of planning and economic policy, it was considered necessary to have social control over banks. In 1969, 14 of the major private sector banks were nationalized. This was an important milestone in the history of Indian banking. This was followed by the nationalization of another six private banks in 1980. This step brought more than 80% of the banking segment in India under the government ownership. Later on, in the year 1993, the government merged New Bank of India with PNB. It was the only merger between nationalized banks and resulted in the reduction of the number of nationalized banks from 20 to 19.

The main purpose of bank nationalization was to check the concentration of economic power in few hands, to bring about sectoral and regional balances through control patterns of allocation, to correct urban bias by providing impetus to branch expansion in unbanked rural and semi-urban areas, and also that banks were considered to be an instrument of social transformation and not only a means of profit maximization. However, this arrangement also saw some weaknesses like reduced bank profitability, weak capital bases, and banks getting burdened with large non-performing assets (NPAs).

Phase III (1991 Onward): The Period of Banking Sector Reforms

As discussed earlier, Indian banking system in the first four decades after independence had turned woefully inefficient. The sector was characterized by administered interest rates, large pre-emption of resources by the authorities through higher SLR, opaque accounting norms, and limited disclosure by the banks; superficial securities market governed by a plethora of complex regulations and extensive restrictions and compartmentalized financial intermediaries. The strong entry barriers in the form of not allowing private and foreign banking thwarted competition from new entrants leading to low level of competition, efficiency, and productivity. The end product was obvious as proved by economic crisis of 1991 which made the reform process in Indian banking inevitable. The transformation of Indian banking during post reform period is discussed in the subsequent sections.

STRUCTURE OF COMMERCIAL BANKING IN INDIA

In India, total number of bank branches has increased from 8,262 in 1969 to 151,420 in 2018. Reserve Bank classifies banks into five categories: Commercial banks, Regional rural banks, Local area banks, Small finance banks and Payment banks. Commercial banks are further classified into Public sector banks, Private sector banks and Foreign sector banks. Public sector banks constitute State bank of India and Nationalized banks (Table 21.1). Let us discuss the structure of Indian banking.

State Bank of India

As mentioned earlier, the Imperial Bank of India was converted into SBI in 1955. In 1959, the government passed the State Bank of India (Associate Banks) Act, which made eight banks that had belonged to princely states into subsidiaries of SBI. Subsidiary banks along with Bharatiya Mahila Bank were merged with the SBI with effect from April 1, 2017. With this merger, SBI joined the league of top 50 banks globally in terms of assets. The merger led to increase the total customer base of the bank to 37 crores with a branch network of around 24,000 and nearly 59,000 ATMs across the country. The merged entity had a deposit base of more than ₹26 lakh crore and advances level of ₹18.50 lakh crore.[2] As on December 31, 2018, there were 24,007 bank

TABLE 21.1 Structure of Banking and Number of Bank Branches

	Commercial Banks								
	Public Sector Banks								
Year	SBI	Nationalized Banks	Private Sector Banks	Foreign Sector Banks	Regional Rural Banks	Local Area Banks	Small Finance Banks	Payment Banks	Total
March 2006	14,441	35,628	7,036	265	14,768	45	–	–	72,183
December 2018	24,007*	68,870	32,521	299	22,176	87	2,818	642	151,420

Source: Database on Indian Economy, RBI.

* Included SBI and its associates.

branches of SBI in the country. SBI has around 190 Foreign Offices in 36 countries serving the international needs of the bank's foreign customers.

Nationalized Banks

A nationalized bank signifies public ownership or government control. In India, major bank nationalization was exercised on July 19, 1969. A second wave of nationalization in banking came into effect in April 1980. In 1993, New Bank of India was merged with PNB. As a result, the number of public sector banks (PSBs) other than SBI declined to 19. The number of nationalized bank branches has increased from 4,553 in 1969 to 68,870 as on December 31, 2018. Among nationalized banks, PNB has maximum number of branches (7,134) followed by Canara Bank (6,506).[3]

August 2019 marked the announcement of four new set of mergers:

1. Punjab National Bank, Oriental Bank of Commerce and United Bank of India will combine to form the nation's second-largest lender (after SBI);
2. Canara Bank and Syndicate Bank will merge;
3. Union Bank of India will amalgamate with Andhra Bank and Corporation Bank;
4. Indian Bank will merge with Allahabad Bank.

The government had already merged Dena Bank and Vijaya Bank with Bank of Baroda in April 2019. Post the mega merger, there are the six PSU banks that will remain independent:

1. Indian Overseas Bank
2. United Commercial Bank
3. Bank of Maharashtra
4. Bank of India
5. Central Bank of India
6. Punjab and Sind Bank

After the second round of merger, the country will essentially have only 12 public sector banks, including State Bank of India. There are various reasons cited by the government for its decision to merge state-owned banks. One of them is that large banks will be able to lend more money and help revive the slowing economy. The government also believes that increased credit growth is necessary to achieve its target of growing India into a $5 trillion economy in the next few years. It is also of the view that the merger will lead to increased operational efficiency that will help these banks lower their costs, thus enabling them to lower their lending rates.[4]

Private Sector Banks

Private sector banks gained prominence in the country after the banking sector reforms of 1990s. There are 22 private sector banks with 32,521 branches across the country. HDFC (4,901) and ICICI (4,868) have maximum number of bank branches as on December 31, 2018.

Foreign Banks

The Oriental Banking Corporation was the first Anglo-Indian commercial bank to be set up in 1842 at Bombay. At the time of independence, there were around 15 foreign banks in the country with nearly one-third of the total deposits of the commercial banking. After independence, however, there was a sharp decline in their overall position in terms of their share of aggregate deposit and credits. During post-reform period, the norms regarding foreign banks were liberalized which saw an upsurge in foreign banking operations in the country. In 2004, the Government of India with a view to liberalize foreign direct investments (FDI) in private sector banks raised the FDI limit to 74% in the private sector banks under the automatic route. RBI unveiled new norms for foreign banks on November 6, 2013 to enable foreign banks compete on a nearly equally footing with Indian banks. To incorporate locally, a foreign bank needs to start out with a capital base of ₹500 crore.[5] Further, all foreign banks who wish to carry banking business in India can only come through a wholly owned subsidiary. However, the banks which commenced banking business in India before August 2010 shall have the option either to continue their banking business through the branch mode* or to convert those branches into a wholly owned subsidiary. The priority sector lending (PSL) requirement will be 40% for foreign banks, such as domestic scheduled commercial banks(see Box 21.1)[6] The foreign banks have contributed in multiple ways, viz., financing of foreign trade, development of banking habits, financing trade and commerce, and so on. There were 130 foreign bank branches in 1969. At present (December 31, 2018), there are 50 foreign banks in the country with 299 bank branches.

Regional Rural Banks

The regional rural banks (RRBs) were established in the year 1976 after the recommendation of working group of rural banks. The RRBs were set up as a part of multi-agency approach to rural credit. The RRBs are owned by the Central Government, the State Government, and the Sponsor Bank whose shares are held in the ratio of 50, 15, and 35%, respectively. In order to consolidate the RRBs, the government is looking at the possibility of merging RRBs operating within the same state and has urged the state-owned banks to explore such options.[7] There were 29 RRBs as on December 31, 2018 as per RBI website.

Local Area Banks

The local area banks (LABs) were established in August 1996. LABs are small private banks having jurisdiction over two or three contiguous districts. The LABs were expected to bridge the gaps in credit availability and strengthen the institutional credit framework in the rural and semi-urban areas. They are supposed to provide efficient and competitive financial intermediation services in the form of mobilization of rural savings and, at the same time, to make them available for investments. LABs were required to have a minimum capital of ₹5 crore.[8] At present, there are three LABs with 87 bank branches across the country.

---

* Earlier, foreign banks in India operated as branches or representative offices of the parent banks. Branch does not have separate legal standing and parent banks are, in principle, responsible for their liabilities. Subsidiaries on the other hand are separate legal entities. They have their own capital base and board of directors.

BOX 21.1 What is Priority Sector Lending Scheme?

The scheme of priority sector lending was introduced by RBI in the year 1974. The scheme was initially introduced in public sector banks but was gradually extended to all commercial banks by 1992. It is a target-based scheme aimed to provide access to credit to the neglected sectors of the economy. Priority Sector includes the following categories: (i) agriculture; (ii) micro, small, and medium enterprises; (iii) advances to weaker section; (iv) export credit; (v) education; (vi) housing; (vii) social infrastructure; (viii) renewable energy; and (ix) others.

Targets and sub-targets for banks under priority sector

Categories	Domestic Scheduled Commercial Banks (Excluding RRBs and Small Finance Banks) and Foreign Banks with 20 Branches and Above	Foreign Banks with Less than 20 Branches
Total priority Sector	40% of ANBC* or CEAOE**, whichever is higher	40% of ANBC or CEAOE, whichever is higher, to be achieved in a phased manner by 2020
Agriculture	18% of ANBC or CEAOE, whichever is higher. Within 18% target for agriculture, a target of 8% prescribed for small and marginal farmers	Not applicable
Micro Enterprises	7.5 percent of ANBC or CEAOE, whichever is higher	Not applicable
Advances to Weaker Sections	10% of ANBC or CEAOE, whichever is higher	Not applicable

*ANBC stands for adjusted net bank credit;
**CEAOE stands for Credit Equivalent Amount of Off-Balance Sheet Exposure

Other areas where lending by commercial banks will be considered as priority sector lending is as follows:

Renewable energy: bank loans up to a limit of ₹150 million.

Education (including vocational courses): loans to individuals up to ₹1 million.

Housing loan: Loans to individuals up to ₹3.5 million in metropolitan centers and up to ₹2.5 million in other centers.

Social infrastructure: Bank loans up to a limit of ₹50 million per borrower.

Sources:

1. RBI (December 28, 2018). *Priority sector lending—Targets and classification.* Retrieved from www.rbi.org.in (accessed on January 5, 2019).
2. RBI revises priority sector lending norms, The Economic Times, June 19, 2018.

Small Finance Banks

Small finance banks were established on the recommendation of "Report of committee on Financial Sector Reforms—A 100 Small Steps" headed by Raghu Ram Rajan in 2009.[9] The small finance bank is a private financial institution (FI) intended to further the objective of financial inclusion by primarily undertaking basic banking activities of acceptance of deposits and lending to unserved and underserved sections including small business units, small and marginal farmers, micro and small industries, and unorganized sector entities. As on December 31, 2018, there are 10 small finance banks with 2,818 branches across the country.

Payment Banks

The payment banks were established on the recommendation of committee (constituted by RBI on September 2013) on "Comprehensive financial services for small businesses and low income households" headed by Dr Nachiket Mor. A payments bank is like any other bank, but operating on a smaller scale without involving any credit risk. In simple words, it can carry out most banking operations but cannot advance loans or issue credit cards. It can accept demand deposits (up to ₹1 lakh) and offer remittance services, mobile payments/transfers/purchases, and other banking services like ATM/debit cards, net banking, and third party fund transfers.[10] A payments bank aims to further financial inclusion, especially through savings accounts and payments services. The six payment banks functioning in India at present are Aditya Birla Payments Bank, Airtel Payments Bank, India Post Payments Bank, Fino Payments Bank, Jio Payments Bank, and Paytm Payments Bank. These banks have 642 branches in the country as on December 31, 2018.[11]

Cooperative Banking

Cooperative banking sector plays an imperative function by providing financial intermediation services to agricultural and allied activities, small-scale industries, and self-employed workers. Since the network of cooperative banks is widespread across different parts of the country, these institutions are considered as a potential instrument to bring people from far-flung areas under the formal banking network.[12] The history of cooperative credit in India can be traced back to 1904 when credit societies were formed under Cooperative Societies Act, 1904. The Act was amended in 1912 with a view to broad basing it to facilitate organization of non-credit societies. Co-operative banks are owned and controlled by their members, who democratically elect the board of directors. The cooperative structure in India can broadly be divided into two segments. While the urban areas are served by Urban Cooperative Banks (UCBs), rural cooperatives operate in the rural parts of the country.

Urban Cooperative Banks (UCBs)

The term UCB, though not formally defined, refers to primary cooperative banks located in urban and semi-urban areas. The first urban cooperative credit society was registered in Kanjivaram in the erstwhile Madras province in October 1904. The banking-related activities of UCBs are governed by the Reserve Bank, whereas the registration and management related activities are governed by the Registrar of Cooperative Societies (RCS) in the case of UCBs operating in single State and Central RCS (CRCS) in the case of multi-State UCBs. UCBs finance urban areas under self-employment, industries, small scale units, home finance consumer finance, personal finance, and so on. As of end-December 2018, there were 1,490 UCBs operating in the country of which majority were non-scheduled UCBs.

Rural Cooperatives

The All-India Rural Credit Review Committee (1969) recommended the establishment of cooperative banks in the country as a part of multi-agency approach. The rural cooperatives are divided into short-term and long-term structures. The structure of short-term cooperatives sector comprises State Cooperative Banks (SCBs) operating as apex level institutions in each state, District Central Cooperative Banks (DCCBs) operating at district level, and the Primary Agricultural Credit Societies (PACS) operating at village level or grass root level. Similarly, the long-term cooperatives are the State Cooperative Agriculture and Rural Development Banks (SCARDBs) at State level and Primary Cooperative Agriculture and Rural Development Banks (PCARDBs) operating at district/block level. Out of the total number of rural cooperatives, short-term cooperatives are in majority while only 1% of the total cooperatives operating in the country were long term in nature.

Non-Performing Assets of Commercial Banks in India

A Non-Performing Asset (NPA) is a loan or advance for which the principal or interest payment remained overdue for a period of 90 days. Banks are required to classify NPAs further into sub-standard, doubtful, and loss assets.

1. *Sub-standard assets*: Assets which have remained NPA for a period less than or equal to 12 months.
2. *Doubtful assets*: An asset would be classified as doubtful if it has remained in the substandard category for a period of 12 months.
3. *Loss assets*: As per RBI, "Loss asset is considered uncollectible and of such little value that its continuance as a bankable asset is not warranted, although there may be some salvage or recovery value."

As of March 31, 2018, provisional estimates suggest that the total volume of gross NPAs in the economy stands at ₹10.35 lakh crore. About 85% of these NPAs are from loans and advances of PSBs. For instance, NPAs in the SBI are worth ₹2.23 lakh crore.[13]

Causes of NPAs During Recent Years

1. *Global financial crisis*: Global financial crisis which occurred in 2007–2008 and Euro-zone crisis of 2009–2010 impacted the production and exports and caused huge losses to Indian companies. The companies failed to repay their loans that turned into bad debts.
2. *Twin balance sheet problem*: Twin balance sheet problem refers to the stress on balance sheets of banks due to NPAs or bad loans on the one hand and heavily indebted corporates on the other. A lot of the loans currently classified as NPAs originated in the mid-2000s, at a time when the economy was booming and business outlook was very positive. Large corporations were granted loans for projects based on the extrapolation of their recent growth and performance. With loans being available more easily than before,

corporations grew highly leveraged, implying that most financing was through external borrowings rather than internal promoter equity. But as economic growth stagnated following the global financial crisis of 2008, the repayment capability of these corporations decreased. This contributed to what is now known as India's twin balance sheet problem.*

3. *Ever-greening*: When the project for which the loan was taken started underperforming, borrowers lost their capability of paying back the bank. The banks at this time took to the practice of "ever-greening," where fresh loans were given to some promoters to enable them to pay off their interest. An evergreen loan is a type of revolving loan. Another example is that as you pay on the loan, the money becomes available to borrow once again. For instance, a bank can lend money to a company to pay off another bank's loan. This way the second bank can save an account from going bad and reduce its NPAs. The second bank can then extend a similar facility to a company which has not been able to repay loans from the first bank.[14]
4. *Frauds*: Recently, there have also been frauds of high magnitude that have contributed to rising NPAs. Although the size of frauds relative to the total volume of NPAs is relatively small, these frauds have been increasing, and there have been no instances of high-profile fraudsters being penalized.
5. *NPAs in Agriculture and MSMEs*: Industrial sickness is rampant in MSMEs. More than ₹32,000 crore is stuck in nearly 4.8 lakh sick MSMEs in the country. Agriculture sector also faces similar concerns as major chunk of money lent to farmers does not come back.

Recent Steps taken by Government to Resolve Problem of NPAs

The measures taken to resolve and prevent NPAs can broadly be classified into two kinds—first, regulatory mean of resolving NPAs according to law, like the Insolvency and Bankruptcy (IBC) Code,** and second, reforming the PSBs. IBC was enacted in May 2016 to provide a time-bound 180-day recovery process for insolvent accounts. The creditors of these insolvent accounts, presided over by an insolvency professional, decide whether to restructure the loan or to sell the defaulter's assets to recover the outstanding amount. If a timely decision is not arrived at, the defaulter's assets are liquidated.

The PSB reforms include measures like: Bank recapitalization, strengthening of bank boards and strengthening of top management. Bank recapitalization is an act of injecting equity capital by the government into PSBs so as to strengthen them financially. In the financial year 2018–2019, the government infused more than ₹1 lakh crore of capital in various PSBs. Bank boards must be strengthened through the induction of quality professionals as independent director. The choice of wrong persons for top management positions has been the principal bane of PSBs in the past decade. The managing director of the bank must be chosen among one of the executive directors of the bank. It will ensure continuity, familiarity with bank culture, and a measure of commitment.[15]

---

* For detailed discussion on Twin Balance Sheet Problem, refer to Chapter 16 "Public, Private and Small Sector in Indian Economy."

** For detailed discussion of IBC, refer to Chapter 16 "Public, Private, and Small Sector in Indian Economy."

Banking Sector Reforms

Banking sector reforms have been the culmination of extensive, well-sequenced, and coordinated policy measures aimed at making the Indian financial sector efficient, competitive, and stable. The government established various committees and implemented their recommendations to improve the overall performance of banking sector. To name few, Chakaravarti Committee on monetary policy (1985), Narsimham Committee-I on financial sector reforms (1991), Padmanabhan Committee to review the supervision of banks (1996), Narsimham Committee-II on the review of banking sector reforms (1997), Verma Committee on weak banks (1998), RH Khan Committee on harmonization of role of FIs and banks (1998) can be mentioned in this regard. The following points can be discussed under banking sector reforms:

1. *Prudential reforms:* Prudential measures include phased implementation of international best practices and norms in order to reduce overall risk of the banking system. Such steps involve the adoption of measures like risk-weighted capital adequacy requirement, appropriate accounting norms, recognition of different components of risk, assignment of risk-weights to various asset classes, application of marked-to-market principle for investment portfolio and limits on deployment of fund in sensitive activities, and migration to advance approaches under Basel II.[16]
2. *Supervisory reforms:* Various steps were taken to enhance the supervisory reforms in the banking sector, viz., establishment of the Board for financial supervision as the apex supervisory authority for commercial banks, FIs, and non-banking financial companies; introduction of CAMELS (C—Capital adequacy, A—Asset quality, M—Management, E—Earnings, L—Liquidity) supervisory rating system, moving toward risk-based supervision and consolidated supervision of financial conglomerates; recasting of the role of statutory auditors; increased internal control through strengthening of internal audit; and inculcating corporate governance in the banking system.
3. *Competition reforms:* In the pre-reform period, banks in India have become uncompetitive and inefficient because of too much government control and limited entry to private sector and foreign sector banks. Under reform measures, the government granted operational autonomy to PSBs and reduced public ownership in such banks by allowing them to raise capital from equity market up to 49% of paid-up capital. Private banks and foreign banks have been allowed to function in India to enthuse the spirit of competition and wider choice. Further permission in the financial sector in the form of FDI as well as FPI has been granted, and banks are allowed to diversify product portfolio and business activities.
4. *Market reforms:* It includes dismantling of administered interest rate measures; reduction in CRR and SLR rates from the erstwhile higher levels; discontinuing the ad hoc treasury bills and market determined pricing for government securities; introduction of pure inter-bank call money market; auction-based repos-reverse repos for short-term liquidity management; and facilitation of improved payments and settlement mechanism.
5. *Institutional and legal reforms:* Institutional reforms in the Indian banking signify the establishment of Lok Adalats (people's courts), Debt Recovery Tribunals, Asset Reconstruction Companies, Settlement Advisory Committees, Corporate Debt Restructuring Mechanism, etc., for quicker recovery/restructuring; Enactment of Securitisation and

Reconstruction of Financial Assets and Enforcement of Securities Interest (SARFAESI), Act and its subsequent amendment to ensure creditor rights; Setting up of Credit Information Bureau for information sharing on defaulters as also other borrowers; setting up of Clearing Corporation of India Limited (CCIL) to act as central counter party for facilitating payments and settlement system relating to fixed income securities and money market instruments. The Banking Ombudsman Scheme launched in 1995 enables an expeditious and inexpensive forum to bank customers for the resolution of complaints relating to certain services rendered by banks. Presently, the Banking Ombudsman Scheme 2006 (as amended up to July 1, 2017) is in operation.

6. *Technology reforms:* Technology reforms include setting up of INFINET as the communication backbone for the financial sector, and introduction of negotiated dealing system (NDS) for screen-based trading in government securities and real-time gross settlement (RTGS) system. The operation of Automatic Teller Machines (ATMs), card-based transactions, internet banking, mobile banking, national electronic fund transfer, express cheque clearing process (ECCS), etc., has metamorphosed the role of Indian banking. A High Level Committee (Chairman: Dr K.C. Chakrabarty) and members from IIT, IIM, IDRBT, Banks, and the Reserve Bank prepared the "IT Vision Document—2011–2017," for the Reserve Bank and banks, which provides an indicative road map for enhanced usage of IT in the banking sector.

Reserve Bank of India

The Royal Commission on Indian Currency and Finance (also known as the Hilton-Young Commission) recommended in 1926 the creation of a central bank to separate the control of currency and credit from the government and to enlarge banking services throughout the country. The Reserve Bank of India was established on April 1, 1935 in accordance with the provisions of the Reserve Bank of India Act, 1934. Since then, the Reserve Bank's role and functions have undergone numerous changes—as the nature of the Indian economy has changed.[17] Though originally privately owned, since nationalization in 1949, the Reserve Bank is fully owned by the Government of India. The Central Office of the Reserve Bank was initially established in Kolkata but was permanently moved to Mumbai in 1937. Sir Osborne Smith was the first Governor of the Reserve Bank for the period 1935–1937.

The Central Board of Directors is at apex of the RBI's organizational structure. It is appointed by the Government for a period of 4 years to govern the affairs of RBI. The Governor is the chief executive of RBI and supervises and directs the affairs and business of the RBI. The management team also includes Deputy Governors and Executive Directors.[18] RBI is made up of 34 Departments which focus on policy issues in the Reserve Bank's functional areas and internal operations. It has 27 Regional Offices and Branches, and they act as Bank's operational arms and customer interfaces, headed by Regional Director.

Functions of RBI

RBI, like other central banks of the world, performs almost all traditional functions of central banking. Let us have a detailed discussion on functions of RBI:

BOX 21.2 Minting and Printing in India

Minting: Coins are minted by the Government of India. The Indian Coinage Act, 1906, governs the minting of rupee coins, including small coins of the value of less than one rupee. One rupee notes (no longer issued now) and coins are legal tender in India for unlimited amounts. Fifty paisa coins are legal tender for any sum not exceeding ₹10 and smaller coins for any sum not exceeding one rupee. The Reserve Bank acts as an agent of the Central Government for distribution, issue, and handling of the coins (including one rupee note) and for withdrawing and remitting them back to the government as may be necessary. The Security Printing and Minting Corporation of India Limited (SPMCIL), a wholly owned company of the Government of India, has four mints at Mumbai, Noida, Kolkata, and Hyderabad for coin production. As per the provisions of Coinage Act, 1906, coins can be issued up to the denomination of ₹1,000.

Printing: For printing of notes, SPMCIL has set up printing presses at Nashik, Maharashtra, Dewas, and Madhya Pradesh. The Bharatiya Reserve Bank Note Mudran Pvt. Ltd. (BRBNMPL), a wholly owned subsidiary of the Reserve Bank, also has set up printing presses at Mysore in Karnataka and Salboni in West Bengal. The Reserve Bank is authorized to issue notes in the denominations of 5,000 rupees and 10,000 rupees or any other denomination, but not exceeding 10,000 rupees that the Central Government may specify.

Sources:
1. Information retrieved from https://www.spmcil.com (accessed on March 31, 2019).
2. Information retrieved from https://www.brbnmpl.co.in (accessed on March 31, 2019).

Currency Issuing Authority

The Paper Currency Act of 1861 conferred upon the Government of India the monopoly of note issues, and between 1861 and 1935, the Government of India managed the issue of paper currency (Box 21.2). However, the RBI Act, 1934, vested with RBI the basic functions of issuing of Bank notes and the keeping of reserves with a view to securing monetary stability in India and generally to operate the currency and credit system of the country to its advantage. RBI issues currency on the basis of minimum reserve system. Minimum reserve system refers to the reserves kept by RBI against its currency liability. According to the RBI (Amendment) Act, 1957, a minimum reserve of ₹200 crore in the form of gold and Foreign Exchange of which at least ₹115 crore should be in gold.

Banker and Debt Manager to the Government

The Reserve Bank of India Act, 1934, requires the Central Government to entrust the Reserve Bank with all its money, remittance, exchange, and banking transactions in India and the management of its public debt. The government also deposits its cash balances with the Reserve Bank. The Reserve Bank may also, by agreement, act as the banker to a State Government. Currently, the Reserve Bank acts as banker to all the State Governments in India, except Jammu & Kashmir and Sikkim. It has limited agreements for the management of the public debt of these two State Governments. The Reserve Bank also undertakes to float loans and manage them on behalf of the governments. It also provides Ways and Means Advances—a short-term interest-bearing advance—to the governments, to meet the temporary mismatches in their receipts and payments. Besides, it arranges for the investments of surplus cash balances of the governments as a portfolio manager. The Reserve Bank also acts as adviser to the government, whenever called upon to do so, on monetary and banking related matter.

Formulation of Monetary Policy

RBI formulates and implements monetary policy of the country so as to regulate the flow of credit into the productive channels. The monetary policy functions with two primary objectives: promoting growth of the economy and maintaining price stability. However, in the wake of the global financial crisis, central banks have expanded their toolkits to deal with risks to financial stability and to manage volatile exchange rates.[19] Monetary policy in India is announced in the month of April every year with the review of same in every quarter. For details see the section of "Monetary Policy" in this chapter.

Regulatory and Supervisory Functions

Traditionally, the Reserve Bank's regulatory and supervisory policy initiatives are aimed at protection of the depositors' interests, orderly development and conduct of banking operations, and liquidity and solvency of banks. With the onset of banking sector reforms during the 1990s, various prudential measures were initiated that have, in effect, strengthened the Indian banking system over a period of time. Improved financial soundness of banks has helped them to show stability and resilience in the face of the recent severe global financial crisis, which had seriously impacted several banks and FIs in advanced countries. However, there is still a need to strengthen the regulatory and supervisory architecture. The Reserve Bank represents India in various international fora, such as the Basel Committee on Banking Supervision (BCBS), Switzerland and the Financial Stability Board (FSB), Switzerland. Its presence on such bodies has enabled the Reserve Bank's active participation in the process of evolving global standards for enhanced regulation and supervision of banks.

Banker to Banks

As banker to the banks, RBI focuses on enabling smooth, swift, and seamless clearing and settlement of inter-bank obligations. It enables banks to maintain their accounts with the Reserve Bank for statutory reserve requirements and maintenance of transaction balances. RBI also acts as a lender of last resort. It can come to the rescue of a bank that is solvent but faces temporary liquidity problems by supplying it with much needed liquidity when no one else is willing to extend credit to that bank. The Reserve Bank extends this facility to protect the interest of the depositors of the bank and to prevent possible failure of a bank, which in turn may also affect other banks and institutions and can have an adverse impact on financial stability and thus on the economy.[20]

Foreign Exchange and Reserve Management

The Reserve Bank plays a key role in the regulation and development of the foreign exchange market and assumes three broad roles relating to foreign exchange: Regulating transactions related to the external sector and facilitating the development of the foreign exchange market; ensuring smooth conduct and orderly conditions in the domestic foreign exchange market; and managing the foreign currency assets and gold reserves of the country. Reserve Bank, as the custodian of

BOX 21.3 What is Market Stabilization Scheme?

Market Stabilization Scheme (MSS) is an intervention by the RBI in the foreign exchange market to withdraw excess liquidity (that is generated as a result of the RBI's purchase of foreign currencies in the foreign exchange market) by selling government securities in the economy. Since the beginning of economic reforms, the country has witnessed large-scale capital inflows. This had resulted in an oversupply of US dollars in the Indian market resulting currency appreciation (supply being greater than demand). Under such circumstances, RBI bought dollars, thus creating an equivalent amount of rupees. Injection of rupees increased money supply, and in order to neutralize it, RBI sold securities and squeezed rupees, a process called *Sterilization*. Thus, RBI was exercising open market operations to sterilize the impact of change in money supply. But continuous resort to sterilization depleted RBI's stock of government securities. On the recommendations of Working Group of RBI on Instruments of Sterilisation, *MSS* was introduced by the way of an agreement between the government and the RBI in early 2004. Under the scheme, RBI issues bonds on behalf of the government (called market stabilization bonds) and the money raised under bonds is impounded in a separate account with RBI. The money does not go into the government account. While these issuances do not provide budgetary support to the government, interest costs are borne by the government. These securities are also traded in the secondary market. By design, the MSS has the flexibility of not only absorbing liquidity but also injecting liquidity, if required, through selling as well as buy-back of securities issued under the MSS. MSS has become the frequently used policy of the RBI during the post-reform period.

Sources:

1. What is sterilisation? *The Hindu Business Line*, February 2, 2003.
2. How RBI intervention changed with a gaining rupee. *The Economic Times*, November 23, 2018.

the country's foreign exchange reserves, is also vested with the responsibility of managing their investment. The Reserve Bank's reserves management function has in recent years grew both in terms of importance and sophistication for two main reasons. First, the share of foreign currency assets in the balance sheet of the Reserve Bank has substantially increased. Second, with the increased volatility in exchange and interest rates in the global market, the task of preserving the value of reserves and obtaining a reasonable return on them has become challenging. Until the balance of payments crisis of 1991, India's approach to foreign exchange reserves was essentially aimed at maintaining an appropriate import cover. The traditional approach of assessing reserve adequacy in terms of import cover has been widened to include a number of parameters about the size, composition, risk profiles, liquidity, and return.

Developmental and Promotional Functions

Apart from traditional and general functions, RBI also undertakes certain specific developmental and promotional functions due to specific nature of Indian economy. These functions are

1. RBI has promoted agriculture finance in the country through establishing Agriculture Refinance and Development Corporation (ARDC) in 1963 and NABARD in 1982.
2. Rapid industrial growth is the key to faster economic development. In this regard, the adequate and timely availability of credit to small, medium, and large industry is very

significant. In this regard, the RBI has always been instrumental in setting up special FIs such as ICICI Ltd. IDBI, SIDBI, and EXIM BANK.

3. RBI collects data and disseminates information on interest rate, inflation, savings and investments, trade, and other macro-economic indicators and such data are quite useful for researchers and policy maker. The Reserve Bank has its separate publication division which regularly publishes important weekly, monthly, half-yearly, and annual reports. It includes RBI weekly reports, RBI Annual Report, Report on Trend and Progress of Commercial Banks in India, Report on Currency and Finance, and RBI Hand Book of Statistics. This information is made available to the public also at cheaper rates.
4. RBI has been instrumental in the mobilization of savings and extending banking in unbanked areas. RBI has been encouraging commercial banks to open new branches in the rural and unbanked areas. Further, RBI has institutionalized savings and taken measures for an expansion of the banking network. It has set up many institutions such as the Deposit Insurance Corporation (1962), UTI (1964), IDBI (1964), NABARD (1982), and NHB (1988) to develop and promote banking habits among the people. At present there are four subsidiaries of RBI, namely, Deposit Insurance and Credit Guarantee Corporation (estb. 1978), National Housing Bank (estb. 1988), Bharatiya Reserve Bank Note Mudran Private Limited (estb. 1995) and Reserve Bank Information Technology Pvt. Ltd (estb. 2016).
5. RBI also established prominent training and academic institutions in the country. For example, National Institute of Bank Management (NIBM) was established in 1969 at Pune. The Institute is engaged in research (policy and operations), education and training of senior bankers and development finance administrators, and consultancy to the banking and financial sector. Indira Gandhi Institute of Development Research (IGIDR) located in Mumbai is an advanced research institute established and fully funded by the Reserve Bank of India for carrying out research on development issues from a multi-disciplinary point of view. Institute for Development and Research in Banking Technology (IDRBT) was established in 1996 in Hyderabad as an Autonomous Centre for Development and Research in Banking Technology.

MONETARY AND LIQUIDITY AGGREGATES

Money is a means of payment, and thus, a lubricant that facilitates exchange. Money also acts as a store of value and a unit of account. In the real world, however, money provides monetary services along with tangible remuneration. It is for this reason that money has to have relationship with the activities that economic entities pursue. Money can, therefore, be defined for policy purposes as the set of liquid financial assets, the variation in the stock of which could impact on aggregate economic activity. Like other countries, a range of monetary and liquidity measures are compiled in India.[21]

Reserve money: Reserve Money is the most important indicator of money supply in the economy. It is also called high powered money, base money, and central bank money.

Reserve money (M0) = Currency in circulation + Bankers' deposits with the RBI + "Other" deposits with the RBI.

Currency in circulation' includes notes in circulation, rupee coins, and small coins. Bankers' Deposits with the RBI represent balances maintained by banks in the current account with the Reserve Bank mainly for maintaining Cash Reserve Ratio (CRR) and as working funds for clearing adjustments. Other deposits with the Reserve Bank for the purpose of monetary compilation includes deposits from foreign central banks, multilateral institutions, financial institutions etc. The reserve money during March 31, 2019 was reported to be ₹27,704 billion. Currency in circulation is 77% of reserve money. Bankers' deposits with the RBI constitute nearly 22% of reserve money. Other deposits with the Reserve Bank constitute 1% of reserve money. Reserve money holds significant position in the RBI's monetary policy because currency in circulation is its biggest component which decides the level of liquidity and price level in the economy.

1. M1 = Currency with the public + Demand deposits with the banking system + "Other" deposits with the RBI. *Currency with the public is currency in circulation less cash held by banks. M1 is called narrow money.*
2. M2 = M1 + Savings deposits of post office savings banks.
3. M3 = M1+ Time deposits with the banking system. M3 is called broad money. *It is considered as the most important indicator of money supply. Money multiplier can be calculated as M3 ÷ M0, where M3 is the broad money and M0 is the reserve money. In India, money multiplier has increased from 1.6 in 1956 to 5.6 in 2019.*
4. M4 = M3 + All deposits with post office savings banks (excluding National Savings Certificates). *It must be remembered that M1 is the most liquid and M4 is least. That is, in terms of liquidity, M1 > M2 > M3 > M4.*

New monetary aggregates: The Working group on money supply chaired by Dr Y.V. Reddy proposed new monetary/ liquidity aggregates in 1998.[22]

1. NM1 = Currency with the public + Demand deposits with the banking system + "Other" deposits with the RBI. *It can be seen that M1 and NM1 are same.*
2. NM2 = NM1 + Short-term time deposits of residents (including and up to the contractual maturity of one year). *NM2 stands in between narrow money (M1) and broad money (M3).*
3. NM3 = NM2 + Long-term time deposits of residents + Call/Term funding from financial institutions.
4. L1 = NM3 + All deposits with the post office savings banks (excluding National Savings Certificates).
5. L2 = L1 +Term deposits with term lending institutions and refinancing institutions (FIs) + Term borrowing by FIs + Certificates of deposit issued by FIs.
6. L3 = L2 + Public deposits of non-banking financial companies.

Monetary Policy

Monetary policy is the regulatory policy of Central Bank (RBI) that involves the management of money supply and interest rate to achieve macroeconomic objectives like inflation, consumption, growth, and liquidity. Earlier monetary policy used to be announced twice in a year in October for October to March and in April for April to September corresponding to agriculture sector seasons. But with the decline of the share of agricultural credit and rise in that of the industrial and services sector credit, the RBI has started making an annual policy statement in April, with a review of the same in every quarter. The monetary policy framework of RBI can be discussed under four heads:

1. the objectives of monetary policy;
2. the analytics of monetary policy (that focuses on the transmission mechanism);
3. the operating procedure (consisting of operating targets and instruments); and
4. the monetary policy reforms.

Objectives of Monetary Policy

The objectives of monetary policy can be categorized as follows:

1. Ensuring adequate flow of credit to the productive sectors for economic growth.
2. Maintaining price stability.
3. Reducing the impact of business cycles (slumps and booms) by manipulation of credit and Interest policy.
4. Stability of exchange rate.
5. Ensure smooth flow of money.

Attaining price stability (or controlling inflation) and promoting economic growth are the most commonly pursued objectives by central banks across the world. While a number of prominent central banks including the European Central Bank, Bank of England, and Bank of Japan have adopted price stability as the single objective of monetary policy, the Federal Reserve of the United States continues to pursue multiple objectives of monetary policy, viz., maximum employment, stable prices, and moderate long-term interest rates. Central banks in several developing countries have also placed exchange rate management as another important policy objective. In 1990s, particularly after the financial crises of 1990s, the concern for financial stability is an integral part of the central bank's activism. In view of large-scale financial crises that occurred in a number of countries in the 1990s (notably in Mexico, South Asia, Brazil, and Argentina), and global financial crisis of 2007–2008, achieving financial stability to prevent such crisis or to protect the national economy from the ill effects of such crisis occurring in another country has become an additional objective of monetary policy. However, it is often not possible to achieve all these objectives by monetary policy alone. It is because the objectives of monetary policy are interrelated, and there is trade-off between cheap money policy and dear money policy (Box 21.4). For example, there is often a conflict between inflation and unemployment—inflation can be reduced at the cost of higher unemployment. Similar trade-offs exist among other objectives as well. To avoid confusion, academicians and policy-makers agree that monetary policy should target price stability, leaving growth and employment to be targeted by fiscal and other policies. India's approach in respect of monetary policy objectives takes into account the ground level realities in the country (such as depending upon the level/stage of development, rate of inflation, nature of financial markets, and relative openness of the economy). Traditionally, maintaining price stability and ensuring an adequate flow of credit to the productive sectors (to maintain the economic growth) of the economy have been the major objectives of monetary policy in India. In the post-reform period, the considerations of financial stability have assumed greater importance in view of the increasing openness of the Indian economy and financial reforms.[23]

BOX 21.4 Cheap Money Policy and Dear Money Policy

Cheap Money Policy: It is the policy by which central bank increases the money supply by lowering the interest rate. The cheaper loans boost up investment activity, growth and employment. Cheap money policy is also called expansionary monetary policy. Cheap money policy can be exercised through reduction in CRR, BR and REPO rates.

Dear Money Policy: It is the policy by virtue of which the central bank reduces the money supply in the economic system by raising the rate of interest. The dearer loans dampen the investment scenario and growth but help to control inflation because of reduction in income and purchasing power. Dear money policy can be exercised through increase in CRR, BR and REPO rates.

Analytics of Monetary Policy

The analytics of monetary policy refers to monetary transmission mechanism by virtue of which monetary policy actions affect output and inflation. In the literature, four sets of transmission channels have been identified:[24] (1) the quantum channel (e.g., relating to money supply and credit), (2) the interest rate channel, (3) the exchange rate channel, and (4) the asset price channel. The functioning and success of these channels depends upon the stage of economic development and the nature of financial structure in the economy. For example, the exchange rate channel would assume significance in an open economy; the quantum channel will play an important role where banks are the major source of finance; the interest rate channel will work effectively in the economy where the interrelationship between money, output, and prices is highly appreciated, and asset price channel is popular where capital market is quite developed. In the modern economies, these channels are highly interdependent and mutually affect each other up to large extent.

Instruments of Monetary Policy

Instruments of monetary policy can be broadly classified into direct and indirect instruments.

Direct Instruments of Monetary Policy

Direct instruments affect the money supply directly and constitute CRR, SLR, and Credit and interest rate directives.

1. *Cash Reserve Ratio* (*CRR*): Cash Reserve Ratio or CRR specifies the amount of reserves, banks need to maintain as cash or with the central bank as percentage of their demand and time deposits. Increase in CRR reduces the money supply from the system and thus leads to rise in interest rate and reduces investment, income, and hence, inflation due to fall in purchasing power. On the contrary, reduction in CRR makes banks richer with cash which leads them to reduce interest rate, and hence, investment and income and purchasing power all rise leading to inflation. RBI is empowered to vary CRR between 3 and 15%.CRR as on July 31, 2019 was 4%.
2. *Statutory Liquidity Ratio* (*SLR*): Statutory Liquidity Ratio or SLR specifies the amount of money banks must invest in government securities (and bonds of PSUs) as proportion of their deposits. Increase in SLR reduces banks' capacity to lend and makes loans dearer which ultimately leads to fall in investment, income, and prices. Conversely, reduction in SLR increases banks' capacity to lend and makes loans cheaper which finally leads to increase in investment, income, and prices. At present (July 31, 2019), RBI has fixed SLR at 19%.

3. *Credit and interest rate directives*: The credit directives entail the priority sector lending norms of RBI which has to be followed by commercial banks. Interest rate directive signifies prescription regarding lending and deposit rates. For example, farmers in India can get agriculture loan up to ₹3 lakh at 7% interest rate. An additional incentive of 3% is being given to farmers for prompt repayment of loans within due date, making the effective interest rate 4%.

Indirect Instruments of Monetary Policy

The indirect instruments affect the money supply via interest rate channel. That is, these instruments first cause the rates of interest/price to change, which, in turn, causes flow of credit to change. They consist of the bank rate, repos/reverse repos, open market operations (OMOs), and marginal standing facility (MSF) of RBI.

1. *Repos/reverse repos*: The repos/reverse repos are used to inject or mop up liquidity for a short duration. Repo rate is the rate at which the central bank of a country (RBI) lends money to commercial banks in the event of any shortfall of funds. In other words, repo rate is the rate at which commercial banks borrow from RBI by pledging securities with it with the option to repurchase them back at a rate called Repo rate. Under reverse repo, the commercial banks can park their surplus funds with RBI and earn a specified interest on it called reverse repo rate. At present, reverse repo rate is lower than repo rate by 25 basis points.*
2. *Open market operations (OMOs)*: OMOs are resorted to by the RBI via the sale/purchase of government securities to/from the market with the primary aim to regulate the flow of money in the market. OMOs are used by RBI to change the liquidity condition for a longer term and are constrained by the stock of government securities available with it at a point of time.
3. *Marginal standing facility (MSF)*: MSF was introduced by RBI in 2011 on the recommendations of the Working Group on Operating Procedure of Monetary Policy (Chairman: Deepak Mohanty). MSF is a window for banks to borrow from the Reserve Bank of India in an emergency situation when inter-bank liquidity dries up completely. Banks can borrow up to 1% of their respective net demand and time liabilities (NDTL). Reverse repo rate < repo rate < MSF rate. The difference in the three rates between one another is 25 basis points. For example, as on July 31, 2019, the repo rate was 6% and Reverse repo and MSF rates were 5.75 and 6.00%, respectively. The fixed interest rate corridor, set by the MSF rate (at the top) and reverse repo rate (at the bottom), reduces uncertainty and avoids difficulties in communication associated with a variable corridor, and thus, helps in keeping the overnight average call money rate** close to the repo rate.
4. *Bank rate*: Bank rate is the rate at which RBI rediscounts the bills of exchange or other commercial papers (CPs) of the commercial banks or in simple language lends to commercial banks. Increase in bank rate reduces the volume of money supply and vice versa. RBI has aligned bank rate to the MSF rate and, therefore, changes automatically as and when the MSF rate changes alongside the change in policy repo rate. Bank rate as on July 31, 2018 was 6%.

---

*In banking, one Basis Point is a unit equivalent to 0.01%, that is, 1/100th of a percent. Thus, 10 bps means 0.10% and 100 bps means 1%.

**Call money rate is the rate at which commercial banks borrow from each other for short term emergencies. Pl refer to section 'Money Market'.

Monetary Policy Reforms

Background

"Financial repression" has been a dominant characteristic of the financial markets in almost all developing economies and India has been no exception.[25] In the pre-reform period, Indian financial market was characterized by complex and inefficient administered interest rate regime, fragile money market (lacking depth, liquidity, and inter-linkage), high CRR, SLR and imprudent control and regulation. In 1955, RBI and ministry of finance agreed to create ad hoc treasury bills (T-bills) as an instrument to raise short-term credit by the Central Government from the RBI. Over time, it became a ritual to roll over the ad hoc T-bills on their maturity, and issuing fresh ad hocs to raise more finance. Since the ad hoc T-bills were held by the RBI, and not sold to the market, every issue of such T-bills amounted to increase in money supply in the economy. Apart from the ad hoc T-bills, the RBI had to purchase dated government securities that were not taken up by the market. These two components (RBI's purchase of ad hocs and dated Government securities) together constitute net RBI credit to the Central Government, and it emerged as the major source of the creation of reserve money, and hence, increases in money supply. This process of financing the fiscal deficits of the government is called automatic monetization of government deficit. The consequence was inflation in almost all the decades of pre-reform period barring some exceptions. CRR was raised steadily from 3% in the early 1970s to 15% in the early 1990s to restrain inflation. Interest rates on government securities purchased by commercial banks (as per SLR requirements) were kept artificially low to reduce the cost of government debt but later on rates were increased to voluntarily attract the banks. The idea did not work and the government increased the limits of SLR to as high as 38.5% by early 1990s. The monetary policy became ineffective and lost its significance in achieving its desired objectives. It is in the background of the above-mentioned facts that monetary policy reforms became unavoidable.

Reform Measures

In 1985, the Chakarvarti Committee was set up to review the working of monetary system. In 1991, Narasimham Committee I (on financial sector reforms), and in 1998, Narasimham Committee II (on review of banking sector reforms) submitted their reports. All the three committees (among others) recommended a fundamental restructuring of the monetary system. The following points can be discussed in this regard:

1. *Adoption of multiple indicator approach*: Though the twin objectives of price stability and ensuring availability of adequate credit to productive sectors of the economy have been retained, the other subsidiary objectives such as financial stability and exchange rate management have also been taken care of. Reflecting development of financial market and liberalization, use of broad money as an intermediate target has been de-emphasized and a multiple indicator approach has been adopted.[26]
2. *Shifting away from direct instruments to indirect instruments*: In the post-reform period, there is a clear cut shift from direct instruments such as CRR, bank rate, and selective credit control measures to indirect instruments such as REPOs and OMOs for the conduct of monetary policy. The rates of CRR, bank rate, and SLR have been remarkably reduced in order to provide more financial autonomy to the banks. The bank rate remained insignificant tool of monetary policy in the decades of 1960s, 1970s, and 1980s because of underdeveloped bill market in the country and also because bank rate signifies voluntary option of the banks to borrow from RBI. RBI re-activated bank rate in April

1997. Initially, all financial accommodation extended by the RBI was linked to this rate. With steady growth of the repo/reverse repo market and introduction of LAF, bank rate is used more to signal the RBI's view of interest rates to the market.

3. *Introduction of Liquidity Adjustment Facility (LAF)*: The LAF was introduced in two phases in April 1999 and June 2000. The Reserve Bank is now able to control liquidity in the system on a daily basis through repos/reverse repos under LAF. This was impossible in the earlier structure when CRR was the primary tool to control liquidity, because CRR could be changed at best on a fortnightly basis. Open Market Operations (OMOs) were re-activated in 1992–1993 in order to develop a market-based mechanism to inject/absorb liquidity from the system. Market Stabilization Scheme (MSS) was introduced in 2004 as an additional instrument to deal with capital inflows without affecting short-term liquidity management role of LAF.
4. *Discontinuing the automatic monetization of fiscal deficit*: The Chakarvarti Committee (1985) and the Narasimham Committee (1991) strongly advocated freeing the monetary policy from the clutches of fiscal policy, stopping (or setting a limit on) monetization of fiscal deficit and hence providing greater freedom to the RBI to regulate the volume of money in the economy. The Central Government and the RBI entered into an agreement to discontinue the ad hoc T-bills from April 1, 1997. However, it was recognized that there could be a temporary mismatch between the receipts and payments of the Government of India, and for that, a scheme of ways and means advances was started with effect from April 1, 1997. Since then, the automatic monetization of fiscal deficit has been stopped and the Central Government has relied on market borrowing to finance the fiscal deficit. This move, apart from creating some independence for the monetary policy, has also given a big boost to the development of the debt market. Further, RBI was precluded from participating directly in the primary market for government securities with effect from April 1, 2006.
5. *Deregulation of interest rate:* Deregulation of interest rate marked an important policy step wherein banks were allowed to set interest rates as per demand and supply forces. In September 1991, the multiple rates for loans to various sectors and various sizes were gradually withdrawn (except for priority sector) and banks were given full freedom to determine their lending rates and allowed to set different prime lending rate (PLR) for different maturities, and also to lend at sub-PLR (below PLR) rates to highly creditworthy borrower. Deposit rate deregulation started in April 1992 with the removal of RBI-prescribed multiple rates for different maturities and replacing these with a single ceiling rate, and afterward, the scope of the ceiling rate was gradually withdrawn by October 1997. The only deposits rate that was determined by RBI was the savings bank rate. However, with effect from 25 October 2011, the RBI deregulated savings bank account interest rates, wherein banks will have to keep a uniform rate of interest for savings accounts with deposits up to ₹1 lakh, while differential interest rates could be set for savings bank deposits over ₹1 lakh. The deregulation is expected to improve the transmission of monetary policy. It is also expected to enhance the attractiveness of savings accounts and encourage thrift behavior in the economy by bringing the savings deposit rate in sync with the changing market conditions.[27]
6. *Stimulating efficiency of financial markets*: The size and efficiency of the financial market is crucial for the fruitful conduct of monetary policy. Larger is the depth and breadth of this market, easier it is for the monetary policy instruments to achieve its goal of influencing the operating target and higher is the speed of adjustment. To enthuse efficiency

in the monetary policy framework, various steps were undertaken in the form of discontinuation of automatic monetization, introduction of primary dealers (PDs) in the government securities market to play the role of market maker, amendment of securities contracts regulation Act, deepening of government securities market by making interest rates on such securities market related, introduction of automated screen-based trading in government securities through NDS; development of pure inter-bank call money market, development of forex market and increased autonomy of authorized dealer.

7. Government constituted *Expert Committee to Revise and Strengthen the Monetary Policy Framework headed by Urjit Patel,* former Governor Reserve Bank of India. The committee submitted its report in January 2014. The following are the key recommendations of committee:[28]
   a. The headline Consumer Price Index (CPI) should be the nominal anchor for monetary policy. The nominal anchor for inflation should be set for a 2-year horizon at 4% with a band of plus or minus 2%.
   b. To bring down inflation, Committee recommended a "glide path" of 8% for January 2015 and 6% for January 2016. Since more than 57% of CPI is food and fuel on which direct influence of monetary policy is limited, the RBI will need to demonstrate commitment to the inflation anchor by responding to risks.
   c. To reduce the fiscal deficit to 3.0% of GDP by 2016–2017, administered prices, wages, and interest rates are impediments to the transmission of monetary policy and should be eliminated.
   d. Monetary Policy Committee (MPC) should be vested with all monetary policy decisions. The committee must comprise the Governor, the Deputy Governor, and Executive Director in charge of monetary policy and two external full-time member. The decisions of the MPC will be taken by voting. Members will be accountable for failure to attain the target—failure being defined as inability to attain the target for three successive quarters.
   e. The real policy rate should be positive. In the first phase, the weighted average call rate would be the operative target and the repo rate would be the single policy rate. The funds available at the repo rate would be restricted and increasingly liquidity would be provided at the 14-day term repo; longer-term repo auctions should be introduced. In the second phase, the 14-day repo rate would be the operative target and recourse to outright two-way OMOs would determine liquidity. OMO should not be used to manage yields on government securities.
   f. There should be a remunerated standing deposit facility at the RBI to sterilize excess liquidity.
   g. With an independent debt management office, the MSS and cash management bills should be phased out.
   h. All sector-specific refinance should be phased out as committed to the Asian Development Bank in 1992.

MONEY MARKET

Money market refers to the market for short-term funds, that is, up to 1-year maturity. This market provides the opportunity to the eligible participants to invest their short-term surplus funds and to borrow short-term funds in the case of deficit, and thus, balances the demand for and supply of short-term funds. The money market plays an extremely important role in Indian Monetary policy framework since RBI intervenes in this market to control the short-term liquidity positions and interest rates in the economy through this market. In modern times, the inter-linkages between the money market, dated government securities market, and foreign exchange market have grown rapidly and it makes the role of RBI more challengeable and demanding. The following are the constituents of money market in India:

1. *Call money market*: The call money market is the market for borrowing and lending for short-term periods (usually up to 14 days, but at times more than that) mostly by commercial banks. It is a telephonic market, that is, deals are struck over telephone and reported to RBI. Commercial banks often face temporary shortages of funds (for example, to meet CRR and SLR requirements, or sudden outgo of funds) or temporary surpluses. When a bank is in shortage of funds, it borrows from another bank which is in surplus. If borrowing (or lending) is made for one day (overnight), it is known as "Call Money." This segment is also called overnight money market. If the maturity of borrowing (or lending) is more than 1 day but up to 14 days, then it is known as "Notice Money." "Term Money" refers to money borrowed (or lent) for more than 14 days but less than 1 year. In Indian money market, most of the transactions are of call money and notice money. In this market, commercial banks and primary dealers (PDs) can both borrow and lend, but FIs (LIC, UTI, GIC, IDBI, NABARD, and ICICI) and mutual funds can only lend. RBI, as regulator, routinely participates in the market to inject liquidity (lend) or to mop up liquidity (borrow). As part of the financial sector reforms, RBI has been progressively moving toward making this market a purely inter-bank market by gradually limiting the scope of participation of non-bank players.[29]
2. *Repos/reverse repos*: In a repo (also known as repurchase option or ready forward contract) transaction, one party say banks borrow funds for a specific period (known as repo period) against the collateral of specific securities at pre-determined rate (known as repo rate) from another party say RBI. On the contrary, banks that need to park (invest) a temporary surplus cash with RBI will enter into an opposite type of transaction with RBI—it will buy the security and will agree to sell it back at a future date at a pre-determined price. This transaction is known as reverse repo transaction. The rate at which RBI borrows money from the commercial banks is called reverse repo rate. In India, apart from the Reserve Bank, only scheduled commercial banks (excluding RRBs) and PDs can participate in repo/reverse repo transactions. Non-bank participants (e.g., FIs) can only lend money to the eligible participants (RBI, commercial banks, and PDs) through reverse repo.
3. *Treasury bills* (*T-bills*): T-bills are the debt obligations of the government that have maturities of 1 year or less, and hence, are short-term obligations of the treasury/government. Currently, T-bills are issued with three maturities—91, 182, and 364 days. These are issued to raise funds for meeting expenditure needs and also provide outlet for parking temporary surplus funds by investor. Being free of default risk, yields on the treasury bills serve as benchmarks for most other short-term rates. The development of this market is crucial for the conduct of OMOs. The investors in T-bills include banks, PDs, FIs, provident funds, insurance companies, NBFCs, FIIs, and State governments. T-bills are issued at a discount to the face value. For example, a 91-day treasury bill of face value ₹100 is issued at a price of ₹98.53. This means that the investor will pay ₹98.53 at the time of purchasing the bill and will receive ₹100 on maturity after 91 days.

4. *Commercial papers*: Introduced in India in 1990 on the recommendation of N. Vaghul Committee, CPs are short-term (up to 1 year) unsecured borrowing instruments issued in the form of a promissory note. CPs were introduced with a view to enable highly rated corporate borrowers to diversify their sources of short-term borrowings and to provide an additional instrument to investor. Corporates, PDs, and the All-India Financial Institutions (AIFIs) are eligible to issue CPs. Currently, CPs can be issued in minimum denomination of ₹5 lakh and multiples thereof. The investors in CPs include individuals, banking companies, other corporate bodies and unincorporated bodies, Non-Resident Indians (NRIs), and Foreign Institutional Investors (FIIs).[30]
5. *Certificate of deposit* (*CD*): Certificate of deposit (CD) was introduced in 1989 on the recommendation of N. Vaghul Committee. It is a negotiable money market instrument and issued in dematerialized form or as a usance promissory note against funds deposited at a bank or other eligible FI for a specified time period. All scheduled commercial banks (excluding RRBs and LABs), selected AIFIs can issue CDs for a minimum period of 7 days and a maximum of 1 year in denominations of ₹1 lakh and in multiple of ₹1 lakh thereafter. The CDs are just like bank fixed deposits, but with the difference that the CDs are freely transferable by an endorsement (just like equity shares or bonds) while bank fixed deposits are not. Like treasury bills, CDs are also issued at a discount to the face value. The discount rate or the yield on CDs can be freely negotiated between the issuer and the investor. CDs can be issued to individuals, corporations, trusts, institutional investors, etc. From the point of view of the issuing bank, CDs are rather high cost source of fund.[31]
6. *Bills rediscounting*: A bill of exchange is a negotiable instrument and is drawn by drawer (seller of the good) on the drawee (purchaser of the good) with the promise by the latter to pay the former within a specified date. The seller if wants funds immediately can get a payment from the bank against the bill but at a discounted rate (called bill discounting). The bank collects the money (as per bill amount) from the purchaser of the goods latter and the difference between the bill amount and the discounted price is the earning of the bank. Since the bills of exchange are negotiable instruments, the bank can sell the bills to another party (for example, another bank or RBI). If the bill is drawn/paid in India, it is called inland bill, if the bill is drawn/paid outside India, it is called foreign bill. Bills can also be classified as demand bill (when the bill is payable by the drawee immediately on presentation before him) or usance bill or time bill (if the bill is payable at a future date). In India, although banks regularly discount a large volume of bills, a secondary market for rediscounting these bills is lacking.
7. *Money market mutual funds* (*MMMFs*): The scheme of MMMFs was introduced in the country in the year 1992. Such funds are short-run liquid investments in high-quality money market instruments and provide investors with a reasonable return along with good liquidity over a period of up to 1 year. Since 2000, the MMMFs have been brought under the purview of SEBI.

Characteristics/Problems of Indian Money Market

1. There is *large scale existence of unorganized money market* besides organized money market causing dichotomy in the functioning of money market instruments. The unorganized market remains outside the ambit of RBI and its regulations as it functions independently.

2. There is *lack of integration* between organized and unorganized segments of money market as well as between sub-markets of Indian money market. There is less co-ordination between co-operative and commercial banks as well as State and Foreign banks. The indigenous bankers have their own ways of doing business.
3. In India, *bill market is restricted* to only a few metropolitan cities. Popularity of cash credit and non-uniform commercial bills provided obstacles to the development of bill market. Further, due to the presence of inter-bank call money, commercial banks never felt the need of an organized bill market.
4. Indian money market is also characterized by *shortage of funds*. Three factors can be attributed to this. First, the lower per capita income results in low savings and higher consumption. Second, the lack of banking habits or inadequate banking habits forces people to save in the form of hoardings, which remain untapped. Third, a vast presence of shadow economy or black money market causes the shortage of financial resources in the money market.
5. The *inadequate banking facility* is an important factor of underdeveloped money market in India. India's adoption of Jan Dhan scheme as well as biometric Aadhaar cards-based account opening has led to a massive opening of bank accounts in the country, but still 20% of population did not have bank accounts till December end 2017.[32] In India, there are 14 bank branches per 1 lakh adult population as compared to 32 in the United States, 45 in Italy, and 72 in Luxemburg.[33]

Reforms in Money Market

1. *Establishment of Primary Dealers (PDs)*: Introduced by RBI in 1995, PDs are a group of highly qualified financial firms/banks, appointed to play the role of specialist intermediaries in the government security market between the issuer on the one hand and the market on the other. The objective of PDs is to meet the government borrowing needs as cheaply and efficiently as possible. Examples of PDs in India are SBI DFHI Ltd., PNB Gilts Ltd., Morgan Stanley Indian Primary Dealer Ltd., and Goldman Sachs (India) Capital Market Pvt. Ltd.
2. *Liquidity adjustment facility* (*LAF*): As part of the move from direct to indirect instruments of monetary policy, and to be able to control the money market rates in an effective manner, the Narasimham Committee on Banking Sector Reforms (1998) recommended the withdrawal of all general and sector specific refinance facilities and move toward LAF through the operations of repos and reverse repos. LAF was introduced in June 2000 and with this RBI began to manage liquidity in the system through the auction of repos and reverse repos. Under the earlier system wherein RBI used to control the liquidity in the system through changes in CRR and OMOs, RBI could either influence the quantum of liquidity (by changing CRR) or the cost of liquidity, that is, the interest rates (through OMO). But after the introduction of the LAF, RBI can control both the quantum of liquidity (by accepting bids up to a certain amount in the repos/reverse repos) and the interest rates.
3. *Establishment of Discount and Finance House in India*: The Discount and Finance House in India was established by the government on April 25, 1988. The objective of establishing DFHI is providing liquidity to money market instruments and developing secondary market. It brings into fold of Indian money market the entire financial system

comprising commercial banks, AIFIs, and helps in equilibrating their short-term surpluses and deficits. It performs various functions such as discounting and rediscounting bills, selling and underwriting marketable securities, treasury bills, commercial bill, and promissory notes.

4. *Introduction of new money market instruments*: During last two to three decades, many money market instruments have been introduced to enhance the efficiency of money market in the country. These instruments are 182-day treasury bills, 364-day treasury bills, certificate of deposit (CD), CP, etc. MMMFs were introduced in 1990s to provide additional short-term avenue to small investor.
5. *Interest rate deregulation*: Money market interest rates have been deregulated since 1989 which proved to be as significant step and ensured dynamism in the money market working. It made interest rates flexible and lent transparency in the transactions of money market.
6. *Replacing sector-specific finance by term money market:* RBI has used in the past a number of sector specific refinance facilities, for example, export credit refinance and food credit refinance. Refinance is used by RBI to meet liquidity shortage in the system, to control monetary and credit conditions, and direct credit to selected sector. But on the recommendation of Urjit Patel Committee, RBI has been withdrawing sector specific refinance facility and is replacing it with term money market. The term money market would provide RBI the flexibility to manage brief episodes of comfortable liquidity. This will help improve the transmission of policy impulses across the interest rate spectrum and engender efficiency in cash and treasury management.[34]

Non-banking Financial Institutions (NBFIs)

Non-banking financial institutions (NBFIs) comprise a heterogeneous group of financial intermediaries and consist of AIFIs, nonbanking financial companies, and PDs. Like ordinary banks, NBFIs do not accept demand deposits and need not cater to various regulations that are mandatory for scheduled commercial banks. Few NBFIs do not come under the domain of RBI but are regulated by SEBI. In the present discussion, we will restrict our self to those NBFIs which come under the domain of RBI (Figure 21.1).

1. *All-India financial institutions* (*AIFIs*): AIFIs were established during planning era to provide long-term financing/refinancing to specific sectors such as agriculture and rural development, trade, housing, and small industries. NABARD and EXIM banks were founded in the year 1982, National housing bank (NHB) in 1988, and SIDBI was established in 1990. AIFIs constituted 23% of total assets of NBFIs.
2. *Non-banking financial companies*: A NBFC is a company registered under the Companies Act, 1956. NBFCs are divided into NBFCs-D—which are authorized to accept and hold public deposits—and non-deposit taking NBFCs (NBFCs-ND)—which do not accept public deposits but raise debt from market and banks. At present, there were 12 activity-based classifications of NBFCs, such as Asset finance company, Loan Company, Investment company, and Mortgage guarantee company. By end-December 2018, there were 108 NBFCs-D and 10,082 NBFCs-ND operating in the country. Industry accounts for

FIGURE 21.1 Structure of Non-banking Financial Intermediaries Under RBI Regulations

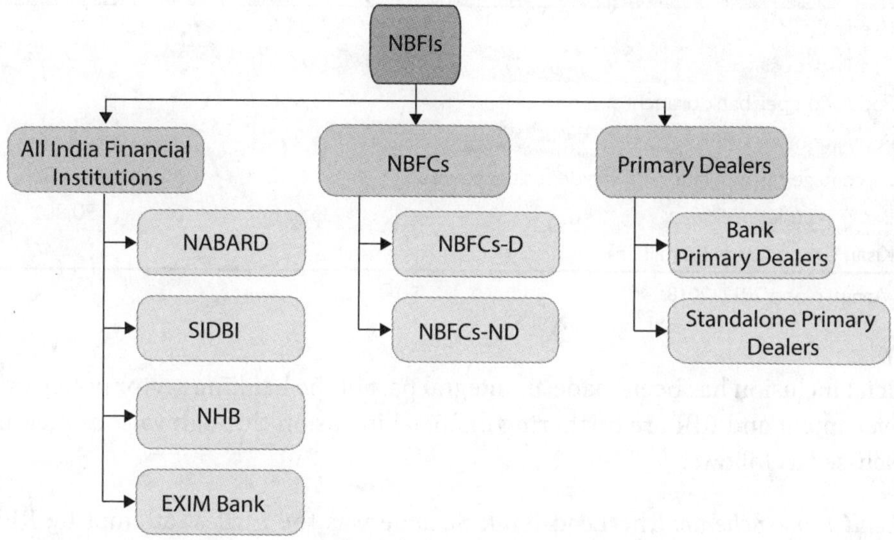

Source: Report on Trend and Progress of Banking in India 2017–2018, RBI.

more than half of total credit extended by NBFCs, followed by retail, services, and agriculture. The major sources of finance of NBFCs-ND have been debentures and bank borrowings, which constitute around 70% of total resource mobilization.

3. *Primary dealers (PDs)*: PDs are the licensed dealers who deal in buying and selling of government securities. PDs are classified as standalone and bank PDs. Standalone PDs function as subsidiaries of banks and established as NBFCs and get license from RBI. Sometimes, banks departmentally undertake PD business with RBI license, and hence, called bank PDs. As on March 31, 2018, there were 21 PDs—14 operating as departments of banks and 7 standalone PDs registered as NBFCs.

Financial Inclusion

Financial inclusion implies providing financial services, viz., access to payments and remittance facilities, savings, loans, and insurance services at affordable cost to those who are excluded from the formal financial system. According to committee on financial inclusion (2008) headed by Dr C. Rangarajan, "Financial inclusion may be defined as the process of ensuring access to financial services and timely and adequate credit where needed by vulnerable groups such as weaker sections and low income groups at an affordable cost."

It is no surprise, then, that India's credit-to-GDP ratio stands at a modest 55.7%, compared to China's 208.7%, the United Kingdom's 170.5%, and the United States' 152.2%. In other words, there is financial under-penetration in India.[35] With just 180 ATMs for a million people, India has among the lowest number of ATMs compared to its population. That is one ATM in India serves around 5,555 number of people in the country. Whereas in South Korea, an ATM serves nearly 400 persons (Table 21.2).[36]

TABLE 21.2 The Progress of Financial Inclusion in India

Sr. No.	Indicator	2010–2011	2017–2018
1	Credit-GDP	54.6	56%
2	Credit-deposit	76.5	76.7%
3	Population per bank branch	13,466	–
4	Population per ATM	16,243	5555
5	Percentage of population having deposit accounts	61.2	80%
6	Banking outlet in villages	33,378	50,805
7	Kisan Credit Cards (in million)	24	46

Source: RBI Annual report 2017–2018.

Financial inclusion has been made an integral part of the banking sector policy in India. The Indian government and RBI are furthering financial inclusion through various measures which can be discussed as follows:

1. *Lead Bank Scheme:* The Lead Bank Scheme was the earliest attempt by RBI to foster financial inclusion. The scheme was introduced by RBI in December 1969 after the recommendation of Committee of Bankers on Branch Expansion Programme of PSBs appointed by RBI under the Chairmanship of Shri F.K.F. Nariman (popularly called Nariman Committee). The lead bank acts as a leader for coordinating the efforts of all credit institutions in the allotted districts to increase the flow of credit to agriculture, small-scale industries, and other economic activities included in the priority sector in the rural and semi-urban areas, with the district being the basic unit in terms of geographical area. The lead bank is entrusted with the responsibility of locating growth centers, assessing deposit potential, identifying credit gaps, and evolving a co-ordinated approach to credit deployment in each district, in concert with other banks and credit agencies. As on June 30, 2018, 20 PSBs and one private sector bank have been assigned Lead Bank responsibility in 714 districts of the country. Over the years, the focus of the Lead bank scheme has shifted to inclusive growth and financial inclusion. The use of Information Technology (IT) and intermediaries has enabled banks to increase the outreach, scale, and depth of banking services at affordable cost.[37]
2. *Service area approach (SAA):* In 1989, the SAA was adopted wherein service area villages were identified and assigned to bank branches based on their proximity and contiguity and by adopting a cluster approach. Credit plans were prepared on an annual basis for the service area of each branch which involved co-ordination between various developmental agencies and credit institutions.
3. *Basic savings bank deposit account (BSBDA):* To achieve the objective of greater financial inclusion, all banks have been advised by the RBI to make available a BSBDA either with "nil" or very low minimum balances. All the earlier existing "No-frills" accounts have been converted into BSBDA as per RBI guidelines.
4. *Pradhan Mantri Jan-Dhan Yojna (PMJDY):* PMJDY was launched on August 28, 2014. It is a programme for financial inclusion to cover all unbanked households in India, whether in urban or rural area, and aims at providing affordable financial services like savings & deposit accounts, banking services, remittance, credit, insurance, and pension. The scheme has been implemented in two phases. Phase I aimed at providing

universal access to banking facilities, basic banking accounts for saving and remittance, and RuPay Debit card with an in-built accident insurance cover of ₹100,000. Phase II incorporated inter alia overdraft facilities of up to ₹5,000, creation of a Credit Guarantee Fund for coverage of defaults in overdraft accounts, and micro-insurance and unorganized sector pension schemes like Swavalamban. PMJDY was extended beyond August 14, 2018 with new features, viz., opening accounts from "every household to every adult"; raising the overdraft limit to ₹10,000 from ₹5,000; overdraft facility up to ₹2,000 without any conditions; and raising accidental insurance cover for new RuPay cardholders from ₹100,000 to ₹200,000, for PMJDY accounts opened after August 28, 2018. Within a span of 4 years, the total number of accounts opened under the PMJDY expanded to 328 million, with ₹851 billion deposits as on September 28, 2018. Of these accounts, 59.1% were opened at branches located in rural and semi-urban center.

5. *Business facilitators (BFs) and business correspondents (BCs)*: With the objective of ensuring a greater financial inclusion and increasing the outreach of the banking sector, the RBI has introduced BF and BC models to enable banks to use the services of NGOs, Self-Help Groups (SHGs), and micro-finance institutions as intermediaries in providing financial and banking services. These intermediaries serve as the facilitators/correspondents of the banks. In the BF model, these intermediaries help the banks facilitate services such as identification of borrowers, collection and preliminary processing of loan applications, creating awareness about savings and other products, processing and submission of applications to banks, and post-sanction monitoring. The BC model includes disbursal of small value credit, recovery of principal/collection of interest, collection of small value deposits, and receipt and delivery of small value remittances.
6. *Adoption of technology*: Technology is the driving force for low-cost inclusion initiatives. The Many initiatives have been taken in this regard. Banks have also been advised to transfer subsidies through Electronic Benefit Transfer (EBT) under different schemes which are in operation and, funded by the Government of India, so that benefit gets credited directly to the account of the beneficiaries. Banks are encouraged to issue KCCs to farmers and GCCs to non-farmer.
7. *Financial inclusion fund*: Based on the recommendations of the Rangarajan Committee on Financial Inclusion, the GOI has set up in NABARD, viz., "Financial Inclusion Fund" (FIF) for meeting the cost of developmental and promotional interventions of financial inclusion and "Financial Inclusion Technology Fund" (FITF), for meeting the cost of technology adoption.
8. *Swabhimaan program*: On the recommendation of Rangarajan Committee Report (Committee on Financial Inclusion), Swabhimaan program was launched in 2011. It is an innovative scheme to take banks to the doorstep of the rural poor instead of the latter having to go in search of banks. The idea is to have BCs, or bank saathis (who may be the local merchant), armed with electronic hand-held devices, which can recognize the bio-markers of bank customer. The customers can then deposit and draw money directly from the bank Saathi, without having to travel long distances to get to the nearest brick and mortar bank branch. The program will be making use of Aadhaar which will make it possible for individuals to establish their identities in any part of India.
9. *Expansion of bank branches*: An important policy initiative to increase the number of bank branches in the Tier 3 to Tier 6 centers was the liberalization of the branch authorization policy in December 2009. RBI has taken several steps to provide banking

facilities in the unbanked villages in the country. The use of information technology and intermediaries has made it possible to increase outreach, scale, and depth of banking services at affordable cost. Upon issuance of revised guidelines on branch authorization policy on May 18, 2017 clarifying on "banking outlet," State Level Bankers Committees' convenor banks were advised to consider opening of a core banking solution (CBS) enabled banking outlet or a part-time banking outlet in the villages with population less than 2,000 that still remain unbanked.[38]

10. *Financial literacy*: Financial literacy is crucial for imparting efficacy to financial inclusion initiatives of the Reserve Bank. In this direction, a number of new initiatives were undertaken during 2017–2018. In order to explore innovative and participatory approaches to financial literacy, a block level Centres of Financial Literacy (CFL) project was initiated in 2017 by the Reserve Bank across 80 blocks in 9 states. The project is currently being implemented by 6 NGOs in collaboration with 10 sponsor banks. In order to create awareness at a large scale on key topics every year, the Reserve Bank had decided to observe one week in a year as "Financial Literacy Week" starting from 2017. In 2018, financial literacy week was observed during June 4–8, with the theme of "Consumer Protection." The week focused on four consumer protection messages, viz., "Know your Liability for Unauthorized Electronic Banking Transactions," "Banking Ombudsman," "Good Practices for a Safe Digital Banking Experience," and "Risk versus Return."[39]
11. *Committee on medium-term path on financial inclusion*: RBI appointed committee on medium-term path on financial inclusion under the chairmanship of Shri Deepak Mohanty, Executive Director, RBI, to make suggestions on strengthening the mechanism for effective credit delivery to the productive sectors of the economy. On the basis of committee's recommendations, the following steps have been taken: (1) BCs registry portal has been launched to enable banks, excluding RRBs, to upload data pertaining to BCs deployed by them. Subsequently, on stabilization of the database, facility of using BC tracker for public shall be made available; (2) a basic certification course for BCs has commenced. The translation of the syllabus into different languages is also under process; and (3) the Certified Credit Counsellors (CCC) scheme for MSMEs which could help bridge the information gap, and thereby help banks to make better credit decisions was launched during 2017–2018.
12. *Extending full financial inclusion in the hinterlands*: RBI has sent a draft National Strategy for Financial Inclusion to the Financial Stability & Development Council (FSDC), headed by the finance minister, for its review. The strategy, which is in the works, will cover a five-year period from 2019. It has the following key points[40]:
    - enhance the penetration of insurance and pension coverage besides bridging the gaps in traditional banking services in the country's rural hinterland;
    - financial inclusion goalposts not only for state-run enterprises, which have traditionally led the initiatives to help achieve the government's social objectives, but also the economic regulators such as the Insurance Regulatory & Development Authority of India, Pension Fund Regulatory & Development Authority, and Securities & Exchanges Board of India;
    - expanding the scope of direct benefit transfer, which is restricted to 23% of total Jan Dhan accounts by the end of 2018.

Summary

1. The evolution of modern Indian banking can be discussed in three phases: Phase I, The colonial period (1786–1947); Phase II, The period of nationalization and social control (1947–1991), and Phase III, The period of banking sector reforms (1991 onwards).
2. In India, total number of bank branches has increased from 8,262 in 1969 to 151,420 in 2018. There are mainly five types of banks: Commercial banks, RRBs, LABs, small finance banks, and payment banks. The commercial banks are further classified into SBI, nationalized banks, private sector banks, and foreign banks. All these banks except LABs are scheduled banks. Cooperatives can be classified into urban cooperatives and rural cooperatives.
3. A NPA is a loan or advance for which the principal or interest payment remained overdue for a period of 90 days. NPAs are classified into sub-standard, doubtful, and loss assets. Factors responsible for NPAs are global financial crisis, twin balance sheet problem, ever-greening, frauds, bad debts in agriculture, and MSMEs. The measures taken to resolve and prevent NPAs can broadly be classified into two kinds—first, regulatory means of resolving NPAs as per various laws, like the IBC Code, and second, reforming the PSBs.
4. Major banking sector reforms initiated during post-reform period are prudential reforms, supervisory reforms, competition reforms, market reforms, institutional and legal reforms, and technology reforms.
5. The RBI was established on April 1, 1935 in accordance with the provisions of the Reserve Bank of India Act, 1934. Major functions of RBI are currency issuing authority, banker and debt manager to the government, formulation of monetary policy, regulatory and supervisory functions, banker to banks, foreign exchange and reserve management, and developmental and promotional functions.
6. Monetary policy is the regulatory policy of Central Bank (RBI) that involves the management of money supply and interest rate to achieve macroeconomic objectives like inflation, consumption, growth, and liquidity. Direct instruments affect the money supply directly and constitute CRR, SLR, and Credit and interest rate directives. The indirect instruments consist of the bank rate, repos/reverse repos, open market operations, and marginal standing facility. Monetary policy reforms in India include multiple indicator approach; shifting away from direct instruments of credit control to indirect measures; introduction of LAF, discontinuing the automatic demonetization of fiscal deficit; deregulation of interest rate; stimulating efficiency of financial markets; and inflation targeting.
7. Money market refers to the market for short-term funds, that is, up to 1-year maturity. The constituents of money market in India are call money market, repos/reverse repos, treasury bills, CPs, CDs, bills rediscounting, and MMMFs. The India money market is characterized by large scale existence of unorganized money market, lack of integration, restricted bill market, shortage of funds, and inadequate banking facility. Reforms in Indian money market includes establishment of PDs, introduction of liquidity adjustment facility, establishment of discount and finance house of India, introduction of new money market instruments, interest rate deregulation, and replacing sector-specific finance by term money market.
8. Non-banking financial institutions (NBFIs) comprise a heterogeneous group of financial intermediaries and consist of AIFIs, nonbanking financial companies, and PDs.
9. Financial inclusion implies providing financial services, viz., access to payments and remittance facilities, savings, loans, and insurance services at affordable cost to those who are excluded from the formal financial system. The major steps taken to promote financial inclusion in India are Lead bank scheme, service area approach, basic savings bank deposit account, PMJDY, establishing BFs and BCs, adoption of technology, financial inclusion fund, Swabhimaan program, expansion of bank branches, promoting financial literacy, implementing recommendations of Committee on medium-term path on financial inclusion and extending full financial inclusion in the hinterlands.

Endnotes

1. Barman, A. (December 16, 2016). Was Indira Gandhi really the economic ogre she's made out to be?. *The Economic Times.*
2. Five associate banks, BMB merge with SBI. *The Hindu*. April 1, 2017.
3. Nationalized banks (2019). *Database on Indian economy*, RBI.
4. How will merger affect Public Sector Banks? The Hindu, September 8, 2019.
5. The Hindu Business Line, November 6, 2013.
6. *Scheme for Setting up of Wholly Owned Subsidiaries (WOS) by foreign banks in India*, retrieved from https://rbi.org.in (Accessed on March 4, 2018).
7. Merger of regional rural banks within same state likely. *The Economic Times*, February 17, 2019.
8. *Report of the review group on the working of the Local Area Bank scheme*. RBI, September 1, 2002.
9. *A hundred small steps report of the committee on financial sector reforms*. New Delhi: Sage Publications, 2009.
10. India Post Payments Bank will deliver banking services to every Indian's doorstep, says PM Modi. *Business Today*, September 3, 2018.
11. Payment Banks. *Database on Indian economy*, RBI.
12. RBI (2011). *Report on trend and progress of banking in India, 2010–2011*. p.105. Retrieved from www.rbi.org.in (Accessed on January 5, 2019).
13. RBI (2018). *Report on trend and progress of banking in India, 2017–2018*. Retrieved from www.rbi.org.in (Accessed on January 5, 2019).
14. RBI warns on evergreening. *Business Standard*, February 6, 2013.
15. Ram Mohan, T.T. (2018). What is the plan for public sector banks? *EPW*. 53 (28).
16. *Report on trend and progress of banking in India*, RBI, 2011. Retrieved from www.rbi.org.in (Accessed on January 5, 2014).
17. RBI: Functions and working. Retrieved from-www. rbi.org.in (Accessed on July 4, 2014).
18. Ibid.
19. Monetary Policy and Central Banking, March 28, 2019 retrieved from https://www.imf.org
20. RBI. *Functions and working*. Retrieved from https://www.rbi.org.in (Accessed on July 14, 2014).
21. RBI Bulletin, May 2019, Vol. LXXIII, No. 5
22. New monetary aggregates: An introduction, retrieved from https://www.rbi.org.in (Accessed on July 12, 2014).
23. Monetary policy framework: An analytical overview (Part 1 of 2), Report on currency and Finance, December 23, 2005.
24. Reddy, Y.V. (2010). The concise oxford companion to economics. In Monetary policy. OUP, p.256.
25. Rangarajan, C. (2010). Two episodes in the reform process. In India's economy: Performance and challenges. OUP. New Delhi., p.108.
26. Mohan, R. (2004). Financial sector reforms in India: Policies and performance analyses. *RBI Bulletin* (October), 858.
27. Economic Survey, 2011–2012, p.107.
28. *Report of the expert committee to revise and strengthen the monetary policy framework*. Mumbai: Reserve Bank of India, January 2014.
29. Master circular on call/notice oney market operations. *RBI*, July 1, 2014.
30. Reserve Bank Commercial Paper Directions, Notifications, August 7, 2017.
31. *Master direction on money market Instruments*. RBI, July 7, 2016.
32. With 1.57 bn accounts, 80% Indians save outside banks: World Bank. *Business Standard*, April 26, 2018.
33. Commercial bank branches (per 100,000 adults). Retrieved from https://data.worldbank.org (Accessed on April 12, 2019).
34. RBI withdraws sector-specific refinance with for liquidity adjustment. *The Economic Times*, June 4, 2014.
35. Credit–deposit ratio improves to 76.7% in FY18. *Business Today*, January 4, 2019.
36. Only 200 ATMs for a million people in India. *The Times of India*, April 2, 2018.
37. *Master circular—Lead bank scheme*. RBI, July 2, 2018.
38. RBI. Annual Report 2017–2018.
39. RBI. Annual Report 2017–2018.
40. RBI prepares for full financial inclusion in hinterland. *The Economic Times*, January 22, 2019.

CHAPTER **22**

Indian Capital Market

The stock market is a device for transferring money from the impatient to the patient.

—Warren Buffett

Introduction

Finance is the life blood of modern economic activities. A Financial market consists of both money market and capital market. While the money market is a market for short-term funds (up to 1 year maturity at the time of issue), the capital market is a market for long-term funds (debt as well as equity shares). We all know that, the money is invested into a business or in land, building, machinery, or equipment, which is used by an entrepreneur in production. All these resources together constitute capital. It must be remembered, however, that money invested is the capital and money not invested or lying idle is not capital. In economics, capital is described as a wealth that produces further wealth. In the modern economic set up, the role of capital has become very important and an efficient financial system is crucial for the overall development of the economy. The nations who have advanced economically are the ones who have accumulated vast amount of capital as more goods can be produced with the aid of capital. As a nation grows, it requires a systematic growth and structure of different financial institutions which can pool capital resources and further lend them to business enterprises and governments. Thus, capital market can be described as any marketplace where trading (buying and selling) of capital takes place. The financial capital constitutes many instruments like securities including equities or shares, bonds, currencies, and derivatives.

The chapter proposes to discuss following topics:

- Components of Capital Market
- Evolution and Growth of Capital Market
- Capital Market Reforms in India
- SEBI and Its Functions

Structure of Capital Market in India

There are three types of participants in the capital market—the issuer of securities, the investors in securities, and the intermediaries. The issuers are the set of borrowers or deficit savers (generally the corporate sector), who issue securities to raise funds. The investors are the set of people, who are surplus savers and deploy their savings by buying or subscribing to such securities. The investors in the capital market include the retail investors (i.e., Indian public), mutual funds, foreign institutional investors (FIIs), financial institutions (such as LIC, GIC, IDBI, and IFCI), banks, etc. The third category consists of intermediaries who provide various services in the Indian securities market. They are the agents who match the needs of users and suppliers of funds for a commission.

Broadly, the capital market is divided into two constituents: (1) security market and (2) development financial institutions (DFIs) (Figure 22.1).

Security Market

The security market is divided into gilt-edged market and corporate security market.

Gilt-Edged Market

It is also called government security market. A government security is a tradable instrument issued by the Central Government or the State Governments. A government security will be money market instrument if it is of short-term nature (usually called treasury bills, with original maturities of less than 1 year). It will be a capital market instrument if it is of longer duration (usually called government bonds or dated securities with original maturity of 1 year or more). In India, the Central Government issues both, treasury bills and bonds or dated securities, while the State Governments issue only bonds or dated securities, which are called the State Development Loans (SDLs). Since the government cannot default on its payment obligation, government securities carry practically no risk of default and, hence, are called risk-free gilt-edged instruments.

FIGURE 22.1 Capital Market Classification

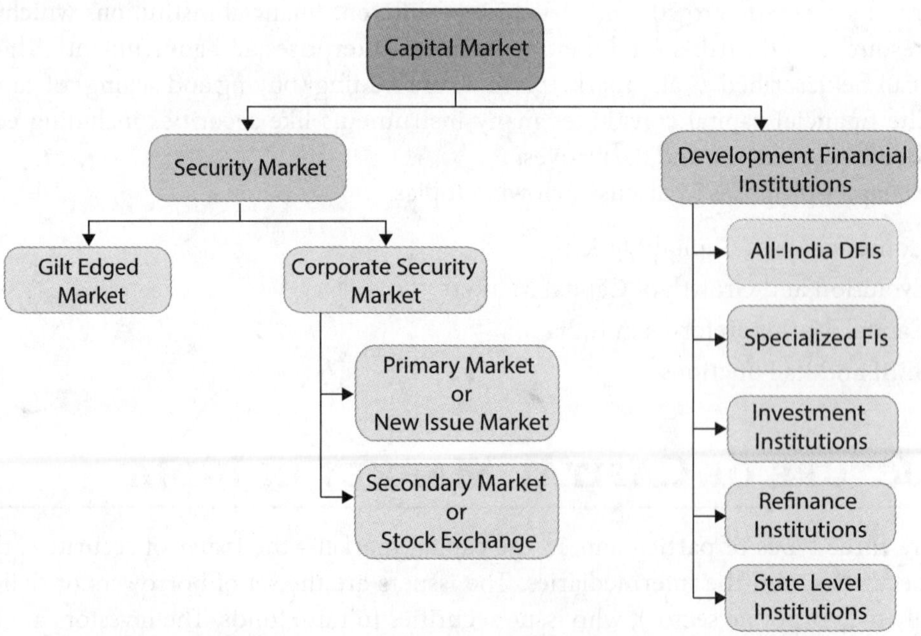

Corporate Security Market

The corporate security market is the market where securities of corporate firms are bought and sold. Such securities are in the form of shares, debentures, and bonds. The corporate securities are traded both in primary as well as secondary market.

The New Issue Market To start or expand the business, the corporate houses often raise funds by issuing bonds, debentures, shares, and so on. The funds are raised by companies with the help of underwriters, merchant banks, and other specialized agencies. There are four methods by which capital is raised by companies in the new issue market.

1. *By Prospectus:* The prospectus is an invitation to the general public for subscribing the capital. The prospectus contains a brief summary of the company's financial information viz. company's profile, its financial position, number of shares, etc.
2. *By Offer for Sale:* Under this, the shares are sold to third parties (mainly the merchant banks) in the bulk who further issue such shares to the public. This method is considered safe by the companies as they already receive money from the third party. Further any premium received from the public goes to third party instead of company.
3. *By Private Placing:* Under this method, the shares are sold to individuals or institutions directly by making a private appeal to them. The method is cost-saving as compared to the other methods as it does not involve issuing the prospectus to the investors.
4. *By Offering Rights Issue:* A rights issue is an issue of rights to a company's existing shareholders that enables them to buy additional shares directly from the company in proportion to their existing holdings. Under this, the shares are sold to them at a discount to the current market price.

Secondary Market or Stock Exchange Secondary market, also called as stock exchange or after markets is the financial market where previously traded financial instruments such as shares, debentures, bonds, options, and future are bought and sold. The importance of secondary market lies in the fact that it provides exit route to the investors. Investors supply capital to the users of capital (corporate and government sector) in the primary market. In the absence of a secondary market, many of the investors would probably not agree to supply capital in the primary market because they would not have an exit route for their investment. Secondary market provides marketability to securities that encourages savers to take risk and make investment in the existing securities. The secondary market thus channelizes the savings of households which become available to public and private corporate houses that stimulates country's gross domestic product (GDP). The history of stock exchange can be traced to as far back as ancient Rome. In medieval times (15th and 16th century), Antwerp in Belgium was considered to be pioneer in the stock trading. Amsterdam Stock Exchange, founded in 1602, is considered as the first stock exchange where shares were traded publicly. The box 22.1 surveys the top five stock exchanges of the world.

BOX 22.1 Top Five Stock Exchanges of the World

New York Stock Exchange

The New York Stock Exchange (NYSE) and nicknamed "The Big Board" is an American stock exchange located in New York. Founded in May 17, 1792, it is world's largest stock exchange in terms of market capitalization. With 2,400 number of listings, its market cap was US$ 23.21 trillion in May 2019. The indices of NYSE are Dow Jones Industrial Average, S&P 500, and NYSE Composite.

National Association of Securities Dealers Automated Quotations

National Association of Securities Dealers Automated Quotations (NASDAQ) was founded on February 4, 1971 and is located in New York. It is the second-largest exchange in the world by market capitalization, behind only the NYSE. With 3,900 number of listings, its market capitalization is US$ 11.22 trillion. The indices of NASDAQ are NASDAQ-100 (NDX), Pre-Market (NDX), After Hours (NDX), DJIA, S&P 500, and Russell 2000.

Japan Exchange Group

Japan Exchange Group (JPX) is an Asian financial services corporation that came into being after the merger of Tokyo Stock Exchange and Osaka Securities Exchange on January 1, 2013. Both Tokyo Stock Exchange and Osaka Securities Exchange were founded in April 1, 1949. With 3,537 companies listed and market capitalization of US$5.61 trillion, it is the world's third-largest stock exchange and Asia's largest bourse in terms of market capitalization. TOPIX and JPX Nikkei 400 and JPX Nikkei Mid Small are the popular indices of JPX.

Shanghai Stock Exchange

Shanghai Stock Exchange (SSE) was founded on November 26, 1990 and is located in the city of Shanghai, China. It has 1,041 listings in its ambit and is world's fourth-largest stock exchange in terms of market capitalization (US$5.01 trillion as of May 2019). The popular indices of SSE are SSE 50 Index (Blue chip), SSE 180 Index, SSE 380 Index, and SSE Composite Index (major Index).

Stock Exchange of Hong Kong Limited

The first stock exchange in Hong Kong was established in 1891. In 1986, the four operational stock exchanges in Hong Kong were merged and the Stock Exchange of Hong Kong Ltd was established. It has 2,062 listings in its fold and with market capitalization of US$4.31 as on May 2019, it stands fifth in international ranking.

Source: Compiled by author from https://www.nyse.com, https://www.nasdaq.com, https://www.jpx.co.jp, http://english.sse.com.cn, https://www.hkex.com.hk. (accessed on May 12, 2019).

Stock Exchanges in India

Stock exchanges are granted recognition for their operations in the securities market by Securities and Exchange Board of India (SEBI) under Section 4 of the Securities Contracts (Regulation) Act (SCRA), 1956. As on March 31, 2019 there are six stock exchanges, out of which three are permanent and three are non-permanent. Besides there are three commodities derivative exchanges which are permanent in status. A commodity market trades in the primary economic sector rather than manufactured products, for example, sugar, pulses and gold, oil, etc. Table 22.1 does a brief survey of stock exchanges in India.

Development Financial Institutions

A DFI is defined as "an institution promoted or assisted by government mainly to provide development finance to one or more sectors or sub-sectors of the economy." Apart from provision of long-term loans, equity capital, guarantees, and underwriting functions, a development bank normally is also expected to upgrade the managerial and the other operational pre-requisites of

TABLE 22.1 Stock Exchanges in India

Sr. No.	Name of Stock Exchange	Year of Inception	Headquarter	About the Stock Exchange	Status
1	Bombay Stock Exchange (BSE)	1875	Mumbai	National level premier stock exchange.	Permanent
2	National Stock Exchange (NSE)	1992	Mumbai	National level premier stock exchange.	Permanent
3	Calcutta Stock Exchange (CSE)	1908	Kolkata	Largest regional stock exchange in India.	Permanent
4	India International Exchange Ltd	2017	Gandhinagar	It is a wholly owned subsidiary of BSE. Diversified portfolio of products and technology services at a more competitive rate to Indian as well as foreign exchanges.	Valid upto December 28, 2019
5	Metropolitan Stock Exchange of India Ltd	2008	Mumbai	Formerly known as MCX Stock Exchange Ltd, it offers an electronic platform for trading in Capital Market, Futures & Options, Currency Derivatives, Interest Rate Futures (IRF), and Debt Market segments.	September 15, 2019
6	NSE IFSC Ltd	2016	Gandhinagar	The stock exchange was launched to grow the financial market as well as expected to bring capital into India. Offers trading in securities in any currency other than the Indian rupee.	May 28, 2019
	List of Commodity Derivative Exchanges				
1	Indian Commodity Exchange Ltd	2008	New Delhi	Deals in commodity trade; it is a public–private partnership with Reliance Capital, MMTC Ltd, Indiabulls Housing Finance Ltd, Indian Potash Ltd, KRIBHCO, and IDFC Bank as major shareholders.	Permanent
2	Multi Commodity Exchange of India Ltd	2003	Mumbai	India's largest commodity futures exchange. It had more than 85% market share in commodity trade in 2016.	Permanent
3	National Commodity & Derivatives Exchange Ltd	2003	Mumbai	Online Commodity Exchange.	Permanent

Source: Annual Report, *SEBI*, 2017–2018.

the assisted projects.[1] DFIs comprise all India DFIs, specialized financial institutions, investment institutions, refinance institutions, state-level institutions, and other financial institutions. Let us discuss all one by one.

All India Development Financial Institutions

Industrial Finance Corporation of India Ltd: Industrial Financial Corporation of India (IFCI) established in 1948 was the first all India DFI in the country. Its objective was to provide medium- and long-term loan to the industry. IFCI was converted into public limited company in July 1, 1993 and since then, known as Industrial Finance Corporation of India Ltd.

Small Industrial Development Bank of India: Small Industrial Development Bank of India (SIDBI) was established in 1990. Headquartered at Lucknow, the main objective of SIDBI is to provide refinance facilities and short-term lending to industries, and serves as the principal financial institution in the Micro, Small and Medium Enterprises (MSME) sector.

Other DFIs: During the past two decades, the distinction between development and commercial banking is getting blurred. Many DFIs have either been converted into banks or closed down. The Industrial Credit and Investment Corporation of India Ltd (ICICI) was founded in 1955 and had been a major dispenser of development finance. It was merged with its offspring ICICI bank in 2002. The Industrial Development Bank of India (IDBI), established in 1964 was converted into a bank in 2004. The Industrial Investment Bank of India (IIBI) established in 1971 to revive the sick industrial units, was closed down in 2012.

Specialized Financial Institutions

Specialized financial institutions provide long-term funds for specialized services such as infrastructure, trade, or venture capital besides provision of technical and managerial advice. Examples are ICICI venture fund, IFCI venture capital fund, Tourism Finance Corporation of India Ltd, Infrastructure Development Finance Corporation, and EXIM bank.

Investment Institutions

Investment institutions in India comprise various organizations that mobilize savings of the people, invest them in the capital market, and distribute the return to such small investors. The investment institutions have notable advantages like diversified portfolio or pooling of risks, professional management, and high degree of liquidity. Government established the Unit Trust of India in 1964 so as to mobilize the small savings of millions of Indian households. Life Insurance Corporation (LIC) was set up in 1956 and provides assistance in term loans, underwriting and direct subscription of equity and debentures, and resource support to financial institutions. General Insurance Corporation (GIC) of India was set up in 1972 and had four subsidiaries, namely (1) National Insurance Company Ltd, (2) New India Assurance Ltd, (3) Oriental Insurance company Ltd, and (4) United India Insurance Company Ltd. With the enactment of General Insurance Business (Nationalisation) Amendment Act 2002, GIC ceased to be a holding company of its subsidiaries. The ownership of the four erstwhile subsidiary companies and also of the General Insurance Corporation of India has been vested with Government of India.[2]

Refinance Institutions

Refinancing institutions give loans to other institutions who ultimately give loans to the end customers. National Housing Bank (NHB) and National Bank for Agriculture and Rural Development (NABARD) are the example of refinance institutions. NHB was established in 1987 and is headquartered at New Delhi. It doesn't give any direct loans to the house loan applicants.[3] Rather, it refinances those banks who give home loans. Similarly, NABARD established in 1982 is another refinancing institution in the field of agricultural credit.

State-Level Institutions

1. *State Financial Corporation*: Indian Parliament enacted the State Financial Corporation Act in 1951 and the first State Financial Corporation (SFC) was set up in Punjab in 1953.

At present, there are 18 SFCs in the country. SFCs cater to the financial needs of small- and medium-sized industrial houses. Generally, operations of SFCs are confined to their respective states but in some cases they extend to neighboring states and UTs as well.[4]

2. *State Industrial Development Corporation*: State Industrial Development Corporations (SIDCs) were set up in different states to accelerate the pace of industrial development in the country. They help in industrialization in multiple ways, like availability of loans on soft terms; allotment of industrial plot/shed in one of the industrial estates or industrial parks developed by the state-level corporation; technical assistance for the preparation of project reports; availability of special incentives provided by the respective state governments for setting up of industries, etc. At present, there are around 56 SDICs throughout the country.[5]

Evolution and Growth of Indian Capital Market

The evolution and growth of Indian capital markets since independence can broadly be divided into four distinct phases.

Phase 1 (1947–1973): The Period of Institution-Building and Legal Framework

The first phase laid the foundation of the new capital market institutions and a legal framework for orderly development of the capital market consistent with the planned industrial development of the country. At the time of independence, Indian capital market was almost non-existent and the lack of availability of long-term finance hampered the industrial development. The banking system which was also too small catered to short-term finances and the corporate debt market did not exist at that time. To fill this gap, a number of DFIs were set up at central level—IFCI (1948), ICICI (1955), IDBI (1964), and UTI (1964). The state-level financial institutions such as SFCs were also set up to complement the efforts of central government. The period also witnessed the development of a solid legal framework for functioning and growth of the capital markets in India. Various legislations, such as Capital Issues (Control) Act, 1947, Securities Contracts (Regulation) Act, 1956, and Companies Act, 1956, were enacted by the government and such laws shaped the capital development of the nation in the following years. Dependence of Indian industry on shares and debentures or public capital markets as a source of finance was insignificant during this period. The reason for less popularity of corporate security market was availability of subsidized credit from the DFIs (long-term) and banks (short-term) and lack of people's participation in such markets.

Phase 2 (1973–1980): The Period of Foreign Exchange Regulation

The enactment of Foreign Exchange Regulation Act (FERA) in 1973 ushered in a new phase of capital market development in the country. The Act required foreign ownership in Indian joint venture companies to be brought down to 40% to be regarded as an Indian company. The MNCs had to offer shares to the Indian public at a very low price in the 1970s because issue price used to be regulated by stringent formula laid down by the Controller of Capital Issues. This not only evoked tremendous response from the public but also taking lessons from the MNCs, a number of domestic companies also made successful public issues to raise equity capital. For the first time, large number of individuals was brought into the capital market and trading in stock markets started gaining popularity.

Phase 3 (1980–1992): The Broadening and Deepening of Capital Market

Liberalization policies of the government in the early 1980s provided impetus to the industrial growth of the country. Riding on buoyant industrial performance resulting from liberalization, the share prices boomed which was followed by another boom in the primary market, and another round of widening of the equity culture among the masses. While only two exchanges were set up during 1946–1980, as many as five stock exchanges were established during the following five years (1980–1985), and another six during the next 5 years (1986–1991). Apart from number of stock exchanges, other parameters of stock market development—the number of companies listed, number of issues of listed companies, and market value of capital—registered a significant growth during the 1980s. Another point to be noted was that debentures became an important source of capital for the corporate sector in the late 1980s. Apart from strong growth in stock markets, the later half of the 1980s witnessed establishment of a few new institutions. The culture of credit rating was introduced for the first time in the country through establishment of three credit rating agencies (CRISIL, ICRA, and CARE) during this phase. The SEBI was also established (1988) during this phase, although the regulator had to wait for 4 more years to obtain statutory power. The securities scam marked the end of this phase and beginning of a new phase. The scam exposed the weaknesses and loopholes of Indian capital market and called for widespread reforms. Incidentally, the need for reforming the capital market was also felt as part of the overall economic reforms program initiated in 1991.

Phase 4 (1992 to Till Date): The Phase of Turbulence and Reforms

The Indian capital markets have shown a remarkable growth during the post-reform period. With its roots laid in socialism for four decades, with stringent control measures over private and foreign sector participation, India opened its gates to the outside world in the early 1990s. Since then, the financial markets underwent radical changes, largely in response to the economic crisis of the late 1980s. However, there is huge potential for the capital markets growth as at present just 2% of the population, account for retail investors and the lowest strata of the pyramid still remains untapped.[6] The post-reform period is marked by various popular stock market scams as well as numerous reformative steps. Table 22.2 summarizes few popular scams that rocked the capital market.

Capital Market Reforms in India

Considerable debate rages about the impact of deregulation on the efficiency of the market. Free market advocates all too often tend to undermine the unruly behavior of stock markets in the post-liberalization scenario. On the other hand, opponents believe that stock market reforms may

TABLE 22.2 Financial Market Scams in India

Year	Name of Scam	Particulars	Key Persons Involved
1992	Securities Scam	Diverted funds of about ₹5,000 crore from the banks to stockbrokers between April 1991 and May 1992. After the scam was exposed, the stock markets crashed.	Harshad Mehta
1995	Roop Bhansali scam	The CRB group owed ₹900 crore to various small investors from which it raised funds over the period of time. The stock market crash of 1995 unearthed the scam.	Chain Roop Bansali
2001	Indian Stock Market Manipulation Scam	Artificially rigged prices of certain chosen securities, using large sums of money borrowed from banks including the Madhavpura Mercantile Co-operative Bank, of which he himself was a director.	Ketan Parekh
2009	Satyam Scam	Manipulation of accounts of Satyam Computer Services by around US$ 1.47 Billion.	Ramalinga Raju
2010	Sahara India Pariwar investor fraud case	Raised several thousand crore through optionally fully convertible debentures that SEBI deemed illegal and failure of Subrata Roy-led Sahara India Pariwar to return ₹24,000 crore plus interests to its investors as directed by the Supreme Court of India.	Subrata Roy
2013	Saradha Scam	Caused by the collapse of a Ponzi scheme in West Bengal.	Sudipto Sen, Debjani Mukherjee, Kunal Ghosh
2013	NSEL Scam	A ₹5,600 crore scam in which a Mumbai-based NSEL (National spot Exchange Ltd) failed to pay its investors in commodity pair contracts. NSEL was a commodity exchange.	Jignesh Shah
2018	Punjab National Bank Scam	The fraud relates to fraudulent letter of undertaking worth ₹11,400 crore (US$ 1.4 billion) issued by the Punjab National Bank at Mumbai branch.	Nirav Modi

Source: Compiled by author

lead to over-speculation, financial crisis, and even misallocation of resources at the cost of real sector growth and stability, as has been seen in the case of India. However, there is now an increasing recognition in LDCs that have given the competition for foreign funding and limited availability of domestic finance, the equity market can play a beneficial role in providing capital to the productive sector as well as facilitate the process of privatization.[7] Government initiated various reformative steps for improvising the performance of Indian capital market. Let us discuss them.

Establishment of SEBI

The reform of the regulatory framework governing the Indian stock market began in the late 1980s with the establishment of the SEBI, but it gained significant momentum with the consolidation of all regulatory authority with SEBI in 1992. SEBI was established with an aim to create an environment which would facilitate mobilization of adequate resources through the security market and its efficient allocation.[8]

Strengthening the Government Security Market

A vibrant secondary segment of the government securities market helps in the effective operation of monetary policy through application of indirect instruments such as open market operations, for which government securities act as collateral. Wide-ranging reforms in the government securities market were largely undertaken in response to the changing economic environment. Reforms, therefore, focused on the development of appropriate market infrastructure, elongation of maturity profile, increasing the width and depth of the market, improving risk management practices, and increasing transparency. Few other remarkable changes include market-based price discovery, widening of investor base, introduction of new instruments, establishment of primary dealers, and electronic trading and settlement infrastructure. Securities Trading Corporation of India (STCI) Ltd in 1994 and Primary Dealers in 1995 were established to streamline and strengthen the security market.[9]

Establishing the National Security Clearing Corporation Ltd

National Securities Clearing Corporation Limited, NSCCL, a wholly owned subsidiary of National Stock Exchange (NSE) was established in 1996. It is responsible for clearing and settlement of all trades executed on NSE and deposit and collateral management and risk management functions. NSCCL was the first clearing corporation to be established in India, introduced settlement guarantee before it became a regulatory requirement. The objectives of NSCC Ltd include:[10]

- to bring and sustain confidence in clearing and settlement of securities;
- to promote and maintain short and consistent settlement cycles;
- to provide counter-party risk guarantee; and
- to operate a tight risk containment system.

Reforms in the Bombay Stock Exchange

The Bombay Stock Exchange (BSE) is Asia's oldest and India's first Stock Exchange and was established in 1875. With 5,439 listings, BSE is among the top ranking stock exchanges in the world in terms of market capitalization ($2.2 trillion in April 2018). The securities scam of 1992 and later Indian stock market manipulation scam of 2001 revealed the vulnerability in the functioning of Indian stock markets. Accordingly various reform measures were undertaken to strengthen the functioning of BSE. The reforms in BSE include introduction of rolling settlement replacing Badla, corporatization of BSE, Demat trading and launching of new indices, and developing a market for derivatives and futures (Table 22.3, Box 22.2).

TABLE 22.3 Important Milestones/Reforms of Bombay Stock Exchange

Year	Landmark
1875	▪ Establishment of Bombay Stock Exchange (BSE)
1957	▪ BSE granted permanent recognition under Securities Contracts (Regulation) Act (SCRA)
1986	▪ SENSEX, country's first equity index launched (Base Year: 1978–1979 = 100)
1995	▪ BSE On-Line Trading (BOLT) system introduced
2000	▪ Equity Derivatives introduced

Year	Landmark
2001	■ New indices like BSE Webx, S&P BSE PSU index, BSE Teck, S&P BSE Dollex 30, S&P BSE PSU index were Launched ■ Stock options & Stock futures were launched ■ 100% book building allowedT+5 settlement Introduced
2002	■ T+3 settlement Introduced
2003	■ India's first ETF on S&P BSE SENSEX—"SPICE" introduced ■ T+2 settlement Introduced ■ Bankex launched
2005	■ BSE becomes a Corporate Entity
2007	■ Singapore Exchange Limited entered into an agreement to invest in a 5% stake in BSE
2008	■ Currency Derivatives Introduced
2009	■ S&P BSE IPO Index launched ■ BSE Launches BSE StAR MF—Mutual Fund trading platform
2010	■ BSE introduced Mobile-based Trading ■ EUREX—S&P BSE SENSEX Futures launched ■ Commencement of S&P BSE Volatility Index and S&P BSE Shariah Index
2011	■ BSE Training Institute Ltd with IGNOU launched India's first 2-year full time MBA program specializing in Financial Market
2012	■ Launch of S&P BSE-GREENEX to promote investments in Green India ■ BSE launched trading in BRICSMART indices derivatives
2013	■ BSE enters into Strategic Partnership with S&P Dow Jones Indices ■ Launch of Currency Derivatives (BSE CDX)
2014	■ Launch of Interest Rate Futures (BSE–IRF)
2015	■ BSE becomes the fastest exchange in the world with a median response speed of 6 microseconds
2016	■ BSE signs Memorandum of Understanding with Korea Exchange (KRX) to launch S&P BSE Sensex-based derivatives contracts at KRX ■ BSE announces commencement of trading of Sovereign Gold Bonds
2017	■ BSE becomes India's first listed stock exchange ■ India's Premier Stock Exchange BSE and World's largest Insurance Exchange Ebix, Inc. sign MOU to launch joint venture company, for Setting up Pioneering Insurance Distribution Network in India
2018	■ BSE launches its commodity derivatives segment making it India's 1st Universal Exchange

BOX 22.2 What is Sensex?

The S&P BSE Sensex (Sensitive Index) was launched in 1986. It comprises 30 prominent stocks derived from all key sectors based on their financial performance. Being an important economic barometer of the economic mood of the nation, Sensex is regarded to be the pulse of the Indian stock market and thus reflects the movement of the Indian stock markets and benchmark for funds performance. The Index Committee meets every quarter to review all the S&P BSE SENSEX. In case of a revision in the Index constituents, the announcement of the incoming and outgoing Securities is made 6 weeks in advance, in accordance with SEBI requirements. The company included in the Sensex must qualify quantitative as well as qualitative criteria. The quantitative criteria include market capitalization, trading frequency, average daily trades, average daily turnover, industry representation, and listed history. The qualitative criteria include track record of the company.

The base period of Sensex is 1978–1979 and it is calculated using the "Free-float Market Capitalization" methodology. Let us understand it with the help of an example. Suppose a company X issues 10,000 shares in total, of which 2,000 are issued to the promoters, and rest 8,000 shares are issued to general public. These 8,000 shares will be called "free-floating" shares. If the price of each share is ₹150, then the "total" market capitalization of the company is ₹1,500,000 (10,000 × 150), but its free-float market capitalization is ₹1200,000 (8,000 × 150). The first step to calculate index will be to get market capitalization of all the 30 companies that form the Sensex. Let us assume that the free-float market capitalization of all the 30 companies arrives at 3,000,000. The free-float market capitalization of the index constituents is then divided by a number known as the Index Divisor. This index divisor is derived from the base period value of the index (1978–1979). Suppose the free-float market capitalization for the base year is 75,000, then index divisor will be 100/75,000. This value provides for comparison of the index over a period of time. In our example, Sensex index value equals 3,000,000×100/75,000 = 40,000 for that day.

Source: Annual Report, SEBI, 2017–2018.

Exit of De-recognized/Non-Operational Stock Exchanges

After the emergence of nationwide trading terminals, developments in technology and abolition of compulsory listing in regional stock exchanges, trading in equity and equity derivative segments were concentrated in two exchanges, namely BSE Ltd and NSE of India Ltd. However, the smaller/regional stock exchanges became defunct due to unsustainable operations and also because the shareholders of companies listed in these stock exchanges did not have an exit option, as these companies were not listed in stock exchanges having nationwide trading terminal.[11] Further, SEBI had to carry out various regulatory, supervisory, and administrative activities of such exchanges which proved to be an unproductive regulatory burden on the resources of SEBI. In its circular dated May 30, 2012, SEBI had given all exchanges 2 years' time to comply with the norms on net worth and trading volumes, failing which they would be de-recognized.[12] Stock exchanges where the annual trading turnover on its own platform is less than ₹1,000 crore can apply to SEBI for voluntary surrender of recognition and exit at any time before the expiry of 2 years from the date of issuance of this circular. If the stock exchange is not able to achieve the prescribed turnover of ₹1,000 crore on continuous basis or does not apply for voluntary surrender of recognition and exit before the expiry of 2 years from the date of this circular, SEBI shall proceed with compulsory de-recognition and exit of such stock exchanges, in terms of the conditions as may be specified by SEBI.[13]

The stock exchanges granted exit by SEBI so far are 19 in number, namely Hyderabad Stock Exchange, Coimbatore Stock Exchange Ltd, Saurashtra Kutch Stock Exchange Ltd, Mangalore Stock Exchange, Inter-Connected Stock Exchange of India Ltd, Cochin Stock Exchange Ltd, Bangalore Stock Exchange Ltd, Ludhiana Stock exchange Ltd, Gauhati Stock Exchange Ltd, Bhubaneswar Stock Exchange Ltd, Jaipur Stock Exchange Ltd, OTC Exchange of India, Pune Stock Exchange Ltd, Madras Stock Exchange Ltd, UP Stock Exchange Ltd, Madhya Pradesh Stock Exchange Ltd, Vadodara Stock Exchange Ltd, Delhi Stock Exchange Ltd, and Ahmedabad Stock Exchange Ltd.[14]

Establishment of NSE

NSE was established in 1992 at Mumbai on the recommendation of MJ Pherwani Committee. The idea behind the establishment of NSE was clear—the newly established body was supposed to complement the operations of BSE and help mitigating the problem of the lack of sufficient liquidity and poor service to the growing number of smaller investors.[15] NSE was the first de-mutualized electronic stock exchange of India. It is the leading stock exchange in India and the fourth largest in the world by equity trading volume in 2015, according to World Federation of Exchanges (WFE). It began operations in 1994 and is ranked as the largest stock exchange in India in terms of total and average daily turnover for equity shares every year since 1995, based on annual reports of SEBI.[16] The electronic screen-based trading was started in NSE in 1994, derivatives trading (in the form of index futures), and internet trading in 2000, which were each the first of its kind in India. The popular indices of NSE are CNX Nifty, CNX Nifty Junior, and CNX 500. With 1,952 listings in its accord, the NSE has market capitalization of US$2.3 trillion as of March 2018.

Development of Corporate Bond Market

While the government security market is now fairly well developed, the corporate debt market needs to be developed so that India can have a well-integrated financial market. Apart from the advantages that it confers for long-term financing, an integrated financial market is necessary for efficient transmission of monetary policy. The foundations for developing an efficient corporate debt market have already been laid as the necessary infrastructure and institutions that have been created for the government security market are already available. The RBI and SEBI have also taken a number of initiatives to ensure that this market develops in a transparent and safe manner. Recent initiatives include announcing guidelines on trading and listing requirements for corporate debt by SEBI and asking banks to invest only in listed and rated corporate paper by the RBI.[17]

Securities and Exchange Board of India

The SEBI was established in 1988 and was provided statutory powers in 1992 as per provisions of the SEBI Act, 1992.[18] Since then, SEBI has gradually adopted many important roles in the area of policy formulation, regulation, enforcement, and market development. Today, SEBI supervises almost every aspect of the capital markets, such as regulation of intermediaries, curbing malpractices like market manipulation and insider trading, development of fair practices by the intermediaries, development of the capital market, creating awareness among investors, and so on. Following are the functions of SEBI[19]:

1. Regulating the business in stock exchanges and any other securities markets;
2. Registering and regulating the working of stock brokers, sub-brokers, share transfer agents, merchant bankers, underwriters, portfolio managers, investment advisers, and such other intermediaries who may be associated with securities markets in any manner;
3. Registering and regulating the working of the depositories, custodians of securities, foreign institutional investors, credit rating agencies, and such other intermediaries as the board may, by notification, specify in this behalf;
4. Registering and regulating the working of venture capital funds and mutual funds;
5. Promoting and regulating self-regulatory organizations;
6. Prohibiting fraudulent and unfair trade practices relating to securities markets;
7. Promoting investors' education and training of intermediaries of securities markets;

8. Prohibiting insider trading in securities;
9. Regulating substantial acquisition of shares and take-over of companies;
10. Calling for information from, undertaking inspection, conducting inquiries and audits of the stock exchanges, mutual funds, other persons associated with the securities market intermediaries;
11. Performing such functions and exercising such powers under the provisions of the Capital Issues (Control) Act, 1947 and Securities Contracts (Regulation) Act, 1947 and Securities Contracts (Regulation) Act, 1956, as may be delegated to it by the central government.

Summary

1. The capital market is a market for long-term funds. Broadly, the capital market is divided into two constituents (1) securities market and (2) development financial institutions (DFIs). The security market is divided into gilt-edged market and corporate security market. Gilt-edged market is the market for government securities. The corporate security market is the market where securities of corporate firms are bought and sold. The corporate securities are traded both in primary as well as secondary market. In the new issue market the shares are sold by prospectus, by offer for sale, by private placing, and by offering rights issue. Secondary markets, also called as stock exchange or after markets, are the financial market where previously traded financial instruments such as shares, debentures, bonds, options, and future are bought and sold. As on March 31, 2019, there are six stock exchanges, out of which three are permanent and three are non-permanent.
2. A DFI is defined as "an institution promoted or assisted by government mainly to provide development finance to one or more sectors or sub-sectors of the economy." DFIs comprise all India DFIs (IFCI, SIDBI, etc.), specialized financial institutions (IDFC, EXIM bank, etc.), investment institutions (LIC, GIC, etc.), refinance institutions (NABARD, NHB, etc.), state-level institutions, and other financial institutions (SFCs, SIDCs, etc.).
3. The evolution and growth of Indian capital markets since independence can broadly be divided into four distinct phases. Phase 1 (1947–1973): the period of institution-building and legal framework; Phase 2 (1973–1980): the period of foreign exchange regulation; Phase 3 (1980–1992): the broadening and deepening of capital market; and Phase 4 (1992 to till date): the phase of turbulence and reforms. Capital market reforms comprise establishment of SEBI in 1988; strengthening the government security market; establishing the National Security Clearing Corporation Ltd; reforms in BSE; exit of de-recognized/non-operational stock exchanges; establishment of NSE in 1992; and development of corporate bond market.
4. The Securities and Exchange Board of India (SEBI) was established in 1988 and was provided statutory powers in 1992 as per provisions of the SEBI Act, 1992. SEBI supervises almost every aspect of the capital markets, such as regulation of intermediaries, curbing malpractices like market manipulation and insider trading, development of fair practices by the intermediaries, development of the capital market, creating awareness among investors, and so on.

Endnotes

1. Chakrabarty, K.C. (2013). *Transformation of development financial institutions into commercial banks: The case of IDBI and the role of employee unions*. Retrieved from https://www.rbi.org.in (Accessed on March 14, 2019).
2. General Insurance Corporation. Retrieved from https://www.gicofindia.com. (Accessed on March 28, 2019).
3. National Housing Bank. Retrieved from https://nhb.org.in (Accessed on March 28, 2019).
4. State Financial Corporation. Retrieved from https://www.india.gov.in(Accessed on March 28, 2019).
5. State Industrial Development Corporation. Retrieved from http://www.cosidici.com. (Accessed on March 28, 2019).
6. A joint study by PWC & ASSOCHAM on *The Indian Capital Market: Growth with governance* (2019). Retrieved from www.pwc.in (Accessed on May 12, 2019). *p.4.*
7. Roy, M.K. (2001). Stock market in a liberalised economy Indian experiences. *Economic and Political Weekly. 36*(04)
8. Gokran, S. (1996). Indian Capital Market Reforms, 1992–1996-An assessment. *Economic and Political Weekly. 31(15)*
9. Securities Trading Corporation of India. Retrieved from http://www.fimmda.org (Accessed on February 14, 2019).
10. National Stock Exchange. Retrieved from https://www.nscclindia.com (Accessed on May 18, 2019).

11. Exit of De-recognized/Non-Operational Stock Exchanges. Retrieved fromhttp://www.sebi.gov.in (Accessed on May 18, 2019).
12. *SEBI scheme may provide easier exit route to regional bourses. Livemint*. July 14, 2014.
13. SEBI circular. Retrieved from www.sebi.gov.in (Accessed on May 18, 2019).
14. Annual Report, SEBI, 2017–2018, p.98.
15. Ego clash, *India Today*, September 30, 1991.
16. NSE. Retrieved from https://www.nseindia.com (Accessed on May 19, 2019).
17. Mohan, R. (2004). A decade of reforms in government securities market in India and the road ahead. *RBI Bulletin*.
18. SEBI. http://www.sebi.gov.in. (Accessed on May 19, 2019).
19. The Securities and Exchange Board of India Act, 1992. Accessed from http://www.sebi.gov.in (Accessed on May 19, 2019).

CHAPTER 23

INFLATION IN INDIA

Inflation is when you pay fifteen dollars for the ten-dollar haircut you used to get for five dollars when you had hair.

—Sam Ewing

INTRODUCTION

Indian economy is no alien to inflation. In fact, it has been subjected to periodic bouts of inflation repeatedly. Inflation has the potency to make and mar the political fortunes of governments. It is because inflation is, at the same time, one of the most dreaded and one of the most misunderstood of economic phenomena. Therefore, in a country like India which boasts of the largest democracy, inflation management is one of the hardest tasks the policymakers have to undertake.

This chapter aims to address following issues:

- Inflation and Its Types
- Wholesale Price Index
- Consumer Price Index
- Cause, Consequences, and Control of Inflation
- Inflation Targeting

INFLATION AND ITS TYPES

Inflation is the general increase in the price level of an economy for a basket of selected goods and services over a period of time. The magnitude of inflation—the inflation rate—is usually reported as the annualized percentage growth of some broad index of money prices.[1] With prices rising, a one-rupee note buys less each year. Inflation, thus, means an ongoing fall in the overall purchasing power of the monetary unit. Inflation can be classified into various types.

Moderate inflation: It is a mild and tolerable form of inflation in the range of 2–4% price rise per annum. It is considered as an efficient and tolerable norm for the Indian economy. It is also called creeping inflation.

Walking inflation: Inflation rate between 5 and 10% can be termed as walking inflation. It is a warning signal for the occurrence of running or double digit and eventually a galloping inflation, if it is not checked in time.

Running inflation: When prices rise by more than 10% a year, it is termed as running inflation. India experienced this kind of inflation during 1970s and 1980s and during 2010 and 2011 in the aftermath of global financial crisis.

Galloping inflation: When prices are rising at double or triple digit rates of 20, 100, or 200% a year, it is termed as galloping inflation. In 1980s, this type of inflation occurred in countries such as Argentina and Israel. Galloping inflation is really a serious problem because if it is not controlled effectively, it soon turns into hyper-inflation.

Hyper-inflation: Under hyperinflation, prices rise by fits and starts. In quantitative terms, if prices rise over 1,000% in a year, it is termed as hyper-inflation. Many European nations witnessed hyper-inflation in the wake of World War I. In Germany, the price index rose from 1 to 10,00,000,000 during January 1922 to November 1923. Hyper-inflation of Zimbabwe in 1990s and Afghanistan in early 2000s are other notable examples.

WHOLESALE PRICE INDEX

Wholesale Price Index (WPI) depicts the price of a representative basket of wholesale commodities. In India, it is a single, unique, and nationwide price indicator that tracks the prices of the commodities in the wholesale market. WPI was first published in January 1942 with base year 1939. In India, Office of Economic Advisor, Department of Industrial Policy and Promotion (DIPP), Ministry of Commerce and Industry calculates the WPI. The Working Group chaired by Late Dr Saumitra Chaudhari recommended new WPI series with base year 2011–2012. The WPI series in India has undergone six revisions in 1952–1953, 1961–1962, 1970–1971, 1981–1982, 1993–1994, and 2004–2005 so far. The current series is the seventh revision. The new series has 697 items and the price data are collected from 8,331 quotations/centers (up from 5,482 quotations/centers in the old series 2004–2005). The 697 commodities have been divided into three major groups (viz. primary articles, fuel and power, and manufactured products) and different sub-groups. Weights are assigned to commodity groups in the proportion of total spending that is devoted to each commodity. For example, while constructing WPI in India the weight assigned to primary articles is 22.62. For fuel and power and manufactured products the weights are 13.15 and 64.23, respectively. A new "Food Index" is being compiled combining the "food articles" under "primary articles" and "food products" under "manufactured products". Together with the Consumer Food Price Index released by Central Statistics Office (CSO), this would help monitor the price situation of food items better.

BOX 23.1 Few Terms Associated with Inflation

Headline inflation: It is overall inflation rate in the economy reported through Consumer Price Index (CPI) combined or CPI (rural +urban). The headline CPI inflation measure is being used as the target rate of inflation as it reflects the prices of essential consumption goods.

Core inflation: The food and fuel are highly volatile and don't represent the true picture of inflation. The core inflation is, therefore, an inflation measure which excludes transitory or temporary price volatility as in the case of some commodities such as food items and energy products.

Hence, Core inflation = Headline inflation – (Food inflation + Fuel inflation).

The core inflation measure is often used by monetary authorities as an input for the conduct of monetary policy.

Retail inflation: It shows the inflation rate at retail level. In India, it is another name for consumer price index.

Protein inflation: Increase in prices of protein-rich food items such as milk, pulses, egg, fish and meat products is called protein inflation. Protein inflation in India was noticed in the recent past during 2011–2012 when increase in income led to structural change in dietary habits of people and they shifted from coarse cereals and other non-protein-rich food items to protein-rich food items.

Sources:

1. Annual Report, RBI, August 2012.
2. Look what is driving core inflation in India, *Business Today*, January 24, 2019.

Consumer Price Index

The Consumer Price Index (CPI) is based on the cost of a basket typically purchased by consumers. The annual percentage change in a CPI is used as a measure of inflation. It is based on household expenditure surveys and thus measures the rise in cost of living. CPI numbers are widely used as a macro-economic indicator of inflation, as a tool by governments and central banks for inflation targeting and for monitoring price stability, and as deflators in the national accounts. CPI is also used for indexing dearness allowance to employees for increase in prices. CPI is therefore, considered as one of the most important economic indicators.[2] In India, four types of consumer price indices (CPI) are released at national level:

1. CPI for Industrial Workers (IW)
2. CPI for Agricultural Laborers (AL)
3. CPI for Rural Laborers (RL)
4. CPI (Rural + Urban or Combined)

CPI-IW: CPI-IW was introduced in 1946 and is released by Labour Bureau in the Ministry of Labour and Employment. The base year of CPI-(IW) is 2016 and it covers 463 items.

CPI-AL: CPI-AL was introduced in 1964 and is released by Labour Bureau. Its base year is 1986–1987 and it covers 182 items.

CPI-RL: CPI-RL was introduced in 1995 and is also released by Labour Bureau. Its base year is 1986–1987 and it also covers 182 items.

Like WPI, all these three indices are calculated on the basis of weighted arithmetic mean as per Laspeyres Index formula.

CPI-Rural + Urban (Combined): National Statistical Commission in 2001 under the chairmanship of Dr C. Rangarajan recommended compilation of national CPI for both rural and urban areas. Based on these recommendations, the all-India CPI series was released for January 2011 for rural (CPI-Rural) and urban (CPI-Urban) areas along with a combined (rural + urban) all-India CPI index (CPI-combined) with 2010 as the base year. CPI combined is published by the CSO in the Ministry of Statistics and Programme Implementation. Since January 2015, the base year has been revised to 2012. The number of items in CPI basket is 299.[3] The CPI-combined

TABLE 23.1 CPI (Rural + Urban) Item Group and Weights

Item Group	Weight
Food and beverages	45.86
Pan, tobacco, and intoxicants	2.38
Clothing and footwear	6.53
Housing	10.07
Fuel and light	6.84
Miscellaneous	28.32
Total	**100**

Source: Ministry of Statistics and Programme Implementation, Govt. of India.

covers 2,300 rural and urban centers and collects 5.5 lakh price quotations from various retail outlets. CPI-combined is calculated on the basis of geometric mean for elementary item index and Laspeyres Index formula for higher level index.[4] In 2013, CPI in India replaced WPI as a main measure of inflation. The RBI too mandated using CPI-combined as the sole indicator of inflation for its monetary policy (Table 23.1).

Causes of Inflation

Inflation takes place due to mismatch between demand and supply. Following are the causes of inflation.

Demand-Pull Inflation

If demand is greater than supply (i.e., demand rises but supply remains constant in the short run), it is called demand-pull inflation. In other words, when the aggregate demand in an economy strongly outweighs the aggregate supply, prices increase. Economists will often say that demand-pull inflation is a result of too many rupees chasing too few goods.

Higher Fiscal Expansion

In the last few years, the government has increased budgetary expenditure on various social development programs and it has resulted into the expansion in money supply in the country resulting into inflation. The government expenditure on various social sector schemes such as education, health, water, poverty removal, employment generation, rural development, and other social infrastructure activities has experienced an increasing trend. Public expenditure as a percentage of gross domestic product (GDP) has increased from around 9 to 30% from 1950–1951 to 2018–2019.[5] But the worrisome part of entire story is increase in unproductive expenditure that includes subsidies on demerit goods, interest payments, and defense expenditure.

Higher GDP Growth and Sticky Core Inflation

India has experienced one of the fastest growth rates in the world in the last few years. Increase in GDP means more income and expenditure and hence more economic activity and inflation.

TABLE 23.2 Trends of Inflation in India

Year	WPI	CPI Combined
2012–2013	6.9	10.2
2013–2014	5.2	9.5
2014–2015	2.0	5.9
2015–2016	–2.5	4.9
2016–2017	3.7	4.5
2017–2018	3.0	3.6
2018–2019	4.3	3.4
2019–2020	1.7	4.8
2020–2021	1.3	6.2
2022–2023	9.6	6.7

Source: RBI Bulletin, April 2024; RBI Report on Currency and Finance, 2021

Higher GDP growth has been accused as the main driver of core inflation in India by the experts. As we have discussed earlier, core inflation signifies non-food and non-fuel segment and thus occupies an unusually large weight (47%) in the CPI and hence has significant bearing on inflation measurement in India. The core inflation has been actually at over 4% in the last 5 years. The key components of core inflation are housing, education, household goods and services, transport and communication, recreational and amusement and personal care, etc. In most of these items, the price pressure remains, this makes the core inflation sticky (Table 23.2).[6]

Income Effect

The post-globalization period has witnessed a tremendous rise in the pay packages of the private sector employees. The government has also provided lofty pay packages to its central government employees as witnessed after the implementation of sixth and seventh pay commission recommendations and subsequent pay hikes in all states of the country to benefit state government employees. Such soaring pay packages have not only regenerated an interest in the minds of youth regarding the government jobs but also contributed into the demand-pull inflation. The introduction of various rural development schemes has generated new avenues of employment and income in rural India contributing to structural shift in the demand patterns among the rural folks causing inflation. For example, India had a normal southwest monsoon during 2011, which had a moderating impact on the prices of select food items, especially cereals and pulses, for which the average inflation during the year was moderate at 3.6%. However, food inflation driven by non-cereal items, whose output is less responsive to monsoon in the short run, remained high. Later, it was found through research that rising per-capita incomes and changes in dietary patterns led to increase in demand for protein-rich items called as food inflation or protein inflation.[7]

Black Money

Inflation is directly correlated to more cash flowing in the system than required to maintain market equilibrium. During 1990s and later, a lot of black money was driven out of India in

Swiss bank and other safe destinations where it used to earn a paltry interest rate of 1–2% a year. This money re-entered the Indian market via the assistance of financial managers who aimed to provide annual returns between 10 and 20% and the money was re-invested via assets such as stocks, bonds, and even real estate. According to experts, black money was biggest reason for inflation in real estate sector.

Increase in Population

The world population is projected to grow to 9 billion by 2042. More population number puts strain on the limited resources and hence naturally gives birth to inflation. In spite of the fact that the average annual growth rate of population has slowed down in India from 1.95% during 1991–2001 to 1.63% during 2001–2011, the net addition to the growth during the period 2001–2011 was around 181.6 million. What makes policymakers worried is that the agriculture growth in India has not been consistent and in the years of low growth (when the agriculture growth rate turns lower), the prices show escalating trend.

Supply-Shock or Cost-Push Inflation

If supply is lesser than demand (i.e., supply falls but demand remains constant in the short run), it is called cost-push or supply-side inflation. It results because of negative supply shock, which is caused by a rise in the cost of oil, imported raw materials, or domestic wage costs per unit of output.

Rise in Wages

Wage-push inflation occurs when wages are increased (as a policy measure or due to trade union pressure) and business must, in order to pay the higher wages, charge more for their products and/or services. The wage increase, then, is not as helpful to employees since the cost of goods has also risen and though their money wage rate seems to be increasing, their real wage rate falls. If prices remain increased, workers will eventually require another wage hike to compensate for the higher cost of living leading to wage price spiral.

Increase in Prices of Basic Materials

The prices of basic materials such as fuel, steel, cement, milk and food products affect the overall prices and hence produce inflation. For example, the sharp rise and volatility of prices of oil and petroleum products in international markets have become a matter of global concern. Crude oil prices turn volatile due to political upheaval in the major oil-exporting countries coupled with increasing uncertainly in the global economic environment. It must be remembered that during the economic crisis of 1990s, burgeoning oil import bill (due to Gulf crisis) led to running inflation in the country. Further, there is unprecedented volatility in global oil prices since the year 2000. A study by International Monetary Fund (IMF) reveals that a 10% increase in global oil inflation, on average, increases domestic inflation by about 0.4 percentage point.[8]

Rise in Administered Prices

The rise in administered prices pushes up the general price level. Food items have a large 45.86% weight in the Consumer Price Index and cereals and products have 9.67% weight. High food inflation can push overall inflation higher. For example, government decision to fix the minimum support price (MSP) may have a direct impact on food inflation and second-round effects on headline inflation, which may force central bank to tighten the monetary policy.[9]

Rise in International Prices

It means inflation in one country spreads to other countries. The latest research has validated a positive relationship between global and domestic inflations. The major source of inflation in the recent past has been price rise in non-food raw materials–dependent manufactured products, much of which has been due to imported global commodity inflation. The high inflation in several commodities globally led to increase in price level of these commodities domestically. For example, international prices of gold and silver, coconut and copra, fertilizers, coffee, and iron are no more country-centric. As a result, domestic manufacturing inflation has also started picking up. Minerals and metal inflation remained at elevated levels thanks to the global impact. Claudio Borio and Andrew Filardo in their research have documented that (1) the growing importance of global factors would call for more intensive monitoring of external developments; (2) failure to appreciate the build-up of global inflationary pressures could result in surprisingly strong inflation in domestic market; and (3) domestic inflation if gets increasingly influenced by global capacity constraints, will make monetary policy ineffective because of its limited (i.e., domestic) reach.[10]

Other Causes

There are other factors as well that lead to supply-shock or cost-push inflation, which includes deficiency of capital equipment, decrease in imports owing to war or restrictions (especially during Gulf war in 1990–1991 and post-Pokhran sanctions in 1998–1999), hoarding of essential articles (onion price hike in 2010), prolonged industrial unrest, drought, famine, etc.

Consequences of Inflation in India

Impact on Balance of Payments

Weakening of Indian rupee is both the cause and effect of inflation. As the domestic inflation increases, imports become relatively cheaper leading to the increased demand of dollars, thus depreciating the currency. A depreciated currency, on the other hand, increases the cost of imported goods too, further fuelling inflation. A weak Indian rupee during the past few years increased the cost of oil and petroleum, which being the major input in many industries seriously affected their profitability.[11]

Impact on Common Man

Inflation reduces the real value of money and hence purchasing power. The section of the society that is most affected by inflation is the consumer. As the salaries and income of the individuals increases with a lag, there is always a time when prices of goods are increasing and they are becoming less and less affordable because income is stagnant. Fixed wage earners are most affected by it as it takes more time for their wages to adjust to rising inflation. If the inflation is high and persistent, the lag between price rise and wage rise increases. Population at the lower end on the spectrum is most affected by inflation.

Impact on Investment and GDP

The consistent increase in prices over the period of time negatively affects the growth and development of a nation. It is because increase in prices for a longer period of time discourages savings. In India, around 60% of gross national savings are done by household sector. With ever-increasing prices, the consumer households find their real savings wiped off and thus precious saving meant for investment are diverted to consumption expenditure. The fall in investment reduces capital formation in the country and thus leads to fall in GDP. In fact, increase in prices during 2009–2011 affected the gross capital formation in the country negatively. Inflation also makes debtors gain and creditors lose. It is because debtors return the same amount of money, but they pay less in terms of goods and services. On the other hand, creditors get back the same amount of money which they lent, but they receive less in real terms because the value of money falls.

So, what must be the ideal rate of inflation in an economy? Unfortunately, this question is hard to answer—developing countries typically have higher inflation, and also have higher growth. India has experienced high inflation since 1970s and witnessed an average of more than 9% inflation between 2006 and 2013. So one might well find a positive correlation between inflation and growth, though this does not mean more inflation causes more growth. For example, high inflation has serious re-distributive effects, destroying the middle class' savings held in bonds and deposits.[12] It needs to be remembered that inflation is good if it occurs at moderate levels. It keeps the business outlook optimistic and thus aids into growth and development of economy.

Inequality

Although inflation erodes the wealth of each and every individual equally, its effects are more pronounced on poor people rather than rich. Big farmers, industrialists, and traders benefit the most from inflation and make the big fortunes. However, the people who are already living at subsistence level are most affected by it. The poor and middle classes suffer because their wages and salaries are more or less fixed but the prices of commodities continue to rise. In terms of capability deprivation, inflation not only leads to increase in inequality but also poverty. On average, countries with the highest levels of inequality will face inflation at least 40% higher than countries with the lowest inequality.[13] A study by Asian development bank revealed that high incidence of food inflation during 2009–2011 pushed around 5 crore Indians below poverty line basket.

MEASURES TO CONTROL INFLATION IN INDIA

There are generally three measures viz. fiscal, administrative, and monetary which have been adopted in the past few years to control inflation in the country.

Fiscal/Trade Measures

Fiscal policy to control inflation comprises measures like change in taxation policy, restraining non-developmental public expenditure, strengthening public distribution system (PDS), and making essential imports and curtailing exports of essential goods.

1. To bridge the mismatch between demand and supply, the government from time to time has imported essential food items from foreign lands. For example, in the eventuality of food inflation during 2010–2012, the import duties were reduced to zero for rice, wheat, onion, pulses, edible oils (crude) and to 7.5% for refined and hydrogenated oils and vegetable oils. The government also permitted certain government agencies such as the State Trading Corporation of India (STC), Minerals and Metals Trading Corporation (MMTC), National Agricultural Cooperative Marketing Federation of India (NAFED), and National Dairy Development Board (NDDB) to make duty-free imports from time to time.
2. To enhance the production of essential goods and services, the government provides tax incentives to the producers in the private sector.
3. The deficit financing which was the chief reason of inflation during 1970s, 1980s, and 1990s is being avoided by the government under new fiscal framework. Enactment of FRBM Act made government responsible in fiscal spending and as a consequence fiscal deficit has come down significantly. Fiscal deficit was reported to be 3.5% of GDP during 2017–2018 and slightly above 4% during 2018–2019.[14]

Administrative Measures

Administrative measures involve rationing and price control. Rationing aims at distributing consumption of scarce goods so as to make them available to a large number of consumers. Effective PDS is the key to supply of essential consumer goods to general public. Enactment of National Food Security Act (NFSA) is the right step toward that direction. Steps have been taken from time to time to procure food grains to poor people through various ways such as providing subsidized food grains through Central issue price and Antyodaya Anna Yojana, allocation under the Open Market Sale Scheme (OMSS) and sale to small traders, ad hoc allocation of food grains to all states/UTs for BPL families at BPL issue price for distribution. The government also provides subsidy to ensure supply of essential items at reasonable prices. Fertilizer subsidy for farmers, capital goods subsidy for MSME sector, and food subsidy for poor can be mentioned in this regard.

Monetary Measures

Drawing from a wider mandate, monetary policy in India has evolved to have multiple objectives of price stability, financial stability, and growth. The appropriate monetary policy stance depends on inflation dynamics, the distribution of exogenous shocks affecting the economy, and the monetary transmission mechanism.[15] The route of monetary policy to control inflation is dear money policy under which RBI tightens expansion of money supply. It can be done by hiking of Repo rate, Bank Rate, CRR, SLR, etc.* In an attempt to rein in inflation, inflation targeting is seen as a paradigm shift in the monetary policy of India.

---

*For detailed discussion, please refer to section "Monetary Policy" in the Chapter 21 Indian Monetary System: Banking, RBI, and Money Market.

Inflation Targeting in India: A Paradigm Shift in Monetary Policy Framework

Inflation targeting is a monetary policy strategy or framework used by RBI for maintaining price level at a certain level or within a range. It signifies the importance of price stability as the key objective of monetary policy. Under inflation targeting, the central bank forecasts the future path of inflation and compares it with the target inflation rate (the rate the government believes is appropriate for the economy). The difference between the forecast and the target determines how much monetary policy has to be adjusted.[16] The basic advantage of inflation targeting is that rising prices create uncertainties in decision making, adversely affecting savings and encouraging speculative investments. Inflation targeting brings in more predictability and transparency in deciding monetary policy. If the central banks could ensure price stability, households and companies can plan ahead, negotiating wages on the basis of expecting low and stable inflation. The policy of inflation targeting was first introduced in some European countries in the 1970s and became a popular approach in the 1990s.[17]

Significance of Inflation Targeting

Inflation targeting was drawn on the backdrop of global financial crisis and their impact on Indian economy. India experienced one of the highest inflation rates among G-20 nations with WPI averaging 7.5% and CPI-IW averaging 10.1% during post-global financial crisis period. It led to the following consequences:

- Erosion of domestic savings as high inflation rates made the real interest rates negative
- Eroding the external competitiveness as high inflation made imports relatively cheaper and exports dearer
- Large demand for gold (through import) as a hedge against inflation contributed into widening of current account deficit
- Weakening of exchange rates as inflation led to depreciation of currency
- Adverse impact on allocative efficiency because of high prices
- Re-distribution of income in the favor of rich.

The Expert Committee to Revise and Strengthen the Monetary Policy Framework, headed by Urjit Patel, former Governor RBI submitted a report in January 2014. On the basis of recommendation of Committee, Government of India and RBI signed a Monetary Policy Framework Agreement on February 20, 2015. Following are the key points of strategy under inflation targeting:

1. The Committee suggested switching over from WPI to CPI as the measure of nominal anchor. Theoretically, reliance on WPI has two problems. First, what the common citizen experiences is retail inflation, that can be better captured by CPI. Second, WPI contains a lot of traded manufactured goods and commodity inputs in the basket, whose prices is determined internationally. In doing so we neglect CPI which is what matters to common man, and is more the consequence of domestic monetary policy.[18]
2. The government has set a target for RBI to bring down inflation below 6% by January 2016, 4% for financial year and all subsequent years with band of ±2%.

3. If RBI fails to meet the target, it will report to the government with the reasons for the failure to achieve the target and propose remedial actions to be taken.
4. The RBI will further estimate the time period within which the failed target would be achieved.

Management of monetary policy and the express objective of inflation targeting have been enshrined as the responsibility of RBI by amending the preamble of the RBI Act, 1934 through the Finance Act 2016. Thus, ensuring price stability through inflation targeting is a legal responsibility of RBI since 2016. Under Section 45ZA(1) of the RBI Act, 1934, the Central Government determines the inflation target in terms of the Consumer Price Index, once in every 5 years in consultation with the RBI. This target would be notified in the Official Gazette. Among other measures, RBI targets inflation primarily by changing the "Policy Rate," which means the rate for repo-transactions. Factors constituting failure to meet inflation target under the Monetary Policy Committee (MPC) Framework was notified on June 27, 2016. In exercise of the powers conferred by the RBI Act, 1934, the Central Government notified the following as factors that constitute failure to achieve the inflation target, namely (1) the average inflation is more than the upper tolerance level of the inflation target notified under the RBI Act for any three consecutive quarters or (2) the average inflation is less than the lower tolerance level of the inflation target notified under the RBI Act for any three consecutive quarters.

Summary

1. Inflation means the general increase in the level of prices over a period of time. Inflation has many types such as moderate inflation (2–4%), walking inflation (5–10%, running inflation (10–20%), galloping inflation (20–100%), and hyper-inflation (1,000% or more).
2. The two popular indices of inflation are Wholesale Price Index (WPI) and Consumer Price Index (CPI). WPI depicts the price of a representative basket of wholesale commodities. The base year of new WPI series is 2011–2012. The new series has 697 items and the price data are collected from 8,331 quotations/centers. In WPI weights assigned to primary articles, fuel and power, and manufactured products are 22.62, 13.15, and 64.23, respectively.
3. CPI is based on the cost of a basket typically purchased by consumers. In India, four types of consumer price indices are released at national level. They are CPI for Industrial Workers (IW), CPI for Agricultural Labourers (AL), CPI for Rural Labourers (RL), and CPI Rural + Urban (Combined). The first three are published by Labour Bureau and the CPI combined is published by CSO. The base year for CPI-IW is 2000–2001, whereas for CPI-AL and CPI-RL, the base year is 1986–1987. CPI combined has base year 2012 and includes 299 items. Food and beverage has maximum weight of 45.86 in CPI combined. RBI uses CPI combined as the sole indicator of inflation for its monetary policy.
4. The two main causes of inflation are demand-pull factors and cost-push factors. The demand-pull inflation takes place when increase in aggregate demand is greater than the aggregate supply. It occurs because of higher fiscal expansion, higher GDP growth and sticky core inflation, income effect, black money, and increase in population. The cost-push factors are supply-side factors and because of supply-side constraints or increase in costs prices go up. It includes rise in wages, increase in prices of basic materials, rise in administered prices, and rise in international prices.
5. Inflation is better for some and worse for others. It leads to increase in imports thus adversely affecting balance of payment, unpleasantly the common man, unfavorably the investment and GDP, and promoting inequality. However, it gives benefits to rich businessmen and creditors.
6. The three measures to control inflation are fiscal, administrative, and monetary. Fiscal policy to control inflation comprises measures like change in taxation policy, restraining non-developmental public expenditure, strengthening public distribution system, and making essential imports and curtailing exports of essential goods. Administrative measures involve rationing and price control. The route of monetary policy to control inflation is dear money policy under which RBI tightens expansion of money supply. It can be done by hiking of Repo rate, Bank Rate, CRR, and SLR. Since 2015, RBI has introduced inflation targeting on the recommendation of the Expert Committee to Revise and Strengthen the Monetary Policy Framework, headed by Urjit Patel, former Governor RBI. Inflation targeting is a monetary policy strategy or framework used by RBI for maintaining price level at a certain level or within a range.

Endnotes

1. White, L.H. *Concise encyclopedia*. (2018). Retrieved from http://www.econlib.org (Accessed on December 12, 2018).
2. Consumer Price Index. Retrieved from www.mospi.gov.in (Accessed from May 28, 2019).
3. Consumer Price Index, Changes in the Revised Series. Retrieved from www.mospi.gov.in (Accessed on May 28, 2019).
4. Das & George. (2017). *Comparison of Consumer and Wholesale Prices Indices in India: An analysis of properties and sources of divergence*. BI Working Paper Series No. 05.
5. *Hand Book of Statistics*. RBI, 2017–2018.
6. Look what is driving core inflation in India. *Business Today*, January 14, 2019.
7. Annual Report, RBI, August 23, 2012.
8. Choi, S., et al. (2017). *Oil prices and inflation dynamics: Evidence from advanced and developing economies*. IMF working paper, WP/17/196.
9. Minutes of the Monetary Policy Committee Meeting July 30–August 1, 2018, RBI.
10. Borio, C.E. V., & Filardo, A.J., (2007). *Globalisation and inflation: New cross-country evidence on the global determinants of domestic inflation*. BIS Working

Paper No. 227. Available at SSRN: https://ssrn.com/abstract=1013577.

11. Kalsie, & Shrivastav. (2017). Inflation and its effects on the Indian economy. *Management Perspective*, 3(1). pp.32–36.
12. Rajan, R.G. (2016). *The fight against inflation: A measure of our institutional development*. Working Papers id:10954, eSocialSciences.
13. Crowe, C. (2004). *Inflation, inequality and social conflict*. CEP Discussion Paper, No. 657 p.28.
14. 'India's 2017/18 fiscal deficit at 3.5% of GDP', Reuters, May 31, 2018.
15. Anand, R., Ding, D., & Tulin, V. (2014). *Food inflation in India: The role for monetary policy*. IMF Working Paper, WP/14/178.
16. Jahan, S. (2019). *Inflation targeting: Holding the line*. Finance and Development., IMF. pp.72–73. Retrieved from https://www.imf.org(Accessed on June 6, 2019).
17. What is inflation targeting in economics? *The Hindu*, January 2, 2019.
18. Rajan, R.G. (2016). *The fight against inflation: A measure of our institutional development*. Working Papers id:10954, eSocialSciences.

CHAPTER **24**

INDIAN TAX SYSTEM

The hardest thing in the world to understand is the income tax.

—Albert Einstein

INTRODUCTION

Tax is a financial charge levied upon by the Government on a product, income, and activity. It is a compulsory payment made by people to the public authority in the absence of quid pro quo.* Tax plays a vital role in the development of a nation by strengthening government's tax capacity, which increases its autonomy and reduces dependence on external assistance as well as redistributing income from haves to have nots. Tax is mentioned as Revenue Receipt in the budget document. In India taxes are levied by both the central and state governments. Some minor taxes are also levied by the local authorities such as the Municipality or the Local Council.

This chapter focuses on the following topics:

- Importance/objectives of taxation in India
- Classification of taxes
- Direct and indirect tax system in India
- Tax reforms in India
- Evaluation of Indian tax system

IMPORTANCE/OBJECTIVES OF TAXATION IN INDIA

There are four main objectives of levying taxes. (1) It leads to the generation of revenue that would be utilized for the public welfare/development of the nation. (2) It helps the state to ensure equity among different sections of society via taxing the rich and distributing that receipt to the poor in the form of essential subsidies. (3) It acts as an important anti-inflationary tool, for example, in the times of demand pull inflation the new tax on income can cut down extra expenditure and bring down inflation. Similarly, in the times of cost push inflation various taxes

* "Quid pro quo" is a Latin phrase, which means something in exchange for something or favor for a favor. You cannot refuse to pay a tax on the ground that you do not use a service. A rich person cannot claim some benefit in return if the taxes he pays are spent on poverty alleviation.

BOX 24.1 Canons of Taxation

Adam Smith in his famous book *Wealth of Nations* enunciated four canons of sound tax system. Let us ponder over them.

1. *Canon of equity or ability:* The subjects of every state ought to contribute toward the support of the Government, as nearly as possible, in proportion to their respective abilities.
2. *Canon of certainty:* The tax that the individual is bound to pay ought to be certain and not arbitrary. The time of payment, the quantity to be paid, ought to be very clear and plain to the contributor and to every other person.
3. *Canon of economy:* Every tax ought to be so contrived as to take out of the pockets as little as possible, over and above that, which it brings into the public treasury of the state.
4. *Canon of convenience:* Every tax ought to be levied at the time, or in the manner, in which it is most likely to be convenient for the contributor to pay it.

Source: Smith, A. (1904) Wealth of Nations, Canon's edition, Bk, V, Ch. II, Part II.

on commodities can be withdrawn. (4) It works as an important fiscal policy/foreign trade policy tool via regulation of custom duty on both exports and imports. For example, reduction in the import tariff on various agriculture items has led to the increase in the availability of foreign agriculture products in India.

Classification of Taxes

Depending upon the nature, the taxes can be broadly classified as single and multiple taxes; direct and indirect taxes; progressive, proportional, and regressive taxes; and central and state taxes.

Single and Multiple Taxes

Promoted by physiocrats in eighteenth century, a single tax is a levy that serves as the Government's only source of revenue. People own what they create, but that things found in nature, most importantly land belongs equally to all. A tax on land value is economically efficient, fair, and equitable; and that it can generate sufficient revenue so that other taxes, which are less fair and efficient (such as taxes on production, sales, and income), can be reduced or eliminated. On the contrary, multiple tax signifies different types of taxes viz. taxes on income, taxes on wealth, corporate taxes, and so on.

Direct and Indirect Taxes

Direct tax is a tax in which impact and incidence are on the same person. Impact is the initial burden of tax and incidence is the final burden of tax. For example, in case of income tax impact and incidence would be on the same individual on whose income the tax is levied. Hence, burden of tax cannot be shifted in case of direct tax. Direct taxes are generally progressive in nature. Income tax, corporate tax, and wealth tax are the types of direct tax.

On the contrary, an indirect tax is a tax in which impact and incidence are on different persons. For example, in case of value added tax (VAT) the impact/initial burden would be on seller and the incidence/final burden would be on buyer. Hence, burden of tax can be shifted in case of indirect tax. Indirect taxes are generally regressive in nature. Goods and Services Tax (GST), custom duty, VAT, and excise duty are the types of indirect tax.

Progressive, Regressive and Proportional Taxes

A *progressive tax* means burden of tax would be more on rich as tax is imposed on the increasing rate as the income increases. For example, the rate of income tax may be zero for ₹0–1.8 lakh of income level and is 10, 20, and 30% for the income bands of ₹1.8–5 lakh, ₹5–8 lakh, and above ₹8 lakh, respectively. The direct taxes are generally progressive in nature. A *regressive tax* is a tax that takes a larger percentage from the income of low-income people than the income of high-income people. If Ram has ₹10 and Sham has ₹5, a tax of ₹1 on a purchase would result in a different percentage of total income applied to taxation, 10% for Ram and 20% for Sham. Thus, a tax that is fixed to the value of the good/service would likely, in effect, result in a higher burden of taxation to people with less money. The indirect taxes are generally regressive in nature. A *proportional tax* is one that imposes the same relative burden on all taxpayers—i.e., where tax liability and income grow in equal proportion. For example, if the tax rate is set at 20%, a taxpayer earning ₹10,000 pays ₹2,000 and a taxpayer earning ₹50,000 pays ₹10,000.

Ad Valorem Versus Specific Tax

An ad valorem tax (Latin for according to value) is a tax based on the value of commodity/property, for example, a 10% import duty on the laptops, drugs, or automobiles. Specific tax on the other hand is a tax based on the quantity of an item, such as 10% per quintal, regardless of price. In India we follow ad valorem tax rates.

Central Versus State Taxes

Article 246 of the Indian Constitution distributes legislative powers including taxation, between the Parliament and the State Legislatures. Schedule VII enumerates these subject matters with the use of three lists:

- List I entailing the areas on which only the Parliament is competent to make laws;
- List II entailing the areas on which only the State Legislature can make laws;
- List III listing the areas on which both the Parliament and the State Legislatures can make laws concurrently.

The land revenue, state excise duty, agriculture income tax, and VAT are purely state taxes.* The central taxes consist of union excise duties, income tax, custom duty, and corporation tax. As per the directions of 11th finance commission, the certain percentage of total proceeds from central taxes is shared between center and state.

---

*There are certain taxes that are levied by local bodies: for example, village panchayat may levy in its area a profession tax, an advertisement tax, an entertainment tax, and land conversion tax. Similarly municipal corporations or urban local bodies levy two types of taxes viz. property tax and professional tax.

India's Direct Taxes

Income Tax

The Government of India imposes an income tax on taxable income of individuals, Hindu Undivided Families (HUFs), companies, firms, co-operative societies and trusts (identified as body of individuals and association of persons), and any other artificial person. Levy of tax is separate on each of the persons. The levy is governed by the Indian Income Tax Act, 1961. The Indian Income Tax Department is governed by the Central Board for Direct Taxes (CBDT) and is part of the Department of Revenue under the Ministry of Finance, Government of India. According to Income Tax Act 1961, every person, who is an assessee and whose total income exceeds the maximum exemption limit, shall be chargeable to the income tax at the rate or rates prescribed in the finance act. Such income tax shall be paid on the total income of the previous year in the relevant assessment year. The total income of an individual is determined on the basis of his residential status in India (Tables 24.1–24.2).

In India, income tax is calculated using income tax slabs and rates for the applicable financial year (FY) and assessment year (AY). For the year 2024–25, the financial year will be 2024–25, and the assessment year will be 2025–26. There are two tax regimes in the country and the

TABLE 24.1 Income Tax Slabs Under New Tax Regime for FY 2023–24, FY 2024–25

Tax Slab	Rates
Up to Rs. 3,00,000	NIL
₹3,00,001 to ₹6,00,000	5% (Tax Rebate u/s 87A)
₹6,00,001 to ₹9,00,000	10% (Tax Rebate u/s 87A up to ₹7 lakh)
₹9,00,001 to ₹12,00,000	15%
₹12,00,001 to ₹15,00,000	20%
Above ₹15,00,000	30%

Source: Budget Documents 2022–23, 2023–24 and 2024–25, Ministry of Finance, Government of India.

TABLE 24.2 Income Tax Slabs Under Old Tax Regime

Old Tax Regime Slabs	Individuals (Age < 60 years)	Resident Senior Citizens (More than 60 but less than 80 years)	Resident Super Senior Citizens (80 years and above)
Upto Rs 2,50,000	Nil	Nil	Nil
₹2,50,001 to ₹3,00,000	5%	Nil	Nil
₹3,00,001 to ₹5,00,000	5%	5%	Nil
₹5,00,001 to ₹10,00,000	20%	20%	20%
Above ₹10,00,000	30%	30%	30%

Source: Budget Documents 2022–23, 2023–24 and 2024–25, Ministry of Finance, Government of India.

Government provides the tax payer an option to choose either of the tax regime. As per the interim Budget 2024–25, the New Tax Regime (which was introduced in 2023) will be considered as the default tax regime if the taxpayer has not opted for any. No changes have been made to the income tax slabs in the interim budget of 2024–25.

Corporation Tax

The corporation tax is levied on the incomes of registered companies and corporations. The rationale for the corporation tax is that a joint stock company has a separate entity, and thus a separate tax different from personal income tax has to be levied upon its income. On September 20, 2019 Government announced new corporate tax rates. Indian companies can opt to pay 22% tax on income if they give up tax exemptions and incentives. With surcharge and cess, effective rate on income will come down to 25.17%, from 34.9% at present. Furthermore, Indian companies formed from October 1 onwards in manufacturing sectors can opt to pay only 15% income tax (17.01% effective) if they don't avail exemptions and incentives and start production by March 31, 2023.* The tax rate for foreign company is 40% (plus surcharge and cess as applicable). Corporate tax is the largest source of tax revenue to the Government of India and constitutes nearly 25% of gross tax revenue.

Minimum Alternate Tax (MAT)

Minimum Alternate Tax (MAT) was introduced in the year 1997–98 and is payable under the Income Tax Act. The concept of MAT was introduced to target those companies that make huge profits and pay the dividend to their shareholders but pay no/minimal tax under the normal provisions of the Income Tax Act, by taking advantage of the various deductions and exemptions allowed under the Act. MAT is levied at the rate of 15% of the book profits (plus surcharge and cess as applicable). If, during a year, a company has paid tax liability as per MAT, it is entitled to claim credit of excess of MAT paid over the normal tax liability (as per corporate tax rate) in the following year.

Gift Tax

Gift tax was introduced in 1958 and is imposed on all donations except the ones given by charitable institutions, government companies, and private companies. Donations like gifts to recognized charitable institutions, gifts to women dependents at the time of their marriage, and gifts to wife are also exempted. The Gift Tax was abolished w.e.f. October 1998 and the donor as well as the recipient was not required to pay taxes on the gifts given/received. Elimination of

---

*Revenue foregone for the reduction in corporate tax rate and other relief measures announced will cost the government ₹1.45 lakh crore per year. The corporate tax has been reduced in a bid to boost the sluggish economy, hurt by slowing demand across sectors, especially manufacturing that is among the highest contributors to the GDP. With this, the new tax rates now bring India broadly in line with its South-East Asian counterparts.

gift tax witnessed distribution of property (both movable and immovable) and income freely, resulting in tax planning and in some cases even tax avoidance. Accordingly, to curb incidents of tax avoidance, gift tax was re-introduced w.e.f. April 1, 2005. This time, however, the emphasis shifted from "donor-based" taxation to a "donee-based" taxation, that is, the income from gift(s) became taxable in the hands of the recipient.[1]

Securities Transaction Tax

Securities Transaction Tax (STT) is a direct tax levied on every purchase and sale of securities that are listed on the recognized stock exchanges in India. Securities are tradable investment instruments such as shares, bonds, debentures, equity-oriented mutual funds, and so on and are issued either by companies or by the Indian government. This tax was introduced w.e.f. October 1, 2004. The rate of STT differs based on the type of security traded and whether the transaction is a purchase or a sale. For instance, while buying or selling an equity share (delivery-based), purchaser and seller both need to pay 0.1% of share value as STT. Similarly, while buying units of an equity-oriented mutual fund, buyer need not to pay any STT; however, while selling units of an equity-oriented mutual fund, seller needs to pay STT at the rate of 0.001% of the unit value. These rates are decided by the Central Government. STT was levied to curb evading of capital gains tax on profits earned by transecting in securities.[2]

Long-Term Capital Gains Tax

It is the tax paid on profit generated by an asset such as shares or share-oriented products (such as equity mutual funds) held for a particular time-frame. Introduced in union budget 2018–19, investors will have to pay 10% tax on profit exceeding ₹1 lakh made from the sale of shares or equity mutual fund schemes held for over 1 year. The Government also introduced the concept of Grandfathering in LTCG tax. When a new clause or policy is added to a law, certain persons may be relieved from complying with the new clause. This is called "grandfathering." The "grandfathering" clause is the exemption granted to existing investors or gains made by them before the new tax law comes into force.[3]

Table 24.3 depicts the trends in tax collection during the past few years.

TABLE 24.3 Tax Revenue as a % of Gross Tax Revenue

	2006–07	2016–17	2017–18	2018–19*	2021–22	2024–25**
Corporation tax (%)	30.5	28.33	29.84	32	25	27.22
Income tax (%)	15.9	20.26	22.54	23	25	30.17
Total direct taxes (%)	46.4	49.65	52.38	55	50	57.49
Custom duty (%)	18.25	13.16	7.15	6	6	6.04
Union excise duty (%)	24.8	22.30	13.51	11	15	8.44
Service tax (%)	7.9	14.87	4.24	–	–	0.026
GST (%)	–	–	22.70	28	29	27.87
Total indirect taxes (%)	51	50.34	47.61	45	50	42.5

*Provisional actuals

**Budget Estimates

Source: (1) Press Information Bureau, Ministry of Finance, December 14, 2018. (2) Economic Survey 2018–19, 2021–22. (3) Budget document 2024–25. Department of Economic Affair Ministry of Finance. Govt. of India.

India's Indirect Taxes

Custom Duty

Custom duties (also called import/export tariff) are taxes on imports and exports of the country. Custom duty performs two main functions. First it yields revenue to the Government and second it regulates the foreign trade of the country as it protects the local industry against foreign competition. During pre-reform period, India was highest taxed nations on the earth. The maximum rate of duty was as high as 300%. But as a part of the policy of liberalization, privatization, and globalization pursued by India particularly since 1991, import duties have been drastically reduced. The peak rate of custom duty has been reduced from 40 to10% since 1999–2000. Since the introduction of GST, the canvass of custom duty has been shortened. In the pre-GST regime, the imports of goods and services were subject to multiple state and federal levies such as customs duty, countervailing duty (equivalent to excise duty), and special additional duty (equivalent to VAT). The single integrated goods and services tax under the GST has replaced all these taxes. However, basic customs duty will continue, and it has been kept outside the purview of GST and will be charged as per the current law only.[4]

Goods and Services Tax

France was the first nation on earth to implement GST way back in 1954. In India, the history of GST can be traced back to the year 2000, when the Late Prime Minister Atal Bihari Vajpayee set up a committee to design a GST model for the country. Since then, governments of both NDA and UPA did certain progress with regard to construction of GST framework. Ultimately, the Goods and Services Tax (GST) Act was passed in the Parliament on March 29, 2017 and the GST regime came into force w.e.f. July 1, 2017. GST is an indirect tax and its implementation is considered as one of the greatest economic breakthrough after independence. At present GST is the single largest tax revenue of the government.

Characteristics of GST

1. *Levied on value addition*: GST is a comprehensive, multi-stage tax that is levied on every value addition.* Let us understand it with the help of an example of bread manufacturing. The baker who makes bread buys flour, sugar, and other materials. The value of the inputs increases when the sugar and flour are mixed and baked into bread. The baker then sells the bread to the warehousing agent who packs bread and labels it. That is another addition of value after which the warehouse sells it to the retailer. The retailer invests in the marketing of the bread (hence makes value addition) thus increasing its value. GST is levied on these value additions, that is, the monetary value added at each stage to achieve the final sale to the end customer.
2. *Subsuming the existing taxes*: GST has replaced many indirect tax laws that previously existed in India. The motto of GST is "One nation, one market, and one tax." GST has subsumed many central- and state-level indirect taxes which are as follows:

*Value addition is equal to cost + profit.

Central taxes: Central excise duty, duties of excise, additional duties of excise, additional duties of customs, special additional duty of customs, service tax, cesses, surcharges, etc.

State taxes: State VAT, central sales tax, purchase tax, luxury tax, entertainment tax, entry tax, taxes on advertisements, taxes on lotteries, betting, gambling, state cesses, surcharges.

3. *Destination-based tax*: GST is a destination-based consumption tax. Under destination-based taxation, tax accrues to the destination place where consumption of the goods or services takes place.[5] Suppose goods manufactured in Punjab are sold to the final consumer in Tamil Nadu. Since GST is levied at the point of consumption, the entire tax revenue will go to Tamil Nadu and not to Punjab.
4. *Three-tier tax system*: There are three taxes applicable under this system: Central GST (CGST), State GST (SGST), and Inter-state GST (IGST).

   CGST: Collected by the Central Government on an intra-state sale (e.g., transaction happening within Punjab).

   SGST: Collected by the State Government on an intra-state sale (e.g., transaction happening within Punjab).

   IGST: Collected by the Central Government for inter-state sale (e.g., Punjab to Tamil Nadu).
5. *Different tax slabs*: Since there is wide socio-economic gap in the country, therefore, it would not be feasible to levy same rate of tax for necessary items like milk and luxury items like BMW car. Therefore, it was critical to set different rates for different class of items. There are four slabs fixed for GST Rates—5, 12, 18, and 28%, apart from exempt category of 0% (Table 24.4).
6. *GST council*: Goods and Services Tax Council is a constitutional body under Article 279 (1) for making recommendations to the Union and State Government on issues related to GST. The GST Council is chaired by the Union Finance Minister and other members are the Union State Minister of Revenue or Finance and Ministers in-charge of Finance or Taxation of all the states. The GST Council is the key decision-making body that will take all important decisions regarding the GST, such as inclusion of new items into GST regime, tax rate, tax exemption, the due date of forms, tax laws, and tax deadlines.

TABLE 24.4 GST Rate Classification

Tax Slabs	Products
0%	Electrical energy, newspapers, milk, duty credit scrips, foodgrains
5%	Household necessities such as edible oil, sugar, spices, tea, and coffee (except instant) are included. Coal, sweets, and life-saving drugs are also covered under this GST slab
12%	Articles of apparels exceeding ₹1,000, bio-diesel, printing ink, specified parts of sewing machine, furniture wholly made of bamboo or cane, computers, and processed food
18%	Hair oil, toothpaste and soaps, capital goods, and industrial intermediaries are covered in this slab
28%	Luxury items such as small cars, consumer durables like AC and refrigerators, premium cars, cigarettes, aerated drinks, and high-end motorcycles are included here.

Source: Budget document, 2017–18, 2018–19, 2019–20. Ministry of Finance, Govt. of India.

Advantages of GST

1. *Removal of multiplicity of taxes*: Before GST, there were multiple taxes at both at center and state level. The multiplicity of taxes led to their cascading effects, which is a situation wherein a consumer has to bear the load of tax on tax and inflationary prices as a result of it. With the introduction of GST, the cascading effects of CENVAT, State VAT, and service tax will be more comprehensively removed with a continuous chain of set-off from the producer's point to the retailer's point than what was possible under the prevailing CENVAT and VAT regime. Certain major central and state taxes will also be subsumed in GST and CST will be phased out. Other things remaining the same, the burden of tax on goods would, in general, fall under GST and that would benefit the consumer.
2. *Increase in tax compliance*: The GST will ensure wider tax base, and increase in tax–GDP ratio. Furthermore, the tax will give more relief to industry, trade, and agriculture through a more comprehensive and wider coverage of input tax set-off and service tax set-off, subsuming of several central and state taxes in the GST and phasing out of CST. The transparent and complete chain of set-offs that will result in widening of tax base and better tax compliance may also lead to lowering of tax burden on an average dealer in industry, trade, and agriculture. Few of the empirical benefits can be mentioned in this regard.
   i. In the first year of implementation of GST, revenues grew by 11.9% and the buoyancy was 1.20. A buoyancy ratio over 1 shows progressiveness in the revenue growth and opens up the prospect of a rising tax-to-GDP ratio. This is a significant improvement over the pre-GST period when the buoyancy ratios for state VAT and central indirect taxes like central excise and service tax were less than 1.[6]
   ii. One of the many benefits of the GST was the voluntary compliance it would elicit. A few numbers highlight this phenomenon. The GST implementation has increased the base of indirect taxpayers by more than 50% with 34 lakh more business entities coming into the tax net. The number of GST registrants rose mainly on account of large increase in voluntary registrations, especially by small enterprises that buy from large enterprises and want to avail of input tax credits.[7]
   iii. Although GST is an indirect tax, yet it has significantly impacted the contribution of direct taxes too in the overall tax revenue of the Government. The provisional direct tax collections for FY 2017–18 is ₹9.95 lakh crore, which is 17.1% higher than the net collections for FY 2016–17. The 2024–25 budget document too highlights direct tax-indirect tax ratio to be around 57:43, which signifies more equitable direct tax system. The increase in direct tax collection can be attributed to the fact that a lot of businesses had become part of formal economic system due to GST, which has led to an impact on direct taxes as well.[8]
3. *Conducive for healthy investment climate:* GST will improve the overall investment climate in the country, which will naturally benefit the development in the states. Uniform CGST, SGST, and IGST rates will reduce the incentive for evasion by eliminating rate arbitrage between neighboring states and that between intra- and inter-state supplies. Average tax burden on companies is likely to come down, which is expected to reduce prices and lower prices mean more consumption, which in turn means more production thereby helping in the growth of the industries. This will create India as a "manufacturing hub."
4. *Tax simplification and ease of doing:* Rationalization of tax structure and simplification of compliance procedures will enhance tax efficiency in the country. Simpler tax regime with fewer exemptions along with reduction in multiplicity of taxes that governed our indirect tax system for long will lead to simplification and uniformity. Reduction in

compliance costs as multiple record-keeping for a variety of taxes will not be needed, therefore, lesser investment of resources and manpower will be required for maintaining records. It will result in simplified and automated procedures for various processes such as registration, returns, refunds, and tax payments. All interactions shall be through the common GSTN portal, therefore, less public interface between the taxpayer and the tax administration. It will improve environment of compliance as all returns to be filed online, input credits to be verified online, encouraging more paper trail of transactions. Common procedures for registration of taxpayers, refund of taxes, uniform formats of tax return, common tax base, and common system of classification of goods and services will lend greater certainty to taxation system.

5. *Hidden benefits of GST:* There are number of hidden benefits associated with the implementation of GST. First, the textile and clothing sector is now fully part of the tax net. Previously, some parts of the value chain, especially fabrics, were outside the tax net, leading to informalization and evasion. Second, one segment of land and real estate transactions has been brought into the tax net: "works contracts," referring to housing that is being built. This, in turn, would allow for greater transparency and formalization of cement, steel, and other sales, which tended to be outside the tax net. The formalization will occur because builders will need documentation of these input purchases to claim tax credit. Third, the GST will rectify the inadequacies of the previous system of domestic taxes levied on imports.[9]
6. *Efficiency in supply chain and logistics:* With the introduction of GST, the check posts in the state have been removed as the whole nation has same tax and compliance structure. Removal of check posts will dramatically reduce transportation costs, fuel use, and corruption. As higher than optimal time is consumed per transportation, logistics costs incurred in India is 2 to 3 times compared to the global benchmarks, according to the World Bank.

   In simple terms, the logistics cost in India is about 13% of GDP as compared to about 8% in Western countries and about 18% in China.[10] A truck in India daily drives just 280 km, whereas the daily distance covered by trucks in the United States is around 800 km. Around 40% of the time is spent on driving and nearly 25% is spent on check posts. With the introduction of GST, India has become a seamless market without any difference between inter- or intra-state sales. The average distance covered by a truck in the country has increased by up to 100–150 km a day as compared to what vehicles were covering in the pre-GST era.[11]

Disadvantages of GST

1. *Higher GST rates:* India's 28% GST rate is the highest among all other countries. There are around 160 countries where GST is in operation, out of which 19 are Asian nations and 53 countries are from Europe. In many countries like Canada, Singapore, Australia, and New Zealand, there is single uniform tax at the rate of 5, 7, 10, and 15%, respectively.[12]
2. *Multiple GST slabs:* GST was implemented with an aim of "one nation, one tax," but Indian GST system with four non-zero slabs is characterized by one of the highest number of slabs in the world. Although most goods fall in the 12, 18, and 28% brackets, there is a case for merging slabs to reduce complexity and classification disputes. The 12 and 18% bracket could be merged into one single slab in the 14–16% range.[13]

3. *Impact on small businesses:* Reforms must bring simplicity and not disruption. GST was an opportunity for India to reform its cobweb like indirect taxation structure and reboot the system afresh. Unfortunately, the ground realities suggest otherwise. The way GST has been introduced is too onerous for small businesses, which may further thwart their growth. The objective to plug the informal economy into formal set-up may have benefits but the cost can outweigh the benefits if done forcefully through radical reforms. Presently, lower exemption threshold coupled with cumbersome compliance has proved to be counterproductive and pushing small businesses toward devising new ways of tax evasion, thereby breeding corruption. The current rate structure is too complicated. This would only perpetuate confusion, corruption, and litigation. Offline utility is the need of the hour to reduce the burden on the platform and make lives simpler for assessees. For small businesses, requirement of filing returns should be made either bimonthly or quarterly.* There is also a great scope for simplification of return forms for small businesses.[14]
4. *Negligible impact on black income:* It is argued that the large number of registrations of businesses under GST would not automatically lead to a rise in the tax to GDP ratio. With the Finance Ministry propounding that 5% of the indirect taxpayers pay 95% of the tax, an increase in the number of registrations is no guarantee of more tax collection. Reports of businessmen evading taxes are coming in daily. Even the income tax data show that a large number of those in the tax net show either nil income or very low income.[15] Earlier businesses generated black incomes via under and over invoicing of their sales and purchases. If person A buys from person B, then A would want to show a higher cost while B would want to show lower revenue. GST and computerization change this by enabling the matching the invoices of sellers and buyer Both have to file returns on the GST network (GSTN). Each business has to register and is allotted a number (GSTIN) and all their invoices carry this number so that they can be cross-checked and the chance of tax evasion is mitigated. However, what if no bill is issued and transactions remain outside the GSTN from beginning to end? Cases of fake billing to claim input credit have been surfacing with regularity. Various exemptions granted under GST make this easy. Reports of evasion of GST are slowly growing, implying that the process of discovery is on. In fact, the chances are that the black income generation process might receive a boost over time.[16]
5. *Cumbersome structure of GST:* The GST in India is levied as VAT, and a VAT can be calculated in a variety of ways. The one chosen in India is in line with the global practice of providing input tax credit to supplier This requires keeping track of all the inputs and the tax paid on them and then of all the outputs and the tax to be paid on them and that is a herculean task for businesses. For the Government it is an even bigger task since it has to aggregate the data from all the activities of all the businesses to ascertain the tax to be collected. The collection and processing of such massive volume of data can only be handled by computerization. Thus, setting up of a large computer network became essential and a GSTN was created. To keep track of all the transactions of businesses, a unique identification number GSTIN has been allotted to all those who have registered. Furthermore, to keep track of the movements of goods so that tax evasion can be mitigated, an e-way bill is required. Each trucker has to register and obtain a 15-digit

*As per budget 2019–20, taxpayers having annual turnover of less than ₹5 crore can now file quarterly returns.

BOX 24.2 Few Important Taxes That Have Been Abolished in the Recent Past

a. **Direct taxes**

Wealth tax: Wealth tax was first introduced on May 1957 on the recommendation of Kaldor and levied on excess of net wealth over exemption limit. The tax is to be paid year after year on the same property on its market value, whether or not such property yields any income. Wealth tax was abolished in the budget of 2015–16 as the cost incurred for recovering taxes was more than the benefit is derived.

Estate duty: Estate duty is levied on the transfer of property of diseased to the heirs of the property. Also sometimes called the "death tax," it was introduced in India in 1953 and was abolished in 1985, when V.P. Singh was the Finance Minister. It is not payable on deaths occurring after March 16, 1985. The policy intention of estate duty is to bring about inter-generation equity, that is, to ensure the children of the rich do not have too much of an advantage in life compared to the less privileged. It was abolished partly because it amounted to double taxation, since stamp duty is in any case levied on transfer of property to heirs.

Fringe benefits tax (FBT): Fringe benefits mean any privilege, service, facility, or amenity directly or indirectly provided by an employer to his employees (including former employees) by reason of their employment. Fringe benefit tax is payable by an employer. The tax was abolished in budget 2009–10.

b. **Indirect taxes**

Excise duty: Excise duty refers to tax on production. The Central Government levies excise duty on numerous items such as tax on textiles, sugar, tea, tobacco, cement, and such other articles. Except alcohol and narcotics (which are subject to state excise), the Central Government has sole right to levy excise duty on all other items. It has been subsumed into GST in the year 2017.

VAT: The state-level VAT was introduced w.e.f. April 1, 2005 and has been introduced by all states/union territories so far. It is the tax on the value addition of the commodities. There were two basic rates of 4 and 12.5%, besides an exempt category and a special rate of 1% for a few selected items. There was also a category with 20% floor rate of tax, for example, VAT on liquor. Since 2017, VAT has become part of GST.

Service tax: This tax was introduced in India in 1994–95 because of increasing role and significance of service sector in country's total GDP. It has been subsumed into GST in the year 2017.

number called TRANSIN. Each consignment transported has to carry an e-way bill and the TRANSIN number, among other things. Thus, billions of pieces of information have to be coordinated every month. Processing this vast amount of data often leads to the systems crashing or slowing down inordinately thus delaying the filing of data by the producer. Businesses, simultaneously, have had to incur additional costs for processing these large amounts of data.

AN ASSESSMENT OF INDIAN TAX SYSTEM

A good tax system is one that is designed on the basis of an appropriate set of principles, such as equality and certainty and guides economy to increase its productive capacity and thereby achieve a higher rate of growth. Let us assess the various characteristics of Indian tax system.

BOX 24.3 Laffer Curve and Its Working in Indian Context

Invented by Arthur Laffer in 1979, this curve shows the relationship between tax rates and tax revenue collected by the governments. The curve suggests that, as taxes increase from low levels, tax revenue collected by the Government also increases. That tax rates increasing after a certain point *T** (maximum tax revenue point) would cause people not to work as hard or not at all, thereby reducing tax revenue. If tax rates reached 100% (the far right of the curve), then all people would choose not to work because everything they earned would go to the Government. Governments would like to be at point *T**, because it is the point at which the Government collects maximum amount of tax revenue while people continue to work hard. The concept of Laffer curve is similar to the notion of tax elasticity, where elasticity refers to changes in tax revenue in response to changes in tax rate. The latest research has verified the effective working of Laffer curve phenomenon in the Indian economy. The tax rates in India have come down dramatically during post-reform period and it has led to widening of tax base and increase in tax-GDP ratio. In Indian context, it needs to be understood that compared to indirect taxes, direct taxes were more buoyant during the post-reform period. Direct tax to GDP ratio was increased from 1.3% during 1990–91 to nearly 6.4% during 2018–19. The introduction of GST is bound to enhance tax elasticity of Indian indirect taxes in the years to come.

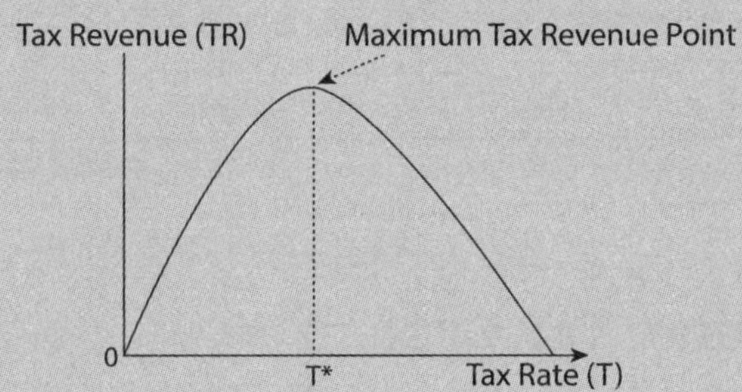

Sources:

1. Mehra, M. Thank you, Mr Laffer, *Business Today*, September 6, 2009
2. Chakraborty, P. (1997). Tax reductions and their revenue implications how valid is the Laffer curve?, *EPW*.
3. Direct tax-GDP ratio of 5.98% in FY18 best in 10 years: Govt, Livemint, January 2, 2019.

Elasticity in Indian Tax System

Elasticity of tax is measured as a ratio of proportionate change in its yield to the proportionate change in its coverage or rate. In other words, elasticity of a tax is referred to its responsiveness to steps taken by authorities in increasing its yield through an extension of its coverage or revision of rates. The idea of elasticity goes well with Laffer curve (see Box 24.3). Today, income tax collections are up from ₹16 thousand crore in 1991–92 to more than ₹11 Lakh crore in 2023–24 in spite of remarkable reduction in rates. Tax elasticity for direct taxes in India is 1.63, whereas for indirect taxes it is 0.89 and for overall taxes it is 1.20. The elasticity calculated is high and more than 1 and thus shows that the tax revenue collections respond better to the changes in tax base and income. The collection always is more than change in the tax base and so either through higher effective tax rates or better compliance, the tax collections exceed changes in the tax base.[17] Table 24.5 explains tax revenue as a percentage of GDP over the past few year.

TABLE 24.5 Tax Revenue as a % of GDP

Year	Direct Tax GDP Ratio (%)	Indirect Tax GDP Ratio (%)
2006–07	5.1	5.6
2016–17	5.57	5.65
2017–18	5.98	5.43
2018–19	5.98	4.94
2021–22	5	4.9
2024–25 (BE)	6.8	3.2

Source: Economic Survey 2018–19, 2021–22. Budget document 2024–25. Ministry of Finance, Government of India.

TABLE 24.6 Tax Buoyancy in India

Tax	Tax Buoyancy (2010–11 to 2016–17)
Gross tax revenue	1.19
Corporation tax	0.78
Income tax	1.21
Custom duty	1.05
Union excise duty	1.80
Service tax	1.84

Source: Reserve Bank of India. *Annual Report 2017–18* and *Economic Survey 2017–18*. Ministry of Finance, Government of India.

Buoyancy in Indian Tax System

An increase in tax revenue on account of increase in GDP is termed its buoyancy. For example, with given rate of a corporation tax, if yield from corporation tax increases as national income increases, it would be termed as buoyant tax. A buoyancy greater than unity over the long run is a desirable feature of a tax system.[18] It needs to be noted that during the period 2010–11 to 2016–17, tax buoyancy was highest for indirect taxes. Even during the first year of implementation of GST, revenues grew by 11.9% and the buoyancy was 1.20.[19] The tax buoyancy of gross tax revenue in India was 1.2 in 2017–18 and projected to be 1.45 in 2018–19. The average buoyancy in personal income tax was higher at 2.5 and 1.2 for 2016–17 and 2017–18, respectively, as against 1.0 during the 7 years from 2009–10 to 2015–16. This is attributable to the ongoing tax-base broadening and enforcement measures (Table 24.6).[20]

Emergence of Progressive Tax Regime

Progressiveness in a tax system can be gauged by direct-to-indirect tax ratio. Higher this ratio, more progressive the tax system is which means more burden falls on richer section of the society and the tax revenue so generated can be utilized for development and hence ensure equity. The direct-to-indirect tax ratio was as lower as 16:84 during 1990–91 reflecting a higher burden of tax on poor. Various tax reforms initiated during the reform period corrected this gap and since 2008–09 the direct-to-indirect tax ratio has turned favorable. During 2021–22 this ratio was reported to be 50:50, which is a welcoming trend.[21] However, for the OECD nations, the direct-to-indirect tax ratio has remained largely constant in the range of 65:35 for the last 40–50 year.

Agriculture Income Tax Is Exempted

Various committees in India have suggested taxing the agriculture income as it will not only reduce sharp inequalities in the agriculture sector but also help the Government to raise its revenue. However, agriculture income is not taxed because of various reasons. *First*, the majority of landholdings (about 80%) in India are marginal in nature. The rest of agriculture that is entrepreneurial in nature and produces surplus for domestic consumption and exports is already reeling under crisis due to various bottlenecks such as farmer suicides, farm debt crisis, and crop failure. Taxing this class of farmers will demotivate them and might aggravate the ongoing crisis in this sector. *Secondly*, research has highlighted that the administrative cost of tax collection would be high and tax yield will be quite insignificant. *Finally*, agriculture falls in the domain of state government and constitution of India has assigned Agriculture Income tax to the state governments, who lack will to implement such taxes due to strong farmer lobby.

Tax Evasion

The wider tax evasion and the spread of black money go hand in hand. There are several factors responsible for tax evasion and main among them are high tax rates, complex tax laws, lack of proper accounts and information, and corrupt tax administration. Among the 3.7 crore individuals who filed tax returns in 2015–16, 99 lakh showed income below the exemption limit of ₹2.5 lakh per annum; 1.95 crore showed income between ₹2.5 lakh and ₹5 lakh; 52 lakh showed income between ₹5 lakh and ₹10 lakh, and only 24 lakh people declared income above ₹10 lakh. Of the 76 lakh individual assesses who declared income of above ₹5 lakh, 56 lakh are in the salaried class. The number of people showing income more than ₹50 lakh in the country is only 1.72 lakh. We can contrast this with the fact that during 2010–15, more than 1.25 crore cars have been sold, and number of Indian citizens who flew abroad, either for business or tourism, were 2 crore in the year 2015. Tax evasion directly affects the tax elasticity and stalls governments' efforts for nation building and development.

Simplicity and Certainty

Simplicity of a tax means that a tax system should not be complicated and difficult to understand, which leads to the problems of misinterpretation of tax laws and increases legal disputes. Certainty means the tax payer should not be subject to arbitrariness and discretion of tax officials, since that breeds a corrupt tax administration. The pre-reform Indian tax system failed miserably on both these counts. In the post-reform period many steps have been taken to inject certainty and simplicity in the Indian tax structure and a lot is yet to be accomplished. Different committees from time to time made recommendations and respective governments have accepted and implemented such measures (Box 24.4). The introduction of VAT in 2005 and GST in 2017 were the steps in right direction. Online filing of tax is another feature that has ensured certainty of tax and made tax filing simpler.

BOX 24.4 Different Committees on Reforms in India Tax System

The Varadacharier Commission (1953) was established by the Government to investigate and report to the Central Government on all matters relating to taxation of income, with particular reference to the extent to which the existing law and procedure was adequate to prevent tax evasion.

Kaldor Committee (1956) headed by noted economist James Kaldor studied the structure of Indian taxation in view of the larger dimensions assumed by the problem of resources for the plan. It recommended introduction of wealth tax.

Tyagi Committee (1958) advised Government on the administration, organization, and procedures vis-à-vis direct taxation.

Law Commission Report (1958) was instrumental to revise the Indian Income Tax Act, 1922.

Boothalingam Committee Report (1967) recommended rationalization and simplification of the tax structure.

Administrative Reform Committee Report (1968) suggested administrative reforms in taxation.

Direct Taxes Enquiry Committee (Wanchoo Committee) Report (1969) was the first committee to delve deeply on the issues of tax evasion and black money in the Indian economy.

The Indirect Taxation Enquiry Committee (L.K. Jha Committee) Report (1976) studied the issue of balance between direct and indirect taxes and thoroughly reviewed the existing structure of indirect taxes of center, state, and local bodies, including their elasticity and buoyancy.

The Direct Taxes Laws Committee (Chokshi Committee) Report (1978) suggested various reforms in the direct tax laws.

Economic Administrative Reforms Commission (Jha Committee) Report (1983) reviewed and made suggestions about the income tax law, procedure, and organization of the department.

The Tax reform Committee (Raja J. Chelliah) Report (1993) examined the tax structure of the economy and gave a comprehensive review on direct and indirect tax reforms.

The Task Force on Direct and Indirect Taxes (Kelkar Committee) Report (2002) suggested simplification and rationalization of both direct and indirect taxes.
Asim Dasgupta Committee (2000) was set up by NDA-I Government to design a GST model.

Source: Compilation by author.

Summary

1. Tax is a financial charge levied upon by the Government on a product, income, and activity. Objectives of levying taxes include: generation of revenue for developmental activities, redistributing income in the favor of poor, using it as an anti-inflationary measure, and its significance as a fiscal policy/foreign trade policy tool. Taxes can be categorized as single and multiple taxes, direct tax and indirect taxes, progressive and regressive taxes, ad valorem and specific taxes, central and state taxes.
2. Direct tax is a tax in which impact and incidence are on the same person. The Government of India imposes income tax on taxable income of individuals, Hindu Undivided Families, companies, firms, co-operative societies and trusts (identified as body of individuals and association of persons), and any other artificial person. The corporation tax is levied on the incomes of registered companies and corporations. Minimum Alternate Tax was introduced in the year 1997–98 to target those companies that make huge profits but pay no/minimal tax under the normal provisions of the Income Tax Act, by taking advantage of the various deductions, and exemptions allowed under the Act. Gift tax introduced since 2005 is a donee-based tax imposed on all donations except the ones given by charitable institutions, government companies, and private companies. Securities Transaction Tax is a direct tax levied on every purchase and sale of securities. Long-term capital gain tax was introduced in union budget 2018–19, wherein investors are required to pay 10% tax on profit exceeding ₹1 lakh made from the sale of shares or equity mutual fund schemes held for over 1 year. Custom duties are taxes on imports and exports of the country.
3. Indirect tax is a tax in which impact and incidence are on the different persons. Examples of indirect taxes are GST, custom duty, and central excise duty. Custom duties are taxes on imports and exports of the country. GST is a comprehensive, multi-stage tax that is levied on every value addition and was introduced in the year 2017. There are four slabs fixed for GST Rates—5, 12, 18, and 28%, apart from exempt category of 0%. Benefits of GST include removal of multiplicity of taxes, increase in tax compliance, incentive to healthy investment climate, tax simplification and ease of doing, efficiency in supply chain and logistics, and hidden benefits of GST. The limitations of GST include higher GST rates, multiple GST slabs, burdensome impact on small businesses, negligible impact on black income, and cumbersome structure of GST.
4. Elasticity of tax is measured as a ratio of proportionate change in its yield to the proportionate change in its coverage or rate. Indian tax system has become more elastic during the post-reform period. An increase in tax revenue on account of increase in GDP is termed its buoyancy. In India tax buoyancy is greater than 1 and for indirect taxes it is higher than direct taxes. The direct-to-indirect tax ratio has increased from 16:84 in 1990–91 to 52:48 in 2017–18. Agriculture income tax that falls in the domain of state government is not levied by states mainly because it is small source of revenue and also because of political lobbying by farmer. In India tax evasion is also rampant as nearly 4 crore people file tax return out of the total population if 135 crore. Indian tax system also fails the test of simplicity and certainty.

Endnotes

1. How are gifts taxed in India? *Livemint*, January 10, 2019.
2. What is securities transaction tax and why is it levied? *Livemint*, January 7, 2019.
3. Long-term capital gains tax, *The Economic Times*, February 3, 2018.
4. GST and interlinkage with customs, *The Economic Times*, May 16, 2017.
5. Goods and Services Tax, Concept and Status, Central Board of Indirect Taxes and Customs (CBIC), Department of Revenue, Ministry of Finance, Government of India, 2019.
6. View: A fair assessment of Good and Services Tax, *The Economic Times*, March 28, 2019.
7. Economic Survey, Part I, 2017–18, pp.33–34. Department of Economic Affairs. Ministry of Finance. Govt. of India.
8. Higher direct tax collections: GST impact? *The Economic Times*, July 1, 2018.

9. *Economic Survey, 2016–17*, Department of Economic Affairs, Ministry of Finance. Govt. of India. p.75.
10. GST in logistics: A game changer, *Business Today*, May 23, 2019.
11. Average distance covered by trucks up by 100–150 km/day post-GST, *The Times of India*, December 31, 2017.
12. GST: Where does India's tax model stand against other prominent countries? *India Today*, December 24, 2018.
13. One year of GST: The successes, failures and what's next on the agenda, *The Economic Times*, June 29, 2018.
14. Banerjee, S., & Prasad, S. Small businesses in the GST regime (2017). *EPW*. 2017, Vol. L II, pp.18–22.
15. Kumar, A. (2019). The structurally flawed GST: Finding an alternative, *EPW*. Vol. l IV, No. 9.
16. Kumar, A. As we debate GST collections, is the new tax regime curbing India's black economy? *The Wire*, 16 August, 2018.
17. Dudine, P., & Jalles, J.T. How buoyant is the tax system? New evidence from a large heterogeneous panel, IMF working paper, WP/17/4, 2017.
18. View: A fair assessment of Good and Services Tax, *The Economic Times*, March 28, 2019.
19. Reserve Bank of India. *Annual Report 2017–18*. p.67.
20. *Press Information Bureau*, Government of India, Ministry of Finance, December 14, 2018.
21. Tax evasion a way of life, The Economic Times, June 18, 2018.

CHAPTER **25**

Public Expenditure, Debt Management, and Fiscal Policy

Government's view of the economy could be summed up in a few short phrases:
If it moves, tax it. If it keeps moving, regulate it. And if it stops moving, subsidize it.
—Ronald Reagan

Introduction

The fiscal affairs of a government unlike a private company are of direct concern to its citizens and to international parties which interact with it. The maxim that "you cannot spend your way to prosperity" is now widely accepted. Fiscal policies must therefore, be embedded in caution than exuberance. A prudent fiscal policy comprises combination of balanced expenditure management, limited public debt, and sound taxation system. The pre-reform period India displayed an unsound fiscal paradigm characterized by low tax–GDP ratio, extravagant non-developmental expenditure, and higher amount of borrowings. Though much has changed since then, yet a prudent fiscal regime is the need of the hour.

The present chapter focuses on the following issues:

- India's Budget and Its Components
- Public Expenditure and Its Causes
- Public Debt: Causes, Sustainability, and Debt Management
- Fiscal Policy and Its Objectives
- FRBM and Suggestions for Sound Fiscal System

India's Budget and Its Components

Budget is a financial forecast of a nation's total receipts and expenditure for an accounting year. It is a comprehensive plan of action designed to achieve the policy objectives set by the government for the coming year. Budget describes the source (rupee comes from) and destination (rupee goes to) of country's finances. In India, the budget is announced before the beginning of financial year and is implemented w.e.f. April 1st. Budget can be classified into two main accounts as revenue and capital. Revenue receipts comprise tax revenue and non-tax revenue. Tax receipts have two components such as direct and indirect taxes.* The non-tax revenue of

*For detailed discussion of taxes, please refer to chapter 24, Indian Tax System.

the government comprises interest receipts, dividends and profits, external grants, fees and fines from economic and social services, receipts of union territories, other revenue receipts, etc. The capital receipts include recovery of loans, other receipts such as disinvestment receipts and borrowing, and other liabilities. The total expenditure in the budget comprises revenue and capital expenditure. The revenue expenditure of the government comprises interest payments, defense expenditure, pensions, subsidies, finance commission transfers, and various central government sponsored schemes. The capital expenditure of the government comprises transfers, centrally sponsored schemes, finance commission transfers, resources of public enterprises, etc.*

In 2018–2019 budget, revenue receipts contributed to 70% of total receipts and capital receipts contributed to 30% of total receipts. On the other hand, revenue expenditure and capital expenditure constituted 87 and 13% of total expenditure of the government, respectively.

Four types of deficits are mentioned in Government of India's budget which are significant for policymaking. Let us have a brief discussion on them.

Revenue deficit: Revenue deficit occurs when revenue expenditure exceeds revenue receipts. If revenue receipts are greater than revenue payments, then it will be revenue surplus.

Effective revenue deficit: Effective revenue deficit (ERD) was introduced in the budget 2011–2012. In India's budget, all grants from the Central Government to the state governments/local bodies are treated as revenue expenditure even if they are used to create capital assets. Such assets created by the state governments/bodies are owned by them and not by the Union Government. Nevertheless, they do result in the creation of durable assets. Therefore, such revenue expenditures contribute to the growth in the economy and therefore, should not be treated as unproductive in nature. Hence,

ERD = Revenue deficit – Transfers from center to states in the form of grants.

ERD was 1.1% of GDP during 2018–2019.

Fiscal deficit: The concept of fiscal deficit was introduced in 1990s on the recommendation of Sukhamoy Chakravarty Committee. Fiscal deficit occurs when a government's total expenditures exceed the receipts that it generates, excluding money from borrowings.

Fiscal deficit = Total expenditure – (Total receipts – Borrowings)

Fiscal deficit reflects the fiscal health of a country and hence considered as an important economic barometer. Higher fiscal deficit reflects government's inability to mobilize resources through revenue receipts as well as non-debt generating capital receipts. The gap has to be filled through borrowings. Fiscal deficit for the year 2018–2019 was 3.4% of GDP.

Primary deficit: Primary deficit is equal to fiscal deficit minus interest payments on the previous borrowings.

That is, Primary deficit = Fiscal deficit – Interest payments

Primary deficit reflects the extent to which such interest commitments have compelled the government to borrow in the current period. It indicates how much of the government borrowings are going to meet expenses other than the interest payments. The difference between fiscal deficit and primary deficit reflects the amount of interest payments. Primary deficit for the year 2018–2019 was 0.2% of GDP.

---

*For better understanding, the reader is advised to refer Table 30.1, of chapter 30, Economic Survey 2018–19 and Budget 2019–20.

Indian Public Expenditure

During the older days of classical school of thought, minimum expenditure by the government was considered to be the best level of expenditure. The analysis of public expenditure was not, therefore, recognized as a worthwhile field of economic research. Public finance concentrated on the study of public revenue and issues relating to taxation rather than the expenditure therefrom. In the post–Second World War period, there has been a phenomenal increase in the level of government or public expenditure both in absolute terms and also in relation to the national income. There has, therefore, been a great amount of scholarly interest in understanding the causes of public expenditure, and its incidence, that is, who benefits from it. The major area of concern has been to channelize public expenditure into those areas of the economy where its effects will be optional in terms of growth, consumption, and distribution. More recently, however, serious concern has been voiced regarding the effective utilization of government funds and the paramount need to avoid wasteful expenditure.

In general usage, public expenditure is classified into following.

Capital Expenditure and Revenue Expenditure

Capital account expenditure signifies the gross and net capital formation in the public sector during the accounting period. The unique characteristic of capital expenditure is that a major portion of the expenditure is made at one point of time and the benefits are realized at different points of time in the ensuing years. Examples of capital expenditure are the acquisition of assets like land, buildings, machinery, etc., construction of canals, roads, dams, and also investment in shares and loans and advances granted by Central Government to state and UT governments, government companies, etc. Expenditure which does not result in creation of assets is treated as "Revenue expenditure." Revenue expenditure is for the normal running of government departments and various services. Examples of revenue expenditure are salaries of the employees, interest payments, subsidies, etc.

Developmental and Non-developmental Expenditure

Developmental expenditure is the expenditure that is directly related to the economic and social developmental of economy. For example, expenditure incurred on education, employment, agriculture, irrigation, transport, and communication can be labeled as developmental expenditure. On the contrary, non-developmental expenditure is incurred on non-development activities of the government in the form of provision of general services of the government. Examples are administrative expenditure, interest payments, defense, external affairs, etc.

Plan and Non-plan Expenditure

Plan expenditure refers to the expenditure incurred by the Central Government on programs/projects, which are recommended by the Planning Commission. Expenditure on Sarv Shiksha Abhiyan, irrigation, housing, construction of dams, etc. can be placed under plan expenditure. Non-plan expenditure, on the contrary, is a generic term used to cover all expenditure of government, not included in the plan. Non-plan expenditure refers to outlays on routine functioning of the government and includes interest payments, subsidies, salary and pension payments, police, defense, etc. Government has scrapped the distinction between plan and non-plan expenditure since budget 2017–2018. The concept has been abolished because of certain reasons. First, non-plan expenditure includes both developmental and non-developmental expenditure components. The government wanted to break the building perception that all non-plan expenditure is either non-developmental or wasteful consumptive expenditure (window dressing). Second, after the abolition of Planning Commission, distinction between plan and non-plan expenditure became irrelevant. Finally, Rangarajan Committee (2012) and Bimal Jalan Committee (2016) recommended removal of the distinction between plan and non-plan expenditure, which had become dysfunctional and obsolete.

Causes of Increase in Public Expenditure in India

Increase in GDP

There is general tendency of increase in public expenditure as GDP of the country goes up. India's GDP since independence has increased by more than 500 times. Adolph Wagner (1835–1917), the noted German economist propounded "The Law of Increasing State Activity," which states that "as the economy develops over time, the activities and functions of the government increase." Further due to the pressure of social progress under the welfare state theory, in addition to the maintenance of law and order, government participation in the economic field for the development of social infrastructure viz. communication, education, medical facilities, etc. becomes inevitable. The employment generation schemes like MNREGA, Education schemes like Sarv Shiksha Abhiyan and Mid Day Meal, and various other welfare programs can be mentioned in this regard. The modern governments are welfare governments. Classical economists were the proponents of laissez faire policy where states had very limited functions.* But now even in the capitalistic economies, there has been increasing state intervention through legislative and administrative measures for augmenting production and distribution.

Size of the Country and Population

Larger the geographical size, larger the role of government activities. India is a diverse topography apart from being the seventh largest country in terms of area. Such a big nation with the second largest number of world's inhabitants requires serious regional planning and development efforts. The population of India has increased from 36 crore in 1951 to more than 120 crore in 2011. There is positive correlation between growth of population and public expenditure because the government needs to spend on health, education, and other essential services for the well-being of its subjects.

Urbanization

In India, urban population has increased from 17% of total population in 1951 to nearly 34% in 2018. The number of mega-sized urban clusters (above 50 lakh population) has remained almost

*Adam Smith wrote in the "Wealth of Nations" that the government should restrict their activities to three things: defence against foreign aggression; maintenance of internal peace and order and public development work.

constant over the years. However, the number of smaller urban clusters has been increasing rapidly.[1] With more and more people migrating to cities, the government needs to strengthen civil and police administration. Further the transportation, road, and health services need to be improved besides planning for urban housing to the increasing population. To mitigate the strains that will develop as cities expand, and to maximize the potential economic opportunity that well-managed cities can offer, India urgently needs a fresh, proactive approach to address the challenges of urbanization. A $1.1 trillion capital investment in Indian cities is necessary to meet projected demand for urban services. In transportation, India needs to build 350–400 km of metros and subways and between 19,000 and 25,000 km of road lanes every year.[2] The smart city mission of the Government of India has envisaged a whopping ₹98,000 crore for the development of 100 smart cities and the rejuvenation of 500 others.

Defense

India is world's fifth largest spender on defense expenditure. The other four nations are the United States, China, Saudi Arabia, and Russia. India's defense budget for 2019–2020 has been envisaged at ₹3.18 trillion. There is demand from several quarters, including the Parliamentary Standing Committee on Defence, to increase expenditure on defense to at least 3% of GDP, from current level of 1.5%. It is widely believed that this will address the problems of national security and underline the government's commitment toward the military. It needs to be mentioned that China spends more than three times in defense than that of India. India's defense expenditure of ₹279,305 crore does not include defense pensions and Ministry of Defence spending. If both are included, the total defense expenditure rises to ₹404,364 crore, or 2.16% of GDP. The Defence Ministry's capital expenditure constitutes 33% of the government's total capital expenditure. Raising the defense budget to 3% of GDP signifies increase in defense capital expenditure which would leave the government with very little money for capital spending, including for infrastructure and asset creation, outside of the procurement for the defense services. Moreover, as most defense equipment are procured from foreign countries, an increased capital budget would raise the defense import bill, and add to the current account deficit.[3]

Interest Payments

Interest payments are the single largest component of India's revenue expenditure. During 2000–2001, Interest payments had climbed to 4.7% of GDP. Though India's interest burden has come down to around 3.2% of GDP, it constitutes nearly 40% of revenue receipts. Almost whatever government borrows is spent on making Interest payments. Interest payments eat up 25% of the budget, 30% is taken by defense, social welfare programs, and subsidies. Remaining 45% is left for everything else—for all the developmental activities which include infrastructure, education, and healthcare.

Subsidies

A study by Andre Blais predicts that public subsidies are higher in those countries, where unemployment is high, agriculture plays a large role in the economy, left-wing parties are in power, and taxes and social security transfers are low.[4] In India, the political economy of subsidies has larger impact on escalation of subsidies from meager ₹140 crore during 1971 to around ₹3 lakh crore during 2018–2019. The share of subsidy in GDP has also escalated to around 1.8%.

SUBSIDIES IN INDIA

A subsidy is a government incentive in the form of financial or non-financial support extended to different economic sectors or individuals with an aim of promoting economic or social welfare.

Kinds of Subsidies

Cash subsidies: It is a poverty reduction measure in which government subsidies and other benefits are given directly to the poor in cash form either by transferring cash in his bank account or charging lesser amount of cash for the goods sold. Examples are direct benefit transfer (DBT) or food subsidy to consumers through public distribution system.

Interest or credit subsidies: Under this the loans are given to beneficiaries at lesser than market rates, for example, interest subvention scheme for farmers and credit-linked capital subsidy scheme extended to MSMEs in India.

Tax subsidies: Under such subsidies the government provides tax exemptions to encourage productive activities or sometimes as a part of fiscal stimulus.* For example, tax benefits are provided for home loans to the units located in special economic zones. The Government of India provided tax subsidies as a part of fiscal stimulus to industry in the aftermath of global financial crisis during 2008–2009.

In-kind subsidies: Subsidies are provided not in cash but in the form of goods and services, for example, free medical services or free medicines at government dispensaries or free mid-day meal to the school students.

Procurement subsidies: It generally takes place in agriculture where food grains are procured by the government (to carry out its PDS operations) from the farmers at price higher than prevailing market price.

Regulatory subsidies: These subsidies are provided to encourage production and consumption of certain categories of goods, for example, subsidies on the production or installation of solar lamps, etc.

Standard Classification of Subsidies

On the basis of standard classification, subsidies are categorized into public goods, merit goods, and non-merit goods.

Public goods: A public good is a product that one individual can consume without reducing its availability to others and from which no one is deprived. Public goods have two distinct aspects such as non-excludability and non-rivalrous consumption.** Examples of public goods are highways, police service, public parks, etc. Such goods cannot be priced and hence are not included while calculating the subsidies.

---

* Fiscal stimulus is an increase in public spending or a reduction in the level of taxation by the government so as to encourage and support economic growth especially during recessionary period.

** A good or service is excludable if it is possible to prevent people who have not paid for it from having access to it. For example, the highways are non-excludable since any person can walk or enjoy ride on it. In economics, a good is said to be rival in nature, if its consumption by one consumer prevents the ability of another party to consume it. For example, an apple consumed by one person eliminates the possibility to consume the same apple by another person. But a broadcast by news channel is available for all the consumers on their respective TV sets.

Merit goods: Merit goods are those goods the social benefit accruing from which is much greater than the sum of private benefits to individual consumers. The consumption of merit goods leads to positive externalities.* Examples of merit good subsidy are public distribution system for below poverty line (BPL) families, free LPG connections to women from BPL families under Pradhan Mantri Ujjwala Yojana.

Non-merit goods: The non-merit goods are the goods whose consumption leads to negative externalities because they affect others without compensating them. Subsiding such goods create more of individual benefits but lesser social benefit. For example, subsidy granted to farmers on electricity and submersible pumps has caused much water extraction and wastage causing lowering of water table.

Central Government Subsidies

The Central Government classifies its subsidies into five different types. Let us briefly discuss them:

1. *Food subsidy*: Food subsidy comprises three components: (1) subsidy to farmers through Minimum Support Price Policy, (2) subsidy to consumers through Public Distribution System, and (3) subsidy to Food Corporation of India in its purchase and maintenance of buffer stock. Food subsidy is the largest component of central government subsidy and constitutes nearly 58% of total subsidy bill.
2. *Fertilizer subsidy*: Fertilizer subsidy constitutes urea subsidy and nutrient-based subsidy.** It constitutes nearly one-fourth of total subsidy bill of the Central Government. Since 2017, the Central Government affected a major change in the mechanism of subsidy payment. Under the new DBT system, 100% of the subsidy is credited into the bank account of a fertilizer manufacturer based on actual sales made by the retailer to the farmer. This is done after the farmer authenticates the purchase with his Aadhaar card through a point-of-sale device at the dealer shop. It constitutes 24% of total subsidy bill.
3. *Petroleum subsidy*: Petrol prices were de-regulated in 2010 by UPA government and diesel prices were de-regulated in 2014 by NDA government. The petroleum subsidy comprises LPG and kerosene. It constitutes 8.5% of total subsidy bill. The recent hike in petroleum subsidy can be attributed to increase in crude oil and depreciation of rupee.[5]
4. *Interest subsidy*: It comprises various sorts of subsidies, for example, interest subvention for farmers, interest subvention on housing loans, credit support to MSME sector, interest subsidy on educational loans, etc. Interest subsidy constitutes 7% of total central government's subsidies.
5. *Other subsidies*: Other subsidies include various kinds of subsidies like price stabilization fund in the department of consumer affairs, subsidy on import of edible oil and pulses, production subsidy to sugar mills, transport/freight subsidy, package for special category states such as Jammu & Kashmir, Himachal Pradesh, Uttarakhand, and so on (Table 25.1).

*Externality refers to a cost or benefit incurred or received by a third party. However, the third party has no control over the creation of that cost or benefit. Externality can be positive or negative. The example of positive externality is government's immunization campaign of pulse polio which ensures better future health and productivity of the citizens of a nation. The example of negative externality is noise pollution which may cause sleep deprivation in the neighbourhood.

**For detailed discussion on NBS, please refer to the chapter 11 Agriculture inputs and Green revolution.

TABLE 25.1 Subsidies in India

Subsidy	2024–25 Budget Estimates* (₹crore)	Percentage of total
Food subsidy	205,250	50
Fertilizer subsidy	163,999.80	40.02
Petroleum subsidy	11,925.01	2.91
Interest subsidy	25,550.34	6.24
Other subsidies	2,997.53	0.73
Grand total	409,722.69	100

*Interim Budget

Source: Statement on subsidies and subsidy related schemes, Ministry of Finance.

Critical Evaluation of Subsidies

Merit Goods Subsidy Versus Demerit Goods Subsidy

National Institute of Public Finance and Policy (NIPFP) has categorized India's subsidies into three parts: Merit 1, Merit 2, and Non-Merit.[6]

Merit 1: Merit 1 subsidies include Elementary education, primary health centers, prevention and control of diseases, and ecology and environment.

Merit 2: Merit 2 subsidies include Education (other than elementary), family welfare, sanitation services, welfare of SC, ST, and OBCs, social welfare and nutrition, food for those below poverty line, plant protection, social and farm forestry, rural development, major and medium irrigation (non-commercial), non-conventional sources of energy (other than atomic energy), and village and small industries.

Non-Merit: It includes subsidies granted for Irrigation (commercial), energy (power), coal and lignite, iron and steel industries, cement and non-metallic industries, petrochemical industries, chemical and pharmaceutical industries, dairy development, engineering industries, transport equipment industries, telecommunications and electronic industries, consumer industries, shipping, civil aviation, road transport, and postal services, food for those above poverty line.

The desired degree of subsidization by the government is broadly indicated as Merit 1 (80–100%), Merit 2 (50–70%), and Non-merit (0–10%). It is very unfortunate than de-merit good subsidies account for major share of subsidies in India. De-merit good subsidies do not generate sufficient positive externalities and should be discouraged. For example, subsidizing higher education is not desirable. It should be a matter of choice. Rather government should subsidize and promote skill-based program which makes the student employable or encourage him to become self-employed.

Subsidies and Inefficiencies

Inefficiencies lead to a higher cost of production which also causes increase in subsidy bill of the government. Also, subsidy interventions by the government distort market prices and often lead to sub-optimal use of inputs in the economy, thereby raising overall costs in the system. Inefficiencies and subsidies, therefore, feed each other. Since inefficiency is neither a public good nor a merit good, the burden of higher cost due to inefficiency should not be passed on to the taxpayer. But when the user (of subsidized good or service) does not pay enough to cover either the legitimate or the inefficiency costs, it is the taxpayer who subsidizes both types of costs. The government's first priority must be to reduce the inefficiency costs without either reducing the level of the service or increasing the user prices.

Mounting Subsidy Burden

During 1971–1972, the Central Government spent just ₹140 crore on subsidies. It reached to ₹12,158 crore during 1990–1991 and peaked to nearly ₹205,250 crore as per 2024–25 Budget estimates. The share of subsidy in country's GDP has increased from 0.3% during 1971 to around 1.8% at present. The food subsidy bill has escalated from 20% during 1990–91 to 50% during 2024–25. Steps must be taken to arrest the burgeoning food subsidy bill which has been growing at a faster pace year after year. Following steps can be suggested in this regard.

First, large stocks of food grains raise the subsidy bill through increased handling and carrying costs along with the losses. There is an urgent need to build storage infrastructure throughout the country. Further, withdrawing such large quantities from the market also results in increasing market prices of food grains, neutralizing much of the consumer benefits that the subsidy provides.

Second, de-centralization of procurement should be pursued as a long-run objective to usher in greater efficiency in the purchase and distribution operations, and to distribute the benefits of the price support operations more evenly across the country.

Third, self-targeting can be brought in by subsidizing coarse grains consumed generally by the poor alone. Two other measures, which may encourage self-targeting are (1) locating of PDS shops in areas where the poor live and (2) allowing/restricting PDS grain purchases on a weekly basis rather than monthly basis. Often the very poor cannot afford purchase of monthly requirements in one go. On the other hand, restricting bulk purchases will discourage the not-so-needy from PDS outlets.[7]

Perverse Subsidies

Perverse subsidies are those subsidies that are harmful to both the economy and the environment. In Germany, for instance, subsidies for coal mining are so large that it would be economically efficient for the government to close down all the mines and send the workers home on full pay for the rest of their lives. The environment would benefit too; less coal pollution such as acid rain and global warming.[8] In their study in 2001, Myers and Kent estimated that globally 60% of direct (conventional) subsidies are perverse. Together with indirect perverse subsidies, this amounts to $1,950 billion annually.[9] Generally de-merit goods subsidies are perverse subsidies. Such subsidies, therefore, create negative externalities. For example, subsidizing tube well irrigation through subsidized electricity has caused lowering of water table at alarming level. Similarly, subsidizing fertilizers and pesticides have many harmful effects on agriculture and environment. Subsidizing kerosene and diesel encourages its use and creates more environment pollution.

Implicit/Hidden Subsidies

There are two kinds of subsidies: explicit and implicit. The explicit subsidies find their mention in annual budget of both central and state governments. The implicit/hidden subsidies on the other hand do not find mention in the government budget. For example, transfers, government guarantees, uncompensated damage to environment, expenditure on tax collection, etc. can be placed under implicit subsidies. Implicit subsidies also take place when the government suppresses supply which leads to increase in prices. Examples are price controls, exchange rate manipulation, quantitative restrictions on trade, etc.[10] It means now the firms in the industry are able to charge higher prices and, therefore, make higher profits, but it usually doesn't burden the government as in the case of explicit subsidies. As per 11th finance commission report, the share of hidden subsidies in total subsidies falls in the range of 63–70% for the Central Government. For states the share of hidden subsidies is as high as 95%.

PUBLIC DEBT IN INDIA

Modern governments are welfare governments. Expenditure of the governments has increased rapidly during recent decades despite role of state in economic activities decreasing considerably. However, there are limits to which revenues from taxes can be raised to meet continuous increasing expenditures. Therefore, the government needs to borrow when current revenue receipts fall short of public expenditure. Such borrowings are called government liabilities. In India, total Central Government Liabilities constitute the following three categories: (1) internal debt, (2) external debt, and (3) public account liabilities.

The first two components, that is, internal plus external debts constitute public debt, whereas all the three components together constitute total liabilities of the government.

Public debt which is the part of government liabilities means debt incurred by the government in mobilizing savings of the people in the form of loans, which are to be repaid at a future date with interest. Public debt constitutes both internal as well as external debts. Article 292 of the Indian Constitution empowers the Government of India to borrow from internal and external sources. Central Government's public debt was ₹61.5 trillion (or 41% of GDP) at the end of March 2018. However it increased to 105.24 Lakh crore (59.3% of GDP) during 2020–21 on account of higher borrowing resorted to due to COVID-19 pandemic as well as sharp contraction in the GDP. Debts of both central and state governments are called general government debt. Let us have a brief discussion on central government liabilities.

Internal Debt

Internal debt of the government is generated by borrowing within the economy, that is, the amount that government owes to lenders within the economy. It comprises marketable and non-marketable securities. It is different from *domestic debt* in the sense that domestic debt is internal debt plus public account liabilities (comprising small savings, provident funds, reserve funds and deposits, etc.). Since internal debt is the major component of domestic debt, all government documents devote their attention toward internal debt and its management. India's internal debt constitutes around 84.7% of total liabilities and nearly 56% of GDP. India's internal debt comprises marketable securities and non-marketable securities.:

Marketable Securities

Marketable securities are securities or debts that are to be sold or redeemed within a year and can be easily converted to cash. Examples are government bonds, common stock, or certificates of deposit. Examples of marketable securities are: Dated Government securities and Treasury bills. Marketable securities constitute around 72% of total liabilities and 33% of GDP.

Non-Marketable Securities

A non-marketable security is not traded on any normal, major secondary market exchanges. Examples are 14-Day Intermediate Treasury Bills, Compensation and other Bonds, Securities issued to International Financial Institutions, Securities against small savings and Special Securities against Postal Life Insurance Fund. Non- marketable securities comprise around 10% of total liabilities and 5.3% of GDP.

External Debt

Under Article 292 of the Constitution of India, the Central Government may borrow from within as well as outside the territory of the country. External debt (₹4.39 trillion, 2.8% of GDP during 2021–22) constituted 5.84% of the total public debt of the Central Government. As State Governments are not empowered to contract external debt, all external debt is contracted by the Central Government and those intended for state government projects are on-lent to States.

Public Account Liabilities

As per Article 266 (2) of the Constitution of India, all public moneys received by or on behalf of the Government of India, other than those which are for credit to the Consolidated Fund of India, are credited to the Public Account of India. The public account liabilities comprise National Small Savings Fund, State Provident Funds, Reserve Funds and Deposits and other accounts. Public Account liabilities, at ₹12.74 trillion during 2020–21, constituted 10.9% of total liabilities and 5.5.% of GDP. The share of public account liabilities has seen a steady decline since 2010–2011 when it accounted for 16.6% of total liabilities.

Causes of Public Debt

1. Public debt or public borrowing is an instrument of fiscal policy. The purpose of borrowing may not always be for obtaining revenue resources only. It may be for influencing aggregate demand, that is, to influence the investment and consumption expenditures for maintaining stability in the economy.
2. The major reason of the increase in public debt is sharp increases in government outlays in public sector projects. Building up the economic infrastructure, like railways, roads, bridges, power plants, etc. that provide the base for economic development, requires huge investments which the government cannot finance just through taxation.
3. The continuous rise in government spending widens the gap of fiscal deficit, and thereby forces the government to depend on public debt from both internal and external sources. Though the government tries hard to reduce the fiscal deficit by promoting an inflow of foreign investment and disinvestment, sustaining a lower fiscal deficit becomes challenging, mainly due to high subsidies and various other developmental and non-developmental expenditures. The economic consequences of high fiscal deficits results in heavy public debt.[11]
4. In times of exigencies like war, or economic crisis, or some natural calamities, the increase in governmental activities results in increasing expenditure that makes the government resort to public borrowing.

5. In recent years, factors, like increase in prices, enlargement of administrative services, increasing expenditure on defense, wages and dearness allowances, etc., have also contributed to increase in public debt.

Burden of Public Debt

The burden of public debt refers to the sacrifice it will impose and have effects on the community through a rise in taxation, necessitated at the time of repayment and for paying the annual interests on the government loans. Whether India's public debt imposes any burden or not, is a debatable issue. It remains a misleading and highly confused concept. Let us have a brief discussion on this.

1. *Classical versus modern views on public debt:* Two different schools (classical and modern) have given their propositions regarding burden of public debt. The classical maintained that if the government expenditure is financed through taxation, the present generation bears the burden. But if government expenditure is financed through public borrowing, the present generation gets relieved from the cost and burden is shifted to the future generation. It is because the present generation reduces its saving in order to meet the debt finance and leave a smaller amount of capital resources for the future. This will reduce the capital formation and hence will reduce the productive capacity of the future generation. However, the modern economists hold the alternate viewpoint. They believe that the public borrowing for the purpose of generating effective demand will not generate any burden. It will help to activate idle savings in the private sector and generate income and employment. During periods of depression, the technique of deficit budget financed through borrowing can be fruitfully utilized to improve employment situation and generating effective demand and thereby raising the level of economic activity. This is what the United States did in the aftermath of twin tower attacks in October 2001 and global financial crisis of 2007–2008. The Indian government too provided fiscal stimulus to the industry so as to help them beat recession (because of global financial crisis and euro zone crisis). For example, in 2002–2003, interest payments amounted to 4.6% of GDP. During the post-FRBM years (2003 onward), interest payments as a proportion of GDP were generally declining. However, the interest payments as a percentage of GDP again increased during the post-crisis period due to factors such as fiscal expansion and fiscal slippage during 2011–2012. A share of the household financial savings went toward government borrowings and consequently household financial savings as a percentage of GDP dropped sharply to 7.1% in 2012–2013 from 12% in 2009–2010. Gross fiscal deficit too rose significantly as a proportion of financial savings, crowding out flow of resources to other sectors.[12]
2. *Primary and secondary burden of debt*: Debt burden is of two types: primary and secondary. When a debt is incurred by the government, the level of taxation in the economy has to be increased in order to meet the interest charges. To the extent of the increase in tax level, the income of the people is transferred to the government. The consequent loss in the income of the people may be called *money burden or primary burden of public debt.* The higher level of taxation caused by the rising public debt may have some repercussions on the economy in the form of adverse effects on the capacity and willingness to work and save. These effects may be called *real burden or secondary burden of public debt.* For

example, in India, interest payments remain a significant component of expenditure of the central government and are often the most inflexible element of revenue expenditure. A substantial amount, nearly one-fifth to one-third of tax collection of the Government of India, is accounted for by interest payments. High interest payments affect the developmental activities as majority of government funds is used for servicing of debt and hence very little is left for the capital formation.[13]

3. *Debt service ratio:* The debt service ratio is the ratio of debt service payments (principal + interest) of a country to its export earnings. Lower this ratio, healthier is the country's international finances. The high external debt poses problems to the government as it has to be repaid in terms of foreign currency and servicing of such debt creates serious problems. The higher amount of debt service payments could potentially strain the exchange rate and also increase the risk of vulnerability to external shocks. The post-reform India has witnessed a remarkable fall in the debt service ratio. The debt service ratio has come down from 35.3% in 1991 to 8.3% in 2017.
4. *Debt trap:* Few economists feel that there is a hidden disease eating into India's Budget and it is quite incurable. It is called a debt trap. A debt trap is a situation in which a borrower is led into a cycle of re-borrowing, or rolling over, his loan payments because he is unable to afford the scheduled payments on the principal of a loan. The Centre's total debt is nearly ₹47 lakh crore and that of states is ₹65 lakh crore, which together accounts for 65% of its GDP. The optimists lament that India's debt–GDP ratio is lower than that of the United States as its debt is 75% of its GDP. But they willfully ignore the crucial fact that the United States borrows money at 1–3% interest rate, while India borrows at 7–9%. So, though the United States's debt is higher than India's, its interest payments are lower. Only 6% of the US federal budget goes to interest payments, while for India it is 25%. The United States also borrows in its own currency, a luxury no other nation enjoys.[14]
5. *Usage of debt:* The usage of funds is another important indicator that cannot be overlooked. If public debt is wasted on unproductive activities, it becomes deadweight. However, the burden of the debt may appear to be much smaller and even nil or negative, if it is utilized in development of nation, building infrastructure, or mitigating poverty and unemployment. Higher government interventions sometimes create crowding out effect in the economy. The crowding out effect in an economy takes place when rising public sector spending drives down or even eliminates private sector spending. It happens when government borrows heavily to invest in some developmental projects and thus takes away the loanable funds which otherwise would have been available to private sector. This in turn raises the interest rates and discourages private investment. The costs of high public debt levels with respect to crowding out of private investment due to large sectoral government interventions such as National Food Security Act, Mahatma Gandhi National Rural Employment Guarantee Act, National highway development project, Pradhan Mantri Gram Sadak Yojna, and Mid-day meal scheme remain debatable and paradoxical.[15]

Is India's Public Debt Sustainable?

The question of "what is a sustainable public debt?" is paramount in the macro-economic analysis of fiscal policy.[16] The question is often understood as asking whether the government is solvent. Public debt has some similarities to a renewable resource. Renewable resources, like fishing grounds, can be used up to a certain threshold. Beyond that point, the reproductive capacity of the resource is harmed; the resource becomes a non-renewable one and is finally used up. In much the same way, public debt, or its servicing, need not be a problem for an economy if it is low enough, but it can lead to default if overused. Debts have the character of a pollutant. Pollutants can be released with no harm up to a certain level given by nature's absorptive capacity. Beyond that level, they may cause negative externalities for other individuals in the short run until the system eventually collapses in the long run.[17] Debt sustainability is often defined as the ability of a country to meet its debt obligations without requiring debt relief or accumulating arrears.

There are various indicators to evaluate the sustainability of public debt in India. Let us discuss one by one.

1. *Debt–GDP Ratio:* The debt–GDP ratio is one of the most important determinants of sustainability of public debt.[18] There is little consensus with regard to a level of debt that may be considered unsustainable. There are countries with debt–GDP ratios close to or higher than 100% without doubt on their ability to service debt and on the other hand, a relatively low debt–GDP ratio can be considered unsustainable for some countries. A secularly rising debt–GDP ratio may nonetheless be considered as leading toward non-sustainability. Symmetrically, a secularly falling debt–GDP ratio can be considered as leading toward stability[19] India's debt level went up consistently during 1980s and 1990s and the combined debt–GDP ratio of the Centre and States reached a peak of 83.3% by the end of 2003–2004. Thereafter, debt–GDP ratio has shown a broadly declining trend. The marginal increase during 2008–09 and 2011–12 was mainly on account of global factors and the increase was significantly lower than what many other countries had witnessed during that turbulent period. Reduction in debt–GDP ratio took place at the level of both Centre and States. For Centre, debt to GDP ratio declined from 58.5% in 2003–04 to 46.1% in 2016–17. Similarly, for States, debt to GDP ratio declined from 31.8% in 2003–04 to 23.7% in 2016–17. Central Government Debt to GDP ratio stood at 67.4% at the end of March 2017.
2. *Interest Payments:* Interest payment is another significant indicator of debt sustainability. It has two important components.
   (a) *Interest payments to revenue receipts*: It simply means capacity to pay interest out of revenue receipts of the government. Lower this ratio, higher is the debt sustainability and vice versa. The ratio of interest payments to revenue receipts IP/RR shows a secular decline for both the Central and State Governments, notwithstanding the marginal increase in recent years due to increased borrowings requirements post-global financial crisis of 2008. Combined IP/RR ratio of Centre and States in 2016–2017 was placed at 21.8% as compared to 35.6% in 2001–2002.
   (b) *Average Interest Cost*: Average interest cost (AIC) is arrived at by dividing interest payments during a year with average debt stock. A continuously declining AIC augurs well for the stability of Government debt. Trend in AIC of both the Centre and States showed a downward movement since 2000. Centre's AIC declined to 6.9% in 2016–17 from 8.1% in 2000–01, while States' AIC declined to 7.5% from 9.4% over the same period. With economy poised for downward interest rate cycle, further lowering of AIC may be expected in coming years. Apart from IP/RR and AIC,

another important criterion of sustainability is whether nominal growth rate of GDP is well above the average interest cost, implying that the growth in revenue generation through higher GDP is likely to exceed the growth in interest obligations. This is likely to further push down the IP/RR ratio providing more fiscal space for other expenditure.

3. *Short-term debt*: Short-term debt is defined as debt with maturity of 1 year or less. Short-term debt of the Central Government includes 14-day intermediate treasury bills, regular treasury bills, dated securities maturing within 1 year, and external debt with maturity of less than 1 year. A greater proportion of short-term debt in total debt increases the risk profile and hence reduces the sustainability of debt. Therefore, higher the period of maturity of a debt, higher is the sustainability and vice versa. Short-term debt declined noticeably during the early 2000s with its share in public debt declining to a low of 6.2% in 2003–2004. It, however, rose consistently thereafter with its share in the public debt increasing to 13.8% in 2008–2009. Since then, it has generally been declining gradually with its share at 11.3% of public debt and 4.6% of GDP during 2017.[20]
4. *External Debt*: Economic literature suggests that foreign borrowing has a positive impact on investment and growth up to a certain threshold level; beyond this level, however, its impact is adverse.[21] Such adverse effect is called "debt overhang." Debt overhang is a situation in which the expected repayment on external debt falls short of the contractual value of debt.[22] But in India, the government debt is mainly raised from internal sources. The share of external debt in total debt is around 7%. The share is not only low but has also declined during past few years. Further, around 70% of the external debt is from multi-lateral agencies, with remaining external debt originating from official bilateral agencies. Multi-lateral debt is owed by developing countries to the international financial institutions viz. IBRD, IDA, IFC, IMF, etc. On the other hand, a bilateral debt is a simple loan arrangement between two nations. Under bilateral loan arrangements, India has taken loan from Japan, Germany, the United States, and few other countries. Loans from multi-lateral institutions are long term and largely on concessional terms, lowering the risk from external borrowings. In 2017–18, 68.4 and 31.6% of total external debt was in the ratio of multilateral and bilateral debt respectively.

   External debt is predominantly borrowed in three currencies viz., SDR (34%), USD (36%), and Yen (25.3%). At the end of March 2017, debt denominated in these three currencies represented 95.9% of total external debt. A small portion (4.8%) is borrowed in Euro and 0.2% in other currencies. External debt (at current exchange rate) as percentage of GDP has consistently declined in the recent years (from 3.6 in 2010–11 to 2.9% in 2017–18), indicating the declining reliance on external debt for financing of fiscal deficit. This implies that debt portfolio of the government has low currency risk and its impact on balance of payments also remains insignificant.

To sum up, India's Government debt portfolio is characterized by favorable sustainability indicators and right profile. Share of short-term debt is within safe limits and it has stabilized after some rise between 2005 and 2012. Most of the Government debt is at fixed interest rates, which minimizes the impact of interest rate volatility on the budget Centre's Debt is mostly of domestic origin implying that currency risk to the debt portfolio is insignificant. Conventional indicators of debt sustainability, that is, debt–GDP ratio and cost of debt, indicate that debt profile of the Government is within sustainable limits, and consistently improving.

Public Debt Management

Fiscal rules as best practice should focus on macro-economic stability and the relevant targets for this are the fiscal deficit, the primary deficit, and the debt–GDP ratio. India's fiscal deficit and debt ratio are much higher than those of other comparable emerging market economies. Markets are knowingly forgiving the government as growth is robust. It may be disaster when things turn bad. There is no hard rule to determine what the debt ratio should be but they should be viewed as "sustainable" by rating agencies and investors.

Government has taken following steps with regard to management of public debt.[23]

1. *Cost of Borrowing*: One of the most important components of debt management strategy is cost of borrowing. Higher the interest rate, higher will be the burden of debt. In spite of increased borrowings over the years, the interest rate (weighted average coupon) has remained broadly stable. For last 10 years, the interest rate of outstanding securities has ranged between 7.81 and 8.55% and was 7.99% in 2016–2017. At the same time, the ratio of interest payments to revenue receipts has shown a secular decline. The Centre's IP/RR was placed at 33.93% during 2016–17 as compared to 53.4% during 2001–02.[24] Steps taken to lower cost of borrowings include planned issuance and offer appropriate mix of instruments to cater to investors' preferences. In line with the international sound practice, transparency and predictability in borrowing plans has ensured cost effectiveness through giving enough time to market players to plan their investments. To prevent any arbitrage in the interest in different maturity buckets, the Government has right to exercise Green Shoe option.*
2. *Rollover Risk*: Rollover risk is associated with the refinancing of debt. A government faces rollover risk when its debt is about to mature and needs to be rolled over into new debt. If interest rates rise adversely, then government would have to refinance the debt at a higher rate and incur more interest charges in the future. Many developing countries and emerging markets generally have large fiscal deficit along with the rollover of debt due for redemption during the year, thus leading to higher gross borrowing requirements. But situation becomes more critical when market conditions are fragile and large amounts are to be rolled over. Indicators such as increasing share of short-term debt to the total debt reflect the rise in rollover risk. In India, rollover risk is managed by elongating maturity, limiting short-term debt issuances, and placing annual issuance limits for maturity buckets as well as individual Government security. Such limits are periodically reviewed keeping in view the macro-economic environment, variations in cash inflows, and cash management considerations of the government.[25]
3. *Redemption Profile of Debt*: Redemption/maturity is a term defined with respect to bonds/securities which have fixed maturities after which they cease to exist on payment of the principal and the stipulated interest. Longer the maturity time of a debt, lesser is the risk. A total of 57% of internal debt in India lies in less than 10-year maturity bucket and 43% lies in more than 10-year maturity bucket. The major reasons for high concentration of outstanding debt in less than 10-year maturity bucket are large issuance of short-term securities during global financial crisis (2008–2010) when market conditions turned

*A greenshoe option is a provision in an IPO underwriting agreement that grants the underwriter the right to sell more shares than originally planned.

**The external short-term debt was the major cause of euro zone crisis.

fragile and demand for long-term securities dwindled significantly; and less appetite in the market for longer term securities.

4. *Risk Management*: An important feature of investor profile of the government is the dominance of domestic investors and limited foreign investor participation. The ability of domestic market to finance government operations is a source of strength of the debt portfolio, which is insulated from the currency risk. Steps are being taken by the government to cap the investment by foreign investors and widen the investor base. This is being done keeping in view the sensitivity of foreign investors to global macro-economic/financial factors** and possible sudden reversals or capital flight, which could potentially impact the economic stability of the host country. The policy stance is oriented toward a calibrated approach to capital account convertibility and gradual opening to foreign investors in the domestic bond markets keeping in view the imperatives of improving demand and market depth as well as maintaining exchange rate stability.[26] The domestic investor base is dominated by commercial banks in short- to medium-tenor securities and by insurance companies and provident funds at the longer duration maturities. However, the share of commercial banks has been declining over the years. With the entry of mutual funds, co-operative banks, regional rural banks, non-banking finance companies, pension funds, the institutional investor base has got diversified reasonably. Mutual funds prefer short-term and liquid securities, co-operative banks prefer short- to medium-term papers, while pension and provident funds prefer longer tenor securities due to longer time horizon of their liabilities.
5. *Reducing Interest Payments: Inflation-indexed Bonds*: Inflation is one of the significant concerns for investors in financial assets as it can quickly erode investors' wealth. Some of the benefits of inflation-indexed bonds (IIBs) are insulation from inflation for the investor, a constant real yield, cost saving for the issuer, risk diversification, and aid in gauging inflation expectations. In the absence of IIBs, investors tend to invest in gold, as this is commonly observed as a hedge against inflation. IIBs may encourage savings and more importantly, these instruments may aid in weaning investors away from gold. The decrease in borrowing cost may also occur due to a strengthened demand for government securities and broader investor base, possibly created by IIBs. The capital-indexed bonds were first issued in India during 1997, in which the principal repayment at the time of redemption was indexed to inflation.[27] No further issuance of indexed bond was made after the 1997 issuance, for nearly a decade and a half, primarily because this instrument received a dull response. In June 2013, IIBs linked to the Wholesale Price Index (WPI) were issued by the Government of India. Unlike capital-indexed bonds, these IIBs provided protection to both, principal and interest payments. Inflation Indexed National Saving Securities were launched for retail investors in December 2013 and linked with Consumer Price Index (CPI).
6. *Restructuring of Existing Debt*: There are two major methods of debt restructuring practiced in India: market buy-backs and debt swaps. Debt buyback is the repurchase by a debtor of its own debt, discounted, or at par. Debt buy-back helps government to reduce borrowing cost over the long period and also lowers rollover risk. With the objective of reducing the government's interest burden and to help banks in off-loading illiquid securities, the government debt buy-back scheme was put into effect in July 2003. Deb swaps or Switch operations are cash-neutral, as these entail simultaneous swapping of government security of a specific maturity with government security of another maturity.[28]

Fiscal Policy

Fiscal policy is the policy regarding receipts and expenditure of the government. It is the policy under which government uses its expenditure and revenue program to produce desirable effects and avoid undesirable effects on the national income, production, and employment. Although the effects of fiscal policy are extensive, they are particularly measurable in areas such as employment, price stability, savings and investment, and the balance of payment.

Objectives of Fiscal Policy in India

Fiscal policy in India has the following primary and additional objectives:

Primary objectives

- Promoting economic growth
- Maintaining price stability in the economy

Additional objectives

- Mobilizing resources
- Promoting allocative efficiency
- Reducing inequality in income and wealth
- Promoting private sector investment

The fiscal policy thus has not one goal but multiplicity of goals. Hence, they cannot be achieved by any one set of policies. A disaggregated approach will be needed. There may be conflicts between allocation and stabilization goals. In the context of economic growth, the fiscal policy has to be framed so as to avoid an inflationary pressure in the economy.

Promoting Economic Growth

Fiscal policy plays a central role in economic development by providing public goods, encouraging private investment, and providing socially optimal direction for economic growth.[29] For example, large-scale investments by the government during second 5-year plan and afterward resulted in huge capital formation in the economy by producing basic and capital goods. The spending under Pradhan Mantri Gram Sadak Yojana, irrigation development programs, and MGNREGS not only results in the creation of rural assets but generates employment opportunity to crores of rural folks throughout the country. In the immediate aftermath of the global financial crisis of 2007–2008, the global economy experienced major deflationary shocks as aggregate demand plummeted owing to the loss of confidence in the financial system. Monetary policy remains ineffective, it was the fiscal policy which helped government to overcome the crisis. In India, government provided huge fiscal stimulus to the industry so as to come out of the crisis.[30]

Maintaining Price Stability in the Economy

Inflation takes place when either demand is more or supply is less. To control the prices, government goes for contractionary fiscal policy that decreases the level of aggregate demand, either through cuts in government spending or increases in taxes. Raising the production is supply-side measure that helps to bring down the prices. The government can channelize credit into certain productive sectors or provide production subsidy to boost production and hence help bringing down the price level. For example, PDS in India works on this principal. Another supply-side measure to arrest inflation is imports. The government also sometimes bans exports or imposes export duty to stabilize the supply and prices. In India, the government has imported essential agriculture items (wheat in 1960s, onion and tomatoes in the recent past) from time to time so as to control inflation. The government imposed 20% duty on export of sugar for promoting availability and moderating price rise during January 2018.[31]

Mobilization of Resources

Resource mobilization is a key development priority and essential to finance investments in human capital and infrastructure. The government mobilizes resources through tax and non-tax revenue receipts and capital receipts. Taxes (both central as well as state) as a percentage of GDP have grown from 6.3% during 1950–51 to nearly 18% during 2018–19. No doubt India's tax–GDP ratio has increased but it must aim to double its tax-to-GDP ratio to achieve the OECD average of about 34%. The tax policy framework needs to address the issue of "missing middle," which includes professionals (like CAs, lawyers, and doctors), which manages a leeway to report actual income and hence gets out of tax net.[32] The non-tax revenue receipts of the government are just 14% of total revenue receipts but there is an ample scope to increase this share. The policy framework must focus on curtailing subsidies and increasing user charges. Similarly, in capital receipts the government needs to gear up disinvestment process, which will not only generate huge capital receipts for the government but also help make PSUs emerge as globally competitive corporates.

Allocating Efficiency

A reasonable definition of allocative efficiency is the production of the best or optimal combination of outputs by means of the most efficient combination of inputs.[33] An efficient and rational allocation of resources is sine qua non for the economic growth of a nation. To promote allocative efficiency, tax policy is one of the most important tools of public finance. For example, custom duties and excise duties in the past were levied mainly for revenue consideration and resulted into efficiency losses. The post-reform period attempted to correct this mistake through rationalization of taxes. Over dominance of public sector, draconian Acts like MRTP, FERA, and patronage extended to small-scale industry (through small-scale reservation policy) during pre-reform period severely affected industrial output. The government tried to rectify it via new initiatives introduced in new industrial policy of 1991. The emergence of strong black market economy which is around 60% of GDP vitiates the allocative impact of fiscal policy on the expenditure side as substantial leakages from the government finances do take place.

Reducing Inequality in Income and Wealth

The experience of advanced countries has shown that fiscal policy can help drive down inequality. For example, public spending for education and healthcare can help equalize economic opportunities. In India, public spending on education amounts to only about 3.8% of GDP, compared to 5.3% for advanced economies and 4.7% for world as a whole. The country trails even far behind public spending for healthcare, at 1.2% of GDP, compared to 8.1% for advanced economies. Clearly, there is a large scope for the country to increase spending in both education and healthcare. In addition to such spending that promotes both growth and equity, there is a case for expanding the social safety net of public transfers and subsidies, as long as the transfers and subsidies are selective and targeted to the most needy and vulnerable groups.[34] Tax policy is another significant tool to improve equity. Direct taxes are considered progressive as burden falls more on rich people. On the other hand, the burden of indirect taxes falls more on common man. Direct–indirect tax ratio which was as low as 16:84 during pre-reform period has increased to around 51:49 and it is a welcome sign. But the country has a long way to go as in advanced nations the ratio is as high as 80:20.

Promoting Private Sector Investment

Fiscal policy can affect indigenous private investment and foreign investment positively. The tax reforms in India since 1991 and the recent introduction of GST have improved country's credentials globally. The easing down of fiscal controls also affects country's performance and output. Government efforts to incentivize special economic zones stem from this principal. Further many empirical studies have highlighted that government capital expenditure in infrastructure has the highest impact on private capital investment since it increases return to private capital. Tax on international trade affects private investment negatively. Import duties, therefore, must be restructured to promote capital technology.[35] The optimal rate of corporation taxes also encourages private investment and leads to increase in tax revenue of the government (through Laffer curve effect).*

Fiscal Responsibility and Budget Management Act

The Fiscal Responsibility and Budget Management (FRBM) Act was enacted in 2003 by Indian Parliament and was brought into effect on July 5, 2004 by the UPA government. During pre-reform period, Indian economy faced the mammoth challenge to curtail ever-increasing fiscal deficit and its monetization spilled over to external sector in the late 1980s and early 1990s. The large borrowings of the government led to such a precarious situation that government was unable to pay even for 2 weeks of imports resulting in economic crisis of 1991. After a good start of the fiscal reforms of early 1990s, the fiscal consolidation faltered after 1997–1998 and the fiscal deficit once again started rising. The Government introduced FRBM Act, 2003 to check the deteriorating fiscal situation.

The main objectives of the FRBM Act were:

1. to achieve long-term macro-economic stability, while generating budget surpluses;
2. to introduce prudential debt management;
3. to introduce transparent fiscal management systems in the country; and
4. to remove fiscal impediments and providing a medium-term framework for budgetary implementation.

Following were the key highlights of FRBM Act[36]:

- Bringing down revenue deficit by 0.5% on annual basis and eliminating it completely by 2008–2009.

*For detailed discussion on Laffer curve, please refer to the chapter 24 Indian Tax system.

- Reduction of fiscal deficit to 3% of GDP at the end of 2008–2009. Revenue deficit and fiscal deficits may exceed the targeted amount only in case of national calamity or national emergency.
- Total liabilities of the Union Government should not rise by more than 9% a year.
- RBI will not subscribe to primary issues of GOI securities w.e.f. 2006–2007. GOI will not borrow from RBI except to meet temporary excess of expenditure over receipts.
- Central Government to lay in each financial year before both houses of parliament three statements viz. medium-term fiscal policy statement, fiscal policy strategy statement, and macro-economic framework statement.
- Finance minister to make a quarterly review of trends in receipts and expenditure and place the review before parliament.

The implementation of FRBM Act improved the fiscal performance of both center and states and even the states had achieved the targets much ahead the prescribed timeline. Government of India was also on the path of achieving this objective right in time. However, by this time the impact of global financial crisis became visible as many sectors of economy, especially manufacturing started witnessing sluggishness. Government in order to revive the economy, announced stimulus packages in December 2008, January 2009, and March 2009, in the form of tax reliefs (central excise duty reduction by 4%), increased expenditure (₹200 billion planned spending), and targeted subsidies (interest subsidies on export finance). Due to this gross fiscal deficit of the country reached 6% of GDP in 2008–2009 (against the target of 2.5%) and rose to 6.4% of GDP in 2009–2010. Revenue deficit shot up to 4.5% of GDP in 2008–2009 and further rose to 5.2% of GDP in 2009–2010. In both the circumstances, the targets set by the FRBM Act, 2003 had been breached significantly.[37]

On the recommendations of 13th Finance Commission, amendments were made to the FRBM Act, 2003, through the Finance Act 2012 through which it was decided that in addition to the existing three documents, Central Government shall lay another document—the Medium Term Expenditure Framework Statement (MTEF)—before both Houses of Parliament. "Medium-Term Expenditure Framework" statement will set forth a 3-year rolling target for expenditure indicators. The Concept of Effective Revenue Deficit (ERD) was also introduced through this amendment. MTEF and ERD are the two important features of amendment to FRBM Act in the direction of expenditure reforms. As per the amendments in 2012, the Central Government had to take appropriate measures to reduce the fiscal deficit, revenue deficit, and effective revenue deficit to eliminate the ERD by March 31, 2015 and thereafter build up adequate effective revenue surplus and also to reach revenue deficit of not more than 2% of Gross Domestic Product by March 31, 2015 and thereafter.

BOX 25.1 Deficit Financing and Debt Monetization in India

Deficit financing: Deficit financing is a practice in which the government spends more money than it receives as revenue, the difference being made up by borrowing from different sources. The government can borrow from internal market while issuing government bonds or selling treasury bills or from external sources. When the government borrows from central bank, it merely transfers its securities to the bank who, on the basis of these securities, issues more notes and puts them into circulation on behalf of the government. In India, the government finances its deficit through both external and internal sources. The internal sources include market borrowings, other borrowings, and draw down of cash balances. The government's recourse to finance its deficit arises because of two reasons: one, its failure to mobilize the desired volume of surplus and second, its rapidly growing expenditures both productive as well as unproductive. Deficit financing can be a useful tool especially during recessionary phase as it raises the effective demand. The machinery and capital equipment lying idle are pressed into operation, which ultimately leads to increase in production and income. But there is a word of caution also. In developing countries, deficit financing generally leads to inflation because in such nations propensity to consume is high, markets are characterized by imperfections and there is little excess capacity in plant and equipment. Further, the resources generated through deficit financing are utilized for producing the consumption goods rather than producer goods. Much of the money also goes into increase in consumption of food products, causing food inflation. However, if resources mobilized through deficit financing are utilized for construction of roads, irrigation development, and creation of social infrastructure, then there is no likelihood of an increase in prices.

Debt monetization in India: In traditional sense, if the government borrows from RBI to finance its total or part of deficit, then it is called debt monetization. For example, RBI can print new currency for the government to finance its deficit. It directly attenuates monetary control. In the modern world, with central banks in charge of controlling the aggregate money supply, the governments typically finance their deficits by issuing government bonds. They can either be purchased by the public from the existing supply of money or by central banks by increasing the monetary base, which ultimately leads to increase in money supply. Now the key question is whether any purchase of government securities by the central bank would tantamount to monetization of debt. In practice, it is still hard to make a black-and-white distinction between what portion of the central bank's purchases of government securities is for the purpose of the conduct of monetary policy and what proportion is in support of government's borrowings. If central bank's purchases of government bonds is in alignment with its target of base money and money supply expansion, then it will not lead to monetization of debt, otherwise it will be debt monetization. Since the late 1980s, several steps were taken to reduce the fiscal dominance of monetary policy.

First, the RBI and the government moved to establish a market-based public debt market during 1986 to 1993. Auctions of 182, 364, and 91-day treasury bills were introduced. As auction-based yields were higher, an increasing part of the government borrowings came to be financed through market sources, enabling a better control of reserve money by the Reserve Bank.

Second, in March 1997, the government and RBI agreed to completely phase out funding through ad hoc treasury bills.

Third, a system of Ways and Means Advances (WMA) was put in place from April 1, 1997. Under this, the Reserve Bank has been extending short-term advances up to the pre-announced half-yearly limits, fully payable within 3 months.

Fourth, enactment of the FRBM Act, 2003 that barred the RBI from subscribing to the primary issuances of the government from April 1, 2006.

Has the monetization been completely phased out in India now that the RBI no longer subscribes to the primary issuances in government auctions? De-facto monetization has been considerably phased out, but not completely. As long as fiscal deficits remain large, the size of market borrowings would also remain large and impinge upon the conduct of monetary policy, no matter how the debt management is conducted.

Sources:

1. Govind Rao, M. (2017) Public finance in India in the context of India's development. NIPFP Working paper series, No. 219.
2. *Fiscal-monetary co-ordination in India: An assessment*, Report on Currency and Finance, RBI, March 4, 2013.

The government revised the FRBM Act further through the Finance Act 2015 to change deadline of March 31, 2015 to March 31, 2018. The ERD which had to be eliminated by March 2015 would now be eliminated only after 3 years, that is, by March 2018. The 3% target of fiscal deficit to be achieved by 2016–2017 had now been shifted by one more year to the end of 2017–2018. The fiscal deficit and revenue deficit registered a sharp rise during covid years. During 2023–24, the fiscal and revenue deficit were recorded to be 5.8 and 2.8% of GDP. The budget 2024–25 has pegged both fiscal and revenue deficit at 5.1 and 2% of GDP respectively. It may, however, be noted that in the new FRBM framework adopted in 2018–2019 budget, revenue deficit is no longer a targeted fiscal indicator in FRBM Act. Effective revenue deficit which is the difference between the revenue deficit and the grants for creation of capital assets has also been removed as a fiscal target.[38] Though revenue deficit is no longer a parameter for measuring fiscal outcomes in the FRBM Act, it is shown as a reference indicator in MTFP Statement. Revenue deficit creates a preference for capital expenditure over revenue expenditure, which may lead to a situation where funds are allotted for creation of capital assets but not for their subsequent maintenance. It is also pertinent to note that even those transfers from Union Government to State Government agencies that create tangible assets under schemes are categorized as revenue expenditure in Union Budget as Grants in-Aid. Then there is the conceptual issue of treatment of expenditures incurred in building human resource capital as revenue expenditure.[39] Human capital and its development by focusing on schools and hospitals and also maintenance of assets, which are in nature of revenue expenditure, are important to improve productivity as buildings and roads which are part of capital expenditure.[40]

N.K. Singh Committee on FRBM

Government of India appointed a high-level committee to review the FRBM Act, 2003. The committee submitted its report in January, 2017. Following are the important recommendations of the committee[41]:

1. Debt should be used the primary target for fiscal policy. A debt-to-GDP ratio of 60% should be targeted with a 40% limit for the center and 20% limit for the states and the targets should be achieved by 2023. To achieve the targeted debt-to-GDP ratio, the committee proposed yearly targets to progressively reduce the fiscal and revenue deficits till 2023 (Table 25.2).
2. An autonomous Fiscal Council must be created with a Chairperson and two members appointed by the center. The role of the Council would include (i) preparing multi-year fiscal forecasts, (ii) recommending changes to the fiscal strategy, (iii) improving quality

TABLE 25.2 Deficit and Debt Targets (as a % of GDP)

Year	Fiscal Deficit	Revenue Deficit	Debt
2017–2018	3	2.1	47.3
2018–2019	3	1.8	45.5
2019–2020	3	1.6	43.7
2020–2021	2.8	1.3	42.0
2021–2022	2.6	1.1	40.3
2022–2023	2.5	0.8	38.7

Source: FRBM review committee report, Volume I, January, 2017.
Ministry of Finance. Govt. of India. Latest Budget Documents.

of fiscal data, (iv) advising the government if conditions exist to deviate from the fiscal target, and (v) advising the government to take corrective action for non-compliance with the Bill.

3. The government may be allowed to deviate from the specified targets upon the advice of the Fiscal Council in the following circumstances: (i) considerations of national security, war, national calamities and collapse of agriculture affecting output and incomes, (ii) structural reforms in the economy resulting in fiscal implications, or (iii) decline in real output growth of at least 3% below the average of the previous four quarters. These deviations cannot be more than 0.5% of GDP in a year.
4. The 15th Finance Commission should be asked to recommend the debt trajectory for individual states. This should be based on their track record of fiscal prudence and health.
5. Government cannot borrow from the RBI except when (i) the center has to meet a temporary shortfall in receipts, (ii) the RBI subscribes to government securities to finance any deviations from the specified targets, or (iii) the RBI purchases government securities from the secondary market.

Summary

1. Budget is a financial forecast of a nation's total receipts and expenditure for an accounting year. Budget has two chief accounts: revenue and capital. Revenue deficit occurs when revenue expenditure exceeds revenue receipts. Effective revenue deficit is revenue deficit minus grants-in-aid to states and local bodies. Fiscal deficit occurs when a government's total expenditures exceed the receipts that it generates, excluding money from borrowings. Primary deficit is equal to fiscal deficit minus interest payments on the previous borrowings.
2. Public expenditure can be classified as capital expenditure and revenue expenditure, developmental and non-developmental expenditure, and plan and non-plan expenditure. There are many causes of increase in government expenditure. There is general tendency of increase in public expenditure as GDP of the country goes up; the larger geographical size and large size of population also causes state to increase expenditure; increase in urbanization also demands state intervention in terms of provision of basic amenities; defense expenditure goes up in the eventuality of external threat and security reasons; interest payment burden inflates because of high public debt; and subsidy bill goes up because of welfare role of the state.
3. A subsidy is a government incentive in the form of financial or non-financial support extended to different economic sectors or individuals with an aim of promoting economic or social welfare. The central government's subsidies comprise food, petroleum, fertilizer, interest, and other subsidies. The total subsidy bill in India has escalated from ₹140 crore during 1970–71 to ₹293,000 crore during 2018–19.
4. In India, total Central Government Liabilities constitute the following three categories: (1) internal debt, (2) external debt; and (3) public account liabilities. The first two components, that is, internal debt plus external debt constitute public debt, whereas all the three components together constitute total liabilities of the government. Internal debt includes marketable and non-marketable securities and is around 38% of GDP. External debt and public account liabilities constitute around 2.9 and 5.5% of GDP respectively.
5. Debt sustainability is often defined as the ability of a country to meet its debt obligations without requiring debt relief or accumulating arrears. The various indicators to gauge the suitability of public debt are debt–GDP ratio, interest payments, short-term debt, and external debt. The public debt management of Government of India comprises various steps such as cost of borrowing, rollover risk, redemption profile of the debt, risk management, inflation-indexed bonds, and restructuring of existing debt.
6. Fiscal policy is the policy regarding receipts and expenditure of the government. There are different objectives of fiscal policy in Indian context. The primary objectives are promoting economic growth and maintaining price stability in the economy. The additional objectives are mobilizing resources, promoting allocative efficiency, reducing inequality in income and wealth, and promoting private sector investment.
7. The Fiscal Responsibility and Budget Management (FRBM) Act was enacted in 2003 by Indian Parliament and was brought into effect on July 5, 2004. The main highlights of FRBM Act were eliminating revenue deficit, reducing fiscal deficit, and introducing transparent fiscal management systems in the country by making government accountable to parliament with regard to expenditure management. FRBM Act has a long journey and was amended in 2012 and 2015. The Government appointed a high-level committee to review the FRBM Act, 2003 under the chairpersonship of N.K. Singh. The committee submitted its report in January, 2017. The committee laid down fiscal targets till 2023, recommended constitution of autonomous Fiscal Council, allowed deviation from fiscal targets only in exceptions, and prohibited government's borrowing from RBI although certain exceptions are there.

Endnotes

1. Urbanisation on the rise in India, *The Hindu*, May 18, 2018.
2. *India's urban awakening: Building inclusive cities, sustaining economic growth.* Mckinsey Global Institute, 2010 Report. Retrieved from https://www.mckinsey.com (Accessed on November 16, 2016).
3. The problem with raising India's defence expenditure to 3% of GDP. *Indian Express*, May 6, 2019.
4. Andre Blais (1986). The Political Economy of Public Subsidies, *Comparative political studies*, Volume 19, Issue 2.
5. Petrol, diesel impact: Oil companies' stocks lose ₹1.25 lakh crore in last two trading sessions. *Business Today*, October 5, 2018.
6. Merit Goods Subsidies. Retrieved from https://www.nipfp.org.in (Accessed on November 27, 2016).
7. Report on Central Government Subsidies in India, Department of Economic Affairs, Ministry of Finance, GOI, 2004, p.13.
8. Myers, N. (2007). *Perverse subsidies.* Retrieved from http://editors.eol.org (Accessed on April 16, 2019).
9. Myers, N., & Kent, J. (2001). *Perverse subsidies: How tax dollars can undercut the environment and the* economy (p.240). Washington, DC: Island Press.
10. Hidden Subsidies. Retrieved from http://www.fao.org (Accessed on April 16, 2019).
11. Bal, D.P., & Rath, B.N. (2014). Public debt and economic growth in India: A reassessment. *Economic Analysis and Policy*, 44, 292–300.
12. Kanagasabapathy, K., Singh, C., & Shimpi, S. (2018). *Need to rationalise rising interest burden on Central Government Public Debt.* EPW, Vol. no. 4.
13. Kanagasabapathy, K., Singh, C., & Shimpi, S. (2018). *Need to rationalise rising interest burden on Central Government Public Debt.* EPW, Vol. 53 Issue 4.
14. Pocha, J.S. (2018). In the end, India will still be trapped in debt. *The Sunday Guardian.*
15. Kaur, B., & Mukherjee, A. (2012). *Threshold level of debt and public debt sustainability: The Indian experience.* Reserve Bank of India Occasional Papers, Vol. 33, No. 1 & 2.
16. D'Erasmo, P., et al. (2015). *What is a sustainable public debt?* Working Paper 21574, National Bureau of Economic Research, p.2.
17. Neck, R., & Sturm, J.-E. (2008). *Sustainability of public debt* (pp.3–4). The MIT Press. Retrieved from https://mitpress.mit.edu (Accessed on December 14, 2016).
18. Blanchard, O. J. (1980). *Suggestions for a new set of fiscal indicators.* OECD, Working Paper, No. 79.
19. *Status paper on government debt. (2016–17).* Ministry of Finance, Department of Economic Affairs, Budget Division, New Delhi, p.40.
20. *Status paper on government debt.* Ministry of Finance, Department of Economic Affairs, Budget Division, New Delhi, p.40.
21. Clements, et al. *External debt, public investment, and growth in low-income countries.* IMF Working Paper, WP/03/249.
22. Krugman, Paul (1988). *Financing vs. forgiving a debt overhang: Some analytical issues.* NBER Working Paper No. 2486. Cambridge, MA: National Bureau of Economic Research.
23. Kanagasabapathy, K., Singh, C., & Shimpi, S. (2018). *Need to rationalise rising interest burden on Central Government Public Debt.* EPW, Vol. no. 4.
24. "Status Paper on Government Debt 2016–17" Ministry of Finance, Department of Economic Affairs, Budget Division, New Delhi.
25. "Status Paper on Government Debt 2016–17" Ministry of Finance, Department of Economic Affairs, Budget Division, New Delhi
26. Kanagasabapathy, K., Singh, C., & Shimpi, S. (2018). *Need to rationalise rising interest burden on Central Government Public Debt.* EPW, Vol. no. 4.
27. Annual Report 2012–2013, *Reserve Bank of India*, Mumbai, p.118.
28. Annual Report 2012–2013, *Reserve Bank of India*, Mumbai, p.85.
29. Engen & Skinner. (1992). *Fiscal policy and economic growth* (p.1). NBER, Working paper no. 4223.
30. Bhattacharyya, I., & Mukherjee, A. (2018). *Does fiscal policy matter for growth? Evidence from EMEs.* RBI Occasional Papers, Vol. 39.
31. Press Information Bureau, Government of India, January 29, 2018.
32. A case for widening the tax base. *The Hindu Business Line*, January 30, 2019.

33. Brumby, J. (2007). Improving allocative efficiency. In Robinson, M. (Eds.), *Performance Budgeting. Procyclicality of Financial Systems in Asia*. London: Palgrave Macmillan.
34. Estrada, et al. (2015). *Fiscal policy and equity in advanced economies: Lessons for Asia* (p.14). ERIA Discussion Paper Series.
35. Soli, V. O., Harvey, S. K., & Hagan, E. (2008). Fiscal policy, private investment and economic growth: the case of Ghana. *Studies in Economics and Finance, 25* (2), 112–130.
36. Fiscal Responsibility and Budget Management Act, 2003 (Act no. 39 of 2003). Retrieved from https://dea.gov.in (Accessed on December 22, 2016).
37. Singh, C., et al. (2017). *A review of the FRBM Act*. Working paper NO: 550, IIM Bangalore.
38. Medium-term fiscal policy cum fiscal policy strategy statement. Retrieved from https://www.indiabudget.gov.in (Accessed on April 29, 2019).
39. Medium-term fiscal policy cum fiscal policy strategy statement. Retrieved from https://www.indiabudget.gov.in (Accessed on April 29, 2019).
40. Government abandons revenue deficit targeting. *Livemint*, February 5, 2018.
41. FRBM review committee report, Volume 1, January 2017. Ministry of Finance. Govt. of India.

CHAPTER 26

CENTER–STATE FINANCIAL RELATIONS IN INDIA

Socialism and federalism are necessarily political opposites, because the former demands that centralized concentration of power which the latter by definition denies.

—**Felix Morley**

INTRODUCTION

There are two types of systems prevalent in the world: Unitary and Federal system. A unitary system is one in which the entire government power is conferred by the constitution on a single central organ and state or other local governments derive authority from this central organ. Examples are France, Germany, and Great Britain. On the contrary, in the federal system, there is clear-cut division and distribution of power between central government and state or local government. Examples are the United States and Canada. However, Indian Constitution is called quasi-federal because it has a unique blend of unitary and federal features. Since resources of the central government yield a substantial surplus, while state governments experience heavy deficits, a mechanism of transfer of resources from the center to the states has been provided. The Indian Constitution envisages that fiscal resources would be transferred from the union to the states on the recommendations of the Finance Commission.

In this chapter, we propose to discuss the following topics:

- Fiscal Federalism and Its Principles
- Finance Commission
- Important Concepts and Definitions Related to Center–State Financial Relations
- 14th Finance Commission and Its Evaluation
- Salient Features of 15th Finance Commission
- Critical Assessment of Center–State Financial Relations

FISCAL FEDERALISM AND ITS PRINCIPLES

The term fiscal federalism was coined by American economist Richard Musgrave in 1959. Fiscal federalism deals with the division of governmental functions and financial relations among levels of government.[1] It has certain principles that become guiding force for the devolution of resources between center and state.

1. There must be a spirit of "independence and responsibility" among the different organs of the state. The division of financial resources and obligations as between the two levels of governments should correspond to the division of powers and functions. Political autonomy will be meaningless unless it is supported by financial autonomy.
2. The federal finance must subscribe to the principle of "adequacy and elasticity." The sources of revenue for each level of government should be such that the revenues generated should not remain static but should be quite elastic. The revenues should increase as the needs of the governments grow.
3. The system of distribution of functions should conform to the requirements of "efficiency and economy." It refers to the nature of tax to be levied at union and state level and administrative efficiency/cost of tax collection.
4. Viewed within the framework of welfare economics, "equitable distribution of wealth and income" of the community is the proper concern of a welfare state. Richer states can be taxed more, and poorer states can get more resources to spend since the sacrifice in extra taxation in richer states is less than the benefit that will be derived if that money were spent in poorer states.
5. "Fiscal equalization" is a systematic process of intergovernmental financial transfers directed toward equalization of the budget capacity or economic performance. Grants-in-aid, subsidies, sharing of taxes, and joint exploitation of a source of revenue are used to bring about fiscal equalization transfers. In India, Finance Commission (FC) deliberates and cooperates between two levels of government and smoothen the process of adjustment in fiscal processes.

Finance Commission

The transfers from center to states take place through three channels, namely Finance Commission, Planning Commission, and Central Ministries, of which the transfers from Finance Commission are predominant.[2] Article 280 of Indian Constitution provides for the appointment of Finance Commission by Indian President. The First Finance Commission was established by the President of India in 1951. The Finance Commission (Miscellaneous Provisions) Act, 1951, additionally defines the terms of qualification, appointment and disqualification, the term, eligibility and powers of the FC. As per the Constitution, the Commission is appointed every 5 years and consists of a chairman and four other members. There have been 15 commissions till date, and so far 14 commissions have submitted their report.

The Finance Commission is entrusted with the task of recommending[3] (Table 26.1):

1. the distribution of net proceeds of taxes to be shared between the union and the states, and the allocation of shares of such proceeds among the states;
2. the principles which should govern the payment of the union grants-in-aid of the revenue of the states; and
3. any other matter concerning financial relations between the union and the states.

TABLE 26.1 Finance Commissions of India

Finance Commission	Year of Estb.	Chairman	Operational Duration
First	1951	K.C. Neogy	1952–1957
Second	1956	K. Santhanam	1957–1962
Third	1960	A.K. Chanda	1962–1966
Fourth	1964	P.V. Rajamannarr	1966–1969
Fifth	1968	Mahaveer Tyagi	1969–1974
Sixth	1972	K. Brahmananda Reddy	1974–1979
Seventh	1977	J.M. Shellet	1979–1984
Eighth	1983	Y.B. Chavan	1984–1989
Ninth	1987	N.K.P. Salve	1989–1995
Tenth	1992	K.C Pant	1995–2000
Eleventh	1998	A.M. Khusro	2000–2005
Twelfth	2003	C. Rangarajan	2005–2010
Thirteenth	2007	Vijay Kelkar	2010–2015
Fourteenth	2013	Y.V Reddy	2015–2020
Fifteenth	2017	N.K. Singh	2020–2025

Source: Previous Commissions. Retrieved from https://fincomindia.nic.in (accessed on November 18, 2016).

Important Concepts and Definitions Related to Center–State Financial Relations

Tax Devolution

Article 280 (3) (a) of the Constitution mandates Finance Commission to make recommendations regarding devolution of taxes, that is, "the distribution between the union and the states of the net proceeds of taxes to be divided between the as well as the allocation between the states of the respective shares of such proceeds".[4] The distribution of the net proceeds of taxes of the Union between the union and the states is called *vertical devolution* and the allocation between the states of the respective shares of such proceeds is called *horizontal devolution.*

Divisible Pool

The divisible pool is that portion of gross tax revenue which is distributed between the center and the states. The divisible pool consists of all taxes, except surcharges and cess levied for specific purpose, net of collection charges.

Grants-in-aid

Apart from tax devolution, horizontal imbalances can also be addressed by the Finance Commission through the system of grants in-aid. Finance Commissions, under Article 275 of the Constitution, are required to recommend the principles as well as the quantum of grants to those states which are in need of assistance and that different sums may be fixed for different states.[5] Over the years, the scope of grants to states has been extended further to cover special problems. Conventionally, Finance Commission recommends grants in-aid for five purposes—revenue deficit, disaster relief, local bodies, sector-specific schemes, and state specific schemes.

Revenue Deficit

Such grants cover the non-plan revenue deficit and had been the largest component of Finance Commission grants. It was only in the 13th Finance Commission that the grants to local bodies formed the largest component of grants-in-aid.

Disaster Relief

It was second Finance Commission that first recommended setting up of specific amounts as grants-in-aid under the "margin money" scheme to meet expenditures on disaster relief. Later different FCs dealt with this issue differently and recommended devolution by establishing different types of funds. With the enactment of the Disaster Management Act, 2005, the 13th Finance Commission recommended establishment of National Disaster Response Fund (NDRF), which was accepted and notified by the Union Government. Since 2010–11, the Union Government has been financing the NDRF through the levy of a cess and the State Disaster Response Fund as grants-in-aid, based on the recommendations of 13th FC.

Local Bodies

It was the 10th Finance Commission which first recommended grants for local bodies. The Finance Commission is required to recommend the measures needed to augment the Consolidated Fund of a State to supplement the resources of the panchayats and municipalities in the state, on the basis of the recommendations made by the Finance Commission of the State.

Sector-specific Grants

Sector-specific grants are being granted by the finance commission on the basis of certain common, as well as specific, needs of the states. There are generally three objectives in recommending grants. The first is to reduce disparities in the standards of various administrative and social services across states. The second is to enable particular states to meet special financial burdens emerging from their peculiar circumstances. The third is to provide resources for specific activities considered to be national priorities.

State-specific Grants

It was the 6th Finance Commission which first recommended grants-in-aid for specified needs of the states. The objectives of such grants are to address the problem of deprivation, generate significant externalities (especially environmental externalities), meet the needs of the marginal groups or areas, and encourage policy innovations. The grants-in-aid recommended for state-specific schemes and projects have steadily increased from ₹1,246 crore (FC-X) to ₹27,945 crore (FC-XIII).

Fiscal Capacity

Fiscal capacity can be defined as the potential ability of the state government to raise revenue from its own sources to provide public goods and other functions of the state. It is an important factor in determining the allocation of intergovernmental grants in order to equalize the amount of resources available to each state.[6]

Income Distance

Income distance is computed by calculating difference between 3-year average gross state domestic product (GSDP) for each state with respect to state with highest per capita GSDP. The income distance criterion was first used by 12th FC, measured by per capita GSDP as a proxy for the distance between states in tax capacity.[7] In the 14th FC, income distance enjoys 50% weightage and Haryana was taken as a benchmark state.*

Fiscal Discipline

Fiscal discipline refers to ideal balance between receipts and expenditure of the government and reflects fiscal health of the state/country over the longer period of time. Fiscal discipline as a criterion for tax devolution was introduced by 11th Finance Commission to provide an incentive to states managing their finances prudently. The criterion continued in the 12th and 13th Finance Commission as well without any change. The index of fiscal discipline is arrived at by comparing improvements in the ratio of own revenue receipts of a state to its total revenue expenditure relative to the corresponding average across all states.[8] Fiscal discipline enjoyed 17.5% weightage in 13th Finance Commission but excluded by 14th FC.

Special Category States (SCS) and General Category States (GCS)

The fifth Finance Commission introduced the concept of a special category state in the year 1969 to provide certain disadvantaged states with preferential treatment in the form of central assistance and tax breaks. The SCS states in India are Assam, Nagaland, Jammu and Kashmir, Arunachal Pradesh, Himachal Pradesh, Manipur, Meghalaya, Mizoram, Sikkim, Tripura, and Uttarakhand. All other states barring these 11 states are treated as General Category States. The rationale for special status is that these states, because of inherent features, have a low resource base and cannot mobilize resources for development. Some of the features required for special status are (1) hilly and difficult terrain; (2) low population density or sizeable share of tribal population; (3) strategic location along borders with neighboring countries; (4) economic and infrastructural backwardness; and (5) non-viable nature of state finances.[9] Following the constitution of the NITI Aayog (after the dissolution of the Planning Commission) and the recommendations of the Fourteenth Finance Commission (FFC), Central plan assistance to SCS states has been subsumed in an increased devolution of the divisible pool to all states (from 32% in the 13th Finance Commission recommendations to 42%) and do not appear in plan expenditure any longer.[10]

---

*Goa had the highest per capita GSDP followed by Sikkim. But since these states are very small, the third highest state, Haryana, was chosen as benchmark.

TABLE 26.2 Gadgil-Mukherjee Formula

Criteria	Weight (%)	Remarks
Population	60	
Per capita income	25	
1. Deviation Method	20	Covering states with per capita SDP below national average
2. Distance Method	5	For all states
Performance in tax effort, fiscal management and progress in respect of national objectives	7.5	Tax policy (2.5%), Fiscal Management (2.0%), National objectives (3%) comprising population control (1.0%), elimination of illiteracy (1.0%), timely completion of Externally Aided Projects (0.5%), and land reforms (0.5%)
Special problems	7.5	

Source: *Report of the working group on state's financial resources for the twelfth five year plan* (2012–2017). Planning Commission, Government of India, May 2012.

Gadgil-Mukherjee Formula

The Gadgil-Mukherjee formula was given by (and also named after) D. R. Gadgil, former Deputy Chairman, Planning Commission in the year 1969. The formula was adopted for distribution of plan assistance among states during Fourth and Fifth Five-year Plans. During the first three five-year plans and three annual plans (1966–1969), the central assistance to states (CAS) was not provided objectively, and it failed to generate balanced regional growth among states. The Gadgil Formula comprised following weights, namely (1) Population (60%); (2) Per Capita Income (10%); (3) Tax Effort (10%); (4) Ongoing Irrigation and Power Projects (10%); and (5) Special Problems (10%). Under the formula, 30% of total plan assistance was in the forms of grants and 70% in the form of loans. The original formula has been subjected to changes from time to time due to reservation of states. Most of the states were unhappy with the modified Gadgil formula, and keeping in view their concerns, a committee was constituted under the chairmanship of Pranab Mukherjee, the deputy chairman of planning commission, to evolve a suitable formula for distribution of central assistance.

The Gadgil-Mukherjee Formula works in two stages. First, 30% of total assistance money is earmarked for the special category states. This may be distributed among these states on the basis of their plan size and past plan expenditures, without using any explicit criteria. The remaining 70% are distributed among the general category states according to a set of criteria with relative weights[11] (Table 26.2).

However, Gadgil-Mukherjee formula has been criticized on the basis of two major reasons. First, there is no explicit basis for a 30% earmarking for the Special Category states; and second, shares determined on the basis of tax effort and fiscal discipline indexes are unscaled implying that if a large state like Tamil Nadu and a small state like Goa had the same tax–effort ratio, they will get the same share regardless of their size. This would lead to a very large per capita share for Goa compared to that for Tamil Nadu, for example, for the same tax effort.

State Fiscal Commission

The State Finance Commission was created by the 73rd and 74th Constitutional (Amendment) Acts. Articles 243 (I) and 243 (Y) of the Constitution provides for State Finance Commission (SFC).*

*Article 243 (I) prescribes State Finance Commission for Panchayats and Article 243 (Y) prescribes State Finance Commission for municipalities.

Accordingly, SFCs are required to recommend (a) the principles that should govern the distribution between the State on the one hand and the local bodies on the other of the net proceeds of taxes, etc., leviable by the state and the inter-se allocation between different panchayats and municipalities, (b) the determination of taxes, duties, tolls, and fees which may be assigned to, or appropriated by the local bodies, and (c) grants-in-aid from the consolidated fund of the State to the local bodies. SFCs are also required to suggest the measures needed to improve the financial position of the panchayats and municipalities. The importance of the SFCs in the scheme of fiscal decentralization is that besides arbitrating on the claims to resources by the state government and the local bodies, their recommendations would impart greater stability and predictability to the transfer mechanism.[12]

Fourteenth Finance Commission and Its Evaluation

The Fourteenth Finance Commission (FFC) of India was constituted by government on January 2, 2013 under the chairmanship of former RBI governor Y. V. Reddy. The Commission submitted its recommendations for the period 2015–16–2020–21. Following are the major recommendations of FFC.

1. *Vertical Devolution:* With regard to vertical distribution, FFC has recommended by majority decision that the states' share in the net proceeds of the Union tax revenues be 42%. The recommendation of tax devolution at 42% (₹3,948,187 crore) is a huge jump from the 32% recommended by the 13th FC. This is the largest ever change in the percentage of devolution. In the past, when FCs have recommended an increase, it has been in the range of 1–2% increase.[13]
2. *Horizontal Devolution:* The FFC has proposed a new horizontal formula for the distribution of the states' share in divisible pool among the states. There are changes both in the variables included/excluded and in the weights assigned to them. Relative to the 13th FC, the FFC has incorporated two new variables: 2011 population and forest cover, and excluded the fiscal discipline variable (Table 26.3).[14]

TABLE 26.3 Horizontal Devolution Formula in the 13th and 14th Finance Commissions

Criteria	Weight (%)	
	13th	14th*
Population	25	17.5
Demographic Change	0	10
Income Distance	47.5	50
Area	10	15
Forest Cover	0	7.5
Fiscal Discipline	17.5	0
Total	100	100

Source: Report of 14th Finance Commission. Retrieved from https://fincomindia.nic.in (accessed on November 23, 2016).

Population is as per 1971 census; demographic changes are changes in population as per 2011 census capturing changes such as migration and age structure since 1971; income distance is computed by calculating difference between 3-year average GSDP for each state with respect to state with highest per capita GSDP; forest cover to take into account the opportunity cost in terms of area not available for other economic activities; area has a floor limit of 2% for smaller states in deciding horizontal devolution.

The table 26.4 provides details about share of different states in tax devolution.

TABLE 26.4 Share of States in Tax Devolution (%)

States	Share of States	States	Share of States
Andhra Pradesh	4.305	Manipur	0.617
Arunachal Pradesh	1.370	Meghalaya	0.642
Assam	3.311	Mizoram	0.460
Bihar	9.665	Nagaland	0.498
Chhattisgarh	3.080	Odisha	4.642
Goa	0.378	Punjab	1.577
Gujarat	3.084	Rajasthan	5.495
Haryana	1.084	Sikkim	0.367
Himachal Pradesh	0.713	Tamil Nadu	4.023
Jammu and Kashmir	1.854	Telangana	2.437
Jharkhand	3.139	Tripura	0.642
Karnataka	4.713	Uttar Pradesh	17.959
Kerala	2.500	Uttarakhand	1.052
Madhya Pradesh	7.548	West Bengal	7.324
Maharashtra	5.521	All states	100

Source: 14th Finance Commission Report, p.95. Retrieved from https://fincomindia.nic.in (accessed on November 23, 2016).

3. *Grants-in-aid:* As mentioned earlier, the previous FCs recommended grants-in-aid for five purposes—revenue deficit, disaster relief, local bodies, sector-specific schemes, and state-specific schemes. Keeping in view the principles adopted by previous FCs, the views expressed by Union and states, the 14th Finance Commission adopted following approach to grants-in-aid:[15]

   (a) The Finance Commission recommended a total revenue deficit grant of ₹194,821 crore during the period 2015–2020 for 11 states.

   (b) For the first time (since its beginning), there is no grant for sector-specific or state-specific schemes. The Finance Commission justified it on the ground that such grants were not based on any formula or any uniform principal and have thus been arbitrary in character. Further, there was duplication of funding in many such schemes.

   (c) Under grant to local bodies, the Finance Commission has used 2011 population data with weight of 90% and area with weight of 10%. The total size of the grant works out at ₹287,436 crore for the period 2015–2020, constituting an assistance of ₹488 per capita per annum to an aggregate level. The share of panchayats and municipalities is in the ratio of 70:30. Further, the grants will be made in two parts—a basic grant and a performance grant. For gram panchayats, 90% of the grant will be basic grant and 10% will be performance grant. For municipalities, this division is in the ratio of 80:20.

TABLE 26.5 Transfers Recommended by 14th Finance Commission

Items	₹Crore
Tax devolution to states	3,948,187
Grants in-aid (A+B+C)	537,354
Post devolution revenue deficit grants to states	194,821
Disaster relief grant to states	55,097
Grants to local bodies to states	287,436
Aggregate transfers to states from finance commission (1+2)	4,485,541
Divisible pool	9,400,444
Fiscal space available with the union government (4−3) of which	4,914,904
Provision for other transfers (expected) to states (7−2)	1,477,943
Total grants from the union to states	2,015,297
Aggregate transfers to states (1+7)	5,963,484
As a percentage of divisible pool	
Tax devolution to states	42
Grants from Finance Commission to states	5.72
Tax devolution and Finance Commission grants to states	47.72
Fiscal space with the union of which	52.28
Provision for other transfers (expected) to states	15.72
Aggregate transfers to states	63.44

Source: 14th Finance Commission Report. Retrieved from https://fincomindia.nic.in (accessed on November 24, 2016).

(d) The 14th Finance Commission observed that NDRF has so far been almost wholly through the levy of cess on selected items, but if the cesses are discontinued or when they are subsumed under the GST in future, the Union Government should consider ensuring an assured source of funding for the NDRF. As mentioned earlier, the 13th Finance Commission had recommended merger of NCCF with NDRF. Similarly, at state level, CRF was merged with SDRF. The 14th Finance Commission recommended that all states contribute 10% to SDRF during award period, with the remaining 90% coming from the Union Government. Commission announced aggregate corpus for all states of ₹61,219 crore under SDRF for the award period (Table 26.5).

4. *Fiscal Environment and Fiscal Consolidation Roadmap:* In the light of approach to fiscal consolidation and the fiscal roadmap as developed through our assessment of Union and State finances, the commission recommend the following set of rules.[16]
   (a) For the Union Government, the ceiling on fiscal deficit will be 3% of GDP from the year 2016–17 onward up to the end of our award period.
   (b) Fiscal deficit of all states will be affixed to an annual limit of 3% of GSDP.
   (c) States will be further eligible for an additional borrowing limit of 0.25% of GSDP in a given year for which the borrowing limits are to be fixed.
   (d) The Union Government should consider making an amendment to the FRBM Act to omit the definition of effective revenue deficit (ERD) from April 1, 2015.
   (e) In order to accord greater sanctity and legitimacy to fiscal management legislation, Union Government should replace the existing FRBM Act with a Debt Ceiling and Fiscal Responsibility Legislation.

5. *Goods and Service Tax:* In the absence of clarity on the design of GST and the final rate structure, the commission was unable to estimate revenue implications and quantify the amount of compensation in case of revenue loss to the states due to the introduction of GST.[17] Therefore, given the scale of reform and the apprehensions of revenue uncertainty raised by the states, the revenue compensation was fixed for five years. The commission recommends 100% compensation to be paid to the states in the first, second, and third years; 75% compensation in the fourth year; and 50% compensation in the fifth and final year. The commission also recommended creation of an autonomous and independent GST Compensation Fund.[18]
6. *Toward Cooperative Federalism:* The commission observed that a compelling case has been made for reforming the existing system of fiscal transfers from the union to the states in a comprehensive manner. The commission felt that the existing arrangements for transfers between the union and the states need to be reviewed with a view to minimizing discretion, improving the design of transfers, avoiding duplication and promoting cooperative federalism. For promoting cooperative federalism, the government can consider the evolution of a new institutional arrangement, for:
   - **(a)** identifying the sectors in the states that should be eligible for grants from the union;
   - **(b)** indicating criteria for inter-state distribution;
   - **(c)** helping design schemes with appropriate flexibility being given to the states regarding implementation; and
   - **(d)** identifying and providing area-specific grants.

FIFTEENTH FINANCE COMMISSION

In pursuance of clause (1) of article 280 of the Constitution, the President has constituted 15th Finance Commission consisting of Shri N. K. Singh, the Member of Parliament and the former Secretary to the Government of India, as the Chairman. The Commission shall make its report available by October 30, 2019, covering a period of 5 years commencing April 1, 2020, till March 31, 2025. Following are the key features of 15th FC.[19]

1. The Commission shall make recommendations as to the following matters, namely:
   - **(a)** the distribution between the union and the states of the net proceeds of taxes and the allocation between the states of the respective shares of such proceeds;
   - **(b)** the principles which should govern the grants-in-aid of the revenues of the states out of the Consolidated Fund of India and the sums to be paid to the states by way of grants-in-aid of their revenues under Article 275 of the Constitution; and
   - **(c)** the measures needed to augment the Consolidated Fund of a State to supplement the resources of the panchayats and municipalities in the State on the basis of the recommendations made by the Finance Commission of the State.
2. The Commission shall review the current status of the finance, deficit, debt levels, cash balances, and fiscal discipline efforts of the union and the states, and recommend a fiscal consolidation roadmap for sound fiscal management. It may ask the Central and State Governments to adhere to appropriate levels of general and consolidated government debt and deficit levels, while fostering higher inclusive growth in the country, guided by the principles of equity, efficiency, and transparency. The Commission may also examine whether revenue deficit grants be provided at all.

3. The Commission may consider proposing measurable performance-based incentives for states, at the appropriate level of government, in following areas:
   (a) efforts made by the states in expansion and deepening of tax net under GST;
   (b) efforts and progress made in moving toward replacement rate of population growth;
   (c) achievements in implementation of flagship schemes of government of India, disaster resilient infrastructure, sustainable development goals, and quality of expenditure;
   (d) progress made in increasing capital expenditure, eliminating losses of power sector, and improving the quality of such expenditure in generating future income streams;
   (e) progress made in increasing tax/non-tax revenues, promoting savings by adoption of direct benefit transfers and Public Finance Management System, promoting digital economy and removing layers between the government and the beneficiaries;
   (f) progress made in promoting ease of doing business by effecting related policy and regulatory changes and promoting labor intensive growth;
   (g) provision of grants-in-aid to local bodies for basic services, including quality human resources and implementation of performance grant system in improving delivery of services;
   (h) control or lack of it in incurring expenditure on populist measures; and
   (i) progress made in sanitation, solid waste management and bringing in behavioral change to end open defecation.
4. The Commission shall use the population data of 2011 while making its recommendations.

Fifteenth Finance Commission Recommendations

The 15th Finance Commission was chaired by Mr. N.K. Singh, and the report was titled '*Finance Commission in COVID times*.' The Commission was required to submit two reports—the first report, consisting of recommendations for the financial year 2020–21. The final report with recommendations for the 2021–26 period. This is the first ever Commission to have given recommendations spanning a period of six years, that is, 2020–26. The Commission was asked to prepare a report on a many new and unique demand via its Terms of Reference (ToR).

The Terms of Reference (ToR) of Fifteenth FC were different from previous commissions on following grounds:

- **Fiscal Consolidation Roadmap:** The Commission was asked to review the current finances of both state and central government and recommend a fiscal consolidation roadmap for sound fiscal management. This task became all the more difficult during the covid times, as fiscal deficit increased all-time high.
- **Indirect Taxation System:** The commission was asked to evaluate the impact of the GST, including the need for payment of compensation for possible loss of revenues for 5 years, and abolition of a number of cesses.
- **Measurable Performance Incentives:** The Commission was asked to consider proposing of measurable performance-based incentives for States, at the appropriate level of government in areas like deepening of tax nets, population control, power sector reforms etc.

- **Using 2011 population against 1971 population data:** The Commission had to use the population data of 2011while making its recommendations. This was tricky as there was an active opposition from Southern States on usage 2011 population data.
- **Other unique demands:**
  1. Analyzing the possibility of creation of a non-lapsable defense fund.
  2. Reviewing the present arrangements on financing Disaster Management initiatives.

Recommendations given by the Fifteenth FC Report for 2021–26 period

Vertical Devolution

- The commission has recommended maintaining the vertical devolution at 41%.
- The idea is to maintain the same level of devolution as recommended by 14th FC (i.e., 42%), the adjustment of about 1% has been made due to the changed status of the erstwhile State of Jammu and Kashmir into the new Union Territories of Ladakh and Jammu and Kashmir.
- Gross tax revenue for 5-year period is expected to be ₹135.2 lakh crore. Out of that, Divisible pool (after deducting cesses and surcharges & cost of collection) is estimated to be ₹103 lakh crore.

Horizontal Devolution

- The horizontal devolution is primarily based on three principles namely need of states, equity among states and performance of states. To balance all three principles, six criteria are used to calculate tax distribution- Income Distance (45%), Area (15%), Population (2011) (15%), Demographic Performance (12.5%), Forest and Ecology (10%) and Tax and Fiscal Transfers (2.5%).
- Income distance: Income distance is the distance of a state's income from the state with the highest income. Income of a state has been computed as average per capita GSDP during the three-year period between 2016–17 and 2018–19. A state with lower per capita income will have a higher share to maintain equity among states.
- Demographic performance: The demographic performance criterion has been used to reward efforts made by states in controlling their population. States with a lower fertility ratio will be scored higher on this criterion.

TABLE 26.6 Criteria for devolution

Criteria	14th FC 2015–20	15th FC 2020–21	15th FC 2021–26
Income Distance	50.0	45.0	45.0
Area	15.0	15.0	15.0
Population (1971)	17.5	–	–
Population (2011)#	10.0	15.0	15.0
Demographic Performance	–	12.5	12.5
Forest Cover	7.5	–	–
Forest and Ecology	–	10.0	10.0
Tax and fiscal efforts*	–	2.5	2.5
Total	**100**	**100**	**100**

Source: 15th Finance Commission Report accessed from https://fincomindia.nic.in, on July 15, 2021.

- Forest and ecology: This is calculated as the share of the dense forest of each state in the total dense forest of all the states.
- Tax and fiscal efforts: This criterion has been used to reward states with higher tax collection efficiency. It is measured as the ratio of the average per capita own tax revenue and the average per capita state GDP during the three years between 2016–17 and 2018–19.

Grants to States

- Revenue deficit grants: 17 states will receive grants worth ₹2.9 lakh crore to eliminate revenue deficit.

TABLE 26.7 Individual share of states in the taxes devolved by the centre (out of 100)

State	14th FC 2015–20	15th FC 2020–21	15th FC 2021–26
Andhra Pradesh	4.305	4.111	4.047
Arunachal Pradesh	1.370	1.760	1.757
Assam	3.311	3.131	3.128
Bihar	9.665	10.061	10.058
Chhattisgarh	3.080	3.418	3.407
Goa	0.378	0.386	0.386
Gujarat	3.084	3.398	3.478
Haryana	1.084	1.082	1.093
Himachal Pradesh	0.713	0.799	0.830
Jammu & Kashmir	1.854	–	–
Jharkhand	3.139	3.313	3.307
Karnataka	4.713	3.646	3.647
Kerala	2.500	1.943	1.925
Madhya Pradesh	7.548	7.886	7.850
Maharashtra	5.521	6.135	6.317
Manipur	0.617	0.718	0.716
Meghalaya	0.642	0.765	0.767
Mizoram	0.460	0.506	0.500
Nagaland	0.498	0.573	0.569
Odisha	4.642	4.629	4.528
Punjab	1.577	1.788	1.807
Rajasthan	5.495	5.979	6.026
Sikkim	0.367	0.388	0.388
Tamil Nadu	4.023	4.189	4.079
Telangana	2.437	2.133	2.102
Tripura	0.642	0.709	0.708
Uttar Pradesh	17.959	17.931	17.939
Uttarakhand	1.052	1.104	1.118
West Bengal	7.324	7.519	7.523
Total	**100**	**100**	**100**

Source: 15th Finance Commission Report accessed from https://fincomindia.nic.in/

- Sector-specific grants: Sector-specific grants of ₹1.3 lakh crore will be given to states for sectors like health, education, implementation of agricultural reforms etc. A portion of these grants will be performance-linked.
- State-specific grants: The Commission recommended state-specific grants of about ₹0.5 lakh crore. These will be given in the areas of social needs, administrative governance and infrastructure etc.
- Grants to local bodies: The total grants to local bodies will be ₹4.36 lakh crore (a portion of grants to be performance-linked). Grants to local bodies (other than health grants) will be distributed among states based on population and area, with 90% and 10% weightage, respectively. Also, no grants will be released to local bodies of a state after March 2024 if the state does not constitute State Finance Commission and act upon its recommendations by then.
- Disaster risk management: The Commission recommended retaining the existing cost sharing patterns between the centre and states for disaster management funds. The cost sharing pattern between centre and states is: (i) 90:10 for north-eastern and Himalayan states, and (ii) 75:25 for all other states. State disaster management funds will have a corpus of ₹1.6 lakh crore (centre's share is ₹1.2 lakh crore).
- Incubation of new cities: Finance Commission has recommended ₹8,000 crore to states for incubation of new cities, granting ₹1,000 crore each for eight new cities. The focus of urban grants for million-plus cities is improvement in air quality and meeting the service level benchmark of solid waste management and sanitation.

Total transfers

- Including total grants of ₹10.33 lakh crore and tax devolution of ₹42.2 lakh crore (41% of ₹103 lakh crore), aggregate transfers to States is estimated to remain at around 50.9% of the divisible pool during 2021–26 period.
- Total transfers (devolution + grants) constitute about 34% of estimated Gross Revenue Receipts of the Union.

Fiscal Management and Consolidation Roadmap

- The Commission suggested that the centre bring down fiscal deficit to 4% of GDP by 2025–26. For states, it recommended the fiscal deficit limit (as % of GSDP) of: (i) 4% in 2021–22, (ii) 3.5% in 2022–23, and (iii) 3% during 2023–26.
- Extra annual borrowing worth 0.5% of GSDP will be allowed to states during first four years (2021–25) upon undertaking power sector reforms including: (i) reduction in operational losses, (ii) reduction in revenue gap, (iii) reduction in payment of cash subsidy by adopting direct benefit transfer, and (iv) reduction in tariff subsidy as a percentage of revenue.
- It recommended forming a high-powered inter-governmental group to: (i) review the Fiscal Responsibility and Budget Management Act (FRBM), (ii) recommend a new FRBM framework for Centre as well as states and oversee its implementation.
- The inverted duty structure between intermediate inputs and final outputs present in GST needs to be resolved. Revenue neutrality of GST rate should be restored which has been compromised by multiple rate structure and several downward adjustments.
- A comprehensive framework for public financial management should be developed. An independent Fiscal Council should be established with powers to assess records from the Centre as well as states.

TABLE 26.8 Transfers Recommended by 15th Finance Commission

Grants	Amount
Revenue deficit grants	**2,94,514**
Local governments grants	**4,36,361**
Urban Local Bodies	*1,21,055*
Rural Local Bodies	*2,36,805*
Health Grants	*70,051*
*Other Grants**	*8,450*
Disaster management grants	**1,22,601**
Sector-specific grants	**1,29,987**
Health	*31,755*
School Education	*4,800*
Higher Education	*6,143*
Implementation of agricultural reforms	*45,000*
Maintenance of PMGSY roads	*27,539*
Judiciary	*10,425*
Statistics	*1,175*
Aspirational districts and blocks	*3,150*
State-specific grants	**49,599**
Total	**10,33,062**

Source: 15th Finance Commission Report accessed from https://fincomindia.nic.in/

Note: *Other grants to local bodies comprise grants for: (i) incubation of new cities (₹8,000 crore), and National Data Centre (₹450 crore).

Other recommendations

- Disaster Management Fund: Setting up the state and national level Disaster Risk Mitigation Fund (SDRMF), in line with the provisions of the Disaster Management Act.
- Defense Modernization Fund: Creation of a separate non-lapsable fund for modernization of defense and internal security. The objective is to bridge the gap between defense budget allocations and the projected budgetary requirements.
- The Commission has also recommended that ₹1,000 crore per annum should be allocated from this fund for the welfare of families of the defense and CAPF personnel who sacrifice their lives in frontline duties.
- Health: States should increase spending on health to more than 8% of their budget by 2022. Primary healthcare expenditure should be two-thirds of the total health expenditure by 2022.
- Centrally sponsored schemes (CSS): A threshold should be fixed for annual allocation to CSS below which the funding for a CSS should be stopped (to phase out CSS which outlived its utility or has insignificant outlay)

Critical Assessment of Center–State Financial Relations

Points in Favor

Balancing Fiscal Autonomy and Fiscal Space

The 14th Finance Commission has made far-reaching changes in tax devolution that will move the country toward greater fiscal federalism, conferring more fiscal autonomy on the states. The share of the states in the net proceeds of central taxes and duties was 29.5% in 11th Finance Commission and 32% in 13th FC. In order to increase the automatic transfers to the states to give them more fiscal autonomy, the 14th Finance Commission raised the share of states from 32–42% of divisible pool. Although there is concern that higher tax devolution may adversely affect the fiscal space or fiscal consolidation path of the Center, to ensure that the Center's fiscal space is secured, Finance Commission has also suggested commensurate reductions in the Central Assistance to States (CAS) known as "plan transfers."[20] Though few have objected about reduced CAS transfers to the states, it must be remembered that CAS transfers per capita are only mildly progressive as compared to tax transfers. It is because CAS transfers had moved away from being Gadgil formula-based to being more discretionary in the last few years. Further apart from higher tax devolution and resultant progressivity, the states will have greater autonomy on the revenue and expenditure fronts (due to reduction in CAS transfer).

Balanced Regional Development

It has always been the endeavor of all the FCs to bring down the regional imbalances. Different FCs recommended devolution of funds so as to reduce regional gaps. All states stand to gain from FFC transfers in absolute terms. However, to assess the distributional effects, the benefits can be measured in terms of population, per capita income, state's own tax revenue receipts and increase in the divisible pool. Following are the observations.[21]

1. The biggest gainers in absolute terms under GCS are Uttar Pradesh, West Bengal, and Madhya Pradesh, while for SCS it is Jammu and Kashmir, Himachal Pradesh, and Assam.
2. The major gainers in per capita terms turn out to be Kerala, Chhattisgarh, and Madhya Pradesh for GCS and Arunachal Pradesh, Mizoram, and Sikkim for SCS.
3. In addition to substantial spending capacity to the states, 14th Finance Commission transfers are highest for Chhattisgarh, Bihar, and Jharkhand among the GCS and for states like Arunachal Pradesh, Mizoram, and Jammu and Kashmir among the SCS.
4. In terms of states' own tax revenues, the largest gains accrue to GCS of Bihar, Jharkhand, and Chhattisgarh and SCS of Arunachal Pradesh, Mizoram, and Nagaland.
5. The 14th Finance Commission transfers are progressive in nature, that is, states with lower per capita Net State Domestic Product (NSDP) receive on average much larger transfers per capita. The correlation between per capita NSDP and 14th FC's transfer per capita is −0.72. This indicates that the Finance Commission recommendations do go in the direction of equalizing the income and fiscal disparities between the major states. However, 14th Finance Commission transfers are less progressive compared to the transfers of 13th FC. The correlation coefficient between the NSDP per capita and 13th

Finance Commission transfers per capita (average of 2011–12, 2012–13, and 2013–14) per capita was –0.84.

6. The decomposition of the resource transfers through tax devolution due to the increase in the divisible pool per se and due to the change in the horizontal devolution formula itself also has a positive bearing on different states. The significant impact due to increase in the divisible pool is on states like Uttar Pradesh, Bihar, Madhya Pradesh, West Bengal, and Andhra Pradesh (United) while states like Arunachal Pradesh, Chhattisgarh, Madhya Pradesh, Karnataka, and Jharkhand are the major gainers due to a change in the horizontal devolution formula which now gives greater weight to a state's forest cover.

Points in Disfavor

Vertical and Horizontal Fiscal Imbalances

Over the years, the center has become stronger in terms of higher revenue potential while states got burdened with greater functional responsibilities in the areas of education, health, economic and social infrastructure, social security and welfare. This has increased vertical fiscal imbalance and also horizontal fiscal imbalances due to differential performance of the states during post-reforms period. As a result, inequality across the states and within the states has increased with respect to providing public services. Such imbalances have occurred because of the following reasons.

First, the fiscal discipline enforced by the center on the states by enacting Fiscal Responsibility and Budget Management Act (FRBMA) has added pressure, particularly in improving productive assets of the poorer states. In the backward states, the fiscal discipline, though necessary, has resulted in decline in the share of capital expenditures, thus affecting the investment in social infrastructure viz. health, education, etc. As a consequence, the states are resorting to more and more on market borrowing on the face of declining central loans to states which no doubt has led to reductions in the tenure but increased the cost of borrowing and worsening state debt burdens. That Commission headed by Rangarajan recommended that if states were to be given debt relief over and above the distribution of tax proceeds, conditions of fiscal discipline should be enforced.[22] Further, it needs to be emphasized that in the present context, the burden of fiscal adjustment should squarely fall on the central government as states are already under the FRBM framework proposed by FFC and implementation of which is monitored by the union government. Any change in that framework in between would be ad hoc and arbitrary.[23]

Second, post the 14th Finance Commission award, aggregate transfers as a percentage of GDP has increased due to the increase in tax devolution, while grants as a percentage of GDP declined. Scope for further increase in the share of transfers from divisible pool is limited given the resource requirement of the union government to finance its own expenditure commitments.[24]

Third, population and geography are considered as the most important criteria for tax devolution as it is perceived to be the most important indicator of the general need of a state. This approach is justified when there are very insignificant differences in area, distribution of population, and per capita income among states. The high weightage given to population may not result in more transfers to states which are underdeveloped and having low population. The criteria such as fiscal performance, tax efforts, prudent fiscal management, and elimination of illiteracy and successful implementation of land reforms, etc., over the time have not helped state Governments.[25]

Increasing Recourse to Cess and Surcharge

It is observed that over the years there has been a proliferation of cess and surcharges in union tax revenues. As these levies are not shareable with the states, this has resulted in effective reduction in the divisible pool of resources available for transfers to states. The share of cess and surcharge in the gross tax revenues of the union government has increased from 9.43% in 2011–12 to nearly 17% in 2017–18. Increasing recourse to cess and surcharge by the union government has become a permanent instrument of resource mobilization. Though the budget 2016–17 abolished 13 cesses, the share of cess and surcharge in gross tax revenues continues to be high. Continuing with this practice would mean denial of national revenue to the states, which is against the spirit of the Constitution. Also when the country has moved toward an integrated GST, it is time these levies are discontinued for a smooth transition to the new tax system.[26] While the 13th Finance Commission had recommended a review of this trend to reduce the share of such levies in the gross tax revenues, the 14th Finance Commission argued that there are two ways to address this concern: by amending the Constitution to include these items in the divisible pool or by increasing the share of the divisible pool to compensate states on this account.

Decentralization Issues

Following the 73rd and 74th Amendments to the constitution, India has become a three-tier multilevel federalism. India has 2.5 lakh local governments comprising over three million elected representatives which makes it the largest democratic and federal country. There are three serious concerns with regard to grant to local bodies and financial decentralization.[27] First, the importance of the local bodies is measured in terms of the percentage of local governments to total public sector expenditure and share of local government expenditure to GDP. Compared to other countries in the world, India stands at the lower end of the spectrum with a share of local governments at only 5.1% of total public sector expenditure (Brazil, 15%; OECD, 20–30%). In fact, this share has declined by over 20% in last 5 years (from 6.4% in 1998–99).

Second, each state is required to establish a State Fiscal Commission (SFC) to review and revise the financial position of panchayat raj institutions (PRIs) and urban local governments. However, it appears that most SFCs do not take their instrumental role seriously in helping to provide the said services and in laying the foundations for participatory democracy in the country. Different union finance commissions (UFCs) have revealed several shortcomings and omission and commission of the SFCs. The main reasons are non-synchronization of the period of recommendation of SFCs and UFCs; lack of clarity in respect of the assignment of powers, authority and responsibilities of the local government; the absence of time limit to take appropriate action; etc.

Third, many studies have documented that PRIs cannot function on their own due to lack of administrative and infrastructural facilities. Given the expenditure decentralization ratio and revenue mobilization by PRIs in the state, local bodies are not in a position to carry out the assigned expenditure responsibilities. Since the amount of grants and share in the taxes given through SFCs is very low, central government needs to transfer more funds to the consolidated fund of the State to fulfill the needs of PRIs. At the same time, as more and more of the states' expenditure of the rural/urban local government is met by transfers from central government, the autonomy of the states diminishes reflecting dependency syndrome.

The Question of State Autonomy

The partition of India and its after effects created a strong public opinion in favor of "strong center and weak states" arrangement. The framers of Indian constitution in a bid to stall divisive forces in the country vested all residuary powers in the center and kept 47 items in the concurrent list. Further, the one-party rule at the center and state further cemented this relationship and the role of states became more and more secondary. In the first five decades after independence, federalism was eroded by the union's arbitrary and partisan exercise of power. In no other democracy does the federal constitution impose a uniform structure, electoral system, and bureaucratic apparatus on states and local governments. In the United States, each of the 50 states has their own constitutions and structure of government. Likewise, in Australia, Canada, and Germany, every states and self-governing territories have their own constitutions.

The time has come for India to move to the third phase of federalism. Many of our states are larger than 90% of nations on earth. We need to allow each state to have its own model of governance, bureaucracy, and local governments, but with firm safeguards to preserve national unity, separation of powers, fundamental rights, and democratic accountability. The one-size-fits-all model cannot deliver the desired outcomes of prosperity, elimination of poverty, and national greatness in a vast and diverse nation of 1.3 billion people. We need more flexible federalism, strengthening India's unity and integrity and allowing us to fulfill our potential.[28]

Summary

1. There are two types of systems prevalent in the world: Unitary and Federal. Indian constitution is quasi-federal as it is the unique blend of both types.
2. Fiscal federalism signifies division of governmental functions and financial relations among levels of government. The guiding principles of fiscal federalism are independence and responsibility, adequacy and elasticity, efficiency and economy, equity and fiscal equalization.
3. Article 280 of Indian Constitution provides for the appointment of Finance Commission by President. The first Finance Commission was established in 1951. The 15 FCs have been established so far, and 14 FCs have submitted their report.
4. Article 280 (3) (a) of the Constitution mandates Finance Commission to make recommendations regarding devolution of taxes. Distribution of taxes between the union and the states is called vertical devolution, and the allocation between the states of the respective shares of such proceeds is called horizontal devolution. Under Article 275 of the constitution, Finance Commission recommends grants-in-aid to those states which are in need of assistance and different sums are fixed for different states. Generally, Finance Commission recommends grants in-aid for five purposes—revenue deficit, disaster relief, local bodies, sector-specific schemes, and state-specific schemes. Fiscal capacity is the ability of the state to generate revenue. Fiscal discipline is the ideal balance between receipts and expenditure of the government. Special Category states are certain disadvantaged states with preferential treatment in the form of central assistance and tax breaks. There are 11 special category states in India, and the rest are general category states. The Gadgil formula was given by D. R. Gadgil, in the year 1969 for distribution of plan assistance among states. The Gadgil Formula was amended by Pranab Mukherjee, and the new formula was called Gadgil-Mukherjee formula.
5. The 14th Finance Commission of India was constituted by government in January 2013 under the chairmanship of former RBI governor Y. V. Reddy for the period 2015–16 to 2020–21. The important recommendations of the 14th Finance Commission are increase in the states' share in the net proceeds of the union tax revenues to 42%; inclusion of two new variables-population and forest cover and exclusion of the fiscal discipline variable; total revenue deficit grant of ₹194,821 crore during the period 2015–2020 for 11 states; ₹287,436 crore for local bodies; creation of aggregate corpus of ₹61,219 crore under SDRF by center and state in the ratio of 90:10; fiscal consolidation through ceiling on fiscal deficit of 3% of GDP for union and 3% of GSDP for states and replacing the existing FRBM Act with a Debt Ceiling and Fiscal Responsibility Legislation; creation of an autonomous and independent GST Compensation Fund and compensation to states to overcome the apprehension of revenue uncertainty due to GST in the form of 100% compensation during first 3 years, 75% compensation in the fourth year and 50% compensation in the fifth and final year; reviewing the existing arrangements for transfers between the union and the states so as to minimizing discretion, improving the design of transfers, avoiding duplication in order to promote cooperative federalism.
6. The 15th Finance Commission was constituted under the chairmanship of Shri N. K. Singh. The Commission shall make its report available by October 30, 2019, covering a period of 5 years commencing on April 1, 2020 till March 31, 2025. The commission is required to make recommendations with regard to tax devolution, grants-in-aid, grants to local bodies, reviewing the current fiscal consolidation efforts of the states and making appropriate recommendations for sound fiscal management; proposing measurable performance-based incentives for states.
7. The working of Finance Commission in India has merits as well as demerits. In order to ensure greater fiscal federalism, the tax devolution has been raised from 32 to 42% of divisible pool. The different FCs through their recommendations have tried to reduce the regional disparities as benefits can be measured in terms of population, per capita income, state's own tax revenue receipts, and increase in the divisible pool. Apart from some convincing merits, India's fiscal federalism suffers from certain serious shortcomings. The vertical and horizontal imbalances have emerged because of excessive pressure on states due to fiscal discipline, decline in grants to states and undue weightage given to certain variables like population. The states have also been denied their share in the divisible pool because of increasing recourse to cess and surcharge by the union which is not

sharable with the states. There are issues related to decentralization due to decline in the share of local government expenditure as a percentage to the total public-sector expenditure, shortcoming in the functioning of state FCs, lack of administrative and infrastructural facilities with PRIs. Union's arbitrary and partisan exercise of power has also eroded fiscal federalism and threatened the states' autonomy.

Endnotes

1. *Encyclopedia Britannica*. Retrieved from https://www.britannica.com (Accessed on November 18, 2016).
2. P. Sahoo, A. Sarkar (June 2013). Changing dynamics of centre-state financial relations, *Yojana.*, p.19.
3. Finance Commission, *Terms of Reference*. Retrieved from https://fincomindia.nic.in (Accessed on November 18, 2016).
4. Jacob, A. (1973 April). The finance commission: Its role in adjustment of union-state financial relations, Seminar on constitutional developments since. New Delhi: Indian Law Institute.
5. M.L. Bhatia. (1956). Federal Grants-in-Aid and Article 275, *EPW*, December 22.
6. J. Martinez and L.F. Jameson. (June 1997). Fiscal capacity: An overview of concepts and measurement issues and their applicability in the Russian Federation. Working Paper 97–3, Policy Research Centre, Georgia State University.
7. Economic Survey. *2014–15*. Department of Economic Affairs. Ministry of Finance. Govt. of India. p.130.
8. *Economic Survey. 2014–15*. Department of Economic Affairs. Ministry of Finance. Govt. of India. p.130.
9. *Economic Survey*, 2014–15, Department of Economic Affairs. Ministry of Finance. Govt. of India. p.130.
10. Ramani, S. (2016, August 6). What is the special category status. The Hindu.
11. Planning Commission (2012). Report of the working group on state's financial resources for the twelfth five year plan. (2012–2017). Retrieved from http://planningcommission.nic.in (Accessed on November 20, 2016).,
12. State Finance Commission. Retrieved from https://fincomindia.nic.in (Accessed on November 23, 2016).
13. Press Information Bureau, Government of India, Ministry of Finance, February 24, 2015.
14. *Economic Survey 2014–15*. Department of Economic Affairs. Ministry of Finance. Govt. of India. p.129.
15. *Report of 14th Finance Commission*, pp.146–147. Retrieved from https://fincomindia.nic.in (Accessed on November 24, 2016).
16. *Report of 14th Finance Commission*, p.203. Retrieved from https://fincomindia.nic.in (Accessed on November 25, 2016).
17. Compensate States for five years: 14th Finance Commission *Hindu Business Line*. February 24, 2015.
18. Finance Commission raises questions on exclusion of goods from GST *Business Standard*. February 25, 2015.
19. *The Gazette of India, (November 27, 2017). PART II—Section 3—Sub-section (ii)*, New Delhi, Govt. of India.
20. *Economic Survey*, 2014–15, chapter 10, p.135. Department of Economic Affairs. Ministry of Finance. Govt. of India.
21. *Economic Survey*, 2014–15, chapter 10, p.135. Department of Economic Affairs. Ministry of Finance. Govt. of India.
22. Vikraman, S. (November 2, 2017). Finance Commission's changing roles, challenges over the years. *Indian Express*.
23. Chakraborty, P. (March 4, 2017). Emerging issues in union–state fiscal relations Vol. 52, Issue No. 9, *Economic & Political Weekly*, p.46.
24. Chakraborty, P., Gupta, M. (April 16, 2016). Evolving centre–state financial relations role of the new framework for grants (Vol. II, No. 16), *Economic & Political Weekly*.
25. Sahoo, P., Sarkar, A. (June 2013) Changing dynamics of centre-state financial relations. *Yojana*, p.19.
26. Chakraborty, P., Gupta, M. (April 16, 2016). Evolving centre–state financial relations role of the new framework for grants (Vol. 2, No. 16). *Economic & Political Weekly*.
27. Sahoo, P., Sarkar, A. (June 2013) Changing dynamics of centre-state financial relations. *Yojana*, p.19.
28. Narayan, J. (March 19, 2018). Re-imagining federalism to fulfil India's potential. *Livemint*.

CHAPTER 27

PLANNING IN INDIA

This is not a dispute about whether planning is to be done or not. It is a dispute as to whether planning is to be done centrally, by one authority for the whole economic system, or is to be divided among many individuals.

—Friedrich Hayek

INTRODUCTION

Many developing countries soon after getting free from centuries of colonial rule adopted some sort of economic planning with a strong conviction that state has to intervene effectively to promote economic development. India was no exception to this trend-in fact it was in many ways frontrunner. Indian policymakers initiated the process of planning in order to attain certain objectives such as speedily raising the levels of living, catching-up with the living standards of the industrially advanced countries, producing product-mix that could sustain growth over a longer period of time, and reducing the extent of the existing inequalities and levels of poverty in the country. More than seventy years of independence, the country's experience with planning presents a mixed picture- it has achieved success in some directions and failed in other.

This chapter addresses the following key components:

- Planning in pre-independent India
- India's five-year plans and their critical assessment
- NITI Aayog and its functions
- NITI Aayog versus Planning Commission
- Strategy for New India @75

PLANNING EFFORTS IN PRE-INDEPENDENCE INDIA

In 1934, M. Visvesvaraya wrote a book, *Planned Economy for India* and proposed a 10-year plan. In 1938, the National Planning Committee (NPC) under the chairmanship of Pt. Jawaharlal Lal Nehru was established by Indian National Congress to prepare a plan for economic development. However, due to outbreak of Second World War the NPC could not move ahead. In 1944, eight industrialists of Mumbai gave "Bombay Plan."* The plan laid down proposals for

*The eight industrialists who scripted the Bombay plan were J. R .D. Tata, G. D. Birla, Purushottamdas Thakurdas, Kasturbhai Lalbhai, Ardeshir Dalal, Lala Sri Ram, John Mathai, and A. D. Shroff.

the development of the post-independence economy of India and aimed at trebling of national income and doubling of per capita income within a 15-year period.[1] In the same year Shriman Narayan and Acharya S. N. Agarwala formulated "Gandhian Plan" that was based on decentralized economic set up and village economy. M.N. Roy gave "People's Plan" that emphasized agriculture and small-scale industries.

PLANNING IN INDEPENDENT INDIA

The planning process formally started when Government of India set up the Planning Commission in March 1950.* The five-year planning model was borrowed from Russia. Let us have a brief survey of five-year plans of India.

First Five-Year Plan (1951–1956): Based on Harrod–Domar model (Box 27.1), the first five-year plan laid emphasis on agricultural development of the country. The plan set the target of 2.1% growth rate but achieved 3.6% growth rate.

Second Five-Year Plan (1956–1961): The second five-year plan was based on P.C. Mahalanobis model and its focus was rapid industrialization with special emphasis on the development of basic and heavy industries. The target growth rate was 4.5% and the actual growth rate was 4.27% (Box 27.1).

BOX 27.1 Economic Models in India

Harrod–Domar Model: The famous Harrod–Domar model was given by Nobel Prize winning economists R. F. Harrod in 1939 and Evsey Domar in 1946 and explains economy's growth rate in terms of the level of saving and productivity of capital. India's first five-year plan was based on this model. Mathematically, this can be expressed as the famous Harrod–Domar growth equation that is as follows: the growth in total output (g) will be equal to the savings ratio (s) divided by the capital–output ratio (k); that is, $g = s/k$. Thus, suppose that 15% of total output is saved annually and that three units of capital are required to produce an additional unit of output: then the rate of growth in output is $15/3 = 5\%$ per annum. This result is obtained from the basic assumption that whatever is saved will be automatically invested and converted into an increase in output on the basis of a given capital–output ratio. Since a given proportion of this increase in output will be saved and invested on the same basis, a continuous process of growth is maintained.

Mahalanobis Model: This model was developed by P.C. Mahalanobis and adopted in the second five-year plan of India. The Mahalanabis model represented an alternative approach to planning that focused on the bottlenecks created by a shortage of capital goods rather than a shortage of aggregate savings as emphasized by the Harrod–Domar model and tried to remove those bottlenecks to rapid economic growth. It is a two-sector model that suggests the allocation of a higher proportion of total investment to capital goods industries rather than to consumer goods industries. It is also called Feldman–Mahalanobis model as both Feldman and P.C. Mahalanobis developed it independently in the year 1928 and 1953, respectively.

Sources:

1. Eltis, W. (1987). Harrod–Domar growth model. In Palgrave Macmillan (Ed.) *The New Palgrave Dictionary of Economics*. London: Palgrave Macmillan.
2. Karmakar, A. K. (2012). Development planning & policies under Mahalanobis strategy: A tale of India's Dilemma. *International Journal of Business and Social Research (IJBSR)*, *2*(2).

*Planning Commission was dissolved by Government of India on August 17, 2014 and has been replaced by NITI Aayog.

It was during this plan that foundation of many public sector enterprises was laid down in the country.

Third Five-Year Plan (1961–1966): The third five-year plan was executed in the backdrop of two wars (Sino-Indian War of 1962) and (Indo-Pak war of 1965–66). The main objectives of the plan were increasing national income over 5% per annum; achieving self-sufficiency in food-grains and increasing agricultural production; expanding basic industries; utilizing manpower resources of the country; ensuring substantial expansion in employment opportunities; and reducing disparities in income and wealth. The target growth rate of third five-year plan was 5.6%, but the actual growth rate was 2.4%.

Annual Plans (1966–1969): Annual plan or plan holiday signifies a period when government abandons regular five-year planning and adopts annual plans. Government may go for annual plans because it does not have enough resources to make allocations as per five-year plan. The two wars with neighbors had weakened the Indian economy. Furthermore, the failure of third plan forced government to go for annual plans for the period 1966–1969.

Fourth Five-Year Plan (1969–1974): Growth with stability and progressive achievement of self-reliance were major objectives of fourth five-year plan. The 1971 slogan of "Garibi hatao" by Prime Minister Indira Gandhi became popular during this period. In the same year Indo-Pak war also took place. The target growth rate of fourth five-year plan was 5.6%, but the actual growth rate was 3.3%.

Fifth Five-Year Plan (1974–1979): The plan laid stress on agriculture and targeted 4.4% overall rate of growth of gross domestic product. In 1978 the newly elected Morarji Desai led Janata Government rejected the plan and introduced its own five-year plan (rolling plan) for the period 1978–1983.

Sixth Five-Year Plan (1980–1985): Indira Gandhi government was once again formed at the center and the newly elected government rejected the plan introduced by Janata Government and introduced its own plan for the period 1980–1985. Major objective of the plan was poverty eradication and technological self-reliance. Many poverty alleviation and employment generation schemes were introduced during this plan. This plan marked the beginning of economic liberalization and end of Nehruvian socialism. The target growth rate was 5.2% and the actual growth rate was 5.5%.

Seventh Five-Year Plan (1985–1990): The main objective of the seventh five-year plan was to establish growth in areas of increasing economic productivity, production of foodgrains, and generating employment through "Social Justice." The target growth rate of plan was 5% but the actual growth rate was 6%.

Annual Plans (1990–1992): Government declared the period of 1990–1992 as plan holiday because of unstable political and economic situation in the country.

Eighth Five-Year Plan (1992–1997): The eighth five-year plan was introduced in the backdrop of economic crisis and marked the beginning of economic reforms. It introduced indicative planning model in the country (Table 27.2). LPG policies (Liberalization, Privatization, and Globalization) were introduced to bring economic transformation. This plan was based on indicative planning. Former Prime Minister P. V. Narasimha Rao, hailed as "father of economic reforms in India" along with Dr Manmohan Singh, then Finance Minister were the chief architect of the plan. The eighth five-year plan as many term it "Rao-Manmohan Singh Model" laid the target of 5.6% GDP growth rate, but the actual growth rate was 6.7%.

BOX 27.2 Types of Planning

Centralized Planning: Under this type of planning, the decision-making is centralized in the hand of state (government) with collective ownership of means of production. The process of central planning is composed of pre-plan studies and forecasts, formulation of aims for given periods of time, establishment of their priorities (order of importance), listing ways and means, and, eventually, the plan's implementation. Such type of planning is prevalent in socialist economies or command economies. It is also called imperative planning.

Decentralized Planning: Under this type of planning, decisions regarding production, investment, and resource allocation are taken through democratic and participatory approach and various stakeholders like state governments, local governments, businessmen, farmers, etc. are involved into the planning process. This is also called planning from below.

Rolling Plan: Under rolling plan every year the performance of the plan is assessed and a new plan will be made next year based upon this assessment. Rolling plan comprises three sub-plans. First is the annual plan that comprises of annual budget. Second is a plan for 3, 4, or 5 years, that is, for fixed number of years. This second plan kept changing as per the requirements of the economy and government. Third is a perspective plan that is for 10, 15, or 20 years. Thus, there is no fixation of dates in respect of commencement and end of the plan in the rolling plans. In India, rolling plan was introduced by Janata Government in the year 1977–78, when it launched its own sixth five-year plan for the period of 1978–1983. Rolling plan is considered to be flexible as it overcomes the rigidities of five-year planning by revising targets, projections and allocations as per the changing conditions in the economy.

Indicative Planning: Indicative planning aims to coordinate private and public investment and output plans through forecasts or targets. Under this planning an attempt is made to promote more stable, rapid and efficient growth via the exchange of forecasts, leading to a generally held set of consistent expectations. India adopted this type of planning since eighth five-year plan.

Sources:

1. Kowalik, T. (1990). Central planning. In Eatwell, J., Milgate, M., & Newman P. (Eds.) *Problems of the planned economy*. London: The New Palgrave. Palgrave Macmillan.
2. Black, J. (1968). The theory of indicative planning. *Oxford Economic Papers*, *20*(3), 303–319.

Ninth Five-Year Plan (1997–2002): Launched in the 50th year of India's independence, the main objective of the ninth five-year plan was "growth with justice and equity." The target of growth rate of ninth plan was 7.1% and the actual growth was 6.8%.

Tenth Five-Year Plan (2002–2007): The main objectives of the tenth five-year plan were to attain high growth rate, reducing poverty rate by 5% (by 2007); providing gainful and high-quality employment, and reducing gender gaps in literacy and wage rates by at least 50% by 2007. Against the target of growth rate of 8.1%, actual growth rate was 7.7%.

Eleventh Five-Year Plan (2007–2012): The main objective of eleventh five-year plan was "faster and more inclusive growth." It laid down the target of 9% but the actual achievement was 7.5%.

Twelfth Five-Year Plan (2012–2017): The main theme of twelfth five-year plan was "faster, more inclusive and sustainable growth." The target laid down by this plan was 8% but the actual achievement was 6.7%.

Critical Assessment of India's Five-Year Plans

Planning and Growth

The basic objective of the Indian five-year plans was to promote national income as well as per capita income of the country. During the planning period, India's national income and per capita income rose, at a snail pace. In India 7 out of 12 five-year plans experienced lower growth rate against the set targets. The average growth rate during first five plans was around 3.55% and per capita growth rate was around 1.3%. The country experienced more than 5% growth rate after sixth plan and in the recent past has become fastest growing major economy in the world. To sum up the growth rate was slow during the first three decades of planning but picked up afterward. But it needs to be mentioned that growth of Indian economy is not that much high as was experienced by China in 1990s and South Korea, Taiwan, Philippines, and other South Asian countries during 1980s and after.

Another feature of growth was massive fluctuations. Unlike South Asian Tiger economies that reflected consistently high growth over a longer period of time, Indian growth registered massive fluctuations. In periods, like 1971–72 and 1991–92, a negative growth of per capita income was registered. The agriculture growth was highly fluctuating as it is linked to changes in exogenous factors.

Planning and Self-reliance

Self-reliance signifies a nation's capabilities to meet all its requirements either from domestic sources or has an ability to import them from abroad. Immediately, after independence India like many other newly liberated countries, could not risk its freedom by opening up its economy to the western world. Indian economy at that time was afflicted by severe problems such as influx of refugees, lower agriculture production, shortage of foodgrains, underdeveloped industrial sector, scarcity of capital, and backward technology. For example, because of lower agriculture production and shortage of food, India had to import foodgrains from foreign lands. Due to scarcity of capital and low saving rate, India had to depend on external foreign aid for meeting its import requirements. The low rate of saving and the persistent deficit in balance of payments were other reasons, which compelled the government to seek foreign aid. Therefore, during the initial phase of planning, government accorded a top priority to the program of industrial development. The second five-year plan was referred to an industrial plan and the number of basic and heavy industries, including iron and steel, non-ferrous metal, coal, cement, heavy chemicals, and others were set up. But a lot has changed since independence.

1. The green revolution of 1960s and government's steps to promote agriculture through different plans have earned rich dividends to the country. Today India has not only become self-reliant in foodgrains but also has become leading exporter of many agriculture products.
2. With the growth of iron and steel, machine tools, and heavy engineering industries, India has attained significant progression toward self-reliance in capital equipment. Engineering goods constitute a large component of India's export and industrial goods comprise around 86% of total merchandise exports of the country.

3. India once a largest borrower of International Monetary Fund (IMF) has now become net lender to IMF. There has been considerable fall in multilateral and bilateral borrowings of the country.

Planning and Employment Generation

One of the basic failures of Planning Commission in India is its inability to reduce the level of unemployment and under-employment, which has been increasing plan after plan. The Planning Commission's emphasis on growth rather than on employment and the adoption of capital-intensive production rather than labor-absorbing production is widely held responsible for the continuous increase of unemployment in India. In spite of the implementation of 12 five-year plans, unemployment in India has remained unabated. The backlog of unemployed persons has been increasing year after year. Agriculture employs nearly 49% while contributing only 15% of the gross value added (GVA), whereas just 29% of China's workforce is employed in agriculture. Furthermore, a large chunk of agriculture workforce is disguisedly unemployed resulting into lower productivity. The planning model failed to make industry and service sector absorb the surplus rural labor force. By some estimates, the Indian economy will need to generate nearly 70 lakh jobs annually to absorb the net addition to the workforce. India exhibits a low and declining female labor force participation rate. The female labor force participation rate in India was 23.7% in 2011–12 compared to 61% in China and 56% in the United States. The planning also failed to formalize Indian economy as India's informal sector employs approximately 85% of all workers.[2] As per the opinion of experts unless and until India adopts an employment-oriented strategy and aims at 3–4% annual increase of employment at higher levels of productivity, the chances of reaching the goal of full employment and alleviating under-employment would remain far from realization.

Planning and Inequality

Reducing inequality was one of the foremost goals of planning but situation remains appalling. According to Oxfam report, 2018, India's top 1% of the population holds 73% of the wealth. Studies have also confirmed that inequality rose sharply along with the growth rate in the post-reform period. In the pre-reform period, the public sector had played a crucial role in maintaining regional equality in the Indian economy by directing resources to backward areas. With a change in the focus of the public sector following the reforms, this process has become weaker. Second, the reforms gave greater freedom and impetus to the private sector and export-oriented production. These sectors, which were attempting to reduce costs and became competitive, were attracted to the areas that were relatively more developed. As a result, investment and activity shifted to these areas, strengthening the forces of divergence.[3]

India experienced a modest growth rate during initial years of planning and therefore, redistribution of income in favor of marginalized section of society and reduction of inequality could not take place effectively. For example, a study by Dandekar and Neelkantha in 1971 concluded that for the period 1951–1971, the condition of the bottom 20% of the population had definitely deteriorated and for the next higher 20% of the population had remained more or less stagnant. Various initiatives like land reforms and area development programs were launched apart from numerous poverty removal and employment generation programs during the planning period but they failed to bring about balanced regional development. Several studies on this issue clearly have shown that inter-state inequality has increased during post reform period as only the better-off states were able to benefit from the economic plans and reforms. The five-year plans have attempted to reduce regional disparities by encouraging industrial development in the interior regions, but industries tended to concentrate in and around urban areas and port cities. Especially, after liberalization, the more advanced states benefited more from them, with infrastructure such as well-developed ports, urbanization, and an educated and skilled work-force, which attracted manufacturing and service sectors.

Planning and Poverty Removal

Poverty removal remained one of their prime objectives in India's planning system especially after fourth five-year plan but the achievement is far from satisfactory and incidence of poverty remains unacceptably high. In 1973–74, the Expert Group under Prof. D. T. Lakdawala estimated about 55% of population was living below the poverty line. However, this proposition came down to about 29.5% in 2011–12 estimates of NSSO as per Rangarajan methodology. According to UN's Millennium Development Goal report, India is a home of one-third of the extreme poor of the world. Around 50 districts in the country are in the erstwhile BIMARU states—Bihar, Jharkhand, Madhya Pradesh, Chhattisgarh, Rajasthan, Odisha, and Uttar Pradesh—and 91 of the poorest 100 are concentrated in these seven states.[4] It was felt by the planning commission that the growth of the economy would be insufficient to eradicate poverty and therefore, poverty removal programs were made an integral part of the five-year plans. There is need to implement anti-poverty, employment generation, and basic services programs effectively besides taking some out of box measures.

Planning and Productivity

Modernization and competitive market is the key to economic development and as an economy matures, it must become competitive and more productive. India has turned productive in certain sectors such as software, gems and jewellery, and textiles, but in overall productivity, we lag behind other emerging markets. China's industrial productivity per worker is three times that of India. Small firms employing less than 20 workers account for 72% of employment but 12% of output in the manufacturing sector. Indian workers are overwhelmingly employed in low-productive and low-wage employment conditions. India's performance in exports is also dismal. In 2015, China accounted for 13.72% of world exports, while India accounted for only 1.67%. Export performance has to be on the basis of higher productivity and that needs scale economies.[5]

One reason for low productivity is that planners failed to sense the actual timing of market reforms in India. South Korea, Taiwan, and China did it earlier in the decades of 1960s and 1970s and hence became frontrunners in the race of economic growth. On the contrary, Indian business enterprises were subject to plethora of regulations and controls. The aim of 1991 economic reforms was freeing the private sector from the innumerable government controls that had existed for a long time. The consequence of this widespread deregulation and introduction of competition in most segments of the economic sphere has been the very visible unleashing of entrepreneurial energies at all levels and in most parts of the country.

NITI Aayog

The National Institution for Transforming India, also called NITI Aayog, was formed via a resolution of the Union Cabinet on January 1, 2015. NITI Aayog is the premier policy "Think Tank" of the Government of India, providing both directional and policy inputs. While designing strategic and long-term policies and programs for the Government of India, NITI Aayog also provides relevant technical advice to the Centre and States.

The Government of India, in keeping with its reform agenda, constituted the NITI Aayog to replace the Planning Commission instituted in 1950. This was done in order to better serve the needs and aspirations of the people of India. An important evolutionary change from the past, NITI Aayog acts as the quintessential platform of the Government of India to bring states to act together in national interest, and thereby fosters Cooperative Federalism. At the core of NITI Aayog's creation are two hubs—Team India Hub and the Knowledge and Innovation Hub. The Team India Hub leads the engagement of states with the central government, while the Knowledge and Innovation Hub builds NITI's think-tank capabilities. These hubs reflect the two key tasks of the NITI Aayog. NITI Aayog is also developing itself as a State of the Art Resource Centre, with the necessary resources, knowledge and skills, that will enable it to act with speed, promote research and innovation, provide strategic policy vision for the government, and deal with contingent issues.

The Prime Minister is the chairperson of NITI Aayog. Rajiv Kumar is the Vice Chairperson of NITI Aayog and Amitabh Kant is Chief Executive Officer. The governing council of NITI Aayog comprises chairperson, ex-officio members NITI Aayog, vice chairperson, full-time members, chief minister of states, Lt. Governor of Andaman and Nicobar Islands (Union Territories), and special invitees of NITI Aayog.

Functions of NITI Aayog

NITI Aayog has following important functions to perform[6]:

1. To evolve a shared vision of national development priority sectors and strategies with the active involvement of states in the light of national objectives
2. To foster cooperative federalism through structured support initiatives and mechanisms with the states on a continuous basis, recognizing that strong states make a strong nation
3. To develop mechanisms to formulate credible plans at the village level and aggregate these progressively at higher levels of government
4. To ensure, on areas that are specifically referred to it, that the interests of national security are incorporated in economic strategy and policy
5. To pay special attention to the sections of our society that may be at risk of not benefiting adequately from economic progress
6. To design strategic and long-term policy and program frameworks and initiatives, and monitor their progress and their efficacy. The lessons learnt through monitoring and feedback will be used for making innovative improvements, including necessary mid-course corrections
7. To provide advice and encourage partnerships between key stakeholders and national and international like-minded think tanks, as well as educational and policy research institutions

8. To create a knowledge, innovation, and entrepreneurial support system through a collaborative community of national and international experts, practitioners, and other partners
9. To offer a platform for resolution of inter-sectoral and inter-departmental issues in order to accelerate the implementation of the development agenda
10. To maintain a state-of-the-art Resource Centre, be a repository of research on good governance and best practices in sustainable and equitable development as well as help their dissemination to stake-holders
11. To actively monitor and evaluate the implementation of programs and initiatives, including the identification of the needed resources so as to strengthen the probability of success and scope of delivery
12. To focus on technology upgradation and capacity building for implementation of programs and initiatives
13. To undertake other activities as may be necessary in order to further the execution of the national development agenda, and the objectives mentioned earlier.

Transition from Planning Commission to NITI Aayog

Before we analyze the transition from Planning Commission to NITI Aayog, let us understand the difference between the two.

- Planning Commission was established in 1950 and dissolved in 2014. NITI Aayog was established in the year 2015.
- Planning Commission was an advisory body and enjoyed power to allocate funds to ministries and states. NITI Aayog is also an advisory body or think-tank but did not enjoy power to allocate funds. It rests with Finance Ministry.
- Planning Commission had deputy chairperson, a member secretary, and full-time members. It did not have any provision for part-time members. NITI Aayog has vice-chairperson, a chief executive officer (secretary-level post), full-time members, and also part-time members.
- Planning Commission reported to National Development Council (NDC) that had state chief ministers and lieutenant governors. The five-year plans would be approved by NDC. NITI Aayog has governing council that has state chief ministers and lieutenant governors.
- Planning Commission was more centralized as policy was formed by the commission and states were then consulted about allocation of funds. NITI Aayog is more democratic as it consults states while making policies. Therefore, states are expected to play more active role under NITI Aayog than Planning Commission.

The case for NITI Aayog

1. *Planning Commission—not in tune with new development strategy:* There were two contradictions between the Indian development strategy and the five-year planning model constraining economic environment over the years. The first is the contradiction between the planning framework and the role of the market. The initial years after independence required planning framework to allocate the low levels of savings to invest in much needed infrastructure and priority sectors to overcome severe infrastructure deficits and

the lack of competitiveness of the economy. However, the framework failed to adapt to the transition after 1991 economic reform period. With fiscal constraints becoming more and more binding and political economy factors crowding out infrastructure spending with subsidies and transfers, the planning exercise lost much of its relevance. The second contradiction was between the centralized command over resource allocation and the developmental role of the states in a federal polity. The end of single party rule and the emergence of coalition governments and regional parties as members of the central coalition brought to the fore the contradiction between centralized planning in a federal framework. The consequence of the above was that the two important sources of economic dynamism, the private sector and the states, had to function in a constrained environment.[7]

2. *Promoting accountability:* The Planning Commission was often charged with an allegation of making discretionary transfers to states to meet non-plan revenue deficits negating the norms set by the Finance Commissions. There was politics and severe distortions in public spending. One of the major challenges of NITI Aayog is to bring about a greater level of accountability in the system. Earlier, under five-year planning model, evaluation was done long after the plan period had ended. Hence, there was no real accountability. But NITI Aayog has established a Development Monitoring and Evaluation Office that collects data on the performance of various ministries on a real-time basis. The data are then used at the highest policymaking levels to establish accountability and improve performance. This performance and outcome-based real time monitoring and evaluation of government work can have a significant impact on improving the efficiency of governance.[8]
3. *Fiscal federalism and inter-governmental coordination:* NITI Aayog is being seen as a platform to promote fiscal federalism among the states through structured support initiatives. First, there is considerable overlap in carrying out legislative and executive functions in concurrent subjects. For example, there is lack of coordination between center and states in areas like energy and environment, education and poverty alleviation where the need for coordinated action and speedy decisions are critical for pursuing the developmental agenda. Second the Union government may have to intervene in the national interest even if they are in the State List or Concurrent List. There may be some public services in the State List, which, for reasons of nationwide externalities or for redistribution require coordinated action to ensure minimum standards throughout the country. The examples include healthcare, urban development, and poverty alleviation.* Third, in the case of union subjects too, the states may be involved in implementation as agencies due to their proximity to the people. In addition, NITI Aayog can facilitate exchange of information and experiences and promote healthy intergovernmental competition through monitoring and regulation. In this direction, NITI Aayog is devising performance-based rankings of states across various verticals to foster a spirit of competitive federalism. Under this the best practices in different states will be identified in various sectors and effort will be made to replicate them in other states.
4. *Promoting innovation:* As a major think tank of the government working on various developmental policies, it should not only have basic research capabilities but also should

*For example, few state governments like West Bengal, Delhi, Odisha and Telangana did not implement Ayushman Bharat Scheme.

access and outsource research on relevant subjects globally. For example, the Atal Innovation Mission, which is also established under NITI Aayog, has already done commendable work in improving the innovation ecosystem in India. It has established more than 1,500 Atal Tinkering Labs in schools across the country and this number is expected to go up to 5,000 by March 2019. It has also set up 20 Atal Incubation Centres for encouraging young innovators and start-ups.

The case against NITI Aayog

NITI Aayog has been confined to writing reports on the Indian economy, preparing draft laws for the Union government, evaluating central schemes, and holding conferences with state government officials. It has no funding role unlike planning commission. The Planning Commission used to disburse around ₹5 lakh crore annually for various plan schemes to states and so it acted as a bridge between states and various central ministries. Now, the money for central schemes, although vastly pruned, is released by the Finance Ministry, which does not have the wherewithal to do it.[9] Thus, as a result the scope and the remit of the NITI Aayog have been expanded and their stature reduced. This has resulted in a vacuum of institutional and procedural arrangements for the interactions between the Union and states. That vacuum has been unfortunately occupied by the ministries in the Union government.[10]

Replacing the Planning Commission, which was promoting regionally balanced growth in India, by NITI Aayog, a think tank, has reduced the Government's Policy reach. This means that currently India's fiscal federalism stands only on one pillar, viz., Union Finance Commission. There is a deep analytical foundation for a case where the NITI Aayog gets significant levels of resources for allocating to the different states. These resource transfers will be aimed at mitigating the development imbalances by promoting accelerated growth of lagging states and sub-regions. Given our political economy, these grants need to be conditional and formulaic. The purpose of these grants would be to enable the lagging states to build capacities in infrastructure sectors such as roads, ports, railways, digital connectivity, supply of power, access to credit, and improving governance. This will serve the objective of helping the lagging states and regions to attain growth acceleration and the reduction in developmental gap.[11]

Strategy for New India @75

NITI Aayog in December 2018 unveiled its comprehensive national Strategy for New India, which defines clear objectives for 2022–23. It is a detailed exposition across 41 crucial areas, which recognizes the progress already made, identifies binding constraints, and suggests the way forward for achieving the clearly stated objectives. Over 800 stakeholders from within the government—central, state, and district levels—and about 550 external experts were consulted during the preparation of the document.[12] The 41 chapters in the document have been disaggregated under four sections: Drivers, Infrastructure, Inclusion, and Governance. Let us have a discussion on these four sections.[13]

Drivers

The first section on Drivers focuses on the engines of economic performance with chapters on growth and employment, doubling of farmers' incomes; upgrading the science, technology, and innovation eco-system; and promoting sunrise sectors like fintech and tourism. Some of the key recommendations in the section on drivers include:

- Accelerating the economy to achieve a GDP growth rate of about 8% on average to make it $4 trillion economy by 2022–23. Gross fixed capital formation will be increased from 29% in 2018 to 36% in 2022.
- To enhance public investment, increasing the tax to GDP ratio to at least 22% of GDP by 2022–23, from the 17% in 2018.
- To raise the export of goods and services to $800 billion a year by 2022–23, as against the $478 billion in 2018.
- Continued exit of the government from non-strategic public sector units and further liberalizing the FDI regime.
- To converting farmers to "agripreneurs" by further expanding e-National Agriculture Markets (NAM) and replacing the Agricultural Produce Marketing Committee Act with the Agricultural Produce and Livestock Marketing Act.
- Promoting "Zero Budget Natural Farming" techniques that reduce costs, improve land quality, and increase farmers' incomes. This has emerged as a tested method for putting environment carbon back into the land.
- Replacing the Commission on Agricultural Costs and Prices (CACP) by an agriculture tribunal.
- To ensure maximum employment creation, complete codification of labor laws and a massive effort must be made to upscale and expand apprenticeships.
- Launch a mission "Explore in India" by revamping minerals exploration and licensing policy.

Infrastructure

The second section on Infrastructure has 11 chapters that elaborate physical foundations of growth that are crucial to enhancing the competitiveness of Indian business and also ensuring the citizens' ease of living. Following are the recommendations under this head:

- Establishing Rail Development Authority (RDA) and the main function of RDA will be advising or making informed decisions on an integrated, transparent, and dynamic pricing mechanism for the railways.
- Doubling the share of freight transported by coastal shipping and inland waterways. Initially viability gap funding will be provided until the infrastructure is fully developed. Developing an IT-enabled platform for integrating different modes of transport and promoting multi-modal and digitized mobility.
- With the completion of the Bharat Net program in 2019, all 2.5 lakh Gram Panchayats will be digitally connected. Aim to deliver all government services at the state, district, and Gram Panchayat levels digitally by 2022–23.

Inclusion

The section on Inclusion deals with the urgent task of investing in the capabilities of all of Indian citizens. The three themes in this section revolve around the dimensions of health, education, and mainstreaming of traditionally marginalized sections of the population. Following are the key recommendations under this head:

- Successfully implementing the Ayushman Bharat program including the establishment of 150,000 health and wellness centers across the country, and rolling out the Pradhan Mantri Jan Arogya Abhiyaan (PM-JAY).
- Creating a focal point for public health at the central level with state counterparts. Promote integrative medicine curriculum.
- Upgrading the quality of the school education system and skills, including the creation of a new innovation ecosystem at the ground level by establishing at least 10,000 Atal Tinkering Labs by 2020.
- Conceptualizing an electronic national educational registry for tracking each child's learning outcomes.
- Providing push to affordable housing in urban areas to improve workers' living conditions and ensure equity while providing a strong impetus to economic growth.

Governance

The fourth and final section on Governance delves deep into how the governance structures can be streamlined and processes optimized to achieve better developmental outcomes. Some of the key recommendations in the section on governance include

- Implementing the recommendations of the Second Administrative Reforms Commission as a prelude to appointing a successor for designing reforms in the changing context of emerging technologies and growing complexity of the economy.
- Setting up a new autonomous body, viz., the Arbitration Council of India to grade arbitral institutions and accredit arbitrators to make the arbitration process cost effective and speedy, and to preempt the need for court intervention.
- Addressing the backlog of pending cases—shift part of workload out of regular court system.
- Expanding the scope of Swachh Bharat Mission to cover initiatives for landfills, plastic waste, and municipal waste, and generating wealth from waste.

Summary

1. Although efforts for planning started during the pre-independence times, the planning process formally started when Government of India set up the Planning Commission in March 1950. India adopted five-year planning model from Russia. India in total had 12 five-year plans. They are: the first plan (1951–1956), the second plan (1956–1961), the third plan (1961–1966), the fourth plan (1969–1974), the fifth plan (1974–1979), the sixth plan (1980–1985), the seventh plan (1985–1990), the eighth plan (1992–1997), the ninth plan (1997–2002), the 10th plan (2002–2007), the 11th plan (2007–2012), and the 12th plan (2012–2017).
2. Five-year plans played a significant role in the initial years as the main task immediately after independence was to give direction to the economy and guide it to become a developed nation. Although the growth rate during initial decades was low but it picked up during sixth five-year plan. A nation that was dependent on foreign aid and essential imports turned into a self-reliant economy over the period of time. Despite being the third largest and fastest growing economy, the rising unemployment and inequalities remain the failure of planning. Even though the poverty headcount ratio has declined, India is still a home for one-third of poor people in the world. Although India has been able to make a mark in certain segments of manufacturing, the productivity level is low as compared to China and other emerging markets.
3. NITI Aayog was founded in the year 2015 as a replacement to Planning Commission, which was dissolved in 2014. With the changing times, the Planning Commission's work had become obsolete. The main task of NITI Aayog is to formulate policies for national development, implement such policies, monitor them, and evaluate their performance. Its other features include fostering cooperative federalism, promoting accountability, and promoting innovation. However, it is being criticized because of its powerlessness in terms of financial allocation, which erstwhile Planning Commission enjoyed.
4. NITI Aayog in December 2018 unveiled its comprehensive national Strategy for New India, which defines clear objectives for 2022–23. Under this it sets the target to achieve average annual growth of 8% during 2018–19 to 2022–23, to generate sufficient jobs and make India a $4 trillion (₹285 trillion) economy. The document titled "Strategy for New India @75" suggested that the growth rate be achieved through increasing the investment rate, improving the ratio of taxes to gross domestic product (GDP), raising export, continued exit of the government from non-strategic public sector units, and further liberalizing the Foreign Direct Investment regime.

Endnotes

1. The Bombay Plan: Blueprint for Economic Resurgence; Edited by Sanjaya Baru and Meghnad Desai, Rupa, 2018.
2. Niti Aayog. (November 2018). Strategy for New India @ 75. pp.12–13. Retrieved from www.niti.gov.in (Accessed on April 19, 2019).
3. 5 Reasons we need to worry about inequality now. *EPW Engage*, February 8, 2019.
4. Rukmini, S. (October 30, 2018). India's BIMARU states developing but not catching up. *Livemint.*
5. Alagh, Y.K. (2018). The next stage of planning in India. *EPW*, Vol. LIII, nos. 26 & 27.
6. Niti Aayog Functions. Retrieved from https://NITI.gov.in (Accessed on May 24, 2019).
7. Govinda Rao, M. (2015). Role and functions of NITI Aayog. *EPW*, Vol. 50, Issue No. 4. pp.13–14.
8. Kumar, R., Kannan, K.P., & Mehrotra, S. Is NITI Aayog relevant? *The Hindu*, September 21, 2018.
9. Sudhaman, K. R. (June 3, 2018). Has NITI Aayog pushed fiscal federalism forward? *Deccan Herald.*
10. Rajadhyaksha, N. (April 3, 2019). NITI Aayog 2.0 should be built on the idea of fiscal federalism, *Livemint.*
11. Kelkar, V. (2019). Towards India's new fiscal federalism, NIPFP working paper series, No. 252.
12. Mukherjee, S. (December 20, 2018). NITI unveils 'Strategy for New India @75' to make India $4-trillion economy. *Business Satandard.*
13. Niti Aayog. (November 2018). Strategy for New India @ 75. pp.12–13. Retrieved from www.niti.gov.in (Accessed on April 19, 2019).

CHAPTER **28**

BLACK MONEY AND DEMONETIZATION

Those who say demonetisation is good in the long run should recall the quote: 'In the long run we are all dead'.

—Dr Manmohan Singh

INTRODUCTION

The black economy (alias the parallel economy, the unaccounted economy, the underground economy, the unreported economy, the shadow economy, etc.) in India has been a matter of grave concern since independence. The issue has become a pan India hot topic of debate during recent times in academic and political circles and media too have given it a due weightage during prime time. The subject matter of black money has both economical and ethical connotations and therefore, affects the social fabric of a nation.

This chapter devotes our attention on the following key issues:

- Meaning, cause, and consequences of black money
- Estimation of black money in India
- Remedies to curb black money menace
- Demonetization: its advantages and disadvantages

WHAT IS ACTUALLY BLACK MONEY?

Black money can be defined as assets or resources that have neither been reported to the public authorities at the time of their generation nor disclosed at any point of time during their possession. In other words, any income can be considered as black, which is illegal, evades taxes, and hence escapes inclusion in national income estimates.[1] In addition to wealth earned through illegal means, the term black money would also include legal income that is concealed from public authorities[2]:

- to evade payment of taxes (income tax, GST, etc.);
- to evade payment of other statutory contributions;
- to evade compliance with the provisions of industrial laws such as the Industrial Dispute Act, 1947 and Minimum Wages Act, 1948; and
- to evade compliance with other laws and administrative procedures.

Therefore, we can say that the black money is amassed by the criminals, smugglers, terrorists, hoarders, tax-evaders, and other anti-social elements of the society.

Causes of Black Money

Non-Compliance of Taxes

Venkatappaiah Committee in 1974 had found high tax rates and complicated tax rate structure and inefficient tax administration as the major factors for tax evasion in the country. High tax rates result in higher net gain from tax evasion and thus provide incentive to evade taxes. India was the highest taxed nation in the world during pre-1991 period with marginal rate of taxes as high as 97.5%. Accordingly, the high rates of taxes were brought down considerably during the post-1991 period. Furthermore, the complexity and loopholes in the tax system have enabled the large businessmen, professionals, and politicians to evade taxes on large scale often with connivance of tax authorities. Widespread corruption in tax departments has led to poor enforcement of tax laws and helped tax evasion. The number of people showing income more than ₹50 lakh in the country is only 1.72 lakh in the year 2017. We can contrast this with the fact that during 2012–2017, more than 1.25 crore cars were sold, and the number of Indian citizens who flew abroad either for business or tourism was more than 2 crore in the year 2017.

Money Laundering

Money Laundering refers to the conversion or "Laundering" of money that is illegally obtained, so as to make it appear to originate from a legitimate source. That is, the illegal, or dirty, money is put through a cycle of transactions, or washed, so that it comes out the other end as legal, or clean money. It is the act of making money that comes from Source A looks like it comes from Source B. In India, money laundering is popularly known as Hawala transactions. It gained popularity during early 1990s when many of the politicians were caught in its net.

Money laundering is accomplished in three basic steps as enumerated below.[3]

1. *Placement:* It refers to the physical disposal of bulk cash proceeds derived from illegal activity. This is the first step of the money laundering process and is accomplished by depositing the cash in domestic banks or in other types of formal or informal financial institutions.
2. *Layering:* It refers to the separation of illicit proceeds from their source by creating complex layers of financial transactions. This is achieved by moving money to offshore bank accounts in the name of shell companies, purchasing high-value commodities like diamonds, and transferring the same to different jurisdictions. The funds might be channeled through the purchase and sale of investment instruments such as bonds, stocks, and traveler's cheques.
3. *Integration:* It refers to the reinjection of the laundered proceeds back into the economy in such a way that they re-enter the financial system as normal business funds. For example, a person can start a business with just a webpage and convert his illegal money to legal by showing profits from the webpage.

Political Funding

Government in February 2017 made two announcements regarding reforms in political funding. First, cash donations to political parties will be capped at ₹2,000 from a single source. Further donations can be made in cash or cheque. Second, amendment to the Reserve Bank of India Act, 1934 was proposed to enable the issuance of electoral bonds.* Regarding first proposal, it needs to be mentioned that earlier Section 29C of the Representation of Peoples Act (RPA), 1951 mandated the political parties to report donations exceeding ₹20,000. Earlier, if a person had to give ₹1 lakh in cash, they would make five receipts by breaking it up and keeping it under ₹20,000. Now, they would have to make 50 receipts. It is a logistical nightmare but it still does not prevent the party from accepting cash donations.[4] In the second proposal regarding electoral bonds, a donor can purchase these bonds from registered bank accounts and give it to a political party of its choice. The party, in turn, would redeem it by depositing it in a specified bank account in the party's name. But the donor will remain anonymous and parties can also accept foreign funding through such bonds. The Foreign Contribution (Regulation) Act that explicitly barred political parties from accepting foreign funding has also been amended.

India has very diverse multi-party political system. As on April 13, 2018 there are three types of political parties in India, that is, national parties (7), state recognized parties (24), and registered unrecognized parties (2044). If we look at the whole picture, the seven national parties have collected close to 75% (₹1,169.07 crore) income from voluntary contributions for the financial year (FY) 2016–2017. Despite constant chatter about the massive (and rising) costs of election campaigns in India, there are a dearth of credible data on the actual costs, the sources of support for candidates, and the implications of campaign costs on governance between elections.[5] A survey conducted by Jennifer Bussell, University of California, of 2,577 politicians of Bihar, Uttar Pradesh, and Jharkhand reveals that parties fund high-level elections, while individuals running for office in local councils rely on their own funds for lion's share of their campaign. Lower level politicians are further inhibited by a lack of access to financing from private sector and bureaucratic actors, which is more prevalent at higher levels. While giving gifts to voters is technically illegal, nearly all at the state and national level respondents report that candidates (MLAs and MPs) are pressured to distribute gifts during electoral campaign. The study revealed that at least 25% of the voters receive gifts during campaign.[6]

Controls on Economic Activity

State control and stringent regulations exacerbate the generation of black money process. There are many components of control that can be underlined as below.[7]

1. Controls on industrial activity
2. Controls on imports through licensing and canalization procedures
3. Foreign exchange controls
4. Controls over prices and distribution of a wide range of commodities
5. Controls on rents and on use of urban land

Entire system of industrial licensing and control in India in pre-1991 period led to considerable corruption and generation of black money. Because of considerable powers vested in

---

* For detailed discussion of electoral bonds, please see the chapter 16 "Public, Private, and Small Sector in Indian Economy."

the regulatory agencies, the whole system tended to promote corruption, rent-seeking, and discrimination based on personalistic relationships. In its report on auction of 2G spectrum in 2007–2008, CAG conclude that the government exchequer incurred a loss between ₹67,364 and 176,645 crore on account of such allotments. As far as the allocation of coal blocks was concerned, it was done in an arbitrary manner and the CAG had alleged that this allocation caused a massive ₹1.86 lakh crore loss to exchequer.

The operation of a complex and discretionary system of controls invites corruption and lobbying of another form. For example, there have been cases where the zoning of urban land has been altered to suit individual developers in return for appropriate considerations. The Adarsh Housing Society scam that was unearthed in November 2010 forced the then Chief Minister of Maharashtra, Ashok Chavan, to resign. The Adarsh Housing Society is a posh, 31-story building constructed on prime real estate in Colaba, Mumbai, for the welfare of war widows and personnel of India's Ministry of Defence.[8] It was a classic case where politicians, bureaucrats, and military officers allegedly conspired to bend several rules concerning land ownership, zoning, floor space index, and membership getting themselves flats allotted in this cooperative society at below-market rates.

Illicit Money Transferred Outside

Deregulation and trade liberalization have accelerated the outflow of illicit money from the Indian economy during the post-reform period of 1991–2008. Opportunities for trade mispricing have grown, and expansion of the global shadow financial system accommodates hot money, particularly in island tax havens. Disguised corporations situated abroad, in secrecy jurisdictions enable billions of dollars shifting out of India to "round trip," coming back into short- and long-term investments, often with the intention of generating unrecorded transfers again in a self-reinforcing cycle. Illicit outflows drain hard currency reserves and reduce tax collection, harming India's poor and widening income gaps.[9] According to 2017 report of US-based think-tank Global Financial Integrity (GFI), an estimated $770 billion in black money entered India during 2005–2014 and nearly $165 billion in illicit money exited the country during the same period. Report further said that only about 28% of illicit assets of India's underground economy are held domestically and rest 72% are held abroad.

About 87% of the global illicit financial flows are happening through trade mis-invoicing. This is how it works: if you want to send money out of the country, you order something from abroad and get an inflated invoice or bill made for it. After paying the inflated bill to your foreign accomplice, the extra money is put away in your name. By reversing this process, by under-invoicing or getting a less-than-actual bill made, you can illicitly allow money to flow into the country. This can be profitably used for a variety of illegal purposes, with no tax to pay.[10]

Standards of Public Morality

The Wanchoo Committee Report way back in 1970s pointed to the general deterioration in moral standards of our people as a significant factor fuelling the growth of tax evasion. In a society where tax evasion and under-reporting of activities and income is perceived to be very common or the norm, such activities may be considered acceptable and honest tax compliance and paying one's due share to the public fund may not be considered a virtue.[11] The Berlin-based NGO, Transparency International (TI), is publishing the Corruption Perceptions Index (CPI) since 1995, annually ranking countries by their perceived levels of corruption, as determined by expert assessments and opinion surveys. The CPI generally defines corruption as the misuse of public power for private benefit. The index ranks countries and territories by their perceived levels of public sector corruption according to experts and business people, uses a scale of 0–100, where 0 is highly corrupt and 100 is very clean.[12] India's ranking is 78 among a group of 180 countries and score is 41/100 as per CPI, 2018.

Inflation

Inflation promotes black income in several ways: First, with a progressive income (and wealth) tax structure, inflation results in "bracket creep,"* which increases the effective burden of taxation, and hence the incentive to evade. Second, general inflation is usually accompanied by pronounced scarcities and windfall gains in certain sectors that are unlikely to be fully declared to the revenue authorities. Third, inflation reduces the real incomes of those (especially fixed salaried employees) whose nominal incomes do not keep pace with rate of change in prices. This includes government servants and many of whom have access to various forms of discretionary authority that can be bartered for money. Thus inflation, especially when it is prolonged and severe, increases the incentive to succumb to such temptations.[13]

Investment in Real Estate

Real estate is one of the major sources of black money in India. National Institute of Public Finance and Policy (NIPFP) in its report in 2012 pointed to the vicious link between real estate sector and the black economy in India. It is hard to value real estate, which makes it suited for undervaluation and an ideal investment for black savings. Understating of the value of immovable properties in the transfer deed is a major way of generating black income.[14] The real registered value of land and building is generally much less than the value agreed upon. The difference between the market value and the declared value of properties at the time of registration gives the extent of under-reported income. In most cases as much as 60% payment is in terms of black money while the white component is merely 40% of the actual value.

Estimation of the Size of Black Money in India

Size of Black Money in India

Kaldor made the first estimate of black money in India. After that different economists and committees have given estimation of the size of black money in India (Table 28.1).

Size of Black Money Outside India

Apart from existence of wide-scale parallel economy with in the country, the sizable chunk of money is also stashed in the foreign lands. According to a study by US-based think-tank GFI, an

*A bracket creep is a situation wherein inflation pushes income into higher tax brackets. The result is an increase in income taxes but no increase in real purchasing power.

TABLE 28.1 Size of Black Money in India: Different Estimates

Economist/Committee/Institutions	Year	Size
N. Klador	1953–1954	₹600 crore (6% of GDP)
Wanchoo Committee (Direct Tax Enquiry Committee)	1961–1962 1965–1966	₹700 crore (4.4% of GDP) ₹1,000 crore (4.2% of GDP)
Rangnekar's estimates	1961–1962 1965–1966	₹1,150 crore ₹2,350 crore
O.P. Chopra's estimates	1960–1961 1976–1977	₹916 crore (6.5% of GDP) ₹8,098 crore (11.4% of GDP)
Poonam Gupta, Sanjeev Gupta	1967–1968 1978–1979	₹3,034 crore (9.5% of GDP) ₹46,867 crore (48.85 of GDP)
National Institute of Public Finance and Policy	1975–1976 1980–1981 1983–1984	₹9,958 to ₹11,870 crore (15–18% of GDP) ₹20,362 to ₹23,678 crore (18–21% of GDP) ₹31,584 to ₹36,786 crore (18–21% of GDP)
Global Financial Integrity Report	2008	$640.7 billion (50% of GDP)
Chandan Sharma, IIM Lucknow	1997–1998 2013–1914	₹7 lakh crore (50% of GDP) ₹60 lakh crore (52% of GDP)
Arun Kumar's estimates	2016–2017	₹93 lakh crore (62% of GDP)

Source: Author's compilation.

estimated $770 billion in black money entered India during 2005–2014. Nearly $165 billion in illicit money exited the country during the same period.[15] NIPFP found that 0.2–7.4% of India's GDP flew outside India in the form of illicit money during 1997–2009. The National Council Applied Economic Research (NCAER) found that the total amount of black money accumulated outside India between 1980 and 2010 was in the range of $384 billion (approximately ₹27 lakh crore) to $498 billion, which was around 2.8% of the GDP. National Institute of Financial Management (NIFM) estimated that the total outflow of black money between 1990 and 2008 was ₹941,837 crore or $217 billion. However, the institutes were unanimous in concluding that the proportion of black money lying within India was much higher than what was present outside, that is, 97% of the total black money was within India.[16] Probably this was the reason that prompted government to go for demonetization.

Impact of Black Money

The following are the impact of black money in an economy:

1. Loss of revenue to the state exchequer as a consequence of tax evasion.
2. Encourages investment in the items of conspicuous consumption, thus channelizing money into unproductive activities, which affects growth.
3. Diversion of resources in the purchases of real estate and investment in luxurious housing by making black money into white, thus pushing up prices of land to astronomical heights and pricing out middle class in the purchase of land for house.
4. Transfer of funds from India to foreign countries through clandestine channels like violating foreign exchange regulations, under invoicing of exports and over invoicing of imports.

5. Increase aggregate demand causing inflationary pressure.
6. Corrupts political system in the most vicious manner and at various levels.
7. Leads to underestimation of GDP as an enormous volume of income is diverted to unaccounted sector.

Government Policies to Curb Black Money

Volunteer Disclosure Scheme (VDS)

Under this scheme, the tax evaders are provided channel to convert black money into white by paying a small amount of money as tax. VDS has been implemented in India from time to time. The 1997–1998 budget introduced volunteer disclosure income scheme (VDIS), under which the amount disclosed either as cash or assets or securities, whether held in India or abroad was charged to tax at 30% for individuals and 35% for companies. The government assured legal immunity to such persons. A total of ₹10,000 crore was collected by the government through VDIS. In 2015, the Black Money (Undisclosed Foreign Income and Assets) and Imposition of Tax Act, 2015 was enacted to provide one time compliance window from July to September 2015 to declarants to declare their undisclosed foreign assets subject to certain prescribed conditions. This measure remained highly unsuccessful as it resulted into around 600 declarations and tax collection of merely ₹2,000 crore. The 2016–2017 budget announced another scheme, income declaration scheme (IDS), that provided people having undisclosed income to come clean through one-time compliance window of 4 months (from June 1, 2016 to September 30, 2016) by paying tax at the rate of 30% along with surcharge of 7.5% and penalty of 7.5%, which would be 45% of the income disclosed. Around 64,275 people declared ₹65,220 crore of income. All VDS schemes had been largely unsuccessful to curb black money menace. For example, VDIS in 1997 collected just 5% of the black income generated that year and IDS in 2016–2017 collected just 0.75 of the black income generated that year.[17]

The Pradhan Mantri Garib Kalyan Yojana (PMGKY) was launched on December 17, 2016 and remained open until March 31, 2017. It is second income disclosure scheme (IDS) to allow tax evaders to come clean with unaccounted wealth by paying 30% tax, 10% penalty, and 33% Pradhan Mantri Garib Kalyan Cess on the tax, all of which add up to around 50%. Furthermore, the declarant was required to deposit of 25% of undisclosed income in the zero-interest Pradhan Mantri Garib Kalyan Deposit Scheme, 2016 with lock-in period of 4 years. The total money collected was ₹2,300 crore, aimed for the welfare of the poor.

Prevention of Money Laundering Act

The Prevention of Money Laundering Act (PMLA), 2002 was enacted by Indian Parliament and came into force with effect from July 1, 2005. The Act was amended in the year 2005, 2009, and 2012 respectively. The Act seeks to combat money laundering in India and has three main objectives:[18]

- To prevent and control money laundering
- To confiscate and seize the property obtained from the laundered money
- To deal with any other issue connected with money laundering in India

Right to Information Act

The Right to Information (RTI) Act was enacted by Indian Parliament in the year 2005 and the Act came into force in the same year. Under RTI Act, 2005 any citizen of the country may request information from a public authority, which is required to reply expeditiously or within 30 days. The Act also requires every public institution/authority to computerize their records and information for wide dissemination so that the citizens need minimum recourse to request for information formally.[19] RTI Act has become a very potent weapon to seek information by public. Everyday 4,800 applications are filed to access information from the government across India and a total of 1.75 crore applications have been filed between 2005 and 2015. A study conducted by Commonwealth Human Rights Initiative (CHRI) reveals that 27.2% (47.66 lakh) of the total RTIs filed between 2005 and 2015 were to the different ministries and departments under the Central Government. Maharashtra (26.40%) and Karnataka (11.83%) hold second and third position, respectively.[20]

Tax Reforms

Government appointed various committees and commissions to suggest tax reforms to curb black money menace, viz. Kaldor Committee in 1956, Administrative Reform Committee in 1969, and Direct Tax Enquiry Committee in 1971. Since the research has provided ample evidence that higher tax encourage tax evasion, the Chelliah Committee in 1993 and Kelkar Committee in 2002 suggested reduction in taxes. It produced a positive impact on tax collection. But few economists have contested this analogy and argued that post-reform period witnessed huge increase in the income of business class (due to LPG policies) and salaried class (due to award of 5th, 6th, and 7th pay commissions), which in fact resulted into higher tax collection.[21] The implementation of GST is going to affect direct taxes, helping in widening of the tax base and increasing the taxes collections. Earlier the tax filers understated incomes by not reporting each and every transaction. By doing this, they saved excise, VAT, Octroi, etc., and more importantly, were able to furnish under reporting of their incomes. Since, GST has a paper trail, which can be accessed by the income tax department. Usage of PAN and Aadhar is more frequent in the present regime, which will help the income tax department to track transactions.[22] Earlier, there were plethora of taxes levied by different authorities on land and real estate, which led to cascading of taxes, thereby increasing the distortionary impact of taxes on efficiency and productivity of the real estate market. The multiple tax system (on transfer, registration, and stamp duties) has been reduced by minimizing the overall tax burden in absolute rupee terms, which will in turn enhance the elasticity and buoyancy of India's indirect tax system, because the audit trail in GST will bring a greater proportion of real estate transactions into the tax net, augmenting the revenue collection.[23]

Demonetization

Demonetization pulls the black money out of the system and is considered as the option of last resort. Demonetization of 2016 in India was also aimed at curbing black money from the system. Demonetization can be sudden or gradual. Different countries of the world have exercised sudden or gradual demonetization from time to time. The sudden demonetization is generally done when authorities do not want to give black marketers sufficient time to get prepared so as to convert their black income to white (Tables 28.2 and 28.3).

DEMONETIZATION IN INDIA

Demonetization is the act of stripping national currency unit of its status as legal tender. There are two methods of demonetization: first, the current form or forms of money are pulled from circulation and retired, often to be replaced with new notes or coins, and second, completely replacing the old currency with new currency.

India has pulled select denominations of its currency three times, that is, in 1946, 1978, and 2016.

Demonetization of 1946: Demonetization was first introduced in India before independence in the year 1946, when the currency notes of ₹1,000 and ₹10,000 were demonetized. The currency ban did not have much impact on the common people and the Indian economy as higher denomination notes were not accessible to common people at that time.

Demonetization of 1978: In 1978, the Janata Government demonetized ₹1,000, ₹5,000, and ₹10,000 notes. The impact of currency ban on common people was again limited as the demonetized notes formed only a small portion of the total money supply.

Demonetization of 2016: The third demonetization in India was announced on November 8, 2016, when government demonetized all ₹500 and ₹1,000 banknotes of the Mahatma Gandhi Series and replaced them with the issuance of new ₹500 and ₹2,000 banknotes in exchange for the demonetized banknotes. India's demonetization of 2016 is unprecedented in international economic history, in that it combined secrecy and suddenness amidst normal economic and political conditions. All other sudden demonetizations (in other parts of the world) have occurred in the context of hyperinflation, wars, political upheavals, or other extreme circumstances. But in Indian case demonetization was announced when the economy was growing at the fastest pace with strong economic fundamentals and an impressive set of reforms.[24]

Objectives of Demonetization

There are different objectives of demonetization:

1. to curb corruption;
2. to check counterfeiting;
3. to dispirit the use of high denomination notes for terrorist activities;
4. to discourage the accumulation of "black money," generated by income that has not been declared to the tax authorities; and
5. to curb inflation.

However, two things are important to worth mention here:

First, research worldwide has found a link between cash and nefarious activities: the higher the amount of cash in circulation, the greater the amount of corruption, as measured by Transparency International. The higher usage of cash leads to diversion of money for illegitimate transactions and corrupt practices. India's currency-to-GDP ratio increased from 9% in 1967–1968 to 12% in 2014–2015. Higher cash dependence of Indian economy is not in tandem with global phenomenon as the empirical evidence has suggested reduction in the use of cash with the level of development.

Second, it is usually the case that high-value notes are associated with corruption because they are easier to store and carry, compared to smaller denominations or other stores of value such as gold.[25] Money can be understood in two dimensions: its function and its nature/origin. Money can be used as medium of exchange (for transaction purpose) or as a store of value (savings for future use) in assets form like gold and real estate. In terms of nature, it can be white or black. How high were India's high-denomination notes in terms of their use for transactions purpose relative to store of value purpose? The research shows that higher a note is relative to nominal per capita income, the less likely it is to be used purely for transactions purposes. In India's case, the denomination/income ratio has fallen sharply over the past quarter century because incomes have been growing rapidly relative to the prevailing highest denomination notes. This suggests that the high-denomination notes have become increasingly useful for transactions over time. The second measure to gauge the use of high-denomination notes (of ₹500 and ₹1,000) for transaction or store of value function is "soil rates,"* that is, the rate at which notes are considered to be too damaged to use and have been returned to the central bank. RBI data shows that in India low-denomination notes had a soil rate of 33% per year. In contrast, the soil rate for ₹500 note was 22%, and for ₹1,000 note was just 11%. One way to estimate black money is to assume that all these notes should soil at the same rate, if they were really being used for transactions. This would yield an estimate of money that is not used for transactions at ₹7.3 lakh crore.[26] In this

TABLE 28.2 Sudden Demonetization Across the World

Country	Year	Objective
Ghana	1982	Very high inflation
Myanmar	1985	Black money
Myanmar	1987	Political
Brazil	1990	Hyperinflation
Brazil	1993	Hyperinflation
Soviet Union	1991	Hyperinflation
Russia	1993	Inflation and control over currency
Iraq	1993	UN sanctions and finance fiscal deficit
North Korea	2009	Black money and inflation
Cyprus	2013	Weak banking system
Greece	2015	Fiscal and banking crisis
Venezuela	2016	Inflation
India	2016	Black money

Source: Economic Survey, Department of Economic Affairs. Ministry of Finance. Govt. of India. 2016–2017.

*Soiled note: means a note which, has become dirty due to usage and also includes a two piece note pasted together wherein both the pieces presented belong to the same note, and form the entire note.

TABLE 28.3 Gradual Demonetization in Different Countries

Country	Year	Objective
Singapore	1967	Independence of Singapore from Malaysia and breakdown of currency union of Malaysia, Singapore, and Brunei
Australia	1988 and 2015	Counterfeiting
Euro	1999	Formation of Eurozone
Singapore	1999 and 2014	Money laundering
Canada	2011	Counterfeiting
Denmark	2012	Counterfeiting
Sweden	2013–2016	Replacement of banknotes
Zimbabwe	2015	Hyperinflation
Pakistan	2015	Black money, corruption, and terrorism
Euro Zone	2016	Replacement of old currency with state of art and secured currency

Source: Economic Survey, 2016–2017. Department of Economic Affairs. Ministry of Finance. Govt. of India.

sense, attempts to reduce the cash in an economy could have important long-term benefits in terms of reducing levels of corruption.

The case for Demonetization

Towards a Tax Compliant Economy

A widely stated comment has been that just because most of the currency came back into the banks, the object of demonetization has not succeeded. According to RBI, 98.96% of ₹500 and ₹1,000 notes (by value) that were invalidated due to the demonetization exercise had been returned by the end of June 2018. As compared to ₹15.44 trillion of the invalidated notes that were in circulation as of November 8, 2016 (date of demonetization), RBI received ₹15.28 trillion.[27] But according to Finance Ministry, the larger purpose of demonetization was to move India from a tax non-compliant society to a tax-compliant society via formalization of economy and making India more tax complaint.[28] In March 2014, the number of income tax returns filed was 3.8 crore. In 2017–2018, this figure has grown to 6.86 crore. In the last 2 years, when the impact of demonetization and other steps is analyzed, the income tax returns have increased phenomenally by 19 and 25%. The income tax collections have increased from the 2013–2014 figure of ₹6.38 lakh crore to the 2017–2018 figure of ₹10.02 lakh crore. The growth of income tax collections in the 2 years of pre-demonetization was 6.6 and 9%. Post-demonetization, the collections increased by 15 and 18% in the next 2 years. The same trend was visible in the third year. The GST was implemented from July 1, 2017, that is, post-demonetization. In the very first year, the number of registered assesses increased by 72.5%. The original 66.17 lakh assesses increased to 114.17 lakhs. When cash is deposited in the banks, the anonymity about the owner of the cash disappears. The deposited cash is now identified with its owner giving rise to an inquiry, whether the amount deposited is in consonance with the depositor's income. Accordingly, post-demonetization about 1.8 million depositors have been identified for this enquiry. Many of them are being fastened with tax and penalties. Mere deposit of cash in a bank does not lead to a presumption that it is tax paid money.[29]

Digitalization of Economy

As discussed earlier, India has a very high predominance of consumer transactions carried out in cash relative to other countries accounting for 68% of total transactions by value and 98% by volume.[30] Besides being convenient and their universal acceptance, cash transactions are also anonymous, helping to preserve privacy, which is a virtue as long as the transactions are not illicit. On the contrary, despite some hardships associated with digital payments (like requirement of special equipment viz. POS machines and smart phones and e-payment charges imposed by firms), they help bring people into the formal economy, thereby increasing financial saving, reducing tax evasion, and leveling the playing field between tax-compliant and tax-evading firms/individuals.[31]

A study by NUS Business School Singapore, Indian Institute of Management, and Hong Kong Baptist University found that India's demonetization, the largest the world has ever seen, effectively stimulated the transition from a cash-based to digitally enabled economy.[32] Digital transactions have increased in volume and value across various modes from wallets to cards and interbank transfers since demonetization. Card transactions at point of sale (POS) terminals at merchant locations have surged, reflecting a positive for the economy as more people start using their debit cards for payments rather than for withdrawing cash at ATMs. Besides plastic, the government has been promoting smartphone-based transactions through the Unified Payments Interface (UPI) and the Bharat Interface for Money (BHIM). Both use the Immediate Payment Service (IMPS) network of the National Payments Corporation of India. Prepaid Payment Instruments or PPIs, which include wallet services such as those offered by MobiKwik and Oxigen, have shown the highest growth in percentage terms since demonetization.[33]

Cleansing of Real Estate

Demonetization could have particularly profound impact on the real estate sector. The sector long known for its cash intensive dealings continues to undergo a cleansing of the system. The sector's transformation toward transparency and formal business practices has impacted the housing sales in the short term but it was a much-needed change. Series of reforms including demonetization, implementation of Real Estate (Regulatory & Development) Act, 2016, and Goods & Services Tax has kept the sector busy during the recent times and the adjustment to the new normal is expected to continue for some more time.[34] In the past, much of the black money accumulated was ultimately used to evade taxes on property sales. To the extent that black money is reduced and financial transactions increasingly take place through electronic means, this type of tax evasion will also diminish.

Impact on GDP

Demonetization in India happened at a time when global economy was suffering from overall subdued demand. India, despite the slowdown in growth following demonetization, still managed to maintain above average global growth rate level.[35] GDP growth rate slowed from 8% in 2015–2016 to 7.1% in 2016–2017 but again rebounded to 7.2% in 2017–2018. Furthermore, growth also lost steam for reasons other than demonetization, such as introduction of GST in July 2017, trade war, lower export growth and the twin balance sheet problem depressing investment in the economy.[36] GDP growth rate for April-June quarter 2019–20 was 5%. In India, the economy is growing, only the rate of growth has slowed down, which is a huge setback for the country as it requires an accelerated growth to provide employment to millions entering the job market every year. A sub-5% GDP growth was last witnessed in the years 2012–13 (4.5%) and 2013–14 4.9%) due to policy paralysis of UPA-II government.

Impact on total output of the country can also be gauged by understanding consumption, investment, government expenditure, and net exports. After demonetization, consumption got temporarily postponed (an aggregate demand shock, because it reduces the supply of money and affects private wealth) during the short term but recovered later. Investment, government expenditure, and net exports remained stable during the short period and increased over the longer period. The one big difference between the growth recession earlier this decade and the current one is that India has more macroeconomic stability. The balance of payments is in better shape, inflation is under control, creating space for an immediate demand stimulus. There is definitely more space right now for a monetary stimulus rather than a fiscal stimulus.

The case against Demonetization

Demonetization Affected the Common Man

Demonetization would never have hit illicit wealth held as real estate, shares, gold, silver, and foreign currency. Only small time concealers of income keep their money in cash. These include women hiding income from their men, to create a stash they could use to buy gold or in a health emergency. Demonetization hit such people hard, not the big fish.[37] Cash is the lifeblood of Indian economy as before demonetization 95% of the transactions were in cash. But when 86% of cash was gone out of the system (due to pulling back of ₹500 and ₹1,000 currency notes), the worst nightmare to the common man had begun. Billions of man-hours were wasted standing in the queues outside bank branches, also causing fall in income of daily wagers and casual/informal workers. Another view point is that government could have issued ₹5,000 notes and ₹2,000 notes in 2014, inducing black money operators to hoard these, and demonetized these in 2016, sparing the ₹500 and ₹1,000 notes held by ordinary folk.[38]

The Question on Impact on Black Money

After the announcement of demonetization, black money hoarders employed various means to convert their black money into white. The intermediaries were offered substantial commissions nearly 35% to exchange their currency. The intermediaries employed daily wagers, laborers, and informal workers who could stand in queue and could deposit cash amount of less than ₹2.5 lakh in banks. The government believed that around one-fourth of currency will not return to the system but the RBI Annual Report 2016–2017 revealed that 98.96% of the ₹500 and ₹1,000 denomination notes that were withdrawn from circulation returned to the banking system, which means on ₹16,000 crore (1.04%) did not return. This could mean that those holding illegal cash were either an insignificant number, or that they found ways of depositing cash into formal banking systems. For context, in the demonetizations of 1946 and 1978, about 14 and 10%, respectively, of high denomination currency did not return to the central bank.[39]

Effect on Informal Sector

India's unorganized sector is an integral part of the process of transition from a traditional economy to a modern economy. While it may not pay taxes and is largely dependent on cash, it plays an important role in providing jobs to millions of first-time workers and to millions of others who are moving out of agriculture to the non-agricultural sector.[40] Demonetization has led to a sharp decline in money supply, so the unorganized sector was adversely affected directly and they have suffered an immediate contraction in transactions and consequently in output. This affects demand in the entire economy since this sector still produces 45% of the output and the impact would spill over to the organized sectors.[41] The negative impact of demonetization was also felt in agriculture. In agriculture, demonetization aggravated the sector's existing stress points by creating new choke points within the supply chain. Cash is a critical input in the agricultural production process and its unexpected shortage had an impact at many levels, including a slowdown in employment of labor and a dip in overall farm incomes.[42]

Summary

1. The black economy in India has been a matter of grave concern since independence. Black money can be defined as assets or resources that have neither been reported to the public authorities at the time of their generation nor disclosed at any point of time during their possession.
2. There are many factors responsible for the generation of black money. The first is non-compliance of taxes. High tax rates, complicated tax rate structure, and inefficient tax administration are the major factors for tax evasion in the country. The second factor is "Laundering" of money that is illegally obtained, so as to make it appear to originate from a legitimate source. Third factor is political funding that takes the form of nexus between political masters and rich businessmen showering benefits on each other on the basis of "quid pro quo." The fourth factor is state control and stringent regulations that exacerbate the generation of black money process. The fifth factor is illicit transfers that take shape in the form of mis-invoicing and round tripping. The sixth factor is fall in public morality that is also revealed by low ranking in India as per corruption perception index. The seventh factor is inflation that reduces real income and results in inflation creep. The eighth factor is investment in real estate in which black income is generated through understatement of property value.
3. Many economists have estimated the extent of black income of India within the country and outside the country. The black income within the country has increased from 6% of GDP in 1950s to 62% of GDP in 2016–2017. There is substantial amount of black income stashed outside the country and global financial integrity (GFI) has estimated that more than $700 billion entered from India during 2005–2014 and around $165 billion exited India during the same period.
4. Black money affects the economy in various ways. Inflation, conspicuous consumption, loss of revenue, and diversion of resources into unproductive activities are among the few consequences of black money.
5. Government launched various schemes under VDS like VDIS in 1997–1998, IDS in 2016–2017, and PMGKY in December 2016. The Prevention of Money Laundering Act (PMLA), 2002 was enacted to combat the problem of money laundering in India. The Right to Information (RTI) Act was enacted in 2005 under which any citizen may request information from a public authority, which is required to reply expeditiously or within 30 days. Tax reforms mainly during the post-reform period were envisaged to discourage tax evasion.
6. Demonetization is an act of stripping national currency unit of its status as legal tender. India has pulled select denominations of its currency three times, that is, in 1946, 1978, and 2016. The objectives of demonetization include curbing corruption, checking counterfeiting, dispiriting terrorist activities, and discouraging the accumulation of black money.
7. The major benefits of demonetization are: increase in tax collection, for example, the number of registered assesses increased from 66.17 lakhs to 114.17 lakhs in the very first year after demonetization. The other factors are increasing trend of digitalization of economy, dramatic reduction in corruption in real estate (apart from demonetization, Real Estate Act, 2016, and GST have also been able to plug loopholes). The GDP growth rate too slowed down from 8% in 2015–2016 to 7.1% in 2016–2017 but again rebounded to 7.2% in 2017–2018. However, there is negative side too. Demonetization affected common man who held major part of money in cash. The impact on the reduction in black money is also debatable as 98.96% of the currency demonetized came back to the system. Finally there is evidence that hints at the impact of demonetization on informal sector mainly agriculture and MSMEs.

Endnotes

1. National Institute of Public Finance (1985). *Report on the aspects of black economy in India*. Retrieved from https://nipfp.org (Accessed on February 4, 2018).
2. *White paper on black money*. (May 2012). Ministry of Finance, Department of Revenue, Central Board of Direct Taxes, Govt. of India. New Delhi. p.2.
3. Singh, V.K. (2006). *Controlling money laundering in India–Problems and perspectives*, IGIDR, Mumbai. Retrieved from www.igidr.ac.in (Accessed on January 5, 2018).
4. *The Wire*, February 6, 2017.
5. Bussell, J. Funding elections in India: Whose money has the most influence? *The Hindustan Times*, July 24, 2018.
6. Bussell, J. Funding elections in India: Whose money has the most influence? *The Hindustan Times*, July 24, 2018.
7. Underlying causes of the black economy: A qualitative review of the principal factors, Accessed from https://www.nipfp.org.in (Accessed on February 14, 2018).
8. *What is the Adarsh scam? Indian Express*, December 22, 2017.
9. Kar, D. The drivers and dynamics of illicit financial flows from India: 1948–2008, November 2010, Global Financial Integrity.
10. Varma, S. $21 billion in black money exited India in 2014: Global Watchdog. *Times of India*, May 3, 2017.
11. White paper on black money, Ministry of Finance, Department of Revenue, Central Board of Direct Taxes, New Delhi, May 2012, p.13.
12. Corruption Perception Index (2017). Accessed from https://www.transparency.org (Accessed on May 4, 1019).
13. Underlying causes of the black economy: A qualitative review of the principal factors, Accessed from https://www.nipfp.org.in (Accessed on February 14, 2018).
14. Real estate under GST: A great weapon in the war against black money. *Business Standard*, January 31, 2017.
15. Finance Ministry declines disclosing black money reports, says probe on, February 4, 2019. Retrieved from www.ndtv.com. (Accessed on March 18, 2019).
16. More black money present within India than outside: Secret govt report, *India Today*, February 21, 2009.
17. Kumar, A. (1999). *The black economy in India*. New Delhi: Penguin Books.
18. Prevention of money laundering. Retrieved from https://dor.gov.in (Accessed on June 18, 2019).
19. The Right to Information Act. Retrieved from https://rti.gov.in (Accessed on June 18, 2019).
20. 1.75 crore RTI applications filed since 2005: Study, *The Economic Times*, October 6, 2016.
21. Kumar, A. (1999). *The black economy in India*. New Delhi: Penguin Books.
22. The GST impact: How this tax will curb black money? *The Hindustan Times*, August 4, 2016.
23. Real estate under GST: A great weapon in the war against black money. *Business Standard*, January 31, 2018.
24. Economic Survey, Department of Economic Affairs. Ministry of Finance. Govt. of India. 2017–2018, p.54.
25. Sands, P. (2016), Making it harder for the bad guys: The case for eliminating high denomination notes. Harvard Kennedy School M-RCBG Associate Working Paper No. 52.
26. Economic Survey, 2017–2018, p.59.
27. Gopakumar, G. RBI says 98.96% of ₹500, ₹1000 notes returned after demonetization. *Livemint*, August 31, 2017.
28. Demonetisation led to more tax collection, higher growth: Arun Jaitley. *The Times of India*, August 30, 2018.
29. Press Information Bureau, Government of India, Ministry of Finance, August 30, 2018.
30. PricewaterhouseCoopers India. (2015). Disrupting cash: Accelerating electronic payments in India. Retrieved from https://www.pwc.in (Accessed on June 14, 2019).
31. Economic Survey, 2017–2018, Department of Economic Affairs. Ministry of Finance. Govt. of India. p.63.
32. Agarwal, S. (2018). India's demonetization drive: A necessary jolt towards a more digital economy? *NUS Business School*, Accessed from https://www.forbes.com (Accessed on June 6, 2019).
33. Bhakta, P. Demonetisation effect: Digital payments India's new currency; debit card transactions

surge to over 1 billion. *The Economic Times*, May 27, 2017.

34. Demonetisation & real estate sector: Positive disruptions. *The Economic Times*, December 1, 2017.
35. Singh, C. (2018). India since demonetization. IIM Bangalore, IIMB-WP No. 567.
36. Arun, T.K. Demonetization: All cost and little benefit. *The Economic Times*, September 2, 2018.
37. Arun, T.K. Demonetisation: All cost and little benefit. *The Economic Times*, September 2, 2018.
38. Anklesaria Aiyar, S.S. Cash in on demonetisation. *The Times of India*, August 16, 2017.
39. An Indefensible Step, EPW, Vol. 52, Issue No. 35, September 2, 2017.
40. Demonetisation, inequality and informal sector. *Livemint*, November 6, 2017.
41. Kumar, A. (2017). Economic consequences of demonetization. *EPW*, Vol. 52, Issue No. 1,
42. How demonetization impacted the Indian economy. *Livemint*, August 30, 2018.

CHAPTER 29

ECONOMIC REFORMS IN INDIA

No force on earth can stop an idea whose time has come.
—Victor Hugo

INTRODUCTION

One of the hallmarks of a modern, vibrant economy as opposed to a traditional, economy is that it is constantly seeking to improve the way it functions. India's economic reforms of 1991 signify a watershed in India's economic development strategy and policies since independence. The reforms constitute a set of economic measures at both micro and macro level to place the economy in a higher trajectory of growth and development. But it was not in 1991 that the first attempt for reforms was made.* Attempts have been made in the decade of 1970s and 1980s but economic reforms began in earnest only in July 1991.

The present chapter will focus on following key issues:

- Genesis of Economic Crisis of 1990s
- Economic Reforms in India: Macroeconomic Stabilization and Structural Adjustment Reforms
- Critical Evaluation of Economic Reforms

*There was one occasion in 1966 when there was a real possibility of significant economic liberalization. Following the suspension of external aid following the Indo-Pakistan War of October 1965 and the severe drought of 1965 that adversely affected agriculture-based exports and increased foodgrain imports, an acute balance of payments crisis emerged. To contain it, India sought the assistance of the International Monetary Fund and the World Bank. These agencies recommended devaluation of the rupee and called for a major liberalization of the control system and relaxation of import controls. The World Bank also promised a substantial setup in non-project loans in support of the liberalization programme. Mrs. Gandhi, who had become the Prime Minister in January 1966, devalued the rupee in June 1966 and announced a modest set of liberalizing measures that extended the hesitant shift toward liberalization that began in 1962. Unfortunately, the Bank reneged on its promise. Besides, a second consecutive drought in 1966 led to inflation and erosion of the potential beneficial effects of devaluation. A politically vulnerable Mrs. Gandhi, who was vehemently criticized by her own party as well as the opposition for devaluing the rupee and allegedly succumbing to external pressure, abandoned the modest liberalization programme and did not attempt any liberalization until the 1980s.

The Economic Crisis of 1990s

Reforms in India have a background and reflect the poor upbringing of Indian economy for decades which ultimately led to the economic crisis of 1990s. Many economists have explained the reasons of India's economic debacle. Jagdish Bhagwati has succinctly summarized the factors that explain Indian economic failure. He divides India's economic failure into three groups: (1) extensive bureaucratic controls over production, investment, and trade; (2) inward-looking trade and foreign investment policies; and (3) inefficient functioning of public sector enterprises.[1] Such policies were very much there for years destroying the capacity of the economy to cope with any external or internal shock. By 1990, economy had become so much vulnerable that the minor oil shock of 1990 (due to Iraq's invasion of Kuwait) made disproportionately larger impact and the country went through one of the worst crisis ever.

The following points can explain the economic crisis of 1990:

1. *Higher fiscal deficit:* Fiscal health of an economy reflects the government's quantity and quality of spending as well as earnings. Imprudent spending leads to higher borrowing and interest payments. The ever-growing non-developmental expenditure of the government deteriorated the fiscal health and ultimately increased fiscal deficit from 5.1% of GDP during early 1980s to 8.4% during 1990–1991. The government borrowed to bring down the fiscal deficit which led to the increase in internal debt from 33.3% of GDP in early 1980s to nearly 50% of GDP at the end of 1990–1991. It raised the burden of servicing the debt from 2% of GDP to 3.8% of GDP.
2. *Adverse balance of payment situation:* India's current account deficit rose from 1.35% of GDP in 1980–1981 to 3.69% of GDP in 1990–1991. The adverse current account situation can be attributed to wrong economic policies of the government like import substitution policy and restricted trade policy over the years. The growing current account deficit was also accentuated by fall in foreign remittances from Arabian countries due to gulf crisis. The unstable coalition government at the center and political uncertainty adversely affected the confidence of external creditors, including in particular non-resident Indians (NRI) led to the outflow of NRI deposits.[2] In order to reduce the foreign exchange deficit, the government accosted to external borrowing, and as a result, India's external debt rose from 12% of GDP in 1980–1981 to 23% of GDP at the end of 1990–1991. The rise in external borrowing led to the increase in debt service burden from 15% of export earnings in 1980–1981 to 30% of export earnings in 1990–1991. Foreign-exchange reserves dwindled to a low of US$1.2 billion (equal to two week's imports). India stared bankruptcy in the face as it struggled to meet external debt obligations.[3]

BOX 29.1 What is Washington Consensus?

The term Washington consensus was coined in 1989 by English economist John Williamson. It encompasses a set of 10 economic policy prescriptions for crisis-wracked developing countries by Washington, D.C.-based institutions such as the International Monetary Fund (IMF), World Bank, and United States Department of the Treasury. The 10 broader points suggested by Washington consensus were reforms in fiscal policy, redirection of public expenditure, tax reform, deregulation of interest rates, competitive exchange rates, trade liberalization, liberal FDI regime, privatization of public sector enterprises (PSEs), free market entry and legal security for property rights. The prescriptions include various micro and macroeconomic reforms so as to produce a paradigm shift in the economic growth and development of such nations. The World Bank and IMF promoted such standard package of advice, known as stabilization and structural adjustment programs, by attaching policy conditions to the loans they made.

Sources:

1. Williamson, J. (2004). The strange history of Washington consensus. Journal of Post Keynesian Economics, 27(2) (Winter, 2004–2005), 195–206.
2. Hurt, S.R. Washington consensus. In Encyclopaedia Britannica. Retrieved from https://www.britannica.com (accessed on August 26, 2018).

3. *High inflation rates:* Indian economy witnessed a sort of double-digit running inflation during 1990–1991. While the average rate of inflation during the period 1980–1989 was around 6.4% per annum, this increased sharply to 11.3% during 1990–1991. The major reason for the large build-up in prices was deficit financing (and consequent growth of money supply) which was carried at the large scale during the decade of 1980s.[4] Poor industrial and agriculture production also created supply side bottlenecks and contributed to supply side inflation.

Economic Reforms in India

The political uncertainty after 1989 resulted in loss in investor confidence. In September 1990, the US credit rating agency Standard and Poor had for the first time placed India at credit rating of BBB, which is the lowest rung of investment grade in its rating scale. Subsequently, in March 1991, the Japanese Bond Research Institute (JBRI) as well as Moody's Investors' Service lowered India's credit ratings to the lowest level in the investment grade.[5] It was the time when P.V. Narasimha Rao* became the Prime Minister of India and he inducted Dr Manmohan Singh into cabinet as the Finance Minister. Further, the immediate task before the government was to explore the means available to finance the deficits.

It was under this situation that India approached IMF for an accommodation under the compensatory and contingency financing facility and the first credit tranche.[6] To overcome the economic crisis, India turned to the International Monetary Fund (IMF), which provided financial assistance on the condition that India embrace a structural adjustment program of which liberalizing trade was a key component. The government too recognized that the time had come to reshape India's economic policies by drawing appropriate lessons from "East Asian Miracle" based on more export-oriented and more globally connected strategies of development, as successfully practiced earlier by Japan and South Korea and also by other South East Asian economies, viz., Hong Kong, Taiwan, Malaysia, Singapore, Indonesia, and Thailand.[7] The Government of India's immediate response was to secure an emergency loan of $2.2 billion from the IMF by pledging 67 tonnes of India's gold reserves as collateral security. The Reserve Bank of India had

* P.V. Narasimha Rao was the ninth Prime Minister of India (1991–1996) and is also hailed as father of economic reforms of India.

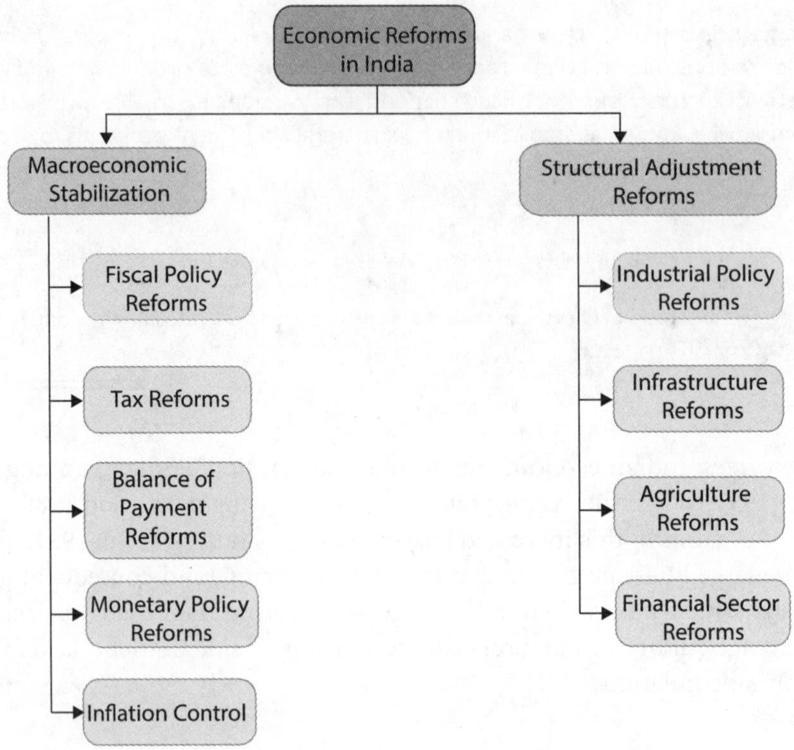

FIGURE 29.1 Economic Reforms in India.

to airlift 47 tonnes of gold to the Bank of England and 20 tonnes of gold to the Union Bank of Switzerland to raise $605 million.[8]

Economic reforms launched since June 1991 may be categorized under two broad areas: Macroeconomic reforms and micro-economic Reforms. Macroeconomic reforms, also called macroeconomic stabilization policies, are demand side measures which constitute returning to low and stable inflation and a sustainable monetary, fiscal, trade, and exchange rate policy. Micro-economic reforms, popularly called structural adjustment reforms, are supply side measures that include industrial, financial, agriculture, and infrastructure sector reforms (see Figure 29.1).

Both macroeconomic stabilization policies and structural reforms go hand in hand. Stabilization is necessary for the accompaniment of structural reform that is crisis driven. This is because the structural reform process can itself add to macro-economic pressures. For example, in the short-run, trade liberalization may worsen the balance of payments and financial liberalization may increase fiscal deficits by raising the cost of government borrowing. In the absence of stabilization policies, such extra macroeconomic strains can bring the reform process to a halt.[9]

Macroeconomic Stabilization

Fiscal Policy Reforms

The fiscal stabilization was conceived as an essential precondition for the success of economic reforms. The design of India's reform program was fully in line with this conclusion and fiscal stabilization was given the highest priority, especially in the initial phase of crisis management when the current account deficit was high and inflation in double digits. As discussed earlier, the

Central Government fiscal deficit experienced a steep rise and reached a peak level of 8.4% of gross domestic product (GDP) in 1990–1991. If the State Governments' deficit is also included, it was around 10% which was high by any standard. A reduction in the Central Government's fiscal deficit was therefore, critical for the reforms to take off.

The government took various steps to permanently strengthen the fiscal situation, for example

1. the abolition of export subsidies in 1991–1992;
2. partial restructuring of fertilizer subsidy in 1992–1993;
3. progressive phasing out the budgetary support to loss making PSUs in the form of government loans to cover their losses;
4. part of the fiscal adjustment in the first 2 years was also achieved by restricting development expenditure, including expenditure on social and economic infrastructure.

The success achieved in fiscal consolidation in the first 2 years was commendable, with the fiscal deficit being reduced by 2.7 percentage points of GDP. In this respect, the management of reforms in the first 2 years was entirely in line with the prevailing consensus on sequencing. The early years of the reforms saw a substantial reduction in the Central Government fiscal deficit from 8.4% of the GDP in 1990–1991 to 5.9% in 1991–1992 and further to 5.7% in 1992–1993.[10]

Tax Reforms

The tax system, both for direct and indirect taxes, had become very complex in India. Maximum marginal personal income tax rates were high, along with a number of rates for different income ranges. The corporate tax rate was high too. Accordingly, the tax code had to be riddled with a number of special provisions for exemption of different kinds of income, and the corporate tax code was full of exceptions and incentives. Because of high rates and complexity, avoidance and evasion was naturally high. Similarly, in the case of indirect taxes, there were high levels of both domestic excise duties and customs tariffs, with a myriad of rates for different commodities. Again, this necessitated a whole range of specific provisions and exemptions for different kinds of producers and end uses, leading to great administrative complexity.[11]

Since 1991, several efforts have been made through the annual budget process to achieve tax reforms. These have focused on[12]

1. expanding the tax base by including services;
2. reducing rates of direct taxes for individuals and corporations;
3. abolishing most export subsidies and lowering import duties;
4. rationalizing sales tax and reducing the cascading effect of central indirect taxes by introducing a MODVAT and VAT;
5. rationalizing both direct and indirect taxes by removing unnecessary exemptions;
6. providing for tax incentives for infrastructure and export-oriented sectors, including setting up special (export) economic zones; and
7. simplification of procedures and efforts for improving the efficiency of the tax administration system especially through computerization.

Balance of Payment Reforms

It is clear from the prior discussion that BOP crisis had been the key trigger for reforms. Therefore, the measures to correct BOP were badly needed. BOP reforms comprised trade policy reforms and reforms in foreign exchange management. In keeping with the objective of greater openness and outward orientation, trade policy was substantially liberalized for all except final consumer goods. The complex import control regime was dismantled, and the policy of freer exports and imports was implemented. The peak rate of customs duty applicable to several items was over 200% in 1991. It was lowered to 65% in 1994 and further to 10% in 2006. Product specific and market linked policies were launched to provide boost to exports, EPZs were given various incentives and SEZ Act was passed in 2005.

Exchange rate policy of the country also underwent a series of transitional reforms since 1991, leading to a total transformation at the end of 3 years. Rupee was devalued by 24% in July 1991 and accompanied by an abolition of export subsidies to help the fiscal position. Adoption of market determined exchange rate system, though somewhat managed was introduced in line with liberalized trade policy.

Monetary Policy Reforms

Over the 1970s and 1980s, monetary policy, as we know it, had become almost non-existent: with a system of credit allocation, administered and different interest rates for different purposes; automatic monetization of fiscal deficits; and financial repression through pre-emption of banks' resources. Hence, a number of measures had to be taken. These include elimination of automatic monetization, reduction of statutory pre-emption of the lendable resource of banks, and interest rate deregulation.[13] The major purpose of such measures was to restore the independence of monetary policy and the central bank. The post-reform period also witnessed a shift from direct to indirect instruments of monetary policy. Such modifications in the monetary policy led to significant reduction in the rates of inflation. Inflation, which was around 7–8% during 1951–1991, had fallen to around 5% in the recent period since the late 1990s.

Control of Inflation

As discussed earlier, prices were alarmingly high in 1990–1991 with the rate of inflation being above 10% mark. There were two solutions to this problem. The short-term and immediate solution was introducing fiscal and monetary discipline and the long-term solution was improving output and supply of goods and services. With fiscal correction and dramatic changes in monetary policy, the inflation was brought down to 8, 4.6, and 4.4% during 1995–1996, 1996–1997, and 1997–1998, respectively.

Structural Adjustment Reforms

Industrial Policy Reforms

Reform of the public sector was a critical element in structural adjustment programs all over the world and was also included on India's reform agenda.[14] With new Industrial Policy, the government announced major package of reforms in July 1991 and an era of liberalization, privatization, and globalization had started (Box 29.2). Industrial licensing was abolished; the existing legislative restrictions on the expansion of large companies were removed; phased manufacturing programs were terminated; and the reservation in the public sector was removed. The list of industries reserved for the public sector was drastically pruned and many critical areas were opened up to private sector participation. Massive de-reservation was launched to make small-scale sector competitive and productive. Restrictions on the import of foreign technology were withdrawn and a new regime welcoming foreign direct investment was introduced. With such massive reforms introduced in one stroke in 1991, the stage was set for a policy framework that

BOX 29.2 Liberalization, Privatization, and Globalization

Few economists describe the economic reforms in India under three heads: Liberalization, Privatization and Globalization.

1. *Liberalization:* Liberalization means the elimination of state control over economic activities. It implies greater autonomy to the business enterprises in decision-making and removal of the government interference. Based on the principle of laissez-faire, market mechanism (demand and supply forces) operates to bring about greater efficiency and guide the path to economic equilibrium. In India, liberalization policies include deregulation of industrial sector, financial sector reforms, tax reforms, foreign exchange reforms, and trade and investment policy reforms.
2. *Privatization:* Privatization is the transfer of control of ownership of economic resources from the public sector to the private sector. It means a decline in the role of the public sector as there is a shift in the property rights from the state to private ownership. In India, privatization involved the disinvestment of PSEs by two ways: (i) withdrawal of the government from ownership and management of public sector companies and/or (ii) by outright sale of public sector companies.
3. *Globalization:* Globalization simply means the integration of national economy with world economy. It means free flow of goods, services, labor, and capital. In other words, globalization refers to the growing economic interdependence of countries worldwide through the increasing volume and variety of cross-border transactions in goods and services and of international capital flows, and also through the more rapid and widespread diffusion of technology. Benefits of globalization include specialization, widening of markets through trade, increase in productivity and competition, and mobilization of large volume of financial savings. The process of globalization takes place through liberal trade and foreign investment policies. The establishment of WTO in 1995 has also augmented the process of globalization.

Source: Citrin, D., & Fischer, S. (2000). Meeting the challenges of globalization in the advanced economies. In H. Wagner. (Ed.), *Globalization and unemployment*. Berlin, Heidelberg: Springer.

encouraged new entry, introduced new competition, both domestic and foreign, which thereby induced the attainment of much greater efficiency in industry over a period of time.[15]

Financial Sector Reforms

Financial sector constitutes both money market as well as capital market. The purpose of reforming the real sector* was to create a new set of incentives which will encourage reallocation of resources toward more efficient uses. This process needed to be underpinned by a parallel process of financial sector reform which would enable the financial sector to mobilize savings and allocate them in a manner which supports the process of restructuring in the real economy.[16] Several initiatives were undertaken to reform the banking system and the capital markets.

As far as banking system reform is concerned, the government announced a package of reforms on the basis of report of Narasimham Committee recommendations. The high reserve requirements applicable to banks in the form of the statutory liquidity ratio (SLR) and the cash reserve ratio (CRR) were lowered to provide financial leverage to the banking system. Interest rate deregulation and market determination of interest on government securities further liberalized banking sector operations. Prudential norms relating to income recognition, provisioning,

* Real sector is the part of the economy that is concerned with actually producing goods and services. For example, agriculture and industry.

and capital adequacy applicable to banks were brought in line with Basle Committee standards. Private sector banks and foreign banks were allowed to operate so as to make Indian banking more competitive.

In the capital market, the government took various steps to remove deficiencies and improve the functioning of capital markets. The Securities and Exchange Board of India (SEBI) was established as an independent statutory authority for regulating the stock exchanges and supervising the major players in the capital markets, viz., brokers, underwriters, merchant bankers, mutual funds, etc. New instruments were introduced in the stock market to provide more depth and transparency in its functioning. Bombay Stock Exchange was corporatized to boost investor confidence and National Stock Exchange was established to widen the capital market spectrum in the country. An important initiative taken as part of the reforms was the opening up of the capital market for portfolio investments. Indian companies were allowed to access international capital markets by issuing equity abroad through the mechanism of Global Depository Receipts. The introduction of new competition led to the introduction of new products and new practices. A new regulator, the Insurance Regulation and Development Authority (IRDA), was founded in 1999 to govern the insurance industry.

Agriculture Sector Reforms

In July 1991 when the devaluation of the Indian rupee presaged the introduction of a whole series of liberalizing economic reforms, agriculture was very far from the minds of most policy makers and commentators. The immediate focus was on the balance of payments, and thereafter on industry and other sectors like the modern services. But later, it was felt that the devaluation of the rupee already provided sufficient incentive to agriculture, because it was expected to make it more attractive to export crops and thereby improve farm incomes. It was believed that freeing agricultural markets and liberalizing external trade in agricultural commodities would provide price incentives leading to enhanced investment and output in that sector, while broader trade liberalization would shift inter-sectoral terms of trade in favor of agriculture.[17] Accordingly, steps were taken to reform Indian Agriculture Sector: the removal of restraints on inter-state movement of foodgrains; the restructuring of the public distribution system (PDS); relaxation of restrictions under the Essential Commodities Act; introduction of forward trading in most agricultural commodities; and removal of some marketing restrictions on crop produce. The trade policy reform in India, in the sphere in agriculture, which sought to dismantle restrictions on trade other than tariffs and to bring domestic prices closer to world prices, represented a fundamental departure from the past.[18]

Infrastructure Sector Reforms

There was worldwide move to reform and develop infrastructure sector during 1990s. The major initiatives for infrastructure development were undertaken after the recommendations of the India Infrastructure Report in the mid-1990s. Off late, it was recognized that infrastructure investment had to be raised by including new legislations and formation of regulatory authorities. The following reform measures were initiated to develop infrastructure sector:

1. The telecom sector was deregulated, private investment in telecom was allowed and Telecom Regulatory Authority of India (TRAI) was formed.
2. In roadways, fuel cess was imposed to finance highway construction. National Highway Development Project (NHDP) and Prime Minister's Gram Sadak Yojana or the Rural

Roads Programme set a new era of road development across the counties and in the far hinterlands.

3. New civil aviation policy was introduced to promote competition, investment, and quality of service via new private airlines, new private airports, and Greenfield FDI.
4. Under port development, private sector and foreign sector entry has been allowed.
5. In electricity sector, comprehensive modern electricity was enacted, which had enabling feature for encouraging private sector entry, enhanced competition, and rational regulation.

Impact of Economic Reforms on Indian Economy

It is a fact that Indian economy has witnessed a remarkable change since the launch of 1991 economic reforms. But as it always happens, there are points in favor and disfavor. There are both the proponents and the opponents of economic reform and their impact on Indian Economy. The protagonists have argued that India's economic progress was not only outstanding during the post-reform period but it also placed India in the higher trajectory of growth. Antagonists, however, have taken a dig on the so-called growth as it failed to deliver in terms of jobs and reducing poverty and inequalities. For example, India's two most-celebrated economists—Nobel Laureate Amartya Sen and Jagdish Bhagwati exchanged sharp notes and views on economic reforms and its impact. The Sen-Bhagwati debate highlights the differences that exist between the prominent thinkers on their visions of economic models and development strategies and the role of state and non-state actors. A strong supporter of the state playing a leading role in funding and providing public goods, Sen has persistently argued for the more inclusive, greater state-driven policy. Bhagwati, on the other hand, is unabashedly laissez faire and a staunch champion of liberal deregulated market-oriented approach and has supported reform measures in India.[19] Keeping in mind the two different strands vis-à-vis economic reforms and their impact on India economy, we will discuss both the viewpoints.

Case for Economic Reforms

India's reforms have been piecemeal and incremental, giving the casual observer the impression that nothing has been happening. If one takes the totality of reforms over the last decade, however, the change is unmistakable. The analogy is with the hour hand of the clock, which looks completely static, and yet completes a full circle every 12 hours.[20]

The Growth Turnaround

Once a poor economic laggard, India now is the world's sixth biggest economy with GDP amounted to $2.597 trillion in 2017. Furthermore, India now has the third-largest GDP (more than $8 trillion) in the world in purchasing power parity terms after China and the United States.[21] Per capita income is up from $375 per year in 1991 to around $2,000 today. India has long ceased to be a low-income country as defined by the World Bank, which uses a threshold of $1,045 and has become a middle-income country. India's annual GDP growth rose from 3.5% in 1950–1980 and 5.5% in 1980–1992 to an average of 8% since 2003.[22] The higher growth rate and per capita income level is helping increase in the market size, creating more opportunities for production and employment.

Industrial and Service Sector Performance

Industrial policy prior to 1991 was laden with controls and state monopoly. The tight control of the government on industry was aptly captured by a leading cartoonist in a 1980s comic strip showing the industry minister tell his staff, "We shouldn't encourage big industry—that is our policy, I know. But I say we shouldn't encourage small industries either. If we do, they are bound to become big...."[23] Indian industry has come a long way since then. Today, the private sector has become an active participant in the economy. Manufacturing and construction sector has experienced a spectacular growth and pulled up the overall growth rate. Service sector too has demonstrated its resilience in software, business services, and financial services. India has become one of the most sought after FDI destination. Introduction of GST, enactment of IBC code, campaign like "Make in India," and numerous entrepreneurship development programs are providing the required depth to the economy.

Attitude Toward Reforms

The greatest change during the post-reform period has been in the attitude toward reforms. Whereas the vocal supporters of reforms within India were rare during the 1980s, virtually every political party today recognizes the need for continued reforms. Differences on which reforms to undertake first and at what pace still exist, but few disagree that reforms must continue. Initial fears that changes in governments will bring the reform process to a halt or even reverse it have proven to be without foundation.[24] The political establishment today agrees to remove hundreds of archaic laws that survived for years like relics in a museum but with no relevance in modern India. From 1947–2013, the successive governments removed 1,301 obsolete laws which came in the way of smooth administration and economic growth in 66 years. The NDA government after it came into power managed to weed out as many as 1,500 Acts during 2014–2017. As many as 2,000 more obsolete central acts not consonant with the times have also been identified for quick termination with useful assistance from the Law Commission.[25]

Case Against Economic Reforms

Impact on Poverty and Inequality

Economic reforms are going to complete their two decades in 2021 and they have failed to affect the common masses. Almost 18 years have elapsed and India is still home for world's largest number of poor. The absolute poverty has decreased but the progress is not that much fast as envisaged. According to National Sample Survey Office (NSSO) 68th round poverty estimates (based on the methodology of Rangarajan committee), 21.9% of population (363 million Indians) was below poverty line (25.7% in rural areas and 13.7% in urban areas). As per multi-dimensional poverty index, around 27.5% of Indians are multi-dimensionally poor. Economic reforms have exacerbated the extent of inequality in India. India is no stranger to income inequality, but the gap is widening further since 1991. According to Oxfam Report, 2018 India's top 1% of the population now holds 73% of the wealth, while 67 crore citizens, comprising the country's poorest half, saw their wealth rise by just 1%. It will take 941 years for a minimum wage worker in rural India to earn what the top paid executive at a leading Indian garment firm earns in a year.[26] In 2017, India's richest 1% held 58% of the country's total wealth, which was higher than the global figure of about 50%.

Jobless Growth

The proportion of unemployed people in India had accentuated during 1993–1994 to 2004–2005 as per the findings of NSSO 61st survey, though it came down slightly in 2011–2012. The country's unemployment rate stood at a 45-year-high of 6.1% in 2017–2018, according to the NSSO's periodic labor force survey.[27] According to the data published in the Business Standard, the labor force participation rate has declined systematically. It was 43% in 2004–2005, 40% in 2009–2010, 39.5% in 2011–2012, and 36.9% in 2017–2018. Further, there is a gender twist to this jobless growth story. Almost the entire decline in the labor participation is triggered due to a sharp reduction of women in the workforce. The labor force participation rate of women was 29.4% in 2004–2005, 23.5% in 2009–2010, 22.5% in 2011–2012, and 17.5% in 2017–2018.[28]

Despite the high growth rate syndrome, India's industrial and service sector has failed to pull workers out of agriculture into gainful employment. Today, approximately 45% of India's workforce still remains in agriculture. The jobless growth syndrome has been far more exclusive than inclusive benefitting the big corporate houses. A total of 99% of MSMEs consist of micro units which fail to grow and evolve into small and medium enterprises proving dent to productivity, employment, and growth.

Structural Bottlenecks

Despite the reform process going on in a snail pace, there are certain structural bottlenecks in the India's economic system that needs to be addressed at the earliest. First, India badly needs reforms in labor laws so as to restore the employer's right to lay-off workers upon adequate compensation to them. Second, privatization of public sector enterprises needs to be speeded up. With almost two-thirds of the industrial output of the organized sector in these enterprises, it will be difficult to stimulate industrial growth in the short run. Third, MSMEs need to be scaled up in terms of growth and productivity. The successful micro units need to be evolved into small and medium enterprises. Fourth, trade liberalization must be continued and emphasis must be to reallocate production toward labor-intensive products in which India has comparative advantage. Fifth, infrastructure is another important area of reforms. Though a lot has happened in infrastructure in the last few years, roads, railways, and ports all need expansion as well as improvement in the quality of service. Sixth, another significant area of reforms is perhaps India's power sector which suffers from the government monopoly at the state level and proverbial inefficiency including large-scale thefts of electricity. Private entry along with the emphasis on renewable energy resource generation must be the priority. Seventh, economic reforms of 1990s virtually bypassed agriculture. The world's highest number of farmers' suicides take place in India. India needs to devise a suitable agriculture policy to increase agriculture productivity and income. Last, but not the least, the reforming bureaucracy is of great significance. The bloated bureaucracy must be downsized and opened up to outside specialists as policymaking increasingly has become sophisticated and specialized activity.

Summary

1. The economic reforms constitute a set of economic measures at both micro and macro level to place the economy in a higher trajectory of growth and development. India's economic crisis is a legacy of imprudent economic policies that were carried over the decades, such as (1) extensive bureaucratic controls over production, investment, and trade; (2) inward-looking trade and foreign investment policies; and (3) inefficient functioning of public sector enterprises. All this resulted into the mounting fiscal deficit (8.4%), adverse balance of payment situation (current account deficit—3.69% of GDP) and high inflation rates (11.3%) in 1991. India approached International financial institutions for help and introduced a set of reforms.
2. Macroeconomic reforms, also called macroeconomic stabilization policies, are demand side measures which constitute returning to low and stable inflation and a sustainable monetary, fiscal, trade, and exchange rate policy. In fiscal front, the government went for fiscal consolidation by cutting down the public expenditure and slashing subsidies. Tax reforms comprised rationalization of taxes, introduction of service tax, VAT, and very recently GST. Balance of payment reforms includes lowering of custom duty, changes in trade policy, and establishment of SEZs. Monetary policy reforms include deregulation of interest rate, reduction in CRR & SLR, and free entry of players. Inflation control measures had two pronged strategy: introducing fiscal and monetary discipline as a short-term solution and improving output and supply of goods and services as a long-term solution.
3. Microeconomic reforms, popularly called structural adjustment reforms, are supply side measures that include industrial, financial, agriculture, and infrastructure sector reforms. Industrial reforms comprised abolishing industrial licensing, introduction of disinvestment program, and doing away with reservation of PSUs. Financial sector reforms included both money market and capital market reforms. Agriculture sector reforms include freeing agricultural markets and liberalizing external trade in agricultural commodities, removal of restraints on inter-state movement of foodgrains, and the restructuring of the PDS. Infrastructure reforms included deregulation of TRAI, launching of NHDP, reforms in port and airport segments, and power sector reforms.
4. The reforms affected growth positively. The per capita income rose over the period of time and India has become sixth largest economy in nominal exchange rate and third largest in terms of PPP. Both industry and services have done remarkable progress during post-reform period. Manufacturing and construction sector in industry and financial and business services in service sector have placed Indian economy in higher trajectory of growth. Over the period of time, there is positive mindset with regard to reform process in the country cutting across the political lines. A huge number of archaic laws have been removed to facilitate reform process.
5. There is another side of reforms as well. Even after the 18 years of reforms, India is still home for world's largest number of poor. The problem of inequality has accentuated with 1% of population holding nearly three-fourth of India's wealth. The other criticism of reforms is jobless growth. Overall LFPR and female LFPR have registered a decline since the beginning of reforms. Both industry and services have failed to absorb surplus manpower of agriculture sector. Further, despite the implementation of reforms, there are structural bottlenecks in industry, agriculture, power sector, infrastructure, trade, and bureaucracy.

Endnotes

1. Bhagwati, J. (1992). *India's economy: The shackled giant*. Oxford: Clarendon Press.
2. Srinivasan, T.N. (1996). *Indian economic reforms: Background, rationale, achievements, and future prospects*. Retrieved from https://www.researchgate.net (Accessed on August 26, 2018).
3. Wadhva, C.D. (1993). *India trying to liberalise: Economic reforms since 1991*. Retrieved from https://apcss.org/Publications/Edited%20Volumes/RegionalFinal%20chapters/Chapter16Wadhva.pdf.
4. Nayyar, D. (1993). Indian economy at the crossroads—Illusions and realities, April 10, *EPW*, p.103.

5. Dholakia, B.H. (1991). India's economic crisis: Nature and remedies. *Vikalpa, 16*(3), July–September 1991.
6. Rangarajan, C. (2010). Two episodes in reform process. In S. Acharya, & R. Mohan (Eds.), *Indian economy Performance and challenges*. New Delhi: OUP.
7. Wadhva, C.D.(2009). *India trying to liberalise: Economic reforms since 1991*, retrieved from https://apcss.org (Accessed on August 27, 2018).
8. Rajghatta, C., & Sinha, P. (2009). Full circle: India buys 200 tons gold from IMF. *The Times of India*, November 4, 2009.
9. Joshi, V., & Little, I.M.D. (1993). Macro-economic stabilisation in India, 1991–1993 and beyond. *Economic and Political Weekly*, December 4, 1993. pp.2659–2665.
10. Ahluwalia, M.S. (1993). *India's economic reforms*, retrieved from http://planningcommission.nic.in (Accessed on September 5, 2018).
11. Mohan, R. (2008). Economic reforms in India: Where are we and where do we go? *RBI Bulletin*, December 2008, p.1478.
12. Wadhva, C.D. (2009). *India trying to liberalise: Economic reforms since 1991*, retrieved from https://apcss.org (Accessed on August 27, 2018).
13. Mohan, R. (2008). Economic reforms in India: Where are we and where do we Go? *RBI Bulletin*, December 2008, p.1478.
14. Ahluwalia, M.S. (1993). *India's economic reforms*, retrieved from http://planningcommission.nic.in (Accessed on September 5, 2018).
15. Mohan, R. (2008). Economic reforms in India: Where are we and where do we go? *RBI Bulletin*, December 2008, p.1478.
16. Ahluwalia, M.S. (1993). *India's economic reforms*, retrieved from http://planningcommission. nic.in (Accessed on September 5, 2018).
17. Ghosh, J, (2016). 25 Years of economic reforms: Agriculture. *Frontline*, August 5, 2016.
18. Nayyar, D. (1993). Indian Economy at the crossroads—Illusions and realities, April 10, *EPW*, p.103.
19. Palit, A. (2013). *Indian economy, Amartya Sen and Jagdish Bhagwati*, ISAS Brief No. 290–26, July 2013.
20. Panagariya, A. (2001). *India's economic reforms what has been accomplished? What remains to be done?*, November 2001, Asian Development Bank, EDRC Policy Brief No. 2, p.1.
21. India becomes world's sixth largest economy, muscles past France. *The Times of India*, July 12, 2018.
22. Aiyar, S. (2016). Twenty-five years of Indian economic reform, A story of private-sector success, government failure, and institutional weakness. *Policy Analysis*, October 26, 2016, No. 803.
23. Panagariya, A. (2001). *India's economic reforms what has been accomplished? What remains to be done?*, November 2001, Asian Development Bank, EDRC Policy Brief No. 2, p.1.
24. Panagariya, A. (2001). *India's economic reforms what has been accomplished? What remains to be done?*, November 2001, Asian Development Bank, EDRC Policy Brief No. 2, p.1.
25. Centre's clean-up Act: Modi government terminates 1,500 archaic laws. *India Today*, July 29, 2018.
26. Income inequality gets worse; India's top 1% bag 73% of the country's wealth, says Oxfam. *Business Today*, January 30, 2019.
27. Unemployment rate at four-decade high of 6.1% in 2017–2018: NSSO survey. *Business Standard, February 6, 2019.*
28. The latest NSSO report creates opportunity for labour reform. *Livemint*, February 4, 2019.

GLOSSARY

CHAPTER 1

Capitalism: Capitalism also called as market economy is an economic system in which private firms and individuals make the major decisions regarding production and consumption. Examples of capitalistic societies are the United States, Australia, and Canada.

Economic Growth: Economic growth is the process by which a nation's wealth increases over time. It is a quantitative change and a short-run phenomenon.

Economic Development: Economic development is the process whereby simple, low-income national economies are transformed into modern industrial economies. It involves qualitative as well as quantitative improvement in an economy over a longer period of time.

Emerging Markets: Emerging markets are countries with low incomes and high growth prospects and are progressing toward becoming more advanced, usually by means of rapid growth and industrialization. India, China, Brazil, and Mexico can be placed in this category.

Factors of Production: Factors of production denote the economic resources, both human and other, which, if properly utilized, will bring about a flow or output of goods and services. They are also called inputs. The four basic factors of production are land, labor, capital, and enterprise.

Frontier Economies: Frontier markets are countries that are better than least developed countries (LDCs) but still less established than the emerging markets. Sri Lanka and Ghana can be placed under this category.

Macroeconomics: Macroeconomics is the study of the aggregates and tries to analyze national or regional economy as a whole. It is concerned with understanding economy-wide events such as the total amount of goods and services produced, the level of unemployment, and the general behavior of prices.

Microeconomics: Microeconomics is a branch of economics that studies the behavior of individual consumers and firms. Examples are determination of pricing and output by a firm or demand and supply pattern of a particular product in a particular market.

Mixed Economy: Mixed economy is a market system of resource allocation, commerce, and trade in which free markets coexist with the government intervention. A combination of free market principles of private contracting and socialist principles of state ownership or planning is common to all mixed economies. All economies of the world are mixed economies, though economies may tilt toward capitalism and socialism.

Socialism: Socialism is a school of thought under which all production and distribution decisions are taken by the government. North Korea, Cuba, and former Soviet Republic can be placed in the category of socialism.

CHAPTER 2

Base Year: The base year is a benchmark year, with reference to which GDP, price inflation and other important indicators are measured. The base year must be a representative year and must not experience any abnormal incidents such as droughts, floods, and earthquakes. It must be a year that is not much far away from the current financial year. In India, the first estimates of national income were published by the Central Statistical Organization (CSO) in 1956 taking 1948–1949 as the base year. In India base year at present is 2011–2012 and before that it was the year 2004–2005.

Capital Formation: The term capital formation means investment and leads to addition to physical stock or productive capacity of the economy. The rate of GDCF is expressed as a percentage of GDP at market price.

Central Statistical Office: The Central Statistical Office (CSO) is a governmental agency in India under the Ministry of Statistics and Programme Implementation (MOSPI) responsible for co-ordination of statistical activities in India, and evolving and maintaining statistical standards. The CSO is located in Delhi. Its major activities are computation of national income, conducting annual survey of industries, economic censuses, human development statistics, gender statistics, etc.

Consumer Goods: Goods used by consumer for consumption are called consumer goods. Consumer goods are of two types. The first type is consumer durables, for example, fans, laptop, car, A.C., etc. The other type is of consumer non-durables and consists of fruits, vegetables, goods for instant consumption, etc.

Final Goods: An item that is meant for final use and will not pass through any more stages of production or transformations is called a final good. For example, a readymade shirt or jeans pant or a notebook purchased from the market. Final goods can be of two types: consumer goods and capital goods.

GDP at Market Price: It is GDP at FC plus indirect taxes minus subsidies.

GDP at Factor Cost: It is GDP at MP minus indirect taxes plus subsidies.

Gross Domestic Product (GDP): Sum total of all the final goods and services produced in a nation in a single accounting year.

Gross National Product (GNP): It is gross domestic product taking into account the net factor income from abroad.

Gross Value Added (GVA): Introduced in January 2015, it is defined as the value of output less the value of intermediate consumption.

Hindu Rate of Growth: Term coined by Professor Raj Krishna in the year 1978 to characterize the slow growth of Indian economy especially the lower annual growth rate of around 3.5% during 1950s to 1980s, while per capita income growth averaged 1.3%.

National Income: The sum value of all goods and services produced in a nation in a single financial year. It is expressed as gross domestic product, gross national product, net national product or gross value added.

National Income at Constant Prices: It is national income of a financial year calculated at base year prices. It is also called real national income.

National Income at Current Prices: It is national income of a financial year calculated at price prevailing in that year only. It is also called nominal national income.

Net National Product (NNP): It is gross national product minus depreciation of capital assets.

Saving: Saving is the part of national disposable income, which is not spent on consumption. Thus, income is identically equal to consumption plus savings. The rate of saving or saving rate is expressed as a percentage of GDP at market price.

CHAPTER 3

Buen Vivir: Buen Vivir means good living, which describes a way of doing things that is community-centric, ecologically balanced, and culturally sensitive.

Easterlin Paradox: Easterlin Paradox (formulated in 1974 by Richard Easterlin) also implies that if each individual in society becomes richer by the same degree then no individual is any better off (in subjective well-being terms) than they were prior to their income increasing.

Gender Development Index: Gender Development Index measures gender inequalities in achievement in three basic dimensions of human development: health (measured by female and male life expectancy at birth), education (measured by female and male expected years of schooling for children and mean years for adults aged 25 years and older), and command over economic resources (measured by female and male estimated GNI per capita).

Gender Inequality Index: Gender Inequality Index reflects women's disadvantages in three dimensions which are: reproductive health (measured by maternal mortality and adolescent fertility rates), empowerment (measured by the share of parliamentary seats held by women and attainment at secondary and higher education by each gender, and economic activity (measured by the labor market participation rate for each gender).

Gross National Happiness: An index used by Government of Bhutan to measure the collective happiness and well-being of its population. The four pillars of GNH's are (1) sustainable and equitable socio-economic development, (2) environmental conservation, (3) preservation and promotion of culture, and (4) good governance.

Human Development: Human development denotes both the process of widening people's choices and the level of their achieved well-being.

Human Development Index: Human Development Index is a comprehensive measure that captures the three essential components of human life—health (measured by life expectancy at birth), knowledge (mean years of schooling and expected years of schooling), and income (GNI- per capita income at PPP US$).

Inequality Adjusted Human Development Index: Inequality Adjusted Human Development Index is a measure of the average level of human development of people in a society once inequality is taken into account.

Multi-dimensional Poverty Index: Global Multi-dimensional Poverty Index identifies deprivations across the same three dimensions as the HDI based on 10 indicators and shows the number of people who are multi-dimensionally poor.

Unhappy Growth Paradox: It is a phenomenon of rapid economic growth associated with declining levels of subjective well-being.

World Happiness Index: Published by World happiness report, it measures happiness across more than 150 countries of the world on the basis of six indicators viz. levels of GDP, life expectancy, generosity, social support, freedom, and corruption.

CHAPTER 4

Composite Water Management Index: Composite Water Management Index was launched by NITI Aayog in 2018 to assess and improve performance in efficient management of water resources. The Index comprises 9 broad sectors covering 28 indicator

FAME India: The Faster Adoption and Manufacturing of (Hybrid) & Electric Vehicles (FAME) India was launched in 2015 to promote eco-friendly vehicles in the country. The scheme will help in addressing the issue of environmental pollution and fuel security.

Paris Agreement: Adopted by more than 190 nations in 2015, the Paris Agreement is an agreement within the United Nations Framework Convention on Climate Change that deals with greenhouse-gas-emissions mitigation, adaptation, and finance.

Soil Conservation: Soil conservation is the practice of preventing soil loss from erosion or reduced fertility caused by over usage, acidification, salinization, or other chemical soil contamination.

Soil Erosion: Soil erosion is defined as the wearing away of topsoil. Soil erosion takes place through wind, water, localized water logging, land salinization, sheet erosion, etc.

Sustainable Development: The term "Sustainable Development" was first defined by Brundtland Commission in 1987 in its report "our common future." It simply means the development that meets the needs of the present without compromising the ability of future generations to meet their own needs.

Sustainable Development Goals: The Sustainable Development Goals (SDGs) are a collection of 17 global goals set by the United Nations General Assembly in 2015 for the year 2030.

Waste Management: Waste management is the collecting, treating, and disposing of solid material that is discarded because it has served its purpose or is no longer useful.

CHAPTER 5

Bharatmala Pariyojana: Launched in 2015 for the development of highways, it focuses on optimizing efficiency of freight and passenger movement by developing economic corridors, inter–corridors, feeder routes, national corridor efficiency improvement, border and international connectivity roads, coastal and port connectivity roads, and green-field expressways.

Conventional Energy: Energy sources that are commonly in use since long time and can be exhausted due to over consumption. Such sources create pollution and add to global warming. Examples are coal, nuclear energy, etc.

Jawahar Lal Nehru National Solar Mission (JNNSM): Launched in 2010, it is an initiative of the Government of India and State Governments to promote solar power in India. JNNSM has been revised twice and now boasts a target of 100 GW of solar PV by 2022.

National Highway Development Project (NHDP): NHDP was launched in 1998 by National Highway authority of India with the objective of developing roads of international standards and represented 49,260 km of roads and highways work. The project was executed in seven phases and the Government planned to end the NHDP program in early 2018 and consume the ongoing projects under a larger Bharatmala project.

National Green Highways Project: Launched in 2015, the project aims at developing green corridors along NH for sustainable environment and inclusive growth. Green Highways Division under NHAI has been entrusted with the task of planning, implementation, and monitoring roadside plantations along 1 lakh km network of NH, which would, in turn, generate 1 lakh direct employment opportunity in plantations sector in next 10 years.

National Gas Grid: The Government has removed regional imbalance within the country with regard to access for natural gas and provide clean and green fuel throughout the country. At present about 16,788 km natural gas pipeline is operational and about 14,239 km gas pipelines are being developed to increase the availability of natural gas across the country.

RCS-UDAN: Launched in 2016, Regional Connectivity Scheme-Ude Desh Ka Aam Naagrik is a flagship scheme of Central Government introduced to enable air operations on unserved routes, connecting regional areas, to promote balanced growth.

Renewable Energy: Sources that are identified few decades ago and are available in abundance. They are environment-friendly and cannot be exhausted. Examples are solar, wind, and bio-mass, etc.

Sagarmala Project: Launched in 2016, the project was launched to promote port-led development in the country through harnessing India's 7,500 km long coastline, 14,500 km of potentially navigable waterways and strategic location on key international maritime trade routes.

CHAPTER 6

Crude Birth Rate: The crude birth rate (CBR) is defined as the number of live births per thousand people. It is usually the dominant factor in determining the rate of population growth.

Crude Death Rate: The crude death rate (CDR) indicates the number of deaths occurring during the year, per 1,000 people estimated at midyear. Subtracting the CDR from the CBR provides the rate of natural increase, which is equal to the rate of population change in the absence of migration.

Demographic Dividend: Demographic dividend is the window of opportunity that results from shifts in a population's age structure, mainly when the share of the working age population is larger than the non-working age share of the population.

Demographic Transition Theory: Demographic transition model was given by Warren Thompson in 1929 and later developed by Adolphe Landry and Frank W. Notestein. There are five stages as per theory: First stage of high birth and death rate; second stage of falling birth and death rate with fall in death rate being steeper; third stage of falling birth and death rates but the fall in birth rate is steeper; fourth stage of low birth and death rate; and fifth stage of negative growth rate where death rate turns greater than the birth rate.

Infant Mortality Rate: Infant mortality rate is the measure of human infant deaths in a group younger than 1 year of age. It is an important indicator of the overall physical health of a country.

Maternal Mortality Rate: The maternal mortality rate (MMR) is the annual number of female deaths per 100,000 live births from any cause related to or aggravated by pregnancy or its management (excluding accidental or incidental causes).

Total Fertility Rate: Total fertility rate (TFR) is the average number of children born to women during her reproductive years. For the population in a given area to remain stable, an overall total fertility rate of 2.1 is needed, assuming no immigration or emigration occurs.

CHAPTER 7

Bank Correspondent: Bank Correspondents (BCs) are individuals/entities engaged by a bank in India for providing banking services in unbanked/under-banked geographical regions. A banking correspondent works as an agent of the bank and substitutes for the physical presence of the bank.

Conspicuous Consumption: Conspicuous consumption is the expenditure incurred on the consumption of luxury goods so as to publicly display economic power.

Crony Capitalism: Crony capitalism is defined as a system where businesses multiply their wealth not by the fair rules of the market, but through their nexus with governments. Examples of crony capitalism are the distribution of legal permits, licenses, land, contracts, tax breaks, and so on.

Gini Coefficient: Given by Italian statistician Corrado Gini in 1921, Gini coefficient is a popular statistical tool to measure the extent to which the distribution of income (or, in some cases, consumption expenditure) among individuals or households within an economy deviates from a perfectly equal distribution.

International Comparison Program: The International comparison program (ICP) is a worldwide statistical initiative led by the World Bank under the auspices of the United Nations Statistical Commission, with the main objective of providing comparable price and volume measures of gross domestic product (GDP) and its expenditure aggregates among countries within and across regions. Through a partnership with international, regional, sub-regional, and national agencies, the ICP collects and compares price data and GDP expenditures to estimate and publish purchasing power parities (PPPs) of the world's economies.

International Poverty Line: International poverty line (IPL) describes the poverty threshold or poverty limit of a country. Given by World Bank, the international poverty line since 2015 is $1.90 a day. The figure is based on ICP purchasing power parity (PPP) calculations and represents the international equivalent of what $1.90 could buy in the United States in 2011.

Mixed Recall Period: Mixed Recall Period (MRP) is a methodology used by NSSO wherein the consumption expenditure data are collected using 365-day recall period for five non-food items and 30-day recall period for remaining items.

Modified Mixed Recall Period: Modified Mixed Recall Period (MMRP) is a methodology used by NSSO wherein the consumption expenditure data are collected using 365-day, 30-day, and 7-day recall period for different items.

National Sample Survey Office: The National Sample Survey Office (NSSO) is headed by Director General and is responsible for conduct of large-scale sample surveys in diverse fields on All-India basis. It collects primarily data through nation-wide household surveys on various socio-economic subjects like employment, consumption expenditure, rural & urban prices, and various other surveys viz. crop estimation surveys, Annual Survey of Industries (ASI), etc.

Poverty Line: Poverty line is a minimum level of individual or family income below which one is classified as poor according to governmental standards. In terms of calorie norms average poverty line per person per day is 2,155 kcal for rural areas and 2,095 kcal for urban areas as per C. Rangarajan committee recommendations.

Universal Basic Income: Universal Basic Income (UBI) is government scheme of regular fixed cash transfer payment to every citizen, regardless of whether he or she is rich or poor and/or wishing to be engaged in paid employment.

Uniform Recall Period: Uniform Recall Period (URP) is a methodology used by NSSO wherein consumption expenditure data are collected using 30-day recall period for all the items.

CHAPTER 8

Current Daily Status: Under this approach, NSSO measures unemployment to ascertain the activity status of an individual for each day of the reference week. A person is classified as employed for the "full day" if he has worked for 4 hours or more, half day if he works for more than 1 hour but less than 4 hours, unemployed if he does not work even for 1 hour.

Cyclical Unemployment: It is an unemployment that takes place due to change in business cycles. Generally, during recession unemployment rises due to fall in economic activity and production.

Current Weekly Status: Under this approach, NSSO measures unemployment using a week as the reference period. A person is considered to be employed if he is employed for at least 1 hour on any day of the reference week, otherwise he is considered unemployed.

Disguised Unemployment: Disguised unemployment signifies unproductive unemployment. The marginal productivity of such workers is zero.

Employment Elasticity: Employment elasticity is a measure of the percentage change in employment associated with one percentage point change in economic growth. For example, employment elasticity for India for the period 1993–94 to 2011–12 was 0.18% which means that for every 10% change in real GDP, there is about 1.8% change in employment.

Jobless Growth: Jobless growth means existence of high growth rate along with high unemployment rate. India is witnessing jobless growth syndrome during post-reform period.

Main Worker: Main workers are those workers who had worked for the major part of the reference period, that is, 6 months. The proportion of main workers in Indian economy has come down.

Marginal Worker: Marginal workers are those workers who had not worked for the major part of the reference period, that is, less than 6 months. The proportion of marginal workers in Indian economy has gone up.

MGNREGS: MGNREGS was launched by government of India in 2006 to provide minimum 100 days of guaranteed employment in a financial year, to those who demand work. It is world's largest employment guarantee program.

Unemployment Rate: The unemployment rate is the total number of unemployed people (calculated as labor force minus work force) divided by the total labor force and the ratio is expressed in percentage.

Usual Principal Status: Under this approach, NSSO uses the major time criterion generally more than 6 months in a principal activity to determine whether the person is in the labor force or out of labor force.

Usual Status: Under this approach, NSSO takes into consideration both the major time criterion and shorter time period (30 days or more in a subsidiary activity) to determine whether the person is employed or not.

CHAPTER 9

Arthashastra: Arthashastra is a classic treatise on politics and economics written in around 300 B.C. by Kautilya. The text incorporates ancient Indian wisdom and includes aspects like agriculture, mineralogy, mining and metals, animal husbandry, medicine, taxes, environment, politics, and trade.

Colonialism: Colonialism is a practice of domination by which a powerful nation subjugates less powerful nation and uses their resources to increase its own power and wealth.

Commercialization of Agriculture: Commercialization of agriculture is defined as a process where peasants start producing primarily for sale in distant markets, rather than for self-consumption. In India, vast scale commercialization took place under British rule as cash crops replaced food grains and crop production became more specialized and regionalized.

Deindustrialization: The decline of India's indigenous industry is called deindustrialization. It got manifest in the form of decay of local industry and craft as well as demise of textile industry and trade.

Drain of Wealth: Drain of wealth signifies the amount of wealth that was siphoned off from India to Britain through remittances, trade, and home charges. The theory was propounded by many Englishmen and Indian nationalists like Dadabhai Naoroji.

Permanent Settlement System: Also called as Zamindari system, Permanent Settlement System was introduced in 1793 by Lord Cornwallis. Under this Landlords or Zamindars were required to deposit a fixed amount of land revenue and were recognized as hereditary owners of land.

CHAPTER 10

Agriculture Production: Agriculture production indicates the volume of output. For example, during the year 2017–18, India's milk production was 176 million tonnes and food grain production was 285 million tonnes. Production can also be measured in terms of value of output.

Agriculture Productivity: Agriculture productivity is the output generated from the resources employed. There are different measures of agriculture productivity and one such measure is crop yield, that is, amount of crop produced per unit or area of land production, generally, in kilograms per hectare of land.

Cash Crops: Cash crops are the crops that are produced by farmers for commercial purpose (and may have industrial use) rather than for self-consumption. Coffee, cocoa, tea, sugarcane, cotton, groundnut, tobacco, and spices are some examples of cash crops.

Cooperative Farming: Under this farmers are encouraged to join hands and pool their land and other resources together so as to benefit from the economies of large scale production.

Cropping Pattern: The cropping pattern means the proportion of area under different crops at a point of time, changes in this distribution over a period of time, and factors determining this change in distribution. The cropping pattern of a country is determined by natural factors like soil type, rainfall and climate conditions, and technological factors.

Kharif Crop: The Kharif crops are the crops that are grown from July to October (during the south-west monsoon). Examples of Kharif crops are rice, maize, sorghum, pearl millet/bajra, finger millet/ragi (cereals), arhar (pulses), soyabean, groundnut (oilseeds), cotton, etc.

Land Ceiling: A ceiling on land holding means statutory absolute limit on the amount of land that a family may hold.

Land Consolidation: Under this, a farmer can be given one consolidated land holding equal to the total of the land in different scattered plots under his/her possession. The major aim of land consolidation is to increase the size of land holding so as to increase agriculture productivity.

Operation Barga: Launched in 1978 by West Bengal Government, Operation Barga was an agricultural tenancy law that regulated rents and security of tenure of sharecroppers (Bargadars). Under these laws, if tenants get registered with the Department of Land Revenue, they would be entitled to permanent and inheritable tenure on the land they sharecropped as long as they paid the landlord at least 25% of output as rent.

Rabi Crop: The Rabi crops are the crops that are grown from October to March (winter). The example of Rabi crops are wheat, barley, oats (cereals), chickpea/gram (pulses), linseed, mustard (oilseeds), etc.

Soil Health Card Scheme: Introduced in 2015, soil health card scheme educates a farmer regarding the status of his soil and provides advice on fertilizer usage and other nutrient recommendations that maintain soil health in the long run. The soil health card is a printed report containing information on soil health on the basis of 12 parameters.

Tenancy Reforms: A component of land reforms in India, the tenancy reforms include regulation of rent to be paid by tenants to landlord, security of land tenure to tenant, and conferment of ownership rights to tenants.

CHAPTER 11

Green Revolution: A phenomenon associated with a general increase in production and productivity of food grains in the late 1950s and 1960s. In India, Green Revolution was launched in the Kharif season of 1966.

Gross Cropped Area: Gross cropped area is the total cropped area under various crops during the whole agricultural year counting the area as many times as the number of crops grown on the same land.

Nutrient-based Subsidy Scheme: Launched in April 1, 2010, the scheme is aimed at improving agricultural productivity, ensuring the balanced use of N, P, and K fertilizers, promoting the growth of indigenous fertilizer industry and containing the fertilizer subsidy bill.

Pradhan Mantri Krishi Sinchayee Yojana: Launched in July 1, 2015, PMKSY was launched as a national mission to improve effectiveness in irrigation and ensure better utilization of the water resources in the country and integrating different irrigations schemes into one scheme. Such schemes are AIBP, IWMP, OFWM, etc.

Rainbow Revolution: A phenomenon related with the integrated development of crop cultivation, horticulture, forestry, fishery, poultry, animal husbandry, and food processing industry.

Second Green Revolution: The second Green Revolution is a transformation in agricultural production/productivity so as to sustain the growing demand by addressing various contemporary issues. It is a smarter revolution that will need to consider many more variables, such as global warming, new types of nonpetroleum energy, better irrigation practices, and inclusive growth while addressing the problems of small and marginal farmers and so on.

Virtual Water: Virtual water is the amount of water used in the production of food, energy, and other products. For example, the average virtual water content of paddy and wheat in India is 2,850 and 1,654 m^3/ton, respectively, against the world average of 2,291 and 1,334 m^3/ton for such crops. The trade of such water-embedded commodities is called virtual water trade.

CHAPTER 12

Agriculture Price Policy: The policy announced by the Government to safeguard the interest of farmers and consumers against price fluctuations of agriculture goods.

Antyodaya Anna Yojana: Launched in 2000, the Antyodaya Anna Yojana (AAY) scheme aims at providing highly subsidized food to poorest of the poor families. The people eligible for the scheme are aged, disabled, pregnant, widow, single or lactating mothers, and tribal families with no support or fixed income.

Buffer Stock: Buffer stock refers to a reserve of a commodity that is used to offset price fluctuations and unforeseen emergencies. The Government builds buffer stock through direct purchase from the domestic market or through imports from outside and releases such stock for sale in the time of distress.

Commission for Agriculture Cost and Prices: Established in 1965as Agriculture Price Commission [renamed in 1985 as Commission for Agriculture Cost and Prices (CACP)], it is an advisory body that determines MSP on the basis of different variables and fixed costs incurred by farmers.

Food Security: Food security is a situation that exists when all people, at all times, have physical, social, and economic access to sufficient, safe, and nutritious food that meets their dietary needs and food preferences for an active and healthy life.

Food Subsidy: Food subsidy is an economic aid providing by the Government and comprises two components, that is, consumer subsidy and cost of maintenance of buffer/strategic buffer. The consumer subsidy is difference between economic cost minus central issue price fixed for TPDS and other welfare schemes. The economic cost consists of two elements: (1) cost of procurement (or MSP), and (2) cost of FCI operations involving handling, storage, administrative, transportation, etc.

Integrated Child Development Services: Launched on October 2, 1975, the Integrated Child Development Services (ICDS) scheme represents one of the world's largest and unique programs for early childhood care and development. The beneficiaries under the scheme are children in the age group of 0–6 years, pregnant women, and lactating mothers.

Issue Price: It is the price at which foodgrains are sold to general public through fair price shops/ration depots.

Mid-day Meal Scheme: Launched in 1997–1998 at all India level, it is world's largest school-feeding program (for primary and upper primary classes) aims at promoting nutritional intake and school enrolment.

Minimum Support Price: Minimum support price (MSP) is the guaranteed price at which the Government purchases foodgrains from the farmers in case market prices fall below it. The Government announces MSP for around 23 crops in the country.

National Food Security Act: Enacted in 2013, the Act makes right to food as fundamental right and aims to provide subsidized foodgrains to approximately two-thirds of India population. It includes the Mid-Day Meal scheme, Integrated Child Development Services (ICDS) scheme, and the Public Distribution System.

Paradox of Plenty: A bumper crop reaped by the farmers brings a smaller total income to them because with greater supply the prices of the crop decline drastically and in the context of inelastic demand for them, bring about fall in the income of the farmers.

Public Distribution System: The public distribution system (PDS) is system of management of scarcity through distribution of foodgrains via fair price shops at affordable prices. PDS is operated under the joint responsibility of the central and the state governments.

The Global Hunger Index: The Global Hunger Index (GHI) is a tool designed to comprehensively measure and track hunger at global, regional, and national levels. GHI scores are based on four indicators: undernourishment, child wasting, child stunting, and child mortality.

CHAPTER 13

Cooperative Credit Society: It is a cooperative bank that provides short-term and long-term loans in the field of agriculture. The short-term credit is financed through PACs, CCBs, and SCBs. The long-term credit is provided through PCARDBs and SCARDBs.

NABARD: An acronym for National Bank for Agriculture and Rural Development which was established on July 12, 1982 on the recommendation of B. Sivaraman Committee. NABARD is fully owned by Government of India and is an apex body for the agriculture credit.

National Commission on Farmers: National commission on farmers was formed by Government of India in 2004. The commission was headed by famous agriculture scientist M.S. Swaminathan (also known as Swaminathan Committee) and submitted five reports on varieties of issues concerning agriculture development, viz., land reforms, agriculture credit & insurance, irrigation, and farmers' suicides.

Kisan Credit Card: Introduced in 1998, Kisan credit card is a credit delivery mechanism that is aimed at enabling farmers to have quick and timely access to affordable credit. Apart from discouraging dependence of farmers on informal sources of credit, the scheme helps farmers in multiple ways like production credit, working capital requirements for allied activities, ancillary credit requirements related to crop production contingent needs, and accidental insurance.

Microfinance: Microfinance is a form of credit that is provided to unemployed or low-income individuals or groups (generally self-help groups) who otherwise would have no other access to financial services.

Regional Rural Banks (RRBs): Established in 1975 on the recommendation of working group on rural banks, the RRBs provide credit in the field of agriculture. RRBs are owned by the Central Government, the State Government, and the Sponsor Bank whose shares are held at the ratios of 50, 15, and 35%, respectively.

Rural Infrastructure Development Fund (RIDF): The fund was created by the government with NABARD in 1995–96 to finance the ongoing projects in different states of the country. The corpus of the fund is raised through commercial banks crediting to the extent of their shortfall in stipulated priority sector lending to agriculture.

CHAPTER 14

Agricultural Marketing and Farmer Friendly Reforms Index: Also called AMFFRI, it is an Index created by NITI Aayog and is based on three indicators in order to rank the states. The indicators are (1) reform the system of agriculture marketing, (2) facilitate and liberalize lease in and lease out of agricultural land, and (3) freedom to fell and sell forest produce grown on private land.

Agricultural Produce Market Committee: It is a statutory market committee constituted by a state government in respect of trade in certain notified agricultural or horticultural or livestock products, under the Agricultural Produce Market Committee Act.

Contract Farming: Contract farming entails an agreement between the buyer and farm producers with regard to quantum of produce based on anticipated yield and contracted acreage at a pre-agreed price.

Co-operative Marketing: Agriculture marketing co-operatives envisages a market form where farm products are marketed collectively for their direct benefit. Co-operatives are formed to organize small and marginal farmers so as to enable them to obtain fair price for their produce.

E-NAM: Launched in 2016, E-NAM or National Agriculture Market is an online trading platform for agricultural commodities in India. The market helps farmers, traders, and buyers with online trading in agriculture commodities.

Retail Markets: Retail markets directly serve the customers and constitute last link in the marketing chain. They can be small agriculture retail outlets or big air-conditioned malls such as Big Bazaar or Reliance Fresh.

Rural Primary Markets: These are periodical markets that serve as focal points to mostly small and marginal farmers to market their farm produce.

Terminal Markets: It is a new experiment in India and functions in hub and spoke format by private enterprises. Terminal market is a central site, often in a metropolitan area serves as an assembly and trading place for commodities.

Wholesale Markets: Also called as secondary markets or wholesale mandis, are located in district headquarters or important trade centers and perform assembling and distribution functions.

CHAPTER 15

Competition Act: On the recommendation of S.V.S. Raghavan Committee, the Indian parliament enacted the Competition Act, 2002 to promote free and fair competition and replaced the archaic MRTP Act, 1969. The objectives of the Act include prohibiting the practices that have an adverse effect on market competition, prohibiting the abuse of dominance in a market, and prohibiting acquisitions, mergers, amalgamations, etc. between enterprises which have or are likely to have an appreciable adverse effect on market competition.

Core Industries: Industries that are necessary for industrialization of a country are called core industries. The eight core industries in India are coal, crude oil, natural gas, refinery products, fertilizers, steel, cement, and electricity.

Ease of Doing Business: It is an index published by the World Bank and advocates for both regulatory quality and efficiency. A nation's ranking on the index is based on the average of 10 sub-indices.

Index of Industrial Production: Published on monthly basis by CSO, it is an index which shows the growth rates in different industry groups of the economy in a stipulated period of time. The base year for the current series of IIP is 2011–12 and it carries 839 items and 407 item groups.

Industrial Licensing: Also called as License Raj, the policy of industrial licensing was introduced by Industries (Development and Regulation) Act, 1951 and sought to regulate the expansion, output, and pricing of both public and private sectors. At present, industrial license is required for only four items.

Make in India: Announced in 2014, it aims at making India a global manufacturing hub, increasing the contribution of the manufacturing sector to 25% of the GDP by 2020, and creating 100 million additional jobs in manufacturing by 2022.

MRTP Act: MRTP Act was enacted in 1969 on the recommendation of Subimal Dutt committee with the objective to ensure that the operation of the economic system does not result in the concentration of economic power in hands of few, to provide for the control of monopolies, and to prohibit monopolistic and restrictive trade practices.

National Investment and Manufacturing Zones (NIMZs): An important component of NMP 2011, the NIMZs are integrated industrial townships with state-of-the-art infrastructure and land use on the basis of zoning; clean and energy-efficient technology; necessary social infrastructure; and skill development facilities to provide a productive environment to persons transiting from the primary sector to the secondary and tertiary sectors.

National Manufacturing Policy: Introduced in 2011 to bring about a quantitative and qualitative change in India's manufacturing sector by targeting the growth rate of 12–14% over the medium term, raising its share to 25% of the GDP by 2022 and creating 100 million additional jobs by 2022.

CHAPTER 16

Central Public Sector Enterprises: CPSEs are joint stock companies owned by the union government of India, with more than 51% stake. Example ONGC, Coal India Ltd. India has 339 CPSEs.

Corporate Social Responsibility: As per the Section 135 of companies Act, 2013, all profit-making corporates, including CPSEs, exceeding prescribed threshold limits, are mandated to spend for social cause at least 2% of average net profits of the company.

Disinvestment: Disinvestment means withdrawal of government equity from PSEs. It was introduced in 1991 as a part of new industrial policy.

Insolvency and Bankruptcy Code: The IBC code was enacted by Indian Parliament in the year 2016 with the objectives of solving the twin balance problem, developing a robust corporate bond market, improving the credit environment, streamlining the corporate insolvency resolution process, preventing value destruction if there is corporate distress, and consequently providing a fillip to India's competitiveness as a business destination.

Maharatnas: Introduced in May, 2010, the scheme aims at empowering mega CPSEs to expand their operations and emerge as global giants. There are eight Maharatnas.

Micro, Small, and Medium Enterprises (MSMEs): MSMEs are defined on the basis of investment in plant and machinery. For manufacturing sector, the microenterprise should have investment up to ₹25 lakh; small enterprise between ₹25 lakh and ₹5 crore; and medium enterprise between ₹5 crore and ₹10 crore. For the service sector, the investment limit for micro, small, and medium unit is ₹10 lakh, ₹2 crore, and ₹5 crore, respectively.

Miniratnas: Launched in 1997, the scheme aims granting enhanced autonomy and delegation of financial powers to some other profit-making companies with an objective making them efficient and competitive. There are two categories Miniratna-I (60 in number) and Miniratna-II (15 in number).

Navratnas: The scheme of navratnas was introduced in the year 1997 for CPSEs, which have comparative advantage and provide them with greater autonomy to compete in the global market, so as, to help them become global giants. There are 16 Navratnas.

Twin Balance Sheet Problem: The twin balance sheet problem refers to the stress on balance sheets of banks due to non-performing assets or bad loans on the one hand, and heavily indebted corporates on the other.

CHAPTER 17

Business Services: These are the services that are primarily consumed by business organizations. For example, outsourcing, consulting, professional services like legal services, business processes, etc.

Financial Services: Products and services offered by financial markets. Examples are the banks, investment banks, insurance companies, credit card companies, stock brokerages, etc.

GATS: GATS stands for general agreement of trade in services and is an agreement of WTO. It suggests four modes of service trade: Mode I, Mode II, Mode III, and Mode IV. In Mode I, while trading in services the supplier and buyer remaining in their respective locations; in Mode-II, service recipient moves to the location of the service provider; in Mode III, there is commercial presence of service provider, and in Mode IV, there is a movement of natural person.

Service-led Growth: A phenomenon that signifies the higher growth rate of service sector and its increasing share in GDP, exports, and foreign investment. India is experiencing this phenomenon since the post-reform period.

Splintering: Fragmentation of economic activities into services of specialized set of institutions or people in the field of banking, accounting, R&D, marketing, transportation, communication, consultancy, etc.

CHAPTER 18

Agriculture Export Zone: Announced in 2001 FTP to promote agricultural exports of the country, AEZs takes a comprehensive look at a particular produce/product located in a contiguous area for the purpose of developing and sourcing the raw materials, their processing/packaging, leading to final exports.

Decanalization: It is a process under which the license to import is granted to a number of importers to promote competition and reduce the cost of imported item.

Export Promotion: The policy of export promotion is based on the principal of comparative advantage, and the country concentrates on the production and exports of products in which it is relatively more efficient.

Foreign Trade Policy: Announced by Ministry of Commerce, it provides direction to country's foreign trade. The Government announces annual or perspective foreign trade policy and lays down broader targets with regard to exports and imports.

Import Substitution: The policy of import substitution signifies replacing imports with indigenous production in order to promote indigenous industry and save valuable foreign exchange reserves. It can be done by imposing quantitative restrictions, tariffs, or other trade barriers.

Special Economic Zone: SEZ is a geographical region that has economic laws different from a country's typical economic laws. The objectives of establishing SEZs are promoting GDP, increasing investment, exports and employment opportunities.

Terms of Trade: It is the ratio at which exports exchange for imports, or in simple words, it is the capacity of exports to buy imports. If the export value in terms of import value rises, the TOT are said to be favorable.

CHAPTER 19

Automatic Route: FDI is allowed under the automatic route without prior approval either of the government or the RBI in specified sectors and the company receiving such FDI needs to report to RBI within 30 days of receipt of share application money.

Balance of Payments: The balance of payments (BOP) is the systematic record of economic transactions of a nation with the rest of the world in a single accounting year.

Balance of Trade: The merchandise trade balance is called balance of trade. If imports are more than exports, it is called a trade deficit. If exports are more than import, it is called a trade surplus.

Brownfield FDI: It is the investment in which the MNC acquires the shares of an existing company in the host country.

Capital Account: The capital account comprises debt or equity of short- and long-term nature. It comprises foreign investment, external commercial borrowings, external assistance, NRI deposits, etc.

Capital Account Convertibility: The capital account convertibility is the freedom to convert domestic currency into foreign currency and vice versa for the capital account transactions (i.e., investments, debts, banking capital, NRI deposits, etc.) at market-determined rates and that also without any restrictions.

Current Account: The current account comprises export and import of goods/merchandise and balance in invisible account. If receipts in the current account are greater than payments, it is called current account surplus. If receipts in the current account are lesser than payments, it is called current account deficit.

Depreciation and Appreciation: Under flexible exchange rate and managed float system, currency depreciates and appreciates depending upon the strength of demand and supply forces. When demand for foreign currency is more (or supply of foreign currency is less), the home currency depreciates. When demand for foreign currency is less (or supply of foreign currency is more), the home currency appreciates. Depreciation provides a boost to exports, whereas appreciation encourages imports.

Devaluation and Revaluation: Devaluation means official lowering of the value of a country's currency vis-a-vis foreign currency. Impact of devaluation and depreciation are same with the difference that devaluation is government induced and depreciation is automatic. Revaluation means official raising of the value of a country's currency vis-a-vis foreign currency. Impact of revaluation and appreciation are same with the difference that revaluation is government induced and appreciation is automatic.

Exchange Rate: Exchange rate is the price of one currency in terms of another currency. It is the rate at which one currency is exchanged for others.

Foreign Direct Investment: FDI is investment made in a country by a foreign investor in order to control the ownership of an entity or business enterprise. FDI inflows are counted from 10% stock or asset ownership in a company.

Foreign Exchange Reserves: Foreign exchange reserves are the international reserve assets held by the central bank in foreign currencies. Such reserve assets are in the form of foreign bank notes (like US$, Euro, Pound Sterling, Yen, etc.), marketable securities/bonds, government securities, gold, Special Drawing Rights (SDRs), and reserve position in the IMF.

Foreign Institutional Investment: FII is short-term capital that goes into short-term equities or hedge funds. It is generally volatile in nature and is also called hot money.

Government Route: Foreign investment in activities not covered under the automatic route requires prior approval of the government. Proposals for foreign investment under government route are considered by respective administrative ministry/department.

Greenfield FDI: It is a type of investment in which a parent company creates a subsidiary in the host country, building its operations from very beginning or scratch.

Tobin Tax: Suggested by James Tobin (Nobel Laureate), it is the tax levied on the capital flight (by foreign institutional investors). The idea behind such tax is to discourage capital flight which can be devastating to a host country.

CHAPTER 20

Agreement on Agriculture (AOA): It is an important WTO agreement and includes three components (1) Market access, (2) Domestic support, and (3) Export subsidies.

Anti-dumping Duty: It is an import duty levied to nullify the impact of dumping by exporter nation. WTO rules provide for imposition of anti-dumping duty if a country can prove the injury caused to local industry by such dumping.

Countervailing Duty: It is an import duty levied to nullify the impact of export subsidy by the exporter nation.

General Agreement on Trade in Services (GATS): GATS are service trade agreements and includes four modes of supplying services (1) cross-border trade, (2) consumption abroad, (3) commercial presence, and (4) presence of natural persons.

International Bank for Reconstruction and Development (IBRD): Established in 1944 as a result of Bretton Woods conference, IBRD lends to governments of middle-income and creditworthy low-income countries.

International Centre for Settlement of Investment Disputes (ICSID): Established in 1966, ICSID provides international facilities for conciliation and arbitration of investment disputes.

International Development Association (IDA): IDA was founded in 1960 and lends to world's poorest countries in the form of interest-free credits and grants. It together with IBRD forms World Bank.

International Finance Corporation (IFC): Established in 1956, IFC promotes the private sector and helps developing countries achieve sustainable growth by financing investment, mobilizing capital in international financial markets, and providing advisory services to businesses and governments.

International Monetary Fund (IMF): Established in 1944, IMF ensures the stability of the international monetary system—the system of exchange rates and international payments that enables countries to transact with each other.

MFN Status: It stands for 'Most favored nations' status. Under this, if one country is granted a trade concession such as lower import duties, then all WTO members must be extended to the same concessions.

Ministerial Conference: Ministerial conference is the highest decision-making body of WTO. It usually meets after every 2 years and is represented by commerce ministers of member countries.

Multilateral Investment Guarantee Agency (MIGA): MIGA was created in 1988 to promote foreign direct investment into developing countries to support economic growth, reduce poverty, and improve people's lives.

Non-tariff Barriers (NTBs): NTBs are trade barriers that restrict imports (or exports) of goods or services through measures other than tariffs. Examples of NTBs are import licensing, SPS, TBT, rules of origin, etc.

Regional Trade Bloc: Regional trade bloc is an intergovernmental agreement of economic integration among participating nations where regional barriers to trade, are reduced or eliminated. For example, ASEAN, NAFTA, and European Union.

Special Drawing Rights (SDRs): The SDR is an international reserve asset, created by the IMF in 1969 to supplement the existing official reserves of member countries. SDRs are allocated to member countries in proportion to their IMF quotas.

Trade-related Aspects of Intellectual Property Rights System (TRIPS): TRIPS agreements introduced intellectual property rules into the multilateral trading system and includes seven types of IPRs: (1) Copyright and related rights, (2) Trademarks, including service marks, (3) Geographical indications, (4) Industrial designs, (5) Patents, (6) Layout-designs (topographies) of integrated circuits, and (7) Undisclosed information, including trade secrets.

World Trade Organization (WTO): Established in 1995, it is an International trade body that facilitates trade among countries and promotes multilateralism. It has 164 members and is headquartered at Geneva, Switzerland.

CHAPTER 21

Bank Rate: Bank rate is the rate at which RBI rediscounts the bills of exchange or other commercial papers of the commercial banks or in simple language lends to commercial banks.

Cash Reserve Ratio: Cash Reserve Ratio or CRR specifies the amount of reserves, banks need to maintain as cash or with the central bank as percentage of their demand and time deposits.

Certificate of Deposits: Introduced in 1989 on the recommendation of N. Vaghul Committee, certificate of deposit (CD) is a negotiable money market instrument and issued in dematerialized form or as a usance promissory note against funds deposited at a bank or other eligible financial institution for a specified time period.

Commercial Papers: Introduced in India in 1990 on the recommendation of N. Vaghul Committee, Commercial papers (CPs) are short-term (up to 1 year) unsecured borrowing instruments issued in the form of a promissory note.

Financial Inclusion: Financial inclusion implies providing financial services, viz., access to payments and remittance facilities, savings, loans, and insurance services at affordable cost to those who are excluded from the formal financial system.

Lead Bank Scheme: Introduced in 1969 on the recommendation of Nariman Committee, the lead bank acts as a leader for coordinating the efforts of all credit institutions in the allotted districts to increase the flow of credit to agriculture, small-scale industries, and other economic activities included in the priority sector in the rural and semi-urban areas, with the district being the basic unit in terms of geographical area.

Liquidity Adjustment Facility: The Liquidity Adjustment Facility (LAF) was introduced in 1999 by RBI to control liquidity in the system on a daily basis through repos/reverse repos.

M_1: M_1 is the currency with the public plus demand deposits with the banking system plus "Other" deposits with the RBI. M_1 is called narrow money.

M_3: M_3 is M_1 plus time deposits with the banking system. M_3 is called broad money and represents money supply in the economic system.

Marginal Standing Facility: Introduced in 2011, Marginal Standing Facility (MSF) is a window for banks to borrow from the RBI in an emergency situation when inter-bank liquidity dries up completely.

Market Stabilization Scheme: Market Stabilization Scheme (MSS) is an intervention by the RBI in the foreign exchange market to withdraw excess liquidity (that is generated as a result of the RBI's purchase of foreign currencies in the foreign exchange market) by selling government securities in the economy

Monetary Policy: Monetary policy is the policy regarding the regulation of flow of credit in the economy. It is executed by RBI.

Money Market Mutual Funds: Introduced in 1992, money market mutual funds (MMMFs) are short-run liquid investments in high-quality money market instruments and provide investors with a reasonable return along with good liquidity over a period of up to 1 year.

Money Supply: Money supply is the total amount of currency in circulation and other liquid instruments that exist in the economy. In India, M_3 is called broad money and is used as a metaphor for money supply.

Nationalized Bank: A nationalized bank signifies public ownership or government control. In India major bank nationalization was exercised in 1969 and 1980. At present there are 19 nationalized banks.

Non-banking Financial Intermediaries: Non-banking financial institutions (NBFIs) comprise a heterogeneous group of financial intermediaries and consist of All-India financial institutions, nonbanking financial companies, and PDs.

Non-performing Assets: A non-performing asset (NPA) is a loan or advance for which the principal or interest payment remained overdue for a period of 90 days.

Pradhan Mantri Jan Dhan Yojana: Introduced in 2014, Pradhan Mantri Jan Dhan Yojana is a program for financial inclusion to cover all unbanked households in India, whether in urban or rural area, and aims at providing affordable financial services like savings & deposit accounts, banking services, remittance, credit, insurance, and pension.

Primary Dealers: Introduced by RBI in 1995, primary dealers (PDs) are a group of highly qualified financial firms/banks are appointed to play the role of specialist intermediaries in the government security market between the issuer on the one hand and the market on the other.

Priority Sector Lending: Introduced in 1974, it is a target-based scheme aimed to provide access to credit to the neglected sectors of the economy. For example, domestic scheduled commercial banks (excluding RRBs and small finance banks) and Foreign banks with 20 branches and above are required to lend 40% of ANBC to priority sector.

Repo Rate: Repo rate is the rate at which commercial banks borrow from RBI by pledging securities with it with the option to repurchase them back at a rate called REPO rate.

Reverse Repo Rate: The commercial banks can park their surplus funds with RBI and earn a specified interest on it called reverse repo rate.

Scheduled Bank: The scheduled commercial banks are those banks which find mention in the second schedule of RBI Act 1934 and which carry out the normal banking business. Examples of Scheduled commercial banks are State Bank of India, nationalized banks, foreign banks, regional rural banks, and other scheduled commercial banks.

Statutory Liquidity Ratio: Statutory Liquidity Ratio or SLR specifies the amount of money banks must invest in the government securities (and bonds of PSUs) as proportion of their deposits.

CHAPTER 22

Bombay Stock Exchange: Bombay Stock Exchange, established in 1875, is the oldest stock exchange in Asia. With more than 5,400 listings and market capitalization of more than $2 trillion, it is among the top ranking stock exchanges in the world.

Capital Market: Capital market is the market for long-term funds. It consists of the primary market, where new securities are issued and sold, and the secondary market, where old securities are traded.

Development Financial Institution: Development financial institutions are specialized institutions set up primarily to provide risk capital for economic development projects. Examples are NABARD, National Housing Bank, etc.

Gilt-edged Market: It is a market for government securities. As they are backed by the government, they are high-quality debt securities with very high credit worthiness.

National Stock Exchange: National Stock Exchange was established in 1992 at Mumbai. NSE is the first de-mutualized electronic stock exchange of India. It is the largest stock exchange in India in terms of total and average daily turnover for equity shares.

Nifty: Nifty is the stock market index of National Stock Exchange. It stands for National Index of 50 and represents the weighted average of 50 Indian company stocks.

Sensex: Sensex is the share price index of Bombay Stock Exchange. Launched in 1986, it comprises 30 prominent stocks derived from all key sectors based on their financial performance.

Security and Exchange Board of India: Established in 1988, Security and Exchange Board of India (SEBI) supervises almost all the aspects of capital market such as regulation of intermediaries, curbing malpractices like market manipulation and insider trading, development of fair practices by the intermediaries, development of the capital market, creating awareness among investors, and so on.

Stock Market: It is the secondary capital market where securities of existing companies are bought and sold. For example, Bombay Stock Exchange.

CHAPTER 23

Consumer Price Index: The Consumer Price Index (CPI) is based on the cost of a basket typically purchased by consumers. In India, four types of CPI released at national level are CPI for Industrial Workers (IW), CPI for Agricultural Labourers (AL), CPI for Rural Labourers (RL), and CPI (Rural/Urban/Combined).

Core Inflation: Core inflation is an inflation measure which excludes volatile component of inflation such as food and fuel prices. It takes into consideration the manufacturing prices.

Cost-push Inflation: Cost push inflation takes place because of supply-side constraints such as increase in input costs, global increase in oil prices or hoarding.

Dear money Policy: It is monetary policy under which central bank tightens the money supply by raising the interest rate via increase in CRR, REPO, or Bank Rate. The motive is to contain inflation.

Demand-pull Inflation: Increase in aggregate demand, supply remaining constant in the short run causes demand-pull inflation. Examples are increase in income, increase in population, and generation of black income.

Headline Inflation: It is the overall inflation rate in the economy reported through CPI combined or CPI (Rural + Urban). The headline CPI inflation measure is being used as the target rate of inflation as it reflects the prices of essential consumption goods.

Hyper-inflation: Hyper-inflation occurs when prices rise every moment, and there is no limit to the height to which prices might rise. In quantitative terms, prices may rise over 1000% in a year.

Inflation Targeting: Inflation targeting is a monetary policy strategy or framework used by RBI for maintaining price level at a certain level or within a range. It was introduced on the recommendation of Expert Committee to Revise and Strengthen the Monetary Policy Framework, headed by Urjit Patel.

Wholesale Price Index: The Wholesale Price Index (WPI) depicts the price of a representative basket of wholesale commodities. In India, WPI is calculated using the 697 commodities from 8,331 centers.

CHAPTER 24

Ad Valorem Tax: An ad valorem tax (Latin for according to value) is a tax based on the value of commodity/property. For example, a 10% import duty on the laptops, drugs, or automobiles. It is more common than a specific tax.

Built-in-flexibility/buoyancy: It reflects the changes in tax revenue because of changes in GDP.

Corporation Tax: A direct tax charged on the net profits of the companies. The rates of corporation tax in India are 30% for Indian companies and 40% for foreign companies. For Indian companies less than ₹400 crore of total revenue, corporation tax rate is 25%.

Custom Duty: An indirect tax levied on imports/exports.

Direct Tax: A tax in which impact and incidence are on the same person. For example, in case of income tax impact and incidence would be on the person whose income is being taxed.

Excise Duty: An indirect tax levied on manufacturing.

Fringe Benefits Tax (FBT): Fringe benefits tax signifies a tax that is levied on any privilege/facility provided by an employer to his employees (including former employees) by reason of their employment. It is a direct tax and was abolished in the budget 2009–10.

Goods and Services Tax (GST): GST is a comprehensive, multi-stage tax that is levied on every value addition. It is an indirect tax and was introduced in the year 2017.

Income Tax: A direct tax charged on the income of individuals and other associations of people.

Indirect Tax: A tax in which impact and incidence are on the different persons and hence burden of tax can be shifted. For example, GST.

Laffer Curve: Propounded by Arthur Laffer (Nobel Laureate), it shows increase in tax revenue with increase in taxes up to a certain point beyond which any increase in tax rate will lead to decrease in tax revenue.

Minimum Alternate Tax (MAT): MAT was introduced in the year 1997–98 to target those companies that make huge profits but pay no/minimal tax by taking advantage of the various deductions and exemptions allowed under the Income Tax Act. The rate of MAT is 18.5%.

Specific Tax: A tax based on the quantity of an item, such as 10% per quintal, regardless of price.

Tax Elasticity: It reflects the change in tax revenue because of changes in tax rate or coverage. Tax elasticity can be explained with the help of Laffer curve.

CHAPTER 25

Burden of Debt: The burden of public debt refers to the sacrifice it will impose and have effects on the community through a rise in taxation, necessitated at the time of repayment and for paying the annual interests on the government loans.

Central Government Liabilities: Central Government Liabilities reflect total debt of Government of India and comprise internal debt, external debt, and public account liabilities.

De-merit Goods Subsidy: The non-merit goods are the goods whose consumption leads to negative externalities because they affect others without compensating them. For example, subsidy on diesel may be good for the receiver but harmful to the society in terms of pollution.

Debt Overhang: Debt overhang is a situation in which the expected repayment on external debt falls short of the contractual value of debt.

Debt Service Ratio: The debt service ratio is the ratio of debt service payments (principal + interest) of a country to its export earnings. Lower this ratio, healthier is the country's international finances.

Debt Trap: A debt trap is a situation in which a borrower is led into a cycle of re-borrowing, or rolling over, his loan payments because he is unable to afford the scheduled payments on the principal of a loan.

Effective Revenue Deficit: Introduced in budget 2011–2012, effective revenue deficit (ERD) is revenue deficit minus transfers from center to states in the form of grants.

Fiscal Deficit: Introduced in 1990s on the recommendation of Sukhamoy Chakravarty Committee, fiscal deficit occurs when a government's total expenditures exceed the receipts that it generates, excluding money from borrowings.

Fiscal Policy: Fiscal policy is the policy regarding receipts and expenditure of the government so as to produce desirable effects on the national income, production, and employment.

FRBM Act: The Fiscal Responsibility and Budget Management (FRBM) Act was enacted in 2003 by Indian Parliament and was brought into effect on July 5, 2004. The main purpose of the Act was to ensure fiscal discipline in the country by eliminating revenue deficit and by lowering fiscal deficit in a stipulated time.

Merit Goods Subsidy: Merit goods are those goods the social benefit accruing from which is much greater than the sum of private benefits to individual consumers. The consumption of merit goods leads to positive externalities. Example of merit good subsidy is public distribution system for BPL families.

Primary Deficit: Primary deficit is equal to fiscal deficit minus interest payments on the previous borrowings. It indicates how much of the government borrowings are going to meet expenses other than the interest payments.

Public Debt: It signifies the debt raised by the government which is to be repaid at a future date with interest. Public debt constitutes both internal debt as well as external debt.

Public Goods: Public goods are a product or service provided by the government (or even the private sector) to all members of a society without any profit motive. Public goods are non-excludable and non-rivalrous in nature. Examples of public goods are highways, police service, public parks, etc.

Revenue Deficit: Revenue deficit occurs when revenue expenditure exceeds revenue receipts.

CHAPTER 26

Decentralization: Decentralization is the transfer of authority and responsibility of public functions from the union to the states and local governments.

Divisible Pool: Divisible pool is the component of gross tax revenue which is distributed between the center and the states.

Grants-in-aid: Grants-in-aid are payments made by central government to state governments, under Article 275 of the constitution. The grants are made to correct horizontal imbalances and cover special problems of the state.

Finance Commission: Finance Commission is a constitutional body which defines the financial relations between center and state. It is provided by Article 280 of Indian Constitution.

Fiscal Capacity: Fiscal capacity is the ability of the state government to raise revenue from its own sources to provide public goods and other functions of the state.

Fiscal Discipline: Fiscal discipline is the ideal balance between receipts and expenditure of the government that ensures smooth financial transactions and long-term fiscal health.

Fiscal Federalism: Fiscal federalism signifies the economic relationship between union, state, and local governments that focuses on the division of finances among these governments.

Gadgil-Mukherjee Formula: Gadgil-Mukherjee formula is named after eminent economist D.R. Gadgil and former president of India Pranab Mukherjee. The formula deals in distribution of planned central assistance to the states.

General Category States: All the states which are not special category states are called general category states.

Horizontal Devolution: Allocation between the states of the respective shares of union's transfers is called horizontal devolution. In India, horizontal devolution is done on the basis of five variables with certain weights.

Income Distance: Income distance is the distance of the GSDP of a particular state from the state with the highest GSDP.

Special Category States: Special category states are certain disadvantaged states in terms of difficult terrain or backwardness and get special financial assistance from the central government.

State Finance Commission: State FC is provided by Articles 243 (I) and 243 (Y) of the Constitution and recommends to the governor with regard to transfer/distribution of resources between state and local bodies.

Tax Devolution: Tax devolution means transfer of tax revenue from center to states.

Vertical Devolution: Distribution of such proceeds between the union and the states is called vertical devolution. For example, 14th FC recommended vertical devolution of 42% of net tax proceeds of the union to the states.

CHAPTER 27

Command Economy: Command economy is an economy where the decisions regarding production, investment, and distribution are taken by central government. It is a "planning from above" model. Cuba, North Korea, and former Soviet Republic can be placed under this type of planning model.

Harrod–Domar Model: The model was given by Nobel Prize winning economists R.F. Harrod and Evsey Domar and explains economy's growth rate in terms of the level of saving and productivity of capital.

Mahalanobis Model: Developed by P.C. Mahalanobis, it is a two-sector model that suggests the allocation of a higher proportion of total investment to capital goods industries.

NITI Aayog: NITI Aayog is an advisory body and think tank of Government of India on economic policy formulation, implementation, monitoring, and evaluation. Established in the year 1915, it has replaced Planning Commission.

Plan Holiday: Government declares plan holiday when it abandons its regular five-year plan and instead adopts annual plan. Government declared plan holiday during 1966–1969 and 1990–1992.

Planning Commission: Planning Commission was an advisory body established in 1950 and dissolved in 2014. Its main task was to formulate five-year plans in India.

Rolling Plan: Rolling plan was introduced in the year 1977–78 by Janata Government. It encompasses three sets of plans. First is the annual plan that comprises of annual budget. Second is a plan for 3, 4, or 5 years, that is, for fixed number of years that keep on changing as per the requirements of the economy and government. Third is a perspective plan that is for 10, 15, or 20 years.

CHAPTER 28

Bracket Creep: It is a situation wherein inflation pushes income into higher tax brackets. The result is an increase in income taxes but no increase in real purchasing power.

Corruption Perceptions Index (CPI): It is an annual publication of Transparency International since 1995 which ranks nations annually by their perceived levels of corruption, as determined by expert assessments and opinion surveys.

Counterfeiting: It means printing fake currency with an objective of executing illegal acts such as money laundering or terrorist-related activities.

Demonetization: Demonetization is the act of stripping national currency unit of its status as legal tender. Objectives of demonetization are to control or curb inflation, counterfeiting, black money or money laundering, etc.

Money Laundering: Money Laundering refers to the conversion or "Laundering" of money that is illegally obtained, so as to make it appear to originate from a legitimate source.

Right to Information (RTI) Act: Enacted in 2005, the RTI Act provides citizens of the country right to seek information from a public authority who is required to reply expeditiously or within 30 days.

Volunteer Disclosure Scheme: In this scheme, tax evaders are provided channel to convert black money into white by paying a small amount of money as tax. Examples are VDIS in 1997 and IDS in 2016.

CHAPTER 29

Globalization: Globalization simply means the integration of national economy with world economy by allowing free flow of goods, services, labor, and capital.

Liberalization: It means the elimination of state control over economic activities and includes several policy measures like deregulation of industrial sector, financial sector reforms, tax reforms, foreign exchange reforms, and trade and investment policy reforms.

Macroeconomic Stabilization: Macroeconomic stabilization, also called as macroeconomic reforms, are demand side measures which constitute returning to low and stable inflation and a sustainable monetary, fiscal, trade, and exchange rate policy.

Privatization: Privatization is the transfer of control of ownership of economic resources from the public sector to the private sector and takes place through the process of disinvestment.

Structural Adjustment Reforms: Structural adjustment reforms, also called as microeconomic reforms, are supply side measures that include industrial, financial, agriculture, and infrastructure sector reforms.

Washington Consensus: The concept developed by John Williamson in 1989 encompasses a set of 10 economic policy prescriptions for crisis-wracked developing countries by international financial institutions like IMF and World Bank in the form of structural adjustment programs and stabilization policies.

INDEX

F

G

H

I

J

K

L

M

N

O

P

Q

R

S

V

W

Y

Z